Patagonia

“”

To my mind there is nothing in life so delightful as that feeling of relief, of escape, and absolute freedom, which one experiences in a vast solitude, where man has perhaps never been, and has, at any rate, left no trace of his existence.

W. H. Hudson, Idle Days in Patagonia (1893)

Highlights...

1. The lakes around Bariloche ▸▸ p116.
2. Los Alerces National Park ▸▸ p137.
3. Whale watching at Península Valdés ▸▸ p152.
4. Glaciar Perito Moreno ▸▸ p191.
5. Trekking around Cerro Fitz Roy ▸▸ p194.
6. Lago Llanquihue and Volcán Osorno ▸▸ p262.
7. A cruise to Glaciar San Rafael ▸▸ p304.
8. Trekking in Torres del Paine ▸▸ p340.
9. Estancia Harberton ▸▸ p367.
10. 24hrs in Buenos Aires ▸▸ p68.

Introduction

Squeezed between two oceans and split by the tail of the Andes, Patagonia is a land of vast horizons and limitless possibilities. Unvanquished by the conquistadors, it has developed in isolation, attracting brave pioneers, hardy Welsh settlers, Wild West outlaws on the run and Che Guevara on a pre-revolutionary jaunt. It remains one of the world's last great wildernesses.

In northern Patagonia, lakes of emerald, blue and indigo nestle among snow-capped volcanoes and ancient monkey puzzle trees. East of the Andes, sheep, not cattle, roam the Argentine steppe and estancias provide a welcome haven of civilization in the emptiness. Head south on the ultimate road trip until, rising up from the flat lands, you see Mount Fitz Roy's spires, or the granite turrets of Torres del Paine. Sculpted glaciers cleave with a roar and the raw power of nature is palpable.

Lumbering seals and migrating whales animate the deserted beaches of the Atlantic, while on the Pacific coast, the land splinters into a labyrinth of islets, fjords and looming icebergs. The oceans meet at the tip of Patagonia, where, surrounded by ice and snow, the Land of Fire is a final frontier at the end of the world.

Contents

Santiago 210

Chilean Lake District 234

Carretera Austral 286

Far South 318

Tierra del Fuego 350

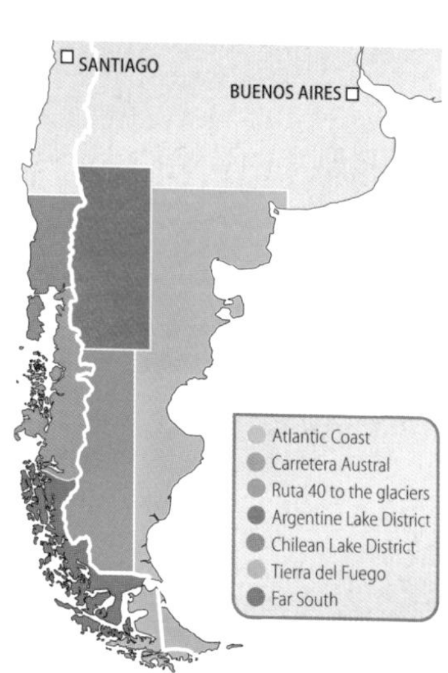

About the guide

Footprint Backpackers' guides are designed for those with a 'backpacker' mindset: interested in the people, culture, wildlife and history of a region and wanting a good value holiday. With over 80 years experience of writing about South America, we hope that you find this guide easy to use, enjoyable to read and good to look at. We especially hope it helps you have the experience of a life-time but please follow the top tips outlined in How big is your footprint? below.

Here is how it works. The boundaries of Patagonia are not very clear but we cover the Argentine provinces of Neuquén, Río Negro, Chubut, Santa Cruz and Tierra del Fuego, and Regions IX to XII in Chile. **Essentials**, the first chapter, deals with practicalities: **Travelling in Patagonia** introduces the region, suggesting where to go, when to go, what to do and how to get around; **A-Z** gives the lowdown on visas, money, health, and so on; **About Patagonia** has overviews of history, landscape and wildlife. For ease, we have divided Patagonia into **seven areas** each of which could form the base for your holiday (see map on previous page). We've also included chapters on the gateway cities of **Buenos Aires** and **Santiago**. At the start of each chapter, a simple rating and a number of 'Don't miss' places on a map give an instant overview of the area and its attractions. Follow the cross reference to the district that interests you to find a more detailed map together with a snapshot showing the timescale you need to allow, how to get there and move around and what to expect in terms of weather, accommodation and restaurants. A range of symbols (for sleeping, for eating, for activities, for transport etc) indicate the facilities in each city, town or area, which are fully described in the listing sections.

Special features include expert travel tips, inspiring travellers' tales, suggestions for blowing the budget and ideas for going that little bit further.

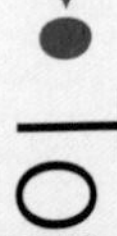

Top tips

How big is your footprint?

1 Where possible choose a destination, tour operator or hotel with a proven ethical and environmental commitment, and if in doubt ask.
2 Spend money on locally produced (rather than imported) goods and services and use common sense when bargaining.
3 Consider staying in local, rather than foreign owned, hotels – the economic benefits for host communities are far greater.
4 Use water and electricity carefully – travellers may receive preferential supply while local communities are overlooked.
5 Don't give money or sweets to children – it encourages begging – instead give to a recognized project, charity or school.
6 Learn about local etiquette and culture – consider local norms and behaviour – and dress appropriately for local cultures.
7 Protect wildlife and other natural resources.
8 Always ask before taking photographs or videos of people.

Ecotourism has expanded astronomically in Chile and Argentina. Useful contacts include **Tourism Concern** (www.tourismconcern.org.uk), the **Eco-Tourism Society** (http://ecotourism.org) and **Conservation International** (www.ecotour.org).

Essentials

Where to go

Possibly the most impressive characteristic of Patagonia is the sense of limitless space and freedom; it takes time to drink in the sheer size of it, the immense skies and the silence. Since it's still a wild and untamed land, allow time for spontaneity – explore a new place mentioned by a *gaucho* you meet on your travels, or take up an offer of Argentine and Chilean hospitality.

One week

The Argentine Lake District is the most easily accessible region for a short visit. Base yourself near **Bariloche** and then either go south to **El Bolsón** and **Los Alerces National Park**, or north to **San Martín de los Andes** and **Pehuenia**, to catch a flavour of a different part of the lakes. Alternatively, fly direct from Buenos Aires to El Calafate for access to **Parque Nacional Los Glaciares**. From here you can either take a bus to El Chaltén to hike around **Cerro FitzRoy**, fly on to **Ushuaia** for the Tierra del Fuego national park and Harberton, or head across the border to Chile's **Parque Nacional Torres del Paine**. Allow time for long bus journeys between each place.

Two weeks

Two weeks in Patagonia will give you time to see the wildlife at **Península Valdés** on the Atlantic coast, including whales in spring, and then fly from Trelew to either **Bariloche** for the lakes or **El Calafate** for the glaciers. Two weeks in summer is perfect for exploring the Lake District in detail, with time for a longer trek, or for visiting two or three different areas. Consider hiring a cabaña and hanging out in Butch and Sundance country, or staying at an estancia to try your hand at riding. Alternatively, cross the border by bus and ferry via Lago Todos Santos to explore the southern **Chilean lakes** or via Los Alerces to the **Carretera Austral**. From Puerto Chacabuco, you may just have time to cruise to the **San Rafael glacier** in the southern Chilean fjords. If you fly in to Santiago, you could catch a plane south to **Puerto Montt** or even all the way down to **Punta Arenas**, in order to hike at Torres del Paine or for access to **Tierra del Fuego**. For a complete contrast, city lovers should spend 24 hours in **Buenos Aires** at the end of their trip, to enjoy clubbing and shopping in civilisation after the wide open spaces.

One month

A month allows you to get a real feel for Patagonia's scale and extraordinary contrasts. You could get off the not very beaten track to some remote estancias in **Santa Cruz**, drive along the isolated **Ruta 40** from Los Antiguos to El Calafate or cycle a stretch of the wild Carretera Austral to **Futaleufú** for whitewater rafting and fishing. From Puerto Montt, head north into the lakes, visit the mystical island of **Chiloe** or take the long ferry south to **Puerto Natales**. Combine short trips to Península Valdes, the glaciers, Ushuaia and Torres del Paine, ending up in the lakes to completely relax by a calm stretch of water surrounded by mountains.

1. Lago General Carrera 2. Estancia Oriental 3. San Rafael glacier
4. Parque Nacional Torres del Paine.

When to go

The Southern Hemisphere summer lasts from December to March. The weather can be positively warm in the Lake District but the far south suffers from very strong winds at this time. **January** and **February** are when Argentine and Chilean schools have their holidays, so the main tourist centres (Bariloche, San Martín, El Calafate, Pucón, Puerto Varas, Puerto Natales and Ushuaia,) can get impossibly busy and prices rise significantly. You should book flights, buses and accommodation as far ahead as possible. However, you'll still find plenty of less popular centres offering a good range of accommodation, close to the national parks. **December** and **March** are good months for trekking, just be aware that transport services may not be running so frequently in rural areas and that the weather may be more unpredictable. **April** and **May** are a spectacular time to visit both the Lake District and Tierra del Fuego, as the leaves turn golden and scarlet, and days can be clear and windless. Rainfall tends to be higher in these months, but the tourist areas are quieter. Easter week is a major holiday in Argentina, however, so book well ahead. Much of southern Patagonia closes down entirely for winter: much accommodation is shut from May to October, transport services run a reduced schedule and many passes across the Andes are closed by snowfall. However, if you like skiing, then this is the season to visit. The best months are **July** and **August**, although many resorts have snow from late June and until September. Ski resort accommodation and transport are generally well organized but bear in mind that July is a school holiday. The rich marine life on the Atlantic coast is most exciting in the spring, with whale-spotting possible from Península Valdés at its best in **September** and **October**. Elsewhere, there are fewer tourists and cheaper accommodation than during the summer but still enough daylight hours for trekking. Winds in the far south are less fierce at this time of year.

Sport and activities

Patagonia might well have been designed for adventure tourism. The spectacular geography offers a huge range of outdoor activities, from whitewater rafting and skiing to some of the finest trekking and fishing anywhere in the world. The infrastructure for 'soft' adventure tourism, such as a half-day's rafting on a Grade III river, or a day spent climbing a volcano, is particularly good in the Lake District. Patagonian estancias provide appealing bases for horseriding and wildife spotting, while further south, the terrain promises hardcore trekking and mountain biking. It is important to check the experience and qualifications of any agency offering expeditions to remote areas and also note that the season for outdoor activities is fairly limited. **CATA** (Consejo de Autoregulación de Aventura), T02-7358034, is an association of more reputable Chilean agencies, which regulates adventure tourism in the country. It works closely with the national park authority, **CONAF**, T02-2361416 (see page 54).

DESTINATION PATAGONIA
Travellers
TRAVEL CONSULTANCY FOR PATAGONIA SINCE 1990
With only one reliable contact in Patagonia you can organise anything. TRAVELLERS is the only English owned and run specialist tour operator based in Chile.
MEMBER OF
ASTA
American Society of Travel Agents
www.travellers.cl
patagonia@travellers.cl
phone/fax +56 (65) 262099

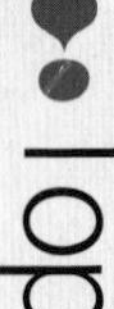

Top tips

Packing for Patagonia

You'll be able to buy most things you'll need once you're in Patagonia – and at cheaper prices than in much of Europe (except imported goods, which are prohibitively expensive) – but along with your basic luggage, bring a waterproof jacket, comfortable walking boots and a lightweight fleece top as a minimum. If you plan to do any outdoor activities, also pack a warm hat, thermal underwear, windproof trousers, wool or fleece jumpers, gloves, waterproof trousers (preferably Gore-Tex), shorts, and walking socks. Bring a smartish set of clothes for the odd night at a good hotel or restaurant, since Latinos tend to dress formally when they go out.

Wear a pouch under your clothes for your money and passport and bring a padlock if you're planning to stay in youth hostels. You should also carry a photocopy of your passport at all times. 35mm film is widely available but you should bring miniDV tapes for video cameras and/or memory cards for digital cameras. You'll also need a universal plug adaptor if you're bringing any electrical equipment. A torch (and spare batteries) can be useful for walking around remote, unlit villages at night and a folding knife is handy for camping, but remember not to carry it in hand luggage. Bring a pen and notebook to record your experiences. You'll need high-factor sun protection cream (particularly in the far south in spring), sun block for lips, sunglasses and insect repellent.

Climbing

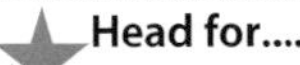

Head for....
Volcán Lanín, Cerro Catedral, Mount Tronador, Cerro Fitz Roy, Volcán Villarrica, Volcán Osorno, Cerro Picada, Torres del Paine.

Contact...
Dirección de Fronteras y Límites, *piso 5, Ministerio de Relaciones Exteriores, Bandera 52, Santiago, T02-6714210*. For permission to climb some mountains in border areas; apply 3 months in advance.
Federación de Andinismo de Chile, *Almte Simpson 77A, Santiago, T02-2220888, www.feach.cl*. Information on permits, expeditions and equipment hire to members. **Escuela Nacional de Montaña** (ENAM) is based at the same address (T02-2220799) for rock- and ice-climbing courses and the *Carnet de La Federación de Chile*, required to climb mountains in CONAF-controlled areas.

Cycling/mountain biking

Mountain biking is popular, particularly on descents from peaks around Bariloche and from *refugios* on volcanoes, such as Osorno. Longer routes include the Siete Lagos in the Lake District and the iconic Carretera Austral. See www.www.andescross.com and www.exchile.com

Head for...
Bariloche, Siete Lagos, PN Los Alerces, PN Villarrica, Puerto Varas, Carretera Austral.

Fishing

Patagonia has arguably the finest fly fishing in the world in incomparably beautiful surroundings. To fish anywhere in Argentina you need a permit costing US$5 per day, US$15 per week, US$50 per year. In Chile, a licence is required, whether for one day or a longer period, and is usually obtained from the local Municipalidad or some tourist offices.

Head for...
Junín de los Andes, Río Baker, Río Grande (Tierra del Fuego), Lago Blanco (Tierra del Fuego).

Contact
Fly Fishing Association of Argentina, *T011-4773 0821*, fishing licences.
Asociación de Pesca y Caza (Sernap), *San Antonio 427, piso 8, Santiago, T02-639 1918, www.sernapesca.cl, Mon-Fri 0900-1400*. Also consult the national park authorities, see p54, and check out www.aapm.org.ar, www.turismo.gov.ar /fishing, www.anglerstdf.com.ar, www.argentinachileflyfishing.com, www.MagallanesFlyFishing.com

Horse riding

A great way to get to the heart of Patagonia's rural tradition and to see some varied and specactular scenery. Expect to pay around US$6 per hour and always check the horses are in good condition. Many *estancias* offer good riding trips. See www.estanciasdesantacruz.com, www.raturstancias.com.ar and www.horsebackridingchile.cl.

Head for...
Estancias throughout Argentine Patagonia (see also p31).

Road trips and 4WD

The sheer size and remoteness of Patagonia means that long-distance road trips are an exhilarating way of exploring the region. What's more, the terrain of endless steppes interrupted by rivers, gorges and gullies, is also ideal for off-roading. The El Calafate area has several companies dedicated to taking tourists on hair-raising trips. Hiring 4WD vehicle, cost from US$1,500 for 10 days. Buy road maps in advance from the Automóvil Club Argentino (ACA) or the Automóvil Club de Chile. For more on driving in Patagonia, see p25.

Head for...
Siete Lagos, Villa Angostura to Puyehue, Trevelín to Futaleufú, Ruta 40 from Los Antiguos to El Calafate, Carretera Austral

Skiing

The season runs from mid-Jun to mid-Oct, but dates vary between resorts. Snow conditions become more slushy the further south you go and facilities in the far south of Chile are fairly basic. However, skiing on an active volcano looking down on five huge lakes (Villarrica/Pucón) or skiing within sight of the sea at the end of the world (Cerro Castor), are memories that will truly last a lifetime.

Head for...

Cerro Catedral (Bariloche), Cerro Bayo (Villa la Angostura), Cerro Chapelco (San Martín de los Andes), La Hoya (Esquel), Termas de Chillán, Villarrica/Pucón, Antillanca, Cerro Castor (Ushuaia).

Contact

www.interpatagonia.com
www.andesweb.com
www.southamericaskiguide.com
www.exchile.com/ski
www.powderquest.com

Trekking

The whole of the Andes region offers superb opportunities for both short and long treks in varied landscapes. The best season for walking is Dec-Apr. National parks in the Lake District are well suited to low-level treks, with signposted trails, guides and plenty of information. It's also worth exploring the lesser known lake regions, such as Pehuenia in the north, Los Alerces National Park and the Seven Lakes in Chile. The most dramatic trekking is in the south of Patagonia in the Parque Nacional los Glaciares, Parque Nacional Torres del Paine and Parque Nacional Tierra del Fuego. In Chile, over 1,000 km of hiking opportunities have been opened up by the building of the Carretera Austral, though heavy rainfall can be a drawback outside summer. The latest plan is the Sendero de Chile (www.senderodechile.cl), a walking route stretching all the way from the Peruvian border to Tierra del Fuego, which is due to be completed by 2010.

You should be reasonably fit before attempting any hikes in Patagonia, especially for overnight treks in the far south. Remember that conditions can be harsh at these latitudes and never overestimate your own abilities. Take account of the season, weather and terrain and make sure you are properly clothed and equipped. If trekking with a tour operator or guide, check their credentials, equipment and experience. You should avoid hiking

...one, even in popular tourist areas, and always register with *guardaparques*, or other authorities before you set out. Hikers have little to fear from the animal kingdom – in fact you are much more of a threat to the environment than vice versa; see How big is your footprint?, p6.

Head for...
Parque Nacional Lanín, Parque Nacional Nahuel Huapi, Cerro Fitz Roy (Parque Nacional Los Glaciares), Cerro Electrico (Parque Nacional Los Glaciares), Parque Nacional Villarrica, Parque Nacional Torres del Paine, Parque Nacional Tierra del Fuego

Contact
The national parks authorities, see p 54. See also www.visit-chile.org.

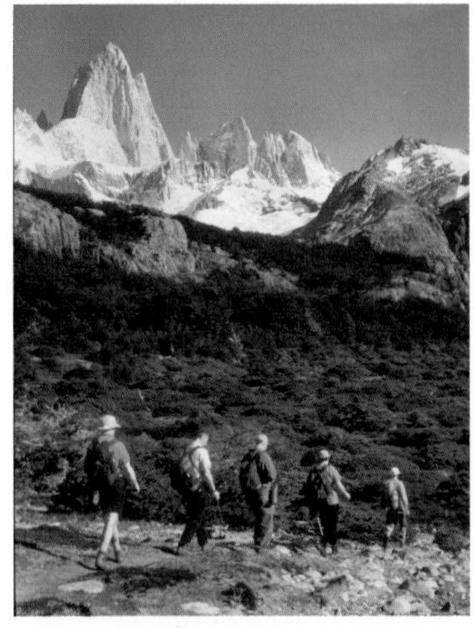

Watersports

Plenty of water and plenty to do including, canoeing, scuba diving, waterskiing, windsurfing and sailing. There's also sea kayaking around the islands off eastern Chiloé or in the fjords around Hornopirén. The tourist resorts in both lake districts offer a wide range of watersports.

Head for...
Bariloche, Río Aluminé, Lago Llanquihue, Villarica, Chiloé, Hornopirén.

Whitewater rafting

Rafting is generally well organized and equipment is usually of high quality. Access to the headwaters of most rivers is easy. Choose a reputable agency who are to be found in nearby towns. Rafts should carry no more than seven plus guide – six is ideal.

Head for...
Río Manso, Río Aluminé, Futaleufú, Pucón, Perohué.

Going further

Travelling

Once you've explored Patagonia there's plenty more of Chile and Argentina to visit for those with the time and the money. In order to experience the archetypal Argentina, head out from the capital, Buenos Aires, to the vast grasslands of the **pampas**, home of the *gaucho* (cowboy) and large *estancias*. In northwest Argentina, a string of cities gives access to the Andean foothills and the higher peaks. From Tucumán, there is a beautiful route through desert foothills to the fine city of **Salta**, departure point for the 'Train to the Clouds', which climbs to 4,475 m. In the northeast are the wetlands of Mesopotamia, the ruined Jesuit missions in Misiones and, of course, the magnificent **Iguazú Falls**, so huge they make Niagara look like a dripping tap.

In Chile, Santiago, is a good base for visiting the vineyards of the Central Valley and the Andean ski resorts. The appealing port city of **Valparaíso** and the Pacific beach resorts are only a couple of hours away or you could even hop on a plane to **Easter Island**. North of the capital, you can star-gaze around **La Serena**, or head into the Atacama desert to experience the lunar landscapes, hot geysers and salt flats around **San Pedro de Atacama**. In the far north is Arica, from where the road to Bolivia passes through the magnificent **Parque Nacional Lauca**, with its wealth of Andean bird and animal life, high lakes and remote volcanoes.

For further information, contact the **Latin American Travel Advisor**, PO Box 17-17-908, Quito, Ecuador; USA/Canada toll-free F888-2159511, international F593-2562566, www.amerispan.com /lata/, which offers a travel information service, country reports by email or fax, and a wide selection of maps. **South American Explorers**, T0800-274-0568, T607 277 0488, www.SAexplorers.org, has details on volunteer programmes, languages courses and guided tours in the region.

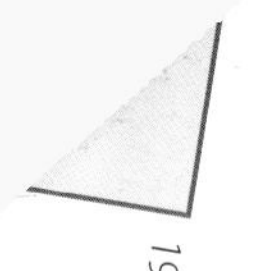

...s offer organized trips to Patagonia, ranging from a whistle-stop tour of ...ecialist trips that focus on a specific destination or activity. The advantage ... reputable operator is that your transport, accommodation and activities are all arranged for you in advance – particularly valuable if you only have limited time in the region or you don't speak Spanish. By travelling independently, however, you can be much more flexible and spontaneous about where you go and what you do. You will be able to explore less visited areas, practise your Spanish and you will save money, if you budget carefully. A list of specialist tour operators can be found in the Essentials A-Z, page 42.

Getting there and flying around

Arriving by air

It is not possible to fly directly to Patagonia from outside Argentina or Chile. Instead you must choose to fly into either Buenos Aires' **Ezeiza International Airport** (officially known as Ministro Pistarini; EZE; see page 59) or Santiago's **Aeropuerto Arturo Merino Benitez** (SCL; see page 213) and pick up any onward transport there. There are dozens of flights per week between Santiago and Buenos Aires, operated by **LanChile**, **Aerolíneas Argentinas**, **Air France**, **American** or **Avianca** (many depart at the same time, check carefully).

Fares vary from airline to airline and according to time of year. In the low season possible to get a return flight from London to Santiago or Buenos Aires for as little as £50 over £50 airport departure taxes), but in the high seasons (December/January and July/Augu this may rise to £750 return. Prices are comparable for flights from the USA, but from Australia and New Zealand they may rise to £1000 return or more. Discounted fares are offered through specialist agencies (see below) but always check the reservation with the airline concerned to make sure the flight still exists. Note that citizens of Mexico, Australia, Canada and the USA are charged a one-off reciprocal entry tax on arrival in Chile, valid for the lifetime of the passport.

Baggage Long-haul flights generally allow two pieces of luggage of up to 32 kg each. These limits are often not strictly enforced if the plane is not full, so if you know you are over the limit, arrive early. However, if you're planning on catching a connecting flight, bear in mind that weight limits for internal services are usually only 20 kg for economy class.

Flights from Europe

Flights to **Buenos Aires** from the UK take around 13 hrs, with **Aerolíneas Argentinas** (T020 7290-7887, www.aerolineas.com), **British Airways** (www.british-airways.com) and other major European carriers. Alternatively, there are daily connecting flights on one of the American carriers via New York or Miami (see below). It is impossible to fly directly to **Santiago** from London, so connections have to be made with **Aerolíneas Argentinas**, **British Airways** or **LanChile** (www.lanchile.com) via Buenos Aires; **Air France** (www.airfrance.com), via Paris; **Iberia** (www.iberia.com) or **LanChile**, via Madrid; **Lufthansa** (www.lufthansa.com), via Frankfurt; **Varig** (www.varig.com.br) via Rio de Janeiro or São Paolo. Flights from the UK take 16-20 hrs, including the change of plane.

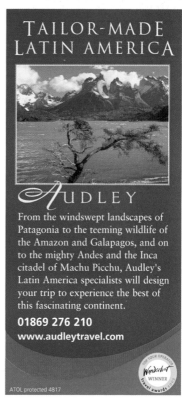

Flights from North America

Aerolíneas Argentinas and other South American and North American airlines fly to **Buenos Aires** from Miami, New York, Washington, Los Angeles, San Francisco, Atlanta, New Orleans, Dallas and Chicago. **Canadian Air International** and **LanChile** fly from Toronto and Montreal. **LanChile** flies to **Santiago** from Miami (9 hrs), New York (12 hrs) and Los Angeles (via Mexico City and Lima) and offers connections with sister airlines from Vancouver via Los Angeles, or from Toronto via New York. Other direct flights are provided by **American Airlines** (www.aa.com) and **Delta** (www.delta.com).

Flights from Australia, New Zealand and South Africa

Aerolíneas Argentinas and **Qantas** fly to **Buenos Aires** from Sydney (via Auckland). **LanChile/Air New Zealand** (www.airnz.co.nz) or **Aerolíneas Argentinas** (via Buenos Aires) fly from Auckland to **Santiago**. **South African Airways** flies from Johannesburg to both cities.

...ight agents

...merica, see Tour operators, p45.

Just the Ticket, *Level 2, 28 Margaret Street, London W1W 8RZ, T020-7291 8111, www.justtheticket.co.uk.* All-purpose ticket agency, often excellent deals.

STA Travel, *Priory House, 6 Wrights Lane, London W8 6TA, T08701-600599, www.sta.co.uk.* Specialists in low-cost student/youth flights, tours, insurance.

Trailfinders, *194 Kensington High Street, London W8 7RG, T020-7938 3939.* Sometimes has good deals to Latin America, especially at peak times. Also at *48 Earl's Court Road, London, W8 6EJ, T020-7938 3366*

In North America

Air Brokers International, *685 Market Street, Suite 400, San Francisco, CA 94105, T01-800-883 3273, www.airbrokers.com* Consolidator and specialist on RTW and Circle Pacific tickets.

Discount Airfares Worldwide On-Line, *www.etn.nl/discount.htm* A hub of consolidator and discount agent links.

International Travel Network/Airlines of the Web, *www.itn.net*, online air travel information and reservations.

STA Travel, *5900 Wilshire Blvd, Suite 2110, Los Angeles, CA 90036, T1-800-777 0112, www.sta-travel.com* Also branches in New York, San Francisco, Boston, Miami, Chicago, Seattle and Washington DC.

Travel CUTS, *187 College St, Toronto, ON, M5T 1P7, T1-800-667 2887, www.travelcuts.com* Student discount fares, IDs and other travel services. Branches in other Canadian cities.

Travelocity, *www.travelocity.com* Online consolidator.

Australia and New Zealand

Flight Centres, *82 Elizabeth St, Sydney, T13-1600; 205 Queen St, Auckland, T09-309 6171.* Branches in other towns and cities.

STA Travel, *T1300-360960, www.statravelaus.com.au 702 Harris St, Ultimo, Sydney, and 256 Flinders St, Melbourne.* In New Zealand: *10 High St, Auckland, T09-366 6673.* Also in major towns and university campuses.

... and leaving again

Check-in two hours before departure. Some airlines will perform check-in at their offices in the city the previous day, after which they require you to be at the airport just 45 minutes before departure. International departure tax (US$28 in Argentina; US$26 in Chile) can be prepaid; you should check if it's included in your ticket when you book.

Onward flights to Patagonia

From Buenos Aires All internal flights from Buenos Aires (as well as some flights to/from neighbouring countries) are handled from Jorge Newbery Airport, generally known as **Aeroparque**, situated 4 km north of the centre of Buenos Aires (see page 59). **Manuel Tienda León** (T011-4314 3636/0800-777 0078) runs very efficient buses between the two airports via the city centre every 30 minutes, 0600-0100, US$5. They have a desk inside the Ezeiza arrivals hall, where you can also book a remise taxi, US$35. From Aeroparque, the main air routes to Patagonia are to Bariloche (US$ 100 one way, 2 hrs 20 mins), to San Martín de los Andes (US$120, 2 hrs), to Trelew (US$100, 2 hrs), to El Calafate (US$120, 3 hrs 15 mins) and to Ushuaia (US$150, 3 hrs 20 mins).

From Santiago You will go through customs and immigration in international arrivals before transferring to the domestic section of the same terminal. **LanChile** (www.lanchile.cl) flies between Santiago and major cities under the banner **Lan Express**. A budget operator called **Sky** (www.skyairline.cl) also serves the main destinations but less frequently. The most important routes from Santiago are to Temuco, Puerto Montt,

Transport

There are no direct flights to Santiago from London and most routes fly via Buenos Aires anyway so, unless you want to focus exclusively on Chile, it makes sense for UK visitors to use the Argentine capital as their base for reaching Patagonia.

Travellers with limited time should consider flying. It offers fantastic views stretching from the Andes to the sea, and in some cases is even cheaper than taking a *salón cama* bus. The disadvantage, of course, is that it reduces your experience of the bits in between.

On long bus journeys, carry small packs of tissues and bottled water, since toilets on buses can be unpleasant. Also take a pullover to combat the fierce air-conditioning.

Diesel (gasoil) cars are much cheaper to run in Argentina and Chile than petrol (nafta) and the fuel is readily available.

Valdivia (via Temuco or Concepción), Osorno (via Temuco or Concepción), Balmaceda (Coyhaique, via Puerto Montt) and Punta Arenas (via Puerto Montt).

Air services in Argentina

Departure tax for domestic flights is US$14, payable at the airport. An additional 5% tax is included in the price of the ticket. The main operator is **Aerolíneas Argentinas** (www.aerolineas.com), which has 178 flights to Patagonia each week. They offer an **Airpass** for multiple flights within Argentina, but each leg of the journey is charged separately; all tickets have to be booked at the time you purchase your international flight, and the dates cannot be changed later. **Southern Winds** (T0810 777 7979 in Argentina, www.sw.com.ar) and **American Falcon** (T0810 222 3252 in Argentina, www.americanfalcon.com.ar) are an excellent alternative for foreign visitors and allow you to book flights once you arrive in Argentina – a few days' notice is generally fine, unless it's December/January, Easter or July. In addition the army airline **LADE** (T0810-810 5233 in Argentina, T+54 11-5129 9000, www.lade.com.ar), provides a weekly service connecting several towns in Patagonia, which is useful to avoid going back to Buenos Aires.

To save you returning to Buenos Aires, there are now frequent flights between Bariloche, Trelew (for Puerte Madryn), El Calafate and Ushuaia. Note that flights to El Calafate, Ushuaia and Bariloche are particularly heavily booked in high season. There also flights to Punta Arenas from Puerto Williams, Ushuaia and Porvenir and to Puerto Natales from El Calafate (summer only). It's wise to leave some flexibility in your schedule to allow for bad weather, which may delay flights in the south. Most provincial airports in Argentina have a desk offering tourist information, banking facilities and a *confitería* (cafeteria) as well as car hire. There are usually minibus services into the nearest town and taxis are available. Don't lose your baggage ticket; you won't be able to collect your bags without it.

Air services in Chile

Departure tax for domestic flights is US$8 each way (credit cards not accepted); additional tourists taxes are included in the price of the ticket. **LanChile** (www.lanchile.cl) is the main domestic operator. It sells a **Visit Chile Airpass**, consisting of three to six flight coupons that can be used on all **LanChile** routes within Chile (not Easter Island). This is only recommended if you are planning on doing several long-distance flights within Chile; visit the website in order to assess the price implications; domestic air taxes are payable in addition for each flight. The airpass must be purchased abroad at the same time as a transatlantic ticket to Chile and is valid for one month after the first flight coupon has been used. Note that the Airpass is more expensive if used in conjunction with an international flight with another carrier. Reservations should be made in advance; flight dates can be altered without penalty but route changes incur a charge of US$30 per change. A refund (minus 10%) can be obtained prior to travel.

LanChile sells cut-price tickets (up to 50% off) either as special promotions or to standby passengers, although availability is often limited. **Sky** may be cheaper on some routes. Note that flight times may be changed without warning; always double check the time of your flight when reconfirming. The most important Patagonian routes are Puerto Montt to Balmaceda or Punta Arenas; Punta Arenas to Puerto Williams, Ushuaia or Porvenir and Puerto Natales to El Calafate (summer only). Destinations in the far south are served by **DAP** (www.dap.cl) based in Punta Arenas. **LanChile** also flies from Santiago to Port Stanley on the Falkland (Malvinas) Islands via Punta Arenas and Río Gallegos.

Getting around by land and sea

Buses in Argentina

The country is connected by a network of efficient long-distance buses, which are by far the cheapest way of getting around. They run all year, are safe and comfortable, and long journeys are travelled overnight, which saves time, as long as you can sleep. The main operators are **Andesmar** (www.andesmar.com), **TAC** (T011-4312-7012), **Via Bariloche** (www.viabariloche.com) and **Tecni Austral** (in the south). You should book seats a day in advance in January. Regional bus services to tourist destinations within Patagonia tend to be much more limited after mid March. For general transport information, consult www.argentinatotal.com.ar. ▸▸ *Choosing your bus, page 25.*

Bus companies may give discounts to students with ID, and to teachers and university professors, with proof of employment. Discounts aren't usually available December to March. Make sure your seat number is on your ticket. Luggage is safely stored in a large hold at the back of the bus, and you'll be given a numbered ticket to reclaim it on arrival. *Maleteros* take the bags off the bus, and may expect a small tip – 50 centavos or a peso is fine.

Buses in Chile

Bus services in Chile are frequent, and on the whole, good, although they are slightly more expensive than equivalent services in Argentina. Buses tend to be punctual, arriving and leaving when they say they will. Along the Carretera Austral, however, services are far less reliable, less frequent and usually in minibuses. Services improve again between Punta Arenas and Puerto Natales in the far south. In addition, there are long-distance international services from Santiago to Buenos Aires, from Osorno to Bariloche, from Coyhaique to Comodoro Rivadavia and from Punta Arenas Río Gallegos.

Apart from at holiday times, there is little problem getting a seat on a long-distance bus and there is no need to reserve far in advance out of season. Prices are highest between December and March but competition between bus companies means you may be able to bargain for a lower fare, particularly just before departure, out of season; discounts are also often available for return journeys. Students and holders of Hostelling International cards may also get discounts out of season. Most bus companies will carry bicycles, but may ask for payment; on **TurBus** payment is mandatory. ▸▸ *Choosing your bus, page 25.*

Choosing your bus

Argentina

commún lots of stops (intermedios), uncomfortable, no recommended for long journeys

semi-cama slightly reclining seat, meals, toilet, loud videos

coche-cama/suite bus fully reclining seats, meals, toilet, loud videos, few stops, definitely worth the small extra expense for a good night's sleep.

Chile

All services travel the same routes and most will show videos on long journeys.

classico/salón-ejecutivo Comfortable enough for daytime travel.

semi-cama more leg room than *classico* and may stop in slightly fewer places. 50% more expensive.

salón-cama the most spacious, dinner available on overnight services. 50% more expensive than semi-cama. A premium service with fully reclining seats runs between Santiago and the lakes (30% more expensive than salón-cama).

Boat

In the Lake District, ferries on Lago Nahuel Huapi and Lago Frías in Argentina link with bus and ferry services across Lago Todos Santos in Chile (see page 119). There are also services across Lago Pirihueico. In the south of Chile, maritime transport is very important. The main transporter/car-ferry operators are **Transmarchilay** and **Navimag**, although there also companies offering more tourist-friendly services in summer. **Puerto Montt** is the hub for boat services south, with regular sailings to Chiloé, Chaitén, Puerto Chacabuco, Puerto Natales (one a week, year round) and the San Rafael glacier. **Punta Arenas** is the departure point for ferry services to Porvenir and Puerto Williams on Tierra del Fuego. Reservations are essential for the ferries in high summer. Details of all routes and booking information are given under the relevant chapters.

Car

Hiring a car is an excellent idea if you want to travel independently and explore the more remote areas of Patagonia, although it can be complicated to take a hire car across the border

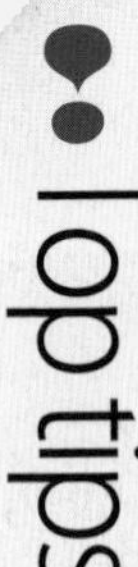

Over the border

The main routes between Argentine and Chilean Patagonia are by boat and bus between Bariloche and Puerto Montt in the Lake District; by road from El Calafate to Puerto Natales and Torres del Paine or by road and ferry from El Calafate via Río Gallegos to Tierra del Fuego. There are many other crossings (some little more than a police post), which are detailed in the appropriate part of the guide. See also http://www.difrol.cl/html/104a.htm. For some crossings, prior permission must be obtained from the authorities. Note that passes across the Andes may be blocked by snow from April onwards. » *Customs and duty free p33. Visas and immigration p47.*

General

✔ Crossing the border is not a lengthy procedure unless you're on a bus, when each individual is checked separately.
✖ It is your responsibility to ensure that your passport is stamped in and out when you cross borders. Do not lose your tourist card; replacing one costs trouble and possibly expense.
✔ Tourist card holders returning across a land border to Argentina will be given a further 90 days in the country. Visa holders should check regulations with the Chilean and Argentine embassies.
✖ Fruit, vegetables, meat, flowers and milk products may not be imported into Chile; these will be confiscated at all borders, where there are thorough searches.
✔ Immigration and customs officials are generally friendly, helpful and efficient, however, the police at Chilean control posts a little further into the country can be extremely bureaucratic.
✖ There are often no exchange facilities at the border so make sure you carry small amounts of both local currencies.
✔ Remember to change your watch if crossing the border from early March to September/October

By car

✔ Obtain an authorization form from the hire company. This is exchanged at the outgoing border control for a quadruple form, one part of which is surrendered on each side of the border. If you plan to leave more than once you will need to photocopy the authorization.
✔ Make sure the numberplate is etched on the car windows.
✔ Ensure that the hire company gives you the vehicle's ownership papers, which have to be shown at police and military checks.
✖ At some crossings, you must pay for the car's tyres to be sprayed with pesticides.

between Argentina and Chile (see above). The most important routes in Argentine Patagonia are Ruta 40, which runs along the west side of the Andes and faster Ruta 3, which runs down the Atlantic coast. Most of Chile is linked by the paved toll road, the **Pan-American Highway** (or Panamericana), marked on maps as Ruta 5, which runs all the way from the Peruvian

Route 40

frontier south to Puerto Montt. (A paved coastal route running the length of Chile is under construction, and should be ready by 2007.) The **Carretera Austral**, a *ripio* (gravel) road marked on maps as Ruta 7, runs south of Puerto Montt, punctuated by three ferry crossings, with a further crossing at Villa O'Higgins for those on the overland route (summer only) from the Carretera to the far south.

Generally, main roads are in good condition but on some *ripio* roads, particularly south of Puerto Montt, a high-clearance, four-wheel-drive vehicle is required, as road surfaces can degenerate to earth *(tierra)*. Most roads in Patagonia are single lane in each direction. There's little traffic and service stations for fuel, toilets, water and food are much further apart than in Europe and the States, so always carry water and spare fuel and keep the tank full. Safety belts are supposed to be worn, if fitted. **Hitchhiking** is relatively easy and safe (although you should always exercise caution) and often involves an exhilarating open-air ride in the back of a pick-up truck. However, traffic is sparse in the south, and roads in places like Tierra del Fuego rarely see more than two or three vehicles per day.

Car hire is more expensive in Chile than in Argentina. There are few hire cars available outside the main tourist centres in either country, although small towns will have cheaper deals. Hiring a car from one place and dropping it off in another is rarely practical since very high penalties are charged. The multinational car hire companies (**Hertz**, **Avis**) are represented all over Patagonia but local companies may be cheaper and tend to be just as reliable. You must be 25 or over in Argentina and 22 or over in Chile to hire a car; a national driver's licence should be sufficient. Vehicles may be rented by the day, the week or the month, with or without unlimited mileage. Rates quoted should include **insurance** and VAT but ALWAYS check first. Note that the insurance excess, which you'll have to pay if there's an accident, is extremely expensive. Check the vehicle carefully with the hire company for scratches and cracks in the windscreen before you set off, so

Fuel facts

In Chile, petrol (*nafta*) becomes more expensive the further south you go, but in Argentine Patagonia, fuel prices are a third lower than in the rest of the country; diesel (*gasoil*) is available in both countries and is much cheaper than petrol. Cars in Argentina are increasingly converting to gas GNC (*gas natural comprimido*), which costs about 25% of petrol. However, you will not be able to hire a GNC car outside Buenos Aires and fuel stations offering GNC are very limited in Patagonia. What's more, if you're taking a gas-run vehicle from Argentina into Chile, check that it will run on Chilean gas: there is a difference.

Travellers' tales

Trucks away

Gastre looked big on the map of central Patagonia, and I was obsessed with getting there. It was 400 miles along the road from Esquel to Puerto Madryn, but the only bus stopped 60 miles short. I got a lift, but arrived in Gastre the day after the weekly bus to the Atlantic coast had departed. I wasn't convinced that the attractive desolation of Gastre's nine square blocks, regularly laid out in an arid plateau at 3,000 ft, justified my trip. With little money and less food, I left the small town on foot, not knowing that for the next day and a half no vehicle would pass in my direction. A big mailbox at the entrance to an estancia was my shelter and a scorpion my only company that night in the desert. Gan Gan was my next destination; two kids and a drunk guy in a small truck picked me up. Beyond Gan Gan I had better luck and eventually reached the coast on a truck, whose cargo of wool 15 ft deep made the best bed I've ever slept on. *Nicholas Kugler*

that you won't be blamed for them on your return. Hire companies will take a print of your **credit card** as their guarantee instead of a deposit but are honourable about not using it for extra charges. Ensure that the hire company gives you the vehicle's ownership papers, which have to be shown at police and military checks (see also page 26).

Useful contacts

Automóvil Club Argentino, *Avenida Libertador Gen San Martín 1850, 1st floor, touring department on 3rd floor, 1425 Buenos Aires, T011-48026061/9, www.aca.org.ar*. This motoring association has fuel stations, hotels and hosterías, as well as offering a useful route service. Members of affiliated motor associations can use ACA facilities and benefit from discounts.

Automóvil Club de Chile, *Av Andres Bello 1863, Santiago, T02-431-1000, acchinfo@automovilclub.cl*, car-hire agency with discounts for members or affiliates. Also provides road maps.

Touring Club Argentino, *Esmeralda 605 and Tucumán 781, third floor, Buenos Aires T011-392-6742*. Similar travel services to ACA but no service stations.

Taxis, *colectivos* and *remises*

Taxis usually have meters and can either be hailed in the street or booked in advance, although they tend to be more expensive when booked from a hotel. Surcharges are applied late at night and at weekends. Agree fares beforehand for long journeys out of city centres or for special excursions; also compare prices among several drivers for this sort of trip.

Collective taxis (*colectivos* in Chile, *remise* taxis in Argentina), operate on fixed routes (identified by numbers and destinations) and are a good way of getting around cities. They are usually flagged down on the street corner and advertise charges in the front windscreen. (Make sure you have small notes and coins to pay the driver.) In Chile, *colectivos* also operate on some interurban routes, leaving from a set point when full; they compete favourably with buses for speed but not for comfort.

Train

A long-distance, overnight train service runs from Santiago to **Temuco**. A bunk in the modern sleeping car costs between US$20 and US$30 (see Chilean Lake District chapter). The only long-distance train within Patagonia runs from **Viedma** on the Atlantic Coast to **Bariloche** in the Lake District (see page 130). Patagonia's best known train, **La Trochita** (www.latrochita.org.ar; made famous by Paul Theroux as *The Old Patagonian Express*), is a purely tourist affair that departs from Esquel in the southern Lake District for the remote Mapuche station at Nahuel Pan (see page 135). Even more touristy is the **Tren del fin del Mundo** (www.trendelfindelmundo.com.ar), which travels from Ushuaia to the Tierra del Fuego national park (see page 366).

Sleeping

Tourist destinations in Patagonia and, especially in the Lake District, have a good range of **hotels** and **hosterías**, although on the Chilean side, there is good-value budget accommodation and some relatively high-end hotels, but not much choice in between. Hosterías have less than 20 rooms, rather than being lower quality; they are often family run and can be very good value in more remote areas. **Residenciales** and **hospedajes** tend to provide simpler accommodation but may also offer services geared specifically towards foreign backpackers, such as internet access, tours, bicycle hire, etc. **Hostales** traditionally offer dorm beds but many now also have double rooms for couples. **Cabañas** are well-equipped self-catering cottages, cabins or apartments, often in superb locations. They're very popular among Argentine holidaymakers and are a great option if you have your own transport and are travelling in a small group. **Camping** is very popular and there are many superbly situated sites with good facilities, although official Chilean campsites can be surprisingly expensive, with no reductions for single travellers or couples. There are also refuges (**refugios**) for walkers in national parks and reserves; standards of comfort and facilities vary hugely. Camping wild is generally safe, even in remote areas, but you should aways consult *guardaparques* before pitching your tent in a national park. ▸▸ *Estancias, p31.*

Accommodation in Argentina is excellent value for visitors from western countries. However, since the devaluation of the peso, a few of the more expensive hotels in major tourist centres charge higher dollar prices to foreigners; it's worth asking if there's a reduction for cash payment in pesos. Accommodation in Chile is just under double the price of equivalent accommodation in Argentina. Prices also tend to be higher in Santiago and the

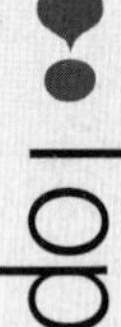

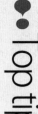

Top tips

A bed for the night

This guide focuses on the best accommodation in the mid-range category (A-D). Bottom-end budget accommodation has only been included if it represents excellent value for money or is the only option in a certain area. 'Budget buster' boxes highlight more expensive options that offer a really unique or special experience. The following price codes are used throughout the guide:

LL (+ **US$151**) and L (**US$101 -150**) Mostly top-quality **hotels**, offering very well-equipped rooms with dataports, plus a restaurant, bar, pool, health suite, business facilities and excellent service. Also luxurious **estancias** (see Home on the range, page 31) and several hotels in Torres del Paine, where you're paying for location not quality.

AL **US$81-100** and A **US$61-80** Comfortable **hotels**, with good facilities, airport transfers, tours, tourist information and buffet breakfasts. Rooms should have TV, minibar, safe and a/c. **Estancias** in these categories may have simpler accommodation than an ordinary hotel, but activities are usually included (see Home on the range, page 31).

A **US$46-60**, B **US$31-45** and C **US$21-30** The quality of **hotels** and **hosterías** in these categories varies widely but most are reliable, with en suite facilities and breakfast.

D **US$12-20** Good quality **residenciales** and **hospedajes**, especially in rural areas, where a lovely setting makes up for the lack of facilities; breakfast included. Also official Chilean **youth hostels** (www.hostellingcl.achatj.html), which charge rates per person; IYHA or Chilean YHA card required.

E **US$7-11**, F **under US$6** Simple **residenciales** and **hospedajes**, sometimes very basic, with shared bathrooms, but usually supplying a towel and toilet paper. In Chile rates are charged per person. Also beds in Argentine **youth hostels** (www.argentina hostels.com, www.hostels.org.ar), either in dorms (often mixed), with large communal bathrooms (US$7) or double rooms (from US$10). Some have cooking facilities, internet access, lockers, laundry and tours. At the very bottom end are Chilean **albergues**: usually just floor space in a school during the summer. They are very cheap (US$2-4 per person), very noisy and offer no privacy.

further south you go from Puerto Montt. However, single travellers do not come off too badly in southern Chile, as many *hospedajes* charge per person (although you may have to share your room). The Chilean government waives the VAT charge (IVA 19%) for bills paid in dollars (cash or travellers' cheques) at designated high-end hotels, but some establishments may get round this apparent discount by offering you a low dollar exchange rate. Prices often rise in high season (*temporada alta*), especially during January and February, but off-season you can often bargain for a discount (*descuento*) if you are staying for two or more days. The ski resorts are more expensive during the winter school holidays. During public holidays or high season you should always book ahead. Few places accept credit cards. In both countries you

Home on the range

Estancias (ranches) are found all over Argentina, especially in the province of Santa Cruz. In Patagonia they're usually devoted to sheep farming although many also offer tourist accommodation, horseriding and other activities, such as birdwatching and trekking, quite apart from the authentic experience of life on the land.

A *dia de campo* (day on the farm) typically includes horseriding (or a ride in a horse-drawn carriage), a lunch of *asado*, and then other farm activities, or time to relax in the peaceful grounds. For a more in-depth experience, choose to stay for a few nights. Estancias can be pricier than hotels, but since devaluation, they are accessible even to travellers on a budget. Rates per night vary between US$50 for two in the most humble places, up to US$150 per person with all meals drinks, transfers and activities included. Reservations should be made about two weeks in advance.

Although estancias are found throughout Argentine Patagonia, they vary enormously in style and activities. **Maipú, Helsingfors** and **Alma Gaucha** are giant sheep farms overlooking glaciers, mountains and lakes. **Viamonte** and **Harberton** on Tierra del Fuego are infused with the compelling history of the early pioneers who built them, while on the mainland nearby, **Monte Dinero** has a colony of Magellanic penguins on its doorstep.
The best estancias are mentioned throughout the guide, but for more information consult **www.estanciasdesantacruz.com, www.tierrabuena.com.ar; www.southtrip.com and www.turismo.gov.ar.**

should establish clearly in advance what is included in the price before booking. For further information on accommodation, consult www.patagonia-chile.com, www.interpatagonia.com, www.backpackersbest.cl, www.backpackerschile.com and www.chile-hotels.com

Eating and drinking

Huge buffet-style 'American breakfasts' are served in international hotels but elsewhere, breakfast (*desayuno*) is a very simple affair. Lunch (*almuerzo*) is eaten any time from 1300 to 1530 and is followed, in Argentina, by a siesta. At around 1700, many Argentines go to a *confitería* for *merienda* – tea, sandwiches and cakes, while Chileans have a snack meal known as *las onces* (literally elevenses). Restaurants open for dinner (*cena*) at about 2000 in Chile but rarely before 2100 in Argentina, where most people don't eat until 2230 or later.

By law, restaurants in Chile have to serve a cheaper fixed-price meal at lunch time (US$2-3), called *la colación* or *el menu*. In Argentina this is known as *el menu fixo*. Those on a tight budget should also try *tenedor libre* (free fork) restaurants, where you can eat all you want for a fixed price.

Food and drink

Eat ...
Patagonian lamb cooked *al asador* on an estancia
Smoked trout in the Lake District
arroz con mariscos (similar to paella) at Puerto Madryn
a Welsh tea at Gaiman in the Chubut valley.
Centolla (king crab) at Punta Arenas
Curanto (seafood and meat stew) on Chiloé

Drink...
Argentine wine from Mendoza
Homemade beer around El Bolsón
Chilean wine from the Maipo valley
Pisco from the Alto del Carmén distillery

Try...
guanaco meat
Mate (a tea made from yerba leaves)
picorocos (giant barnacles) on the Pacific coast

Avoid...
Eating shellfish that you have bought unofficially in the far south of Chile because of the poisonous 'marea roja' (see page 329).
Ordering *café* in Chile - you'll get hot water and some instant coffee granules.
Being vegetarian; your diet will be very limited unless you self-cater.

Food and drink

Argentina may not have a particularly sophisticated cuisine, but it doesn't really need one: the meat is legendary. The classic meal is the *asado* – beef or lamb (in Patagonia) cooked over an open fire. In rural areas, a whole lamb is splayed out on a cross-shaped stick at an angle over the fire (*al asador*). *Parrilla* restaurants, found all over Argentina, grill cuts of meat in much the same way; they can be ordered as individual dishes or as *parrillada* (basically a mixed grill). Other meat to try includes wild boar in Bariloche and even guanaco. Italian immigration has left a legacy of pizza, *pasta casero* (homemade pasta) and *ñoquis* (gnocchi). Perhaps the most outstanding ingredient in Chilean cuisine is the seafood. Some of the best is to be had at Angelmo (Puerto Montt). The most popular fish are *merluza* (a species of hake), *congrio* (ling), *corvina* (bass – often served marinated in lemon juice as *ceviche*), *reineta* (a type of bream), *lenguado* (sole) and *albacora* (sword fish). There is an almost bewildering array of unique shellfish, particularly *erizos*, *machas*, *picorocos* and *locos*. The local *centolla* (king crab) is also exquisite.

Both Argentine and Chilean wine is excellent, and even the cheapest varieties are very drinkable. The best are from Mendoza in Argentina and from the Central Valley in Chile. Also try the home-brewed beer around El Bolsón in Argentina. Cider (*chicha de manzana*) is popular in southern Chile. The most famous spirit in Chile is *pisco*, made with grapes and usually drunk with lemon or lime juice as *pisco sour* or mixed with coca cola or sprite. The great Argentine drink is *mate* (pronounced mattay), an important social convention (see The mate ritual, page 40).

Accidents

Contact the relevant emergency service and your embassy (see p34). Make sure you obtain police/ medical reports required for insurance claims.

	Argentina	Chile
Ambulance	107	131
Coastguard		138
Fire service	100	132
Police	101	133
Air Rescue Service		138

Children

Chileans and Argentines are incredibly warm and receptive to children and will go out of their way to make them welcome. More expensive hotels provide a baby-sitter service; children's meals are offered in many restaurants and most have high chairs. Self-catering *cabañas* may be the best sleeping option for families as they are good value and well-equipped.

For most tourist attractions, there are cheaper prices for children; on sightseeing tours try and bargain for a family rate. Chilean domestic airlines charge around 66% for children under 12 but fares on long-distance buses in both Argentina and Chile are calculated for each seat, so you'll have to seat small children on your knee to save money. Bear in mind that distances are long; consider flying if possible. Trekking and adventure tourism in Patagonia are not really suitable for young children and the climate is often too cold, wet and windy for them.

Advice

→ Be very careful about sunburn in the south, due to the lack of ozone.
→ If your child has special dietary needs, learn the appropriate Spanish phrases.
→ Order mineral water rather than tap water
→ Take water, fruit, biscuits, tissues, games and books on long bus journeys; the videos shown on board are generally action movies, not suitable for under 12s.

Customs and duty free

Argentina

Visitors coming from countries not bordering Argentina are exempt from taxes on articles brought into the country, including new articles up to US$300, and an additional US$300, if goods are purchased at duty free shops within Argentina. You can claim back tax (IVA) at the airport when you leave the country, if you've bought goods over the value of US$23 and have the receipts. Ask for the necessary form when you buy goods, and take it to the IVA desk at check in.

Chile

The following may be brought into Chile duty free: 500 cigarettes or 100 cigars or 500 g of tobacco, plus three bottles of liquor, and all articles for personal use, including vehicles, radios, portable tape recorders, cameras, personal computers, and similar items. Fruit, vegetables, meat, flowers, seeds and milk products may not be imported into Chile; these will be confiscated at all borders, where there are thorough searches.

Disabled travellers

Facilities for the disabled in Argentina and Chile are sorely lacking. Wheelchair users won't find many ramps or even lowered kerbsides; pavements tend to be shoddy and broken even in big cities, and only a few upmarket hotels have been fully-adapted for wheelchair use. Tourist sights, particularly in National Parks, generally only have limited access for disabled visitors. However, the best museums have ramps or lifts and some may offer special guided tours for the visually- or hearing-impaired: the superb dinosaur museum in Trelew is setting the pace here. Boat trips to some of the glaciers should also be possible with prior arrangement. Airlines are extremely helpful, especially if you let them know your needs in advance; long-distance buses can't accommodate wheelchairs but drivers will help those with some mobility. Argentines and Chileans generally go out of their way to help you, making up for poor facilities with kindness and generosity. Speaking Spanish is obviously a great help, and travelling with a companion is advisable.

Useful organizations

Directions Unlimited, *123 Green Lane, Bedford Hills, NY 10507, T1-800-533-5343, T914-241 1700*. A tour operator specializing in tours for disabled US travellers.

Disability Action Group, *2 Annadale Ave, Belfast BT7 3JH, T01232-491011*. Information about access for British disabled traveller.

Disabled Persons' Assembly, *PO Box 27-524, , Wellington 6035, New Zealand, T04-801-9100, gen@dpa.org.nz*. Has lists of tour operators and travel agencies catering for the disabled.

Drugs

Using drugs, even soft ones, without medical prescription is illegal and penalties are severe – up to 10 years' imprisonment – even for possession. In this connection, the planting of drugs on travellers by traffickers or the police is not unknown. If offered drugs on the street, make no response at all and keep walking. Note that people who roll their own cigarettes are often suspected of carrying drugs and can be subjected to intensive searches. It is advisable to stick to commercial brands of cigarettes.

Electricity

220 volts AC. Either 2 or 3 flat-pin plug. You are advised to bring a universal adapter, as these not readily available.

Embassies and consulates

Argentine

Australia, *100 Miller Street, Suite 6, Level 30, North Sydney, New South Wales 2060, T02-922 7272, F02-923 1798*.

Canada, *90 Sparks Street, Suite 910, Ottawa KIP 5B4, T1-613-236 2351, F1-613-235 2659*.

Chile *Miraflores 285, Casilla 9867, Santiago de Chile, T02-639 8617/638 0890/633 1076, F02-639 3321*.

New Zealand, *11th Floor, Harbour View Building, 52 Quay Street, PO Box 2320, Auckland, T09-309757*.

United Kingdom, *27 Three Kings Yard, London, W1Y 1FL, T020-7318 1340, F020-7318 1349*.

United States, *12 West 56th Street, New York 10019, T1-212-603 0400, F1-212-3973523*.

Chilean

Find Chilean embassies and consulates around the world at www.minrel.cl/pages/misiones/index.html

Argentina, *Tagle 2762, Buenos Aires 1425, T011-4802 7020, F011-4804 5927, data@embajadadechile.com.ar* Also consulates up and down the country.

Australia, *10 Culgoa Circuit, O'Malley Act 2606, PO Box 69, Canberra, T02-6286 2430, F02-6286 1289, chilemb@embachile australia.com* Also in Melbourne and Sydney.

Canada, *50 O'Connor Street, Suite 1413, Ottawa, Ontario K1P 6L2, T1-613-235 4402, F1-613-235 1176, echileca@chile.caglobalx.net* Also in Montreal, Toronto and Vancouver.

Ireland, *44 Wellington Road, Ballsbridge, Dublin 4, T 01-2692575, embachileirlanda@eircom.net*
New Zealand, *19 Bolton Street, Wellington, T04-471 6270, F04-472 5324, echile@embchile.co.nz*
UK, *12 Devonshire Street, London, W1G 7DS, T020-7580 6392, F020-7436 5204., cglonduk@congechileuk.demon.co.uk*
USA, *1732 Massachusetts Ave NW, Washington DC 20036, T1-202-785 1746, F1-202-887 5579, embassy@embassy ofchile.org* Also consulates across the Union.

Gay and lesbian travellers

In a macho culture, it is no surprise that there is quite a lot of homophobia in Chile and Argentina. Away from the capital cities, gay men and lesbian women are not encouraged to be open about their sexuality, and there are few places where you can go to meet other gay/lesbian friends.

Useful contacts

www.pride-travel.com.ar, a helpful Argentine agency, organizing tours and trips, nights out in Buenos Aires and travel advice for the rest of the country.
www.thegayguide.com.ar, tips on Buenos Aires gay scene
www.gaychile.com, gay-friendly hotel reservations and info on gay-friendly shops and other establishments.
Novellus *Almirante Pastene 7, Of 54, Providencia, Santiago, T02-2518547, novellus@tempotravel.cl*, a specialist travel agency for gays and lesbians.

Health

No vaccinations are demanded by immigration officials in Chile or Argentina, but you would do well to be protected by vaccination against typhoid, polio, hepatitis A and tetanus. Children should, of course, also be up-to-date with any immunisation programmes in their country of origin. See your GP or travel clinic at least six weeks before departure for general advice on travel risks and vaccinations. Try ringing a specialist travel clinic if your own doctor is unfamiliar with health in the region. Make sure you have sufficent medical travel insurance, get a dental check, know your own blood group and if you suffer a long-term condition such as diabetes or epilepsy, obtain a Medic Alert bracelet/ necklace (www.medicalalert.co.uk).

Health risks

Temperate regions of South America, like Patagonia, present far fewer health risks than tropical areas to the north. However, travellers should take precautions against the following: **diarrhoea/intestinal upset**; **hanta virus** (carried by rodents and causing a flu-like illness); **hepatitis A**; **hypothermia**; **marea roja** (see Fishy business, p329); **rabies**; **sexually transmitted diseases**; **sun burn** (a real risk in the far south due to depleted ozone); **ticks**.

Further information

www.btha.org British Travel Health Association.
www.cdc.gov US government site that gives excellent advice on travel health and details of disease outbreaks.
www.fco.gov.uk British Foreign and Commonwealth Office travel site has useful information on the country, people, climate and a list of UK embassies/consulates.
www.fitfortravel.scot.nhs.uk A-Z of vaccine/health advice for each country.
www.travelscreening.co.uk Travel Screening Services gives vaccine and travel health advice, email/SMS text vaccine reminders and screens returned travellers for tropical diseases.

Insurance

Always take out comprehensive insur- before you travel, including full cover and extra cover for any activities (hiking, rafting, skiing, riding etc) that you may undertake. Check exactly what's being offered, the maximum cover for each element and also the excess you will have to pay in the case of a claim. Keep details of your policy and the insurance company's telephone number with you at all times and get a police report (*constancia*) for any lost or stolen items.

Internet

The best way to keep in touch is undoubtedly by email. Broad band is widely available in Argentina, even in remote areas and, although connection speeds tend to be slower in Chile, most services are adequate for a traveller's needs. Dedicated centres/internet cafés are widespread, particularly in towns and tourist centres and most *locutorios* ('phone centres) also have an internet connection. Prices vary from US$0.30 to US$1 per hour in Argentina, rising up to US$3 per hour in Chile. To access the @ symbol, you usually press the ctrl and alt keys together with q.

Language

Although English is understood in many major hotels, tour agencies and airline offices (especially in Buenos Aires and Santiago), travellers are strongly advised to learn some Spanish before setting out. Argentines and Chileans are welcoming and curious, and they're very likely to strike up conversation on a bus, shop or in a queue for the cinema. They're also incredibly hospitable (even more so away from the capital cities), and are quite inclined to invite you for dinner, to stay or to t... vel with them, and your attempts to ... panish will be enormously ...d. Spanish language classes are ... ow cost in a number of ... and Argentina. ... Box 58129, Philadelphia, ... 1100 (worldwide) *T1-800-879 6640 (USA, Canada) F215-751 1986, www.amerispan.com*, runs Spanish immersion programmes, educational tours, volunteer and internship positions throughout South America.

Spanish Abroad, *5112 N 40th Street, Suite 103, Phoenix, AZ85018, T1-888 722 7623 (toll free)/1-602 778 6791/0800-028 7706 (UK freephone), www.spanishabroad.com*, offers courses in Buenos Aires and Santiago, with tailor-made programmes, airport pickup and excursions.

Argentina

The distinctive pronunciation of Argentine Spanish is Italian-influenced – in Buenos Aires, you might even here the odd word of *lunfardo* Italian-orientated slang. It varies from standard Spanish chiefly in the replacement of the 'll' and 'y' sounds by a soft 'j' sound, as in 'beige'. The 'd' sound is usually omitted in words ending in 'd' or '-ado', and 's' sounds are often omitted altogether at the ends of words. 'S' before a consonant is usually pronounced as a Scottish or German 'ch', so that *mosca* becomes a kind of *moch-ka*. In the conjunction of verbs, the accent is on the last syllable. The big change, grammatically, is that the Spanish 'tú' is replaced by 'vos' and is used almost universally instead of 'usted'.

Chile

Chilean pronunciation is very quick and lilting, with final syllables cut off and can present difficulties to the foreigner, even those that speak good standard Spanish. Chileans also have a wide range of unique idioms that even other Latin Americans find difficult to understand, In rural areas of Region IX, travellers may encounter Mapudungu, the Mapuche language.

Media

Newspapers and magazines

The *Buenos Aires Herald* (www.buenosairesherald.com) is a daily English-language paper, with domestic

Cash in hand

- At ATMs, withdraw $99 instead of $100 to give you a supply of small notes.
- ATMs in Argentina give out the cash and receipt before the card is returned: don't walk away without your card.
- Make sure you have the card emergency number to hand in case your credit/debit card is lost or stolen: Mastercard T0800-5550507; Visa T0800-32222.

news and a brief digest of world news. *News Review* (newsrevi@mcl.cl) is a similar Chilean publication. Few foreign-language newspapers are available outside Buenos Aires and Santiago but Spanish speakers may want to check out the national dailies, especially *La Nación* (www.lanacion.com.ar) and *Clarín* (www.clarin.com.ar), both of which have good websites and excellent Sunday travel sections. Visitors should also look at *Lugares*, a glossy but informative monthly travel magazine with superb photography. It often has an English translation at the back.

Radio and television

The **BBC World Service** broadcasts at 97.1Mhz from noon to 0500 in Argentina, but no longer transmits to Chile. Many hotels have cable TV in the rooms, but rarely have any English news channels.

Money

The unit of currency in **Argentina** is the peso ($) = 100 centavos. Peso notes in circulation are 2, 5, 10, 20, 50 and 100. Coins in circulation are 1, 5, 10, 25 and 50 centavos and 1 peso. US dollar bills are also widely accepted. In **Chile**, the unit is also the peso ($). Peso notes in circulation are 1,000, 2,000, 5,000, 10,000 and 20,000 (only in Santiago); coins come in denominations of 1, 5, 10, 50, 100 and 500 pesos.

Exchange rates in Argentina £1 = Arg $5.64; €1 = Arg $3.92; US$1 = Arg $2.95; Chilean $100 = Arg $0.50.
Exchange rates in Chile £1 = Ch $1,125; €1 = Ch $783; US$ = Ch $588; Arg $ = Ch $200.

ATMs and credit cards

In general, the easiest way to get cash while you're in Patagonia is to use an international credit or debit card at an ATM (*cajero automático*). These can be found in every town or city (with the notable exceptions of El Chaltén in Argentina and along the Carretera Austral, where the only ATM is in Coyhaique), with instructions available in English. Maestro, Mastercard, Plus/Visa and Cirrus are all widely accepted. In Chile, ATMs operate under the sign **Redbanc** and will accept daily transactions of up to US$400. A full list of Redbanc machines in Chile is listed by town at www.redbanc.cl. Commission is usually around 2-3%, but check with your card company before leaving home. You may also be charged a cash handling fee.

Credit cards are generally accepted for payment only in large hotels, city shops and restaurants and for expensive tours. In shops, identification is usually necessary. Credit card use does not usually incur a commission or higher charge in Chile, and places accepting Visa and Mastercard usually display a 'Redcompra' sticker in the window, but in parts of Argentina commission of 10% is often charged.

Changing money

Most major towns in both countries have **bureaux de change** (*casas de cambio*). They are often simpler and quicker to use than banks but may not have the best rates, so shop around. US dollars (US$) and euros (€) are usually easier to change than other currencies but will only be accepted if clean and unblemished. Travellers to rural areas of Chile should carry supplies of 1,000-peso notes, as higher denominations are difficult to change. **Traveller's cheques** are not very convenient for travel in Patagonia. The exchange rate for traveller's cheques is often lower than for cash and the commission can be very high (usually 10% in Argentina).

Cost of travelling

Since devaluation of the peso, Argentina has become relatively cheap for foreign visitors from most western countries. Long-distance bus travel on major routes is very cheap (see Getting around, page 24), comfortable accommodation with a private bathroom and breakfast costs no more than US$25 for two people, while dinner in the average restaurant will be around US$8 per person including wine. Having said that, touristy areas such as El Calafate, Ushuaia and Buenos Aires can be much pricier than the rest of the country.

Chile is more expensive than Argentina and southern Chile is even more expensive from 15 December to 28 February. You should budget on a minimum of US$250 per person per week for basic accommodation, food, overland transport and an occasional tour. With a budget of US$500 a week, you will be able to stay in nice hotels, eat in smart restaurants and not stint yourself on excursions and nightlife.

Police and the law

The police in Chile and Argentina are usually courteous and will be helpful to tourists. However, you should always be wary of anyone who claims to be a plain clothes policeman. If you get into trouble, the worst thing that you can do is offer a bribe, as this will be seen as both an insult and an admission of guilt.

Legal penalties for most offences are fairly similar to what you might expect in a western European or North American country, although the attitude towards possession of soft drugs, such as cannabis, is very strict. If you get into trouble, your first call should be to your consulate, which should be able to put you in touch with a lawyer who speaks your language.

Post

Argentina

The post service is reliable, but for assured delivery, register everything. Letters take 10-14 days to get to Europe and the USA. Post (including small parcels up to 2kg) can be sent from the *Correo* (post office) or through the private postal service Oca from any shop displaying the purple sign. Larger parcels must be sent from the town's main post office, where they are examined by customs and then taken to 'Encomiendas Internacionales' for posting. All incoming packages are also opened by customs. Poste restante (*lista de correo*) is available in every town's main post office.

Chile

The Chilean postal system is usually efficient. Letters to Europe/North America cost US$0.65 (add US$0.80 to register them). Surface mail rates for parcels to Europe cost US$16 for less than one kilo; US$20 for one to three kilos. The *lista de correos* (poste restante) service only holds mail for 30 days, then returns it to sender. The Central Post Office in Santiago is good and efficiently organized, but letters are kept separately for men and women so poste restante envelopes should be marked Sr or Sra/Srta.

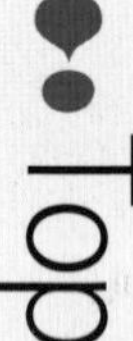

Top tips

The mate ritual

Wherever you go in Argentina, you'll see groups of people sharing a *mate* (pronounced mattay). Whatever their class, or job, everyone, from students and upwards, drinks several *mates* a day. Dried yerba leaves, similar to tea, are placed in a hollowed out gourd into which hot water (not boiling) is poured, and the resulting infusion is drunk through a metal straw with a filter at the bottom. The cup is filled with water for each person in the group, who then drinks in turn. If offered, give it a go, but be prepared for the bitter taste; you can add a little sugar to make it more palatable. The experience of sharing a *mate* is a great way to make Argentine friends and also to find out what really makes the country tick.

Public holidays

The main holiday period is in January and February when schoolchildren are on holiday and most families go away for a few weeks. All popular tourist destinations become extremely busy at this time and you should book transport and accommodation in advance. Banks, offices and most shops close on public holidays although transport should run as normal, except on 25 and 31 Dec.

Argentina

1 Jan, Good Friday, 2 Apr (Veteran's Day), 1 May, 25 May, 10 Jun, 20 Jun, 9 Jul, 17 Aug, 12 Oct (Columbus Day), 8 Dec (Immaculate Conception Day), 25 Dec.

Chile

1 Jan, Good Friday, 1 May, 21 May, 15 Aug, 1st Mon in Sep (Day of National Unity), 18-19 Sep (Independence), 12 Oct (Columbus Day), 1 Nov, 8 Dec, 25 Dec.

Safety

Following the economic breakdown of 2001/2, petty crime in Argentina increased dramatically, especially in Buenos Aires. Recently, improved stability has meant that crime is less prevalent but security remains a concern in certain areas of Buenos Aires, especially La Boca. Chile is generally a safe country to visit but, like all major cities, Santiago does have crime problems. Elsewhere, the main threats to your safety are more likely to come from natural hazards and adventure activities than from incidents of crime. Don't hike alone in remote areas and always register with *guardaparques* (rangers) before you set off.

General advice

→ Keep valuables out of sight.
→ Keep all documents and money secure.
→ Split up your main cash supply and hide it in different places.
→ Lock your luggage together with a chain/ cable at bus or train stations.
→ At night, take a taxi between transport terminals and your hotel.
→ Use the hotel safe deposit box and keep an inventory of what you have deposited. Notify the police of any losses and get a written report for insurance.
→ Look out for tricks, used to distract your attention and steal your belongings.
→ Don't fight back – it is better to hand over your valuables rather than risk injury.

Student travellers

If you are in full-time education you are entitled to an International Student Identity Card, which is distributed by student travel offices and travel agencies in

77 countries. The **ISIC** (www.isic.org) gives you special prices on all forms of transport and access to a variety of other concessions and services, including an emergency helpline (T+44-20-8762-8110). In Chile, alternative student ID cards can be obtained from Providencia 2594, Local 421, Santiago, and cost US$8 (photo and proof of status required).

Telephone

In both countries, avoid calling from hotels, which charge very inflated prices.

Argentina

Locutorios (phone centres) are abundant in Argentina and are the easiest way to make a call. They have private booths where you can talk for as long as you like and pay afterwards, the price appearing on a small screen in your booth. They often have internet, photocopying and fax services too.

For local calls, if you can't find a locutorio, use a public payphone, minimum 25 centavos. For long-distance and international calls, use phone scratch cards, available from kioskos and *locutorios* for 5 or 10 pesos; two good brands are Argentina Global and Hable Mas. Dial the free 0800 number on the card, followed by the code on the card (scratch the silver panel to reveal it) and then the international number. These cards can usually be used in *locutorios* too, but the rates are more expensive.

If calling to Argentina from abroad, dialy the country code (54) and then the area code of the place you want to call. Once in Argentina, dial 0 before each area code. For international calls form Argentina, dial 00, the country code and city code. Note that tariffs are reduced from 2200 to 0800.

Chile

There are eight main phone companies (carriers) offering competing rates, which are widely advertised. The cheapest call centres (known as *centro de llamados*) tend to be run by CTC or by small independent operators. National calls cost around US$0.10 per min. A call to a mobile costs US$0.25-0.30 per min.

Telephone boxes (more widespread than call centres) are programmed to direct calls via one carrier and can be used for local, long-distance and collect calls. They accept coins or pre-paid phone cards (CTC are the most common). To make a local call, simply dial the number you require and pay the rate charged by the carrier who owns the booth. To make an inter-urban call, dial '0' plus the area code (DDD) and the number; if you wish to select a carrier, dial its code before the area code (leaving out '0'), then the number. To make an international call, you will need a phone card; dial '00' before the country code.

Mobile phones

If you plan on using a mobile phone on your travels, you're advised to hire one locally, as international roaming is not available in all areas. Major airports and hotels often have rental desks, or can advise on local outlets.

Phone facts

	Argentina	Chile
IDD	+54	+56
International access code	00	00
Operator	19	130
International operator	000	n/a
Directory enquiries	110	103
International directory enquiries	110	n/a
Mobile phone prefix	area code +15	08 or 09

Time

Argentina is 3 hrs behind GMT. Chile is 4 hrs behind early Mar-Sep/Oct and 3 hours behind mid Sep/Oct-early Mar.

Tourist information

For national parks, see p54.

Argentina

Tourism authorities in Argentina are generally better equipped than their Chilean counterparts. You might have to be patient in some parts of the country, even when requesting the most basic information, but the major centres of Bariloche, San Martín del los Andes, Villa la Angostura, Puerto Madryn, El Calafate and Ushuaia, all offer good tourist resources and reliable websites. Staff in these popular tourist areas usually speak at least some English and opening hours are long – typically 0800-2000 in summer although they may close at weekends or during low season. Provincial websites, with information on sights and accommodation, can be accessed via the excellent government tourist website: www.turismo.gov.ar. Also consult www.patagonia.com.ar and www.interpatagonia.com. For free information anywhere in the country phone T0800-555 0016 (0800-2000 daily).

Chile

The national secretariat of tourism, **Sernatur**, (www.sernatur.cl), has provincial offices in Temuco, Osorno, Puerto Montt, Ancud, Coyhaique, Punta Arenas and Puerto Natales (addresses are given under the relevant destination). These can provide town maps, leaflets and other useful information, otherwise contact head office in Santiago. Other towns have municipal tourist offices.

For information, contact **Tourism Promotion Corporation of Chile**, *Antonio Bellet 77, Oficina 602, Providencia, Santiago, T02-2350105*. Useful websites : www.visit-chile.org, www.gochile.cl, www.chile-outdoors.cl, plus region-specific sites: www.patagoniachile.cl and www.chileaustral.com.

Tour operators

In Europe

Audley Travel, *6 Willows Gate, Stratton Audley, Oxfordshire, OX27 9AU, T01869 276210, www.audleytravel.com*
Tailor-made tours to Patagonia and other Latin American destinations.

Austral Tours, *20 Upper Tachbrook St, London SW1V 1SH, T020-72335384, F72335385, www.latinamerica.co.uk*
Interesting and imaginative tours of Chile and Argentina.

Condor Journeys and Adventures,

2 Ferry Bank, Colintraive, Argyll, PA22 3AR, UK, T 01700 841318, www.condorjourneys-adventures.com Adventure and ecological tour specialist including expeditions, Magellan Strait cruises and estancia visits.

Encounter Overland, *2002 Camp Green, Debenham, Stowmarket, Suffolk, IP14 6LA, UK, T0870-499 4478, www.encounter overland.co.uk* Adventurous expeditions in groups across wild terrain. Slide shows in London to give you an idea.

Exodus, *Grange Mills, Weir Rd, London SW12 0NE, T870-240 5550, www.exodus.co.uk* Excellent, well-run tours of Patagonia, with trekking and climbing included.

Experience Chile, *T07977 223 326, www.experiencechile.org* Itineraries and accommodation in the region, especially Torres del Paine.

Explore, *1 Frederick St, Aldershot, GU11 1LQ, T0870 333 4002, www.explore.co.uk* Highly experienced and well respected tour operator: small groups. Well executed.

Galapagos Classic Cruises, *6 Keyes Rd, London NW2 3XA, T020 8933 0613, www.GalapagosCruises.co.uk* This outfit offers good tailor-made tours.

Fidibus Tours, *Postfach 178, CH-3033 Wohlen, Switzerland, T+41 79 4325904, F+41 1 2742736, www.fidibustours.de* Not a travel agency as all tours are organized on a private basis in off-road campers for up to 4 people. Tents provided.

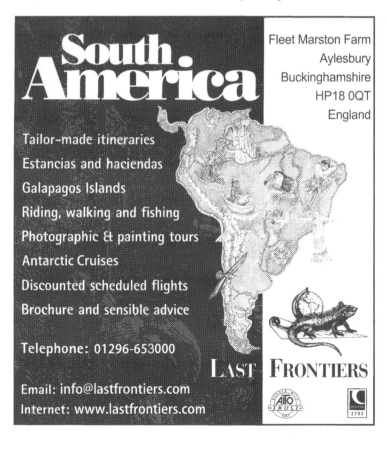

Journey Latin America, *12-13 Heathfield Terr, Chiswick, London, W4 4JE, T020-8747 8315, and 12 St Ann's Square (2nd Floor), Manchester, M3 7HW, T0161-832 1441, www.journeylatinamerica.co.uk* Deservedly well-regarded, this long-established company runs adventure tours, escorted groups and tailor made tours to Patagonia and other destinations in South America. Also cheap flights and expert advice.

Last Frontiers, *Fleet Marston Farm, Aylesbury, Buckinghamshire, HP18 0QT, T01296-653000, www.lastfrontiers.com* Wide range of tours in Argentina and Chile including great estancias and remote expeditions from Carretera Austral to Torres del Paine. Also fishing, skiing, birdwatching holidays.

Latin America Travel, *103 Gainsborough Rd, Richmond TW9 2ET, T0870-4424241, www.latinamericatravel.co.uk* Offers a tour taking Península Valdés and the glaciers.

Select Latin Amercia (incorporating **Galapagos Adventure Tours**), *79 Maltings Pl, 169 Tower Bridge Rd, London SE1 3LJ, UK, T0207 407 1478, www.selectlatinamerica.com*. Quality tailor-made holidays and small group tours.

South American Experience, *47 Causton Street, Pimlico, London SW1P 4AT, T020-79765511, www.southamerican experience.co.uk*. Will book flights and accommodation, also offers tailor-made trips.

Steppes Latin America, *51 Castle St, Cirencester, Glos GL7 1QD, T01285-885333, www.steppeslatinamerica.co.uk* Tailor-made escorted tours to Patagonia , including riding trips and bird watching.

Trips Worldwide, *14 Frederick Place, Clifton, Bristol, BS8 1AS, T0117-311 4400, www.tripsworldwide.co.uk* Specialists in tailor-made holidays.

The Travel Company, *15 Turk St, Alton,*

Hampshire, GU34 1AG, T0870-7941009, www.adventurecompany.co.uk For trips exploring Patagonia.

In North America

4StarSouthAmerica.com *T1-800-747-45 40 (US), T0871-711 5370 (UK), T+49 700 4444-7827 (rest of the world).* Tour operator and flight consolidator based in Washington DC, Stuttgart, Germany and Rio de Janeiro, offering escorted tours in Patagonia and South America. For flights, www.4starflights.com

International Expeditions, *1 Environs Park, Helena, AL 35080, USA, T1-800-6334734 (toll free), T205-428 1700, www.international expeditions.com* Travel company specializing in nature tours.

Ladatco Tours, *2200 S Dixie Highway, Suite 704, Coconut Grove, FL 33133, T1-800-3276162 (toll free), www.ladatco.com* Specialist operator based in Miami, runs explorer tours themed around mysticism, wine, etc.

Lost World Adventures, *337 Shadowmoor Drive, Decatur, GA 30030, T800 999 0558, F404 377 1902, www.lostworld.com* Long time tour operator in the region. Has interesting itineraries for all budgets.

Mila Tours, *T1-800-3677378 (toll free), www.milatours.com* Arrange a wide range of tours from rafting to photography.

Myths and Mountains, *976 Tee Court, Incline Village, NV 89451, T1-800-670-6984 (toll free), T775-832 5454, www.mythsandmountains.com* Cultural, wildlife and environmental trips.

Wilderness Travel, *1102 Ninth St,*

Berkeley, CA 94710-1211, T510-5582488, T1-800-3682794 (toll free), www.wildernesstravel.com Organizes trips worldwide, including very good tours of Patagonia.

In Australia and New Zealand

Australian Andean Adventures, *Suite 601, Level 6, 32 York Street, Sydney, NSW 2000, T02-9299 9973, www.andean adventures.com* The specialists in trekking in South America for Australians.

South America Travel Centre, *104 Hardware St, Melbourne, T03-96425353, www.satc.com.au* Good, individual tailor-made trips to Chile.

Visas and immigration

Visa and immigration regulations change frequently so always check with the Argentine and Chilean embassies before you travel. Keep photocopies of essential documents and some additional passport-sized photographs, and always have a photocopy of your passport with you.

Argentina

Visitors from neighbouring countries only need to provide their ID card to enter Argentina. Citizens of the UK, western Europe, USA, Australia, New Zealand and South Africa (among other countries) require a **passport**, valid for at least six months, and a **tourist card**, which is given to you on the plane before you land. This allows you to stay for a period of 90 days, which can be renewed for another 90 days (US$35), either by leaving the country at a border (see page 26) and immediately re-entering, or by paying US$35 at the National Directorate of Migration, *Antártida Argentina 1365, Buenos Aires, T011-4312 8663*. No renewals are given after the expiration date.

Other foreign nationals should consult with the Argentine embassy in their home country about visa requirements.

Chile

For the latest information, c… www.minrel.cl/pages/consulare… index.html

Carry your passport at all times; it is illegal not to have identification handy and thorough searches are normal procedure. Citizens of the UK, western Europe, USA, Canada, Australia, New Zealand and South Africa (among other countries) require only a **passport**, valid for at least six months, and a **tourist card**, which is handed out as a matter of routine at major land frontiers and at Chilean airports. This allows visitors to stay for 90 days and must be surrendered on departure from Chile.

Other foreign nationals should consult with the Chilean embassy in their home country about visa requirements. Ninety day tourist card extensions (US$100) can be obtained from the Ministerio del Interior (Extranjería) in Santiago or (preferably) from any local *gobernación* (government) office, where the procedure is slightly less time-consuming.

Women travellers

Argentine and Chilean men here are generally respectful of a woman travelling alone and don't tend to make improper suggestions, although you may hear the traditional *piropo* as you walk past: it's an inoffensive compliment that you can ignore. You can discourage unwanted attention by wearing a ring on your wedding finger and, when accepting a social invitation, ask if you can bring a friend, to check the intentions of whoever's inviting you. In other respects, women travellers should follow the safety tips given on p40 and never go hiking alone.

Women travelling in Chile should be aware that tampons and towels must never be flushed down the pan, since the water pressure is too low to cope. Carry a supply of plastic bags in case bins aren't provided.

rough history

50,000 years ago, the first people cross the temporary land bridge between Asia and America at the Bering Straits and begin a long migration southwards, reaching Tierra del Fuego 12,000 years ago. Many Patagonian peoples remain nomadic until the encroachment of European settlers on their land in the 19th century.

The Incas expand their empire into central Chile. They are stopped by hostile forest tribes at the Rio Maule, near present-day Talca. Due to its topography, Patagonia is not touched by Inca incursions.

1516 Juan de Solis arrives in the Plata estuary. He and his men are killed by the indigenous Querandí peoples. Other Europeans follow, including Portuguese explorer Ferdinand Magellan who ventures south into the Pacific via the straits north of Tierra del Fuego. The straits become an important trade route until the building of the Panama Canal in the 20th century. Towns like Punta Arenas and San Julián are later developed as stopover ports.

C15-16th Following the overthrow of the Incas by a tiny force of Spaniards led by Francisco Pizarro, Pedro de Valdivia is given the task of exploring and conquering Chile. He reaches the fertile Mapocho Valley and founds Santiago. The settlements of Concepcion, Valdivia and Villarica soon follow.

1580s Buenos Aires is established, but the discovery of precious metals in Peru and Bolivia, focuses colonial attention elsewhere, and it remains a backwater for 200 years. Meanwhile, a group of settlers led by Pedro de Sarmiento seeks to found a colony on the north banks of the Magellan Straits. The colony is a disaster, and only two people survive. This is the end of attempts at European settlement in southern Patagonia for centuries.

1598 A rebellion by the Mapuche tribe in Chile drives the Spanish back to the north of the Rio Biobío, leaving isolated groups of settlers in Valdivia and on the island of Chiloe, and ensuring that European influence in Patagonia will remain marginal. It is not until 1881 that the treaty ending Mapuche Independence from Chile is signed.

1776 Buenos Aires is made the capital of the new Viceroyalty of the Rio de la Plata and becomes an important trade route for European goods and contraband. Estancias are formed to farm and export cattle in the area around Buenos Aires.

1808-16 Napoleon invades Spain and deposes King Ferdinand VII. Argentine independence from Spain is declared on 9 July 1816

Background

The original big foots

The dry Patagonian plateau was originally inhabited by one principle indigenous group, the Tehuelches, who lived along the eastern side of the Andes, as far north as modern-day Bariloche, and were hunters of guanaco and rheas. In the 18th century, they began to domesticate the wild horses of the region and sailed down the Patagonian rivers to reach the Atlantic coast.

The Tehuelches were very large: it is said that when the Spanish first arrived in this area, they discovered Tehuelche footprints in the sand, exclaiming 'qué patagón' ('what a large foot'), hence the name Patagonia.

In the 18th and early 19th centuries, the Tehuelche interacted with European whalers and were patronizingly described as 'semi-civilized'. The granting by the Chilean government of large land concessions in the late 19th century, combined with Argentine President Julio Roca's wars of extermination against Patagonian native peoples in the 1870s, spelled the end for the Tehuelches. They were hunted and persecuted by settlers and only a few survived diseases and the radical change of lifestyle.

Towards the end of the 20th century, a belated sense of moral guilt arose among the colonizers, but it was too late to preserve the Tehuelche way of life. Today only a few isolated groups remain in Argentine Patagonia. For details of the indigenous groups further south and in the Patagonian fjords, see page 356.

by Jose de San Martin, who goes on to lead armies of freedom fighters into Chile with Simon Bolivar. But independence brings neither stability nor unity in Argentina, with fighting by federalist groups.

1832-3 General Rosas, dictator of Argentina and military supremo, leads a campaign against the Pampas Indians, destroying their independence and their way of life. This is the beginning of the incursion of European forces into Patagonia. On seeing Rosas's army, Charles Darwin wrote that he doubted any indigenous Pampas people would be left within a generation.

1843 Alarmed by widespread naval activity in the region, the Chilean navy sends a cutter to the Magellan Strait and erects a fort at Fuerte Bulnes, to claim the Magellan Straits for Chile – the rest of Patagonia between here and the Chilean mainland now falls under Chilean jurisdiction.

1845-80 The Chilean government encourages settlement around Lago Llanquihue, provoking extensive immigration to the area by German colonists. Legacy of this settlement can be seen in the German-looking buildings around Puerto Octay, Frutillar and Puerto Varas.

1853 Juan de Rosas, a powerful governor of Buenos Aires, brings order, gaining support by seizing lands from indigenous peoples and handing them to friends in the 'Campaign of the Desert'. This is followed by a new era of growth and prosperity. Buenos Aires at last grows as a city.

1865-1915 Welsh immigrants arrive in Puerto Madryn on the Atlantic Coast and settle inland along the Chubut Valley. They learn from the indigenous Tehuelche people and successfully irrigate the valley for agriculture.

1879 President Julio Roca sends a force against the indigenous peoples of Patagonia, exterminating many of them and herding the rest into settlements. This 'Conquest of the Wilderness' is the beginning of the process of European settlement in Patagonia.

Late C19th Argentina is transformed by a newly stable economy based on cattle farming, foreign investment and mass European immigration. Thomas Bridges founds a mission in Tierra del Fuego.

Early C20th Rural poverty in both countries leads to urbanization and high unemployment, wealth is concentrated in the hands of the very few. The wool boom encourages the creation of large farms for sheep-raising in Patagonia. Many migrants come from the island of Chiloé to work at farms in Argentine Patagonia and on Chilean Tierra del Fuego.

1940s-50s Following a military coup in 1943, Juan Peron wins the presidency in 1946 and 1952. An authoritarian and charismatic leader, he institutes stringent reforms against the economic elite and in favour of the workers. In 1955 he is ousted and exiled to Spain, but remains popular with the people, making a brief return to power in 1973.

1960s-70s Chile's politics become increasingly polarised. The Marxist coalition led by Salvador Allende, introduces sweeping reforms, such as redistribution of income and the takeover of many private enterprises. The country is plunged into economic chaos.

11 Sep 1973 General Pinochet seizes power in a bloody coup. Allende allegedly commits suicide and thousands of his supporters are murdered. During the dictatorship which follows, an estimated 80,000 are tortured, murdered or exiled; one of the early detention centres is on Isla Dawson in the Magellan Straits.

1976-83 In Chile, the building of the Carretera Austral begins. The new military government in Argentina institutes a reign of terror known as the 'Dirty War'. Any vaguely left-wing thinking, opposition or criticism of the military is met with violent torture and elimination by death squads. Up to 30,000 people 'disappear'. Internal conflict ends with the war against Britain over the disputed Malvinas (Falkland Islands). Democracy of a kind returns, when Alfonsín becomes president in 1983.

1978 Argentina and Chile nearly go to war over a territorial dispute over three islands – Lennox, Nueva and Picton – in the Beagle Channel. The Pope has to intervene, and the islands are awarded to Chile.

1973-90 Pinochet dissolves Congress in Ch[illegible] opposition. His economic policies brin[illegible] in 1988 sees him rejected by a major[illegible] Christian democrat, Patricio Aylwin is elec[illegible]

1990s In Argentina, Peronist president Carlos Mene[illegible] reforms, selling off nationalized industries, an[illegible] foreign investment. The country falls heavily int[illegible] Fernando de la Rua of the UCR centre-left Alliance, p[illegible] corruption and tough measures to balance Argentina[illegible]

2001 In December, nationwide demonstrations erupt whe[illegible] access to bank accounts is restricted in the 'corralito'. Argentina is plunged into serious economic and political crisis. Rioting, looting and widespread civil chaos result in the death of 27 people.

Jan 2002 Eduardo Duhalde becomes Argentina's fifth president in 2 weeks. He is forced to devalue the peso in order to borrow money from the International Monetary Fund. The middle class is devastated, many losing their life savings. Widespread poverty becomes a reality, with child malnutrition, and unemployment over 20%.

2003 Argentine elections threaten to return Menem to power, even though he bankrupted the nation by selling off national industries. Kirchner wins by a narrow lead, promising to reduce corruption and reduce the burden of government employees. The country recovers some stability. Tourism flourishes - both from foreigners enjoying low prices, and Argentines realising that their own country is more magnificent than Miami holidays which became the aspirant norm under Menem.

Today Patagonia remains very much an extremity of both Argentina and Chile. Historically absent from the national boundaries until the 19th century, it still feels very different to the rest of the countries. Some long for the utopia of a united Patagonia, free of the internal wranglings of the power bases of Buenos Aires and Santiago.

Land and environment

Landscape

Patagonia stretches roughly from Rio Colorado (39°) to the Magellan Straits and covers some 780,000 sq km. Shaped by tectonic pressures, volcanic activity and the ice age, it is made up of three main geographical features: mountain, steppe and coast.

Mountain The Andes, which form a natural frontier between Chile and Argentina, diminish in size south of Santiago (eroded by glacial action), but become increasingly volcanic in nature. Geographical faults associated with the mountains, lead to frequent volcanic eruptions and earthquakes. In the Lake District, the mountain passes are low enough in places for crossing. However, further south the increase in precipitation and latitude lead to larger snowfalls and more glaciation. The U-shaped valleys that can be seen throughout the

Background

…alafate

According to local lore, whoever eats the fruits of the Calafate, *Berberis buxifolia*, will return to Patagonia. Certainly, he or she is likely to have purple-stained lips and fingers thanks to the plant's edible berries. This spiny, hardy shrub grows to 2 m in height and has single bright yellow or orange flowers dotted along its arching branches in spring. Also known as the Magellan barberry, its wood is used for making red dye.

south are typical of a glacial landscape. Though of modest height, Cerro Fitzroy and other peaks on the fringes of the Patagonian ice cap are among the most dramatic on the continent.

Some of Patagonia's richest national parks are to be found in mountain areas. As the glaciers melted, lakes were left in the foothills on both sides of the Andes. Frequent rainfall and fertile soil has led to large expanses of southern beech forest, with some areas of magnificent virgin Valdivian rainforest. Here you will see *coihues* (evergreen beeches) ove 450 years old and *alerces* over 1,500 years old, with the ancient species of bamboo cane (*caña colihue*) growing everywhere. The rivers and lakes have abundant trout and salmon.

Steppe Lying in the eastern shadow of the Andes and sheltered from the rain, this area is characterized by an arid, wind-swept plateau with terraces, which drop in altitude from west to east. The surface of the ancient rocks has been subjected to endless erosion; the dry conditions and strong winds strip the surface of cover, and fill the air with dust. Only where rivers have scored deep valleys in the rock base can soil accumulate. Overgrazing by sheep has produced serious desertification in many parts of the steppe, creating a dramatic and desolate landscape. Plant life in the steppe has had to adapt to the severe climatic conditions. The northwest of this area is covered by bushy scrublands, such as the *coiron* grasses and calafete (*berberis buxifolia*). All have deep roots to access the water deep below, and many have small leaves or spines. Nearer the mountains where the climate is less severe and the soil more fertile, there is a herbaceous steppe which includes *coiron blanco* and shrubs such as the *neneo*.

Background

The monkey puzzle tree

The Araucaria Araucana, is known in Argentina and Chile as the *araucaria* or *pehuén* and elsewhere called variously the Chilean pine, the umbrella tree, the parasol tree and the monkey puzzle tree. The species has flourished on both sides of the Andes between 37° and 39° south for 200 million years, although, it is much more widespread in Chile than in Argentina. Very slow growing, it can reach up to 40-m high; and live for 1,200 years. The characteristic cones can weigh up to 1 kg. The *araucaria* was revered by the Mapuche, who ate both its cones and its sharp leathery leaves. Some isolated trees are still seen as sacred by the Mapuche who leave offerings to the tree's spirit.

Coast In the far south of Patagonia the coastline has been dissected by Ice Age glaciers into a maze of islands and channels. The ice that once covered the southern Andes was so heavy that it depressed the relatively narrow tip of South America. When the ice melted and the sea level rose, water broke through leaving the western Andes as islands and creating the Chilean fjords, glaciated valleys carved out by the ice and now drowned. Much of the coastal area and the archipelagic islands are covered with lichen, moss and fern, as well as wildflowers including orchids, and trees such as the antarctic beech (*nothofagus moorei*).

Climate

Patagonia is generally thought of as a temperate climate with cool summers and mild winters, but it is well-known for its unpredictable weather. Two factors have a major effect on climatic conditions: the Andes and the Humbolt current. Cold air which accompanies the current sweeps in from the Antarctic and meets with warmer air over the land, creating rainfall in Chile, but very little of the moisture reaches the Argentinian side of the mountains. Further south, coastal temperatures are moderated by the ocean; there is no real summer, but the winters are rarely severe, although there are frequent storms.

Patagonia national parks

Patagonia has an extensive network of reserves and protected areas, the most important of which are designated national parks (PN). Additional areas have been designated as natural monuments (MN) and natural reserves (RN).

Argentina
The main office of the **Administracion de Parques Nacionales** is at Santa Fe 680, near the Plaza San Martín in central Buenos Aires, T011-4311 8853/0303. Most parks have *guadaparque* (ranger) offices at the main entrance, where you can get advice and basic maps. They are usually knowledgeable and happy to explain the wildlife and good walks. Parks in the lake district are particularly well set up for trekking, with signed trails, refugios and campsites.

Chile
All reserves and national parks in Chile are managed by **CONAF** (the Corporación Nacional Forestal), Avenida Bulnes 285, piso 1, Santiago, T/F02-697-2273, www.conaf.cl. It maintains an office in each region of the country, and kiosks in some natural areas. Most of the parks have public access; details are given in the text. Camping areas are usually clearly designated, wild camping is discouraged and frequently banned.

Wildlife

The varied geography of Patagonia has created a number of different ecosystems, so it's no surprise that the wildlife is extremely varied, as animals and plants have been forced to adapt to the severe climatic conditions. Chile in particular is an ecological island: fauna that is commonplace in neighbouring countries has not been able to migrate here because of the Andes, the desert, the ice and the sea, and the country's isolation has contributed to a range of endemic wildlife. Specialist wildlife and birdwatching tours led by experts are available in most areas and are detailed throughout the guide.

Land mammals Typical of Patagonia, is the **guanaco** – a coffee-coloured, cousin of the llama, with a long neck and small head. Standing at 1.5 m tall and weighing 55 kg, they are very agile and fast runners. Both grazers and browsers, they live in deserts, shrub land, savannah and occasionally on forest fringes. An estimated 20,000 now survive. Two species of deer found in Patagonia are the **huemul** and the **pudú**. The huemul appears on Chile's coat of arms, along with the condor. Both the huemul and the pudú are very rare and difficult to spot, see page 313, Deer, oh deer. A large, reddish-brown species of **puma** can still be found in the mountain valleys, although it's a solitary, nocturnal creature and understandably shy of humans. Other land mammals typical of Patagonia include a small hairless vole called the **tucotuco**, unique to Tierra del Fuego; a type of chinchilla called a **vizcacha**; a rodent called a **mara**; as well as the **otter**, **cougar**, **armadillo**, **skunk** and several species of **fox**.

Marine mammals Numerous colonies of **seal** (including the elephant seal which can weigh up to three tonnes) and **sea-lion** live all along the Patagonian coast and come ashore to mate in December and January. Five species of **dolphin**, including the Fitzroy, Commerson and Peale, can be spotted, frequently off the coast of Chiloé. Types of **whale** include the southern right whale, which comes to breed off the coast of Península Valdés and can be spotted from June to December; and the killer whale, which arrives to feed on the young seal pups from March to April.

Birds The **choique**, known as 'Darwin's rhea', is a large, flightless, ostrich-like bird, which roams the Patagonian steppes. Once hunted for its feathers, it is now farmed for meat and protected in the wild. Another long-legged bird is the southern **flamingo**, most commonly seen around lake shores, it also inhabits coastal areas on the Península Valdés and the Isla de los Pájaros. From the coast to the mountains, **geese** can be seen flying in pairs; other species to look out for are the black-necked **swan**, the Andean **duck**, the austral **parakeet** and the Magellanic **woodpecker**. Birds of prey include the **condor**, with a wingspan of more than four metres; and various species of **eagle**, **hawk**, and **buzzard**. Two regional birds of prey, the **jote** and the **tiuque**, are also common. Half the world's species of **penguin** can be found along the coast of Chile, including the Humbolt, Magellanic and King species. They live in the sea for most of the year, but colonize Patagonia and Tierra del Fuego by the thousand, as they come onto land from October to March in order to breed. Other coastal birds include the **petrel**, **oystercatcher**, **cormorant**, **heron** and **albatross**.

Buenos Aires

Introduction

Buenos Aires might look European but its passions are entirely Argentine: the nostalgic tango danced in *milongas* and bars, the passion of crowds at La Boca stadium, and the steaks you smell grilling on *parrillas* all over the city. The city's inhabitants – fashion-conscious, fast-talking Porteños – know how to party. They start dancing in the early hours and they don't stop for a siesta.

Stroll past baroque buildings and Italianate palaces on Avenida de Mayo and Plaza San Martín, and laze in the beautiful parks of Palermo; admire contemporary art at MALBA, or shop in chic malls. Visit Eva Perón in Recoleta's labyrinthine cemetery, or buy crafts from the market outside. San Telmo is the city's most atmospheric barrio, and its narrow streets of crumbling old buildings come alive on Sundays when musicians strike up everywhere and tango dancers strut their stuff in Plaza Dorrego.

If the pace becomes too much, escape into the jungly maze of rivers at the Tigre Delta, or hop across the River Plate to Uruguay's colonial town of Colonia. Buenos Aires provides the perfect contrast to the peace and wilderness of Patagonia.

Ratings

Landscape
★

Chillin'
★

Activities
★★

Culture
★★★★★

Costs
$$$$

Ins and outs

» p78

Getting there

Air Ezeiza (T011-5480 6111) 35 km southwest of the centre is the city's international airport. It has two terminals: B for **Aerolíneas Argentinas**, and the larger A for all other airlines, with casas de cambio, Banco de la Nación (open 24 hrs), ATMs, pharmacy, left luggage (24 hrs, US$1 per piece), *locutorio*, and a tourist office immediately as you enter the Arrivals hall, open 0700-2000, with a free hotel booking service. An efficient bus service, run by **Manuel Tienda León** (desk in arrivals, T0800 888 5366, www.tiendaleon.com), links Ezeiza with the centre every 30 minutes 0600-0100, US$7.40 for the 40-minute journey, with free hotel transfer/pick up. Ordinary taxis charge US$12; more reliable are *remise* taxis, fixed fare US$18, which are booked in advance from a desk at the airport, for example, *La Terminal*, T011-4312 0711.

Aeroparque (T011-4576 5111) 4 km north of Palermo, is the domestic airport. It is smart and modern, with bars and restaurants, shops, airport tax counter, tourist information, car rental, bank, ATMs, exchange facilities, post office, *locutorio* and luggage deposit (US$ 1.30 per piece a day). From Aeroparque *Manuel Tienda León* buses charge US$3 for the 20-minute journey to the centre, *remises* US$4 and ordinary taxis US$3. » *For flights to and from both airports, see Essentials, pp20-23.*

Bus The long-distance bus terminal is **Retiro** at Ramos Mejía y Antártida Argentina, five blocks north of Plaza San Martín, T011-4310 0700. There are left-luggage lockers, US$2.50, but large baggage should be left at *guarda equipage* on the lower floor. City tourist information is at desk 83 on the upper floor; local bus information is at the Ramos Mejía entrance on the middle floor. Ordinary taxis leave from the official rank on the lower floor but these are unreliable. The area is unsalubrious so take a *remise* taxi into town (**Remise La Terminal** T011-4312 0711, booked from 1 of 2 booths on the bus platform) or call a radio taxi (see Transport, page 78) and ask the company to pick you up from one of the five bridges leading from the arrivals level.

Getting around

There is a good network of **buses** (colectivos), which are frequent, efficient and very fast, plus five **metro** (Subte) lines, labelled 'A' to 'E' – four link the outer parts of the city to the centre; the fifth ('C') links Plaza Constitución with Retiro station and connects with all the other lines. The central stations of 9 de Julio ('D'), Diagonal Norte ('C') and Carlos Pellegrini ('B') are linked by pedestrian tunnels. **Taxis** are painted yellow and black and carry "Taxi" flags, but for security always 'phone a radio taxi. Alternatively, *remise* taxis charge a fixed rate to anywhere in town and are very reliable, although they can work out more expensive for short journeys.

Tourist information

National tourist office ⓘ *Av Santa Fe 883, open Mon-Fri 0900-1700, T011-4312 2232/5550, www.turismo.gov.ar*. There are also tourist kiosks at Aeroparque and Ezeiza airports, and city-run touist kiosks open 1200-2000 on Avenida Florida, junction with Roque Sáenz Peña; at Abasto Shopping Mall (Av Corrientes 3200); in Recoleta (on Av Quintana, junction with Ortiz); in Puerto Madero, Dock 4, and at Retiro Bus Station (ground floor). The website www.bue.gov.ar has useful information in English. The tourist police can be contacted at Corrientes 436, T011-4346 5748 and T0800 9995000. **Auto Mapa**'s pocket-size *Plano guía* of the Federal Capital is available at news stands, US$2.70. *Buenos Aires Day & Night* is a free bimonthly magazine with a city map available together with other publications at tourist kiosks and some hotels.

Sights

The formal centre is around Plaza de Mayo, from where the broad Avenida de Mayo heads west to the congress building. Halfway, it crosses the 22 lanes of Avenida 9 de Julio, which heads north to Avenida del Libertador, the main road leading out of the city to the north and west, via the fashionable suburbs of Recoleta and Palermo. East of the centre are the city's vibrant, renovated docks at Puerto Madero, while to the south are the green spaces of Costanera Sur and the city's most atmospheric barrio, San Telmo.

Getting there International and domestic flights. Excellent long distance buses.

Getting around Metro and radio taxis.

Time required 2 days at the start of your trip.

Weather Sweltering in summer, mild in winter, perfect in spring and autumn.

Sleeping Great range from utterly luxurious to cheap and friendly.

Eating Steak and international cuisine.

Activities and tours Watch tango, dance tango.

★ **Don't miss...**Sunday market at San Telmo.

City centre

» pp 69-81

Plaza de Mayo

This broad open plaza is the historic heart of the city, surrounded by some of the major public buildings including the famous pink Casa de Gobierno or **Casa Rosada** ⓘ *T011-4344 3802, Mon-Fri 1000-1800, Sun 1400-1800, free. Tours from Hipólito Yrigoyen 219 (passport required), changing of the guards every 2 hrs 0700-1900.* The colour derives from President Sarmiento's desire to symbolize national unity by blending the colours of the rival factions which had fought each other for much of the 19th century: the Federalists (red) and the Unitarians (white). The building has been the site of many historic events: from its balcony, Perón appeared before the masses, and when the economy crumbled in December 2001, angry crowds of *cacerolazas* (middle-class ladies banging their saucepans) rioted outside. Since 1970, the Mothers of the Plaza de Mayo (*Madres de los Desaparecidos*) have marched every Thursday at 1530 anti-clockwise around the central monument in silent remembrance of their children who disappeared during the 'dirty war'.

Opposite the Casa Rosada, on the west side of the plaza is the white-columned **Cabildo**, originally the 18th-century administrative centre. Inside is the **Museo del Cabildo y la Revolución**, ⓘ *T011-4334 1782, Tue-Fri 1130-1800, Sat 1400-1800,* Sun *1300-1800, US$0.30,* good for an overview of Argentine history. The **Cathedral Metropolitana**, on the north side of the plaza, lies on the site of the first church in Buenos Aires, built in 1580, ⓘ *check times for Mass at entrance.* The current structure was built in classical style between 1758 and 1807, and inside, in the right-hand aisle, is the imposing tomb of General José de San Martín (1880) Argentina's greatest hero, who liberated the country from the Spanish.

La City

Just north of the Plaza de Mayo lies the main banking district known as La City, with some handsome buildings to admire. The **Banco de Boston**, Florida 99 and Avenida R S Pena, dates from 1924 and boasts a lavish ceiling and marble interior. Also worth seeing is the marvellous art deco **Banco de la Provincia de Buenos Aires** at San Martín 137, built in 1940, and the **Bolsa de Comercio**, 25 de Mayo y Sarmiento, which dates from 1916 and houses the stock exchange. The **Basílica Nuesta Señora de La Merced,** ⓘ *J D Perón y Reconquista 207, Mon-Fri 0800-1800,* founded in 1604 and rebuilt 1760-1769, has a highly decorated interior and an altar with an 18th-century wooden figure of Christ, the work of indigenous carvers from Misiones. Next door, the **Convento de la Merced**, originally built in 1601, has a peaceful courtyard in its cloisters.

South of Plaza de Mayo

To the south west of the Plaza de Mayo is an entire block of buildings built by the Jesuits between 1622 and 1767, called the **Manzana de las Luces** (Enlightenment Square) – bounded by streets Moreno, Alsina, Perú and Bolívar. The former Jesuit church of **San Ignacio de Loyola**, ⓘ *guided tours Sat-Sun 1700 but open at other hours,* begun in 1664, is the oldest colonial building in Buenos Aires and the best example of the baroque architecture introduced by the Jesuits. Its splendid golden nave dates from 1710-1734. Worth seeing are the secret **18th-century tunnels** ⓘ *T011-4342 3964, guided tours from Perú 272, Tue, Wed, Fri 1200-1500, Sat-Sun 1500-1900, in Spanish (or English by prior arrangement), arrive 15 mins before tour, US$1.30,* which are thought to have been used by escaping Jesuits or for smuggling contraband from the port. For centuries the whole block was the centre of intellectual activity, and although little remains today, the history of this area is fascinating.

The **Museo de la Ciudad,** ⓘ *Alsina 412, T011-4331 9855, Mon-Fri 1100-1900, Sun 1500-1900, US$ 1, free on Wed,* is a historical house with a permanent exhibition covering social history and popular culture, and gives an insight into 19th-century life in Buenos Aires. The **church of San Francisco,** ⓘ *Alsina y Defensa, Mon-Fri 0700-1300, 1500-1900, guided visits Tue 1530 and 1630, Sat 1630 and 1730,* was built by the Franciscan Order 1730-1754 and given a new façade in 1911 in German baroque style.

Palacio Barolo

The small, but beautifully designed **Museo Etnográfico J B Ambrosetti,** ⓘ *Moreno 350, T011-4345 8196, Tue-Sun 1430-1830 (in summer 1600-2000), US$0.30,* contains fascinating anthropological and ethnographic collections from all over Argentina, charting the development of various indigenous groups. One block further south at Defensa y Belgrano, the **church of Santo Domingo**, founded in 1751, where General Belgrano, a major figure in Argentine independence, is buried.

Avenida de Mayo

From the Plaza de Mayo, take a stroll down this broad leafy avenue which links the Presidential Palace to the Congress building to the west. Constructed between 1889 and 1894 and inspired by the grand design of Paris, it's filled with elaborate French baroque and art nouveau buildings. At Perú and Avenida de Mayo is the **subte station Perú**, furnished by the Museo de la Ciudad to resemble its original state, with posters and furniture of the time. You'll need to buy a US$0.25 ticket to have a look.

Along the avenue west from here, you'll see the splendid French-style **Casa de la Cultura** at number 575, home of the newspaper *La Prensa* and topped with bronze statues. At number 702 is the fine Parisian-style **Edificio Drabble**, and at number 769, the elegant **Palacio Vera**, from 1910. Argentina's most celebrated writer, Jorge Luis Borges, was fond of the many cafés which once lined Avenida de Mayo, of which **Café Tortoni**, at number 825, is the most famous. It has been the haunt of illustrious writers, artists and poets since 1858 and its high ceilings and art nouveau stained glass plunge you straight back into another era. It's an atmospheric place for coffee, but particularly wonderful for the poetry recitals, tango and live music, which are still performed here in the evenings (see also Eating, page 72).

Continuing west over Avenida 9 de Julio, look out for the 1928 **Hotel Castelar** at number 1152 (see Sleeping, page 69), the beautiful art nouveau **Hotel Chile** at number 1297 and **Palacio Barola** at number 1370. Avenida de Mayo culminates at the Italian academic-style **congress building,** ⓘ *guided visits T011-4331 4633, Thu only, free.*

Plaza San Martín and around

Ten blocks north of the Plaza de Mayo is the splendid Plaza San Martín, designed by Argentina's famous landscape architect Charles Thays, and filled with luxuriant mature palms and plane trees. It's popular with runners in the early morning and office workers at lunchtimes. At the western corner is an equestrian **statue of San Martín**, 1862, and at the northern end of the plaza is the **Falklands/Malvinas memorial** with an eternal flame to those who fell in the War,

The obelisk on Avenida 9 de Julio

1982. The city's main shopping street, **Avenida Santa Fe**, starts from Plaza San Martín, crosses Avenida 9 de Julio and heads through Retiro and Recoleta to Palermo. Around the plaza are several elegant mansions, among them the **Palacio San Martín**. Most striking, however, is the elegant art deco **Edificio Kavanagh**, east of the plaza, once the tallest building in South America. The **Plaza de la Fuerza Aérea**, northeast of Plaza San Martín was until 1982 called the Plaza Británica; in the centre is a clock tower presented by British and Anglo-Argentine residents in 1916, known as the Torre de los Ingleses.

Three blocks northwest of Plaza San Martín is one of the city's most delightful museums, the **Museo de Arte Hispanoamericano Isaac Fernández Blanco**, ⓘ *Suipacha 1422, Tue-Fri 1400-1900, Sat, Sun and holidays 1500-1900, Thu free, closed Jan. Guided tours in English T011-4327 0272; guided tours in Spanish Sat-Sun 1600.* Housed in a beautiful 1920s neo-colonial mansion with tiled Spanish-style gardens, it contains a fascinating collection of colonial art, with fine Cuzqueno school paintings, and dazzling ornate silverware.

Avenida 9 de Julio

This is one of the world's widest thoroughfares, with 11 lanes of traffic in each direction and the city's famous landmark at Plaza de la República: a 67-m-tall **obelisk** commemorating the 400th anniversary of the city's founding, where football fans traditionally congregate to celebrate a victory.

Just a block north of the obelisk on 9 de Julio is **Teatro Colón**, ⓘ *tour tickets from Toscanini 1168 (on C Viamonte side) or from Tucumán 1171, www.teatrocoln.org.ar, in Spanish and English, T011-4378 7132/33, US$2.50.* The theatre is characterized by exquisite opulence and an almost perfect acoustic, due to the horseshoe shape and the mix of marble and soft fabrics. Workshops and rehearsal spaces lie underneath the Avenida 9 de Julio itself, and there are stores of costumes, including 22,000 pairs of shoes. The theatre is home to three orchestras, as well as the city's ballet and opera companies (see page 76).

Four blocks west of Plaza de la República, **Centro Cultural San Martín**, ⓘ *Av Corrientes 1530. Tango desk open daily 1400-2100, for classes see www.tangodata.com.ar*, houses good photography exhibitions, a theatre and modern art museum. It's a great centre of tango, too.

Buenos Aires centre

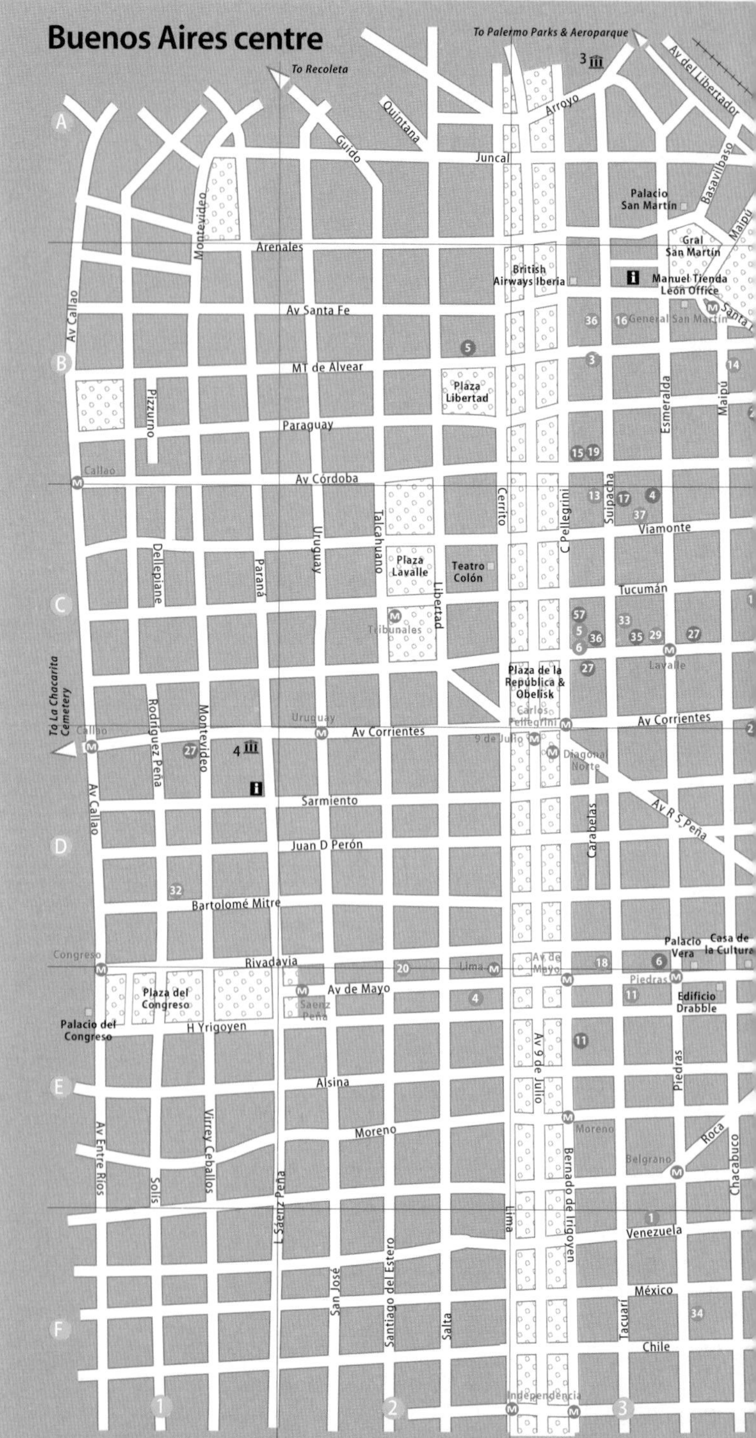

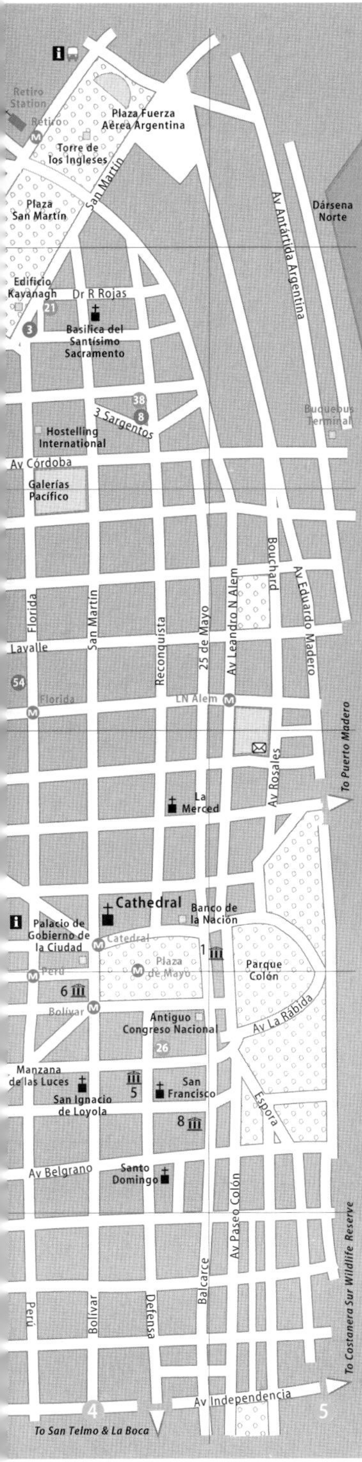

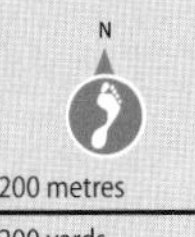

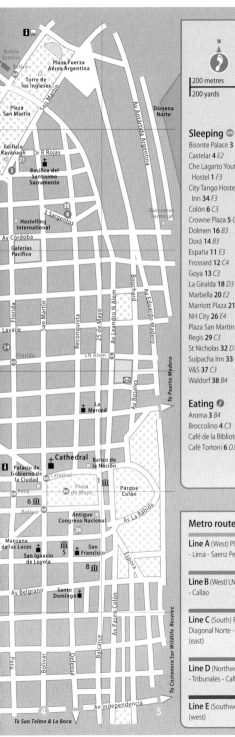

Sleeping

Bisonte Palace **3** *B3*
Castelar **4** *E2*
Che Lagarto Youth Hostel **1** *F3*
City Tango Hostel Inn **34** *F3*
Colón **6** *C3*
Crowne Plaza **5** *C3*
Dolmen **16** *B3*
Dorá **14** *B3*
España **11** *E3*
Frossard **12** *C4*
Goya **13** *C3*
La Giralda **18** *D3*
Marbella **20** *E2*
Marriott Plaza **21** *B4*
NH City **26** *E4*
Plaza San Martín **36** *B3*
Regis **29** *C3*
St Nicholas **32** *D1*
Suipacha Inn **33** *C3*
V&S **37** *C3*
Waldorf **38** *B4*

Eating

Aroma **3** *B4*
Broccolino **4** *C3*
Café de la Biblioteca **5** *B2*
Café Tortoni **6** *D3*
Catalinas **8** *B4*
Club Español **11** *E3*
El Palacio de la Papa Frita **27** *C3/D1*
Exedra **15** *B3*
Gran Victoria **17** *C3*
La Casona del Nonno **35** *C3*
La Chacra **19** *B3*
La Estancia **36** *C3*
La Taska **20** *B4*
Richmond **54** *C4*
Sorrento **25** *C4*
Tomo Uno **57** *C3*

Museums

Casa de Gobierno (Casa Rosada) **1** *D5*
Centro Cultural San Martín **4** *D1*
Museo de Arte Hispanoamericano Isaac Fernández Blanco **3** *A3*
Museo de la Ciudad **5** *E4*
Museo del Cabildo y la Revolución **6** *E4*
Museo Etnográfico JB Ambrosetti **8** *E4*

Metro routes

Line A (West) Plaza de Mayo - Perú - Piedras - Av de Mayo - Lima - Saenz Peña - Congreso

Line B (West) LN Alem - Florida - Carlos Pellegrini - Uruguay - Callao

Line C (South) Retiro - General San Martín - Lavalle - Diagonal Norte - Av de Mayo - Moreno - Independencia (east)

Line D (Northwest) Catedral - Diagonal Norte - 9 de Julio - Tribunales - Callao

Line E (Southwest) Bolívar - Belgrano - Independencia (west)

North of the centre » pp 69-81

Recoleta

Situated north of Plaza San Martín, beyond Avenida 9 de Julio, Recoleta became a fashionable residential area when wealthy families started to move here from the crowded city centre after the yellow fever outbreak of 1871. Its streets, lined with French-style mansions, cafés, art galleries and museums make for a pleasant stroll. At its heart is the **Plaza de la Recoleta**, and running down its southeastern side is Calle Ortiz. At weekends, **Plaza Alveas** has an art and craft market from 1100 until 1800, when the whole place is lively, with street artists and performers. There's a helpful **tourist information** booth at Ayacuco 1958, T011-4804 5667.

The **Cementerio de la Recoleta**, ⓘ *0700-1745, tours 1430 on the last Sun of month (not in summer), T011-4803 1594*, is a labyrinth of ornate shrines, with a vast congregation of angels on their roofs. Eva Perón is buried here in the Duarte family vault, among other illustrious figures from Argentina's history. The former Jesuit church of **El Pilar**, next to the cemetery dates from 1732 and was restored in 1930. There are stunning 18th-century gold alterpieces made in Alto Peru and an interesting, small museum of religious art downstairs.

Close to the cemetery is the **Buenos Aires Design Centre**, where you can buy stylish contemporary designs and well made handicrafts from all over Argentina. There are also lots of good restaurants here, some with open terraces. To the north, the **Museo de Bellas Artes** ⓘ *Av del Libertador 1473, T011-4801 3390, www.mnba.org.ar, Tue-Fri 1230-1930, Sat-Sun 0930-1930, closed Jan*, houses a fine collection of Argentine 19th and 20th-century paintings and examples of European works, particularly post-Impressionist paintings and Rodin sculptures. In nearby **Plaza San Martín de Tours**, you're likely to spot one of Buenos Aires' legendary dog walkers, managing an unfeasible 20 or so dogs without tangling their leads.

The wide and fast avenue **Avenida del Libertador** runs north from Recoleta towards Palermo past parks, squares and several major museums. **Museo de Motivos Populares Argentinos José Hernández**, ⓘ *Av Libertador 2373, T011-4802 7294, www.malba.org.ar for exhibitions, www.malbacine.org for film screenings, Wed-Sun 1300-1900, US$0.30, free Sun, closed in Feb*, has an extensive collection of gaucho artefacts, including ornate silver *mates*, plaited leather *talebartería* and decorated silver stirrups, together with pre-Hispanic artefacts, and paintings from the Cusco school. The museum not to be missed, however, is the **Museo de Arte Latinoamericano (MALBA)**, ⓘ *Av Figueroa Alcorta 3415, T011-4808 6500, Mon, Thu, Fri 1200-1930, Wed 1200-2100, Sat-Sun 1000-2100, closed Tue, free, (cinema tickets US$1.30, book in advance)*, which opened in 2001 to house a collection of Latin American art. It's a great building, vibrant and accessible, with stunning art and a good cinema.

Palermo

Northwest of Recoleta is the attractive sprawling barrio of Palermo, named after Giovanni Domenico Palermo who transformed these lands into productive orchards and vineyards in the 17th century. It has a series of great parks, designed by Charles Thays in the early 20th century. The **Parque Tres de Febrero** ⓘ *winter Mon-Fri 0800-1800, Sat-Sun 0800-2000; summer 0800-2000 daily*, is the largest, with lakes, tennis courts, a rose garden and the **Museo de Arte Moderno Eduardo Sivori**, ⓘ *Tue-Fri 1200-2000 (winter 1800), US$0.70, Sat-Sun 1000-2000 (winter 1800), US$0.30, Wed free, T011-4774 9452*, where you can immerse yourself in a fine collection of Argentine art. South of here is the beautifully harmonious **Japanese garden** ⓘ *1000-1800, US$0.70, T011-4804 4922, guided visits Sat 1500, 1600*, a charming place to walk, with koi carp to feed and little bridges over ornate streams. The **Jardín Zoológico Las Heras y Sarmiento** ⓘ *1000-1900, guided visits US$2, under 13s free*, to the west, occupies impressive buildings in spacious grounds landscaped by Charles Thays, while the **Municipal Botanical Gardens** ⓘ *west of the zoo at Santa Fe 2951, 0800-1800 daily, free,* designed by Thays in 1902 has areas planted with characteristic specimens representing the various regions of Argentina.

The oldest and most appealing part of Palermo is between avenidas Córdoba and Santa Fe, south of Juan B Justo and north of Avenida Scalabrini Ortiz. It's a very seductive place, with cobbled streets of tall bohemian houses bedecked with flowers and plants, and leafy plazas and gardens. Many bars, cafés and chic boutiques have opened up around Calle Honduras, making it a relaxing area for an afternoon stroll. The focus is **Plaza Serrano**, recently renamed **Plaza Cortázar**, after the Argentine writer, whose novel *Rayuela* (Hopscotch) is set around here.

Puerto Madero

Puerto Madero and the docks ›› *pp 69-81*

East of the city centre at Puerto Madero, the 19th-century docks have been successfully transformed into attractive modern developments of restaurants, shops, housing and even a university campus. Walk along the waterside of the old warehouses lining Avenida Alicia M de Justo from the northern end of Dique No 4, where you'll find a helpful tourist information kiosk in a glass construction under one of the cranes.

Walking south, by Dique no 3, is the **Fragata Presidente Sarmiento**, ⓘ *Av Dávila y Perón, T011-4334 9386, Mon-Fri 0900-2000, Sat-Sun 0900-2200, US$0.70, free for children under 5*, which was the Argentine flagship from 1899 to 1938, and is now an interesting museum. Also over Dique 3 is the striking harp-like construction of the **Puente de la Mujer** (Bridge of Women), suspended by cables from a single arm.

South of the centre ›› *pp 69-81*

San Telmo

The city's most atmospheric barrio is also its oldest. Formerly one of the wealthiest areas of the city, it was abandoned by the rich during the great outbreak of yellow fever in 1871, and it's one of the few areas where buildings remain un-modernized and crumbling. San Telmo is a delightful place to stroll, with artists' studios, cafés, antique shops and small museums hidden away in its narrow streets. On Sundays a bric-a-brac market and free tango demonstrations are held in the central **Plaza Dorrego**. This is a good place to start meandering. Behind the plaza, on Carlos Calvo, there's a wonderful indoor market – **Mercado de San Telmo** built in 1897. Walk south along Calle Defensa to the white stuccoed church of **San Pedro González Telmo** ⓘ *Humerto 1, T011-4361 1168, guided tours Sun 1500, 1600, free.* Begun by the Jesuits in 1734, but only finished in 1931, it's a wonderful confection of styles with ornate baroque columns and Spanish-style tiles.

Top tips

24 hours in the city

Start with a traditional Buenos Aires breakfast of strong coffee and *medialunas* at **Café Tortoni**, lapping up the atmosphere of leather chairs and art nouveau loved by poets and intellectuals. Then wander down Avenida de Mayo with its splendid buildings to **Plaza de Mayo** where you can admire the bright pink **Casa Rosada**, and pop into the **Cabildo** for a taste of history. Take a taxi to **MALBA**, the stunning gallery of Latin American art, and have tea at its chic café before strolling through the airy galleries. From here take a taxi to **Palermo Viejo** for French, Vietnamese, Armenian or Italian food at any of the great new restaurants. Choose *Azafran* perhaps, for its views of the leafy Plaza.

If it's a sunny day, take a stroll around the **botanical gardens** in Palermo and cool off with an ice cream at *Persicco*, watching fashionable Porteños wander by. If you'd rather shop for stylish clothes instead, jump into a taxi and head to **Patio Bullrich** or **Palermo Alto**. At around 1700, it's time for *merienda* – a very English affair of sandwiches and fancy cakes at *Café Victoria* in **Recoleta**. While you're here, visit the colonial church **El Pilar**, and the cemetery next door, where Eva Perón is buried. Just outside, there's a huge **craft market**, selling cheap chic jewellery and handcarved *mate* pots, or you could pop into the **Buenos Aires Design Centre** for some Argentine handicrafts.

By now you'll be ready to relax in your hotel for an hour to get ready for the night out. At nine-ish, take a taxi to **Las Cañitas** in Palermo and choose a restaurant that appeals from a huge range along Calle Baez. Try *Novecento*, for a legendary steaks. Hold back from eating too much though, because your **tango** class at the **milonga** starts at 2230. Head for *Confitería Ideal or La Virutia*, and let the experts take you in hand. If that's too daunting, sit back and watch the city's best dancers' breathtaking display at *El Viejo Almacén*. If you've caught the infectious Porteño rhythm, have a cosy cocktail at a **Palermo Viejo** bar until the nightclubs open at 0200, perhaps El *Divino* or *El Living*. You'll emerge at dawn, when you can appreciate Buenos Aires' beautiful architecture in the crisp early light before staggering to *Clasico y Moderno* for a laid-back breakfast.

At the end of Defensa, is the **Parque Lezama** ⓘ *Defensa y Brasil, Sat-Sun 1000-2000*, originally one of the most beautiful parks in the city, but now a little run down and not a safe place to wander at night. On the west side is the **Museo Historico Nacional** ⓘ *Defensa 1600, T011-4307 4457, Tue-Fri 1100-1700, Sat 1500-1800, Sun 1400-1800, US$0.40*, which presents the history of the city and the country through key figures and events, with some impressive artefacts, portraits and paintings, particularly of San Martín. Among the ever-growing number of cheap and lively restaurants along Defensa, several venues offer tango shows. The best is the historical **El Viejo Almacén**, where the city's finest tango dancers demonstrate their extraordinary skills in a small atmospheric theatre, with excellent live music and singing from some the great names of tango (see page 75).

La Boca

The distinctive houses of the La Boca suburb.

East of the Plaza de Mayo, Paseo Colón, runs south towards the old port district of La Boca, where the Riachuelo flows into the Plata. An area of heavy Italian immigration in the early 1900s, La Boca is known for its brightly painted zinc houses, a tradition started by Genoese immigrants who used the leftover paint from ships. It's a much-touted tourist destination, but there's really only one block to see on the pedestrianized street **El Caminito**, and the houses here are reconstructions. Despite the tango demonstrations and tourist souvenirs, the area has become dangerous for foreign tourists, with police are on hand to stop visitors straying from El Caminito. Always take a radio taxi to and from La Boca, never the bus.

Vivid paintings of La Boca's ships, docks and workers, painted by Benito Quinquela Martín (1890-1977) can be seen in the **Museo de Bellas Artes 'Benito Quinquela'**, ⓘ *Pedro de Mendoza 1835. Tue-Fri 1000-1730, Sat-Sun 1100-1730, closed Jan, US$0.35, T011-4301 1080*, along with his own collection of paintings by Argentine artists. There's a roof terrace with superb panoramic views over the whole port, revealing the marginalized poverty behind the coloured zinc façades.

La Boca is home to one of the country's great football teams, Boca Juniors, and the area is especially rowdy when they're playing at home. Tours can arrange a ticket as part of a group, and fans will be entertained by the **Museo de la Pasión Boquense** ⓘ *Brandsen 805, T011-4362 1100, www.boquense.com, daily 100-1900, US$3.*

Sleeping

The tourist offices at Ezeiza and Jorge Newbery airports book rooms. Hotels and guest houses may display a star rating, but this does not match up to international standards. Many more expensive hotels charge different prices for *extranjeros* (non-Argentines), in US dollars, and there's not much you can do to get around this, since a passport is required as proof of residency. Make it clear that you'll pay in pesos in cash and you may get a reduction.

Centre *p61, map p64*

LL **Alvear Palace**, *Alvear 1891, T/F4808 2100, reservations 4808 7777, www.alvear palace.com*. The height of elegance, an impeccably preserved 1930s Recoleta palace. A sumptuous marble foyer, with Louis XV-style chairs, and a charming orangerie where you can take tea with superb patisseries (US$10). Antique-filled bedrooms. Unique. Recommended.

LL **Crowne Plaza Panamericano**, *Carlos Pellegrini 551, T011-4348 5250, www.panameri cano-bue.com.ar*. Extremely smart and modern city hotel, with luxurious and tasteful rooms, a lovely covered rooftop pool, and superb restaurant, Tomo 1. Excellent service too.

LL **Four Seasons**, *Posadas 1086, T011-4321 1200, www.fourseasons.com/ buenosaires*. An entirely modern palace in traditional style, offering sumptuous luxury in an exclusive atmosphere. Pool and health club.

LL **Marriott Plaza**, *Florida 1005, T011-4318 3000, www.marriott.com*. With a superb location overlooking Plaza San Martín, built in Parisian style in 1909, and retaining period elegance in the public rooms and bedrooms, excellent restaurant, the *Plaza Grill*, and very good service throughout.

LL **NH City Hotel**, *Bolivar 160, T011-4121 6464, www.nh-hoteles.com*. Very chic minimalist design, one of three in the Spanish-owned chain in central Buenos Aires, luxurious rooms. .

AL **Dolmen**, *Suipacha 1079, T011-4315 7117, www.hoteldolmen.com.ar*. In a good location, this has a calm relaxing atmosphere, good professional service, comfortable modern well-designed rooms, and a little pool.

AL **Etoile**, *R Ortiz 1835 in Recoleta, T011-4805 2626, www.etoile.com.ar*. Outstanding location, rooftop pool, rooms with kitchenette.

AL **Plaza San Martín Suites**, *Suipacha 1092, www.plazasanmartin.com.ar*. Neat modern self-contained apartments, comfortable and attractively decorated, with lounge and little kitchen, so that you can relax in privacy, right in the city centre, with all the services of an hotel. Sauna, gym, room service. Good value.

A **Colón**, *Carlos Pellegrini 507, T011-4320 3500, www.colon-hotel.com.ar*. With a splendid location overlooking Av 9 de Julio and Teatro Colón, in the heart of the city, extremely good value. Charming bedrooms, comfortable, pool, gym, great breakfasts, and perfect service. Highly recommended.

B **Bisonte Palace**, *MT de Alvear 910, T011-4328 4751, www.hotelbisonte.com*. A rather charming place, thanks to courteous staff. The rooms are plain, but spacious, breakfast is ample, and this is in a good location. Very good value.

B **Castelar**, *Av de Mayo 1152, T011-4383 5000, F4383 8388, www.castelarhotel.com.ar*. A wonderfully elegant 1920s hotel which retains all the original features in the grand entrance and bar. Small but good bedrooms. Also a spa with turkish baths and massage.

B **Dorá**, *Maipú 963, T011-4312 7391, www.dorahotel.com.ar*. Charming old-fashioned place with comfortable rooms, good service, an attractive lounge decorated with paintings. Warmly recommended.

C **Frossard**, *Tucumán 686, T011-4322 1811, www.hotelfrossard.com.ar*. A lovely old 1940s building with high ceilings and the original doors, attractively modernized, and though the rooms are small, the staff are welcoming, and this is good value, near C Florida.

C **Regis**, *Lavalle 813, T011-4327 2605, www.orho-hoteles.com.ar*. Good value in this old-fashioned but modernized place, with good breakfast and friendly staff. Good beds and spacious bathrooms. Full breakfast.

C **Waldorf**, Paraguay 450, T011-4312 2071, www.waldorf-hotel.com.ar. Welcoming staff and a comfortable mixture of traditional and modern in this centrally-located hotel. Good value, with a buffet breakfast, English spoken. Recommended.

D **Goya**, *Suipacha 748, T011-4322 9269, www.goyahotel.com.ar*. A range of rooms offered in this friendly welcoming and central place, worth paying C for the superior rooms, though all are comfortable and well maintained. Good breakfast, English spoken.

D **Marbella**, *Av de Mayo 1261, T/F4383 3573, info@hotelmarbella.com.ar*. Modernized, and central, though quiet, breakfast included, English, French, Italian, Portuguese and German spoken. Highly recommended.

D **Suipacha Inn**, *Suipacha 515, T011-4322 0099, www.fullmen.com.ar*. Good value, neat small rooms with a/c, basic breakfast.

E **España**, *Tacuarí 80, T011-4343 5541*. Delightful, old-fashioned and full of character, run by a charming eccentric old couple. Recommended.

E **La Giralda**, *Tacuarí 17, T011-4345 3917, F4342 2142*. Nicely maintained and good value. Popular with budget travellers, with discounts for students and for long stays.

Youth hostels

Most youth hostels are in San Telmo, (see below) but there are a few in Recoleta and Palermo. Price codes are per person:

E **St Nicholas**, *B Mitre 1691 (y Rodríguez Peña), T011-4373 5920/8841, www.stnicholas hostal.com.ar*. Beautifully restored old house, spotless rooms, cooking facilities, large roof terrace, luggage store; also D double rooms. Discounts for HI members. Recommended.

E **V&S**, *Viamonte 887, T011-4322 0994, www.hostelclub.com*. The best and very central. Also C in attractive double room with bath. Tiny kitchen, internet access, tours arranged. Highly recommended.

F **Che Lagarto**, *Venezuela 857, T011-4343 4845, www.chelagarto.com*. Central, lively atmosphere and bar, breakfast (D double rooms), kitchen, internet access, travel desk, airport pick-up. Each room has its own bathroom. Recommended.

Palermo p66

A **Malabia House**, *Malabia 1555, Palermo Viejo,T011-4831 2102, www.mala biahouse .com.ar*. An elegant bed and breakast with individually designed bedrooms and lovely calm sitting rooms. Highly recommended.

F **Tango Backpackers Hostel**, *Thames 2212, T011-4776 6871, www.tangobp.com*. Well situated to enjoy Palermo's nightlife, this is a friendly hostel with shared rooms, and all the usual facilities.

San Telmo p67

D **La Casita de San Telmo**, *Cochabamba 286 T/F4307 5073/8796, guimbo@pinos.com*. 6 rooms in restored colonial house, rooms rented by day, week or month.

E **Victoria**, *Chacabuco 726, T/F011-4361 2135*. Rooms with bath, fan, kitchen and laundry facilities, good meeting place.

Youth hostels

Worldwide chain Hostel-Inn has opened hostels in Buenos Aires, www.hostel-inn.com. **Buenos Aires Inn**, *Humberto 1 No. 820, T011-4300 7992*, E pp in double room. Also E **The Tango City Hostel Inn**, *Piedras 680, T011-4300 5764*. Both are well organized, lively, and offer lots of activities, and the usual facilities.

E **Buenos Ayres**, *Pasaje San Lorenzo 320, San Telmo, T011-4361 0694, www.buenosayres hostel.com*. A new hostel also has double rooms with bath, kitchen, laundry, internet access with breakfast included.

E/F **El Hostal de Granados**, *Chile 374, T011-4362 5600, www.hostaldegranados.com.ar*. Small well-equipped rooms for 2 to 4, with bath, breakfast included, kitchen, free internet, laundry service.

F/E **Sandanzas**, *Balcarce 1351, T011-4300 7375, www.sandanzas.com.ar*. Arty hostel, small but frinedly, with lounge and patio, internet, kitchen, breakfast included.

Eating

Eating out in Buenos Aires is one of the city's great pleasures, with a huge variety of restaurants from the chic to the cheap. To try some of Argentina's excellent steak, choose from one of the many *parrillas*, where your huge slab of lean meat will be expertly cooked over a wood fire.

Argentines are very sociable and love to eat out, so if a restaurant is full, it's usually a sign that it's a good place. Remember, though, that they'll usually start eating between 2130 and 2230. If in doubt, head for Puerto Madero, where there are lots of good mid-range places serving international as well as local cuisine. In many mid- to upper-range restaurants, lunch is far cheaper than dinner. A portion at a *comidas para llevar* (take away) place costs US$1.50-2.50. Many cheaper restaurants are *tenedor libre*: eat as much as you like for a fixed price. Alternatively, try a slice of pizza at any of the fast food joints on and around Lavalle. The following list, for reasons of space, gives only those restaurants easily accessible for people staying in the city centre.

Retiro, and the area between Plaza de Mayo and Plaza San Martín *p62*

🍴🍴 **Club Español**, *B de Irigoyen 180 (on Av 9 de Julio, near Av de Mayo)*. Luxurious ambience in a fine building, recommended for a quiet dinner, with very good food.

🍴🍴 **El Palacio de la Papa Frita**, *Lavalle 735 and 954, Corrientes 1620*. Great place for a filling feed, with a large menu, atmospheric.

🍴🍴 **La Casona del Nonno**, *Lavalle 827*. Popular with tourists for its cheap set price menu, Italian-style food.

🍴🍴 **La Chacra**, *Av Córdoba 941 (just off 9 de Julio)*. A superb traditional *parrilla* with excellent steaks brought sizzling to your table (US$13 for complete parrilla and salads for 2), impeccable old-fashioned service, and a lively buzzing atmosphere.

🍴🍴 **La Estancia**, *Lavalle 941*. A slightly touristy but reliable *parrilla*, popular with business people at lunchtime, and serving good grills, US$13 for two.

🍴🍴 **La Taska**, *Paraguay between Maipú and Florida*. Really authentic Basque food, delicious dishes: recommended.

🍴🍴 **Sorrento** *Corrientes 668, (just off Florida)*. Intimate, elegant atmosphere, traditional menu with good fish dishes and steak.

🍴🍴 **Tomo Uno**, *Crowne Plaza Hotel, Carlos Pellegrini 521, T011-4326 6695*. Argentine regional dishes and international cuisine of a high standard in a sophisticated modern atmosphere.

🍴🍴 **Broccolino**, *Esmeralda 776*. Good Italian food, very popular, try *pechuguitas*.

🍴 **Catalinas**, *Reconquista 850*. Recommended for fish and seafood.

🍴 **Exedra**, *Carlos Pellegrini and Córdoba*. A welcoming traditional-style café right on Av 9 de Julio, serving cheap set-price menu for US$4, including a glass of wine.

🍴 **Gran Victoria**, *Suipacha 783*. Good value *tenedor libre*, including *parrilla*, in a cheery atmosphere.

Cafés

Aroma, *Florida y Alvear*. A great place to relax in the centre, with a huge space upstairs, comfortable chairs by big windows onto C Florida, so you can read the papers, and watch the world go by.

Café Tortoni, *Av de Mayo 825-9, T011-4342 4328 www.cafetortoni.com.ar*. This famous Buenos Aires café has been the elegant haunt of artists and writers for over 100 years, with marble columns, stained glass ceilings, old leather chairs, and photographs of its famous clientele on the walls. Excellent coffee and cakes, and good tea, all rather pricey, but worth a visit for the interesting *peña* evenings of poetry, music, tango and Dixieland, Fri 2100.

Café de la Biblioteca, *M T de Alvear 1155* (Asociación Biblioteca de Mujeres). Coffee and light snacks, and lots of books.

Confitería Ideal, *Suipacha 384*. One of the most atmospheric cafés in the city. Wonderfully old-fashioned 1930's interior, almost untouched, serving good coffee and excellent cakes with good service. Upstairs, tango is taught: Mon-Thu 1200-1500, and Tue, Wed, Sat, 1500-2100, and there's tango dancing at a *milonga* here, Mon, Wed, Thu, Sun 15-2200, and Fri at 1400-2030. Highly recommended.

Richmond, *Florida 468, between Lavalle and Corrientes*. Genteel, old fashioned and charming place for tea with cakes, and a basement where chess is played between 1200-2400 daily.

Clásica y Moderna, *Callao 892*. One of the city's most welcoming cafés, with a bookshop at back, lots of brick and wood, this has a great atmosphere, good for breakfast through to drinks at night, with live music Thu to Sat. Highly recommended.

Recoleta *p66*

ΨΨΨ **Lola**, *Roberto M Ortiz 1805*. Well known for superb pasta dishes, lamb and fish. Recommended.

ΨΨ **El Sanjuaniño**, *Posadas 1515*. Atmospheric place offering the best of Argentina's typical dishes from the northwest: *humitas*, *tamale*, and *empanadas*, as well as unusual game dishes.

ΨΨ **Empire Bar**, *Tres Sargentos 427*. Serves Thai food in a tasteful atmosphere.

ΨΨ **Morizono**, *Reconquista 899*. Japanese sushi and sashami, as well as other dishes. Also delivery, T011-4314 4443.

ΨΨ **Rodi Bar**, *Vicente López 1900*. Excellent *bife* and other dishes in this typical *bodega* (wine cellar), a welcoming unpretentious place.

ΨΨ **Sirop**, *Pasaje del Correo, Vte Lopez 1661, T011-4813 5900*. Delicious French-inspired food, superb patisserie too. Highly recommended.

Ψ **Grants**, *Junín 1155*. *Tenedor libre*, which serves mainly Chinese but also *parrilla*, pasta, seafood, very good value.

Ψ **Güerrín**, *Corrientes 1368*. A Buenos Aires institution, serving incredibly cheap and filling slabs of pizza and *faina* (chick pea polenta) which you eat standing up at a zinc bar, or at tables, though you miss out on the colourful local life that way. Wonderful.

Cafés

Café Victoria, *Roberto M Ortiz 1865*. A wonderful old-fashioned café, popular with marvellous perfectly-coiffed ladies sipping tea in a refined atmosphere, great cakes.

Persicco, *Salguero y Cabello, Maure y Migueletes and Av Rivadavia on 4900 block*. The best ice cream in town. Superb chocolate, delicious mascarpone all served in chic style. Unmissable, highly recommended.

San Telmo *p67*

There are plenty of restaurants along C Defensa, and in the surrounding streets, and new places are opening all the time.

ΨΨΨ **La Brigada**, *Estados Unidos 465, T011-4361 5557*. The best choice in San Telmo, this is a really superb and atmospheric *parrilla*, serving excellent Argentine cuisine and wines in a cosy buzzing atmosphere. Very popular and highly recommended. Always reserve.

Ψ **El Desnivel**, *Defensa 855*. Popular for cheap and basic food, jam packed at weekends, good atmosphere.

Ψ **La Trastienda**, *Balcarce 460*. Theatre café with lots of live events, also serving meals and drinks from breakfast to dinner, great music. Relaxed and cool place hang out, with an arty crowd. Recommended.

Ψ **La Vieja Rotiseria**, *Defensa 963*. Cheap café for bargain *parrilla*, US$4 for two, packed at weekends, so come early.

Puerto Madero *p67*

An attractive place to eat, and to stroll along the waterfront before dinner. There are many restaurants along Av Alicia Moreau de Justo (from north to south), these are recommended. The cheapest places are next to the boat, **Fragata Sarmiento** on *Dique 3*.

ŸŸŸ **Katrine**, *No 138*. Delicious fish and pasta.

ŸŸŸ **La Parolaccia**, *Nos 1052 and 1160*. Pasta and seafood, does bargain executive lunch for US$4 Mon-Fri only.

ŸŸŸ **Las Lilas**, *No 516*. Excellent *parrilla*, popular with Porteños.

ŸŸ **El Mirasol del Puerto**, *No 202*. Well known and loved for a broad menu.

Palermo *p66*

This sprawling area of Buenos Aires is very popular, with many chic restaurants and bars in Palermo Viejo and the Las Cañitas district, (see below). Take a taxi to one of these restaurants, and walk around he area before deciding where to eat. There are lots of restaurants around the *Plaza Cortázar*, and along *Honduras*.

ŸŸŸ **Te Mataré Ramirez**, *Paraguay 4062, T011-4831 9156*, (also at San Isidro). Buenos Aires' only aphrodisiac restaurant. Red velvet, cupids on the walls, mellow live jazz, and excellent cuisine. Try the marinaded prawns, or fillet steak in oyster sauce. Highly recommended.

ŸŸ **Azafrán**. *On the plaza at Honduras 5143*. Lovely relaxed place for modern Mediterranean cooking. Recommended.

ŸŸ **Katmandu**, *Córdoba 3547*. Tasty Indian dishes in an exotic atmosphere.

ŸŸ **Kayoko**, *Gurruchaga 1650*. Sushi and other Japanese dishes.

ŸŸ **Luciana**, *Amenabar 1202, T011-4788 4999*. Excellent Italian trattoria.

ŸŸ **Sarkis**, *Thames 1101*. Serves delicious Arabic cuisine, superb couscous and meat dishes, with belly dancers later on at weekends. Recommended.

ŸŸ **Social Paraiso**, *Honduras 5182*. Delicious dishes, relaxed chic atmosphere. A Palermo secret.

Cafés

Palermo has lots of good cafés opposite the park, including the fabulous ice creams at **Volta**, *Av del Libertador 3060, T011-4805 1818*.

Las Cañitas *p66*

This area of Palermo is fashionable for a wide range interesting restaurants mostly along C Baez, most open around 2000 and for lunch at weekends.

ŸŸ **Campo Bravo**, *Baez y Arevalo*. A stylish minimalist place serving *parrilla* in a friendly atmosphere. Recommended.

ŸŸ **De la Ostia**, *Baez 212*. A small and chic bistro for tapas and Spanish-style food, with a good atmosphere.

ŸŸ **Eh! Santino**, *Baez 194*. A trendy small joint for Italian-style food and drinks.

ŸŸ **Morelia**, *Baez 260*. Superb pizzas on the *parilla* or in wood ovens, and has a lovely roof terrace for summer.

ŸŸ **Novecento**. Across the road from *De la Ostia*. Lively French-style bistro, stylish but unpretentious. Good fish dishes among a broad menu. Popular and recommended.

Ÿ **El Primo**, *on the opposite corner from Campo Bravo*. Popular *parrilla*. Cheap set menus, relaxed atmosphere.

Ÿ **La Fonda del Polo**, *on the opposite side of Baez*. Standard meat dishes in an intimate environment with lots of polo bric-a-brac on the walls.

Entertainment

Details of most events are given in the Espectáculos section of newspapers, *La Nación* and *Clarín*, and the Buenos Aires Herald (English) on Fri, and also in www.laguia.clarin.com. For tango shows, see p75.

Bars and clubs

There are lots of bars and restaurants in San Telmo, Palermo Viejo and Las Cañitas districts, with live music (usually beginning 2330-2400). The latest, highly recommended trend is the supper club, a fashionable restaurant serving dinner

Top tips

Tango round the city

Argentina's tango revival continues, as 20- and 30-somethings fill the city's trendy *milongas* – lively informal dance venues where anyone can join in. National Tango Day is 11 December, with events all over the city, while Buenos Aires' fabulous tango week takes place in early March, with free classes and performances. Free guided tours themed around legendary tango singer Carlos Gardel (pictured) are offered by the **tourist office**, T011-4373 2823, and tour operator, **Tangol**, *Florida 971, www.tangol. com*, runs tango outings and classes. For further details, visit the tango desk in the **Centro Cultural San Martín**, *Sarmiento 1551, T011-4373 2823, www.tangodata.com.ar*. See also *www.elfueyetango.com.ar.*

Tango shows These may be tourist-oriented but the dancing is superb: **El Viejo Almacén**, *Balcarce y Independencia, T011-4307 7388, www.viejoalmacen.com, US$50 for dinner/show*, is the city's finest (see p68). Also recommended are **La Esquina de Carlos Gardel**, *Carlos Gardel 3200, T011-4867 6363*, and **La Ventana**, *Balcarce 431, T011-4331 0217, US$45 for dinner/show*. There are also demonstrations at **Café Tortoni** (see page 62) and free shows at San Telmo's Sunday market (see page 67).

Tango classes *Milonga* classes start at 2000, followed by dancing from 2200, sometimes with a live orchestra. Even with a few basic steps, it's a pleasure being whisked around the floor. Try the **Confitería Ideal**, *Suipacha 384, T011-4605 8234*; fashionable **La Viruta** in Palermo Viejo, *Armenia 1366, T011-4774 6357, www.lavirutatango.com*; and **Centro Cultural Torquato Tasso**, *Defensa 1575, T4307 6506, www.tango-tasso.com*.

around 2200, which clears the table at 0100 for all-night dancing. Generally it is not worth going to nightclubs before 0230 at weekends. Dress is usually smart. **Pride Travel**, *Paraguay 523, T5218 6556*, www.pride-travel.com. Organizes gay nights out in Buenos Aires.

Cinemas

Films range from new Hollywood releases to Argentine and world cinema; details are listed daily in all main newspapers. Films are shown uncensored and most foreign films are subtitled in Spanish, though children's films are often dubbed. Tickets are best booked in the early afternoon to ensure good seats (average price US$2-4; there are discounts on Wed and for first show daily. There are several good cinemas on Lavalle, also in shopping malls, in Puerto Madero (dock 1) and in Belgrano (Av Cabildo and environs). On Fri and Sat nights many central cinemas have *trasnoches*, late shows starting at 0100. At **Village Recoleta**, *Vicente López y Junín*, there is a cinema complex with **trasnoche** programme on Wed, Fri and Sat. Independent foreign and national films are shown during the *Festival de Cine Independiente*, every Apr.

Theatre

About 20 commercial theatres play all year, and there are many amateur theatres, with a theatre festival at the end of May. You are advised to book early for a seat at a concert, ballet, or opera. Tickets for most popular shows (including rock and pop concerts) are sold through **Ticketek**, *T011-5237 7200*, **Entrada Plus**, *T011-4324 1010* or **Ticketmaster**, *T011-4321 9700, www.tm.com.ar*.
Teatro Colón, see p63, ticket office Tue-Sat 1000-2000, Sun 1000-1700. Opera and ballet tickets sold 2 days before performance. Good opera tickets are around US$35, with the cheapest seat at US$1.30; 'El Paraíso' tickets are available for standing room in The Gods – queue for a good spot
Teatro San Martín, *Corrientes 1530, T011-4371 0111/8 or 0800-333 5254, www.teatrosanmartin.com.ar*. Organizes many cultural activities, often free, including concerts, 50% ISIC discount for Thu, Fri and Sun events (only in advance at 4th floor, Mon-Fri). The theatre's **Sala Leopoldo Lugones** shows international classic films, daily, US$1.

Shopping

The main shopping streets are the pedestrianized C Florida, stretching south from Plaza San Martín, and Santa Fe, especially going west from Av 9 de Julio to Av Pueyrredon. Along Florida, **Galerias Pacificos** is a recommended mall with a good range of clothes and a cheap food court. Designer clothes shops can be found in exclusive shopping mall **Patio Bullrich** and along Arenales and Santa Fe, between 9 de Julio and Callao. Cheaper clothes can be found in the **Abasto** shopping mall, Subte Carlos Gardel.

Handicrafts

Leather is cheap and of very high quality.
All Horses, *Suipacha 1350*. **Aida**, *Galería de la Flor, shop 30, Florida 670*. Here you can have a leather jacket made to measure in the same day.
Arte y Esperanza, *Balcarce 234, Alhué, Juncal 1625 and Artesanías Argentinas, Montevideo 1386*. Very good aboriginal-style crafts.
El Boyero, *Galería Larreta, Florida 953, T011-4312 3564*. High quality silver, leather, wood work and other typical Argentine handicafts.
Galería del Caminante, *Florida 844*. A variety of good shops with leather goods, arts and crafts, souvenirs, etc.
Kelly's, *Paraguay 431*. A very large selection of reasonably-priced Argentine handicrafts in wool, leather, wood, etc.
Regionales La Rueda, *Paraguay 728*. Gaucho artefacts, woollen goods, silver, leather, good prices.

Bookshops

Foreign books are hard to find, and prices are very high, try **Librería Rodríguez**, *Sarmiento 835*; **Kel Ediciones**, *MT de Alvear 1369 and Conde 1990 (Belgrano)*. Foreign newspapers are available on Florida, in Recoleta and the kiosk at Corrientes y Maipú. **El Viajero**, *Carlos Pellegrini 1233, T011-4394 7941, www.elviajero.com*, has travel books, a library and an information service.

Camping equipment

Cacique Camping, *Esteban Echeverría 3360, Munro, T011-4762 4475*. Clothing and equipment.
Ecrin, *Mendoza 1679, T011-4784 4799, info@ escalada.com*. Imported climbing equipment.
Imperio Deportes, *Ecuador 696*. Also repairs. Recommended.

Markets

Plaza Dorrego, *San Telmo*. A wonderfully atmospheric market for souvenirs, antiques, and all kinds of curious bric-a-brac. Free tango performances and live music, Sun 1000-1700.
Plaza Italia, *Santa Fe y Uriarte (Palermo)*. Second-hand textbooks and magazines are sold daily, handicrafts on Sat 1200-2000, Sun 1000-2000.
Parque Centenario, *Díaz Vélez y L Marechal*. Sat, local crafts, good, cheap hand-made clothes.
Mercado de las Luces, *Manzana de las Luces, Perú y Alsina, Mon-Fri 1100-1900, Sun 1400-1900*. Handicrafts.

Activities and tours

Polo

Argentina has the top polo players in the world. The high handicap season is Sep to Dec, but it is played all year round (low season Mar-May). A visit to the national finals at Palermo in Nov and Dec is recommended. **Asociación Argentina de Polo**, *T011-4342 8321*.

Football

Soccer fans should go to see **Boca Juniors** at La Bombonera, *Brandsen 700, La Boca, buses 29, 33, 53, 64, 86, 152*, open Mon-Fri for visits, matches Sun 1500-1900 and sometimes Fri or Sat, cheapest entry US$3-5. Their arch-rivals are **River Plate**. The soccer season Mar-Jun, Aug-Dec. Rugby season Apr-Oct/Nov.

Tour operators

Three-hour city tours or longer tours with dinner and a tango show, or a gaucho fiesta at an estancia (farm or ranch) are bookable through most travel agents.
Buenos Aires Tur (BAT), *Lavalle 1444, T011-4371 2304*. City tours (US$6) twice daily; Tigre and Delta, daily, 5 hrs (US$13).
Buenos Aires Vision, *Esmeralda 356 p 8, T011-4394 4682*. City tours, Tigre and Delta, Tango (US$ 33, cheaper without dinner) and Fiesta Gaucha (US$27).

Class Adventure Travel, *Av Pres Roque S Peña 615, Buenos Aires, www.cat-travel.com*. Head office in Peru. Dutch-owned and run. Highly recommended. **Eternautas**, *Arcos 2514, T011-4781 8868, www.eternautas.com*. Historical, cultural and artistic tours of the city and Pampas. **Eves Turismo**, *Tucumán 702, T011-4393 6151*. Helpful and efficient, for flights. **Exprinter**, *San Martín 170, T011-4341 6600, Galería Güemes, www.exprinterviajes.com* Especially 5-day, 4-night tour to Iguazú and San Ignacio Miní.
Flyer, *Reconquista 621, p 8, T011-4312 9194/95*. English spoken, repeatedly recommended, especially for estancias, fishing, polo, motorhome rental.
Say Hueque, *Viamonte 749, 6th floor, of1, T011-5199-2517, www.sayhueque.com* Fun trips for budget travellers.
Tripping, *Marcos Dartiguelongue and Leonardo Kawakami, T011-4791 6769, T15-4993 3848 (mob), trippingbsas @hotmail.com*. Tours to dance clubs, football matches, parachute jumps, horseback trips and city bike tours.
Turismo Feeling, *San Martín 969 p 9, T011-4313 5533*. Excellent and reliable horseback trips and adventure tourism.

Transport

Air

For flight details, see p20-23. For transport to and from the centre, see p59.

Airline offices Aerolíneas Argentinas, *Perú y Rivadavia, Av LN Alem 1134 and Av Cabildo 2900, T0810-2228 6527, www.aerolineas.com.ar*. Extremely helpful and efficient. **Air Canada**, *Av Córdoba 656, T011-4327 3640*. **Air France**, *San Martín 344 p 23, T011-4317 4700 or T0800-222 2600*. **Alitalia**, *Av Santa Fe 887, T011-4310 9910*. **American**, *Av Santa Fe 881, T011-4318 1000, Av Pueyrredón 1889*, branches in Belgrano and Acassuso. **Avianca**, *Carlos Pellegrini 1163 4thfl, T011-4394 5990*. British Airways, *T011-4320 6600, Carlos Pellegrini 1163 10th fl*. **Iberia**, *Carlos Pellegrini 1161 1st fl, T011-4131 1000*. **Lan Chile**, *Cerrito y Paraguay, T011-4378 2200, www.lan chile.com*. **Líneas Aéreas del Estado** (LADE), *Perú 714, T011-4311 5334, Aeroparque T011-4514 1524, reservas@ lade.com.ar*. Erratic schedules. **Lufthansa**, *M T Alvear 636, T011- 4319 0600, www.lufthansa-argentina.com*. **Qantas**, *Av Córdoba 673 13th fl, T011-4514 4726, www.qantas argentina.com.ar* **Southern Winds**, *Av Santa Fe 784, T0810-777 7979, www.sw.com.ar*. **United**, *Av Madero 900, T0810-777 8648*. **Varig**, *Florida 1, T011-4342 4420, www.varig.com.br*.

Boat

Connections to the north of Argentina and Uruguay with Buquebus, www.buquebus.com.ar. To **Colonia de Sacramento**, 3 daily, 3 hrs, US$22 return (cars US$ 23-30); the faster boat takes 1hr, US$60 return (cars US$39-44).

Bus

Local Collectivos basic fare US$0.30 or US$0.40 to the suburbs, paid with coins into a machine behind the driver. Check that your destination appears on the bus stop, and in the driver's window.

Long distance Boats and buses are heavily booked Dec-Mar, especially at weekends. See also Essentials, p24. Ticket offices are on the upper floor of **Retiro** bus terminal, *Ramos Mejía y Antártida Argentina*, and are organized by colour-coded regions of the country.

Car hire

Driving in Buenos Aires is no problem if you have eyes in the back of your head and nerves of steel. **Avis**, *Cerrito 1527, T011-4326 5542*. **AL International**, *San Luis 3138, T011-4312 9475*. **Budget**, *Santa Fe 869, T011-43119870*. ISIC and GO 25 discount. **Hertz**, *Ricardo Rojas 451, T011-43121317*. **AVL**, *Alvear 1883, T011-48054403*. **Ricciard Libertador**, *Av del Libertador 2337/45, T011-47998514*. **Localiza**, *Paraguay 1122, T011-43143999*. **Unidas**, *Paraguay 864, T011-43150777*.

Metro

Trains run Mon-Saturday 0500-2250, Sun 0800-2200. Free maps are available from subte stations and the tourist office. Single fare to anywhere US$0.25 payable in pesos only at the ticket booth.

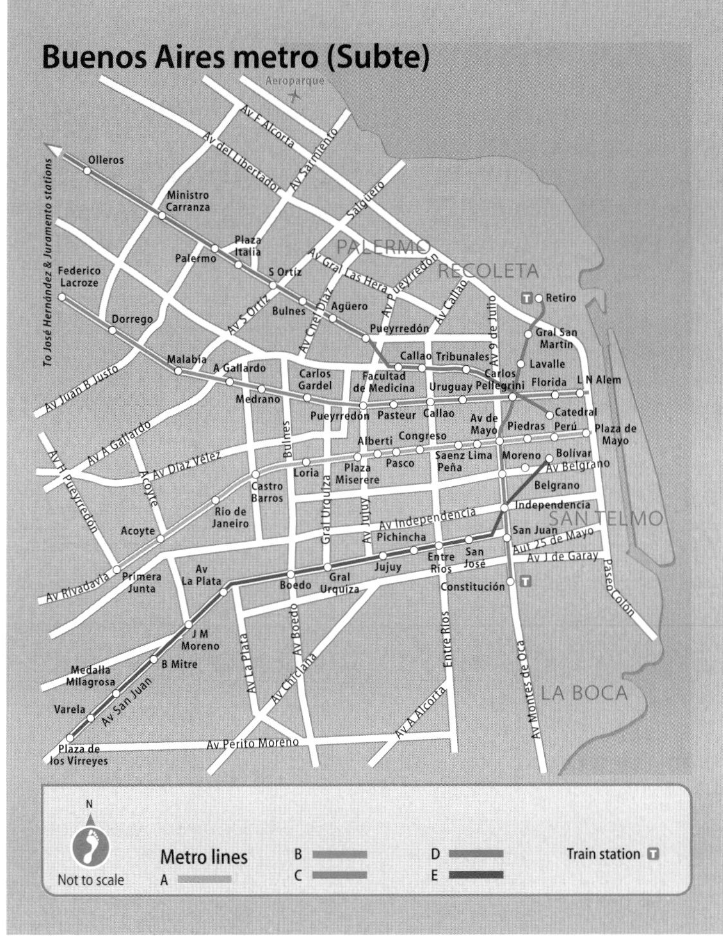

Taxi

For security, phone for a radio taxi: **Radio Taxi Sur**, *T011-4638 2000*; **Radio Taxi 5 Minutos** *T011-4523 1200*; **Radio Taxi Diez** *T011-45855007*; **Onda Verde** *T011-4867 0000*. Fares are shown in pesos, starting at US$0.35, plus US$0.04 for every 200 m or one-minute wait. A charge is sometimes made for hand luggage. Remise taxi **La Terminal**, *T011-4312 0711*, is recommended for journeys from Retiro bus station. About 10% tip is expected.

Directory

Banks and currency exchange

ATMs are widespread. Visa and MasterCard ATMs at branches of **Banco de la Nación Argentina**, **ABN Amro Bank**, **BNP**, **Itaú** and others. MasterCard/Cirrus also at **Argencard** offices. For lost of stolen cards, Mastercard *T011-4340 5700*, Visa *T011-4379 3333*. Casas de cambio on *San Martín* and *Corrientes*. Major credit cards usually accepted but check for surcharges. General **MasterCard** office at *Perú 151*, *T011-4348 7070*. **Visa**, *Corrientes 1437, p 2, T011-4379 3333*.

Embassies and consulates

All open Mon-Fri unless stated otherwise. For other embassies, consult the phone book. **Australia**, *Villanueva 1400 y Zabala, T011-4777 6580, www.argentina.embassy.gov.au 0830-1100*. **Canada**, *Tagle 2828, T011-4808 1000, www.dfait-maeci.gc.ca/bairs, Mon-Thu 1400- 1600*, tourist visa *Mon-Thu 0845-1130*. **Chilean Consulate**, *Tagle 2762, T011-4801 2761, 0900-1300*. **New Zealand**, *C Pellegrini 1427 5th fl, T011-4328 0301, T011-4328 0747, kiwiargentina @datamarket.com.ar. Mon-Thu 0900-1300, 1400-1730, Fri 0900-1300*. **US Embassy and Consulate General**, *Colombia 4300, T5777 4533/34* or *T011-4514 1830, 0900-1800*.

Internet

Broadband Speedy is widely available, prices US$0.30-US$0.65 per hr. Many *locutorios* (phone centres) have internet access. Several on Florida and Lavalle. **De la City**, *Lavalle 491*. **Cybercafé**, *Maipú 486 (basement)*. **Comunicar**, *Lavalle y Cerrito*.

Language schools

For Spanish lessons try: **Encuentros**, *T/F4832 7794*; **Argentina I.L.E.E**, *T011-4372 0223, www.argentinailee.com*; **IBL**, *T011-4331 4250*; **PLS** *T011-4394 0543, www.pls.com.ar*; **Instituto del Sur** *T011-4334 1487, www.delsur. com.ar*. **Universidad de Buenos Aires**, *T011-4334 7512 or T011-4343 1196, idlab@filo.uba.ar*. **Cedic** *T/F4315 1156*. Enquire also at **Asatej** (see Useful addresses).

Medical services

For free ambulance service to an emergency department (day and night) call **Sala de guardia**, *T107, or T011-4923 1051/58*. **Hospital Argerich**, *Almte Brown esq Pi y Margall 750, T011-4362 5555/5811*. **Hospital Juan A Fernández**, *Cerviño y Bulnes, T011-4808 2600*. **Hospital de Clínicas José de San Martín**, *Av Córdoba 2351, T011-5950 8000*.

Post office

Correo Central – Correos Argentinos, *Sarmiento y Alem, Mon-Fri, 0800-2000, Sat 0900-1300. Poste restante* on ground floor (US$0.50 per letter). **UPS**, *Bernardo de Irigoyen 974, T011-4339 2877*.

Safety

If robbed or attacked, call the tourist police, **Comisaría del Turista**, *Av Corrientes 436, T011-4346 5748 (24 hrs)*. English spoken. Keep this number in your pocket. Street crime is on the rise, especially in the tourist areas of La Boca, San Telmo and Recoleta, and individuals walking alone are more at risk than couples or groups. Be careful when boarding buses, and near the Retiro train and bus stations. Do not change money on the street. If your passport is stolen, call your embassy for emergency help.

Going further

If you have more than a few days to spend in the city, here are three tips for perfect escapes - all possible in a day, or overnight:

The Tigre Delta
Take the coastal train – **Tren de la Costa** – from the suburb of **Olivos** (local train from Retiro to Olivos) to the little resort of **Tigre** in the jungly overgrown river delta, 29km north. Popular with families and the jet set in summer, it has lots of hotels and restaurants, a fruit market, excellent fishing, and you could hire a kayak if you're feeling energetic, see www.tigre.gov.ar /turismo, T011-4512 4495. Or take a river bus down the tranquil canals to stay at a luxurious riverside retreat, such as **La Pascuala** (www.lapascuala.com.ar US$125 per person for 24 hours).

Colonia de Sacramento
East across the Río de la Plata, on the shores of Uruguay, lies **Colonia del Sacramento**, whose Portuguese colonial centre is beautifully preserved. Hire a bike (US$3 per day), or a scooter (US$4) to see the whole place at your leisure. Boats leave from Puerto Madero three times daily, 3 hrs (US$22 rtn) or 1 hr (US$60 rtn) – see www.buquebus.com. Take your passport, no visa required, pesos and dollars accepted everywhere.

Estancias in the Pampas
The immense flat lands stretching out from the capital are dotted with grand cattle estancias. Either visit for the day or spend the night to enjoy riding, walking, fishing, or just relaxing in complete peace and luxury. **San Antonio de Areco** 113km northwest (www.sanantoniodeareco.com), is a good base with a lively gaucho feel, a couple of great museums and three estancias on its doorstep. Alternatively, head 126km south to the cowboy town of **Chascomús** where **Dos Talas** offers the most exquisite estancia stay in a historic house, www.dostalas.com.ar, from US$120 per person per night, everything included.

Telephone
Locutorios are available on almost every block (see Essentials, p41). Public telephone boxes use coins (25 centavos minimum for local calls). Pre-paid cards can also be used (available at *kioskos*), don't accept cards without a wrapper or with a broken seal. International telephone calls from hotels may incur a 40-50% commission plus government tax of about the same amount.

Useful addresses
Asatej: Argentine Youth and Student Travel Organization, *Florida 835, p 3, oficina 320, T011-4114 7500, www.asatej.com*. Student discounts, flights, hotels, information, ISIC cards, English spoken. Asatej Travel Store, sells travel goods. Central Police Station: *Moreno 1550, Virrey Cevallos 362, T011-4370 5911/5800*. Migraciones: (Immigration), *Antártida Argentina 1335/55, edificios 3 y 4, T011-4317 0200, F4317 0282*. Visas extended mornings.

Argentine Lake District

Los Angeles
Parque Nacional Laguna de Laja
Piedra del Indio
Chos-Malal
Rincón de los Sauces
Río Colorado
El Hueco
Santa Bárbara
Copahue
Mulchén
Termas de Copahue
Cavíahue
CHILE
Ralco
40
Loncopué
Parque Nacional Tolhuaco
Termas de Tolhuaco
Reserva Nacional Malalcahuello
Lonquimay (2,865m)
Río Neuquen
NEUQUÉN
Curacautín
Sierra Nevada
Malacahuello
Lonquimay
Bajado del Agro
Añelo
Las Lajas
Vilcún
Llaima
Lago Conguillio
Paso Pino Hachado
Parque Nacional Conguillio
Cherquenco
Vol Llaima (3,050m)
Emb Cerros Colorados
Temuco
Icalma
Mariano Moreno
Melipeuco
Paso de Icalma
Los Laureles
Cunco
Zapala
Lago Alumine
Plaza Huincal
Playa Negra
Río Colico
Lago Colico
Moquehue
PN Laguna Blanca
22
Neuquén
Lago Huilipilún
Lago Caburga
Cutral-Có
Caburga
Parque Nacional Huerquehue
22
Villarrica
Lago Villarrica
Pucón
237
Las Penas
Termas de Palquin
Quillén
Aluminé
Villarrica (2,840m)
Villa El Chocón
Lican-Ray
Quetrupillán (2,009m)
Puesco
40
Lago Calafquén
Parque Nacional Villarrica
Paso Mamuil Malal
Emb Ezequiel Ramos Mexia
Coñaripe
Picún Leufú
Lago Panguipulli
Liquiñe
Lanín (3,768m)
Lago Neltume
Paso Carirriñe
Lago Riñihue
Puerto Fuy
Lago Huechulafquen
Choshuenco
Parque Nacional Lanín
Junín de los Andes
Piedra del Aguila
Lago Pirehueico
Futrono
Paso Hua Hum
El Cuy
Llifén
Lago Lacar
Lago Ranco
Lago Maihue
San Martín de los Andes
ARGENTINA
p86
p96
RIO NEGRO
Lago Ranco
Lago Huishue
Confluencia
Lago Gris
Río Limay
Mencué
Lago Constancia
Río Golgol
215
Portezuelo de Puyehue
237
Termas de Puyehue
Villa La Angostura
Parque Nacional Puyehue
Parque Nacional Los Arrayanes
Parque Nacional Nahuel Huapi
Lago Nahuel Huapi
La Picada
Petrohué
Peulla
Paso Pérez Rosales
Bariloche
Catedral
Lago Todos los Santos
Tronador (3,460m)
Lago Mascardi
Aguada de Guerra
Comallo
Pilcaniyeu
Cayutué
Parque Nacional Vicente Pérez Rosdales
Ingeniero Jacobacci
Ralún
Villa Mascardi
p108
23
Lago Chapo
Los Juncos
Maquinchao
Cochamó
Las Bayas
Parque Nacional Alerce Andino
258
40
Puelo
p116
El Bolsón
Norquinco
Los Repollos
Parque Nacional Hornopirén
El Maitén
Parque Pumalín
Parque Nacional Lago Puelo
Epuyén
Cholila
Leptepu
Parque Pumalín
Leleque
La Bolsa
Lago Menéndez
Parque Nacional Los Alerces
Gualjaina
Lago Futulaufquen
Esquel
Amarillo
Trevelin
40
Lago Espolo
Futaleufú
Paso Futaleufú
Río Chubut
Colán Conhué
Lago Yelcho
Puerto Piedra
Paso Palena
Corcovado
Tecka
Puerto Ramírez
Palena
p131
Don't miss...
1 Pehuenia ▶▶ p89.
2 Volcán Lanín ▶▶ p96.
3 Parque Nacional Los Arrayanes ▶▶ p111.
4 Hiking around Bariloche and Pampa Linda ▶▶ p118.
5 A boat trip on Lago Menéndez ▶▶ p138.
N
40 km
40 miles

Introduction

Argentina's best-loved region has astonishingly beautiful lakes and rivers, deep green forests and snow-capped mountains. It's vast, unspoilt and ideal for adventures of all kinds. You can walk in the perfectly preserved footprints of dinosaurs around northern Neuquén, admire ancient monkey puzzle trees in tranquil Pehuenia and hook a magnificent rainbow trout at Junín de los Andes. San Martín de los Andes is an appealing base for exploring Parque Nacional Lanín, where the perfect cone of Volcán Lanín turns every snapshot into a Japanese woodcut. Climb to the top for a challenging hike or admire its reflection in Lago Paimún. With a dramatic lakeside setting, Bariloche is the main centre in Parque Nacional Nahuel Huapi. Trek for days in the surrounding peaks, sail through the lakes to Chile, or wander around the fairy tale wood of arrayanes trees at Villa la Angostura. Further south, you can sample the local cerveza in laidback El Bolsón, track down Butch and Sundance's hide out in sleepy Cholila or catch the old Patagonian Express from Esquel. Finally, enjoy the silence and beauty of Los Alerces national park, where forested mountains drop steeply into pristine lakes.

Ratings

Landscape
★★★★★

Chillin'
★★★★★

Activities
★★★★★

Wildlife
★★★★

Costs
$$$

Northern Neuquén

The province of Neuquén contains the northern part of the Lake District, an enormous region stretching from just north of Bariloche to the border with Mendoza province. The gateway is the pleasant city of Neuquén on the province's eastern border. This is an important fruit-growing area, providing most of Argentina's apples, pears and grapes. To the southwest, enormous dinosaur footprints mark the landscape around Villa El Chocón; the skeleton in the museum there is proof that the largest carnivores ever known roamed around this area 100 million years ago.

The unspoilt wilderness in the northwest of the province is only now opening up to visitors, although it is just as spectacular as better known destinations to the south. The area west of Zapala, known as Pehuenia has large forests of ancient pehuén or monkey puzzle trees. Further north, Caviahue is a good base for walking and skiing in a rugged and unspoilt landscape, while bleaker Copahue is known for its high-quality thermal waters.

Getting there Frequent flights and buses to Neuquén from Buenos Aires and other major cities.
Getting around Bus services to/from Neuquén; hire car for Pehuenia.
Time required 4 days.
Weather Warm in summer, snowy in winter, bright and chilly in spring, mild in autumn.
Sleeping Few hotels outside Neuquén but lots of lovely cabañas in Pehuenia, no hostels.
Eating Fresh, locally grown apples, cherries and pears in summer.
Activities and tours Rafting in Río Aluminé, skiing, trekking
★ **Don't miss...** Pehuén forests at Villa Pehuenia

Neuquén and around » pp 92-95

The provincial capital is an attractive industrial town, founded in 1904, just after the arrival of the railway. It has no major tourist attractions but is a useful stopping point en route to the lakes and a good base for exploring the dinosaur finds in the area to the southwest.

Ins and outs

Getting there There are daily flights from Buenos Aires to the airport 7 km west of town, T0299-444 0245. Take a local bus 10 or 11 into town for US$0.40 (*tarjeta* bus card needed), or taxi US$4. There are frequent long-distance buses to the central terminal at Mitre 147 from Buenos Aires and towns throughout the Lake District as well as west to Temuco and Puerto Montt in Chile. **Tourist information** ⓘ *Félix San Martín 182, T0299-442 4089, www.neuquentur.gov.ar, turismo@neuquen.gov.ar, daily Mon-Fri 0700-2000, Sat-Sun 0800-2000.* The office hands out helpful lists of accommodation and a good map.

Sights

At the northern end of Av Argentina at the Parque Centenario there is the **Mirador Balcon del Valle** with panoramic views over the city and the confluence of the rivers (be sure not to take the bus to Centenario industrial suburb). In the university buildings at the entrance of the park is the **Museo Paleontológico de Ciencias Naturales**, Argentina 1400, which includes exhibitions of dinosaur fossils found in the region. The former railway station, at Olascaoga y Pasaje Obligado, has been converted into a cultural centre and exhibition centre. The **Museo de la Ciudad Paraje Confluencia**, Independencia y Córdoba, T0299-442 9785, has a small display on the Campaign of the Desert, colonial annihilation of indigenous groups, (see box, page 48). South of the centre there is also a pleasant walk along the Río Limay. Facing Neuquén and connected by bridge is **Cipolletti**, in Río Negro province, a prosperous fruit-growing centre of the region. All the towns in the valley celebrate the *Fiesta Nacional de la Manzana* (apples are the main local crop) in the second half of March. Two lakes nearby, **Lago Pellegrini**, 36 km north, and **Embalse Cerro Colorado**, make a pleasant excursion from the city, with daily buses in summer.

Villa El Chocón and around

To the southwest of Neuquén lies the huge **Embalse Ezequiel Ramos Mexía** in an area that has become famous in recent years for the wealth of dinosaur fossils that have been found here. Villa El Chocón lies at the northern end of the lake, 72 km from Neuquén, on the most direct route to Bariloche. It's a neat, rather uninspiring town, but worth a stop for the amazing evidence of **dinosaurs** nearby (take Route 237 towards Piedra del Aguila, and turn left at Barrio Llanquén to the lake shore). Red sedimentary rocks have preserved bones and even footprints of the creatures that lived in this region during the Cretaceous period, about 100 million years ago. Some of these can be seen at the **Museo Paleontológico Ernesto Bachmann** ⓘ *T0299-490 1223, www.interpatagonia.com/paseos/ernestobachmann, daily 0900-1900 winter 0800-2100 summer, guided tours, website has information in English.* Exhibits include fossils of the mighty 10-ton, 15-m long *Gigantosaurus Carolinii*, a carnivorous dinosaur larger than the more famous Tyrannosaurus Rex. There's a well laid out and informative display with information on these quite mind-boggling finds.

In the **Valle Cretacico**, 18 km south of Villa El Chocón, near the Dique with its pedestals of eroded pink rock, there are two walks beside the lake to see more dinosaur footprints, amazingly well preserved.

Background

Dinosaurs

Few countries are as important as Argentina for palaeontologists. The relative abundance of fossils near the surface has made the country one of the most important for the study of dinosaur evolution. Patagonia was home to Jurassic dinosaurs (180-135 million years old) and outstanding examples have been found here. Cerro Cóndor in Chubut is the only site of Middle Jurassic dinosaurs found in the Americas, and has given palaeontologists an important breakthrough in understanding the evolutionary stages of the period. At least five examples of patagosaurus have been found there, indicating that these dinosaurs at least were social creatures, perhaps for purposes of mutual defence. In Santa Cruz traces of dinosaurs from the Upper Jurassic period have been found in rocks which indicate that the climate was arid and desert-like at the time, surprising palaeontologists with the news that dinosaurs could live and breed in such adverse conditions.

The most important discoveries of dinosaurs from the Cretacic period (135-70 million years ago) have been made in Neuquén and Chubut. Dating from the period of separation of the continents of South America and Africa, these provide evidence of the way in which dinosaurs began to evolve in different ways due to geographic isolation. The *Carnotaurus sastrie* has horns and small hands, for example. The Patagonian dinosaurs are relatively huge, the *Argentinosaurus huiculensis* is one of the largest herbivorous dinosaurs found on earth, while the carnivorous *Gigantosaurus carolinii* found near Neuquén city was larger even than the better known *Tyranosaurus Rex*, discovered in North America.

Dinosaur spotting in Patagonia: **Villa Chocón**, southwest of Neuquén city, boasts huge and perfectly preserved dinosaur footprints next to the lake. Further finds from the site can be seen in Neuquén's palaeontological museum. **Trelew** on the Atlantic coast, has the country's finest dinosaur museum, and as part of the same foundation, there's an excellent site with 40 million years of history near the Welsh village of **Gaiman**. Many of the most interesting finds are to be seen in **Buenos Aires**.

Plaza Huincul

There are more dinosaur remains at a quite impressive little museum in the otherwise rather dull town of **Plaza Huincul**, 107 km west of Neuquén. The **Museo Municipal Carmen Funes** includes the vertebrae of *argentinossaurus huinclulensis*, believed to have weighed over 100 tons and to have been one of the largest herbivorous dinosaurs ever to have lived on earth, as well as a nest of fossilised dinosaur eggs.

Zapala and around

Zapala (1,012 m) lies in a vast dry plain with views of snow-capped mountains to the west. It's modern and unappealing, but a useful place to stop on the RN40, to cross the border into Chile at the Icalma Pass (see page 90), or to explore the less-visited northern end of the Lake

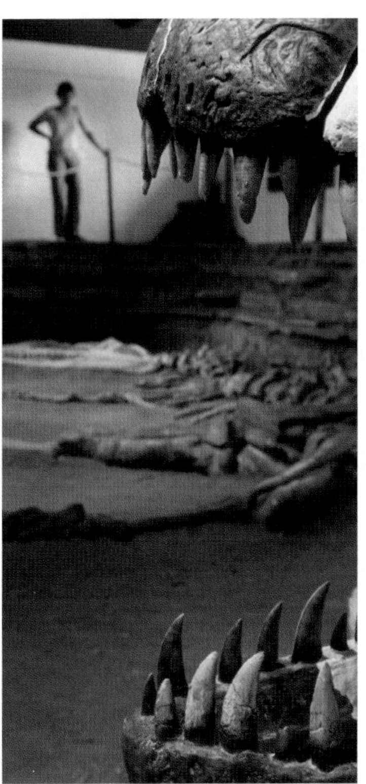

District. **Tourist information** is available at San Martín y Mayor Torres ⓘ *T02942-421132, open (summer) Mon-Fri 0700-1930, Sat/Sun 0800-1300, 1600-1900, closes earlier off-season.*

The **Museo Mineralógico Dr Juan Olsacher** ⓘ *Etcheluz 52 (next to the bus terminal), neumin@zapala.com.ar, Mon 0900-1500, Sat and Sun 1600-2000, free,* is one of the best museums of its type in South America; it contains over 2,000 types of mineral and has the finest collection of fossils of marine reptiles and marine fauna in the country. On display is the largest turtle shell from the Jurassic period ever found and an ophthalmosaur, as well as photos of an extensive cave system being excavated nearby.

Southwest of Zapala is the **Parque Nacional Laguna Blanca** ⓘ *entrance 10 km from the junction of RN46 and RN40, www.parquesnacionales.gov.ar, entry US$2, no public transport,* a reserve covering large areas of high arid steppe and a vast lagoon that is one of the most important nesting areas of the black-necked swan. The landscape is very dry, and rather bleak, so take drinking water and a hat if you decide to visit.

Pehuenia » *pp92-95*

The magical and unspoilt area of Pehuenia is named after the country's unique forests of *pehuén* trees (see page 53), which grow here in vast numbers. Covering a marvellous open mountainous landscape, these ancient, silent trees create a mystical atmosphere, especially around the lakes of Aluminé and Moquehue. Daily buses from Zapala and Aluminé make this area accessible by public transport, though having your own vehicle is an advantage. The *ripio* is rough but cycling is perhaps the best way to appreciate the peace and beauty of the area.

Villa Pehuenia and around

Reached by *ripio* road, the eastern shores of Lago Aluminé lie 107 km west of Zapala. A **tourist kiosk** is signposted, T02942-498027, by the turning for Villa Pehuenia. This small, isolated village on the northern shore is picturesquely sited among steep, wooded hills. The **Mapuche** (see page 239), the largest indigenous group in the south of the continent, chose this area for settlement because of its chain of eight volcanoes and its sacred *pehuén* trees. Infrastructure is slowly building here so that, at the moment, you can have the best of both worlds: an unspoilt feel combined with comfortable accommodation, thanks to a rapidly growing cluster of *cabañas*. The peninsula stretching out into the lake from the village offers wonderful walks along the araucaria-fringed shore and fabulous views from the **mirador del Cipres**.

Just a few kilometres further along the main road from Villa Pehuenia, signposted to the right, is the **Batea Mahuida**, a reserve created to protect an area of *pehuén* trees and the majestic volcano, regarded by the Mapuche peoples as sacred. This is a lovely for walking in summer, with tremendous views of all seven volcanoes around. There's also a winter sports centre here, Parque de Nieve, administrated by the Mapuche people, offering snowmobiles, snowshoe walks and husky rides. Delicious homecooked food is served.

Lago Moquehue

Another 10 km on Route 13 brings you to the sprawling village of Moquehue,on the shores of its lake. It's a wilder more remote place than Villa Pehuenia with a lovely wide river that's famous for trout fishing. This is a beautiful and utterly peaceful place to relax and walk. A short stroll through araucaria forests brings you to a waterfall, while a longer hike to the top of Cerro Bandera (four hours return) gives wonderful views over the area as far as Volcán Llaima. You should also head along Route 13, 11 km to Lago Ñorquinco, past mighty basalt cliffs with *pehuéns* all around. There are fine camping spots all around and a couple of comfortable places to stay.

Aluminé and around

On Route 23 between Pehuenia and Junín lies the area's self-proclaimed rafting capital. There is indeed superb rafting (grades two-six) on Río Aluminé, but despite the grand setting, the town is a drab little place with earth roads. There's a very friendly **tourist office** ⓘ *Calle Christian Joubert 321, T0294-496001, www.alumine.net, open 0800-2100 all year*, and a service station – the first one you'll reach driving south from Villa Pehuenia. In March, the harvest of the *piñones* is celebrated in the Fiesta del Pehuén with horse riding and live music. ▲▸▸ *p94.*

Border with Chile

Paso Pino Hachado (1,864m) lies 115 km west of Zapala via Route 22. On the Chilean side the road runs northwest to Lonquimáy, 65 km west and Temuco, 145 km southwest. Buses from Zapala and Neuquén to Temuco use this crossing. **Argentine immigration and customs** ⓘ *9 km east of the border, open 0700-1300, 1400-1900.* **Chilean immigration and customs** ⓘ *at Liucura, 22 km west of the border, open Dec- Mar 0800-2100, Apr-Nov 0800-1900.* Very thorough searches and two- to three-hour delays reported.

A more tricky route is via **Paso de Icalma** (1,303 m), 132 km west of Zapala, reached by Route 13 (ripio). On the Chilean side this road continues to Melipeuco, but is often impassable in winter. Permission to cross must be obtained from the Policía Internacional in Temuco (Prat 19, T045-293890). **Argentine immigration and customs** ⓘ *9 km east of the border, open 0800-2000 in summer, 0900-1900 approximately in winter.* All paperwork to be carried out at the customs office. **Chilean immigration and customs** ⓘ *open Dec-Mar 0800-2100, Apr-Nov 0800-1900.*

From Aluminé there is access to **Lago Rucachoroi**, 23 km west, in the Parque Nacional Lanín. This is the biggest Aigo Mapuche community inside the national park and is set in gentle farmland surrounded by ancient *pehuen* forests. Access is by a rough *ripio* road, spectacular in autumn when the deciduous trees are a splash of orange against the bottle green araucarias. The *guardería* can advise about a possible trek to Quillén (see below). » *For information on the rest of Parque Nacional Lanín, see page 96.*

Lago Quillén

At the junction by the small town of **Rahue**, 16 km south of Aluminé, a road leads west to the valley of the Río Quillén and the exquisite Lago Quillén, from where there are fine views of Volcán Lanín peeping above the mountains. The lake itself is one of the region's most lovely, jade green in colour, with beaches along its low-lying northern coast. Further west, where annual rainfall is among the heaviest in the country, the slopes are thickly covered with Andean Patagonian forest. There's no transport, and accommodation only is at the **Camping Pudu Pudu** (with food shop and hot showers) on the lake's northern shore, just west of the *guardería*.

Caviahue and around » *pp92-95*

Located 150 km north of Zapala and with an attractive lakeside setting, **Caviahue** is an excellent base for walking and riding in summer and for winter sports from July to September, when it is one of cheaper ski resorts in the Lake District. **Tourist information** ⓘ *8 de Abril, bungalows 5/6, T02948-495036, www.caviahue-copahue.com.ar.*

The arid, dramatic and other-wordly landscape of the **Reserva Provincial Copahue** is formed by a giant volcanic crater, whose walls are the surrounding mountains. The park was created to protect the araucaria trees that grow on its slopes and provides the setting for some wonderful walks through unexpectedly stunning scenery. **Copahue** (altitude 1,980 m) is a thermal spa resort enclosed in a gigantic amphitheatre formed by mountain walls. It boasts the best thermal waters in South America, although it's decidedly bleaker than Caviahue. Tourist information is available on Route 26, on the approach into town.

Volcán Copahue last erupted, smokily, in 2000, destroying the bright blue lake in its crater, but the views of the prehistoric landscape are still astounding. Even more highly recommended, however, is an excursion to **El Salto del Agrio**, on RN 27. This is the climax in a series of delightful waterfalls, between ancient araucaria trees poised on basalt cliffs. Other walks will take you to **Las Máquinas**, 4 km south of Copahue, where sulphurous steam puffs through air holes against a panoramic backdrop. And to **El Anfiteatro**, where thermal waters reaching 150°, are surrounded by a semicircle of rock edged with araucaria trees. Just above Copahue, is **Cascada Escondida**, a torrent of water falling 15 m over a shelf of basalt into a pool surrounded by a forest of araucaria trees; above it is magical **Lago Escondida**

Sleeping

Neuquén p87

AL **Hotel del Comahue**, *Av Argentina 377, T0299-443 2040, www.hoteldel comahue.com.ar* Quite the most comfortable by a long way is this international-style, elegant modern 4-star, with spa and pool, an excellent restaurant, very good service and business facilities.
D **Alcorta**, *Alcorta 84, T0299-442 2652*. With breakfast, TV in rooms, good value. Also flats for 4.
D **Royal**, *Av Argentina 145, T0299-448 8902, www.hotelguia.com/hoteles/royal* A smart modern hotel, but with welcoming rooms, car parking and breakfast included, good value.
E **Res Neuquén**, *Roca 109 y Yrigoyen, T0299-442 2403*. Pleasant, with bath, breakfast and TV.

Villa El Chocón and around p87

B **La Posada del Dinosaurio**, *Costa del Lago, Barrio 1, Villa El Chocón, T0299-490 1200, www.posadadinosaurio.com.ar* Convenient for dinosaur hunting, this has very plain but comfortable rooms, with views over the lake, and a restaurant.
D **La Villa**, *Club Municipal El Chocón, T0299-490 1252*. Decent budget choice.

Plaza Huincul p88

C **Hotel Tortorici**, *Cutral-Co, 3 km west, Av Olascoaga y Di Paolo, T0299-496 3730, www.hoteltortorici.com* The most comfortable option is this newly built hotel with neat rooms and a restaurant.

Zapala p88

A **Hostal del Caminante**, *Outside Neuquén 13 km south towards Zapala,T02942-444 0118*. A popular place in summer, with a pooland garden.
C **Hue Melén**, *Brown 929, T02942-422414*. Good value 3-star hotel, with decent rooms, restaurant serves the town's best food, including local specialities.
C **Huincul**, *Av Roca 311, T02942-431422*. A spacious place with a cheap restaurant, serving good home-made regional food.
D **Pehuén**, *Elena de Vega y Etcheluz, T02942-423135*. Comfortable, 1 block from bus terminal, with an interesting display of local maps.

Villa Pehuenia p90

There's plenty of *cabañas*, many with good views over the lake, and set in idyllic woodland. Ask the tourist office for directions, as the tracks are unnamed.
C **Cabañas Bahía Radal**, *T02942-498057, bahiaradal@hotmail.com*. Luxurious *cabañas* in an elevated position with clear lake views.
C **Cabañas Puerto Malén**, *Club de Montana, T011 4226 8190 (Buenos Aires), www.puerto malen.com* Well-built wooden *cabañas* with clear lake views from their balconies.
C **Las Terrazas**, *T02942-498036, lasterrazasvillapehuenhia@yahoo.com.ar* Warmly recommended. Beautiful, architect-designed *cabañas* in Mapuche style. Tasteful, warm and with perfect views over the lake. Also D bed and breakfast. The owners know the area intimately and can direct you to magical places for walking, and to Mapuche communities to visit.
D **La Serena**, *T011-547940319, www.complejolaserena.com.ar* Beautifullly equipped and designed *cabañas* with great uninterrupted view,

gardens going down to beach, sheltered from wind, furnished with rustic-style handmade cypress furniture, and wood stoves, all very attractive.

Camping

Camping Agreste Quechulafquen, *at the end of the steep road across La Angostura*. Situated among lovely steep hills and dense vegetation, run by Mapuche Puels.

Camping El Puente, *at La Angostura*. US$2pp, with hot showers; a simpler site, in beautiful surroundings.

Las Lagrimitas, *just west of the village, T02942-498063*. A lovely secluded site on the beach, with food shop, US$2pp, hot showers and fireplaces.

Lago Moquehue *p90*

C **Hostería Moquehue**, *T02946-156 60301, www.hosteriamoquehue.netfirms.com* Set high above the lake with panoramic views, cosy, stylish, rustic rooms, nicely furnished. Excellent food: try the superb Moquehue trout and local *chivito*. Charming family hosts.

C/D **Cabañas Melipal**, *T02942-432445, T02942-156-61549*. Very attractive, rustic stone-built *cabañas* in secluded sites right on lake side, 1 for 4 the other for 12. Lovely old-fashioned style, well equipped and warm, fabulous views from balcony, use of boats. Highly recommended.

D **Cabañas Huerquen**, *T02942-156 4700, huerquen_patagoni@hotmail.com* Beyond Moquehue on the road to Ñorquinco are lovely secluded stone *cabañas* in beautifully tranquil setting.

F **Ecocamping Ñorquinco Norquinco**, *11 km from Moquehue, towards Ñorquinco, T02942-496155* One amazing rustic *cabaña* right on the lakeside, with a café, $6.50 pp per night, Dec-Easter. Great fishing, hot showers and a *proveduría*.

Camping

Camping Trenel, *on the southern shore of Lago Moquehue*. Beautiful shady sites in a fabulous elevated position surrounded by *nirre* trees; seats and *parrillas* overlooking lake. Recommended, smart, hot showers, restaurant, shop, information and trips.

Aluminé *p90*

D **Pehuenía**, *just off Route 23, Crouzeilles 100, T02942-496340, pehuenia2000@yahoo.com.ar* A huge tin chalet-style building, not attractive, but with great views over the hills opposite. The rooms are comfortable and simple, the staff are friendly, and it's good value. Horse riding, bike hire and canoeing at the owner's campsite, Bahía de los Sueños, 6km from the red bridge north of Aluminé.

Camping

La Vieja Balsa, *T02942-496001, just outside Aluminé on Route 23 on the Río Aluminé*. A well equipped site, that also offers rafting and fishing, US$1 pp per day to camp, hot showers, food shop, fireplaces, tables, open Dec to Easter.

There are 2 campsites before and after **Lago Rucachoroi**; open all year, but really ideal only Dec-Feb. The first has more facilities, with toilets, but no hot water, some food supplies, including wonderful Mapuche homemade bread and sausages, and offers horse riding.

Caviahue *p91*

B **Nevado Caviahue**, *8 de Abril s/n, T02948-495042, www.caviahue.com*. Plain rooms, but modern, and there's a restaurant, and cosy lounge with wood fire. Also A-B for 6 *cabañas*, well equipped but not luxurious.

C **Lago Caviahue**, *Costanera Quimey-Co, T02948-495110, www.hotellagocaviahue.com* Better value than the Nevado above; comfortable lakeside apartments with kitchen, good restaurant, great views, 2km from the ski centre.

Camping

Copahue, *T02948-495111, Hueney Municipal, 495041*.

Copahue *p91*

A-C **Hotel Copahue**, *Olascoaga y Bercovich, T02948-495117*. Lovely old place where you'll be warmly welcomed. Recommended. Well built wood and stone *cabañas*, price depends on season.

Eating

Neuquén *p87*

Anonima This supermarket has a good *patio de comidas* (food hall), and games to amuse the kids.

El Reencuentro, *Alaska 6451*. A popular *parrilla* recommended for delicious steaks in a warm atmosphere.

Fatto Dalla Mama, *9 de Julio 56*. Fabulous filled pasta.

La Birra, *Santa Fe 23*. Lots of choice, and is very welcoming, with chic modern surroundings.

Rincón de Montaña, *9 de Julio 435*. Recommended for delicious local specialities and cakes.

Tutto al Dente, *Alberdi 49*. Recommended for tasty home made pasta.

Cafés

Café El Buen Pan, *Mitre y Corrientes, open 0600 to 2300*. A bright modern place for snacks and good bakery too.

Living Room, *Pte Rivadaria*. A lovely comfortable bar-café, with armchairs and table outside, a great place to relax.

Villa Pehuenia *p89*

Costa Azul, *located on the lakeside, T02942-498035*. The village's best restaurant, where you can taste delicious local dishes and pasta; *chivito* (kid) *al asado* is the speciality of the house.

Aluminé *p90*

Apart from **La Posta del Rey**, the only other decent choice is **Parrilla Aoniken**, near the bus terminal at *Av 4 de Caballería 139*, with pizzas and *milanesas*, and a cheap set menu, US$3 for 3 courses.

Caviahue *p91*

The most recommendable places to eat are mostly in the hotels:

Copahue Club Hotel, *Valle del Volcán*. Serves good *chivito al asado* and locally caught trout.

Hotel Caviahue. The hotel restaurant serves kid, along with pastas.

Hotel Lago Caviahue. The most stylish place to eat with an inspired *chivo a la cerveza* (kid cooked in beer) on the menu, along with more traditional favourites and local specialities.

Activities and tours

Neuquén *p87*

Aventura Jurasica, *Centro Comercial Local 3, T0299-126321863*. Dinosaur tours. Also in Villa El Chocón at *Alejandro París, T0299-490 1243*.

Gondwana Tour, *Córdoba 599 T496 3355, geoda@copelnet.com.ar* Excursions to dinosaur sites nearby, and accommodation.

Villa Pehuenia *p90*

Expedicion Llienan Mapu, *Rute 11 km 17.5, T02942-156 64705*. Horse riding, 4WD excursions, husky rides and cross country skiing in winter. Recommended.

Aluminé *p90*

Aluminé Rafting, *Ricardo Solano, T02942-496322*. US$9-15, depending on grade of difficulty, for 3 hrs rafting, grades 2-6. All equipment included. *Circuito Abra Ancha* 2,5 hours, grade 2, 6km very entertaining, suitable for everyone. *Circuito Aluminé Superior*, 12 or 15km run, 5-6 hours, grade 3/4, very technical river leaving Lago Alumine, for those who like a thrill, passing little woods of araucarias and nirres, family trips grades 1 and 2, costs $20pp for Abra Ancha, $60pp for higher level. Trekking $80 per day, trekking in Cordon de Chachil, $120 per day, 2 days minimum, but can be up to a week, also kayaking, and biking.

Caviahue *p91*

The ski resort has 3 lifts and excellent areas for cross-country skiing; contact Caviahue Base, T02948-495079.

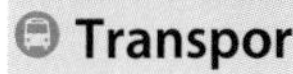

Transport

Neuquén *p87*

Air

To **Buenos Aires**, daily with Austral/Aerolíneas Argentinas, *Santa Fe 52, T0299-442 2409*. Southern Winds, *Argentina 237, T0299-442 0124*.

Bus

The terminal is at *Mitre 147*. Left luggage: US$0.70 a day per item. Andesmar, *T0299-442 2216*, Via Bariloche, *T0299-442 7054*, El Valle, *T0299-443 3293*.

About a dozen companies to **Buenos Aires**, daily, 12-16 hrs, US$25-35. To **Zapala** daily, 3 hrs, US$4.50. To **San Martín de los Andes**, 6 hrs, US$10. To **Bariloche**, 7 companies, 5-6 hrs, US$11, best views if you sit on left. To **Mendoza**, Andesmar, and 3 others, daily, 12 hrs, US$17. To **Junín de los Andes**, 5 hrs, US$8, many companies.

To **Aluminé**, 6 hrs, US$8, many companies. To **Zapala**, 2-3 hrs, US$4.30, Albus, Centenario. To **Plaza Huincul**, 1½ hrs, US$2, same companies. To **Caviahue** (6 hrs, US$10) and **Copahue**, 6½ hrs, US$11, Centenario.

To **Chile** Services to **Temuco** stop for a couple of hours at the border, 12-14 hrs, US$17. Some companies offer discount for return, departures Mon-Thu and Sat; 7 companies, some continuing to destinations en route to **Puerto Montt**.

Zapala *p88*

The bus terminal is at Etcheluz y Uriburu, *T02942-423191*. To **Neuquén**, 2-3 hrs, US$4.50, Albus, Centenario, several daily. To San Martín de los Andes, 3-4 hrs, US$8. To **Junín de los Andes**, 3hrs, US$8 with Albus, Centenario, several daily. To **Aluminé**, 2 1/2 hrs, US$4.50, several companies, daily. To **Villa Pehuenia**, 2½hrs, US$5, 4 a week, go on to **Moquehue** 3 hrs, US$7. To **Caviahue**, (3 hrs, US$7) and **Copahue** (3½-4 hrs, US$7.50) daily with Centenario. To **Bariloche**, Albus, TAC, Vía Bariloche via San Martín. To **Buenos Aires**, 18 hrs, US$25-30, many companies. To **Temuco** (Chile), US$16, Mon/Wed/Fri, Centenario (buy Chilean pesos in advance).

Villa Pehuenia *p90*

There are 3 buses weekly to Villa Pehuenia and **Moquehue** from **Neuquén** (less predictable in winter, when the roads are covered in snow) and **Aluminé**.

Aluminé *p90*

Buses daily to/from Zapala, with either Aluminé Viajes (*T02942- 496231*), or Albus (*T02942-496368*), 3hrs, US$4. Twice a week to Villa Pehuenia 1 hr, US$2. Twice a week to San Martín de los Andes, 4 hrs, US$5, with Tilleria *T02942-496048*.

Caviahue *p91*

Buses to/from **Neuquén**, El Petroleo and Centenario. Daily, 6 hrs, US$11, via Zapala (US$5). El Centenario *T02948-495024*.

Directory

Neuquén *p87*

Banks and currency exchange Lots of ATMs along Av Argentina, plus casas de cambio. **Consulates** Chile, *La Rioja 241, T0299-442 2727*. **Internet** Near the bus terminal at *Mitre 43 T0299-443 6585*, a block from bus station. **Post office** *Rivadavia y Santa Fe*. **Telephone** Many *locutorios* in the centre, often with internet access. Telecom, *25 de Mayo 20*, open daily till 0030, and *Olascoaga 222*, open till 2345. Cheap.

Zapala *p88*

Banks Three banks including Banco de la Nación Argentina, *Etcheluz 465*, but difficult to change TCs. **Internet** Instituto Moreno, Moreno y López y Planes. CPI, *Chaneton y Garayta*.

Parque Nacional Lanín

Some of the most beautiful sights in the Lake District are to be found in Parque Nacional Lanín, which stretches along the border with Chile for 200km. The park covers 379,000 ha and includes 24 glacial lakes, one of which (Lago Lacar) drains into the Pacific.

Vegetation is varied throughout the park, due to differences in rainfall and altitude. In the north between Lagos Ñorquinco and Tromen, araucaria trees dominate, mixed here and there with lenga and ñire. But further south, you'll find a combination of the southern beech species: roble, rauli and the majestic grey-trunked coihue. Bamboo grows in profusion along Lago Huechulafquen at the centre of the park; this prehistoric species dies off en masse once every 20 to 30 years, when all the plants simultaneously rot, and new life begins the following year. Wildlife includes wildcats and foxes, the elusive pudu and some red deer.

Getting there Flights to Chapelco airport or long distance buses from Buenos Aires, Bariloche, Puerto Madryn and Temuco.

Getting around Frequent buses and plenty of tours. Ideal cycling area. Boats across Lago Lacar.

Time required Upto a week to really see the park and chill out.

Weather Warm in summer, snowy in winter, chilly in spring, mild in autumn.

Sleeping Plentiful in San Martín de los Andes, but heavily booked in Jan/Feb. Junín de los Andes is quieter.

Eating grilled trout, chocolate.

Activities and tours Fishing, trekkin, skiing.

★ **Don't miss...** Volcán Lanín

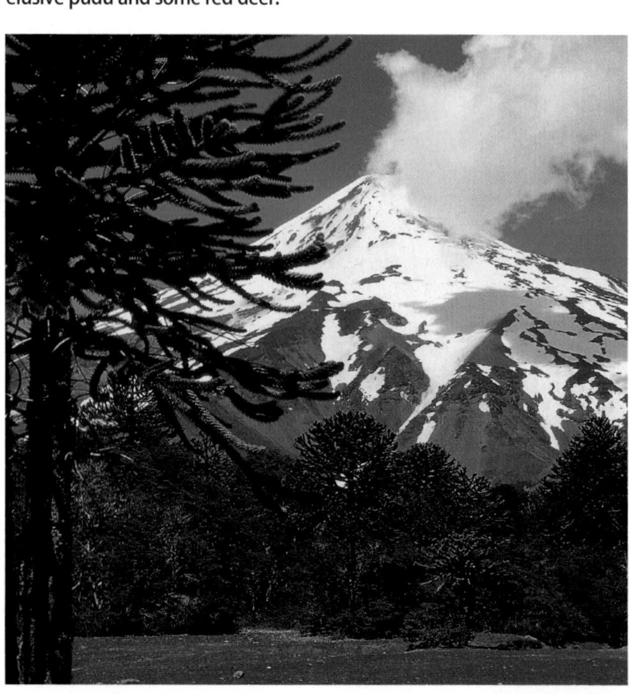

Ins and outs

Access The park can be entered at various points; the most significant are 3, 4, 7 and 8, where there are *guardaparques* who can advise on hikes. Other entrances are more remote.

1 Route 18 from Aluminé to Lago Rucachoroi (see page 91)
2 Route 46 from Rahue to Quillén (see page 91)
3 Route 60 to Lago Tromen, for the ascent of Lanín and Paso Tromen
4 Route 61 from north of Junín de los Andes to Lago Huechulafquen. The easiest entry, with regular buses in summer, fabulous walks and great camping.
5 Route 62 from Junín de los Andes to Lago Currhué for good walking and thermal pools.
6 Route 48 from the junction with route 62 to Puerto Arturo and Lago Lolog
7 Along route 48 to Lago Lacar and Paso Hua Hum
8 Route 234 via San Martín de los Andes.

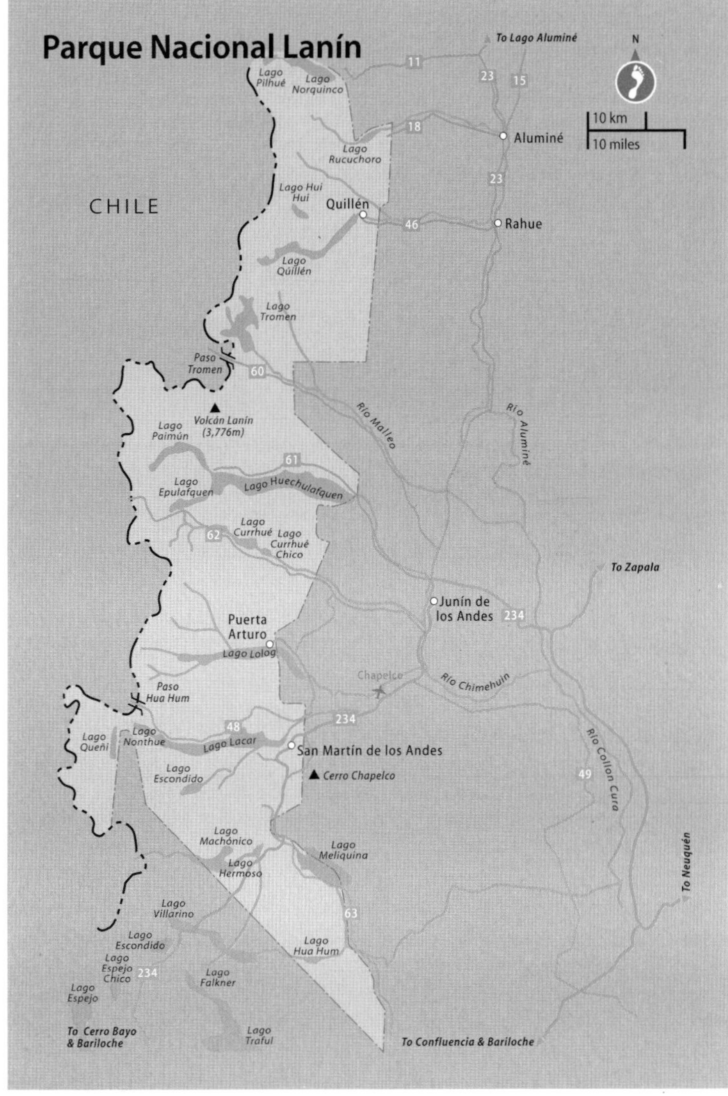

Park information ⓘ *Administration: Emilio Frey 749, San Martín de los Andes, T02972-427233, laninupublico@smandes.com.ar, entry US$2*. There is also a helpful information office in Junín de los Andes, in the same building as the tourist office, T02972-491160. You're supposed to register at the administration in San Martín de los Andes before setting out on any major treks in the park, although this is obviously impractical. However, *guardaparques* at Lago Huechulafquen should always be notified before you set off, and will advise on routes. Having a good map is essential: try to get hold of the excellent Parque Nacional map in Junín or San Martín de los Andes before you arrive at the park. Wherever you are in the park, fires are a serious hazard: always put out campfires with lots of water, not just earth. Pack up all rubbish and take it away with you.

Exploring the park

Lago Huechulfaquen

In the centre of the park, Lago Huechulafquen stretches from smooth lowland hills in the east to steep, craggy mountains in the west, heavily clad in native beech trees, overlooked by the magnificent extinct snow-capped Lanín on the Chilean border. The northern shore of the lake, with its grey volcanic sand, shelter beautiful, if basic, camping grounds.

Around Lago Paimún

It's worth the trek to view the sugary peak of Lanín from the exquisitely pretty crescent-shaped Lake Paimún, further west. There is a range of excellent walks here, along paths marked with yellow arrows. Ask *guardaparques* for advice on routes before setting off and allow plenty of time for return before dark. Guides are only required for longer unmarked treks; for these, ask in the Junín park office or at San Martín de los Andes. You can also explore much of the area on horseback, including the trek to the base of Volcán Lanín. Five places along the lake hire horses: ask *guardaparques* for advice, or ask at Mapuche communities. To cross to other side of Lago Paimún there's a boat operated by the Mapuche: just ring the bell.

Lago Curruhué and Termas de Lahuen-Co

Lago Curruhué and the thermal pools at **Termas de Lahuen-Co** are a two-day hike from Lago Paimún. Alternatively, drive there along Route 62 from either Junín or San Martín de los Andes. You'll pass ancient pehuén forests along the south shore of the Lago Currhue Grande

Walks around Lago Paimun

1 El Saltillo Falls (2 hrs return) fabulous views en route to the waterfall. Start from the campsite at Lago Paimún.
2 Termas at Lahuen-Co (12 hrs) 8 hrs to the end of Lago Paimún, then four more to reach the Termas, best done over two days. A beautiful walk, and you'll be rewarded by a soak in the simple rustic pools. First cross the lake from Puerto Canoa.
3 Volcán Lanín (8 hrs return) a satisfying walk to the base of the volcano and back. Start from Puerto Canoa.
4 Cerro El Chivo (7 hrs return), a more challenging walk through forest to the summit at 2,064 m. Note that heavy snow can lie till January. Set off early, and register at the campsite at Bahía Cañicul.

and the impressive lava field at Escorial. The pools are 8 km further on, with rustic camping and a *guardería*. Trips to Lago Curruhué and the termas are offered by tour companies in San Martín but there's no public transport to these places at present.

Paso Tromen and around

Paso Tromen, known in Chile as **Paso Mamuil Malal**, is situated 64 km northwest of Junín de los Andes and reached by *ripio* Route 60 which runs from Tropezón on Route 23, through Parque Nacional Lanín. Along this route there are several Mapuche communities, which can be visited. Some 3 km east of the pass a turning leads north to **Lago Tromen**, a lovely spot where there is good camping, and south of the pass is the graceful cone of the **Lanín** volcano. This is the normal departure point for climbing to the summit (see below). Paso Tromen is a beautiful spot, with a good campsite, and lovely walks. From the *guardería*, footpaths lead to a *mirador* (one-and-a-half-hours round trip), or across a grassy prairie with magnificent clear views of Lanín and other jagged peaks, through *ñirre* woodland and some great araucaria trees to the point where Lago Tromen drains into Río Malleo (4 km).

Climbing Lanín

One of the world's most beautiful mountains, Lanín (3,768 m) is geologically one of the youngest volcanoes of the Andes; it is now extinct. It is a three-day, challenging climb to the summit; crampons and ice axe required. The ascent starts from the Argentine customs

Border with Chile

The **Paso Tromen** (aka Paso Mamuil Malal) crossing is less developed than the Hua Hum and Puyehue routes further south (see page 101 and 112); although this is the route used by international buses between Junín and Temuco, it is unsuitable for cycles and definitely not usable during heavy rain or snow (June to mid-November), as parts are narrow and steep. For up-to-date information, contact the gendarmería, T02972-491270, or customs, T02972-492163. On the Chilean side the road continues through glorious scenery, with views of the volcanoes of Villarrica and Quetrupillán to the south, to Pucón on Lago Villarrica (see page 240). **Argentine immigration and customs** ⓘ *3 km east of the pass, open 0800-2000 all year.* **Chilean immigration and customs** ⓘ *at Puesco, 17 km from the border, open Dec-March 0800-2100; Apr-Nov 0800-1900.*

post at the Tromen pass, where you must register and where all climbers' equipment and experience are checked. A four-hour hike leads from here to two free *refugios* at 2,400 m, sleeping 14 to 20 people.

It's vital to get detailed descriptions of the ascent from the *guardaparques*. To climb the north face, follow the path through lenga forest to the base of the volcano, over arroyo Turbio and up the *espina de pescado*. From here there are three paths to the *refugios*: **1** straight ahead, the espina de pescado is the shortest but steepest (four to five hours), **2** to the right, the camino de mulas is the easiest but longest (seven hours) and is marked; and **3** to the left, *canaleta* should be used only for descent. From the refugios, it is six to seven hours over ice fields to the summit. Because of Lanín's relative accessibility, the risks of climbing it are often underestimated. An authorised guide is absolutely necessary for anyone other than the very experienced. Crampons and ice-axe are essential, as is protection against strong, cold winds. Climbing equipment and experience is checked by the *guardaparques* at the Tromen pass.

Junín de los Andes » *pp102-107*

Situated on the beautiful Río Chimehuin, the quiet town of Junín de los Andes (773 m) is justifiably known as the trout capital of Argentina. It offers some of the best fly fishing in the country in world renowned rivers, and the fishing season runs from mid November to the end of April. Junín is also an excellent base for exploring the wonderful virgin countryside of Parque Nacional Lanín and for climbing the extinct volcano itself.

Founded in 1883, Junín is not as picturesque or tourist-orientated as its neighbour, San Martín – there are definitely no chalet-style buildings, and few chocolate shops here – but it's a quiet neat place with genuinely friendly people.

Sights

Most of what you need can be found within a couple of blocks of the central Plaza San Martín with its fine araucaria trees among mature *alerces* and cedars. The small **Museo Salesiano** ⓘ *Ginés Ponte y Nogueira, open Mon to Fri 0900-1230, 1430-1930, Sat 0900-1230*, has a fine collection of Mapuche weavings, instruments and arrowheads, and you can buy a whole range of excellent Mapuche handicrafts in the *galería* behind the tourist office. There's an impressive sculpture park **El Via Christi** ⓘ *just west of the town,T02972-491684, from the plaza walk up Av Ant. Argentina across the main road RN 234, to the end*. Situated among pine forest on a hillside, the stations of the cross are illustrated with touching and beautifully executed sculptures of Mapuche figures, ingeniously depicting scenes from Jesus's life together with a history of the town and the Mapuche community. The sculptures are to be found along trails through the pine woods. A lovely place to walk, and highly recommended. The church, **Santuario Nuestra Senora de las Nieves y Beata Laura Vicuña**, also has fine Mapuche weavings, and is a pleasing calm space. The best fishing is at the mouth of the river Chimehuin on the road to Lago

Huechulafquen, although there are many excellent spots around; see guides below. In the town itself, there are pleasant picnic sites along the river. The **tourist office** ⓘ *T02972-491160, www.junindelosandes.com.ar, open 0800-2200 summer, 0800-2100 rest of year,* on the plaza is staffed by friendly people, who can advise on accommodation and hand out maps.

San Martín de los Andes and around ›› pp 102-107

San Martín de los Andes is a charming tourist town nestled in a beautiful valley surround by steep mountains on the edge of Lago Lacar, with attractive chalet-style architecture and good but expensive accommodation. It's a good centre for exploring southern parts of the **Parque Nacional Lanín** and lakes **Lolog** and **Lacar**, where there are beaches for relaxing and good opportunities for water sports, mountain biking and trekking. **Cerro Chapelco** (2,394m), 20 km south of San Martín, offers superb views over Lanín and many Chilean peaks. In summer, this is a good place for trekking, archery, horse riding or cycling (take your bike up on the cable car, and cycle down), while in winter it transforms into a well organized ski resort (see page 106). The other most popular excursions are south along the **Seven Lakes Drive** to Lagos Traful, Meliquina, Filo Hua Hum, Hermoso, Falkner and Villarino (see below) and north to the thermal baths at **Termas de Lahuen-Co**.

Ins and outs

Tourist information ⓘ *San Martín y Rosas 790, on the main plaza, T02972-427347. Open 0800-2100 all year.* The office has lists of accommodation, with prices up on a big board, hand-out maps and good advice. Staff speak English and French, but are very busy in summer, when it's advisable to go early in the day, before they get stressed. Also check www.chapelco.com.ar and www.smandes.gov.ar

Sights

Running perpendicular to the *costanera*, along the lake, is Calle San Martín, where you'll find most shops and plenty of places to eat. There are two plazas, of which Plaza Sarmiento is lovely, wooded, nicely maintained and illuminated by little lamps at night. The more functional Plaza San Martín, has a sporadic crafts market, and is more of a public space. It's a pleasant one-and-a-half hour walk to **Mirador Bandurrias** with great views, and a *quincho*-like restaurant run by a Mapuche community. There's a good little museum on local history, **Museo Primeros Pobladores** ⓘ *1000 to 1500, 1800 to 2100 Mon-Fri, Sat and Sun 1300 to 2200.*

Lago Lacar and around

Lago Lacar can be explored by car along much of its length, as there's a *ripio* road, Route 48, leading to the Chilean border at **Paso Hua Hum**, 41 km. You can cycle or walk all the way

Border with Chile

Paso Hua Hum (659 m) lies 47 km west of San Martín de los Andes along Route 48 (*ripio*), which runs along the north shore of Lago Lacar. It is usually open all year round and is an alternative to Paso Tromen (see page 99). The road (*ripio*, tough going for cyclists) continues 11 km on the Chilean side to **Puerto Pirehueico** (see page 247). Buses from San Martín de los Andes, connect with the boat across Lago Pirehueico to Puerto Fuy or there are buses to Panguipulli for onward connections.

Argentine immigration ⓘ *2km east of the border, open summer 0800-2100, winter 0900-2000.* Chilean immigration ⓘ *Puerto Pirehueico, open summer 0800-2100, winter 0900-2000.*

 around the lake and on to **Lago Escondido** to the south. There are beaches at **Hua Hum**, at the western end of the lake, and rafting on the nearby Río Hua Hum. On the southern shore, 18 km away, there is a quieter beach at **Quila Quina**, where you can walk either to a waterfall, along a guided nature trail, or to a tranquil Mapuche community in the hills above the lake. Both lakeshore villages can be reached by boat from the pier in San Martín. ›› *p107*.

Sleeping

Lago Huechulafquen *p96*
There are superb campsites and 3 overpriced *hosterías* (LL), all rather taking advantage of their lakeside positions. Hostería Paimún, is the most luxurious but not the most welcoming; try instead, Huechulafquen, *T0972-426075, T02944-156 0973, www.7lagos.com/huechulafken*, for comfortable rooms, peaceful gardens and expert fishing advice or the basic Refugio del Pescador, *T02972-491319*.

Camping
Camping Lafquenco, *just after the sign to Bahía Coihues*. Highly recommended for its friendly welcome, with a good spot on the lakeside and lots of room, $3pp.
Piedra Mala, *beyond Hostería Paimún*, beautiful wooded site with 2 beaches, hot showers, *parrillas* and a *proveduría* (food shop) $4 adults, $2 children.

Paso Tromen *p99*
There's a municipal campsite on the Río Curi Leuvú; a free CONAF site in Puesco (Chile), with no facilities, and a superb campsite, Agreste Lanín, at Puesto Tromen, open Dec to Apr US$1 per person, with shaded areas, hot showers, toilets, *parilladas* and places to wash. Well run by friendly people. Take food.

Junín de los Andes *p100, map p103*
D **Hostería Chimehuín**, *Suárez y 25 de Mayo, T02972-491132, hosteriachimehuin @jandes.com.ar* A long-established fishing *hostería* with beautiful gardens, and friendly owners, quaint decor, and comfortable rooms all with bath and TV. Ask for the spacious rooms with balconies in the block next to the river. Good breakfasts, open all year. Recommended.
D **Milla Piuke**, *off the RN234, at Gral Roca y Av los Pehuenes, T/F02972-492378, millapiuke@jandes.com.ar* Delightful and welcoming new *hostería*, with tastefully decorated and stylish rooms all with bath and TV, and apartments for families, warm hospitality from the radiant owner Vilma. Breakfast included. Highly recommended.
D **San Jorge**, *at the very end of Antártida Argentina, T/F02972-491147, www.7lagos.com/ hotelsanjorge open Nov-Apr*. A big, recently modernized 1960s hotel, beautifully located with lovely views and large gardens, homely well furnished rooms, all with bath and TV. Very good value, with good restaurant and internet access. English spoken.
E **Res Marisa**, *Juan Manual de Rosas 360, T02972-491175, www.residencial marisa.com.ar*. Simple, good value, with plain clean rooms, and cheery family owners. *Confiteria* downstairs, breakfast is US$0.70 extra. It's on the main road, so a little noisy during the day, but handy for the bus terminal and cheap eating places.

Estancias
L **Estancia Huechahue**, *southeast of town (reached from the Junín-Bariloche bus), T02972-491303, www.ridingtours.com*, Self-sufficent, English-run estancia, with comfortable, farmhouse accommodation, offering horse riding, wonderful 3-5 day trips into Lanín National Park where you camp, with everything included, also fishing, river trips, and farm activities.

Camping
Beata Laura Vicuña, *Ginés Ponte 861, T02972-491149, campinglv @jandes.com.ar* Located on the river, with hot showers, electricity, small shop, discounts for stays over two days, also very good value *cabañas* for 4 or 7.

San Martín de los Andes *p101, map p104*
Single rooms and rates are scarce. Rates are much higher in Jan/Feb and July.

A **Hotel Del Viejo Esquiador**, *San Martin 1242, T02972-427690*. Very comfortable rooms with good beds, in traditional hunting lodge-style, excellent service. English spoken. Recommended.

A **La Raclette**, *Pérez 1170, T02972-427664*. Delightful characterful rooms in a charming old building, with an excellent restaurant, in a quiet part of town.

B **Hostería Walkirias**, *Villegas 815, T02972-428307, www.laswalkirias.com* A lovely place, homely but smart, with very spacious and well furnished, tasteful rooms with big bathrooms, breakfast and free transfer from the airport included, sauna and pool room, charming owners. Great value off season.

B **La Masia**, *Obeid 811, T02972-427879*. Spacious high-ceilinged rooms, chalet style with lots of dark wood, and nice little bathrooms, lots of cosy places to sit in the evenings in bar and lounge.

C **Casa Alta**, *Obeid 659, T02972-427456*. Deservedly popular bed and breakfast, with charming multilingual owners. Comfy rooms, most with bathrooms, lovely gardens, delicious breakfast. Closed in low season, book in advance.

C **Crismalu**, *Rudecindo Roca 975, T02972-427283, crismalu@smandes.com.ar*

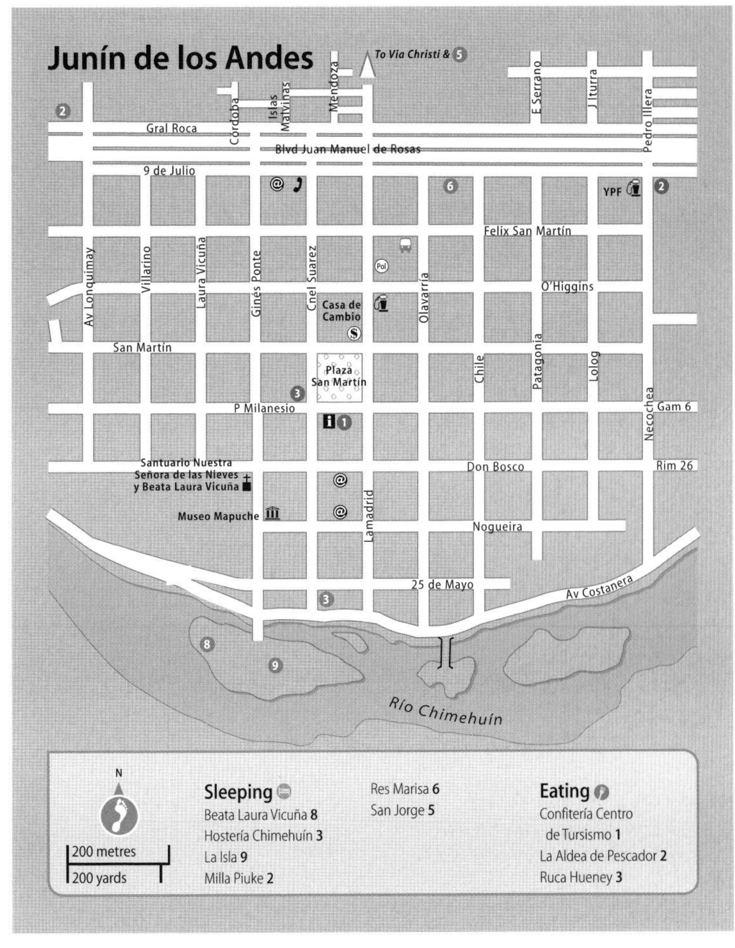

Simple rooms in attractive chalet-style place, good value, breakfast included.

C Hostería Las Lucarnas, *Pérez 632, T02972-427085*. Really good value, this central and pretty place with simple comfortable rooms, and friendly owner, who speaks English.

D-E pp **Hosteria Bärenhaus**, *Los Alamos 156, 5 km outside town, Barrio Chapelco (8370), T/F02972-422775, www.baerenhaus.com* Welcoming English-and German-speaking owners have thought of everything to make you feel at home here: excellent breakfast, very comfortable rooms with bath and heating, or great value shared dorms. Highly recommended. Free pick-up from bus terminal and airport.

E pp **Hostel Puma**, *Fosbery 535, T02972-422443, puma@smandes.com.ar* Hostelling International discounts. Excellent, lovely hostel, warm, friendly, and clean, run by an enthusiastic guide who organizes treks to Lanín, rooms for 4 with private bathroom, also doubles **D**, kitchen facilities, laundry, information on local trails, internet, cycle hire. Taxi US$0.80 from terminal. Recommended.

Cabañas

Plentiful *cabañas* are available on the hill to the north of town, and down by the lakeside. Prices increase in high season, but are good value for families or groups.

Antuen, *Perito Moreno 1850, T/F02972-428340, www.interpatagonia.com/antuen*. Modern well equipped and luxurious for 2 to 7, jacuzzi, pool, games room, views from elevated position above valley.

Cabañas del Lago, *Costanera 850,*

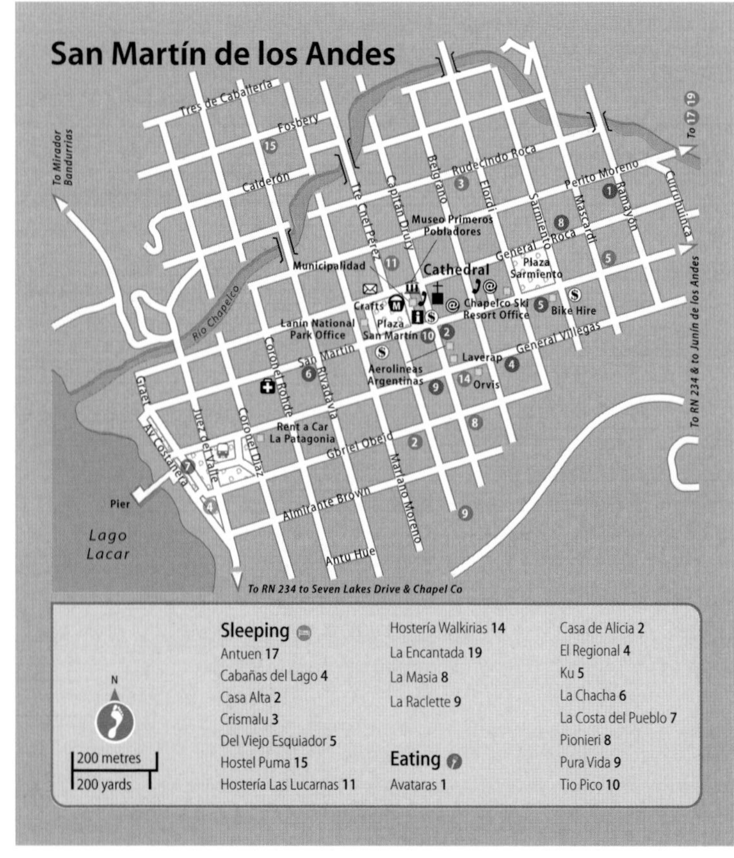

T/F02972-427898, www.interpatagonia.com/*cabanasdellago* The main attraction is that they're right on the lakeside, simple rustic *cabañas*, not the most luxurious, but great location, and a bit cheaper than most. English spoken.
La Encantada, *Peritor Moreno y Los Enebrs, T/F02972-428364, www.laencantada.com*. In a spectacular position above town in wooded surroundings, large, beautifully furnished cosy *cabañas* for two or more families, with all possible comforts, and pool, games room, fishing guides offered too.

Camping

Catritre, *Route 234 km 4. Southern shore of the lake, T02972-428820*. Good facilites in a gorgeous position on the shore.
Quila Quina, *T02972-426919*. A pretty spot and a peaceful place (out of peak season) with beaches and lovely walks.

Eating

Lago Huechulafquen *p96*

There are lots of places to eat here, with *provedurías*, selling good *pan casero*, home-made bread, at Bahía, Piedra Mala and Rincon, and light meals served at **La Valsa**, at Población Barriga.

Junín de los Andes *p100, map p103*

¶¶ **Ruca Hueney**, *on the plaza at Col Suárez y Milanesio*. The best place to eat in town, this popular place serves a broad menu: the 'famous' *bife de chorizo Ruca Hueney* and locally caught trout are delicious, US$8 for 2 courses.
¶ **Confitería Centro de Tursismo**, *next to the tourist office*. A café-restaurant good for coffee and sandwiches.
¶ **La Aldea de Pescador**, *Route 234 y Necochea, on the main road by the YPF station*. A great place for *parrilla* and trout, very cheap.

San Martín de los Andes *p101, map p104*

¶¶¶ **Avataras**, *Teniente Ramon 765, T02972-427104, open only Thu Fri Sat from 2030*. The best in town, this pricey, inspired place is absolutely marvellous. The surroundings are elegant, the menu imaginative, US$13 for three courses and wine, an excellent treat.
¶¶ **La Chacha**, *Rivadavia y San Martín*. A much-recommended traditional *parrilla* for excellent steaks, and good pasta for vegetarians, with good old-fashioned service to match.
¶¶ **Pionieri**, *General Roca 1108*. Excellent Italian meals in a cosy house, with good service, English and Italian spoken. Recommended. The same owners run *Los Patos* (next door) for take-away food, *T02972-428459*.
¶¶ **Pura Vida**, *Villegas 745*. The only vegetarian restaurant in town, small and welcoming, also fish and chicken dishes.
¶ **El Regional**, *Villegas 955*. Hugely popular for regional specialities – smoked trout, patés and hams, and El Bolsón's home-made beer, all in cheerful German-style decor.
¶ **Ku**, *San Martín 1053*. An intimate *parrilla*, also serving delicious home-made pastas and superb mountain specialities, with excellent service and wine list.
¶ **La Costa del Pueblo**, *on the costanera opposite pier, T02972-429289*. This is one of the best value places overlooking the lake. A big family-orientated place, where kids running around give the place a cheerful atmosphere, offering a huge range of pastas, chicken and trout dishes. Cheap dish of the day (US$4 for 2 courses), good service, recommended.
¶ **Tio Pico**, *San Martin y Capitan Drury*. For a drink or lunch on the main street, this is a great bar-café, serving tasty *lomitos* in a warm atmosphere.

Teashops

Casa de Alicia, *Drury 814, T02972-425830*. Delicious cakes and smoked trout.

Shopping

San Martín de los Andes *p101, map p104*
There's a handicraft market in summer in Plaza San Martín. Lots of outdoor shops on San Martín sell clothes for walking and skiing, all pricey, **Mountain Ski Shop**, *San Martín 861*. There are two recommended places for chocolates, among the many on San Martín: **Mamusia** which also sells home-made jams, and **Abuela Goye**, which also serves excellent ice creams.

Activities and tours

Junín de los Andes *p100, map p103*

Fishing

The season runs from 2nd Sat in Nov to Easter. For fly casting and trolling, visit lagos Huechulafquen, Paimún, Epulaufken, Tromen, Currehue and ríos Chuimehuin, Malleo, Alumine and Quilquihue. For further information, consult www.turismo.gov.ar /pesca.
Alquimia Viajes and Turismo, *Padre Milanesio 840, T02972-491355, www.interpatagonia.com/alquimia* Fishing excursions and a range of adventure tours, including climbing.
Flotadas Chimehuin, *Gines Ponte 143, T02972-491313, www.todo-patagonia.com /chimehuin*. Expert guidance or tuition for novices; all inclusive packages with food, transport and accommodation.
Río Dorado Lodge, *Pedro Illera 448, T02972-491548, www.riodorado.com.ar* The luxury fishing lodge at the end of town, has a good fly shop, and organizes trips, run by experts.

San Martín de los Andes *p101, map p104*

Adventure tours

El Claro, *Villegas 977, T02972-428876, www.interpatagonia.com/elclaro* Trips to the lakes, also paragliding, horse riding, and other adventure trips.
Lucero Viajes, *San Martín 946, T02972-428453, www.luceroviajes.com.ar* Rafting at Hua Hum (US$20) horse riding (US$20), including transfers, 4WD trips, and tours to Hua Hum (US$10), Quila Quina (US$7), and Termas de Lahuen-Co (US$17), ski passes in winter.
South Temptations, *San Martín 1254, T02972-425479, www.geocities.com/ southtemptations* Fishing trips, tours and 3-10 day trips around the lakes. Office in the bus terminal, *T02972-457422, or in Chile T56-63311647*.
Tiempo Patagónico, *San Martín 950, T02972-427113, www.tiempo patagonico.com*. Both conventional excursions, including the Seven lakes drive, and adventure tourism.

Bird watching

Juan Carlos Lizaso, *T02972-421553*. Tours in Lanín national park, all year round.

Cycling

Many places rent mountain bikes in the centre, reasonable prices, maps provided.
HG Rodados, *San Martin 1061*. Rents mountain bikes at US$6 per day, also spare parts and expertise.

Flying

Aeroclub de los Andes, *T02972-426254, aeroclubandes@smandes.com.ar* For flights in light aircraft.

Horse riding

Las Taguas, *Perito Moreno 1035, T02972-427483, www.lastaguas.com* Marvellous horse riding trips over the surrounding areas of great beauty. Recommended.

Skiing

Cerro Chapelco, *20 km south of San Martín de los Andes, T02972-427845, www.chapelco.com.ar*. The resort is well organized, with 22 pistes and an overall drop of 730 m. There's a ski school and snowboards for hire, plus restaurants and a small café at the top. **Transportes Chapelco**, T02944-425808, run buses from San Martín, US$2 return.

Transport

Junín de los Andes *p100, map p103*

Bus

The terminal is at Olavarría y Félix San Martín, T02972-492038, (do not confuse with Gral San Martín). To **San Martín de los Andes**, 45 mins, US$4, several a day, Centenario, Ko Ko, Airén. To **Neuquén**, 7 hrs, US$23, several companies. To **Tromen**, Mon-Sat 1 1/2 hrs, US$5. To **Caviahue** and **Copahue**, change at Zapala. 3 1/2hrs, US$11. To **Bariloche**, 3 hrs US$7, Via Bariloche, Ko Ko. To **Buenos Aires**, 21 hrs, US$30, several companies.

To Chile To **Temuco** (5 hrs) US$9 via Paso Tromen, with either Empresa San Martín or Igi-Llaima.

San Martín de los Andes *p101, map p104*

Air

Chapelco airport, T02972-428388, is northeast on the road to Junín de los Andes; taxi US$7. Flights to **Buenos Aires**, Aerolíneas Argentinas, also LADE weekly from **Bahía Blanca**, **Esquel**, and **Bariloche**. **Airline offices** Aerolíneas Argentinas, *Drury 876, T02972-427003*. LADE, *in the bus terminal at Villegas 231, T02972-427672*. Southern Winds, *San Martín 866, T02972-425815*.

Boat

Boats from San Martín pier, T02972-428427, depart to **Quila Quina** hourly, 30 min each way, US$5 return, and to **Hua Hum**, US$15 return, three daily in season.

Bus

The bus terminal is reasonably central, at Villegas 251, information T02972-427044.

To **Buenos Aires**, 20hrs, US$40 *coche cama*, daily, 6 companies. To **Bariloche**, 4 hrs, US$7, many daily: Via Bariloche, *T02972-425325*; Albus, *T02972-428100* (via Traful and La Angostura); Ko Ko, *T02972-427422*, daily (fast route via Confluencia, or via the Seven Lakes in summer only). To **Puerto Madryn** (via Neuquén) US$30.

To Chile Buses to **Puerto Pirehueico** via Paso Hua Hum leave early morning daily, 2 hrs, US$4; they connect with boat across Lago Pirehueico to Puerto Fuy. To **Temuco** with Empresa San Martín, *T402972-27294*, Mon, Wed, Fri, Igi-Llaima, *T02972-427750*, Tue, Thu, Sat, US$9 , 6-8 hrs (heavily booked in summer).

Car hire

Rent a Car La Patagonia, *Villegas 305, T02972-421807, 15557669*.
Localiza, *El Claro Turismo, Villegas 977, T02972-428876*.

Directory

Junín de los Andes *p100, map p103*

Banks and currency exchange

Travellers cheques can be cashed at **Western Union**, *Milanesio 570, 1000-1400, 1600-1930*; change money at **Banco Provincial Neuquén**, *San Martín y Lamadrid*, also has ATM. **Internet** in the *galería* behind tourist office. **Post office**, *Suárez y Don Bosco*. **Telephone**, *locutorio near tourist office on plaza at Milanesio 540*.

San Martín de los Andes *p101, map p104*

Banks and currency exchange Many ATMs along San Martín, also exchange at Banco de la Nación, *San Martín 687*, and Banco de la Provincia de Neuquén, *Obeid y Belgrano*. **Internet** Lots of fast services, Cybercafe Patagonia, good place at back of *galería around San Martín 850*. **Laundry** Laverap, *Drury 880*, 0800-2200 daily. Marva, *Drury y Villegas*, and *Perito Moreno 980*. Fast, efficient and cheap. **Medical services** Hospital Ramón Carrillo, *San Martín y Coronel Rodhe, T02972-427211*. **Post office** *General Roca y Pérez*, Mon-Fri 0800-1300, 1700-2000, Sat 0900-1300. **Telephones** Cooperativa Telefónica, *Drury 761*.

Parque Nacional Nahuel Huapi

This is the oldest national park in Argentina. It was created in 1934, but originated from a donation made to the state in 1903 by Francisco Perito Moreno of 7,500 hectares of land around Puerto Blest. The park now covers 750,000 hectares of dramatic scenery along the Chilean border, encompassing lakes, rivers, glaciers, waterfalls, rapids, virgin forest and snow-clad mountains, including the mighty Tronador (3,478m).

The outstanding feature of the park is the splendour of its lakes. North of Villa La Angostura, Lagos Correntoso and Espejo offer some stunning walks and tranquil places to stay. The largest lake is Lago Nahuel Huapi, a huge 531 sq km and 460 m deep in places, with long fjord-like arms of water, or 'brazos'. A peninsula on the northern shore encompasses the Parque Nacional Los Arrayanes, which contains a rare woodland of arrayán trees, with cinnamon-coloured flaky bark. South of Lago Nahuel Huapi, Lagos Mascardi, Guillelmo, and Gutiérrez have even grander scenery, with horseriding, trekking and rafting along Río Manso.

Tourism is most developed around the city of Bariloche on the southeast shore of Nahuel Huapi; it is dealt with in its own section, see page 116. Villa Traful and Villa La Angostura make pleasant alternative bases for exploring the northern portion of the park.

Getting there Bariloche is the main access point (see p116) but there are also direct buses to Villa Angostura. Ruta de los Siete Lagos is the best driving route into the park.

Getting around A hire car is an advantage.

Time required 4 days to explore the northern portion of the park.

Weather Warm in summer, snowy in winter, bright and chilly in spring, mild in autumn.

Sleeping Pricey hotels and a couple of hostels in Villa La Angostura; a few hosterias at Villa Traful. Good campsites.

Eating Pricey tourist restaurants in Villa La Angostura.

Activities and tours Cycling, fishing and riding.

★ **Don't miss...** Parque Nacional los Arrayanes

Ins and outs

Park information Bariloche is the main centre for entering the park, where you can equip yourself with information on transport, walks and maps. The **Nahuel Huapi National Park Intendencia** ⓘ *San Martín 24, T02944-423111, www.parquesnacionales.com.ar, open 0900-1400*, is very helpful. Also useful for information on hiking is **Club Andino Bariloche** (CAB; see page 129), which sells hand-drawn walking maps, showing average walking times and *refugios*, although note these are sometimes out of date, so always check with *guardaparques* that paths are open before you set out. CAB can also advise on transport within the park. More detailed maps are available from Buenos Aires, at the Instituto Geográfico Militar. The tourist office in Villa La Angostura is another useful resource. There are many refugios in the park run both privately and by **Club Andino Bariloche**, who charge US$5 per night, plus US$2 for cooking, or US$2.50 for breakfast, US$5 for dinner. Take a good sleeping bag. Most areas of the park are free to visitors, but you must pay entry, US$4, at Puerto Pañuelo, Villa La Angostura and Pampa Linda.

Flora and fauna

Vegetation varies with altitude and climate, but includes large expanses of southern beech forest an,d near the Chilean border, where rainfall is highest, there are areas of magnificent virgin Valdivian rainforest. Here you will see *coihues* (evergreen beeches) over 450 years old and *alerces* over 1,500 years old, with the ancient species of bamboo cane *caña colihue* growing everywhere. Eastern parts of the park are more steppe-like with shrubs and bushes. Wildlife includes the small *pudú* deer, the *huemul* and river otter, as well as foxes, cougars and guanacos. Among the birds, Magellan woodpeckers and austral parakeets are easily spotted as well as large flocks of swans, geese and ducks.

La Ruta de los Siete Lagos

The Seven Lakes Drive is the most famous tourist route in the Argentine Lake District. It follows Route 234 through the Lanín and Nahuel Huapi National Parks from San Martín de los Andes to Villa La Angostura and passes seven magnificent lakes, all flanked by mountains clad in beech forest. It is particularly attractive in autumn (April/May) when the trees turn red and yellow. Although the road is only partially paved, the hard earth surface is usually only closed after heavy rain or snowfall. There's limited facilities for camping along the route but plenty of perfect picnic spots, especially at Pichi Traful or Lago Espejo. Five-hour, round-trip excursions along the Seven Lakes Route are operated by several companies. Buses will stop at campsites on the route, but it's better to have your own transport, as you'll want to stop and explore. The route is good for cycling, although there's more traffic in January and February. The seven lakes are (from north to south) Lácar, Machónico (in PN Lanín), Falkner, Villarino, Correntoso, Espejo and Nahuel Huapi.

San Martín de los Andes to Bariloche

There's an alternative direct route south to Bariloche, via **Confluencia**, that's also appealing. Follow route 234 then take Route 63, unpaved, southeast along the tranquil shore of **Lago Meliquina** and over the Paso de Córdoba, Km 77, (1,300 m) where you enter the **Parque Nacional Nahuel Huapi**. (You could turn off along an unpaved track to isolated **Lago Filo-Hua-Hum** at Km 54, before continuing to Confluencia.) From Confluencia, take the paved Neuquén-Bariloche highway, through the astounding **Valle Encantado**, 100 km from Bariloche. Here, the road winds through mountains, whipped into jaggy peaks and rising surprisingly from rolling scrubby land by the milky turquoise waters of the Río Limay. The weird rock formations include El Dedo de Dios (The Finger of God) and El Centinela del Valle (The Sentinel of the Valley). The road reaches Bariloche, 157 km from San Martín de los Andes.

Villa Traful

If you want to get off the beaten track, Villa Traful is ideal. The quiet pretty village sprawls alongside the narrow deep-blue sliver of **Lago Traful**, enclosed on both sides by stunning sharp peaked mountains. Approaching from the west, you'll pass forests of lenga and coihue, their elegant tall trunks creating a woody cathedral, with idyllic spots to camp all along the

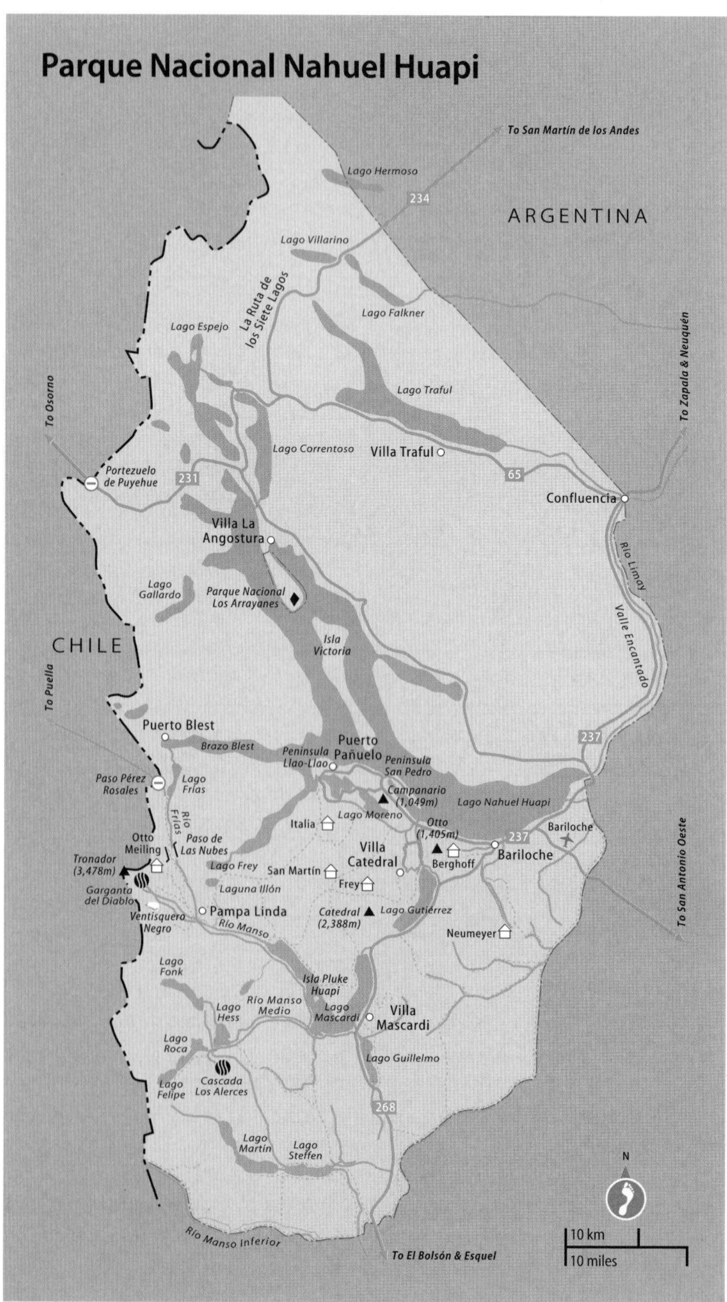

shore. There are also some wonderful walks and waterfalls to see here, and little else to do here but unwind. There's a small but very helpful **tourist office** further along the lakeshore, just past Aiken cabañas, T02944-479020, www.7lagos.com/traful, with information on walks, riding and fishing. The *guardería* opposite the pier is open only in high season, with advice on walks. A one-and-a-half hour walk (quicker by horse or bike) from the village centre will bring you to the lovely **cascadas del Arroyo Coa Có y Blanco**, which thunder down through beech forest and cañas colihues bamboo.

Villa La Angostura and around » pp 112-115

This pretty town with a villagey feel is a popular holiday resort for wealthier Argentines on the shores of Lago Nahuel Huapi and provides access to the wonderful **Parque Nacional Los Arrayanes** (see page 111) at the end of the **Quetrihué Peninsula**. The town has two centres: **El Cruce**, where there are countless restaurants, hotels and *cabaña* complexes, and the picturesque port, known as **La Villa**, 3 km away at the neck of the Quetrihué Peninsula. The **tourist office** ⓘ *Av Siete Lagos 93, T02944-494124, www.villalaangostura.net.ar, www.turismoangostura.com, high season 0800-2100, low season 0800-2000*, is opposite the bus terminal north of town and is busy and helpful, with good maps, and accommodation information; English spoken.

Bus company **15 de Mayo** runs buses between El Cruce and la Villa every two hours, but it's also a pleasant walk. About halfway between the two centres is a chapel (1936), designed by Bustillo, the architect who gave this region's buildings their distinctive chalet style. There's also the tiny **Museo Regional** ⓘ *Mon 0800-1400, Tue- Fri 0800-1630, Sat 1430-1700*, with interesting photos of the original indigenous inhabitants. Fom La Villa, a short walk leads to **Laguna Verde**, an intense emerald green lagoon surrounded by mixed *coihue*, cypress and arrayán forests, where there's a self-guided trail.

Around Villa La Angostura

There are fine views of Lagos Correntoso and Nahuel Huapi from **Mirador Belvedere**, 3 km drive or walk up the old road, northwest of El Cruce. From the *mirador* a path to your right goes to **Cascada Inacayal**, a waterfall 50 m high, situated in an area rich in native flora and forest. Another delightful walk leads to beautiful 35-metre **Cascada Río Bonito**, lying 8 km east of El Cruce off Route 66. One of the country's most popular ski resorts is at **Cerro Bayo** (1,782 m), further along the same path. Alternatively, 1 km further along the road, take the ski lift to a platform at 1,500 m, where there's a restaurant with great views. The ski lift functions all year; cyclists can take bikes up and cycle down.

Parque Nacional Los Arrayanes

ⓘ *12 km south of La Villa via a clear path that can be walked (3 hrs one-way) or cycled (2 hrs one-way). Boats run from La Villa twice daily in summer (in winter only if there's sufficient demand). US$7 return with the more attractive boat* Huemul II, *T02944-494233 (tickets from Hotel Angostura), or US$9.30 return with the catamaran. Boats also sometimes run from Bariloche, via Isla Victoria.*

One of the most magical spots in the Lake District, this park was created to protect a rare forest of *arrayán* trees. It is one of the few places where the *arrayán* grows to full size and some of the specimens are 300 years old. *Arrayán* grow in groves near water and have extraordinary cinnamon-coloured peeling trunks that are cold to the touch. They have no outer bark to protect them, but the surface layer is rich in tannins, which keep the tree free from disease. They have creamy white flowers in January and February, and produce blue-black fruit in March. The most rewarding way to see the park is to take the boat trip

across the lake and to stroll along the wooden walkways through the trees, once the guided tour has left. Then walk back to the port through the mixed forest. There's a *confiteria* in the park, selling drinks and confectionery.

Sleeping

La Ruta de los Siete Lagos *p109*

C **Hostería Lago Villarino**, *Lago Villarino.* A lovely setting, good food, also camping.

C **Lago Espejo Resort**, *Lago Espejo.* A beautifully situated hotel and simple camping area, on the tranquil shore of the lake, surrounded by *coihue* trees.

D **Hostería Lago Espejo**, *Lago Espejo.* Old fashioned and comfortable, with good food in the restaurant, open Jan-Mar only.

D pp **Hosteria Los Siete Lagos**, *Lago Correntoso.* A lovely simple *hostería* in a secluded spot, with just five small, simple rooms, but some great views. There is only electricity in the evenings but full board is possible. Good restaurant with home-made bread for sale. Also a free campsite summer only. No phone; book through Villa la Angostura tourist office.

Border with Chile

Officially known as **Paso Samore**, Paso Puyehue (1,280 m) lies west of Villa La Angostura via unpaved Route 231 – a spectacular six-hour drive. Some travellers think this route is even more scenic than the ferry journey across Lago Todos Los Santos and Lago Frías (see page 119) and it's certainly far cheaper and more reliable, although it's liable to closure after snow. Heading east to west, the best views are from the southern side of the bus. From Villa La Angostura, Route 231 passes the junction with 'Ruta de Los Siete Lagos' for San Martín at Km 94. The pass itself is at Km 125. On the Chilean side the road continues via Parque Nacional Puyehue and Entre Lagos to Osorno.

Argentine customs and immigration ⓘ *Km 109, 14 km east of the border, open winter 0900-2000, summer 0800-2100.* **Chilean immigration** ⓘ *at Pajaritos, Km 146, 22 km west of the border, open 2nd Sat in Oct to 1 May 0800-2100, winter 0900-2000.* For vehicles entering Chile, formalities take about 30 minutes and include the spraying of tyres and the wiping of shoes on a mat, for which you pay US$2 to *Sanidad* (have Chilean pesos ready).

“” Perhaps one day, tired of circling the world, I'll return to Argentina and settle in the Andean lakes... (Ernesto 'Che' Guevara, *The Motorcycle Diaries*)

Camping

The campsite at Lago Espejo Resort is open all year, US$1pp. Further along an earth track is the lovely **Lago Espejo Camping**, open all year, US$1pp, no showers, but toilets, drinking water and fireplaces. Also picnic spots, busy Jan.

Villa Traful and around *p110*

B/D **Ruca Lico**, *T02944-479004, 15-553960, www.interpatagonia.com/rucalico* Luxurious *cabañas*, in woodland above the lake shore, lavishly furnished in rustic chic style, with jacuzzi and balcony with splendid views. Good value for 6, a treat for 2. Recommended. Horse riding.

D **Aiken**, *T02944-479048, www.aiken.com.ar* Rustic and compact, but well decorated *cabañas* in spacious gardens with old trees, and open views of the lake below. All have *parrilladas* outside. Cheap for 4 or 5. Recommended.

D **Hostería Villa Traful**, *T02944-479005.* A delightful place to stay above the lake, in pretty gardens. Separate little cabins, with comfortable furnishings, and ample bathrooms. There are also pretty *cabañas* for up to 6, US$50. Charming hospitality, also organizes fishing and boat trips.

Camping

Camping Traful Lauquen, *on the shore, T02944-479030, www.interpatagonia.com/trafullauquen* With 600m of beach, this is among the loveliest of the sites along the lake. Hot showers, fireplaces, restaurant, US$2.30 pp, open Nov to Mar. Calm and beautifu, favoured by families.

Costa de Traful, *T02944-479023.* If you're under 30 and you've got a guitar, or would like to meet somebody who has, camp at this lively place, US$2.30pp, open Dec to Apr. 24-hr hot showers, restaurant, fireplaces, *proveduria, cabañas*, fishing, horse riding, treks to see cave paintings on the other side of the lake, boat trips, diving for those with experience.

Villa La Angostura *p111*

Accommodation is good, but pricey in peak seasons.

L **Las Balsas**, *on Bahía Las Balsas (off Av.Arrayanes), T02944-494308, www.lasbalsas. com.ar* The most famous and exclusive hotel in the area, fabulous rooms and service, in a lakeside location.

A **Portal de Piedra**, *N231 y Río Bonito, T02944-494278, www.portaldepiedra.com* A welcoming *hostería* and tea room in the woods, with tastefully decorated wood-panelled rooms, and attractive gardens. Guests only restaurant, excursions and activities.

B **Casa del Bosque**, *T02944-595229, www.casadelbosque.com* Luxury and style in wonderfully designed *cabanas*, lots of glass, with jacuzzis and all possible comforts, in secluded in woodland at Puerto Manzana. Recommended.

B **Hostería Pichi Rincón**, *Route 231, km 64, 2 km northwest of the Cruce, T02944-494186, www.pichirincon.com.ar* Attractive wood and stone chalet in woodland elevated above the lake, with cottagey wood-lined rooms, and comfortable lounge with wood fire. Attentive service, and good restaurant.

B **Hotel Angostura**, *T02944-494233, www.hotel laangostura.com.ar* Open all year, beautifully situated on the lakeside at the port,handsome stone and wood chalet was designed by Bustillo in 1938, charming old-fashioned feel, with lovely gardens, and an excellent restaurant.

B **La Posada**, *Route 231, km 65, west of town, T02944-494450,T02944-494450, www.hosteriala posada.com* In a splendid elevated position off the road and with clear views over the lake, this is a welcoming, beautifully maintained hotel in lovely gardens, with pool and fine restaurant; a peaceful place to relax.

D **Verena's Haus**, *Los Taiques 268, T02944-494467.* A quaint and welcoming wooden house, with accommodation for adults and non-smokers only, cosy rooms with a pretty garden, delicious breakfasts. English spoken. Recommended.

F **Hostel la Angostura**, *T02944-494834, www.hostellaangostura.com.ar* 300m up the road behind the tourist office is this warm, luxurious and cheap hostel, all small dorms have bathrooms, and the friendly young owners organize trips. Highly recommended.

F pp **Lo del Francés**, *Lolog 2057, T02944-15564063, www.lodelfrances.com.ar.* Comfortable chalet-style hostel on shore of Lago Correntoso, with great views from all the rooms. Argentina Hostels Club (www.hostels.org.ar). Recommended.

Camping

There are many sites along Route 231.

Osa Mayor, *signposted off main road close to town, T02944-494304, osamayor@uol.com.ar* Highly recommended is this delightful leafy site on a hillside with good, shaded levelled camping spots, and all facilities and clean bathrooms, run by a friendly family. US$2.30pp. Also rustic, rather basic *cabañas*. Lovely apart from Jan, when the place is packed.

Eating

Villa Traful and around p110

† **Ñancu Lahuen**, *T02944, 479179.* A delightful tea room and restaurant serving trout and home made pastas, cakes and delicious home made chocolates. A homely place, with a big open fire.

† **Parrilla La Terraza**, *T02944-479077.* Recommended for delicious locally produced lamb and kid on the *asado*, with panoramic lake views.

Villa La Angostura p111

†† **Hora Cero**, *Av Arrayanes 45.* Hugely popular, a big range of excellent pizzas, and *pizza libre* (as much as you can eat for US$2) on Wed and Sat is a great deal.

†† **Los Troncos**, *Av Arrayanes 67.* Great local dishes like trout-filled ravioli, and fabulous cakes and puddings. Warm atmosphere and live music at weekends.

†† **Nativa Café**, *Av Arrayanes 198.* Most relaxed and welcoming eaterie on the main drag with a high-ceilinged chalet feel, good music and an international menu. Excellent pizzas. Friendly efficient staff and a mixed clientele. Recommended.

†† **Rincon Suizo**, *Av Arrayanes 44.* Open only in high season for delicious regional specialities with a Swiss twist, in a rather more authentic chalet-style building.

† **El Esquiador**, *Las Retames 146 (behind the bus terminal).* Best budget meal is the *parrilla*, with fixed price 3-course menu.

† **Gran Nevada**, *opposite Nativa café.* Good for cheap *parrilla* US$2, and *noquis* US$1.20 in a cheery friendly atmosphere.

Activities and tours

Villa Traful and around p110

Cycling

Bikes for hire at **Del Montanes** T02944-479035, up the road behind the centre of the village.

Fishing

The season runs mid Nov-end Apr.

Andres Quelin, *Hostería Villa Traful, T02944-479005.* A fishing guide who organizes boat trips to see a submerged cypress wood.

Osvaldo A Brandeman, *Bahía Mansa, T02944-479048, pescaosvaldo @mail.com* Fishing expert and guide.

Villa La Angostura p111

Adventure tours

Club Andino Villa La Angostura, *Cerro Bayo 295*. Excursions and information.
Lengas Tour, *Av Arrayanes 173, T02944-494575, turismo@lengas.com* Horse riding, fishing, hunting, all with bilingual guides.
Rucan Turismo, *Av 7 Lagos 90, T02944-495075, www.rucanturismo.com* Skiing, riding, mountain biking and tours.
Terpin Turismo, *Los Notros 41, T02944-494551, terpinturismo@netpatagon.com* Trips to Chile and surroundings, car hire.
Turismo Cerros y Lagos, *Av Arrayanes 21, T02944-495447, www.patagonian adventures.com*. Skiing, adventure sports.

Fishing

For permits and a list of fishing guides, ask the tourist office. The following fly shops also arrange fishing trips: **Angler's Home Fly Shop**, *Belvedere 22, T02944-495222*. **Class**, *Av Arrayanes 173, T02944-494411*.

Horseriding

Cabalgatas Correntoso, *T02944-15552950, cabalgatascorrentoso@cybersnet.com.ar* Horseback excursions in the surrounding area and to Villa Traful, about US$5 per hr.

Skiing

Cerro Bayo, *T02944-494189, www.cerrobayoweb.com*, is one of Argentina's pricier resorts (adult ski pass US$20 for 1 day in high season). It has 24 pistes, many of them fabulously long, covering 20 km in total, and all with excellent views over the lakes below; it's also a great area for snowboarding.

Transport

Villa Traful and around p111

In high summer, a daily **bus** between **Villa la Angostura** and **San Martín** stops here, but in low season, buses run only 3 times a week. *Kiosko El Ciervo*, by the *YPF* service station, sells tickets and has the timetable.

Villa La Angostura p111

Bus

The terminal is at the junction of Av 7 Lagos and Av Arrayanes, opposite the *ACA* service station. For bus network information, contact **Andesmar**, *T02944-495247*; **Via Bariloche/El Valle**, *T02944-495415*; **Albus**, *T02944-156 17578*; 15 de Mayo *T02944-495104*.

To/from **Bariloche**, 1¼ hrs, US$3, several companies, several daily. Daily buses to **San Martín de los Andes** with **Ko Ko** and **Albus**. To **Osorno** (Chile), US$7; arrange for the bus from San Martín to pick you up in Villa la Angostura. For other destinations, change at San Martín de los Andes or Bariloche.

Car hire

Terpin Turismo, *Los Notros 41, T02944-494551, terpinturismo@netpatagon.com.ar*
Giminez Vidal, *Las Muticias 146, T02944-494336*.

Directory

Villa La Angostura p111

Banks and currency exchange
Andina, *Arrayanes 256, T02944-495197*, for cash and TCs. ATMs at Banco de Patagonia, *Av Arrayanes 275*, and Banco Prov de Neuquén, *Av Arrayanes 172*. **Internet** Punta Arrayanes, *Av Arrayanes 90, T02944-495288*. **Post office** *Siete Lagos 26*. **Telephone** Several *locutorios* along *Av Arrayanes*. **Medical services** Hospital Rural Arraiz, *Copello 311 (at barrio Pinar), T02944-494170*.

Bariloche and around

Sitting on the steep and wooded southern shore of Lago Nahuel Huapi at an altitude of 770 m, San Carlos de Bariloche is one of Argentina's most beautifully sited cities, and a good base for exploring the stunning scenery of Nahuel Huapi National Park.

It has long been popular among Argentine tourists and is well set up for visitors, with many hotels and restaurants in the town centre, and more along the shore of the lake west towards Llao Llao, where Argentina's most famous hotel enjoys a spectacular setting. The city provides access to some great trekking country and is also the starting point for the three lakes route to Puerto Montt in Chile.

West of Bariloche, Pampa Linda, is the base for climbing Mt Tronador and for the trek through Paso de las Nubes to Lago Frias. Skiing is available at Cerro Catedral and water sports are possible on many of the lakes. Horse riding is widely available and is a wonderful way of exploring the area.

Getting there Regular flights from Buenos Aires and other towns, including Santiago. Extensive bus connections, plus bus/boat from Puerto Montt.
Getting around Excellent bus services along Lago Nahuel Huapi, plentiful tours.
Time required At least a week for trekking.
Weather Warm in summer, snowy in winter, chilly in spring, mild in autumn.
Sleeping Huge range in Bariloche and along Lago Nahuel Huapi. Good campsites. Refugios in the mountains. Everywhere heavily booked in Jan/Feb.
Eating Wild boar, chocolate, fondu, raspberries, strawberries and calafate berries.
Activities and tours Trekking, mountain biking, ice climbing, horse riding, skiing.
★ **Don't miss...** Trekking around Bariloche and Pampa Linda.

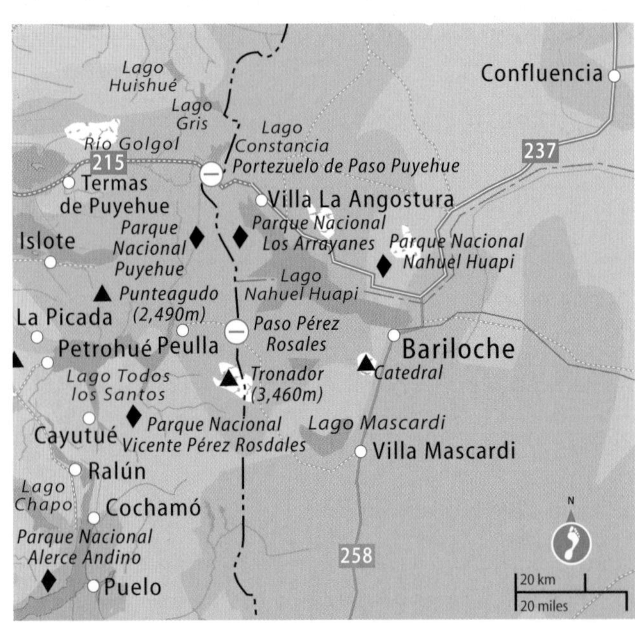

Ins and outs

Getting there The airport is 15km east of town, taxis charge US$5 to the centre. A bus service run by **Del Lago Turismo**, Villegas 222, T02944-430056, meets each arriving/departing flight, US$1. Bikes can be carried. Bus and train stations are both 3 km east of town; taxi US$1.50, frequent buses 10, 20, 21. If you are staying in one of the many hotels on the road to Llao-Llao, west of town, expect to pay a little more for transport to your hotel.

Getting around Bariloche is an easy city to walk around and to orient yourself in, since the lake lies to the north, and the mountains to the south. The main street is Calle Mitre, running east from the Centro Cívico. More accommodation and many restaurants are spread along Avenida Bustillo, which runs along the southern shore of Lago Nahuel Huapi for some 25 km, as far as **Hotel Llao-Llao**, and an area known as Colonial Suiza. Frequent local buses, run by **3 de Mayo**, shuttle along its length.

Tourist information The tourist office is in the **Centro Cívico** ⓘ *T02944-423122, T02944-423022, www.bariloche.com, www.bariloche.org, daily 0900-2100*. Helpful staff speak English, French and German, and have maps showing city buses, and can help with accommodation and campsites.

Sights

At the heart of the city is the **Centro Cívico**, designed by Bustillo in the 1930s in 'Bariloche Alpine style' and made of local wood and stone. It was inspired by the Swiss and German origins of Bariloche's early settlers. On the attractive plaza above the lake, there's the **Museo de La Patagonia** ⓘ *Tue-Fri 1000-1230, 1400-1900, Mon/Sat 1000-1300, US$1*, which apart from stuffed animals, has indigenous artefacts and material from the lives of the first white settlers. Next to it is **Biblioteca Sarmiento** ⓘ *Mon-Fri, 1000-2000*, a library and cultural centre. From the plaza, the chalet style (bordering on kitsch) continues along the tourist-orientated main street, Mitre, in a proliferation of chocolate shops and restaurants serving fondue as well as delicious local trout and wild boar. The **cathedral**, built in 1946, lies six blocks east of the centro civico. Opposite the main entrance, there is a huge rock deposited here by a glacier during the last glacial period. On the lakeshore at 12 de Octubre y Sarmiento is the **Museo Paleontológico**, which has displays of fossils mainly from Patagonia including an ichthyosaur and replicas of a giant spider and shark's jaws.

West of Bariloche » pp122-130

Avenida Bustillo runs parallel to the lakeshore west of Bariloche, with **Avenida de los Pioneros** running parallel above it. From these roads, with good bus services, there's access to the mountains above. **Cerro Campanario** (1,049 m) ⓘ *chairlift at Km 17.7 on Av Bustillo, T02944-427274, daily 0900-1200, 1400-1800, extended opening in summer, US$4*, offers a superb panorama of the lake, edged with mountains. There are more great views from **Cerro Otto** (1,405 m) ⓘ *cable car at Km 5 on Av de los Pioneros*, with its revolving restaurant. To climb Cerro Otto on foot (2-3 hrs): turn off Avenida de los Pioneros at Km 4.6, then follow the trail past Refugio Berghof; don't walk this route alone, as the paths can be confusing. For a much longer trek or a good day-long cycle route, tackle **Circuito Chico**, one of the 'classic' Bariloche tours (see page 128). **Cerro Catedral** ski resort (2,388 m), 21 km southwest of Bariloche, is one of the major ski resorts in Argentina (see page 127), and in summer, the **cable car** ⓘ *T02944-460090, open 0900-1700, US$7*, is useful for starting walks » p114.

Llao Llao

Península Llao Llao, 25 km west of town, is a charming area for walking (see Top tips, p128) or for just appreciating the gorgeous views. The beautiful **Hotel Llao-Llao**, designed by Bustillo, is superbly situated on a hill with chocolate-box views. The hotel opened in 1937 as a wooden construction, but burned down within a few months and was rebuilt using local stone. It overlooks the **Capilla San Eduardo**, also designed by Bustillo, and **Puerto Pañuelo**, where boats leave for Puerto Blest (see page 118). You can also take a **boat trip** from Puerto Pañuelo across Lago Nahuel Huapi to **Isla Victoria** and the **Parque Nacional Los Arrayanes**, on the Quetrihué peninsula (see page 111) ⓘ *half-day excursion 1300-1830; full-day excursion 0900-1830 or 1300-2000 in season, US$15, take picnic lunch.*

Puerto Blest

ⓘ *Tours by Catedral and Turisur (see Activities and tours, page 114). Departure time 0900. US$16, plus US$4 for bus transfer – a cheaper alternative is to take the 0730 '3 de Mayo' bus (US$0.70) to Puerto Pañuelo.* The all-day boat trip from Puerto Pañuelo to Puerto Blest, at the western end of Lago Nahuel Huapi, is highly recommended. Boats are comfortable but fill up entirely in high season, so are much more pleasant in December and March. There's a good but expensive *cafeteria* on board. The boat sails down the fjord-like Brazo Blest, with *coihue*-clad mountains dropping steeply into theprussian blue water; it's usually raining, but very atmospheric. When you get to Puerto Blest, walk through beautiful forest to the **Cascada de**

Hotel Llao Llao

los Cántaros (one hour); set off while the rest of the party stops for lunch and you'll have time for your picnic by the falls before the crowd arrives by boat. The *guardaparques* can advise on other walks but the seven-hour 15-km trek to **Lago Ortiz Basualdo** is particularly recommended (summer only). From Puerto Blest, the tour continues by short bus ride to **Puerto Alegre** on Lago Frías and then crosses the peppermint-green lake by launch; for the continuation of the route into Chile, see below.

The lakes crossing to Chile

ⓘ *Cruce de Lagos, www.lakecrossing.cl. Book by 1900 the day before and further in advance during the high season. US$140 per person, plus lunch at Peulla (US$20). Credit cards accepted. Take your passport when booking. No cars carried.*

This popular route to **Puerto Montt** in Chile, involving passenger ferries across Lago Nahuel Huapi, Lago Frías and Lago Todos Los Santos, is outstandingly beautiful whatever the season, though the mountains are often obscured by rain and heavy cloud. It's a long and tiring journey, however, and is not recommended in torrential downpours. The route is from Bariloche to Puerto Pañuelo by road, Puerto Pañuelo to Puerto Blest by boat (1½ hours), Puerto Blest to Puerto Alegre on Lago Frías by bus, Puerto Alegre to Puerto Frías by boat (20 mins), then 1½ hours by road from Puerto Frías, via **Paso Pérez Rosales**, to Peulla in Chile. Cross Lago Todos Los Santos in the afternoon from Peulla to Petrohué (2½ hours), then continue by bus, via the Petrohué falls, Ensenada and Puerto Varas, to Puerto Montt.

Tickets are available from various operators (see page 127), but all trips are run by **Cruce de Lagos**, who own the exclusive rights, in collaboration with **Andina del Sud** on the Chilean side (see page 272). The journey can be done in one or two days: the one-day crossing (1 Sep-30 Apr) includes a two-hour lunch stop in Peulla during the summer (see Eating, page 114, for options) but does not allow you to return to Bariloche the next day. For the two-day crossing (all year round), there is an overnight stop in Peulla. Alternatively, you could do the first section from Puerto Pañuelo to Puerto Blest and Lago Frías, on a regular day trip (see Puerto Blest, page 118). Note that the launches (and hence the connecting buses) on the lakes serving the direct route via Puerto Blest to Puerto Montt generally do not operate at weekends. You can't take a bike from Puerto Blest to Lago Frias, 'due to the highest level of eco protection'. ▸▸ *For details of onward or return transport from Puerto Montt, see page 282.*

Towards Mount Tronador » pp122-130

Lago Gutiérrez

From Bariloche, route 258 passes the picturesque **Lago Gutiérrez**, which feels like a fjord, with mountains dropping steeply into its western side and spectacular views all around. There are many ways to access the lake, including hiking/cycling trails from Cerro Catedral or Refugio Frey, and it can be explored on foot or bike almost all the way round. Watersports can be practised here in summer.

Lago Mascardi

Route 258 continues to Lago Mascardi with its backdrop of grand jagged mountains, around which there are many places to stay and to walk, all easily reached by car (or by bus in summer). There are also boat trips across Lago Mascardi with **Del Lago Turismo** (see Activities and tours, page 114). At the southern end of the lake, **Villa Mascardi** is a small village from where a *ripio* road 81 with a **one-way system** ⓘ *access going west 1000-1400, going east 1600-1800, two-way 1900-0900, times may vary, so check with the tourist office, T02944-423022*, runs towards Cerro Tronador and Cascada Los Alerces. A few kilometres west of the Lago Mascardi turn-off is an entrance into the national park, US$4 for foreigners. At Km 10 is the lovely straight beach of Playa Negro, handy for launching boats and fishing; opposite is the peaceful **Camping La Querencia**. Shortly afterwards, the road forks, with the right-hand branch following a narrow arm of Lago Mascardi towards Tronador. There's a viewpoint in pretty woodland, from where you can see **Isla Piuke Huapi** at the centre of the lake.

Lago Hess and around

The left-hand fork meanwhile runs for 18 km through the beautiful valley of the **Río Manso Medio** to **Lago Hess** and on to the nearby **Cascada Los Alerces**. Lago Hess is a beautiful spot for a picnic, with good camping at **Camping Los Rapidos**. It is also the starting point for trekking excursions in a remote area of small lakes and forested mountains, including lagos Fonck, Roca, Felipe and Cerros Granito and Fortaleza. Check with *guardaparques* at Lago Hess about conditions on the paths. Río Manso offers some of the best rafting in Argentina, with sections of river suitable for all levels (see Activities and tours, page 114).

Pampa Linda

The quiet hamlet of Pampa Linda lies 40 km west of Villa Mascardi in the most blissfully isolated location, with spectacular views of Mount Tronador towering above. There's a *guadería* (ranger station) with very helpful *guardaparques*, who can advise on the state of the trails and with whom you must register before trekking in the area. A good way to make the most of the area is to take a tour with an agency from Bariloche, and then stay on

Border with Chile

Paso Pérez Rosales is west of Puerto Frías and is the crossing used by buses on the 'Three Lakes' route between Bariloche and Puerto Montt (see page 119). If you plan to make this crossing independently be prepared for some long walks, as cars are not carried on the ferries and it is impossible to buy a separate bus ticket from the border to Peulla, 26 km west.

Argentine immigration and customs ⓘ *at Puerto Frías, open all year.* Chilean immigration and customs ⓘ *at Peulla, open daily 0800-2100 summer, 0800-2000 winter.* Chilean currency can be bought at Peulla customs at a reasonable rate.

Traveller's tales

Tronodor treats

We made our base the out-of-season Hostería Pampa Linda, whose staff were very welcoming, if slightly embarrassed that we were the only guests. Next day, with the cloud beginning to lift we cut walking sticks from the local bamboo and began our climb of Mount Tronador. After a 1000 metre ascent through beautiful autumn beech forest we reached the tree line and saw the magnificent peak bathed in sunlight and below it a bright-white glacier. We spent a cold but beautifully starry night at the refugio and early next morning in hot sunshine we traversed our first glacier, roped to our experienced guide. With the silence, the sunshine, a cloud inversion below us, the other peaks of the Andes poking through and the odd growl of ice tearing free from the glacier, the crossing was remarkable and the highlight of our stay in every way. After descending, we hitched a lift with an old folks' outing back to Bariloche, stopping en route so that two of the sprightly passengers could climb an apple tree and poach delicious apples for the whole bus. *Eddie Pullman and Alison Macaulay*

at Pampa Linda for more trekking, before returning to Bariloche with the minibus service run by **Transitando lo Natural** ⓘ *T02944-156 08581, T02944-423918, 3½ hrs, US$8.*

From Pampa Linda, a lovely track (*ripio*) leads to **Ventisquero Negro**, a rather filthy-looking glacier, which hangs over a fantastically murky pool in which grey icebergs float. The colour is due to sediment and, while not exactly attractive, the whole scene is very atmospheric. The road ends at the **Garganta del Diablo**, one of the natural amphitheatres formed by the lower slopes of Mount Tronador. A beautiful walk (90 mins there and back) from the car park through beech forest takes you to a more pristine glacier and up to the head of the gorge, where thin torrents of ice water fall in columns from the hanging glacier above.

Mount Tronador

Mighty Mount Tronador, (3,478 m), overshadows Pampa Linda, and can be visited in a good day's tour from Bariloche, taking in the beautiful Lagos Gutierrez and Mascardi and stopping for lunch at **Hostería Pampa Linda**. From Pampa Linda two paths head up the mountain: the first leads to a *refugio* on the south side, while the other leads to **Refugio Otto Meiling** (15 km, 5 hours each way), situated at 2,000 m on the edge of the eastern glacier. Follow the path for another hour from the *refugio* for a view over Tronador and the lakes and mountains of the national park. Otto Meiling is a good base camp for the ascent, with lots of facilities and activities, including trekking and ice climbing; always ask the *guardaparques* in Pampa Linda if there's space (capacity 60).

Paso de los Nubes

Pampa Linda is also the starting point for a 22 km walk over Paso de los Nubes (1,335 m) to **Laguna Frías** and **Puerto Frías** on the Chilean border. You'll see a spectacular glacial landscape, formed relatively recently (11,000 years ago). The pass lies on the continental divide, with water flowing north to the Atlantic and south to the Pacific. Views from the Río Frías valley are tremendous, and from Glacier Frías you enter Valdivian rainforest. Allow at least two days for the whole route: camping is available after 4 hours or after 7 hours; then it's another five hours to Puerto Frías. You must register with *guardaparques* at Pampa Linda before setting out and check with them about conditions. The route should only be attempted if there is no snow on the pass (normally December to February only) and when the path is not excessively boggy. For further information, refer to the excellent leaflet produced by Parque Nacional Nahuel Huapi. From Puerto Frías a 30-km road leads to Peulla in Chile on the shore of Lago Todos Los Santos (see page), or you can take a boat back across lagos Frías and Nahuel Huapi to Bariloche; three times a day in summer (check this before you leave Bariloche; see page 129).

Lago Steffen and Lago Martín

About 20 km south of Villa Mascardi, a one-way dirt road leads to Lago Steffen, where a footpath runs along both northern and southern shores (of Lago Steffen) to Lago Martín. Both lakes are quite outstandingly lovely, fringed with beech and *alamo* trees, with far-off mountains in the distance and pretty beaches where you can sit at the waters' edge. There's also great fishing here. Further south, a road leads west along the **Río Manso Inferior** towards Chile. There is excellent rafting on the river (grade 2 or 3), through lush vegetation, towards the Chilean border. Contact **Del Lago Turismo** or **Aguas Blancas** for details of full-day trips and three-day expeditions from Bariloche; see Activities and tours, page 114.

Sleeping

Bariloche *p116, map p123*

Prices rise in Jul and Aug for skiing, and mid-Dec to Mar for summer holidays. Prices given are lake-view high-season prices where applicable. If you arrive in the high season without a reservation, consult the listing published by the tourist office. There's also a booking service in Buenos Aires, at *Florida 520 (Galería), room 116*. In Jul and Oct-Dec, avoid these hotels, which specialize in schooltrips: *Ayelén, Bariloche Ski, Interlaken, Millaray, Montana, Piedras* and *Pucón*.

B **La Pastorella**, *Belgrano 127, T02944-424656, F02944-424212, www.lapastorella.com.ar* A cosy, quaint little *hostería*, whose very welcoming owners speak English. Recommended.

B **Tres Reyes**, *12 de Octubre 135, T02944-426121, F02944-424230, hreyes@bariloche.com.ar* Traditional lakeside hotel with spacious rooms and lounge with splendid views, all recently modernized, and with friendly professional staff who speak English. It's cheaper on the spot than if you reserve by email.

D **El Radal**, *24 de Septiembre 46, T02944-422551*. Small, very clean, comfortable, restaurant.

D **Güemes**, *Güemes 715, T02944-424785*. A lovely quiet bed and breakfast in a residential area, with lots of space, very welcoming, all the simple rooms have bath, breakfast is included, and the owner is a fishing expert.

D **Piuké**, *Beschtedt 136, T02944-423044*. A delightful little bed and breakfast, with simple nicely decorated rooms with bath, breakfast included. Excellent value. German, Italian spoken.

D **Premier**, *Rolando 263, T02944-426168. www.premierhotel.com.ar* Good economical choice in centre of town, with a light spacious entrance and gallery, with neat modern rooms with bath and TV, friendly owners, internet access, English spoken. Recommended.

E **Res No Me Olvides**, *Av Los Pioneros Km 1, T02944-429140, 30 mins' walk or Bus 50/51 to corner of C Videla then follow signs*. Beautiful house in quiet surroundings, use of kitchen, camping. Recommended.

Youth hostels

E pp **Aire Sur**, *Elflein 158, T02944-522135, airesur@abari.com.ar* Also well run, light airy peaceful place with dorms sleeping 3-7, and one E double. There is a terrace and garden with climbing-wall. Breakfast extra, internet laundry, cycle hire.

Knowledgeable owner also runs mountain bike excursions and kayaking.

E pp **Hostel 1004**, *in the Bariloche Centre building, San Martín y Pagano, 10th floor, T02944-432228, www.lamoradahostel.com* Fantastic views from this penthouse flat, where there are rooms sleeping 3-4, a central and friendly place, with kitchen facilities, lots of helpful information, English spoken. Recommended.

E pp **La Bolsa**, *Palacios 405 (y Elflein), T02944-423529, www.labolsadeldeporte.com* Recommended for its friendly relaxed atmosphere, and homely rustic rooms – some with great lake views, and a sunny deck to sit out on.

E **Patagonia Andina**, *Morales 564, T02944-421861, www.elpatagonia andina.com.ar* A quiet place with double/twin rooms with shared bath and dorms. Well equipped small kitchen, TV area, sheets included, breakfast extra, internet, advice on trekking, good atmosphere.

Epp **Periko's**, *Morales 555, T02944-522326, www.perikos.com* A warm and friendly atmosphere, quiet, with an *asado* every Fri, otherwise calm. Towels and sheets included, but breakfast extra. Use of kitchen, and washing machine, nice airy rustic rooms for 4, either all girls or boys, with their own bathroom. Also E double with own bath. Garden, free internet access, can also organize horse riding, rent mountain bikes. Highly recommended.

E pp **Ruca Hueney**, *Elflein 396, T02944-433986, rucahueney@bariloche.com.ar* A lovely calm place, with comfortable beds and duvets! Spotless kitchen, quiet place to sit and eat, and very welcoming owners. Fabulous double room E with extra bunk beds, bathroom and great view. Also Spanish school. Highly recommended.

West of Bariloche p118

There are many *hosterías*, *cabañas* and campsites along Av Bustillo on the shore of Lago Nahuel Huapi. Take buses 10, 11, 20, 21.

Budget buster

LL **Llao Llao**, *Bustillo Km 25, T02944-448530, www.llaollao.com* Deservedly famous, this is one of the world's top hotels. It's in a superb location, with panoramic views from its perfect gardens. The hotel has an excellent restaurant, a golf course, gorgeous spa suite and swimming pool, and organizes watersports on the lake. The terrace is a great place for afternoon tea. Worth every peso.

L **Edelweiss**, *San Martín 202, T02944-426165, F425655, www.edelweiss.com.ar* Far more than just a smart international 5-star. Real attention to detail, with excellent service, and well furnished, spacious and comfortable rooms. *La Tavola* restaurant serves excellent food, there's a superb indoor pool and beauty salon, and good suites for families. Highly recommended.

A **Cabañas Villa Huinid**, *Bustillo Km 2.5, T02944-523523, www.villahuninid.com.ar* Recommended luxurious *cabanas* for 2-8, beautifully furnished, and well equipped.
A **Tunquelén**, *Bustillo Km 24.5, T02944-448400, www.maresur.com.ar.* This is a comfortable 4-star hotel, on the lakeside neary Llao Llao, with really splendid views and a secluded feel – wilder and closer to nature than Llao Llao. Nicely decorated cottage-style rooms, attentive service, superb food, warmly recommended. Much cheaper if you stay 4 days.
B **La Caleta**, *Bustillo Km 1.9, T02944-441837. Cabañas* sleep 4, open fire, excellent value.
C **Katy**, *Bustillo Km 24.3, T02944-448023 adikastelic@yahoo.com* Delightful peaceful place in a garden full of flowers, charming family, breakfast included. Also offers adventure tourism, *www.gringos patagonia.com*
C **Hosteria Santa Rita**, *Bustillo Km7.2, T/F02944-461028, www.santarita.com.ar* Close to the centre, but with peaceful lakeside views, comfortable rooms, lovely terrace, and great service from the friendly family owners. Warmly recommended. Bus 10, 20, 21, to km 7.5.
C **Puerto Blest**, *Puerto Blest*. A small cosy hotel built in 1904, with homely rather than luxurious rooms. It's worth staying a night if you want to try any of the treks from here, or fish trout, and the only other option is free camping with no facilities.
E pp **Hostel Alaska** *(Hostelling International), Bustillo Km 7.5, T02944-461564, www.alaska-hostel.com To get there, take bus 10, 20, 21, to km 7,5).* Well run, cosy chalet-style hostel open all year, doubles and dorms. Kitchen facilites, internet access, rafting and riding.
E pp **Refugio Lynch**, *on the slopes of Cerro Catedral*. Refugio, restaurant and *confiteria*.

Camping

Complete list of campsites is available from the tourist office, with prices and directions, www.bariloche.org.
Petunia, *Bustillo Km 13.5, T02944-461969*. Well protected from winds by trees, a lovely shady lakeside site with beach, all facilities and restaurant, and shop, recommended, also *cabañas*.
Selva Negra, *Bustillo Km 2.9, T02944-441013*. Very attractive well-equipped site, highly recommended.

Lago Gutiérrez p120

AL **El Retorno**, *Villa Los Coihues, on the northern shore, T02944-467333, www.hosteria elretorno.com* With a stunning lakeside position, this is a traditional family-run hotel in tasteful hunting lodge style, with lovely gardens running down to the beach, tennis courts, and comfortable rooms. Also a restaurant. Very relaxing.

Camping

Villa los Coihues, *Lago Gutierrez, T02944-467479*. Well equipped and beautifully situated.

Lago Mascardi and around *p120*

A pp **Hotel Tronador**, *T02944-441062, hoteltronador@bariloche.com.ar* A lakeside paradise, open mid-Nov to Easter, the lovely rooms have terrific lake views from their balconies, there are beautiful gardens, and the charming owner is truly welcoming. It's a really peaceful place, (especially out of peak season). Riding, fishing and excursions on the lake. Highly recommended.

B **Mascardi**, *km 36,8, towards Tronador, T02944-490518, www.mascardi.com* Just a few kilometes from the turning is this luxurious place with a delightful setting in lovely gardens on its own beach by the lake, restaurant and tea room, horse riding, mountains bikes, rafting fly fishing in Río Guillelmo also arranged.

Camping

Camping La Querencia, *T02944-426225, Ruta 258, km 10*. A pretty and peaceful spot on the side of a river, opposite the lovely straight beach of Playa Negro.

Camping Las Carpitas, *km 33, T02944-490527*. Set in a great lakeside position, summer only, *cabañas* and restaurant.

Camping Los Rapidos, *T/F02944-461861, T02944-422266*. Attractive site going down to the lake, with *confitería*, food store and all facilities, US$2.50pp. Also basic *albergue* US$3pp (sleeping bag needed). Trekking, kayaking, fishing and mountain bikes.

Pampa Linda *p121*

D **Hostería Pampa Linda**, *T02944-442038, www.tronador.com* Comfortable retreat from which to trek in the area. Simple rooms, all with bath and stunning views. The owners are charming; Sebastian de la Cruz is one of the area's most experienced mountaineers. Horse riding can be organized, as well as trekking and climbing courses. Full board, and packed lunches for hiking available.

G **Refugio Otto Meiling**, a good base camp for the ascent of Tronador, with lots of facilities and activities, including trekking and ice climbing; always ask the *guardaparques* in Pampa Linda if there's space (capacity 60), US$3.40 pp per night, dinner US$5, let them know in advance if you're vegetarian.

Camping

Pampa Linda, *T02944-424531*. Idyllic lakeside site, *confitería* and food shop.

Eating

Bariloche *p116, map p123*

♈♈ **Kandahar**, *20 de Febrero 698, T02944-424702*. Highly recommended for its excellent food and intimate warm atmosphere. Reserve in high season. Dinner only. Argentine dishes, and other imaginative cuisine served in style, in a cosy place, run by ski champion Marta Peirono de Barber, superb wines and the pisco sour are recommended. US$7 for two courses. Wonderful.

♈♈ **La Marmite**, *Mitre 329*. A cosy place with good service, perfect for a huge range of fondues, good wild boar and delicious cakes for tea too. Recommended, US$5.

♈♈ **Vegetariano**, *20 de Febrero 730, T02944-421820*. Also serves fish in its excellent set menu, beautifully served in a warm friendly atmosphere. Highly recommended, US$5 for three courses.

♈♈ **Familia Weiss**, *also Palacios y V.A.O'Connor*. Excellent local specialities in chalet-style splendour, with live music. The wild boar is particularly recommended. US$6, menu US$4.

♈ **El Boliche de Alberto**, *Villegas 347, T02944-431433*. Very good steak and live folklore music.

El Viejo Munich, *Mitre 102*. A traditional café serving great coffee and good local dishes, a very comfortable place to hang out for a couple of hours.

Friends, *Mitre 302*. A good lively café on the main street, convenient for lunch, open 24 hrs, US$3 for dinner.

Jauja, *Quaglia 366, T02944-422952*. A quiet welcoming place, recommended for trout, in a friendly atmosphere, and good value. (also take away round the corner at Elflein128).

La Jirafa, *Palacios 288*. A cheery family run place for good food, good value, US$3.

Pilgrim, *Palacios 167, between O Connor and Mitre*. One of two Irish pubs in town, serves a good range of beers in a pub atmosphere, also regional dishes, reasonably priced too.

Rock Chicken, *Quaglia y Moreno*. Small, busy, good value fast food (also take away).

Simoca, *Palacios 264*. Recommended for delicious and cheap Tucumán specialities, such as *humitas* and *locro*, and huge *empanadas*, US$3.

West of Bariloche *p118*

Bellevue, *Bustillo Km24.6, T02944-448389, open 1600-2000, Wed to Sun*. The best tea room, perched high up among lovely gardens with incredible views. It's worth a special trip on the bus to taste Karin's raspberry cheesecake and chocolate cake. An unmissable treat.

Cerveceria Blest, *Bustillo Km 11.6, T02944-461026, open 1200-2400*. Wonderful brewery with delicious beers (try *La Trochita* stout), imaginative local and German dishes in a warm rustic atmosphere. Recommended.

El Patacón, *Bustillo Km 7, T02944-442898*. Good *parrilla* and game.

La Raclette, *Cerro Catedral ski resort*. Highly recommended, family place.

Meli Hue, *Bustillo Km24,7, T02944-448029*. Tearoom and bed and breakfast, in a lavender garden and selling fragrant produce, also has lovely views.

Shopping

Bariloche *p116, map p123*

Bookshops

La Barca Libros, *Quaglia 247, T02944-423170, www.patagonia libros.com*. Wonderful range on Patagonia, good selection in English.

Clothing and outdoor equipment

Arbol, *on Mitre in the 400 block*. Good quality outdoor gear, clothes and gifts.

Martin Pescador, *Rolando 257, T02944-422 2275*, Also at Cerro Catedral in winter. Fishing, camping and skiing gear.

Patagonia Outdoors, *Elflein 27, T02944-426768, www.patagonia-outdoors.com.ar* Maps and loads of equipment, plus adventure tours, trekking and rafting.

Food and drink

The local chocolate is excellent; try **Abuela Goye**, *Mitre 258*; **El Turista**, *Mitre 252*, touristy, and **Mamushka**, *Mitre 216*. Also **Fenoglio**, *Mitre 301 y Rolando*, for superb ice cream.

Activities and tours

Bariloche *p116, map p123*

Adventure tourism

Aguas Blancas, *Mitre 515, T02944-429940, www.aguasblancas.com.ar* Rafting on the Manso river (see p120 and p122), all grades, with expert guides, all equipment provided, also bikes, horse riding and longer expeditions, lunches included.

Aire Sur hostel, *Elflein 158, T02944-522135, lionsauma@yahoo.com.ar* Biking, paragliding and canyoning.

Cumbres Patagonia, *Villegas 222, T02944-423283, cumbres@bariloche.com.ar* Rafting, horse riding, trekking, fishing.

Del Lago Turismo, *Vilegas 222, T402944-30056, cordille@bariloche.com.ar* The best in town, helpful and friendly, and speaking fluent English. Conventional tours and adventurous options, horse riding and kayaking. Also a summer boat trip up Lago Mascardi to Cascada de los

Césares and Hotel Tronador.

Extremo Sur, *Morales 765, T02944-427301, www.extremosur.com* Rafting and kayaking, all levels, full day all-inclusive packages offered, US$30 to US$50, or a three-day trip for US$180 includng accommodaton.

Gringos Patagonia, *T02944-448023, www.gringos patagonia.com*. Friendly English-speaking owners, rafting, mountain biking, paragliding, cross country skiing. Recommended.

Refugio Neumeyer, *18km from Bariloche, also office in town at 20 de Julio 728, T02944-428995, www.eco-family.com*. Family-run, child-friendly and a good base for trekking, climbing (and tuition), nightwalking with lanterns.

San Carlos Travel, *Mitre 213 piso 2, T02944-432999, sancartrav@bariloche.com.ar* Birdwatching and specialist tours.

Transitando lo Natural, *20 de Febrero 28, T02944-423918, transita@bariloche.com.ar*. Buses to Pampa Linda, and nature trips.

Tronador Turismo, *Quaglia 283, T02944-421104, tronador@bariloche.com.ar* Tours, trekking to Refugio Neumeyer, rafting, expeditions to the Chilean border and winter sports.

Boat trips

Catedral Turismo, *Palacios 263, T02944-425444* Tickets for the Cruce de Lagos crossing to Puerto Montt in Chile, www.lakecrossing.cl, see p119 and Transport, p129. US$178 for one day; US$220 for two days, including dinner, bed and breakfast in Peulla.

Turisur, *Mitre 219, T02944-426109, www.bariloche.com/turisur*, offers trips from Puerto Pañuelo to Isla Victoria and Bosque de Arrayanes full or half-day US$11/US$16; to Puerto Blest and Lago Frías full day, including buses, US$20. Also offers conventional tours.

Cycling

This is a great area for mountain biking, with some challenging descents from the peaks around Bariloche (see Top tips, p128). **Club Andino** (address above) has detailed maps and advice on where to go. Also contact Diego Rodriguez, *www.adventure-tours-south.com*. Bicycles can be hired from: **Aire Sur**, *Elflein 158, T02944-522135*. US$5 per day; **Bike Way**, *VA O'Connor, 867, T02944- 424202*; **Dirty Bikes**, *V O'Connor 681, T02944-425616, www.dirtybikes.com*

Fishing

Excellent trout fishing Nov-Mar (permits required); arrange boat hire with tackle shops. For guides, consult **AGPP**, *T02944-421515, www.guiaspatagonicos.com/guias*

Baruzzi Deportes, *Urquiza 250, T02944-424922*. Guided fishing excursions (flycast, trolling, spinning) for experts and newcomers; US$150-300.

Martin Pescador, *Rolando 257, T02944-422275, martinpescador @bariloche.com.ar* Great shop for fishing supplies (as well as camping and skiing), experts can organize fishing expeditions.

Horseriding

Estancia Fortín Chacabuco, *T02944-441766, www.estanciaspatagonicas.com* Superb riding for all levels, biliingual guides, lovely landscape east of Bariloche.

Tom Wesley, *Bustillo km 15.5, T02944-448193, tomwesley@bariloche.com.ar* Relaxed ranch. Tuition and day rides.

Paragliding

Parapente Bariloche, *T02944-462234, 15552403, parapente@bariloche.com.ar* Gliding at Cerro Otto.

Skiing

Cerro Catedral, *T02944-460125, open mid-Jun to end Aug, ski lifts open 0900-1700, lift pass adults US$15 per day, see also p118*. One of South America's most important ski resorts, with 70 km of slopes of all grades, a total drop of 1,010 m and 52 km of cross-country skiing routes. There are also snowboarding areas and a well equipped base with hotels, restaurants and equipment hire, ski

Top tips

The best walks and cycle routes around Bariloche

1 Circuito Chico (trek/cycle route) The classic 60-km circular route begins on Av Bustillo at Km 18.3, runs around Lago Moreno Oeste, past Punto Panorámico and through Puerto Pañuelo to Llao Llao. You could extend this circuit, by returning via Colonia Suiza and the Cerro Catedral ski resort or along the Península de San Pedro. Traffic on this route can be a nuisance in high summer, but the views are great.

2 Around Llao Llao (walk) choose from an easy circuit in virgin Valdivian rainforest; an ascent of Cerrito Llao Llao, for wonderful views (2 hrs), or a 3 km trail to Braza Tristeza, via Lago Escondido.

3 To Refugio López Walk (5 hrs return) from the south-eastern tip of Lago Moreno and climb up Arroyo López (2076 m) for views or cycle to Colonia Suiza from a path at Av Bustillo km 10,5, and continue up to Refugio Lopez via a steep track.

4 Cerro Catedral to Refugio Frey (walk; 4 hrs each way) via Rio Piedritas. The refugio at 1,700m has a beautiful setting on a lake

5 Cerro Catedral to Bariloche (walk 6 hrs/cycle) descend down a rocky path to the shores of Lago Gutiérrez and then follow the RN258 back into town. Buses to Catedral will carry bikes.

6 Bariloche to Cerro Otto (cycle) Up a track from Av Bustillo, km 2. From the summit, the very hardy could descend to Lago Gutiérrez.

7 Around Refugio Neumayer Cycle to Refugio Neumayer southeast of Bariloche then hike to Laguna Verde or through Magellanic forest to a mirador at Valle de los Perdidos (see page 127).

8 Pampa Linda to Mount Tronador (walk) See page 120.

schools (US$30 per person per hour) and nursery care for children. The resort is busiest from mid-Jul to mid-Aug during the school holidays.

Xtreme Snow Solutions, *at the resort, T02944-460309, www.skipacks.com*, has a ski school and equipment hire. Equipment can also be rented by the day from **Robles Catedral**, *T02944-460062, www.roblescatedral.com*; **Martín Pescador** (see Fishing, above); **Cebron**, *Mitre 171*, or **Milenium**, *Mitre 125*.

Tours

Most agencies in Bariloche charge the same price for tours. They get very booked up in season, and many trips only run in Jan and Feb or when there is enough demand. Check the itinerary before you book.

Tours include: **San Martín de los Andes**, via the Seven Lakes Drive, returning via Paso de Córdoba and the Valle Encantado, 12 hrs, US$10; **Circuito Chico** (60 km), half-day, US$5-7; **Cerro Tronador/Cascada los Alerces**, full day (255 km), U$12; **El Bolsón** including Lago Puelo, full day (300 km), US$12; **Lagos Gutiérrez, Mascardi and Hess**, the Cascada Los Alerces and Cerro Tronador, full day leaving at 0800, US$10, lots of time spent on the bus but useful as a way to get to Pampa Linda if the bus from CAB isn't running.

Trekking and climbing

There's a good range of peaks around Bariloche, offering walks ranging from 3 hrs to several days (see Top tips, p128). The season runs from Dec to Apr; winter storms can begin as early as Apr at higher levels, making climbing dangerous. **Club Andino Bariloche**, *20 de Febrero 30, T02944-422266, www.clubandino.com.ar (the website lists areas to walk, in Spanish), open Mon-Fri 0900-1300, and also 1600-2100 in high season only*. The club arranges guides; ask them for a list. Its booklet *Guía de Sendas y Picadas* gives details of climbs and provides 4 maps (1:150,000) and details of *refugios* and paths. There's also a book *Excursiones, Andinismo y Refugios de Montaña en Bariloche*, by Tonchek Arko, available in local shops, US$2.

Recommended trekking guides include: **Andescross.com**, *T02944-467502, www.andescross .com*; **Angel Fernandez**, *T02944-524609, 156 09799*; **Daniel Feinstein**, *T/F02944-442259*; and the owner of Pampa Linda Hostería, **Sebastian de la Cruz**, *T02944-490517, 442038, 15557718, pampalindaa @bariloche.com.ar*, a renowned and knowledgeable mountaineer.

Transport

Bariloche *p116, map p123*

Air

Many flights a day to **Buenos Aires**, with Aerolíneas Argentina, Southern Winds, American Falcon and Lapa. Aerolíneas also flies twice a week to **El Calafate** (2 hrs) and **Ushuaia** (2 hrs). American Falcon flies to **Puerto Madryn** and **Montevideo**. Southern Winds to **Córdoba**. LADE weekly to many destinations, including **Bahía Blanca, Comodoro Rivadavia, Mar del Plata, Puerto Madryn**; book well in advance in peak seasons. There are LanChile flights to/from **Santiago** (2hrs) and **Puerto Montt** (45 mins). **Airline** offices Aerolíneas Argentinas, *Quaglia 238, y Mitre, T02944-422425*. American Falcon, *Mitre 159, T02944-425200*. LADE, *Quaglia 238, T02944-423562*. Southern Winds, *Quaglia 262, T02944-423704*.

Bus

The bus terminal, T02944-432860, has toilets, small *confiteria*, *kiosko*, no *locutorio* but public phones. Left luggage US$0.50 per day. Frequent buses 10, 20, 21 from bus /train station to centre of town, US$0.60, and along Av Bustillo, run by 3 de Mayo.

Bus company offices in town: Vía Bariloche/El Valle, *Mitre 321, T02944-429012, www.viabariloche.com*; Andesmar/Albus, *Mitre 385, T02944-430211*; Chevallier/La Estrella/Ko Ko, *Moreno 105, T02944-425914*; TAC, *Moreno 138, T02944-434727*; Cruz del Sur, *T02944-437699*, Don Otto/Río de La Plata, *12 de Octubre T02944-437699*; Flechabus, *Moreno 107, T02944-423090, www.flechabus.com*; 3 de Mayo, for local services, *Moreno 480, T02944-425648*.

Local 3 de Mayo buses leave from the big bus stop on Moreno y Rolando. Useful routes include: bus 20 to **Llao Llao**, for lakeside hotels and restaurants, every 20 mins, journey 45 mins, US$0.70; bus 10 to **Colonia Suiza** and **Bahia Lopez** for trekking; bus 50 to **Lago Gutiérrez**.

Bus marked 'Catedral' for **Cerro Catedral**, leaves from terminal or from Moreno y Palacios, every 90 mins, journey 35 mins, US$1. Bus to **Cerro Otto**, *T02944-441031*, leaves from hut at the Civic Centre, hourly 1030-1730 to connect with cable car, returning hourly 1115-1915, combined ticket for bus and cable car US$8pp.

Long distance To **Buenos Aires**, 6 companies daily, 22½ hrs, US$50 *coche cama*, **Andesmar**. To **Bahía Blanca**, 3 companies, US$30. To **Mendoza**, US$30, **TAC** and **Andesmar**, 19 hrs, via Piedra de Aguila, Neuquén, Cipolleti and San Rafael. To **Esquel**, via El Bolson, Don Otto, Mar y Valle, Vía Bariloche, Andesmar, 4hrs, US$6 . To **Puerto Madryn**, 14 hrs, US$25 with **Mar y Vale** and **Don Otto**. To **San Martín de los Andes**, Ko Ko, 4 hrs, US$8. No direct bus to **Río Gallegos**; you have to spend a night in **Comodoro Rivadavia** en route: **Don Otto** daily, US$38, 14½ hrs. To **El Calafate**, ask at youth hostel *Alaska*, or *Periko's* about **Overland Patagonia's Safari Route 40**, a 4-day trip down Ruta 40 to **El Calafate** via the Perito Moreno national park, Cueva de Las Manos and Fitz Roy, staying at Estancia Melike and Río Mayo en route. US$95 plus accommodation at US$5 per day. *www.visitbariloche.com/alaska*

To **Chile** To **Osorno** (4-6 hrs) and **Puerto Montt**, 7-8 hrs US$18-20, daily, **Bus Norte, Río de la Plata, TAS Choapa, Cruz del Sur, Andesmar** (sit on left side for best views). For **Santiago** or **Valdivia** change at Osorno.

Taxi

Radio Taxi Bariloche, *T02944-422103, 431717*; **Remises Bariloche**, *T02944-430222*. **Remises del Bosque**, *T02944-429109*. **Puerto Remises**, *T08009-990885 (freephone), 02944-435222*, **Melipal Remises**, *T02944-442300*.

Car hire

Hertz, *Quaglia 352, T02944-423457, 15581186, hertz@bariloche.com.ar* Efficient. **Localiza**, *San Martín 463, T02944-424767, localizabrc@ bariloche .com.ar* Reliable, English spoken. **Open Rent a Car**, *Mitre 171, T02944-426325, opencar@bariloche.com.ar* **Bariloche Rent a Car**, *Moreno 115, T02944- 327638, rentacar@bariloche.com.ar*. Tell your car hire company if you plan to enter Chile.

Train

Booking office *T02944-423172*. Closed 1200-1500 weekdays, Sat afternoon and all Sun. Information from the tourist office. Tourist service to **Viedma**, *www.trenpatagonico.com.ar*, with sleeper section and carries cars, 16 hrs, US$18 *semi cama*.

Lago Mascardi *p120*

Buses from Bariloche to **El Bolsón** pass through **Villa Mascardi**. Buses to **Los Rapidos** from the terminal in Bariloche, 0900, 1300, 1800 daily in summer.

Pampa Linda/Mount Tronador *p120*

Bus marked 'Tronador' departs from outside Club Andino Bariloche, *20 de Febrero 28*, daily Jan-Apr, and according to demand in Dec. Run by **Transitando lo Natural**, T02944-156 08581, T02944-423918, 3½ hrs, US$8. From Pampa Linda you can often get a lift with an excursion trip returning to **Bariloche**, US$7.

Directory

Bariloche *p116, map p123*

Banks and currency exchange ATMs at many banks along Mitre; best exchange rates and service at casas de cambio, eg **Sudamérica**, *Mitre 63, T02944-434555*. **Consulates** Austria, *24 de Septiembre 230, T02944-424873*. Brazil, *Moreno 126 piso 5, T02944-425328*. Chile, *Rosas 180, T02944-422842*. France, *T02944-441960*. Germany, *Ruiz Moreno 65, T02944-425695*. Italy, *Beschtedt 141, T02944-422247*. Lebanon, *Quaglia 242 piso 3, T02944-431471*. Switzerland, *Quaglia 342, T02944-426111*. **Customs** Bariloche centre *T02944-425216*, Rincon (Argentina) *T02944-425734*, Pajarito (Chile) *T0056-64 236284*. **Immigration office** *Libertad 191, T02944-423043, Mon-Fri 0900-1300*. **Internet** Many places along Mitre, and in the first block of Quaglia. **Language schools** **La Montana**, *Elflein 251, 1st floor, T02944-156 11872, www.lamontana.com*. **Medical services** Dial 107 for emergencies, or San Carlos Emergencias, *T02944-430000*, Clinic: **Hospital Zonal**, *Moreno 601, T02944-426100*. **Post office** *Moreno 175, Mon-Fri 0800-2000, Sat 0830-1300*. **Telephone** Many locutorios along Mitre, Telecom at Mitre y Rolando is helpful.

The southern end of the lake district offers quite different scenery from that further north, with dense forests hugging the Andean foothills and contrasting with the Patagonian steppe further east. At the pretty and easy-going town of El Bolsón, there are beautiful rivers, waterfalls and mountains to explore, and a small national park, Lago Puelo, for fishing and walking. The pioneer town of Esquel is the southernmost centre in the lakes and can be reached via Cholila, a wild small settlement where Butch Cassidy hid out. From Esquel, you can explore the magnificent Parque Nacional Los Alerces, go skiing in winter, take a ride on La Trochita or visit the appealing Welsh pioneer village of Trevelin.

Getting there Daily flights, long distance buses to Esquel.

Getting around Daily buses from Esquel to El Bolsón, and to Chile via Trevelin and Futuleufú.

Time required A week for trekking in Los Alerces or 3 days for a brief tour of the area.

Weather Mild in summer, snowy in winter, chilly in spring.

Sleeping Plenty of options in El Bolsón, less choice in Esquel. An excellent hostel in Trevelin.

Eating Calafate ice cream, local beer, trout-filled pasta.

Activities and tours Trekking, mountain biking.

★ **Don't miss...** The boat trip across Lago Menéndez in Parque Nacional Los Alerces.

El Bolsón and around

El Bolsón is situated in a broad fertile valley 130 km south of Bariloche, surrounded by the mountains of the *cordillera* on either side, (hence its name: the big bowl), and dominated by the dramatic peak of **Cerro Piltriquitrón** (2,284m). With a river running close by and a warm sunny microclimate, it's a

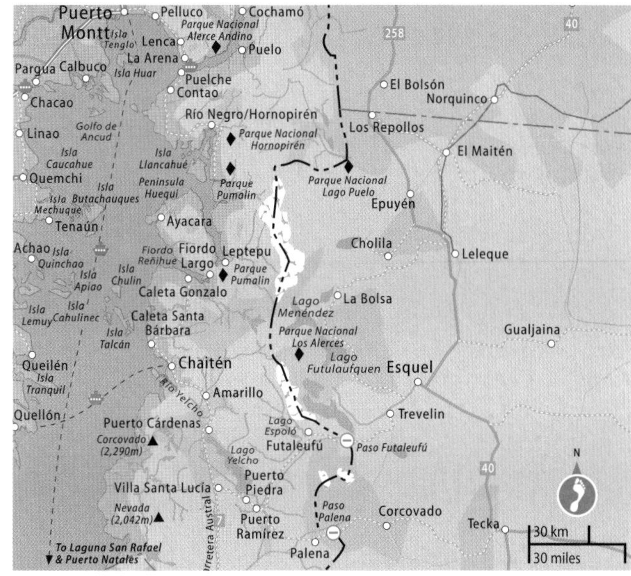

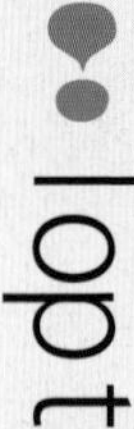

The best walks around El Bolsón

1 Cerro Piltriquitrón (6-7 hrs round trip if you walk all the way) Walk or drive 10 km east up winding earth roads towards the jagged peak that looms over the town. Then it's an hour's walk through the sculpture park of the Bosque Tallado to the mirador with fabulous views over the valley to the Andes beyond. Food and shelter are available at the refugio (1,400 m).
2 Cerros Lindo and Hielo Azul (2 days) Hike up Río Motoco, with Refugio Motoco at the top of the path, up Arroyo Lali to Cerro Lindo (2,135 m), with Refugios Cerro Lindo at the top, and up to Cerro Hielo Azul (2,270 m), also with a refugio. Club Andino Piltriquitrón has details of routes and transport.
3 Cajón de Azul (4 hrs one way) Walk up Río Azul, which flows from a deep canyon to the refugio along a well marked path. It's a bit hairy crossing the two wood and wire bridges, but worth it for a dip in the sparkling turquoise water on the way down. Set off early to allow for a leisurely lunch at the top, or spend the night in the refugio, with its lovely gardens. To start the walk, take a Nehuén minibus from Belgrano y Perito Moreno to Wharton, leaving El Bolsón at 0900. You'll be collected at 2000.

magical setting which inspired thousands of hippies to create an ideological community here in the 1970s. They've built a laid-back town with a welcoming, rather nonchalant atmosphere, and still produce the handicrafts, home-brewed beers, fruit and jams for which the town is famous. There are many beautiful mountain walks and waterfalls nearby and swimming and rafting on Río Azul. The small national park of Lago Puelo is within easy reach, with fishing and walking, but if you'd rather just sit and relax, this is a wonderful place to spend a few days. The helpful and friendly **tourist office** ⓘ *San Martin y Roca, T02944-492604, www.bolsonturistico.com.ar, open 0900-2000 daily in winter, 0900-2300 daily in summer*. tourist office (with plenty of English speakers) is on the side of the semicircular plaza. They'll give you an excellent map of the town and the area and suggest places to stay. **Club Andino Piltriquitrón** ⓘ *Sarmiento y Roca, T02944-492600, open daily during peak season, otherwise Tue and Fri only 1730-1930*, can advise on hikes; all walkers must register here before setting off.

Around El Bolsón

There's an impressive long sweep of waterfalls at **Cascada Escondida**, 10 km northwest of town, a good place for a picnic, with a botanical garden and *casa de te* (tea room) nearby, serving delicious homemade beer, cakes and waffles. All along **Río Azul** are lovely places to bathe, camp and picnic. For a pleasant hour-long walk, with views over the town, climb **Cerro Amigo**. There are also good views from **Cabeza del Indio**, so called because the rock's profile resembles a face. It's a good 6km drive or bike ride from the centre; take Azcuénaga west to cross the bridge over Río Quemquemtreu and follow signs. See also Top tips above.

Parque Nacional Lago Puelo

This lovely green and wooded national park is centred around the deep turquoise-coloured Lago Puelo, 18 km south of El Bolsón on the Chilean border,

Butch Cassidy's cabin near Cholila

surrounded by southern beech forest. With relatively low altitude (200 m) and high rainfall, the forest is rich in tree species, particularly the *arrayán* and the *pitra*, *coihues* (evergreen beech) and cypresses. The lake is glorious in April, when the trees turn a vivid yellow. There's lots of wildlife, including the *huemul*, *pudu* and foxes, and the lake is known for its good fishing for trout and salmon. There are gentle walks on marked paths around the northern shore area, boat trips across the lake and canoes for rent.

The main entrance is along a pretty road south from El Bolsón, through *chacras* (small farms) growing walnuts, hops and fruit, to **Villa Lago Puelo**, 3 km north of the park, where there are shops, plenty of accommodation and fuel. From here the road is unpaved. The administration centre is 500 m north of the lake (all year round Mon-Fri 0800-1500), with a booth at the pier in summer. They have a helpful leaflet and can advise on walks. To the left of the entrance, **Bosque de las Sombras** or Forest of the Shadows, is a delightful overgrown forest, which you wander through on wooden walkways, on the way to the shingle beach at 'La Playita'. **Senda a los Hitos** (10-km; 3 hours each way) is a walk through marvellous woods to the rapids at Río Puelo on the Chilean border (passport required).

Entrance is also possible at **El Desemboque**, on the eastern side of the park: take the bus from El Bolsón to Esquel, alight at El Hoyo, then walk 14 km to El Desemboque. From El Desemboque, you can hike (7 hrs) to **El Turbio**, where there's a *guardaparque*, and on to **Cerro Plataforma** (12 hrs); allow three days for the whole trip. There's also a three-day trek through magnificent scenery to **Glaciar y Cerro Aguaja Sur**: get advice and directions from the *guardaparques*. ▸▸ *For boat trips and fishing in the park, page 141.*

South towards Esquel ▸▸ *pp 138-143*

Cholila

Cholila lies 76 km south of El Bolsón on Route 71, which branches off Route 258 at Km 179. The peaceful village is spread out in a wonderful, broad, open landscape, with superb views of Lago Cholila, crowned by the Matterhorn-like mountains of Cerros Dos and Tres Picos. There's excellent fishing, canoeing and kayaking on rivers nearby and you can visit the evocative wooden **cabins** ⓘ *13 km north of town along Ruta 71, entry US$3, if there's anyone around*, where Butch Cassidy, the Sundance Kid and Etta Place lived between 1901 and 1905.

Background

Butch and Sundance

Butch Cassidy (real name Robert LeRoy Parker) and the Sundance Kid (born Harry Longabaugh) pursued careers in which periods of legal employment was mixed with distinctly illegal activity. In the late 1890s the two were part of a gang known variously as the Train Robbers' Syndicate, the Hole in the Wall Gang and the Wild Bunch, which operated out of a high valley on the borders of Utah, Colorado and Wyoming. Gang members specialized in hold-ups on railway payrolls and banks. In 1900 they celebrated the wedding of one of their colleagues by having their photo taken: a big mistake. The photo was recognised and, with their faces decorating 'Wanted' posters across the land, Cassidy, Sundance and his girlfriend Etta left for Argentina in February 1901.

Using the names Santiago Ryan and Harry Place, the outlaws settled on government land near Cholila but Pinkerton detectives soon tracked them down and informed the Argentine authorities. They lay low, in the house which you can now visit (see page 133); but by 1905 it was time to move on. The gang raided banks in Villa Mercedes and Río Gallegos, posing as ranching company agents. They opened a bank account with US$7,000, spent two weeks at the best hotels and socialised with the city's high society, and then entered the bank to close their accounts and empty the safe before escaping to Chile. Shortly afterwards, Etta returned to the States.

No longer welcome in Argentina, Butch and Sundance moved to Bolivia, finding work at the Concordia tin mine. In 1908 they seized an Aramayo mining company payroll; with military patrols in pursuit and the Argentine and Chilean forces alerted, they rode into the village of San Vicente where they were besieged. The 1969 movie showed Butch and Sundance gunned down by the Bolivian army, but rumours have persisted that, having faked their deaths, they returned to the USA. Butch was said to have become a businessman, a rancher, a trapper and a Hollywood movie extra, while Sundance had run guns in the Mexican Revolution, migrated to Europe, fought for the Arabs against the Turks in the First World War, sold mineral water, founded a religious cult, and still found time to marry Etta. (Adapted from *Digging up Butch and Sundance* by Ann Meadows, London, 1996).

It's easy to understand why they hid out here for so long: Cholila still feels remote and untouched and the views from their land are breathtaking. The cabins can't be seen from the roadside, but there is a small sign. Go out of season and you'll have them to yourself.

Leleque

Route 40 (paved) is a faster way to get from El Bolsón to Esquel and is the route that the bus takes. Stop off at Leleque to see the **Museum of Patagonia** ⓘ *off the RN 40 at km 1440, museoleleque@ciudad.com.ar, open Mar, Apr, Sep-Dec 1100-1700, Jan/Feb 1100-1900. Closed Wed. US$1*, located in the vast estate owned by **Benetton**, the Italian knitwear company.

There's a beautifully designed exhibition on the lives of indigenous peoples, with dwellings reconstructed of animal skins, using the original construction techniques, a huge collection of delicate arrowheads and the original *boleadoras* for catching cattle. Another moving exhibit highlights the first pioneers in Patagonia, especially the Welsh. And there's an attractive café in a reconstructed *boliche* (provisions shop and bar).

Esquel

» *pp 138-143*

Esquel is a pleasant breezy town in a fertile valley with a dramatic backdrop of mountains. It was originally an offshoot of the Welsh colony at Chubut, 650 km to the east and still has a pioneer feel to it, thanks to the old-fashioned general stores and architecture from the early 1900s. It's a busy country town, not at all touristy and with few sights, but all the more appealing for that. It's the best base for visiting the Parque Nacional Los Alerces and for skiing at La Hoya in winter. Esquel is also famous for the steam train *La Trochita*, immortalised by Paul Theroux as the 'Old Patagonian Express'. The very basic **tourist office** ⓘ *Alvear y Sarmiento, T02945-451927, www.esquel.gov.ar, www.esquelonline.com.ar, open daily 0800-2000, summer 0730-2200. Closed weekends off-season*, is friendly but staff have little, or incorrect, information. They do hand out a useful town map, however, with a plan of Los Alerces national park on the other side.

Ins and outs

Getting there and around There's an **airport** 20 km east, reached by bus or taxi, and a smart modern bus terminal on Avenida Alvear, six blocks from the main commercial centre around Avenida Fontana. Buses arrive here from Comodoro Rivadavia and Bariloche, with connections from those places to all other destinations in Patagonia and to the north. Buses also run daily into Los Alerces National Park. » *Transport, p143.*

Sights

The town has two mildly interesting musems: the **Museo Indigenista y de Ciencias Naturales** ⓘ *Belgrano 330 y Chacabuco, open daily except Tue, 1600-2000*, which has indigenous artefacts, and the **Museo de Arte Naíf**, Av Fontana y Av Alvear, which displays Argentine 'modern primitive' paintings. It's also the departure point for the famous narrow gauge steam train, **La Trochita** ⓘ *Estacion Viejo Expreso Patagonico, T02945-451403, www.latrochita.com.ar, 0900/1000 daily Jan/Feb, 1000 Sat only for rest of year, 2½ hrs, US$35, children US$10, tickets from tour operators, or from station office*. Although it's obviously a tourist experience, this is a thoroughly enjoyable trip, taking in the lovely valley and mountains of the *precordillera* framed through the windows of the quaint old train, with its wood stoves and little tea room. There's Spanish commentary along the way, and homemade cakes and handicrafts for sale at the Mapuche hamlet **Nahuel Pan**, where the train stops en route to El Maitén at the northern end of the line. Sometimes there's an extra service from **El Maitén**, T02945-495190, on Saturday, taking 6 hrs, US$7, with a dining car.

La Trochita (Old Patagonian Express)

Traveller's tales

Christmas in the Andes

It was a crisp, clear Boxing Day when my good friend Wig and I headed off for Futaleufú on our bikes. We left Trevelin thoroughly entertained by the sight of Father Christmas on horseback: a gaucho Santa, giving sweets out to the local children. We headed gently out of the village towards the border and were immediately swept up into the arms of the mighty Andes. We'd expected long climbs and tight ravines but were instead greeted by easy slopes weaving through broad and devastatingly beautiful terrain, slowly shifting mile by mile. The sun gloriously warmed these majestic peaks and as we stopped to drink from a clear running roadside stream we were grinning like Cheshire cats. You couldn't dream up such a staggering range of snow clad mountains nestling in between huge tranquil lakes. It was like Scotland with the lights on. *Diarmid Scrimshaw*

Trevelin ▸▸ *pp 138-143*

The pretty village of Trevelin, 22 km southwest of Esquel, was once an offshoot of the Welsh colony in the Chubut valley (see box page 156). With a backdrop of snowcapped mountains, it's an appealing place to stay, with fishing and rafting on **Río Futuleufú**, and beautiful waterfalls at **Nant-y-fall**. The enthusiastic English-speaking **tourist office** in the central plaza, T02945-480120, www.trevelin.org, offers maps, accommodation and fishing advice.

Sights

The Welsh chapel of 1910, **La Capilla Bethel**, is now closed but the building can be seen from the outside. There is also a fine old flour mill dating from 1918, which houses the **Museo Histórico Regional** ⓘ *daily 1100-1800, US$1*, with fascinating artefacts from the Welsh colony. **El Tumbo del Caballo Malacara** ⓘ *200 m from main plaza, guided tours US$2*, is a private house and garden that belonged to John Evans, one of the first settlers. The house contains all his belongings and outside is the grave of his horse, Malacara, who once saved his life. Eisteddfods are still held in Trevelin every year and *Té Galés* (Welsh tea), including an amazing excess of delicious cakes, is served at Nain Maggie tea rooms.

Around Trevelin

Molino Nant Fach ⓘ *Route 259, 22 km southwest towards the Chilean border, US$0.40*, is a beautiful flour mill built by Merfyn Evans, descendant of the town's founder Thomas Dalar Evans. It's an exact replica of the first mill built in 1899. Merfyn's fascinating tour (in Spanish, but English booklets are available) recounts a now familiar tale of the Argentine government's mismanagement of natural resources and industry, through the suppression of the Welsh prize-winning wheat industry. It's a beautiful spot and Merfyn tells the rather tragic story in a wonderfully entertaining way. The **Nant-y-fall Falls** ⓘ *US$0.25 pp including guide to all seven falls (1½-hr walk)*, lie 17 km southwest on the road to the border and are reached via an easy trail through lovely forest. The series of waterfalls is spectacular and the area makes a good picnic spot, too. Both Molino Nant Fach and Nant-y-fall Falls are accessible only by private car or organised tour.

Parque Nacional Los Alerces

» pp138-143

ⓘ *60 km west of Esquel, access via ripio RN17, between Cholila and Trevelin, T02945-471020, alerces@ciudad.com.ar, park entry US$2, daily bus along RN 71 stops at campsites and hosterías.* One of the most magnificent and untouched expanses of the whole Andes region, this national park was established to protect the tall and stately *alerce* trees (Fitzroya cupressoides) that grow deep in the Valdivian rainforest. In order to protect this fragile environment, access is possible only at the eastern side of the park, via *ripio* Route 71, which runs along Lagos Futalaufquen, Verde and Rivadavia. The western side of the park, where rainfall is highest can only be accessed by boat or by hiking to Lago Krügger. The park offers several good treks, rafting and fishing, plus idyllic lakeside campsites and *hosterías*.

The park contains four major lakes: **Lago Rivadavia** at the northern entrance; vivid blue **Lago Futalaufquen**, with some of the best fishing in the area; **Lago Menéndez**, which can be crossed by boat to visit the ancient *alerce* trees, and the emerald-green **Lago Verde**. At the southern tip of Lago Futalaufquen is **Villa Futalaufquen**, a village with a visitors' centre with useful information on the park. Helpful *guardaparques* at the *Intendencia* here give out maps and advise on walks. There is a service station, *locutorio*, two food shops and a restaurant.

There are two border crossings south of Esquel. On the Chilean side, these crossings both link with route 7 north to Chaitén.

Paso Futaleufú lies 70 km southwest of Esquel via RN259 (ripio from Trevelin) towards Futaleufú (see page 297). The border is a bridge over the Río Futaleufú. When entering Chile, change money in Futaleufú and then continue towards Puerto Ramírez; outside Ramírez, take the right turn to Chaitén, otherwise you'll end up at Paso Palena. **Argentine immigration and customs** ⓘ *on the Argentine side of the bridge*; **Chilean immigration and customs** ⓘ *at the border 9 km east of Futaleufú*. Formalities should take no longer than an hour

Paso Palena lies 120 km southeast of Esquel and is reached by ripio RN17, 26 km west of Corcovado. On the Chilean side, the road continues to Palena (see page 297). **Argentine immigration and customs** ⓘ *at the border, open daily 0900-1800*. **Chilean immigration and customs** ⓘ *at Palena, 8 km west of the border.*

Exploring the park

From Puerto Limonao, there are boat trips across Lago Futulaufquen and along the pea-green **Río Arrayanes**, which is lined with extraordinary cinnamon-barked *arrayán* trees. Even more spectacular, is the unforgettable trip from **Puerto Chucao** across **Lago Menéndez** (one and a half hours) to see the majestic 2,600 year old *alerce* tree, known as 'El Abuelo' at the lake's northwestern tip. From El Abuelo, walk to the hidden and silent, jade-green **Lago Cisne** and then back past the rushing white waters of Río Cisne. If walking, register with *guardaparques* before you set off, bear in mind that it takes 10 hours to reach the *refugio* at Lago Krügger, and camping is possible (one night only) at Playa Blanca, where fires are not permitted.

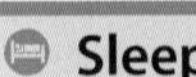

Sleeping

El Bolsón *p131*

There are *cabañas* and *hosterías* in picturesque settings with lovely views, in the Villa Turismo, 3 km southeast of the centre. Buses run by *Comarca Andina*, opposite *Via Bariloche T02944-455400*.

C **La Casona de Odile**, *Barrio Lujan, T02944-492753, www.bolsonturistico .com.ar /odile* A really special place to stay, in rustic wooden cabins in this idyllic lavender farm by a stream, with delicious cooking by the charismatic Odile. Reserve ahead. Recommended.

D **Sukal**, *Villa Turismo, T02944-492438, www.sukal/elbolson.com* Gorgeous bed and breakfast, a haven of peace in a flower-filled garden, with glorious views. Also a *cabana*, US$20 for 4. Delightful.

D **La Posada de Hamelin**, *Int Granollers 2179, T02944-492030, www.bolsonturistico .com.ar/hamelin.* Very welcoming, run by charming German-speaking owners, who make a really outstanding breakfast. Lovely chalet-style house with quaint and comfortable rooms all with bathroom, and lovely garden. Highly recommended.

D **Hostería Steiner**, *San Martín 670, T02944-492224.* A little way out of the centre is this peaceful place with huge lovely gardens. Simple plain rooms, wood fires, German spoken. Recommended.

E pp **Refugio Patagónico**, *Islas Malvinas y Pastorino, T02944-156 35463*. High quality youth hostel, with small dorms all with bathrooms, in a spacious house set in open fields, where you can also camp, with great views of Piltriquitrón, and just 5 blocks from the plaza. Recommended.

Cabañas

The following cost around US$40 per night for 5 people in the Villa Turistica.

Cabañas Paraíso, *T02944-492766, www.bolsonturistico.com.ar/paraiso/* Lovely wooden cabins in a gorgeous setting amongst old trees.

Cabañas Piltri Hué, *T02944-492711, www.bolsonturistico.com.ar/piltrihue* Very alpine-style setting for these picturesque little *cabañas*.

La Montana, *T02944-492776, www.montana.com.ar* Well equipped smart *cabañas* with pool and play area.

Camping

Arco Iris, *T02944-15558330*. Blissful wooded site near Rio Azul, helpful owners.

La Chacra, *Belgrano 1128, T02944-492111*. 15 mins walk from town, well shaded, good facilities, lively in season.

Quem Quem, *Rio Quemquemtreu, T02944-493550, quemquem @elbolson.com* Well kept site with hot showers, good walks, pick-up from town.

Parque Nacional Lago Puelo *p132*

There's no accommodation in the park itself, but plenty in Villa Lago Puelo, with *cabañas*, restaurants and campsites spread along Route 16.

A-D **Puelo Ranch**, *T02945-499411, www.interpatagonia.com/elbolson/caban as* Hidden from the road is a superb complex of very comfortable *cabanas*

D **Hostería Enebros**, *T02945-499413*. On the road, comfortable.

D **Posada los Ninos**, *T02945-499117*. In a pretty rural setting, very peaceful.

Cabañas

La Granja, *km 13, T02945-499265.* Set in lovely woodland, with a pool.
Villa Antares, *Km 11, T02945-499334.* Well equipped and attractive cabins.

Cholila *p133*

A-B pp **Hostería La Rinconada**, *T02945-498091, larinconada @interlink.com.ar* Offers excursions, riding, kayaking. Full board available.
C pp **El Trébol**, *Lago Los Mosquistos, T/F02945-498055, eltrebol@teletel.com.ar* Comfortable rooms with stoves, meals available, popular with fishing expeditions, reservations advised.
D **Cabanas Cerro La Momia**, *RN71 in Villa Rivadavia, T0297-446 1796, www.cabanas cerrolamomia.com.ar* Peaceful setting, basic *cabañas*, but breakfast is included.

Esquel *p135*

A-B **Cumbres Blancas**, *Ameghino 1683, T/F02945-455100, www.cpatagonia.com/ esq/cblancas* A little out of the town centre, with great views of surrounding hills, comfortable traditional rooms and an airy restaurant serving dinner US$7.
B **Angelina**, *Alvear 758, T02945-452763.* A warm welcoming place, open high season only, serving good food.
B **Canela**, *C Los Notros, Villa Ayelén, T/F02945-453890, www.canela-patagonia.com* Comfortable bed and breakfast and tearoom. Helpful English-speaking owners.
C **La Tour D'Argent**, *San Martín 1063, T02945-454612, www.cpatagonia.com /esq/latour* With breakfast, the bright plain modern rooms are very good value in this friendly family-run hotel.
D **La Chacra**, *Km 4 on Ruta 259 towards Trevelin, T02945-452471.* Tranquil place with spacious modern rooms and huge breakfast, Welsh/English spoken.
D **La Posada**, *Chacabuco 905, T02945-454095 laposada@art.inter.ar* A real gem. Welcoming tasteful *hostería* in a quiet part of town, with a lovely lounge and good, spacious rooms, breakfast included. Excellent value.
E **Lago Verde**, *Volta 1081, T02945-454396, patagverde@teletel.com.ar* A modern comfortable hostel, with rooms for 2, breakfast extra, kitchen, laundry. Handy for the bus terminal, 2 blocks from La Trochita. Excursions. Recommended.

Camping

El Hogar del Mochilero, *Roca 1028, T02945-452166.* Summer only (Jan-Mar), laundry facilities, 24-hr hot water, friendly owner, internet, free firewood.
La Colina, *Darwin 1400, Laguna Zeta, T02945-454962.* US$1.75 pp, hot showers, kitchen, lounge, log fire, cheap rooms.

Trevelin *p136*

C **La Granja**, *on the road to Esquel 3km from Trevelin, T02945-480096.* In a lovely open setting, comfortable *cabañas* and camp site, as well as macrobiotic meals and good Italian cooking. Horses for hire.
D **Pezzi**, *Sarmiento 353, T02945-480146.* Open Jan-Mar only, an attractive small hotel, English spoken, and a garden.
D-E **Casa Verde Hostal**, *Los Alerces s/n, T/F02945-48009, casaverdehostel @ciudad.com.ar.* Superb HI hostel in a spacious log cabin. Comfortable dorms for 4-6, with bathrooms, kitchen, laundry, lounge, meals, trekking, rafting.

Parque Nacional Los Alerces *p137*

A **Hostería Quimé Quipan**, *Lago Futalaufquen, T02945-471021.* Delightful, comfortable rooms, impeccably clean, with uninterrupted lake views, dinner included. Wonderfully peaceful. Paths lead down to a small rocky beach.
C **Bahía Rosales**, *Lago Futalaufquen, T02945-471044.* A welcoming family-run place. Spacious *cabañas* in an elevated position above the lake, also *refugio*-style *cabañas* to share and camping in open ground, fireplaces and tables and hot showers; restaurant and *quincho.*
D **Cabañas Tejas Negras**, *Lago Futalaufquen, T02945-471046.* Comfortable. Also good camping facilities and tea room.

D **Pucón Pai**, *Lago Futalaufquen, T02945-471010, puconpai@ciudad.com.ar* Spartan rooms, but a good restaurant with lovely views, recommended for fishing; also campsite, US$2pp.

Camping

Several campsites at Lagos Rivadavia, Verde and Río Arrayanes, ranging from free to US$3 depending on facilities. All have marvellous views, lake access and fireplaces; can be busy in high season. **Krügger Lodge** has a *refugio* and campsite, with hot showers, food shop, meals provided, fishing guides, boat trips.

Eating

El Bolsón p131

Acrimbaldo, *San Martin 2790*. Good value *tenedor libre*, smoked fish and beer.

Cerro Lindo, *San Martín y Hube*. An elegant place for dinner, delicious pastas.

Dulcinea, *on the road to El Hoyo*. This delightful tea room is not to be missed. Famous for cakes and rose hip tea, and fondu at nights in season.

Il Rizzo, *San Martin 2500*. Good value pizzas and draught beer in a lively café.

Jauja, *San Martín 2867*. A great meeting place, welcoming atmosphere, good music and tasty food. Try the trout-filled pasta and the hand-made ice cream.

La Calabaza, *San Martín y Hube*. Inexpensive food, with inventive delicious vegetarian dishes, relaxed atmosphere.

Parrilla Patagonia, *on the road 258 2 km out of town*. Superb *parrilla* for steak, and excellent Patagonian lamb and kid on the *asado* at weekends. Also a cheap set menu and *parrilla libre*.

San Jorge, *3 km from town towards Cascada Escondida, T02944-491313*. Cakes, beer and *picadas* in pretty gardens.

Esquel p135

Don Chiquino, *behind Av Ameghino 1649*. A fun atmosphere: the walls are lined with number plates, and there are magic and mind-teasing games while you wait for your pasta and pizzas.

La Española, *Rivadavia 740*. Serves excellent beef, with salad bar, and tasty pastas. Recommended.

La Tour D'Argent, *San Martin 1063*. Delicious local specialities, good value set meals, and a warm atmosphere.

Maria Castaña, *Rivadavia y 25 de Mayo*. Popular for excellent coffee, reading the papers and watching street life.

Shangai, *25 de Mayo 485*. Chinese and everything else *tenedor libre*. Great value.

Tango Gourmet, *Alvear 949*, A restaurant/bar with tango shows and lessons, open 1100-2400.

Vascongada, *9 de Julio y Mitre*. Good trout and local specialities.

Trevelin p136

The best tea room, offering a huge *té galés* and excellent *torta negra* is **Nain Maggie**, *P Moreno 179*. Recommended.

Parrilla Ruca Laufquen, *Av San Martin y Libertad*. Recommended for *parrilla* and also home-made pasta in a relaxed family atmosphere with the TV on.

Patagonia Celta, *25 de Mayo s/n*. The best place to eat by a long way. Really delicious local specialities, superbly cooked fresh trout, steaks and vegetarian dishes too in elegant stylish surroundings. Very welcoming, and reasonably priced.

Shopping

El Bolsón p131

The handicraft and food market is on Tue, Thu, and Sat in season 1000-1600 around the main plaza, for leather and jewellery, carved wood and organic produce.

Centro Artesanal, *Av San Martín 1059, open daily 1100-1900*. If the market's not open, crafts can be bought here.

Granja Larix, *RN 258, Km 118.5, T02944-498018, alejandra@bariloche.com.ar* For fabulous smoked trout, homemade jams.

Esquel p135

Casa de Esquel, *25 de Mayo 415*. Rare books on Patagonia, also souvenirs.

Librería Patagonica, *25 de Mayo 415, T452544.* Rare books on Patagonia and recent editions, with friendly service.
Braese, *at 9 de Julio 1959.* Home-made chocolates and regional specialities.

Activities and tours

El Bolsón p131

Cabalgatas de Cerro, *T02944-492967*, Horseriding in the surrounding hills.
Ernesto Hecker, *O Nelli 3217, T02944-156 37560.* Great walking trips in the mountains and in the national parks, with detailed expertise on vegetation, geology and local history. Recommended.
Patagonia Adventures, *P Hube 418, T02944-492515, www.argentinachile flyfishing.com* Rafting, paragliding, fishing, boat trip on Lago Puelo to Chile.
Viva Mas Patagonia, *Av San Martín 2526, T02944-156 37665, lamaroma @hotmail.com* Rafting on Río Azul, grade 1 or 3.

Parque Nacional Lago Puelo p132

Boat trips

Juana de Arco, *T02945-493415, T02945-1 56-02290, juanadearco@red42.com.ar.* Boat trips across Lago Puelo,US$2 for 45mins, US$6 to the Chilean border, including walk through woodland. Recommended. Also fishing trips.

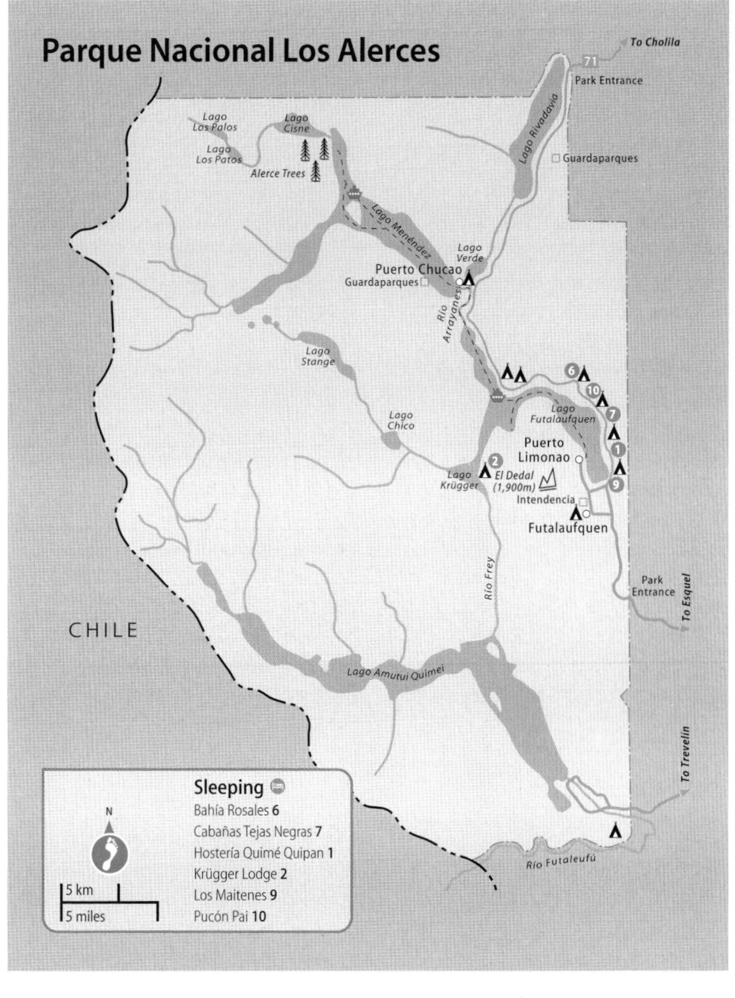

Top tips

Best walks in Los Alerces national park

1 Around the Intendencia (40 mins) a gentle trail to see cave paintings, a waterfall and a mirador with views over the lake.
2 To Puerto Limao (2 hrs) Easy stroll along Lago Futalaufquen.
3 Río Arrayanes (50 mins) Easy walk to Lago Verde, via the suspension bridge over the Río Arrayanes. Another self-guided trail leads to Puerto Chucao on Lago Menéndez where boat trips begin.
4 Cerro El Dedal (8hrs return) A steep climb for wonderful views from the summit at 1,900 m. Register with guardaparques and get detailed directions; start before 1000 and carry plenty of water.
5 Lago Krügger (2 days) Hike though coihue forest to the tip of Lago Krügger (10 hrs). The refugio here is open only Jan/Feb. Then catch a boat back to Puerto Limonao.

Fishing

Zona Sur, *T02945-156 -15989, alemaca @yahoo .com.ar* All inclusive fishing trips Nov-Apr, US$100 for 3, with equipment.

Esquel *p135*

Adventure tours

Esquel Expeditions, *T02945-451763, moranjack@ciudad.com.ar* Experienced guide leads adventure trips, trekking, mountain biking and canoeing in Los Alerces, nearby mountains and up Río Futaleufu into Chile. Recommended.

Patagonia Verde, *9 de Julio 926, T/F02945-454396, patagoniaverde @ciudad.com.ar* Excellent tour to Los Alerces, including the boat across Lago Menéndez. Also adventure trips. Helpful.

Fishing

Sebastián Ferrer, *T02945-452292*. English spoken, 1-day guided excursion for 2 people in the national park, US$150, including boat and meals (licence US$50).

Skiing

La Hoya, 15km north, 22km of pistes for beginners and experienced skiers, 7 ski-lifts. Popular and cheap. Ski pass US$7 per day in high season, equipment hire US$4 a day. Contact **Club Andino Esquel**, *Volta 649, T02945- 453248, www.esquelonline.com.ar*.

Trevelin *p136*

Adventure tours

Gales al Sur, *Patagonia s/n, T/F02945-480427, correo@galesalsur.com.ar* Tours to Chilean border, Los Alerces national park and Futaleufú dam; also La Trochita. Recommended for rafting, trekking, bike, 4WD and horse riding excursions. Friendly, English spoken.

Fishing

Fishing is popular in many local rivers and lakes, most commonly in ríos Futuleufú and Corintos and lagos Rosario and Greda. The season runs from mid-Nov to mid-Apr, and the tourist office can advise on guides and where to go.

Parque Nacional Los Alerces *p137*

Boat trips

Boat trips, US$16-27 run frequently in high season, and can be booked through **Safari Lacustre**, *T02945-471008, www.brazosur.com*, **Patagonia Verde** in Esquel, or **Gales al Sur** in Trevelin. US$5 extra for transport from Esquel.

Fishing

Lago Futalaufquén has some of the best fishing in this part of Argentina; local guides offer trips and boat transport. Ask in the *Intendencia* (park office), or at **Hostería Cume Hue**, T02945-453639 (am) or T02945-450503 (pm). Fishing licences can be obtained either from the food shops, the *kiosko* or **Hosteria Cume Hue**.

Transport

El Bolsón p131

Several buses daily from **Bariloche** and **Esquel**, with **Don Otto, Via Bariloche**. Heavily booked in high season. US$5-6.50, 2 hrs. **La Golondrina** runs 3 buses daily Mon-Sat from the plaza to Mallin Ahogado, from where you'll have to walk to reach the waterfalls.

Parque Nacional Lago Puelo p132

Buses from **El Bolsón** with **Via Bariloche** every 2 hrs Mon-Sat, 4 on Sun, 45mins, US$1.40. **Transportes Esquel** daily connecting Lago Puelo with **Cholila, PN Los Alerces** (4-5 hrs) and **Esquel**.

Esquel p135

Air

Airport, 20 km east of town, U$9 by taxi, US$1.50 by bus. To **Buenos Aires**, 3 per week, **Aerolíneas Argentinas** (agent) *Huala Av Fontana y Av Amedhino, T02945-453614*. **LADE**, *Alvear 1085, T02945-452124*, to **Bariloche** and elsewhere.

Bus

The modern terminal at *Alvear 1871, T02945-451566*, has toilets, kiosko, *locutorio*, left luggage and taxis. 3 daily buses to **La Hoya**, US$5 return.

Long distance To **Bariloche**, 4-5hrs, US$5, **Don Otto, Andesmar, Mar y Valle** (T02945-453712), **Vía Bariloche** (T02945-453528). To **El Bolsón**, 2 hrs, US$3, on bus to Bariloche, or via Los Alerces National Park, see below. To **Trelew**, 9 hrs, US$11, **Mar y Valle, Emp Chubut, Don Otto**, daily. To **Trevelin**, **Via Trevelin** (T02945-455222), Mon-Fri, hourly 0700-2100, every 2 hrs weekends, US$1.05. To **Buenos Aires** travel via Bariloche: **Andesmar** (T02945-450143), including change in Bariloche, 24 hrs, *semi cama* US$50. To **Comodoro Rivadavia**, 9 hrs US$13, **Don Otto** (T02945-453012), 4 times a week (but usually arrives full in season).

To Chile From Esquel to **Paso Futaleufú**, 0800 daily in Jan/Feb, otherwise Mon, Fri, sometimes Wed, with **Jacobsen** US$3. From the border, **Transportes Cordillera** T02945-258633, and **Ebenezer**, to **Futuleufú** and **Chaitén**, 4 times a week, and daily Jan/Feb. From Chaitén there are services to **Coyhaique**.

Trevelin p136

Buses to **Esquel**, with **Via Trevelin** (T02945-455222), Mon-Fri, hourly 0700-2100, every 2 hrs weekends, US$1.20. To **Chilean border**, **Jacobsen** bus from Esquel runs through Trevelin, 0830 daily in Jan/Feb, otherwise Mon, Fri, sometimes Wed, US$3, connecting bus at border to **Futuleufú** and onto **Chaitén.**

Parque Nacional Los Alerces p137

From **El Bolsón**, Transportes Esquel, daily, 4-5 hrs, via Cholila and Epuyen. From **Esquel**, Transportes Esquel, T02945 -453529, daily at 0800 (returning 2115) along the east of **Lago Futalaufquen**, and continuing to **Cholila**, **El Bolsón** and **Lago Puelo** (return 1500). You can stop at any point on the road, US$3 each way.

Directory

El Bolsón p131

Banks and currency exchange

Banco Patagonia, *San Martín y Roca*, with ATM outside. **Internet** Ciber Café La Nuez, *Av San Martín 2175, T02944-455182*. **Post office** *San Martín 1940*.

Esquel p135

Banks and currency exchange

ATMs at Banco de la Nación, *Alvear y Roca*; Banco Patagonia, *25 de Mayo 739*; Bansud, *25 de Mayo 752*. **Internet** lots in the centre. **Post office**, *Alvear 1192 y Fontana*. Mon-Fri 0830-1300, 1600-1930, Sat 0900-1300. **Telephone** many *Locutorios* in centre and at bus terminal.

Atlantic Coast

BUENOS A
Bahía Blanca
Moquehue
PN Laguna Blanca
Cutral-Có
Huincal
Cipolleti
Neuquén
General Roca
Villa Regina
Chichinales
Chimpay
Pichi Mahuida
Juan de Garay
La Adela
Río Colorado
Montes de Oceá
Aluminé
Villa El Chocón
Puesco
Picún Leufú
Emb Ezequiel Ramos Mexía
Lamarque
Choele Choel
Junín de los Andes
Piedra del Aguila
Trica-Có
Río Limay
Río Colorado
Pedro Luro
San Martín de los Andes
El Cuy
Río Negro
General Conessa
RIO NEGRO
Confluencia
Mencué
Sierra Colorado
Nahuel Niyeu
Villalonga
Teniente General Frías
Parque Nacional Nahuel Huapi
Aguada de Guerra
Los Menucos
Valcheta
San Antonio Oeste
Cubanea
San Javier
Carmen des Patagones
Bariloche
Comallo
Aguada Cecillo
Las Grutas
Vicealmirante E O'Connor
Viedma
Pilcaniyeu
Mascardi
Las Bayas
Ingeniero Jacobacci
Los Juncos
Maquinchao
RIO NEGRO
Balneario El Cóndor
Arroyo los Berros
Arroyo de la Ventana
Sierra Grande
Golfo San Matías
Norquinco
El Maitén
Gastre
Punta Norte
Leleque
Can-Gan
Telsen
Golfo San José
Península Valdés
Gualjaina
Istmo Carlos Ameghino
Paso del Sapo
Puerto Madryn
Puerto Pirámides
Esquel
Golfo Nuevo
Trevelin
Colán Conhué
CHUBUT
Punta Delgada
Río Chubut
Dolavon
Trelew
Tecka
Gaiman
Rawson
Pampa de Agria
El Pajarito
Vinttner
Las Plumas
Río Chubut
Alto Río Pico
José de San Martín
Paso de Indios
Los Altaires
Dique F Ameghino
Florentino Ameghino (Merayo)
Gobernador Costa
Embalse Florentino Ameghino
Reserva Natural Punta Tombo
Uzcudún
Tapera
Garyalde
Alto Río Sanguer
Río Chico
Camarones
Buen Pasto
Los Tamariscos
Reserva Natural Cabo Dos Bahías
p148
Facundo
Lago Musters
Alto Río Mayo
Sarmiento
Pico Salamanca
Lago Colhué Huapí
Río Mayo
Colhué Huapí
Astra
General Mosconi
Lago
Río Guenguel
Comodoro Rivadavia
SANTA CRUZ
Atlantic Ocean
Golfo San Jorge
Perito Moreno
Las Heras
Koluel Kayke
Caleta Olivia
Estancia Telken
Río Deseado
Cañadón Seco
Pico Truncado
ARGENTINA
Fitz Roy
Cueva de las Manos
Jaramillo
Monumento Natural Bosque Petrificados
Bajo Caracoles
Antonio de Biedma
Río Deseado
Puerto Deseado
N
Reserva Natural San Julián
Las Horquetas
Estancia La Maria
100 km
100 miles
Gobernador Gregores
Estancia La Angostura
Río Chico
Puerto San Julian
La Julia
Laguna Grande
Piedrabuena
Rincón Grande
Santa Cruz
Puerto de Punta Quilla
Estancia Monte León
Parque Nacional Monte León
SANTA CRUZ
Cañadón de las Vacas
Atlantic Ocean
Cerrito
Puerto Coig
Río Coig
Estancia Hill Station
Bahía Grande
Río Gallegos
Güer Aike
Laguna Azul
Parque Nacional Pali Aike
Estancia Monte Dinero
p168
Punta Delgada
Punta Espora
Cerro
Don't miss...
1 Whale watching at Península Valdés ▸▸ p152.
2 Museo Paleontológico Egidio Feruglio ▸▸ p155.
3 Welsh tea at Plas y Coed in Gaiman ▸▸ p163.
4 Petrified forests ▸▸ p169 and ▸▸ p171.
5 Parque Nacional Monte León ▸▸ p171.

Introduction

Marine life abounds along Patagonia's seemingly endless virgin coastline. Stop off on your way south at the friendly city of Bahía Blanca or at the quaint town of Carmen de Patagones and then head down to Puerto Madryn. This pleasant seaside town is a great base for the Península Valdés, where sealions and penguins gather in their thousands, and southern right whales cavort with their young in the spring. Take a walk on the shore and then try the excellent seafood. Nearby, Trelew has a superb dinosaur museum, while Gaiman keeps the Welsh pioneer heritage alive with a fascinating museum, Eisteddfods and overwhelming Welsh teas.

Further south, you'll find colonies of cormorants in Ría Deseado and dolphins frolicking in the beautiful bay at Puerto San Julian. Leaving the sublime shorelines behind, venture inland to explore the weird lunar landscapes of the Bosques Petrificados – an unforgettably eerie sight. There are quiet towns for rest at Piedrabuena and Río Gallegos, and the new national park Monte León offers superb accommodation in a wild and splendidly isolated setting.

Ratings

Landscape
★★★

Chillin'
★★★

Activities
★★★

Wildlife
★★★★★

Costs
$$$

Bahía Blanca to Camarones

Many visitors to Patagonia head for Península Valdés, a splay of land stretching into the Atlantic which hosts an array of wildlife, most famously Southern right whales, which come here to breed in spring. The seaside town of Puerto Madryn makes a good base for exploring the area. Just south, Trelew is worth a visit for its superb palaeontological museum, and for access to the old Welsh pioneer villages of Gaiman and Dolavon in the Chubut Valley to the west. Half way from Buenos Aires you could break your journey at the friendly town of Bahía Blanca, spend a night at historic Carmen de Patagones on the Río Negro, or go shark fishing at Bahía San Blas. Viedma has a direct train to Bariloche and Bahía Blanca has excellent transport links everywhere.

Getting there Fly direct to Trelew.

Getting around Good bus services and tours.

Time required 3 days at Península Valdés, 1 day for the Chubut Valley.

Weather Pleasant in summer, cold winds in winter.

Sleeping Good hotels in Puerto Madryn, less choice elsewhere. Fine coastal estancias.

Eating Excellent seafood in Puerto Madryn, decadent Welsh teas in Gaiman.

Activities and tours Wildlife watching, diving, fishing.

★ **Don't miss...** Southern right whales at Península Valdés, Jun-Dec

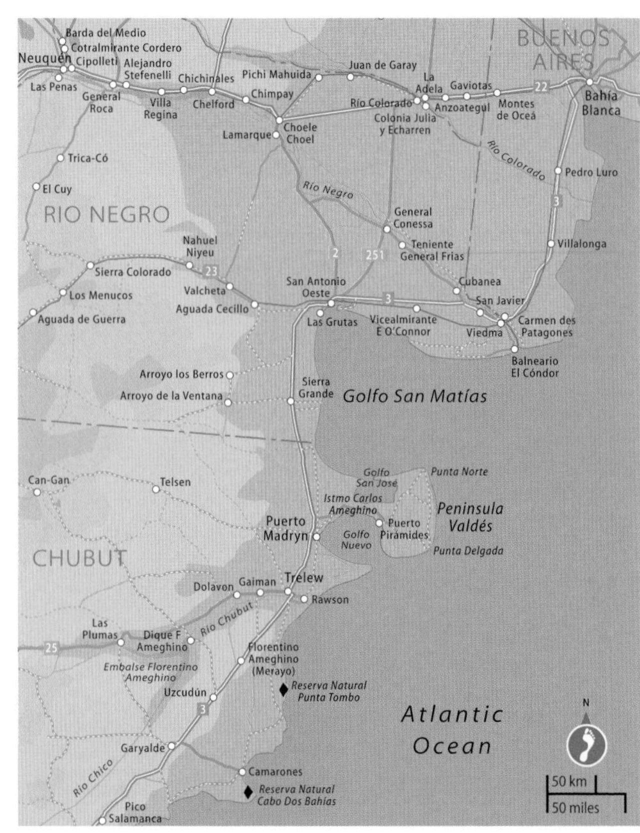

Bahía Blanca » pp 158-167

Bahía Blanca is the best stopping point on the route south. It's a busy city, and yet it's a relaxed and attractive place with superb early 20th-century architecture around its large plaza.

Ins and outs

Getting there and around There are several **flights** daily from Buenos Aires to **Airport Comandante Espora**, T0291-486 1456, 11 km northeast of centre, US$3 in a taxi. Also weekly flights with **LADE** to many places in Patagonia. Bahía Blanca is an excellent transport hub with **buses** from all over the country to the terminal, Estados Unidos y Brown, T0291-481 9615, 2 km east of the centre, connected by local buses 512, 514, or taxi US$2. There are also **trains** from Buenos Aires to the station 6 blocks east of the plaza at Av Gral Cerri 750, T0291-452 9196. Use local buses, taking *tarjebus* cards rather than cash, to get to the shopping mall 20 blocks north. Taxis are cheap, plentiful and safe. » *Transport p166.*

Sights

At the city's heart is the large **Plaza Rivadavia**, a broad, well kept leafy space, planted with a wide variety of trees, with a striking sculpture at its centre. On the west side is the Italianate **Municipalidad** (1904), which houses the **tourist office** ⓘ *Alsina 65, T0291-459 4007, www.bahiablanca.gov.ar, Mon-Fri 0730-1900, Sat 1000-1300*. To the south is the impressive French-style **Banco de la Nación** (1927). Three blocks north there's the classical **Teatro Colón** (1922), which hosts regular theatre, live music and dance, T0291-456 3973. At the side of the theatre, at Dorrego 116, the **Museo Histórico** ⓘ *T0291-456 3117, Tue-Sun 1500-2000*, has interesting displays on the city's history. Outside is a statue of Garibaldi, erected by the Italian community in 1928. There are lively, changing exhibitions at the **Museo de Arte Contemporánea** ⓘ *Sarmiento 450, Tue-Fri 1000-1300, 1600-2000.*

To the northwest of the centre, along the attractive Avenida Além, the **Parque de Mayo**, is filled with eucalyptus trees, with children's play areas, bars, and a fine golf course and sports centre nearby.

Not to be missed is the **Museo del Puerto** ⓘ *Torres y Carrega, open weekends, summer 1700-2030, winter 1500-2000, and weekdays for schools, and public by arrangement, free, take bus 500A or 504 from the plaza, running hourly at weekends, or a taxi; US$3*, located 7 km away at the port area, which is known as *Ingeniero White*. Set in a former customs building, this has entertaining and imaginative displays on immigrant life in the early 20th century, with witty photographs, evocative music and sound. And there's a great café in one of the exhibition spaces on Sundays. The port also has a couple of fine fish restaurants in its red light district.

Carmen de Patagones and Viedma » pp 158-167

These two pleasant towns straddle the broad sweep of the Río Negro, 250 km south of Bahía Blanca. Viedma, on the south bank, was founded in 1779, but destroyed almost immediately by floods, after which Carmen de Patagones was founded on higher ground to the north. The **Fiesta de 7 de Marzo** (for a week around the 7th March) is worth a visit, although accommodation is heavily booked. » *Festivals and events, p164.*

Ins and outs

There are comfortable **buses** direct from Buenos Aires several times a day to the terminal at Av Pte Peron y Guido, 15 blocks from plaza in Viedma, taxi US$1, and a **train** three times a week between Viedma and Bariloche in the the Lake District. Patagones (as it's known) and Viedma are linked by two bridges and a very small **ferry**, which takes 4 minutes and leaves every 15 minutes, US$0.20. Patagones has a helpful and dynamic **tourist office** ⓘ *Bynon 186, T02920-462054, www.vivalaspampas.com*. Viedma has a rather impoverished **tourist office** ⓘ *on the costanera, 3 blocks east of Plaza Alsina, T02920-427171, www.rionegrotur.com.ar, open 0900-2100*.

Carmen de Patagones

Carmen de Patagones is by far the most picturesque of the two towns. Its town centre, just east of the river, lies around the Plaza 7 de Mayo, and just west is the **Iglesia del Carmen**, built by the Salesians in 1880. Take a stroll down the pretty adobe streets winding down to the river, to find many early pioneer buildings, including the **Casa de la Tahona**, a disused 18th-century flour mill, that now houses the **Casa de la Cultura**. Nearby is the fascinating **Museo Historico** ⓘ *Biedma 4, T02920-462729, open daily 0930-1230, 1900-2100, Sun pm only*, which gives a great insight into early pioneer life.

Viedma

Viedma is the provincial administrative centre and a duller place than Carmen de Patagones. However, it does have better accommodation and a pretty bathing area on the river, with large grassy banks shaded by willow trees, where everyone hangs out to swim and drink *mate* on warm summer afternoons. The river water is pleasantly warm in summer and completely uncontaminated.

There are two plazas, with the cathedral, built by the Salesians in 1912, on the west of Plaza Alsina. Two blocks east, on the Plaza San Martín, are the French-style **Casa de Gobierno** (1926) and, opposite, the **Museo Gobernador Tello** ⓘ *open 0900-1230, 1700-1930 in summer*, with fossils, rocks and indigenous *boleadoras*. Along the attractive *costanera*, the **Centro Cultural**, opposite Calle 7 de Marzo houses a small **Mercado Artesenal** selling beautifully made Mapuche weavings and wood work.

South and west of Viedma

This whole stretch of coast is great for shore fishing, with *pejerrey, variada* and even shark among many other species. At **El Cóndor** ⓘ *30 km from Viedma, 3 buses a day in summer*, there is a beautiful beach, with the oldest *faro* (lighthouse) in the country, dating from 1887. **Playa Bonita**, 12 km further south is known as a good fishing spot, with pleasant beaches. The sealion colony at **Lobería Punta Bermeja**, 60 km south, is visited by some 2,500 sealions in summer. You can see the animals at close range and get further information at the impressive visitor centre. There's another stretch of lovely coastline at **Bahia San Blas** (www.bahiasanblas.com), a well-established shark fishing resort 100 km from Patagones.

Puerto Madryn and around » *pp 158-167*

Puerto Madryn is a pleasant breezy seaside town with a grand setting on the wide bay of Golfo Nuevo, the perfect base for seeing the extraordinary array of wildlife on Península Valdés, just 70 km east. During breeding seasons you can see whales, penguins and seals at close range or go diving to explore life underwater. If you want to stay on the peninsula itself, there's the small popular resort of Puerto Pirámides as well as several *estancias* to choose from, but Puerto Madryn makes a good place to enjoy the sea for a couple of days. The town was the site of the first Welsh landing in 1865 and is named after the Welsh home of the colonist, Jones Parry. It is a modern, relaxed and friendly place and hasn't been ruined by its popularity as a tourist resort.

Ins and outs

Getting there The airport, 10 km west of centre, taxi US$5, has regular flights to/from Buenos Aires and El Calafate plus weekly flights with **LADE** to other towns in Patagonia (see Essentials, page 23). There are more frequent services to/from Trelew airport, see page 154. An hourly bus with **Mar y Valle** links Trelew airport with Puerto Madryn's bus terminal; a taxi will cost US$20. Puerto Madryn is connected to all the main tourist destinations by long-distance buses from Buenos Aires, Bahía Blanca and south to Río Gallegos. The terminal, T02965-451789, is at Irigoyen y San Martín (behind the old railway station). Walk three blocks down R S Pena to get into town. » *Transport, p166.*

Tourist information ⓘ *Av Roca 223, off 28 de Julio, T02965-453504, www.turismo .madryn.gov.ar, open Mon-Fri 0700- 2100, Sat/Sun 0830-1330, 1530-2030.* This is one of the country's best tourist information centres, located on the seafront next to the shopping complex. Its staff are friendly, extremely well organized and speak both English and French. They have leaflets on Península Valdés, accommodation lists and can advise on tours.

Around Puerto Madryn

You're most likely to be visiting the town to take an excursion to Península Valdés (see page 152) but there are other worthwhile destinations along the coast nearby. You can stroll along the long stretch of town beach to **El Indio**, a statue marking the gratitude of the Welsh to the native Tehuelche people, whose shared expertise ensured their survival. As the road curves up the cliff here, there's the splendid **EcoCentro** ⓘ *Julio Verne 784, T02965-457470, www.ecocentro.org.ar, 1000-1800 daily (check with tourist office), US$2.50, reductions for students, children and retired, bus linea 2 from 25 de Mayo y Belgrano, then 5-min walk from the university*, an inspired interactive sea-life information centre that combines an art gallery, café and fabulous reading room with comfy sofas at the top of a turret. The whole place has fantastic views of the bay; great for an afternoon's relaxation or for finding out about whales.

Less exciting is the **Museo de Ciencias Naturales y Oceanográfico** ⓘ *Domecq García y J Menéndez, Mon-Fri 0900-1200, 1430-1900, Sat 1430-1900 entry US$1.* It's an old-fashioned museum but its displays on local flora and wildlife are informative and worth a look.

You can spot whales from the *ripio* road at the long **Playa El Doradillo**, 16 km northeast of Puerto Madryn, and sea lions 15 km southeast at the **Punta Loma Reserve** ⓘ *open during daylight hours, US$3, but free with ticket to Península Valdés.* Access is via the coastal road from town and, like the road to the north, makes a great bike ride – allow 1½ hours to get there. The reserve is best visited at low tide in December and January.

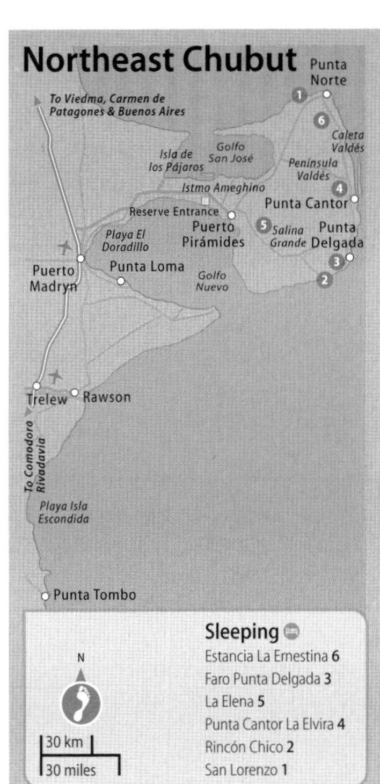

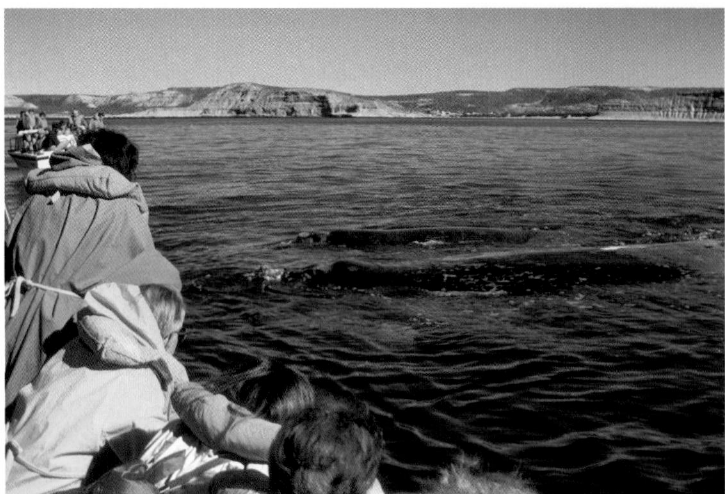

Whale watching around Península Valdés

Península Valdés » *pp 158-167*

Whatever time of year you visit Península Valdés, you'll find a wonderful array of marine life, birds and a profusion of Patagonian mammals such as guanacos, rheas, patagonian hares and armadillos. But in spring, this treeless splay of land is host to a quite spectacular numbers of whales, penguins and seals, who come to breed in the sheltered waters of the gulf and on beaches at the foot of the peninsula's chalky cliffs. The land is almost flat, though greener than much of Patagonia, and at the heart of the peninsula are large saltflats, one of which, **Salina Grande**, is 42 m below sea level. The peninsula is privately owned – many of its *estancias* offer grand places to stay in the middle of the wild beauty – but it is also a nature reserve and was declared a World Heritage Site by UNESCO in 1999. The beach along the entire coast is out of bounds and this is strictly enforced. The main centre for accommodation and whale trips is **Puerto Pirámides**, on the southern side of the isthmus.

Ins and outs

Getting there Península Valdés is best visited by taking one of the well-organized full-day excursions from Puerto Madryn but you could also hire a car relatively inexpensively for a group of 4, and then take just the boat trip to see the whales (Sep-Nov) from Puerto Pirámides. Note that distances are long on the peninsula, and roads beyond Puerto Pirámides are *ripio*, so take your time. A cheaper option is the daily bus to Puerto Pirámides. » *Transport, p166.*

Tourist information The **entrance** ⓘ *US$3, tickets are also valid for Punta Loma*, is on a narrow isthmus, 79 km east of Puerto Madryn. Here, there's an interesting **interpretation centre** with stuffed examples of the local fauna, many fossils and a wonderful whale skeleton. Ask for the informative bilingual leaflet on southern right whales. Contact the tourist office in **Puerto Madryn** (see above) or the small office on the edge of **Puerto Pirámides**, T02965-495084, which has useful information on hikes and driving tours.

Whale watching

Puerto Pirámides, 107 km east of Puerto Madryn, is the main centre for visits to the peninsula and whale-watching boat trips leave from its broad sandy beach. Every year

Península Valdés

✓ Take an organized tour rather than hiring a car. The excess charged for turning them over is huge and you'll be too tired after driving on the *ripio* roads to enjoy the wildlife to the full.

✓ To spend more time on the peninsula and see more of the wildlife, stay at one of several *estancias* there: Rincón Chico, Faro Punta Delgada, La Elena, are all right in the middle of the land.

✗ Whale watching trips in boats from Puerto Pirámides are not for the easily sea sick. If it's a rough day and you're prone to sickness, bring good binoculars and head for the Playa El Doradillo, 16km north of Puerto Madryn where you can often spot whales close to

between June and December 400-500 **southern right whales** migrate to the Gulfo Nuevo to mate and give birth. It is without doubt one of the best places in the world to watch these beautiful animals, as, in many places the whales come within just a few metres of the coast. Take a boat trip and, with luck, you'll be very close to a mother and baby. Sailings are controlled by the Prefectura, according to weather and sea conditions (if you're very prone to sea sickness think twice before setting off on a windy day).

Wildlife colonies

Isla de los Pájaros in the Golfo San José, 5 km from the entrance. Bird Island's **seabirds** can only be viewed through fixed telescopes (at 400 m distance). Only recognized ornithologists can get permission to visit. Between September and April you can spot wading birds, herons, cormorants and terns.

Punta Norte, at the northern end of the peninsula, 97 km from the entrance, is not often visited by the excursion companies, but it has colonies of Magellanic penguins and sea lions. Killer whales (orca) have also been seen here, feeding on sea lion pups at low tide in March and April. **San Lorenzo estancia** is nearby (see Sleeping, page 158).

Caleta Valdés 45 km south of Punta Norte in the middle of the eastern shore, has huge colonies of **elephant seals**, which can be seen at close quarters. During the first half of August the bull-seals arrive to claim their territory, and can be seen at low tide engaging in bloody battles for their women. From September to October, you'll see them hauling their blubbery mass up the beach to breed. At Punta Cantor, just south of here, you'll find a good café and clean toilets. There are also three marked walks, from 45 minutes to two hours. A short distance inland is **Estancia La Elvira** (see Sleeping, page 158).

Punta Delgada, at the southeastern end of the peninsula, 91 km from the entrance, is where **elephant seals** and **sea lions** can be seen from the high cliffs in such large numbers that they seem to stretch out like a velvety bronze tide line on the beautiful beach below. It's mesmerising to watch as the young frolic in the shallow water, and the bulls lever themselves around the females. There's a hotel nearby, **Faro Punta Delgada** (see Sleeping, page 158), a good base for exploring this beautiful area further.

Trelew and the Chubut Valley »» *pp 158-167*

The Río Chubut flows a massive 820 km from the foothills of the Andes to enter the Atlantic at Rawson. Welsh pioneers came to this part of the world in 1865 and their irrigation of the arid land around the river enabled them to survive and prosper. You can trace their history west along the valleyfrom the pleasant airy town of Trelew, past little brick chapels sitting amidst lush green fields, to the villages of Gaiman and Dolavon (see also 'A little Wales beyond Wales', page 156). If you're keen to investigate further into the past, there's a marvellous museum full of dinosaurs at Trelew and some ancient fossils in the Parque Palaeontológico Bryn-Gwyn near Gaiman.

Ins and outs

There are daily flights from Buenos Aires, El Calafate, Ushuaia and Bariloche in high season to Trelew's airport, 5 km north of the town. A taxi into the centre costs US$3 and local buses to Puerto Madryn will stop at the airport entrance if asked. The bus terminal is north of the centre on the east side of Plaza Centenario, T02965-420121. A 10-minute walk south is the main plaza, where you'll find the very helpful **tourist office** ⓘ *Mitre 387, T02965-420139,* *www.trelewpatagonia.gov.ar, open Mon-Fri 0800-1400, 1500-2100, Sat/Sun 0900-1300, 1500-2000.* They'll give you an excellent map, directing you to the town's older buildings. Visit in mid-October for the Eisteddfod.

Trelew

Located some 70 km south of Puerto Madryn, Trelew (pronounced *'Trel-Yeah-Oo'*) is the largest town in the Chubut valley. Founded in 1884, it was named in honour of Lewis Jones, an early settler, and the Welsh colonization is still evident in a few remaining chapels in the town's modern centre and in the Welsh language still spoken by some residents.

The lovely, shady Plaza Independencia in the town centre is packed with mature trees and hosts a small handicraft market at weekends. Nearby is the **Capilla Tabernacle**, on Belgrano between San Martín and 25 de Mayo, a red-brick Welsh chapel dating from 1889. Heading east, rather more impressive is the **Salon San David**, a Welsh meeting hall first used for the Eisteddfod of 1913 and now, sadly, used for bingo. The most wonderful building in the town, however, is the 1920s **Hotel Touring Club**, Fontana 240. This was the town's grandest hotel in its heyday; politicians and travellers met in its glorious high-ceilinged mirrored bar, which is now full of old photographs and relics. You can eat lunch here and there's simple accommodation (see Sleeping and Eating below); you should also ask the friendly owner to see the elegant meeting room at the back.

The town's best museum – and indeed one of the finest in Argentina – is the **Museo Paleontológico Egidio Feruglio** ⓘ *Fontana 140, T02965-432100, www.mef.org.ar, Mon-Fri 1000-2000 spring and summer, 1000-1800 rest of year, Sat/Sun 1000-2000, US$2.50, reductions for students, the retired and children under 12.* Imaginatively designed and beautifully presented, the museum traces the origins of life through the geological ages, displaying dynamically poised dinosaur skeletons, with plentiful information in Spanish. Tours are free and are available in English, German and Italian. There is also a reasonably cheap café and shop. Ask for information about the **Parque Paleontológico Bryn Gwyn** near Gaiman, see page 157.

The **Museo Regional Pueblo de Luis** ⓘ *Fontana y 9 de Julio, T02965-424062, Mon-Fri 0800-2000, Sat closed, Sun 1700-2000, US$2,* is appropriately housed in the old railway station, built in 1889. It was Lewis Jones who founded the town and started the railways that exported Welsh produce so successfully. The museum has interesting displays on indigenous societies, on failed Spanish attempts at settlement and on Welsh colonization.

Just outside town, on the road to Rawson, you'll find one of the oldest standing Welsh chapels, **Capilla Moriah**. Built in 1880, it has a simple interior and a cemetery with the graves of many original settlers, including the first woman born in the Welsh colony.

Gaiman

West of Trelew, route 25 heads through the beautifully green and fertile floodplain of the Río Chubut to Gaiman and Dolavon before continuing through attractive scenery all the way to Esquel (see page 135) and the Welsh colony of Trevelin (see page 136).

Gaiman is a small pretty place with old brick houses, retaining the Welsh pioneer feel, and hosts an annual *Eisteddfod* (Welsh festival of arts) in October. The **tourist office** ⓘ *T02965-491571, www.gaiman.gov.ar, Oct-Mar, Mon-Sat 0900-2100, Sun 1400-2000, Apr-Sep, Mon-Sat 0900-1700, Sun 1100-1700, near the old railway on Belgramo between 28 de Julio and Rivadavia,* is housed in the Casa de Cultura. Around the town plaza are several **tearooms**, many of them run by descendents of the original settlers, serving delicious and 'traditional' Welsh teas (see Eating, page 163). It's hard to imagine their abstemious ancestors tucking into the vast plates filled with seven kinds of cake and scones, so for a reminder of the spartan lives of those idealistic pioneers, visit the wonderful, tiny **Museo**

Background

A little Wales beyond Wales

Among the stories of early pioneers to Argentina, the story of the Welsh emigration, in search of religious freedom, is courageous. The first 165 settlers arrived in Patagonia in July 1865. Landing on the bay where Puerto Madryn now stands, they were forced by lack of water to walk south across the parched land to the valley of the Chubut river, where they found cultivatable land and settled. The first ten years were harsh indeed, and they were saved by trade with local Tehuelche indigenous peoples, who taught them essential survival skills. The British navy also delivered supplies, and there was support from the Argentine government, eager to populate its territory.

The settlement was partly inspired by Michael D Jones, a non-conformist minister who provided much of the early finance and recruited settlers through the Welsh language press and through the chapels. Jones, whose aim was to create a 'little Wales beyond Wales', far from the intruding influence of the English, took particular care to recruit people with useful skills such as farmers and craftsmen. Between 1865 and 1915, the colony was reinforced by another 3,000 settlers from Wales and the United States. The early years brought persistent drought, and finding that the land was barren unless irrigated, the pioneers created a network of irrigation channels. Early settlers were allocated 100 hectares of land, and when, by 1885 all irrigable land had been allocated, settlement expanded westwards along the valley. The charming town of Trevelin (near Esquel, see page 136), where Welsh is still spoken, was the result of this westward migration.

The success of the Welsh colony was partly due to the creation of their own successful Cooperative Society, which sold their produce and bought necessities in Buenos Aires. Early settlers were organised into chapel based communities of 200-300 people, which were largely self-governing and organized social and cultural activities. The colony thrived after 1880, growing prize-winning wheat in the valley, and exporting successfully to Buenos Aires and Europe, but was badly weakened by the great depression in the 1930s, and the poor management of the Argentine government. Many of the Welsh survived, however, and most of the owners of Gaiman's extraordinary Welsh tea rooms are indeed descendants of the original settlers. Welsh language is kept alive in both Gaiman and Trevelin, and musical Eisteddfods are held every October. So, as you tuck into your seventh slice of Welsh cake, spare a thought for the harsh conditions endured by those brave early pioneers.

Histórico Regional Galés ⓘ *Sarmiento y 28 de Julio, T02965-491007, open Tue-Sun 1500-1900, US$1.* Its impressive collection of Welsh artefacts, objects and photographs is an evocative and moving testimony to extraordinary lives lived in harsh conditions. Curator Mrs Roberts is helpful and hugely knowledgeable.

Many older buildings remain: the low, stone **Primera Casa** 'first house' (1874) ⓘ *on the corner of main street Avenida Tello and Evans, open daily 1400-1900*; the old **railway station** (1909), which now houses the regional museum (see above); the **old hotel** (1899), at Tello y 9 de Julio, and the **Ty Nain tea room** (1890), on the Plaza at Yrigoyen 283 (see below). On the south side of the river there are two old chapels: **Capilla Bethel** (1913) and the **Capilla Vieja** (1888). A far more recent monument to human energy and inspiration is the extraordinary **El Desafío** ⓘ *two blocks west of plaza, daily until 1800, US$1.50*, an imaginative sculptural world, made entirely from rubbish by the eccentric Joaquín Alonso – painted plastic bottles, cans and wire form pergolas and dinosaurs, sprinkled liberally with plaques bearing words of wisdom and witty comments. It's beginning to fade now, but still good fun.

Some 8 km south of town, there are fossil beds dating back 40 million years at the **Parque Paleontológico Bryn Gwyn** ⓘ *T02965-432100, www.mef.org.ar, open 1000-1900, end Sept to end March, daily, US$2 adults, taxi from Gaiman US$1.70*. A mind-boggling expanse of time is brought to life by the guided tour. It takes one and a half hours to do the circuit, with fossils to see, as well as a visitors' centre where you can experience some fieldwork in palaeonthology.

Dolavon and around

Founded in 1919, the most westerly Welsh settlement in the valley, is quiet and not as inviting as Gaiman, although if you stroll around its two intersecting streets, you'll find a few buildings reminiscent of the Welsh past.

If you're in your own transport, it's worth driving from Dolavon back towards Gaiman through the neat squared fields of the beautiful irrigated valley, where you'll see Welsh chapels tucked away among poplar trees and silver birches. The **San David chapel** (1917) is a beautifully preserved brick construction, with an elegant bell tower and sturdy oak-studded door, in a quiet spot surrounded by birches, an impressive testimony to Welsh pioneer spirit.

South of Trelew » pp 158-167

Reserva Natural Punta Tombo

ⓘ *107 km south of Trelew, access from ripio route 1 towards Camarones. Open Sep-Mar, US$4. Tours from Trelew and Puerto Madryn, US$20, including 45 mins at the site, where there's a café and toilets.*

There is a lovely rock and sand beach with birds and other wildlife at **Playa Isla Escondida**, 70 km south of Trelew, with secluded camping but no facilities. Head south from here to see the penguin colony at the **Reserva Natural Punta Tombo**. This reserve is the largest breeding ground for Magallenic penguins in Patagonia. The birds come here in September, chicks hatch from mid-November and first waddle to the water in January-February. It's fascinating to see these creatures up close, but noisy colonies of tourists dominate the place in the morning; it's quieter in the afternoon. You'll see guanacos, hares and rheas on the way.

Camarones and the Reserva Natural Cabo dos Bahías

Camarones is a quiet fishing port on Bahía Camarones, 275 km south of Trelew, whose main industry is harvesting seaweed. This is prime sheep-rearing land, and Camerones wool is world-renowned for its quality. Aside from the salmon festival around 7-9 February, the only real attraction is the penguin colony at the **Reserva Natural Cabo Dos Bahías**, ⓘ *28 km southeast of Camerones at the southern end of the bay and reached by a dirt road, open all year, US$5*. It protects around 12,000 pairs of penguins, which you can see close up, but also lots of other marine life. You can see seals and sea lions any time, plus whales from March to November and even killer whales from October to April.

Sleeping

Bahía Blanca *p149*

B **Argos**, *España 149, T0291-455 0404, www.hotelargos.com.ar* Three blocks from the plaza, the city's finest is a 4 star business hotel with comfortable rooms, and good breakfast. Also a restaurant.

B **Austral**, *Colón 159, T0291-456 1700, www.hoteles-austral.com.ar* A friendlier 4-star with plain spacious rooms, good bathrooms, and good views over the city, attentive service, and decent restaurant.

C **Bahía Hotel**, *Chiclana 251, T0291-455 0601, www.bahia-hotel.com.ar* A new modern business hotel, this is good value, with well-equipped rooms, a bright airy bar and *confitería* on street level.

C **Italia** *Brown 181, T0291-456 2700*. Set in a lovely 1920s Italianate building, this is one of the town's oldest, full of character, but some rooms are badly in need of a face lift.

D **Barne**, *H Yrigoyen 270, T0291-453 0294*. A friendly, low-key family-run place that's good value.

Viedma *p149*

C **Austral**, *25 de Mayo y Villarino, T02920-422615, viedma@hoteles -austral.com.ar* Along the *costanera*, this modern hotel has well equipped, if slightly old-fashioned, rooms.

C **Nijar**, *Mitre 490, T02920-422833*. Very comfortable, smart modern rooms, a quiet relaxed atmosphere, and good attentive service. Recommended.

D **Peumayen**, *Buenos Aires 334, T02920-425222*. An old-fashioned friendly place on the plaza.

E **Hotel Spa**, *25 de Mayo 174, T02920-430459*. A real find, this is a great-value hotel in a quiet complex with steam baths, a very relaxing atmosphere and welcoming staff.

Puerto Madryn *p150,map p159*

Accommodation often gets full in spring and summer, when prices rise; book in advance. Watch out for the 'international tourist' price in more expensive hotels.

AL **Tolosa**, *Roque Sáenz Peña 253, T02965-471850, F02965-451141, www.hoteltolosa.com.ar* An extremely comfortable modern place with faultless personal service and great breakfasts. Note that the superior rooms are much more spacious and have full wheelchair access. Free use of bicycles and internet. Highly recommended. International tourist prices.

A **Bahía Nueva**, *Av Roca 67, T/F02965-451677, www.bahianueva.com.ar* One of the best seafront hotels, with a welcoming reception area and high standards in all details. Rooms are on the small side, but comfortable, breakfasts are generous, and staff are helpful and professional. International tourist prices but cheaper in low season. Recommended.

B-C **Villa Pirén**, *Av Roca 439, T/F02965-456272, www.piren.com.ar* Excellent modern rooms and apartments in smart seafront building with great facilities. Ask for the junior suite, or rooms with a view.

C **Playa**, *Av Roca 187, T02965-451446, www.playa hotel.com.ar* Good central sea front location with spacious entrance and airy *confiteria*. All good value and comfortable, there is a range of rooms and it's worth paying extra for the larger, more modern rooms with sea view. Parking costs US$2 per night.

C **Santa Rita**, *Gob Maiz 370, T02965-471050, www.hostelsantarita.com.ar.* Welcoming place and comfy rooms with wash basin – this is good value with dinner included or you can use the kitchen facilities. Helpful hosts. Often recommended by travellers.

D **Hostería Torremolinos**, *Marcos A Zar 64, T02965-453215*. Nice modern place with simple, well decorated rooms.

D **Gran Palace Hotel**, *28 de Julio 400, T 02965-471009*. Attractive entrance to this central and economical place, but rooms are a bit squashed and rather dark, thanks to the mahogany effect wallpaper.

But they're clean and have bathroom and TV, making this good value.

D **Muelle Viejo**, *H Yrigoyen 38, T02965-471284, www.muelleviejo.com* Ask for the stylish, comfortable modernized rooms in this funny old place. Excellent value large rooms sleep 4 and there are *parrilla* and kitchen facilities if you want to cook.

D-E **La Posta**, *Roca 33, T02965-472422. Residencial laposta@infovia.com.ar* You'll find small but very clean rooms in this welcoming little place on the sea front. Also simple self-catering apartments, all popular in high season. Recommended.

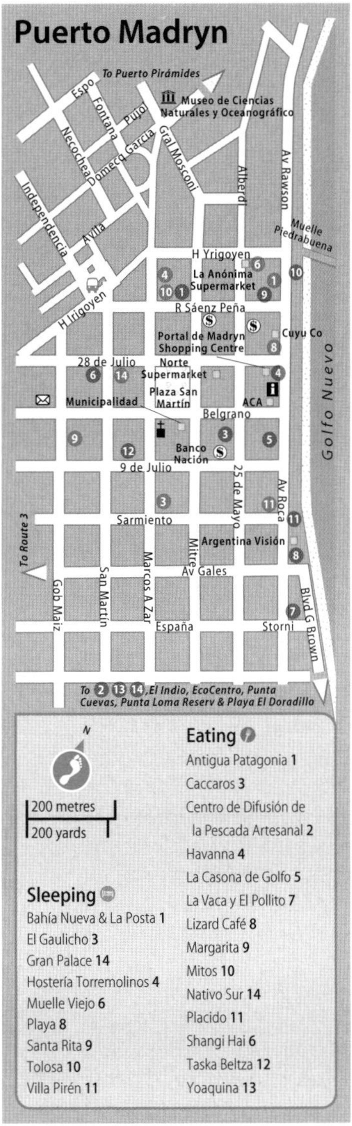

F **El Gualicho**, *Marcos A Zar 480, T02965-454163, www.elgualicho.com.ar* By far the best budget place, this new hostel is beautifully designed and run by a friendly and enthusiastic owner. Free pick up from bus terminal, parrilla, garden, some attractive double rooms, and bikes for hire – book ahead. Highly recommended.

Puerto Madryn

200 metres
200 yards

Sleeping
Bahía Nueva & La Posta 1
El Gaulicho 3
Gran Palace 14
Hostería Torremolinos 4
Muelle Viejo 6
Playa 8
Santa Rita 9
Tolosa 10
Villa Pirén 11

Eating
Antigua Patagonia 1
Caccaros 3
Centro de Difusión de la Pescada Artesanal 2
Havanna 4
La Casona de Golfo 5
La Vaca y El Pollito 7
Lizard Café 8
Margarita 9
Mitos 10
Nativo Sur 14
Placido 11
Shangi Hai 6
Taska Beltza 12
Yoaquina 13

Península Valdés p152, map p151

Accommodation is good quality, but can be pricey. The following are all in Puerto Pirámides unless otherwise stated.

B **The Paradise**, *far end of the main street, T02965-495030, www.hosteria paradise.com* Huge very comfortable light rooms, smart bathrooms, and splendid suites with jacuzzis. Also a fine restaurant, serving delicious squid, among other seafood.

C **Cabañas del Mar**, *Av Roca s/n, T02965-495049, cabanas@piramides.net*
5 comfortable 4 bed cabañas, well equipped, but no heating.

C **Motel ACA**, *on beach front, at Av Roca s/n, T02965-495004, 02965-156 61629, curti@satlink. com.ar* Slightly old fashioned, this has welcoming rooms, handy for the beach. Also a good seafood restaurant, from whose terrace you might even spot whales.

Estancias

To really appreciate the space and natural beauty of the peninsula, staying at an *estancia* is an appealing (if slightly expenisve) option. Ask the tourist office for advice. Day trips to *estancias* can also be arranged, with access to some of the most beautiful places.

AL **Faro Punta Delgada**, *T02965-15406304, www.puntadelagada.com* Comfortable accommodation right on the cliffs, offering half and full board, excellent food, and horse riding, guided walks, English speaking guides, recommended.

AL La Elena, *near Salina Grande, T02965-421448, alcamar@ciudad.com.ar* An old Spanish settlement, price is for full board, and horse and bike excursions are offered.
AL La Ernestina, *T02965-471143, www.laernestina.com.ar* A smaller estancia at Punta Norte, ideal for spotting killer whales.
AL Punta Cantor La Elvira, *T02965-474248, T02965-15-698709, www.laelvira.com.ar* Traditional Patagonian dishes and comfortable accommodation.
AL Rincón Chico, *south of Puerto Pirámides, T02965-471733, www.rinconchico.com.ar*. A working sheep farm, still owned by the original pioneer family who built it. Luxurious, beautifully situated, great for walking. Recommended.
AL San Lorenzo, *T02965-456888, www.puntanorte.com* See penguins close up, with wonderful walks to the coast.

Trelew *p155, map p161*

Trelew is not a touristy town, but there are a few reasonable places to stay and a good campsite.
B Rayentray, *San Martín y Belgrano, T/F02965-434702, www.cadena rayentray.com.ar* Huge modernized 1960s place with comfortable rooms and professional staff – the spacious 'superior' rooms are worth the extra, with sitting area and good bathrooms, and splendid 70s leather panelling. Swimming pool on top floor is free for guests, but gym, sunbed and sauna are extra.
C Centenario, *San Martín 150, T02965-420542, www.hotelcentenario.com.ar* This vast 1970s relic is worth seeing for the untouched décor, though it's more amusing than comfortable, and service is poor. Popular with Argentines, but you can always get a room here; not great value.
C Libertador, *Rivadavia 31, T/F02965-420220, www.hotellibertadortw.com.ar* Breakfast is included in this large modern place, highly recommended for its friendly service and comfortable rooms – the newer more spacious rooms are slightly pricier but worth it. Book ahead.
E Galicia, *9 de Julio 214, T02965-433802, www.hotel-galicia.com.ar* Breakfast included in this recently refurbished and central hotel, whose smallish rooms don't quite live up to the grand entrance, but are extremely comfortable and well decorated, and the staff are friendly. Excellent value and recommended.
E Touring Club, *Fontana 240, T02965-433997, F02965-425790, htouring@ar.inter.net* The best budget option. Gorgeous, faded bar, vast staircase and light corridors. The rooms are on the plain side, but they're quiet and spacious, with big bathrooms, and well kept. Breakfast is extra, but this is still good value.
F pp Rivadavia, *Rivadavia 55, T02965-434472, www.cpatagonia.com/rivadavia* Simple, comfortable rooms with TV and bath, and some even cheaper rather spartan rooms without, in this well-located place. This is the best value in town, if you can ignore the grumpy owner. Breakfast extra.

Camping

Camping Patagonia, *11 km south on Ruta 7 towards Rawson, T02965-428968*. US$2. Pretty site with *parrillas*, hot showers, football pitch and *proveduría* (food shop).

Gaiman *p155*

B Unelem, *Av Tello y 9 de Julio, T02965-491663, www.unelem.com.ar* Priciest, but very comfortable, is this restored old hotel from 1867, whose restaurant serves Welsh cooking.
C Casa de Té Ty Gwyn, *9 de Julio 111, T02965-491009, tygwyn@cpsarg.com* The next best option in town are the smart new rooms above this tea house.
D pp Gwesty Tywi, *Jones 342, T02965-491292, gwestywi@infovia.com.ar* Pretty and well kept bed and breakfast.
D Plas Y Coed, *Jones 123, T02965-491133*. Marta Rees' delightful tea room also has

double and twin rooms with bath and TV including breakfast.

Camarones *p157*

B **Kau I Keu Kenk**, *Sarmiento y Roca*. Good food, recommended, owner runs trips to penguin colony.

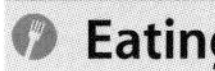

Eating

Bahía Blanca *p149*

El Mundo de la Pizza, *Dorrego 53*. Fabulous pizzas, thin bases loaded with toppings, lots of choice in this big atmospheric place, the city's favourite.

For You, *Belgrano 69*. Cheap *tenedor libre parrilla* and Chinese food, as much as you can eat for US$3.

Lola Mora, *Av Alem and Sarmiento*. The city's most sophisticated restaurant serves delicious Mediterranean-style food, in an elegant colonial-style house. US$8 for 3 courses and wine. Excellent.

Micho, *Guillermo Torres 3875, Ingeniero White, T0291-457 0346*. There are several good fish restaurants in the port area, but this elegant restaurant is the best. Be sure to take a taxi at night.

Santino, *Dorrego 38*. Italian-influenced, with a relaxed but sophisticated atmosphere and a welcoming glass of champagne, very good value. US$6 for 2 courses and wine.

Viedma *p149*

Camilla's Café, *Saavedra and Buenos Aires*. A smart and relaxing place for coffee, to watch Viedma trundle by on its errands.

La Balsa, *on the river at Colon y Villarino*. By far the best restaurant, inexpensive with a pleasant atmosphere. Delicious seafood, and a bottle of superb Río Negro wine, Humberto Canale Merlot, are highly recommended.

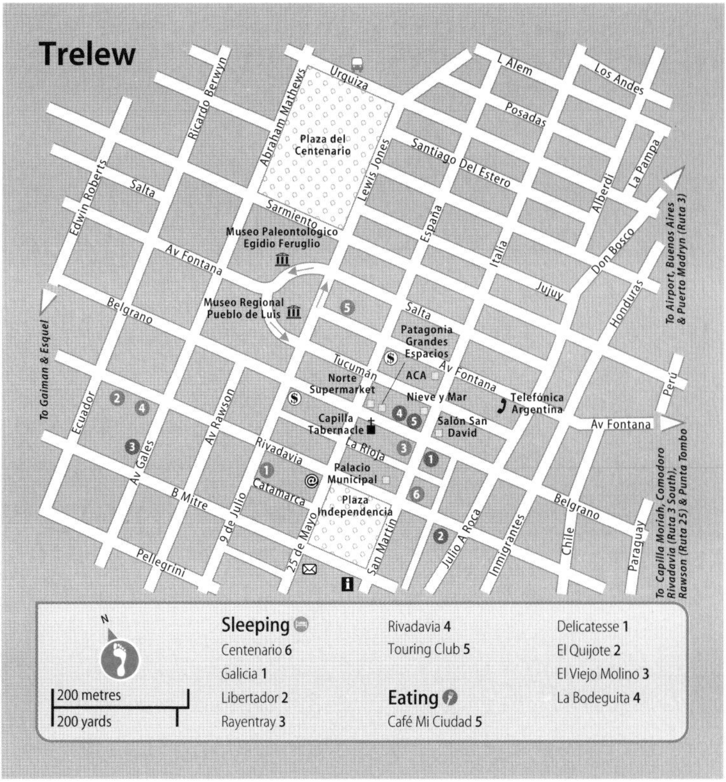

Trelew

200 metres
200 yards

Sleeping
Centenario **6**
Galicia **1**
Libertador **2**
Rayentray **3**
Rivadavia **4**
Touring Club **5**

Eating
Café Mi Ciudad **5**
Delicatesse **1**
El Quijote **2**
El Viejo Molino **3**
La Bodeguita **4**

Ⲯ **Parrilla Libre**, *Buenos Aires and Colón*. Cheap *tenedor libre* steaks in a cheerful atmosphere, US$2.50 for dinner.

Puerto Madryn *p150, map p159*

One of the unmissable pleasures of Puerto Madryn is the great seafood served in its beachfront restaurants. While you're here, try at least one plate of *arroz con mariscos* (rice with a whole selection of squid, prawns, mussels and clams). Most restaurants are mid-range and charge around the same price, but differ widely in quality. Without doubt, the best place to eat in town is the wonderful Taska Beltza, though there's plenty of choice along the coast road.

ⲮⲮⲮ **Nativo Sur**, *Blvd Brown 2000, T02965-457403*. Smarter than its more popular sister restaurant *Yoaquino*, this is a good place for a quiet dinner on the beach front, with an imaginative menu of local Patagonian produce and seafood.

ⲮⲮⲮ **Placido**, *Av Roca 508, T02965-455991*. Overlooking the sea and beautifully designed, with stylish tables and intimate lighting, this is perfect for a romantic dinner. Excellent service and a good range of seafood, with cheaper pasta dishes too, lots of options for vegetarians.

ⲮⲮ **Antigua Patagonia**, *Mitre y RS Pena, T02965-458738*. Large welcoming *parrilla* and seafood restaurant with a warm buzzing atmosphere, array of old objects on the brick walls, and good-value set menu. Popular with families and couples alike. Small play area for kids. Recommended.

ⲮⲮ **Caccaros**, *Av Roca 385, T02965-453767*. Stylish simple place on sea front with relaxing atmosphere, good value seafood menu, and cheap lunch menu.

ⲮⲮ **Cantina El Nautico**, *Av Roca 790, T02965-471404*. Long-established and now resting on its laurels, this is still popular for its seafood, and family atmosphere. The set menu isn't great value, and you're better off choosing individual dishes.

ⲮⲮ **Centro de Difusion de la Pescada Artesanal**, *Blvd Brown, 7th roundabout, T02965-15-538085*. Grandly named, but with no sign outside, this is a basic *cantina* on the coast road east, opposite the municipal campsite, where the fishermen's families cook delicious meals with their catch. Hugely popular with locals, so come early. Far more authentic than *El Nautico*.

ⲮⲮ **La Vaca y el Pollito**, *Av Roca y A Storni, T02965-458486*. You can't miss this place as it's partly built into the wooden hull of a boat. A big place but with a cosy atmosphere, the speciality is *parrilla*, very reasonably priced, but there's seafood and pastas too. Great for families, with a big soft play area for kids.

ⲮⲮ **Taska Beltza**, *9 de Julio 345, T02965-15-668085, closed Mon*. Chef and owner 'El Negro' cooks superb seafood with great passion and a Basque influence. The *arroz con mariscos* is cheap and superb. Highly recommended. Book ahead.

ⲮⲮ **Yoaquina**, *Blvd Brown between 1st and 2nd roundabouts, T02965-456058*. Great in the summer when you can eat outside, this is a relaxed spacious beachfront place, serving good seafood, if slightly pricey, and open from breakfast to after dinner. Cheap lunch menu, play area for kids, attentive service. Recommended.

Ⲯ **Havanna**, *Av Roca y 28 de Julio*. Smart, buzzing café selling the famous *alfajores* you see all over Argentina, coffees and sandwiches *de miga*. Very central, and open from breakfast to the early hours.

Ⲯ **La Casona de Golfo**, *Av Roca 349, T02965-15-511089*. Good value *tenedor libre* with lots of choices including good *parrilla* and seafood, and 'helados libre' – as much ice cream as you can eat. Great for families – kids pay half price.

Ⲯ **Shang Hai**, *28 de Julio y San Martín, T02965-457496*. Bright jolly place for cheap *tenedor libre* with a Chinese slant.

Península Valdés *p150*

The following are all on the beach in Puerto Pirámides. There are also reasonably priced restaurants at Punta

Norte, at Punta Cantor and at the Faro in Punta Delgada.

¥¥ **El Salmon**, *T02965-495065*. Closest to the beach on the right hand side, this has great views from its open deck and serves good seafood.

¥¥ **Paradise**. Just off the beach, good atmosphere and seafood.

¥¥ **Patagonia Franca**, *T02965-495006*. Good seafood restaurant in the new hotel on the beach front, with perfect sea views.

¥¥ **Quimey Quipan**, *T02965-156 93100*. By the beach, and next to *Tito Bottazzi*, this family-run place specializes in delicious seafood with rice and has a cheap set menu. Recommended. Always open for lunch, ring to reserve for dinner.

¥ **Mc Pato**. Just off the beach, a friendly place with a good atmosphere that serves huge sandwiches. Recommended.

¥ **Mi Sueno**. Close to the beach, good cheap pizzas to share.

Trelew *p157, map p161*

¥¥ **Delicatesse**, *Belgrano y San Martín*. Serves pizzas in a cheery atmosphere, good for families.

¥¥ **El Quijote**, *Rivadavia 463, T02965-15-402937*. Traditional *parrilla*, popular with locals.

¥¥ **El Viejo Molino**, *Gales 250, T02965-428019, open 1130-0030, closed Mon.* The best restaurant in town, and well worth a visit to see the first flour mill that was built here in 1886. It is now beautifully restored as a fine restaurant and café in relaxed and stylish surroundings. There's an imaginative menu with Patagonian lamb and homemade pastas, good value set menu with wine included, and Welsh teas. Recommended.

¥¥ **La Bodequita**, *opposite the cinema on Belgrano*. Serves superb homemade pastas, in a warm and lively atmosphere. Recommended.

¥ **Hotel Touring Club**, *Fontana 240*. Open from breakfast to the small hours for sandwiches and drinks, worth a visit to see the splendid 1920s bar.

¥ **Café Mi Ciudad**, *Belgrano y San Martín*. A smart café serving great coffee; read the papers watching street life.

Gaiman *p155*

¥ **El Angel**, *Jones 850*. A stylish, small restaurant serving delicious food in an old-fashioned, intimate atmosphere.

Welsh teas

You're unlikely to be able to resist the scrumptious Welsh teas for which Gaiman has become famous. Tea is served from 1500, all the tea rooms charge about the same – US$4 – and include the most well

known of the Welsh cakes *Torta Negra* – a delicious dense fruit cake.

Plas Y Coed, *Jones 123*. The first house to start serving tea, has lovely gardens, and the owner Marta Rees is a wonderful raconteur and fabulous cook who can tell you all about her Welsh forebears, married in this very house in 1886. Highly recommended.

Ty Cymraeg, *down by the river*. Set in a lovely spot, with room for big groups, and selling good cakes.

Ty Gwyn, *9 de Julio 111*. This large tea house serves a very generous tea in a more modern place with traditional features; the owners are welcoming. Recommended.

Ty Nain, *Yrigoyen 283*. Quite the prettiest house and full of history. Owner Mirna Jones is charming; her grandmother was the first woman to be born in Gaiman.

Ty Te Caerdydd, *Finca 202, 2 km from the centre, but well sign posted*. A quite staggering theme park of its own, with manicured lawns and dressed-up waitresses; its main claim to fame is that Princess Di took her tea here. The atmosphere is entirely manufactured.

Bars and clubs

Puerto Madryn *p150, map p159*

Disco Rancho Cucamonga, *Blvd Brown y Jenkins*. Near beach, young crowd.

Lizard Café, *Av Roca y Av Gales, T02965-458333*. Lively funky place with friendly people. Good for cheap and plentiful pizzas or for late night drinks on the seafront.

Margarita, *RS Pena, next to Ambigu on RS Pena and Av Roca*. Late night bar for drinks and live music.

Mitos, *28 de Julio 64*. Friendly and welcoming stylish café with good atmosphere, and pictures of tango stars and jazz musicians on the walls. Great for breakfast, or lunch and open until the early hours. Recommended.

Festivals and events

Carmen de Patagones *p150*

Fiesta de 7 de Marzo, *T464360, subcom@patagones.mun.gba.gov.ar*, celebrates the victory at the Battle of Patagones with a week of music and handicrafts, fine food, a huge procession, horseriding displays, and lots of meat on the *asados*. Great fun. Book accommodation ahead.

Shopping

Puerto Madryn *p150, map p159*

The sleek new indoor shopping centre **Portal de Madryn**, *28 de Julio y Av Roca*, has all the smart clothes shops, *Café Havanna* on the ground floor, and a kids games area with a fast, but not cheap, food place *Mostaza* on the top floor. *Cardon*, is recommended for regional goods and leather bags.

You'll find lots more posh clothes, whale and penguin T-shirts, high quality Patagonian handicrafts, leather goods, and artesanal *alfajores* and cakes in streets *28 de Julio and Av Roca*.

Activities and tours

Viedma *p150*

Fishing

Fishing equipment is available in Viedma at **Patagonia Out Doors Life**, 25 de Mayo 340, and **Tiburón**, Zatti 250, among others. Ask the tourist office for a leaflet, T02920-427171.

Puerto Madryn *p150, map p159*

Diving and watersports

Golfo Azul, *Mitre y H Yrigoyen, T02965-451181*, windsurf boards, kayaks, jet ski, sailing boats for hire.

Hydro Sport, *Balneario Rayentray, 5th roundabout, T02965-495065, hysport@infovia .com.ar* Rents scuba equipment and boats, and organizes land and sea wildlife tours to see whales and dolphins.

Juan Benegas, *T02965-495100*. Offers diving expeditions and provides equipment. Tours do not run after heavy rain in the low season.
La Oveja Negra Safari Submarino, *Blvd Brown 1070, T02965-474110*.
Na Praia, *Blvd Brown y Perlotti, T02965-473715*, windsurf boards, kayaks, jet ski, sailing boats for hire.
Ocean Divers, *Blvd Brown (between 1st and 2nd roundabout), T02965-472569*. Advanced courses (PADI) and courses on video, photography and underwater communication.

Mountain biking

Bikes can be hired from: **Future Bike**, *Juan B Justo 683, T02965-15-665108*; **Na praia**, *on beach at Blvd Brown and Perlotti, T02965-473715*; **XT Mountain Bike**, *Av Roca 742, T02965-472232*.

Tours

Many agencies in Puerto Madryn do tours to **Península Valdés**, usually taking in the same places: the interpretation centre and viewing point for the Isla de los Pajaros, and then Puerto Pirámides, where the boat trip to see the whales costs US$12 extra. Then either Punta Delgada or Caleta Valdés, with time to look at wildlife or other variations. Trips take 12 hrs, so you should bring water and lunch, although there are places to eat in Puerto Pirámides. All charge US$17, plus US$3 entrance to the Peninsula – but shop around to find out how long you'll spend at each place, how big the group is, and if your guide speaks English. Most tour companies (addresses below) stay 50-60 mins on location. Usually half price for children under 10, free for under 6s.

Tours are also offered to see the penguins at **Punta Tombo**, or the Welsh village of **Gaiman** with Ameghino Dam thrown in, but these are both 400 km round trips and better from Trelew. New agencies are opening all the time, the following are reliable.

Alora Viagio, *Av Roca 27, T02965-456563, www.aloraviagio.com.ar* A helpful company which also has an office at the bus terminal.
Argentina Visión, *Av Roca 536, T02965-451427, www.argentinavision.com* Offers 4WD adventure trips and can arrange estancia accommodation at Punta Delgada. English, French, German, Italian, Portuguese spoken.
Cuyun Co, *Av Roca 165, T02965-451845, www.cuyunco.com.ar* Offers a friendly personal service and a huge range of more imaginative tours beside Península Valdés: guided walks with biologists, 4WD expeditions, and also arrange estancia accommodation. Bilingual guides. Recommended.
Flamenco Tour, *Av Roca 331, T02965-455505, www.flamencotour.com.ar* For slightly more sedate trips and charming staff.
Jorge Schmid, *at Puerto Pirámides itself, or through agencies*, is the main whale-watching operator, May to Dec, with other wildlife trips Dec-Mar.
Tito Botazzi, *Blvd Brown 1070, T/F02965-474110, www.titobottazzi.com* Particularly recommended for small groups, well informed bilingual guides.

Trelew *p155, map p161*

Tours

Agencies run tours to **Punta Tombo**, US$18, **Chubut Valley** (half-day), US$10, both together as a full day US$22. Tours to **Península Valdés** are best done from Puerto Madryn (see above).
Nieve y Mar, *Italia 20, T02965-434114, www.nievmartours.com.ar* Punta Tombo and Valdes, bilingual guides (reserve ahead). Organized and efficient.
Patagonia Grandes Espacios, *Belgrano 338, T02965-435161, www.surturismo.com.ar* Good excursions to Punta Tombo and Gaiman, but also palaeontological trips, staying in *chacras*, whale watching. Recommended.

Transport

Bahía Blanca *p149*

Air

Several daily flights to **Buenos Aires** with AR/Austral (*T0291-456 0561/0810-2228 6527*). LADE has weekly flights to various Patagonian destinations (see Air services in Argentina).

Airline offices Aerolíneas Argentinas, *San Martín 198, T0291- 426934*. LADE, *Darregueira 21, T0291-437697*.

Bus

Local Buy *tarjetas* (Tarjebus cards) from kiosks for 1 (US$0.40), 2, 4 or 10 journeys. **Long distance** To **Buenos Aires** frequent, 8½ hrs, several companies – most comfortable by far is **Plusmar** suite bus US$20, otherwise US$10-15, shop around. To **Neuquén**, 6 a day, 8 hrs, US$10. To **Viedma**, **Ceferino**, **Plusmar** and **Río Paraná** (to **Carmen de Patagones**), 4 hrs, US$5-6. To **Trelew**, **Don Otto** and others, US$28, 10½ hrs. To **Río Gallegos**, **Don Otto** US$34.

Bus companies Andesmar *T0291-4815462*; **Ceferino** *T0291-481 9566*; **Don Otto** *T0291-481 8585*; **Plusmar** *T0291-456 0616*; **Rápido del Sur** *T0291-481 3118*.

Train

To **Buenos Aires**, 3 weekly, 12½ hrs, Pullman US$30, first class US$15, tourist class US$10, not comfortable.

Carmen de Patagones/Viedma *p149*

Air

Aeropuerto Gobernador Castelo is 5 km south of Viedma. LADE (*Saavedra 403, T/F02920-424420*) flies to **Buenos Aires** and Patagonian destinations.

Bus

To **Buenos Aires**, 3 daily, 14 hrs, US$20, **Don Otto/La Estrella/Cóndor**. To **Bahia Blanca**, 4 daily, 4 hrs, US$5, **Rio Parana**.

Train

A sleeper train, *Viedma T02920-422130, Bariloche T02944-423172, www.tren-patagonico.com.ar*, which also carries cars, departs from Viedma Fri 1800, to **Bariloche**. Restaurant and a cinema car showing videos. US$30 for a bed, US$18 for a *semi-cama* seat. Book ahead.

Puerto Madryn *p150, map p159*

Air

Puerto Madryn Airport is served by **Aerolíneas** and **American Falcon** to/from **Bariloche**, **Buenos Aires** and **El Calafate**. Also weekly services by **LADE** to other destinations (see Essentials). More frequent flights serve Trelew airport (see below). **Airline offices** LADE, *Roca 117, T02920-451256*. **Aerolíneas Argentinas**, *Roca 303, T02920-421257/0800-2228 6527*.

Bus

To **Buenos Aires**, 18 hrs US$17-20, several companies, **Andesmar** recommended. To **Río Gallegos**, 18 hrs; US$18, **El Pingüino** (connecting to El Calafate, Punta Arenas, Puerto Natales), **Andesmar**, **TAC**, **Don Otto**. To **Trelew**, 1 hr, every hr, US$4 with **28 de Julio**, **Mar y Valle**. To **Puerto Pirámides**, 1 hr, US$2, daily, 28 de Julio. To **Bariloche**, 15 hrs, US$46, daily, except Wed, **Mar y Valle**.

Bus companies Andesmar, *T02965-473764*; **Don Otto**, *T02965-451675*; **El Pingüino**, *T02965-456256*; **TUS**, *T02965-451962*; **28 de Julio/Mar y Valle**, *T02965-472056*.

Car hire

More expensive than other parts of Argentina, large insurance excess, so drive slowly on *ripio* roads. Try **Localiza**, *Roca 536, T02965-456300, 0800 9992999*, for efficient, helpful service, or **Puerto Madryn Turismo**, *Roca 624, T02965-452355*.

Taxi

Outside the bus terminal, *T02965-452966/474177*.

Península Valdés p152
Join a full day excursion from Puerto Madryn (see above), hire a car (see above) or catch the daily bus from Puerto Madryn to **Puerto Pirámides**, departs 1000 daily, **28 de Julio**, 1 hr, returns 1800, US$2 each way. Then take the boat trip to see the whales (Sep-Nov) from Puerto Pirámides with **Jorge Schmidt**, *T02965-451511/495012*.

Trelew p155, map p161
Air
Aerolíneas Argentinas flies to/from **Buenos Aires**, **Río Gallegos**, **Ushuaia** and Río Grande; **Lapa** (and TAN) fly to **Comodoro Rivadavia**. LADE also flies to several Patagonian airports.

Airline offices Aerolíneas Argentinas, *25 de Mayo 33, T02965-420170*. LADE, *Terminal de Omnibus, of. 12 /13, T02965-435925*.

Bus
Bus companies Andesmar, *T02965-433535*; TUS, *T02965-421343*; El Pingüino, *T02965-427400*; Don Otto, *T02965-432434*; TAC, *T02965-431452*; El Cóndor, *T02965-433748*; 28 de Julio/ Mar y Valle, *T02965-432429*; Que Bus, *T02965-422760*; El Ñandú, *T02965-427499*.

Local Mar y Valle and 28 de Julio both go frequently to **Rawson**, 30 mins, US$0.50; to **Gaiman**, 30 mins, US$1, and **Dolavon** 1 hr, US$1.50. Mar y Valle also daily to **Puerto Madryn**, 1hr, US$2, and to **Puerto Pirámides**, 2½ hrs, US$5.

Long distance To **Buenos Aires**, 20 hrs, US$20, several companies, daily; to **Comodoro Rivadavia**, 5 hrs, US$8, many companies; to **Río Gallegos** (for connections to **El Calafate**, **Puerto Natales**, **Punta Arenas**) 17 hrs, US$20. To **Esquel**, 10 hrs, US$14, Mar y Valle, Empresa Chubut, Don Otto.

Car hire
Car hire companies at the airport desks are staffed only at flight arrival times and cars are taken quickly. All have offices in town: AVIS, *Paraguay 105, T/F02965-434634*; Localiza, *Urquiza 310 T02965-435344*; Hertz, *airport, T02965-436005*.

South of Trelew p157
Bus
Don Otto from Trelew to **Camarones**, Mon and Fri, 2½ hrs, return 1600. Also El Nañdu, Mon, Wed, Fri 0800 to **Reserva Natural Cabo Dos Bahías**, 2½ hrs, return 1600, US$4.20.

Directory

Bahía Blanca p149
Consulates Chile, *Güemes 102, T0291-455 0110*; Italy, *Colón 446, T0291-454 5140*. Spain, *Drago 70, T0291-422549*. **Internet** Try places along Estomba and Zelarray and near plaza. **Laundry** Laverap, *Av Colón 197*; Las Heras, *Las Heras 86*. **Post office** *Moreno 34*. **Telephone** Big *locutorio* at *Alsina 108*, also internet. **Travel agent** ASATEJ, *Zelarrayán 267, T0291-456 0666, bblanca@ asatej.com.ar*

Viedma p149
Travel agencies Mona Tour, *San Martín 225, Viedma*. Sells flights and tickets for the train to Bariloche, www.tren-patagonico.com.ar.

Puerto Madryn p150, map p159
Internet Internet Centro Madryn, *25 de Mayo y Belgrano*, US$0.60 per hour. Re Creo, *Roque Sáenz Peña 101*. **Post office**, *Belgrano y Maiz, 0900-1200, 1500-1900*. **Telephone** Many *locutorios* in centre.

Trelew p155, map p161
Internet *25 de Mayo 219*. **Post office** *25 de Mayo and Mitre*. **Telephone** Telefónica, *Roca y Pje Tucumán*, and several locutorios in the centre. **Travel agent** Turismo Sur (aka Patagonia Grandes Espacios), *Belgrano 338*, also currency exchange.

South to Río Gallegos

Lovers of marine life will want to head south towards Río Gallegos and beyond, where the Atlantic coastline is extraordinarily rich in sea birds, penguins, whales and sealions. The southernmost town, Río Gallegos, is a quiet but pleasant place, with accommodation and tours offered. Beyond, on the last spit of land before Tierra del Fuego, is Cabo Vírgines. Inland, route 26, known as the Bioceanic Corridor, runs west across the steppe amid oil wells, towards Río Mayo, the border and the Chilean towns of Coyhaique and Puerto Aisén and provides access to two petrified forests of ancient araucaria trees. Comodoro Rivadavia is a rather dull base for exploring these forests, but the little town of Sarmiento is far more pleasant.

Getting there Flights to Río Gallegos or long-distance buses along the coast.

Getting around Good bus services, allow for long journeys.

Time required: A week to travel to both the coastal nature reserves and the petrified forests.

Weather Pleasant in summer, cold winds in winter.

Sleeping Decent hotels in large towns, few budget options. Some fine coastal estancias.

Eating: Excellent seafood all along the coast.

Activities and tours Wildlife watching, coastal walks, tours to the petrified forests.

★ **Don't miss...**The petrified forests around Sarmiento and Parque Nacional Monte León.

Comodoro Rivadavia and inland » pp173-177

This is a useful transport hub for all areas of Patagonia – if you have the time to travel by bus. It is the largest city in the province of Chubut and was established primarily as a sheep-exporting port but flourished when oil was discovered here in 1907. However, since the petrol industry was privatised in the 1990s, there's been unemployment here and now the town has a slightly sad, unkempt feel. There's little to make you want to stay, although there's a popular beach at **Rada Tilly**, 12 km south, where you can see sea lions at low tide.

If you're fascinated by oil, you could visit the **Museo del Petroleo** ⓘ *T02967-4559558, Tue-Fri 0900-1800, Sat/Sun 1500-1800, taxi US$43 km north of the centre at San Lorenzo 250*, for a good history of local oil exploitation, or the **Museo Paleontológico** ⓘ *20 km north, open weekends, 1400-1800*, to look at fossils and reconstructions of dinosaurs. There's a good view of the city from **Cerro Chenque** (212 m), a dun-coloured hill, unattractively adorned with radar masts, whose cliffs give the town its drab backdrop. The **tourist office** ⓘ *Rivadavia 430, T02967-446 2376, www.comodoro.gov.ar, Mon-Fri 0900-1400, or in the bus terminal, daily 0800-2100*, is very helpful, English spoken.

Sarmiento and around

Sarmiento lies on the Río Senguer, 150 km west of Comodoro and just south of two great lakes, **Lago Musters** and **Lago Colhué Huapi**, both of which offer good fishing in summer. Founded in 1897, it's a quiet and relaxed place, sitting in fertile, well-irrigated land, and little visited by tourists, despite being close to two areas of petrified forest.

Most accessible is the huge park, **Bosque Petrificado de Sarmiento (José Ormachea)** ⓘ *32 km south along a ripio road, entry US$2.50*. Less easy to reach is the rather bleaker **Bosque Petrificado Víctor Szlapelis** ⓘ *40 km further southwest along the same road; minibus from Sarmiento twice daily Dec-Mar, taxi US$16*. These 60-million-year-old forests of fallen araucaria trees, nearly 3 m in circumference and 15-20 m long, are a remarkable sight, best visited in summer as the winters are very cold. **Sr Juan José Valero**, the *guardaparque* (Uruguay 43, T0297-4898407) can give guided tours and provide camping information. Otherwise contact Sarmiento's helpful **tourist office** ⓘ *Avenida San Martín, almost at Alberdi, T0297-489 8220, see also www.interpatagonia.com/sarmiento*. There is also a small museum – ask the tourist office for directions.

Monumento Natural Bosques Petrificados

Puerto Deseado and around » pp173-177

Puerto Deseado is a pleasant fishing port on the estuary of the Río Deseado, which drains, strangely, into the Lago Buenos Aires in the west. The estuary encompasses a wonderful nature reserve, and provides easy access to more reserves, protecting sea lions and penguins. Outside the former railway station is the **Vagón Histórico** ⓘ *San Martín 1525, T0297-487 0220, T0297-156 234351, turismo@pdeseado.com.ar, www.scruz.gov.ar*, an 1898 carriage, now used as the tourist office.

Reserva Natural Ría Deseado

The submerged estuary (*ría*) of the Río Deseado is an important nature reserve and a stunning area to visit. Among many varieties of seabird, there's a colony of Magellanic penguins, and the crumbling chalky cliffs, mauve and ochre, splattered with guano, are home to four species of cormorants including the unique red-legged cormorant, most appealing with their smart dinner-jacketed appearance. These birds nest from October to April on four offshore islands. The reserve is also the breeding ground for Commerson's dolphins, beautiful creatures, who frolic playfully around the tour boats which run from the town's pier (see page 176).

Around Puerto Deseado

North of Puerto Deseado, on the shore of the peninsula, is **Cabo Blanco**, the site of the largest fur seal colony in Patagonia. It's another magnificent area, a rocky peninsula bursting out from flat lands, with one of the oldest lighthouses on the coast perched on top, and thousands of seals resting on the rocks below. The breeding season is December to January. A little further west, you should also visit **Reserva Cañadón de Duraznillo** in the *estancia* of La Madrugada (see Sleeping, page 173). Here you'll see lots of guanacos, ñandues, foxes and birds, as well as the largest seal colony in the province on spectacular unspoilt beaches.

South of Puerto Deseado are two more reserves: **Isla Pingüino**, an offshore island, with a colony of Magellanic penguins, as well as cormorants and steamer ducks, and the **Reserva Natural Bahía Laura**, an uninhabited bay 155 km south along *ripio* and dirt roads, where black-necked cormorants, ducks and other seabirds can be found in abundance. Darwin Expediciones and Los Vikingos run tours.

Cormorants at Puerto Deseado

Monumento Natural Bosques Petrificados

ⓘ *Route 49, 86km south of Fitz Roy, T0297-4851000, www.parquesnacionales.gov.ar/MNbosquespetrificados, Oct-Mar 0900-2000, Apr-Sep 1000-1700. Donations accepted. No services or water anywhere close by, and no accommodation.* Extending over 10,000 hectares in a bizarre, wind-wracked landscape surrounding the **Laguna Grande**, this park contains much older petrified trees than the forests further north around Sarmiento. The trunks, mainly of giant araucaria trees, are up to 35 m long and 150 cm in diameter and were petrified in the

Jurassic period 140 million years ago by intense volcanic activity in the Andes *cordillera* which covered the area in ash. The place is more eerie than beautiful, but it does exert a strange fascination, especially when you consider that the fossils of marine animals that you see on the site are a mere 40 million years old, belonging to a sea that covered the land long after the trees had turned to stone. There is a small visitor centre and a well signposted 2 km nature walk. Please do not remove souvenirs.

Puerto San Julián and around » pp173-177

The quiet port town of Puerto San Julián, lying on the Bahía San Julian, is the best place for breaking the 834 km run from Comodoro Rivadavia to Río Gallegos. The first Mass in Argentina was held here in 1520 after the Portuguese explorer Magellan had executed a member of his mutinous crew. Then in 1578, Francis Drake also put in here in order to behead Thomas Doughty. In 1780, Antonio Viedma founded the colony of Florida Blanca here but it failed due to scurvy; you can visit the ruins 10 km west of the present town. Puerto San Julián was finally founded in 1901 to serve as a port for the sheep *estancias* in this part of Santa Cruz. A small regional museum, **Museo Regional at Rivadavia and Vieytes**, houses the amazingly well preserved dinosaur footprint found in the town. Enquire at the **tourist office** ⓘ *Av Costanera y 9 de Julio, or San Martín 1126, T02962-454396, centur@videodata.com.ar, www.scruz.gov.ar/turismo*, about tours to see the wildlife in the Reserva San Julian. It's also worth visiting **Estancia La María**, 150 km west, which incorporates one of the main archaeological sites in Patagonia: a huge canyon with 87 caves of paintings including human hands and guanacos, 4,000-12,000 years old.

Reserva San Julián

The **Reserva San Julián**, on the shores of Bahía San Julián, includes the islands **Banco Cormorán** and **Banco Justicia** (thought to be the site of the 16th-century executions), where there is a colony of Magellanic penguins and nesting areas for several species of cormorants and other birds. You're also very likely to spot Commerson's dolphins in the bay. It's a lovely location and the concentration of marine life is stunning. December is the best time for spotting dolphins and cormorants, although there's plenty to see through to April. **Cabo Curiosa**, 15 km north, has 30 km of spectacular coastline and fine beaches.

Piedrabuena

Known officially as Comandante Luís Piedrabuena, this quiet town is named after the the famous Argentine explorer and sailor, Piedra Buena, who built his home on an island in the Río Santa Cruz here, in 1859. On the island is **Casa Histórica Luis Piedra Buena**, a reconstruction of the original building where he carried on a peaceful trade with local indigenous groups. In recent years, **Isla Pavón**, T02966-15623453, has become most popular as a weekend resort for those fishing steelhead trout, with a smart 4-star *hostería* as well as an attractive campsite. In March there's a national trout festival. Piedrabuena is a good base for exploring the **Parque Nacional Monte León**; the **tourist office** ⓘ *Av Gregorio Ibáñez 388, T02962-497498*, can provide further information.

Parque Nacional Monte León

ⓘ *Access along 23 km of poor ripio road that branches off Route 3, 36 km south of Piedrabuena, 210 km north of Río Gallegos. Contact Vida Silvestre in Buenos Aires, T011-43116633, www.parquesnacionales.gov.ar, www.vidasilvestre.org.ar* Monte León incorporates 40 km of coastline, where there are many species of seabirds and an enormous penguin colony. Sea lions occupy the many caves and bays, and the tiny island Monte León is an important

Estancia Monte León

breeding area for cormorants and terns. The park is owned by US millionaire Douglas Tompkins and looked after by the organization **Vida Silvestre**, but so far access is difficult. Your efforts to get here will be rewarded by wonderful walks along wide isolated beaches, with extraordinary rock formations and cliffs riven with vast caverns, fabulous at low tide. The old house at the heart of the park has been converted to a *hostería*, which is the best way to enjoy the park in comfort (see Sleeping below). There are also plans to turn the old shearing shed into a visitor centre.

Río Gallegos and around » *pp 173-177*

The capital of Santa Cruz province lies on the estuary of the Río Gallegos, the river famous for its excellent brown trout fishing. It's a pleasant airy town, founded in 1885 as a centre for the trade in wool and sheepskins, and is by far the most appealing of the main centres on southern Patagonia's east coast. It was once the main access point for trips to the Parque Nacional Glaciares (see page 188) but receives fewer visitors since the airport opened at El Calafate. However, you may well come here to change buses, and could visit the penguin reserve at Cabo Vírgenes some 130 km south, or Monte León 210 km north. The town itself has a couple of museums, and boasts a few smart shops and restaurants.

Border with Chile

From Río Gallegos, Route 3 continues south to the Chilean border at **Paso Integración Austral**. On the Chilean side, the road continues as Route 255 to Punta Arenas via Punta Delgada, where ferries cross to Tierra del Fuego (see page 154). For bus passengers the border crossing is easy, but hire cars will need special documentation.

Argentine immigration and customs ⓘ *open 24hrs in summer, Apr-Nov 0800-2200.* Chilean immigration and customs ⓘ *open 0800-2200 daily.*

Ins and outs → *Río Gallegos is pronounced rio ga-shay-gos*

Getting there Flights arrive at the airport, 10 km from centre, from Buenos Aires, El Calafate and Ushuaia. There are also **LADE** flights connecting all major Patagonian towns, see Essentials, page 23. A taxi into town costs US$2.50. The crowded bus terminal is 3 km from the centre, at the corner of Route 3 and Av Eva Perón. Buses 1 and 12 will take you into town, or take a taxi for US$1.

Tourist information ⓘ *Av Roca 863, T/F02966-438725, www.scruz.gov.com.ar/turismo, turismo@spse.com.ar, open Mon-Fri 0900-2100, Sat 1000-2000, Sun 1000-1500, 1600-2000.* An excellent and well-organized office with information for the whole province. The staff are extremely helpful, speak English and have a list of *estancias* in Santa Cruz. There's also an office at the airport and a small desk at the bus terminal, T02966-442159.

Sights

The tidy, leafy Plaza San Martín, two blocks south of the main street, Avenida Roca, has an interesting collection of trees, many planted by the early pioneers, and a diminutive corrugated iron cathedral, with a wood-panelled ceiling in the chancel and stained glass windows. The best of the town's museums is the small **Museo de los Pioneros** ⓘ *Elcano y Alberdi, open daily 1000-2000, free*, housed in a building that was shipped here from Britain in 1890. The museum has interesting photographs and artefacts telling the story of the first Scottish settlers, who came here in 1884 from the Falkland Islands/Las Malvinas to take up government grants of land. Also stimulating is the **Museo Malvinas Argentinas** ⓘ *Pasteur 74, open Mon and Thu 1300-1800, Tue, Wed, Fri 1300-1800, third Sun in the month 1530-1830*, which aims to inform visitors about Argentine claims to Las Malvinas.

Reserva Provincial Cabo Vírgenes

ⓘ *branch off Route 3, 15 km south of Río Gallegos, onto Route 1 (unpaved) for 119km, 3½ hrs, US$2.30.* This nature reserve protects the second largest colony of Magellanic penguins in Patagonia. There's an informative self-guided walk to see their nests amongst the *calafate* and fragrant *mata verde* bushes. It's good to visit from November, when the chicks are born and there are nests under every bush. You can climb the Cabo Vírgenes **lighthouse** (owned by the Argentine Navy) for wonderful views and there's a *confitería* close by for snacks and souvenirs. **Estancia Monte Dinero**, 13 km north of Cabo Vírgenes, is a wonderful base for visiting the reserve (see Sleeping, below).

South of Cabo Vírgenes are the ruins of **Nombre de Jesús**, one of two doomed settlements founded by Pedro Sarmiento de Gamboa in 1584. **Laguna Azul**, near the Monte Aymond border crossing, is a perfect, royal blue lagoon in the crater of an extinct volcano. It's set in an atmospheric and arid lunar landscape and is a good place for a walk. Take a tour, or get off the bus along Route 3, which stops on the main road.

Sleeping

Comodoro Rivadavia *p169*

Hotels are either luxurious or basic, with little in between:

B **Lucania Palazzo Hotel**, *Moreno 676, T02967-449 9338, www.lucania-palazzo.com* A stylish and luxurious business hotel, with a lovely airy spacious reception, and superb rooms, many with sea views, good value. A huge American breakfast, and use of the sauna and gym are included. Recommended.

D **Hotel Azul**, *Sarmiento 724, T02967-447 4628.* This is a nice quiet old place, with lovely bright rooms, friendly owners, and great panoramic views from the *confiteria*, though breakfast is extra.

D **Hotel Victoria**, *Belgrano 585,*

T02967-446 0725. An old fashioned city *hostería*, mostly used by workers in the oil industry, but it's friendly, and clean and comfortable enough. Breakfast US$1.20.

D **Rua Marina**, *Belgrano 738, T02967-446877*. All rooms have TV and bath and breakfast; newer rooms are particularly comfortable. Friendly welcome.

E **Hospedaje Cari Hue**, *Belgrano 563, T02967-472946*. Sweet rooms, with separate bathrooms off a central hallway. Very nice owners who like backpackers. Breakfast extra. Best budget choice.

Sarmiento *p169*

C **Chacra El Labrador**, *10 km from Sarmiento, T0297-489 3329, agna@coopsar.com.ar* This is an excellent place to stay on a small *estancia*, breakfast included, other meals extra and available for non-residents. English and Dutch spoken, runs tours to petrified forests at good prices, will collect guests from Sarmiento (same price as taxi).

Puerto Deseado *p170*

A **La Madrugada**, *120 km from Puerto Deseado, via the RN 281 to km 79, then RN68, T155-94123, T011-537 155 55, www.vidasilvestre.org.ar, walker@caminos turismo.com.ar* Good Patagonian cooking and comfortable accommodation, with splendid views and plenty of places to spot wildlife from the *estancia* itself. The owners also arrange excursions to the sea lion colony and cormorant nesting area. English spoken, recommended.

C **Isla Chaffers**, *San Martín y Mariano Moreno, T0297-487 2246, www.islachaffers .wm.com.ar* Modern and central.

C **Los Acantilados**, *Pueyrredón y España, T0297-487 2167, www.pdeseado.com .ar/acantour* Beautifully-located hotel, popular with anglers, comfortable rooms with bathrooms, good breakfast.

Puerto San Julián *p171*

B **Bahía**, *San Martín 1075, T02962-454028, nico@sanjulian.com.ar* Modern and comfortable rooms, good value.

B **Estancia La María**, *150 km west, contact Fernando Behm, Saavedra 1163, T02962-452328*. Simple accommodation in a modern house, with amazing cave paintings. The owners also organize trips to see marine and birdlife.

C **Municipal**, *25 de Mayo 917, T02962-452300*. Attractive rooms, well-run, good value, no restaurant.

Piedrabuena *p171*

A-B **Hostería El Alamo**, *Lavalle 08, T02962-47249*. Quiet, breakfast extra. Good.

A-B **Hostería Municipal Isla Pavon**, Isla Pavón,*T02966-15-638380*. Luxurious 4-star catering to fishermen of steelhead trout.

A-B **Motel Sur Atlanticoil**, *3 km away on Route 3, T02962-497008*. Comfortable.

C **Res Internacional**, *Ibáñez 99, T02962-47197*. Recommended.

Parque Nacional Monte León *p171*

Estancia Monte León, *on RN3, www.vida silvestre.org.ar*, open Nov-Apr. Beautifully modernized but traditional *estancia* with 4 impeccably tasteful rooms, decorated with Tompkins' considerable style. See also www.estanciasdesantacruz.com/monteleon

Río Gallegos *p172*

Most hotels are situated within a few blocks of the main street, Av Roca.

C **Apart Hotel Austral**, *Roca 1505, T/F02966-434314, www.apart austral.com.ar* A smart new apart hotel, with bright rooms, with attractive sunny décor, and very good value, particularly the superior duplexes. Kitchen facilities are a bit basic, but adequate for a couple of nights. Breakfast US$1.50 extra.

C **Comercio**, *Roca 1302, T02966-422458, hotelcomercio@informacionrgl.com.ar* Good value, nicely designed comfortable rooms with bathrooms, and breakfast included. Cheap *confitería* on the street.

C **Croacia**, *Urquiza 431, T02966-421218*. Cheaper, with comfortable beds, bright spotless rooms with bath, huge breakfasts, and helpful owners. Recommended.

C **Santa Cruz**, *Roca 701, T02966-420601, www.advance.com.ar/usuarios/htlscruz,* This modern city-style hotel is excellent value. Go for the slightly pricier new rooms with excellent bathrooms and full buffet breakfast. Highly recommended.

D **Covadonga**, *Roca 1244, T02966-420190.* Attractive old 1930s building, the basic rooms have bath and TV, and come off a long corridor to a courtyard. Breakfast is included, and though rooms are small, it's all clean and well maintained.

D **Nevada**, *Zapiola 480, T02966-435790.* A good budget option, with clean, simple spacious rooms, nice beds and good bathrooms, and welcoming owners.

D **París**, *Roca 1040, T02966-420111.* Fairly simple rooms with bath, set back from the street, a good value choice, though breakfast is extra.

Estancias

A **Hill Station**, *63 km north of Río Gallegos, contact the tourist office for details.* An estancia with 120 years of history, run by decendents of the founder, William Halliday. A sheep farm, also breeding criollo horses, this offers wonderful horse riding to see flora and fauna of the coast, and simple accommodation.

A **Monte Dinero**, *near Cabo Vírgines, T02966-428922, www.montedinero.com.ar* Comfortable accommodation on a working sheep farm. The house is lined with wood rescued from ships wrecked off the coast, and the food is delicious and home grown. Friendly English-speaking owners will take you on a tour of the reserve and give an impressive sheep dog demonstration. Highly recommended. See also www.estanciasdesantacruz.com/montedinero

Eating

Comodoro Rivadavia p169

‡‡ **Cayo Coco**, *Rivadavia 102.* A welcoming little bistro, with very cheery staff, and excellent pizzas. Recommended.

‡‡ **Dionisius**, *9 de Julio y Rivadavia.* A smart and elegant parrilla, popular wth a more sedate clientele, serving excellent set menus for US$5.

‡‡ **La Barra**, *San Martín 686.* A pleasant bright café for breakfast, very good coffee or a light lunch.

‡‡ **La Tradición**, *Mitre 675.* Another popular and recommended *parrilla*.

‡‡ **Peperoni**, *Rivadavia 348.* A cheerful modern place with good range of home made pastas, filled with exciting things like king crab, as well as serving seafood and *parrilla*. US$4-7, for main dish.

‡ **La Barca**, *Belgrano 935.* Welcoming and cheap *tenedor libre*.

Puerto Deseado p170

‡ **El Pingüino**, *Piedrabuena 958.* Established *parrilla* which serves fabulous rice pudding.

‡ **Puerto Cristal**, *Espana 1698.* Panoramic views of the port, a great place for Patagonian lamb and *parrilla*.

Puerto San Julián p171

‡ **El Muelle Viejo**, *Mitre 1.* Good seafood on this seafront restaurant. The *pejerrey* is recommended. Also bars and tearooms.

‡ **Sportsman**, *Mitre y 25 de Mayo.* Excellent value.

Río Gallegos p172

There are lots of good places to eat here, many serving excellent seafood.

‡ **Buena Vista**, *Sarmiento y Gob Lista, T02966-444114.* Most chic, and not expensive. Near the river, with open views across the Plaza de la Republica, this has an imaginative menu.

‡ **El Club Britanico**, *Roca 935.* Doing its best to look like a London gentleman's club, though lacking in atmosphere, serves cheap set lunches.

‡ **El Dragon**, *9 de Julio 29.* Cheap and varied *tenedor libre*.

‡ **El Horreo**, *Roca 863.* Next door to *Puesto Molino*. A more sophisticated option, rather like a bistro in feel, serving delicious lamb dishes and good salads. Recommended.

Puesto Molino, *Roca 862, opposite the tourist office*. A relaxed airy place, its design inspired by life on estancias, with bold paintings, wooden tables and excellent pizzas (US$5 for two) and *parrilla* (US$10 for two). Recommended.

Activities and tours

Comodoro Rivadavia *p169*

Aonikenk Viajes, *Rawson 1190, T02967-446 6768, aonikenk@satlink.com* Tours to the petrified forests, with 2 hrs at the site.
Marco Sur, *San Martín 263 Local 9, Galeria San Martín, T/F02967-4477490, www.marcosur.com.*

Puerto Deseado *p170*

Both companies offer excursions by boat to Río Deseado reserve and Reserva Provincial Isla Pinguino, 2 hrs.
Darwin Expediciones, *España 2601, T0297-15-6 247554, www.darwin-expediciones.com.*
Los Vikingos, *Estrada 1275, T0297-15-6245141/ 4870020, vikingo@puertodeseado.com.ar* Also day trips to the Monumento Natural Bosques Petrificados.

Puerto San Julián *p171*

Tur Aike Turismo, *Av San Martín 446, T02962-452086.* Excellent zodiac boat trips, lasting 90 min.

Río Gallegos *p172*

Fishing

The southern fishing zone includes the ríos Gallegos, Grande, Fuego, Ewan and San Pablo plus Lago Fagnano, near Ushuaia. It is famous for runs of sea trout. Ask the tourist office for fishing guides and information on permits, www.scruz.gov.ar/pesca

Tours

Macatobiano Turismo, *Roca 908, T/F02966-422466, macatobiano@macatobiano.com* Day tours to Cabo Vírgenes, US$15; half-day tours to Laguna Azul, Estancia Monte León, plus air tickets to El Calafate and Ushuaia.
Transpatagonia Expedicion, *airport, T02966-422504, 442013, transpatagonia@infovia.com.ar.* Day tours to Reserva Provincial Cabo Vírgines, US$30, including lunch at Estancia Monte Dinero.
Tur Aike Turismo, *Zapiola 63, T02966-422436.* Day tours to Estancia Monte Dinero and Cabo Vírgines.

Transport

Comodoro Rivadavia *p169*

Air

The airport is 9 km north; take bus No 6 to from bus terminal, hourly (45 mins), US$0.40; taxi US$3. To **Buenos Aires**, with Aerolíneas Argentinas/Austral, *9 de Julio 870, T0297-444 0050.* Also **LADE**, *Rivadavia 360, T0297-447 6565*, once a week to other towns in Patagonia.

Bus

The terminal, *Pellegrini 730, T02967-3367305*, has an excellent tourist office 0800-2100. To **Buenos Aires**, 2 daily, 28 hrs, US$45. To **Bariloche**, 14 hrs, US$19 (Don Otto, *T02967-447 0450*). To **Esquel** (paved road) 8 hrs direct with ETAP and Don Otto, US$18; in summer buses usually arrive full, so book ahead. To **Río Gallegos**, Don Otto, Pingüino and TAC, *T02967-444 3376*, daily, 11 hrs, US$9. To **Puerto Madryn**, US$8. To **Trelew**, Don Otto 3 daily 4 hrs US$6. To **Caleta Olivia**, La Unión hourly, US$1.50. To **Sarmiento**, US$4, 2½ hrs, 3 daily.

To Chile To **Coyhaique**, US$15, 12 hrs, and **Santiago**, 35 hrs $155, Etap Angel Giobbi, twice a week.

Car rental

Patagonia Sur Car, *Rawson 1190, T02967-446 6768.* Avis, *9 de Julio 687, T/F02967-496382.*

Sarmiento *p169*

There are 3 buses daily to **Comodoro** with Etap, *T0297-447 4841*, and overnight services to **Esquel**, *T0297-454756*, daily except Sat. To **Chile** via Río Mayo, Giobbi, 0200, 3 weekly; seats are scarce.

Puerto Deseado *p170*
Bus terminal, *T0297-155 928598*. Sportman and La Unión, daily to **Caleta Olivia**, US$5, for connections to Comodoro Rivadavia.

Puerto San Julián *p171*

Air

LADE, *San Martín 1552, T02962-452137*, flies each Mon to various Patagonian destinations (see Essentials).

Bus

To **Buenos Aires**, Transportadora Patagónica, T02962-452072, Pingüino, T02962-452425. To **Río Gallegos**, Pingüino, 6 hrs, US$7.

Río Gallegos *p172*

Air

Río Gallegos used to be the nearest airport to **El Calafate**, but there are fewer flights now that Lago Viedma airport has opened. Both Pingüino and Interlagos can arrange packages to El Calafate including accommodation and trip to Moreno glacier from offices at the airport.

Regular flights to/from **Buenos Aires**, **Ushuaia** and **Río Grande** direct with Aerolíneas Argentinas. Also LADE to **Río Turbio**, **El Calafate**, **Ushuaia** and **Comodoro Rivadavia** once a week (book as far in advance as possible). The Ladeco service from **Punta Arenas** to **Port Stanley** on the **Falkland Islands/Islas Malvinas** stops here once a month in either direction.

Airline offices Aerolíneas Argentinas, *San Martín 545, T02966-422020/0810-222 86527, also at airport T02966-442059*. LADE, *Fagnano 53, T02966-422316*. Southern Winds, *San Martín 661, Local 9 T02966-437171*.

Bus

To **El Calafate**, 4-5 hrs, US$9, Taqsa and Interlagos. To **Los Antiguos**, Sportman daily at 2100, US$20. To **Comodoro Rivadavia**, Pingüino, Don Otto and TAC, 10 hrs, US$10. To **Bariloche**, Transportadora Patagonica, daily at 2130. To **Buenos Aires**, 33 hrs, several daily, Pingüino, Don Otto, TAC, US$35. To **Río Grande** and **Ushuaia**, Tecni Austral, Tue, Thu, Sat, 1000, US$18-23, 8-10 hrs.

To Chile To **Puerto Natales**, Pingüino, Sat, 7 hrs, US$7 or Bus-Sur Tue and Thu 1700. To **Punta Arenas**, Pingüino and others, US$11, daily.

Car

Book car rental in advance in high season. Hire companies include Localiza, *Sarmiento 237, T02966-424417*; Cristina, *Libertad 123, T02966-425709*, Taxi Centenario, *Maipú 285*, T02966-422320.

Taxis

For group excursions taxis may be the same price as a tour bus. *Remise* cheaper.

Directory

Comodoro Rivadavia *p169*
Consulates Belgium, *Rivadavia 283*. Chile, *Sarmiento 936*. Italy, *Belgrano 1053*. **Internet/telephone**, *Rivadavia 201* and several along San Martín. **Post office** *San Martín y Moreno*.

Río Gallegos *p172*
Banks Change TCs here if going to El Calafate. 24-hr ATMs are plentiful. Banco Tierra del Fuego, *Roca 831*, Cambio El Pingüino, *Zapiola 469*, and Thaler, *San Martín 484*, will change Chilean pesos and US$. **Consulates** Chile, *Mariano Moreno 136*, Mon-Fri, 0900-1300; tourist cards issued at the border. **Internet/telephone** J@va cybercafe (next to British Club on Roca); also various *locutorios* offer internet services US$0.60 per hr. **Post office** *Roca 893 y San Martín*.

Ruta 40 to the glaciers

CHILE
ARGENTINA
SANTA CRUZ
REGION XI
REGION XII
Hudson
Atravesado
Río Ibáñez
Reserva Nacional Cerro Castillo
Cerro Castillo
Balmaceda
Lago Blanco
Paso Huamules
Lago Blanco
Río Guenguel
Villa Cerro Castillo
Puerto Ibáñez
Puerto Grosse
Río Murta
Levicán
Bahía Murta
Lago General Carrera
Lago Buenos Aires
Fachinal
Río Tranquillo
Reserva Nacional General Carrera
Chile Chico
Los Antiguos
Perito Moreno
Laguna San Rafael
Río Tranquilo
Mallín Grande
Pico del Sur (2,190m)
Estancia La Serena
520
Lago Bertrand
Reserva Nacional Lago Jeinemeni
Puerto Guadal
Río Deseado
Lago Bertrand
El Maitén
Jeinemeni (2,600m)
Cevallos (2,743m)
Estancia Telken
Río Pinturas
Campo de Hielo San Valentín
Puerto Bertrand
Río Chacabuco
Reserva Nacional Tamango
Paso Roballos
Cochrane
Lago Cochrane
40
Lago Pueyrredón
Cueva de las Manos
Campo de Hielo Norte
Río Baker
Lago Posadas
Lago Salitroso
Bajo Caracoles
Caleta Tortel
Estancia La Oriental
Puerto Yungay
Parque Nacional Perito Moreno
Herros (2,770m)
San Lorenzo (3,706m)
Villa O'Higgins
Las Horquetas
L Strobel
p182
Lago O'Higgins
Gobernador Gregores
Lago San Martín
L Cardiel
Estancia La Maipu
Estancia La Angostura
Río Chico
Fitz Roy (3,405m)
El Chaltén
Glaciar Viedma
Lago Viedma
La Julia
Estancia Helsingfors
Tres Lagos
Laguna Grande
Estancia La Leona
Cerro Norte
Parque Nacional Los Glaciares
Glaciar Upsala
Leona
N
Rincón Grande
Lago Argentino
Río Santa Cruz
Puerto Bandera
Estancia Arice
Río Bote
Gendarme Barreto
40 km
40 miles
Glaciar Perito Moreno
El Calafate
Estancia Alta Vista
Estancia Nibepo Aike
El Cerrito
p188
Fuentes del Coyle
Lago Sarmiento
Parque Nacional Torres del Paine
La Esperanza
Paso Cancha Carrera
Cerro Castillo
Gobernador Mayer
Monumento Nacional Cueva Milodón
Río Coig
Seno Ultima Esperanza
Balmaceda (2,035m)
Paso Dorotea
Río Turbio
Paso Casas Viejas
Puerto Natales
El Turbio
Río Gallegos
Cordillera Sarmiento
Bella Vista
El Zurdo
Morro Chico
9
Pali Aike
Don't miss...
1 Cueva de las Manos p184.
2 Staying at a remote estancia p186.
3 Upsala Explorer p193.
4 Mount Fitz Roy p194.
5 Minitrekking on the glaciers p197.

Introduction

The southernmost part of Argentina's iconic road, the Ruta 40, penetrates the remotest heart of Patagonia, running alongside the Andes, with access to peaks, glaciers and two national parks – perfect terrain for your wildest adventure.

There's less than one person per square kilometre in this part of Patagonia and you'll drive for hours without seeing a soul. Head south to the mysterious Cueva de las Manos, where thousands of handprints were painted by pre-historic people or west to the Perito Moreno national park, a virgin wilderness, where jagged peaks are reflected in limpid lakes and condors wheel overhead. For a little civilization in your wilderness, stay at an estancia, where you can experience the timeless life on the land and feast on Patagonian lamb.

At the northern end of Parque Nacional Los Glaciares, El Chaltén is the base for trekking around the magnificent peaks of Fitz Roy, where you can climb on ice or hike for days. Further south, El Calafate is the gateway to the spectacular Perito Moreno and Upsala glaciers. Get your crampons on and explore, then watch with wonder as ice castles cleave off with a mighty roar.

Ratings

Landscape
★★★★★

Chillin'
★★★

Activities
★★★★

Wildlife
★★

Costs
$$$

South on the Ruta 40

Route 40 (paved) heads south from Esquel across a deserted landscape that gives you a taste for the full experience of Patagonia. The main reason for travelling along this route is to visit the extraordinary Cueva de las Manos, south of Perito Moreno but the journey itself will also leave a lasting impression: you might not see a soul all day, and passing a car is a major event. However, there are estancias hidden in the emptiness, where a night or two can give you a wonderful flavour of Patagonian life. When at last you arrive at Mount Fitz Roy, you may think you've imagined it. The sight of the great turrets of granite is made all the more spectacular by days spent crossing endless flatlands, with only condors and clouds for company.

Getting there direct flights to Perito Moreno; buses are limited.
Getting around 4WD or organized tour; buses are limited.
Time required From 1 day to 1 week.
Weather Windy all year round but warm in summer. Incredibly cold in winter.
Sleeping A great hotel in Los Antiguos, remote estancias off Ruta 40, otherwise very limited.
Eating Try the homecooked fare at Hostería Lagos del Furioso.
Activities and tours Horse riding, best arranged from a typical estancia.
★ **Don't miss...** Cueva de las Manos.

Ins and outs

Getting there and around Chalten Travel and Itinerarios y Travesías run a daily bus service between Los Antiguos and El Chaltén; you're unlikely to stop in between, except to see the Cueva de las Manos from Perito Moreno. Various companies organize tours, with *estancia* stays included (www.tierrabuena.com.ar or www.estanciasdesantacruz.com.) For drivers travelling south, the road is paved

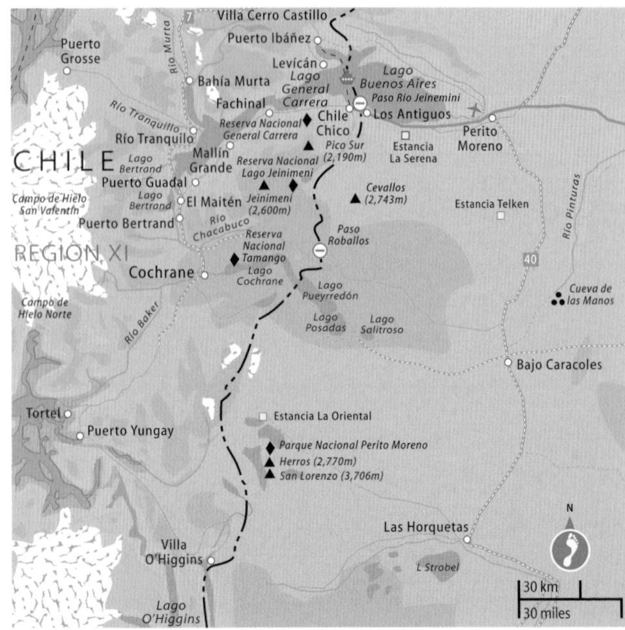

A view along the Ruta 40

as far as Perito Moreno, and then good *ripio*, improving greatly after Las Horquetas. Fuel is available in most places but carry extra to avoid a 72 km detour to Gobernador Gregores. If cycling, note that food and water stops are scarce, the wind is fierce and there is no shade.

Perito Moreno and around

Your most likely stop on the long road south is the spruce little town of Perito Moreno, 25 km west of Lago Buenos Aires and accessible by bus from Esquel or Comodoro Rivadavia. It's the nearest base for exploring the mysterious cave paintings at the **Cueva de las Manos** to the south. The town has no sights as such, but southwest of the town is **Parque Laguna**, where you can see varied bird life, including flamingos and black-necked swans, and go fishing. You could also walk to the crater of **Cerro Volcan**, from a path 12 km outside Perito Moreno: ask at the friendly **tourist office** ⓘ *San Martín 1059, T02963-432020, www.scruz.gov.ar, open 0700-2300*, for directions. Staff can also advise on tours and *estancia* stays.

Border with Chile

Two roads cross the border into Chile west of Río Mayo to take you to Coyhaique (see page 299). Further south, the road from Perito Moreno to Los Antiguos leads to a border on the shores of Lago Buenos Aires.

Coyhaique Alto is reached by a 133 km road (87 km *ripio*, then dirt) that branches off Route 40 about 7 km north of Río Mayo, continuing on the Chilean side 50 km west to Coyhaique. **Chilean immigration** ⓘ *Coyhaique Alto, 6 km west of the border, open May-Aug 0800-2100, Sep-Apr 0700-2300.*

Paso Huemules is reached by a road which branches off Route 40, some 31 km south of Río Mayo and runs west 105 km via Lago Blanco (fuel), 30 km from the border. This crossing has better roads than Coyhaique Alto. On the Chilean side, this road continues via Balmaceda airport, 61 km to Coyhaique. **Chilean immigration** ⓘ *3 km from the border, open winter 0800-2000, summer 0800-2200.*

From **Los Antiguos** a bridge crosses the border heading towards Chile Chico, (see page 311). **Chilean immigration** ⓘ *20 km from the border, open winter 0800-2000, summer 0800-2200.*

Los Antiguos

From this part of Argentina, the easiest and most commonly used route to Chile is via the pretty little village of Los Antiguos, which lies just 2 km east of the border, on the southern shore of **Lago Buenos Aires**. This is the second largest lake in South America and extends into Chile as Lago General Carrera (see page 310). The landscape is very beautiful and unspoilt and the Río Baker, which flows from the lake, is world-renowned for excellent trout fishing. The main reason to enter Chile here is to take the ferry over the lake to Puerto Ibáñez with bus connections to Coyhaique on the Carretera Austral. (You can also drive to Puerto Ibáñez from Perito Moreno, via the paved road around the north-east side of Lago Buenos Aires.)

Los Antiguos is a sleepy little place, but has a rather pleasant quiet atmosphere, thanks largely to its warm microclimate. It's a rich fruit-growing area with a popular cherry festival in early January that attracts national *folclore* stars. There's a small but willing **tourist office** ⓘ *Av 11 de Julio 446, www.losantiguos-sc.com.ar, summer 0800-2200, at other times 0800-1200 only*. While you're here, visit two local *chacras* (small farms). You can walk to **Chacra Don Neno**, where strawberries are grown and good jam is sold, or (if you have transport) head further afield to idyllic **Chacra el Paraiso**, which grows and sells perfect cherries.

Cueva de las Manos

ⓘ *Access via an unpaved road east off Route 40, 3 km north of Bajo Caracoles, US$1.50, under-12s free. 6 hrs return journey by car from Perito Moreno. Estancia Los Toldos (80 km from Perito Moreno, 18 km from the caves) organizes trips, p186.* Situated 163 km south of Perito Moreno and 47 km northeast of Bajo Caracoles, the canyon of the **Río Pinturas** contains outstanding examples of handprints and cave paintings, estimated to be between 3,000 and 9,300 years old. In the cave's four galleries are over 800 paintings of human hands, as well as images of guanacos and rheas, and various geometrical designs painted by the Toldense peoples. The red, orange, black, white and ochre pigments were derived from earth and calafate berries and fixed with a varnish of guanaco fat and urine. The canyon itself is also worth seeing: 270 m deep and 480 m wide, with strata of vivid red and green rock; it's especially beautiful in the early morning or evening light. A *guardaparque* living at the site provides helpful information.

Cueva de las Manos

66 99 Of the more than 800 handprints painted in the Cueva de las Manos, all but 31 depict left hands

Bajo Caracoles and beyond

After hours of spectacular emptiness, even tiny Bajo Caracoles is a relief. It's nothing more than a few houses, facing into the wind, with an expensive grocery store and very expensive fuel. Route 41 (unpaved) heads 99 km northwest from here, past Lago Ghio and Lago Columna, to the **Paso Roballos** border and on to **Cochrane** (see page 312). Although it's passable in summer, the route is often flooded in spring and there's no public transport. **Chilean immigration** ⓘ *11 km from border, winter 0800-2000, summer 0800-2200.* Route 39, meanwhile, heads west for 72 km to **Lago Posada** and **Lago Pueyrredón**, two beautiful lakes with contrasting blue and turquoise waters, separated by a narrow isthmus, where guanacos and rheas can be seen.

South of Bajo Caracoles, Route 40 crosses the Pampa del Asador and then, near **Las Horquetas**, swings southeast to follow the Río Chico. There is a turning off west to Lago Belgrano and **Parque Nacional Perito Moreno** (see below). South of this junction, Route 40 improves considerably. At Km 464, Route 25 branches off towards **San Julian** on the Atlantic coast, via **Gobernador Gregores** (72 km, fuel), while Route 40 continues southwest towards Tres Lagos. There is no food between Bajo Caracoles and Tres Lagos, although there are estancias roughly every 25 km.

Parque Nacional Perito Moreno

ⓘ *Entrance 90 km west of Las Horquetas via ruta 37, open Nov-Mar, free, no public transport. The nearest information centre is in Gobernador Gregores, 220 km away: Av San Martín 409, T02962-491477, peritomoreno@apn.gov.ar.* Situated southwest of Bajo Caracoles on the Chilean border, this is one of the wildest and most remote parks in Argentina. The large, interconnected system of lakes and glaciated peaks offers good trekking and abundant wildlife but much of the park is dedicated to scientific study and inaccessible.

Ten kilometres beyond the park entrance, the *guardaparque*'s office has maps and leaflets on walks and wildlife. The most accessible section of the park is a little further on, around turquoise **Lago Belgrano**. Several good hikes are possible from here, around the peninsula with fine views of Cerro Herros; to **Cerro Léon**, starting from Estancia La Oriental, good for spotting condors; and the one- or two-day hike to **Lago Burmeister**, via Cerro Casa de Piedra, 16 km. At the foot of **Cerro Casa de Piedra** is a network of caves containing paintings, accessible only with a guide. For longer routes, consult the *guardaparques*.

The **Sierra Colorada** dominates the northeast of the park and the erosion of its multicoloured rocks is responsible for the lakes' vibrant colours. Between the lakes are snow-covered peaks, the highest of which is **Cerro Herros** (2,770 m), while outside the park itself, but towering over it to the north is **Cerro San Lorenzo** (3,706 m), the highest peak in southern Patagonia. Vegetation changes with altitude: dense *coiron* grasses and shrubs cling to the windswept steppe, while beech forest, *lenga* and *coihue* occupy the higher slopes. Wildlife includes guanacos, foxes and the rare huemul, plus flamingos, ñandus, steamer ducks, grebes, black-necked swans, Patagonian woodpeckers, eagles and condors. The lakes and rivers are unusual for Argentina in that they contain only native species of fish.

Sleeping

Perito Moreno p183

D **Austral**, *San Martín 1327, T02963-42042*. Bath, breakfast and a decent restaurant.
D **Belgrano**, *San Martín 1001, T02963-42019*. Also pleasant, with simple rooms.

Estancia

L pp **Telken**, *RN40, 28 km south of Perito Moreno, T02963-432079/432303, T011-4797 7216, www.estanciasde santacruz.com/telken.* Formerly a sheep station, now aimed at tourism. Comfortable accommodation in the farmhouse, wood-lined rooms, and charming bedrooms. All meals shared with the welcoming owners, who also offer horse riding. Highly recommended.

Los Antiguos p184

A **Hostería La Serena**, *29 km east of Los Antiguos, T02963-432340.* Comfortable accommodation, excellent home-grown food, fishing and trips to Chilean and Argentine Lake District, open Oct-Jun.
B **Antigua Patagonia**, *on the lakeside, signposted from Ruta 43, T02963-491038 /491055, www.antiguapatagonia.com.ar* Los Antiguos has one really great hotel, and it's really worth a detour. Luxurious rooms with beautiful views on the shore of the lake. There's also an excellent restaurant. The owner arranges tours to the Cueva de los Manos and nearby Monte Cevallos. Recommended.
D **Argentino**, *11 de Julio 850, T02963-491132*. Comfortable rooms, and a decent restaurant.
F pp **Albergue Padilla**, *San Martín 44 (just off main street) T02963-491140*. Big shared rooms for 4-8 with bathrooms, *quincho* and garden, where you can also camp. Very friendly. El Chaltén travel tickets sold.

Camping

Municipal, *T02963-491308, /156-211855*. Outstanding site with every facility, lovely grounds 2 km from centre, US$1.25 pp.

Cueva de las Manos p184

L **Los Toldos**, *7 km off the RN40, 60 km south of Perito Moreno, T02963-432856, 011-4901 0436, www.estanciasde santacruz.com/lostoldos*. The closest *estancia* for visiting the Cueva de las Manos. A modest building, set in a wonderful landscape. The owners organize trips by horse or 4WD to see the cave paintings, as well as to the lakes and the PN Perito Moreno. They also have an albergue, the **Hostería Cueva de Las Manos** (B), open Nov-Easter.

Bajo Caracoles and beyond p185

There are some superb *estancias* around Gobernador Gregores, tricky to get to without your own transport, but offering an unforgettable slice of Patagonian life.
A pp **La Angostura**, *T02962-452010, F02962-454318, 55 km south of Gobernador Gregores*. Horse riding, trekking, fishing, recommended.
D **Hostería Lagos del Furioso**, *between lagos Posadas and Pueyrredón, Route 39, T02963-490253, T/F011-48120959, www.lagos delfurioso.com*. Open Mid Oct-Easter. Comfortable accommodation in cabins by the lake shore, superb Patagonian cooking with home produced food, and good wines. Horse-riding, trekking and excursions in 4WD vehicles.
D **Hotel Bajo Caracoles**, *Bajo Caracoles, T0297-434963*. Very old fashioned, 1920s building, with plain spacious rooms and meals, but a rather insitutional feel. Given the wilderness all around you'll probably be glad of a bed.

Parque Nacional Perito Moreno p185

Camping 4 free sites inside the park: Lago Burmeister, Mirador Lago Belgrano, Cerro de Vasco and Alberto de Agostini. No facilities; fires not permitted.
B **Estancia La Oriental**, *T02962-452196, elada@uvc.com.ar*. Open Nov-Mar, full board. In a splendid setting, rooms are comfortable, and superb horse riding is offered. Recommended.

Eating

Perito Moreno p185
There's good food at **Pipach**, *next to Hotel Austral*, **Parador Bajo Caracoles**, or pizzas at **Nono's**, on *9 de Julio y Saavedra*. **Rotiseria Chee's I**, is a cheap and cheery place to eat and does takeaways.

Los Antiguos p184
La Perla del Lago, *Fitzroy y Perito Moreno*. The best *parrilla*.

Activities and tours

Perito Moreno p183
Tour operators
Señor Sabella, *Av Perón 941, T02963-432199*. Trips to Cueva de las Manos, including a spectacular 2-hour along the river valley.
Transporte Terrestre Guanacondór, *Juan José Nauto 432079* and **Transporte Lago Posados**, *T02963-432431*. Both offer the 'Circuito Grande Comarca Noroeste', which includes Perito Moreno to Bajo Caracoles, Cueva de los Manos, Lago Posada, Paso Roballos, Monte Cevallos and Los Antiguos. Also day tours to Cueva de los Manos, with option of collecting from Bajo Caracoles, US$30-40.

Transport

Perito Moreno p185
Air
The airport is 7 km east out of town, and the only way to get there is by taxi. LADE, *Av San Martín 1207, T02963-432055*, has flights to/from **Río Gallegos**, **Río Grande**, **Ushuaia**, **El Calafate** and **Gob Gregores**.

Bus
The terminal is on the edge of town, T02963- 432072. La Union, T02963-432133, to **Comodoro Rivadavia**, 6hrs US$12, and to **Chile** via Los Antiguos, 2 buses daily in summer, 1hr, US$2. Co-op Sportman also daily to **Comodoro Rivadavia**. To **El Chaltén**, Chaltén Travel, www.chaltentravel.com, depart 1000 on even dates (ie 2nd, 4th, 6th); Itinerarios y Travesias, www.elchalten.com/ruta40, 1800 on odd dates (ie 1st, 3rd, 5th), US$30. It's a14 hr, 582 km journey over bleak emptiness; see also p209.

Los Antiguos p184
Bus
Co-op Sportman to **Comodoro Rivadavia**, via Perito Moreno and Caleta Olivia, daily, 7½ hrs, US$9. Chaltén Travel and Itinerarios y Travesias to **El Chaltén** and **El Calafate**, US$40, see above for details. Tickets from Albergue Padilla, *San Martín 44 Sur, T02963-491140*. La Union across the border to Chile Chico (Chile), 45 mins, US$1; also Transportes VH, US$2.

Cueva de las Manos p184
Northbound buses run by Itinerarios y Travesias stop here at dawn for a couple of hours en route between **El Chaltén** and **Los Antiguos**, see p209. It's a great way to see the caves. Tickets are available from Albergue Patagonia in El Chaltén, *Av San Martín 495, T02962-493088, alpatagonia@infovia.com.ar*. Otherwise, the Perito Moreno tourist office, T02963-432222 can advise on tours, see above.

Parque Nacional Perito Moreno p185
There is no transport into the park but it may be possible to get a lift with *estancia* workers. Also consult www.parquesnacionales.com.

Directory

Perito Moreno p183
There are two ATMs in the main street, at Banco de la Provincia de Santa Cruz and Banco de la Nación, but nowhere to change traveller's cheques.

Parque Nacional Los Glaciares

Of all Argentina's impressive landscapes, the sight of the immense glaciers in this national park may stay with you longest. This is the second-largest national park in Argentina, extending along the Chilean border for over 170 km; almost half of it is covered by ice fields from which 13 glaciers descend into two great lakes: Lago Argentino in the southeast and Lago Viedma to the northeast.

East of the ice fields, there's southern beech forest before the land flattens to the wind-blasted Patagonian steppe. Bird life is prolific: you may spot black-necked swans, the magallenic woodpecker, and, perhaps, even the torrent duck, diving in the streams and rivers. Guanacos, grey foxes, skunks and rheas can be seen on the steppe, and the rare huemul inhabits the forest.

There are two main areas to explore: the glaciers can be visited by bus and boat trips from El Calafate, while from El Chaltén, 230 km northwest, there is superb trekking around the dramatic Fitz Roy massif and ice climbing near its summit. The central section, between Lago Argentino and Lago Viedma, is the Ice Cap National Reserve, inaccessible to visitors apart from a couple of estancias.

Getting there By air to El Calafate for access to the glaciers or by bus to El Chaltén for Cerro Fitz Roy.

Getting around Plenty of organized tours and treks.

Time required At least 5 days trekking around Fitz Roy, 3 days in El Calafate for the glaciers.

Weather Very cold in winter with heavy snowfall, mild in summer; strong winds all year.

Sleeping Pricey in El Calafate and booked up in high season. Overpriced and unattractive in El Chaltén. Many estancias.

Eating Lots of choice in El Calafate, less in El Chaltén. All expensive as everything has to be imported.

Activities and tours 'Minitrekking' on the glaciers and hiking around Cerro Fitz Roy.

★ **Don't miss...** Glaciar Perito Moreno.

Perito Moreno glacier

Ins and outs

Getting there Access to the national park is via **El Calafate**, for glaciers, on Lago Argentina, 50 km from the park's eastern boundary, or via **El Chaltén**, for trekking, near Fitz Roy on the northeastern edge of the park. There are regular flights to El Calafate airport, 20 km east of town, as well as buses from Río Gallegos and Puerto Natales. El Chaltén is reached by several buses daily from El Calafate and Río Gallegos, or from the north along the Route 40 from Los Antiguos. » *Ins and outs, p189-194, Transport, p208-209.*

Best time to visit Although this part of Patagonia is generally cold, there is a milder microclimate around Lago Viedma and Lago Argentina, which means that summers can be reasonably pleasant, with average summer temperatures between 5 and 22°C, though strong winds blow constantly at the foot of the *cordillera*. Precipitation on the Hielo Sur, up to 5,000 mm annually, falls mainly as snow. In the forested area, around 1500 mm of rain falls annually, mainly between March and late May. In winter, the whole area is inhospitably cold and most tourist facilities are closed. The best time to visit, therefore, is between November and April, avoiding January and early February, when Argentines take their holidays, campsites are crowded and accommodation is hard to find. Park entry US$3. For further information contact T02962 491477, peritomoreno@apn.gov.ar.

El Calafate » *p 199-209*

El Calafate sits on the southern shore of Lago Argentino, a new town existing almost entirely as a tourist centre for visiting the glaciers in the Parque Nacional, 50 km west. From El Calafate you can get to **Glaciar Perito Moreno** by bus and boat and even go trekking on its surface, or travel by boat along the western arms of Lago Argentino, between stately floating icebergs, to see **Glaciares Spegazzini** and **Upsala**. All are breathtakingly beautiful and will be an unforgettable part of your trip to Patagonia.

Founded in 1927, the town has expanded rapidly and many of its hotel owners are new arrivals from Buenos Aires, here to escape the economic stress of the city. El Calafate is expensive and not particularly attractive, but it's the only place to stay to see the glaciers, unless you camp in the park itself, or can afford an *estancia*. Despite the growing number of hotels, hostels and *cabañas*, it can't quite accommodate the hordes of visitors that descend during January and February. In contrast, it's empty and quiet all winter but extremely cold, so it's best to come in March or April if you can.

Ins and outs → *Airport charge for departing passengers is US$18.*

Getting there The easiest way to get to El Calafate is by **air**, with several daily flights in summer from Buenos Aires to its airport, Lago Viedma, 22 km east of town. You can also fly here from Ushuaia in Tierra del Fuego or from Puerto Natales in Chile in order to combine a trip to the glaciers with trekking in Torres del Paine. The **Aerobus** minibus service, T02902-492492, meets all flights and charges US$3 for the journey into town; a taxi, T02902-491655/492005, will cost you US$7.

Bus travel is convenient too, with buses from Río Gallegos and Ushuaia and from Puerto Natales, via Cerro Castillo, if you want to get directly to/from Torres del Paine. The bus terminal is centrally located up a steep flight of steps off the main street, and has a small tourist office. » *Transport, p208.*

Getting around From El Calafate, access to the park is very straightforward, with regular bus services as well as organized tours that combine access with boat trips, walking and even ice trekking on Glaciar Moreno. El Calafate's shops, restaurants and tour operators can mostly be found along its main street, Av del Libertador, running east-west. Hotels lie within two blocks north and south and smaller *hosterías* are scattered throughout the newly built residential area sprawling up the hill. There are many *estancias* nearby, on the way to the national park, and also several campsites.

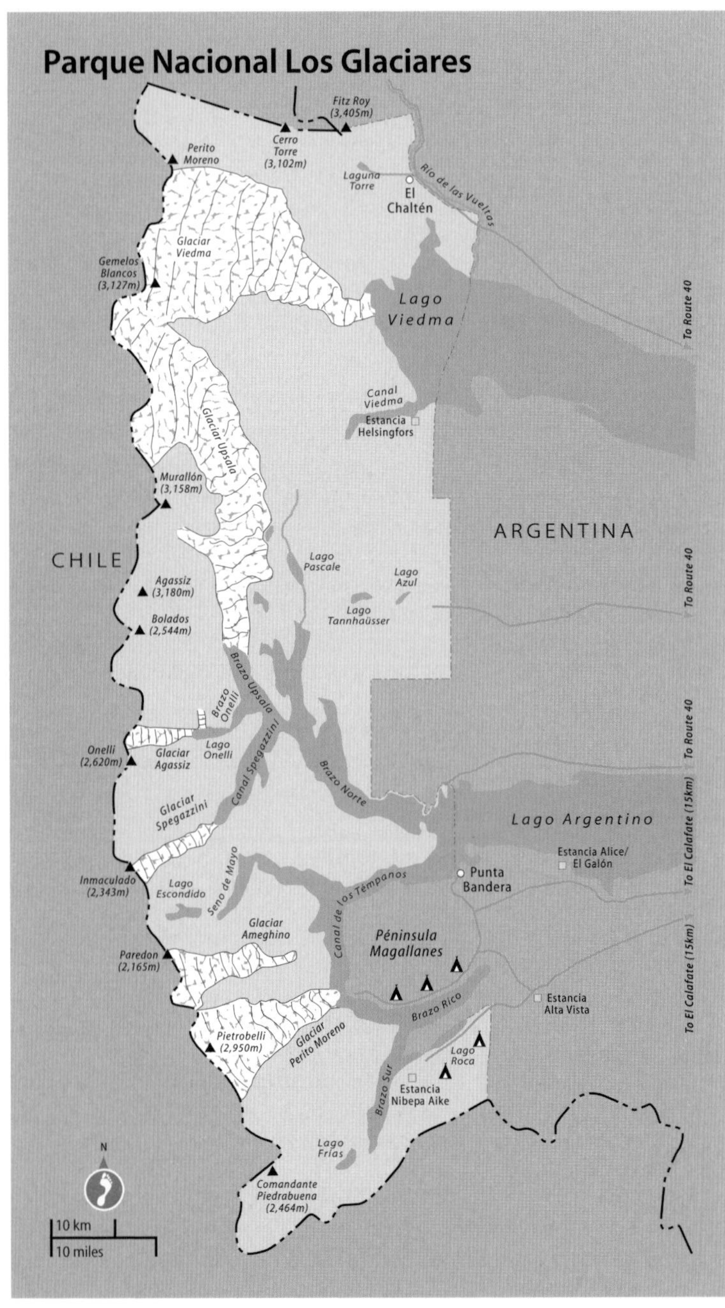

Tourist information El Calafate **tourist office** ⓘ *in the bus terminal, T02902-491090, www.elcalafate.com or www.interpatagonia.com in English, open Oct-Apr daily 0700-2200*, may look disorganized, but the efficient staff speak several languages and have a good map with accommodation shown, as well as helpful information on *estancias* and tours. There's another branch at the airport, T02902-491230. There's also an **Intendencia del Parque** (park office) ⓘ *Libertador 1302, T02902-491005, open Mon-Fri 0800-1600, apnglaciares@cotecal.com.ar.*

Around El Calafate

Just west of the town centre is **Bahía Redonda**, a shallow part of Lago Argentino that freezes in winter, when ice-skating and skiing are possible. From the **Intendencia del Parque**, Libertador 1302, an hour's stroll will take you to **Laguna Nimez** at the eastern edge of this bay, where there's a bird reserve with flamingos, black-necked swans and ducks. To get there, follow Calle Bustillo up the new road among cultivated fields and orchards to cross the bridge. Keep heading north: the laguna is signposted. At **Punta Gualicho** (or Walichu) on the shores of Lago Argentino, there are cave paintings, and though they're rather badly deteriorated, the 30-min walk is worthwhile. Walk to the top of the **Cerro Calafate**, behind the town, 2½-3 hrs, for views of the silhouette of the southern end of the Andes, Bahía Redonda and Isla Solitaria on Lago Argentino. There is also scope for good hill-walking to the south of the town, while **Cerro Elefante**, to the west, on the road to the Moreno glacier, is good for rock climbing.

In addition to the glaciers, El Calafate provides access to some other good places for trekking, horse riding and exploring by 4WD, if you're here for a few days. There are several *estancias* within reach of the town, which offer a day on a working farm, a lunch of superb Patagonian lamb, cooked *asado al palo*, and outdoor activities. '**El Galpón del Glacier**' (formerly Estancia Alice) offers displays of sheep shearing, walking and horse riding trips to the Perito Moreno glacier and Cerro Frias. Overnight accommodation is available in the lovely house with views of Lago Argentino.

Lago Roca, 40 km southwest of El Calafate, is set in beautiful open landscape, with hills above offering panoramic views. The lake is perfect for lots of activities, including trout and salmon fishing, climbing and walking, and there are several *estancias*, where you can see farm activities, such as the branding of cattle in summer. There is also good camping in a wooded area and a restaurant.

Lago Argentino and the glaciers » p202-209

Perito Moreno glacier

The sight of this expanse of ice, like a frozen sea, its waves sculpted by wind and time into beautiful turquoise folds and crevices, is unforgettable. You'll watch the immense and silent mass in awe, until suddenly a mighty roar announces the fall of another hunk of ice into the water below. Moreno was, until recently, one of the few glaciers in the world that was still advancing. Some 30 km long, 5 km across and 60 m high, it reaches the water at a narrow point on one of the fiords, **Brazo Rico**, opposite Peninsula Magellanes. It used to advance right across Brazo Rico, blocking the fiord roughly every three years. As the water pressure built up behind it, the ice would break, reopening the channel and sending giant icebergs (*témpanos*) rushing down the **Canal de los Témpanos**. This hasn't happened since February 1988, causing concern that global warming may be to blame. Walking on the ice itself is a wonderful way to experience the glacier; the steeply curved peaks, with mysterious chasms below, are lit by refracted bluish light.

Background

Francisco Moreno, El Perito

You can't miss the name of Argentina's favourite son as you travel around Patagonia. Francisco Pascasio Moreno (1852-1919) is commemorated by a national park, a town, and a world famous glacier. Moreno, a naturalist and geographer, travelled ceaselessly in Patagonia, exploring areas previously unknown to the authorities in Buenos Aires. At the age of 20, he paid his first visit to Patagonia, travelling up the Río Negro to Lago Nahuel Huapi, along the Río Chubut, and then up the Río Santa Cruz to reach the giant lake which he named Lago Argentino. Expeditions such as these were dangerous: apart form the physical hardships, relations with the indigenous populations were poor. On one expedition, Moreno was seized as a hostage, but escaped on a raft which carried him for 8 days down the Río Limay to safety.

His fame established, Moreno was elected to congress and appointed Director of the Museo de Ciencias Naturales in La Plata. In 1901 he became an expert (*perito*) adviser to the Argentine side in the negotiations to draw the border with Chile. His reward was a grant of lands near Bariloche which he handed over to the state to manage, the initial act in creating the national parks system in Argentina, and an inspiring gesture towards sharing the country's spectacular natural beauty at a time when anyone who could was buying it up as fast as possible. Moreno's remains are buried in a mausoleum on Isla Centinela in Lago Nahuel Huapi.

Viewing the glacier There are various ways to approach the glacier. All excursions (and the regular bus service) will take you 85 km from El Calafate direct to the car park on Peninsula Magallanes, where you begin the descent along a series of wooden walkways (*pasarelas*) to see the glacier slightly from above, and then, as you get lower, directly head-on. There are several wide viewing areas, where, in summer, crowds wait expectantly, cameras poised, for another hunk of ice to fall from the vertical blue walls at the glacier's front. Never walk down to the rocks overlooking the channel; there is a real danger of being washed away, if a large chunk of ice breaks off the glacier. However, you can also approach the glacier by walking around the tranquil lake shore. From the restaurant at the car park, a path leads over big bald rocks, carved smooth by ancient glaciers, until the Perito Moreno appears through rich *lenga* forest. *Guardaparques* (park rangers) guide an hour-long walk along the lake shore, leaving from the park ranger's office in the car park (check for times T02902 491005). There are also boat trips which leave constantly during the day from the tourist pier (well-signposted from the carpark), to survey the glacier from the water below, giving you a chance to appreciate its magnitude and its varied sculptural forms. To get closer still, there are guided treks on the ice itself, known as *minitrekking*, which allow you to walk along the crevices and frozen crests in crampons. This is possible for anyone with a reasonable level of fitness and is not technically demanding. Tour companies in El Calafate offer all of these options. ▸▸ *Activities and tours, p206.*

Budget buster

Upsala Explorer

Although it's expensive, the Upsala Explorer, must be recommended as one of the best ways to visit the Upsala glacier. A bus leaves from El Calafate at 0700 and takes you to Puerto Bandera, where you catch the boat through Brazo Norte. From the boat you will gain your first glimpse of the glacier's front, passing through a lake strewn with icebergs. The boat lands at remote Estancia Cristina (also open to paying guests), where a traditional asado lunch is served and optional horse riding is offered. From here, you're taken in sturdy 4WD vehicles to a point high above the lake to walk alongside massive rocks polished smooth by the path of glaciers, to see Upsala from above. This is an overwhelmingly beautiful sight: the glacier stretches apparently endlessly away from you, with the deep still prussian blue lake below and fire-coloured rocks all around.

US$90-105 depending on your seat in the boat (including all food), bus transfer US$11, park entry US$2, book through agencies in El Calafate. For further details, see www.upsalaexplorer.com.ar.

Upsala glacier

The fiords at the northwestern end of Lago Argentino are fed by four other glaciers. The largest is the Upsala glacier, named after the Swedish university which commissioned the first survey of this area in 1908. It's a stunning expanse of untouched beauty, covering three times the area of the Perito Moreno glacier, and is the longest glacier flowing off the Southern Patagonian icefields. Unusually it ends in two separate frontages, each about 4 km wide and 60 m high, although only the western frontage can be seen from the lake excursion. It can be reached by motor-boat from Punta Bandera on Lago Argentina, 50 km west of Calafate, on a trip that also goes to other, much smaller, glaciers. **Spegazzini**, further south, has a frontage 1½ km wide and 130 m high. In between are **Agassiz** and **Onelli** glaciers, both of which feed into **Lago Onelli**, a quiet and very beautiful lake, full of icebergs of every size and sculpted shape, surrounded by beech forests on one side and ice-covered mountains on the other.

Upsala glacier, Lago Argentina

Cerro Fitz Roy

Around Cerro Fitz Roy » p 199-209

At the northern end of Parque Nacional Los Glaciares, the soaring granite of Mount Fitz Roy (3,405 m) rises up from the smooth baize of the steppe, more like a ziggurat than a mountain, surrounded by a consort of jagged snow-clad spires, with a stack of spun cotton cloud hanging constantly above them. It is one of the most magnificent mountains in the world and towers above the nearby peaks: **Torre** (3,128 m), **Poincenot** (3,076 m) and **Saint-Exupery** (2,600 m). Its Tehuelche name was El Chaltén, ('smoking mountain' or 'volcano'), perhaps because at sunrise the pink towers are occasionally lit up bright red for a few seconds in a phenomenon known as the *amanecer de fuego* ('sunrise of fire'). Perito Moreno named the peak after the captain of the *Beagle*, who saw it from afar in 1833, and it was first climbed by a French expedition in 1952. It stands in the northern end of Parque Nacional Los Glaciares at the western end of Lago Viedma, 230 km north of El Calafate, in an area of lakes and glaciers that makes marvellous trekking country. The base for walking and climbing around Fitz Roy is the modern town of El Chaltén, which has been built right next to the mountains.

Ins and outs

Getting there and around The quickest way to reach El Chaltén is to fly to El Calafate (see page 189) and then catch one of the frequent buses for the 220-km journey north. There are also daily buses to El Chaltén from Los Antiguos along Route 40, useful if you've come from the Lake District. Access to the park is free and it is not necessary to register before you set out. Most paths are very clear and well worn but a map is essential, even on short walks: the park information centre has photocopied maps of treks but the best is one published by *Zagier and Urruty*, 1992, US$6 (F011-45725766) and is available in shops in Calafate and Chaltén.

Best time to visit Walking here is only really viable mid-October to April, with the best months usually March to April when the weather is generally stable and not very cold, and the autumn colours of the beech forest are stunning. Mid-summer, December and January, and spring, September to October, are generally very windy. And in December/January the campsites can be full to bursting, with many walkers on the paths.

Tourist information The **Intendencia del Parque** (park office) is in El Chaltén, across the bridge at the entrance to the town, T02962-493004. It hands out helpful trekking maps of the area, with paths and campsites marked, giving distances and walking times. El Chalten's **tourist office** ⓘ *Güemes 21, T02962-493011, www.elchalten.com, open Mon-Fri 0900-2000, Sat-Sun 1300-2000*, has an excellent website, with accommodation lists, but no email.

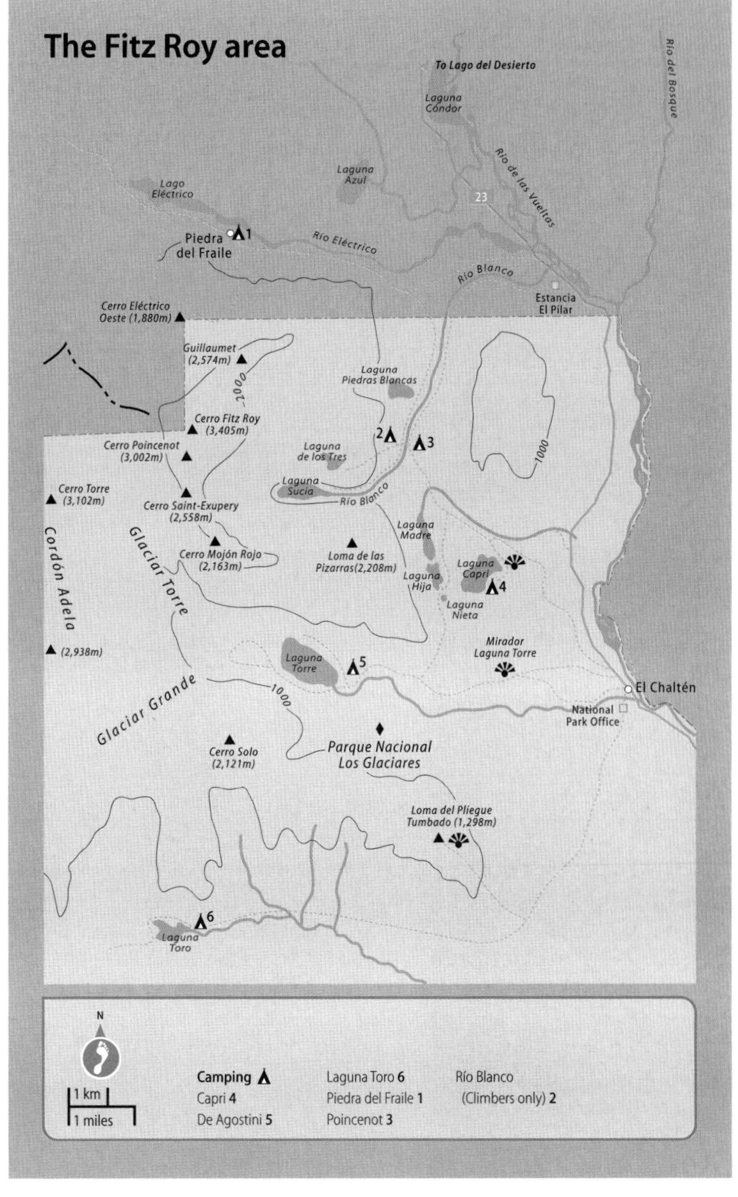

El Chaltén

The small modern town of El Chaltén is set in a wonderful position at the foot of Cerro Fitz Roy and at the mouth of the valley of the Río de las Vueltas but, having been founded in 1985 in order to pre-empt Chilean territorial claims, it has grown with little thought for aesthetics. Now hugely popular as a centre for trekking and climbing in summer, and for cross country skiing in winter, it's an expensive place and its concrete and tin buildings are unattractive, especially when the harsh wind blows. But the steady stream of visitors create a cheerful atmosphere and, from the town, you can walk directly into breathtaking landscapes. Tourist infrastructure is still developing in El Chaltén and, so far, there are no ATMs (or internet cafés), so take sufficient cash. Accommodation ranges from camping and hostels to not-quite-luxurious *hosterías*, all hideously overpriced. Food, too, is expensive, though there is increasingly plenty of choice. Credit cards are accepted in bigger establishments.

▲ Hiking around Fitz Roy → *These are the most popular walks from El Chaltén.*

Laguna Torre (2 hrs each way) Walk west to Mirador Laguna Torre (90 mins) for views of Cerro Torre then continue to busy **Camping De Agostini** (30mins) on the lake shore, where there are fantastic views of the dramatic peaks of Cordon Torre.

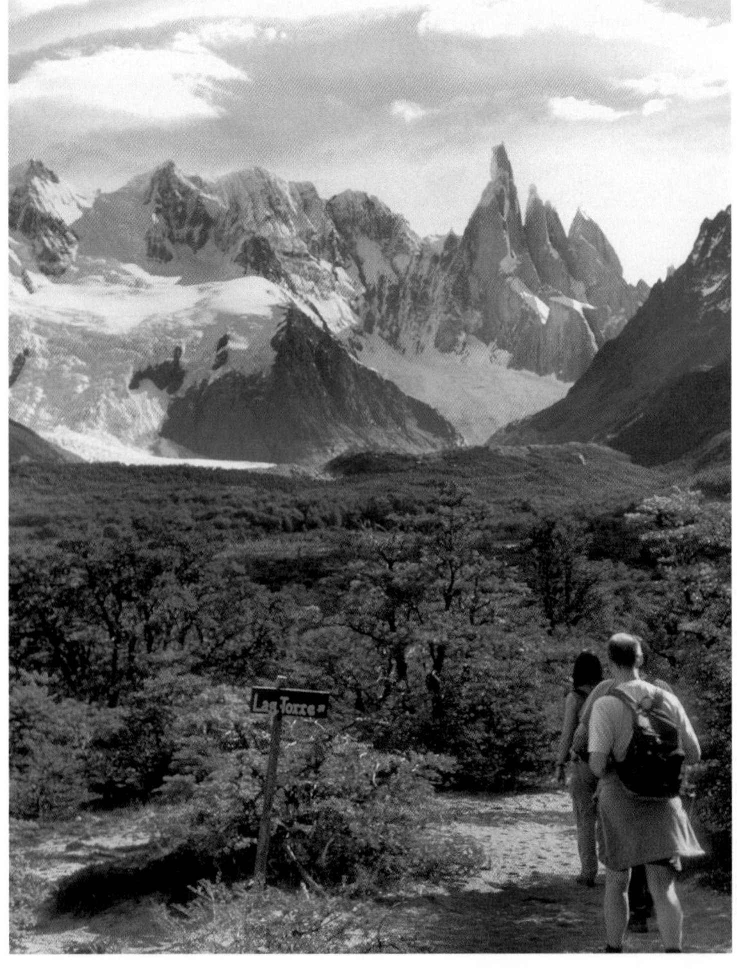

Top tips

Hike right

General advice for anyone trekking around El Chaltén and Cerro Fitz Roy:

→ **Equipment** A map is essential, even on short walks. Also take plenty of warm clothes and a four-season sleeping bag, if you're camping. A gas/alcohol stove is essential for camping, as fires are prohibited everywhere in the National Park. It is possible to rent equipment in El Chaltén; ask at the park office or Rancho Grande.
→ **Information** The park's Intendencia provides a good photocopied map, recommending lots of walks, and giving times for walking (one way) and locations for campsites. The *guardaparques* can advise on walks and, although you're not required to register, it's a good idea to check with them about the state of the paths and conditions in the mountains. Some speak English.
→ **Paths** Paths are well marked. Stick to the centre of the path so as not to make it any bigger and walk in single file (this means at times that you're walking in a rut). Do not stray from the paths.
→ **Rubbish** Take all rubbish back down the mountain with you.
→ **Water** All river water in the National Park is drinkable. Don't bathe in rivers and lakes; do not wash or bury waste within 70 m of a water source. Never go to the toilet near water sources.
→ **Weather** Be warned that the weather changes hourly, so don't wait for a sunny day to go hiking and be prepared for a sudden deterioration in conditions. Always wear sun screen (factor 30 at least).
→ **Wildlife** As you leave El Chaltén, don't let the dogs follow you, as they frighten the rare *huemules* (an endangered species of deer).

Laguna de Los Tres (4 hrs each way) Walk up to Laguna Capri (2 hrs), with great views of Fitz Roy, then continue to **Camping Poincenot** (1 hr) and **Camping Río Blanco** (only for climbers, by arrangement). From Río Blanco you can head southwest to Laguna de los Tres, where you'll get a spectacular view on a fine day (1 hr) but in bad weather, you're better off walking to Piedras Blancas (1 hr).

Laguna Torre (7 hrs each way) A marvellous walk offers views of both mountain groups. By climbing past Laguna Capri and taking the signed path to your left, passing two lakes, Laguna Madre and then Laguna Hija, to reach the path that leads to Laguna Torre.

Loma del Pliegue Tumbado (4 hrs each way) A marked path from the *guardería* (park ranger's office) leads southwest to this viewpoint where you can see both cordons and Lago Viedma. This is a good day walk, best in clear weather. More experienced trekkers can continue to the glacial Laguna Toro (6 hrs from El Chaltén).

Río Blanco to Piedra del Fraile (7 hrs each way) This beautiful walk starts at **Camping Río Blanco** (see above) and runs north along the Río Blanco and then west along the Río Eléctrico to **Camping Piedra del Fraile** (4 hrs), just outside the national park. From here a path leads south, up Cerro Eléctrico Oeste (1,882 m) towards the north face of Fitz Roy (2 hrs); it's tough going but with spectacular views. You should take a guide for the last bit. Ask at El Pilar estancia and outdoor centre, www.elpilar.com.ar.

Climbing Fitz Roy

Base camp for ascents of Fitz Roy (3,375 m) is **Campamento Río Blanco** (see above). Other peaks include Cerro Torre (3,102 m), Torre Egger (2,900 m), Cerro Solo (2,121 m), Poincenot (3,002 m), Guillaumet (2,579 m), Saint-Exupery (2,558 m), Aguja Bífida (2,394 m) and Cordón

Border with Chile

Three crossings provide access to Puerto Natales and Torres del Paine. They are open, subject to weather conditions, 24 hrs daily from September to May and 0700-2300 daily at other times. Most buses use the Río Turbio crossing but Cancho Carrera is quicker if you're driving to the national park from El Calafate. Note that Argentine pesos cannot be exchanged in Torres del Paine.

Paso Cancha Carrera 129 km west of La Esperanza and 42 km north of Río Turbio. The most northerly of the crossings is the most convenient (though desolate) crossing between Argentina and Torres del Paine but it is often closed in winter. On the Chilean side the road continues to Cerro Castillo, where it meets the good ripio road that runs between Puerto Natales (65 km south) and the national park. **Argentine customs and immigration** ⓘ *at Cancha Carrera, 2 km east of the border*, is fast and friendly. **Chilean customs and immigration** ⓘ *at Cerro Castillo, 7 km west of the border, open 0800-2200.*

Paso Dorotea 14 km south of Río Turbio, 27 km from Puerto Natales. On the Chilean side the road runs south for 11km to join Route 9 between Puerto Natales and Punta Arenas. **Chilean customs and immigration** ⓘ*2 km from the border, open winter 0800-2400, for summer times, check in Puerto Natales.*

Paso Casas Viejas 33 km south of Río Turbio via 28 de Noviembre. On the Chilean side, the road continues west to join Route 9 east of Puerto Natales at Km14. **Argentine customs and immigration** ⓘ *open winter 0800-2200, summer 0800-2400.* **Chilean customs and immigration** ⓘ *1 km from the border, open winter 0800-2200, summer 0800-2400.*

Adela (2,938 m): most of these are for very experienced climbers only, as is the **Campo de Hielo Continental** (Continental Icefield), which marks the border with Chile (no access from Chile). The best time to climb is mid-February to the end of March; November and December are very windy and the winter months are extremely cold. Permits for climbing are available at the national park information office and guides are available in El Chaltén; ask Sr Guerra about hiring mules to carry equipment.

Around El Chaltén

The main attraction here is clearly the trekking around Fitz Roy, but there is also stunning virgin landscape to explore outside the park, around the **Lago del Desierto**, 37 km north. The long skinny lake is fiord-like and surrounded by forests. It's reached by unpaved Route 23, which leads along the Río de las Vueltas via **Laguna Condor**, where flamingos can be seen. A *mirador* at the end of the road gives fine views over the lake and a path runs along the east side of the lake to its northern tip, from where a trail leads west along the valley of the Río Diablo to **Laguna Diablo**, and north to Lago O'Higgins in Chile, see page 313.

En route to the lake is *estancia* **El Pilar** in a stunning position with views of Fitz Roy. Accommodation is available here (see page 199) but you can also visit for tea or use it as an excellent base for trekking up **Río Blanco** or **Río Eléctrico**.

Lago Viedma to the south of El Chaltén can also be explored by boat. The trips usually pass Glaciar Viedma, with the possibility of ice trekking on some excursions. ›› *Activities and tours, p206.*

Towards Torres del Paine ›› *p 199-209*

From El Calafate

Tof Routes 11, 40 and 5 to **La Esperanza** (165 km), where there's fuel, a campsite and a large but expensive *confitería*. From La Esperanza, *ripio* Route 7 heads west along the valley of the Río Coyle towards the border crossing at Cancha Carrera (see below). A shorter route (closed in winter) misses Esperanza and goes via El Cerrito direct to **Estancia Tapi Aike**, T02966 420092, bvdesing@fibertel.com.ar. ›› *Transport, p208.*

Río Turbio

A charmless place you're most likely to visit en route to or from Torres del Paine in Chile. The site of Argentina's largest coalfield hasn't recovered from the recent depression hitting the industry. It has a cargo railway connecting it with Punta Loyola, and visitors can see Mina 1, where the first mine was opened. There's a small ski centre nearby, **Valdelén**, which has six pistes and is ideal for beginners, also scope for cross-country skiing between early June and late September. There is tourist information in the municipal building on San Martín.

Sleeping

El Calafate *p189, map p201*

L **Kosten Aike**, *Gob Moyano 1243, T02902-492424, www.kostenaike.com.ar*. A special place, relaxed and yet stylish with large elegant rooms, king sized beds throughout, jacuzzi and gym. The tranquil restaurant is open to non residents (US$10 for 3 courses) and has an excellent chef, there's a cosy bar with a wood fire, and a garden. The staff are extremely attentive and speak English. Recommended.

L **Los Alamos**, *Moyano y Bustillo, T02902-491145, www.posadalosalamos.com*. Located in 2 separate buildings, extremely comfortable, with charming rooms, beautifully decorated and equipped, good service, lovely gardens and without doubt the best restaurant in town, La Posta. Recommended.

AL **El Quijote**, *Gob Gregores 1181, T02902-491017, www.hieos.com.ar*. This spacious, modern hotel is Italian-owned and designed. An elegant entrance lounge, and very tasteful comfortable rooms with excellent bathrooms, all beautifully decorated with traditional touches, TV, phone and minibar. Great restaurant. Italian and English spoken. Recommended.

AL **Hostería Kau-Yatún**, *25 de Mayo (10 blocks from town centre), T02902-491259, F491260, www.kauyatun.com*. A comfortable old estancia house offering many facilities, a restaurant and *asados*, and horse riding tours with guides.

A **Michelangelo**, *Espora y Gob Moyano, T02902-491045, michelangelohotel@cotecal.com.ar*. Quiet and welcoming, modern and stylish in design, with a really excellent restaurant, US$10 for 2 courses, such as hare, steak, and ink squid ravioli. All rooms have TV, bath and minibar, breakfast included. Recommended.

B **ACA Hostería El Calafate**, *1 de Mayo 50, T02902-491004, F491027*. Modern, with good views from a slightly elevated position above the town centre, and open all year. Good value.

C **Amado**, *Libertador 1072, T02902-491134, familiagomez@cotecal.com.ar*. Breakfast is included; all rooms have bath TV and phone. The décor is clean and plain; functional but nothing special.

C **Hospedaje Sir Thomas**, *Cte. Espora 257, T02902-492220, www.sirthomas.com.ar*. A modern house with comfortable and spacious wood-lined rooms, with private bathrooms, breakfast $5 extra.

C **Vientos del Sur**, *a little way up the hill at Calle 54 2317, T02902-493563, www.vientosdelsur.com*. One of the most welcoming places in town, worth the short taxi ride for the views over the lake, comfortable modern rooms with bath and TV, and the kindest attention you could wish for. Recommended.

D **Cabañas Nevis**, *Libertador 1696, T02902-493180, www.cabanasnevis.com.ar*. Well-spaced, A-shaped *cabañas* for 5 and 8, some with lake views. Great value.

C **del Norte**, *Los Gauchos 813, T02902-491117*. Open all year, kitchen facilities, comfortable, owner organizes tours.

E **Hospedaje Alejandra**, *Cte. Espora 60, T02902-491328*. Great value in this homely place, rooms with shared bath but no breakfast – you can make it yourself, very friendly owner. Also E pp, one flat for 5, equipped with TV. Recommended.

Youth hostels

B-F **Hostels del Glaciar**, *Los Pioneros 251 , T/F02902-491243 (reservations in Buenos Aires T/F03488-469416, off season only); and Av Libertador, T02902 491792,* www.glaciar.com. The most appealing budget option. Discount for ISIC or IYHA members, open mid-Sep to end May. **Hostel Pioneros** is the original and best hostel in town (often recommended), with a whole range of accommodation for all budgets; shared dorms (F pp), double rooms with shared bath (C double) and more luxurious double rooms with bathrooms (B double). Many languages are spoken by the friendly and helpful staff, there are lots of bathrooms, and also internet access and kitchen facilities. The cosy restaurant *Punto de Encuentro* has a good value fixed menu, and vegetarian options. They also run the much loved *Alternative Glaciar Tour* (see below), and organize a booking service for Navimag and hotels and transport throughout Patagonia, and run free shuttle service from bus terminal. The newly-opened **Hostel Libertador** is of the same standard. Both are highly recommended. Book in advance in summer.

E **Albergue Buenos Aires**, *Buenos Aires 296, 200 m from terminal, T02902-491147, hospbuenos aires@cotecal.com.ar*. Comfortable, kitchen facilities, helpful, hot showers, luggage store.

E pp **Calafate Hostel**, *Gob Moyano 1226, 300 m from bus terminal, T02902-492450, www.interpatagonia.com/hostelspatagonia*. The other big hostel, this is a huge rangey place, with well-built dorms for 4-6 with shared bath, and C double rooms with private bath. Also has G pp *refugio* space for those with sleeping bags, kitchen facilities, internet access and a huge lively sitting area. Friendly staff can arrange tours

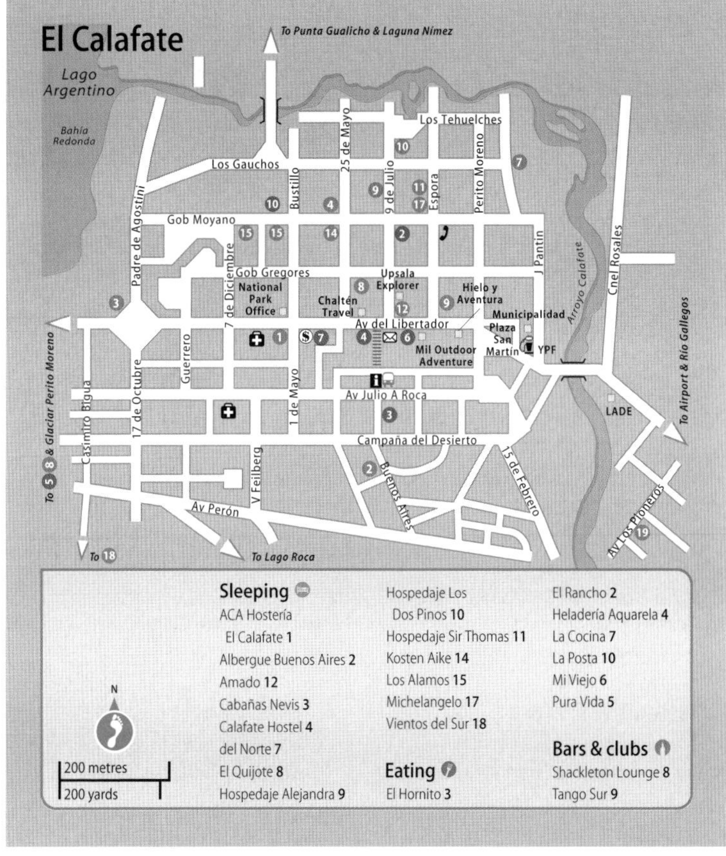

and accommodation in the sister hostal **Albergue Patagonia** in El Chaltén. Book a month ahead for Jan and Feb. They also run the helpful travel agency **Chaltén Travel**.

E **Hospedaje Los Dos Pinos**, *9 de Julio 358, T02902-491271*. A popular place offering the whole range of accommodation, from dorms, rather cramped (E), cheap cabañas for 7 (C), tiny little studio flats for 2 (B) and a campsite (F), all sharing a nice friendly TV room where you can cook. The helpful owner also arranges tours to glacier.

Around El Calafate *p191*

Estancias

LL **Estancia Alta Vista**, *33 km west of El Calafate, T02902-491247, altavista@cotecal.com.ar*. The area's most expensive, absurdly exclusive. An attractive place in lovely gardens, with excellent cuisine and wines and good service.

L **El Galpón del Glaciar**, formerly **Estancia Alice**, *22 km west of El Calafate, T/F02902-491793, or contact in Buenos Aires T011- 4312 7206, www.estanciaalice.com.ar*. Lovely house with views of Lago Argentino. Very comfortable accommodation, 16 rooms. Sheep shearing, birdwatching and horse riding. Trips to the Perito Moreno glacier and Cerro Frias. All meals and excursion to glacier included, US$240 pp.

E pp **La Leona**, *106 km north of Calafate near east end of Lago Viedma, T02902-491418, info@estancias desantacruz.com*. A simple *estancia* in wide open country, popular with anglers.

Parque Nacional Los Glaciares: Lago Argentino *p191*

LL **Los Notros**, *Perito Moreno Glacier, T/F02902-499510, T011-4814 3934, www.losnotros.com*. Luxurious accommodation in spacious, well designed rooms with wonderful views of the Perito Moreno glacier, where you can walk, hike, trek, and ride horses. With breakfast and free transfers to the glacier *passarelas* included, but transport from airport and other meals extra.

L **Estancia Helsingfors**, *T/F02966-420719, T/F011-4824 4623/3634, www.helsingfors.com*. A fabulous place in a splendid position on Lago Viedma, 150 km from El Calafate, with stylish rooms, a welcoming lounge, delicious food, and excursions directly from there to glaciers and to Laguna Azul, by horse or trek, plus boat trips. Recommended.

A pp **Estancia Nibepo Aike**, *in the far south of the park on the shores of Brazo Sur of Lago Argentino, T02902-436010, www.estanciasdesantacruz.com/nibepoaike*. Open Oct-April for horse riding, expeditions, fishing, boat tours to glacier, recommended.

Camping

Bahía Escondida, *7 km east of the glacier*. The only one with all facilities, fireplaces, hot showers and shop. Crowded in summer, US$3pp.

Correntoso, *10 km east of the glacier*. An unmarked site with no facilities but a great location. No fires. US$2pp.

Lago Roca, *50 km from El Calafate, T02902-499500*, beautifully situated, US$3 pp, bike hire, restaurant/*confitería*.

El Chaltén *p196, map p201*

The tourist office website has a full list, www.elchalten.com.

AL **Hostería El Puma**, *Lionel Terray 545, T02962-493095, www.elchalten.com/elpuma*. The most desirable place in town, set a little apart, and with splendid views up the valley. Welcoming, stylish, comfortable rooms and plush bathrooms. Transfers and a big American breakfast are included. They can also arrange tours through their excellent agency **Fitz Roy Expeditions** (see Activities and tours, below). Recommended.

AL **Hostería Posada Lunajuim**, *Trevisán s/n, T/F02962-493047, www.elchalten.com/lunajuim*. Stylish, relaxed and welcoming place, with comfortable rooms (thick duvets on the beds!) with bathrooms, a lovely big lounge with wood fire, full American breakfast is included. Run by a very friendly family, charming hosts. Recommended.

A **Fitz Roy Inn**, *T02962-493062, caltur@cotecal.com.ar*. An overpriced place that seems to have stopped making an effort, this has pleasant but small rooms, often filled with package tour clients. Breakfast included. Also travel agency Cal Tur.

C **Hospedaje La Base**, *Lago de Desierto 97, T02962-493031*. A friendly little place, has basic double rooms with bath rooms. For 3 or 4 (E). Tiny kitchen for guests to use, self service breakfast included, and a great video lounge.

C **Northofagus**, *Hensen s/n T02962-493087, www.elchalten.com/northofagus*. A small cosy bed and breakfast, with simple double rooms with shared bath, including breakfast. Welcoming and good value.

Youth hostels

E **Albergue Patagonia**, *T/F02962-493019, www.elchalten.com/patagonia*. Sister establishment of Alberque Calafate in El Calafate, this is the most appealing of several hostels in El Chaltén. It is IYHA-affiliated, and a small friendly place, with kitchen, video room, bike hire, laundry. Helpful information on Chaltén and excursions to Lago del Desierto. Next door is their restaurant *Fuegia*, with Patagonian dishes, curries and vegetarian food.

E **Albergue Rancho Grande**, *San Martín s/n, T02962-493005, www.elchalten.com/ranchogrande*. HI-affiliated, in a great position at the end of town with good open views, and a welcoming attractive restaurant and lounge. This accommodates huge numbers of trekkers in rooms for 4, with shared bathrooms, and is well run, with friendly staff who speak several languages between them. Breakfast and sheets extra. There are also C private double rooms, breakfast extra, and one family room, with private bath. Recommended. Reservations can also be made in the sister businesses in El Calafate: Calafate Hostel and Chaltén Travel.

E **Cóndor de los Andes**, *Av Río de las Vueltas y Halvorsen, T02962-493101, www.condorde losandes.com*. Friendly, small and modern, with nice little rooms for 6 with bathrooms en suite, sheets included, breakfast US$2 extra. Washing service, library, kitchen. Quiet atmosphere, calm place. Recommended.

Parque Nacional de los Glaciares: Cerro Fitz Roy *p194*

There are campsites in the national park at Confluencia, Poincenot, Capri and Lago Toro. Río Blanco is only for climbers with prior permission arranged. Campsites have no services but all have latrines, apart from Toro. A gas/alcohol stove is essential for camping, as fires are prohibited everywhere in the National Park. See also Hike right, p197.

Camping Piedra del Fraile, *on Rio Electrico, just north of the park boundary*. It is privately owned and has *cabañas* with hot showers (E pp) as well as camping (US$5pp).

Around El Chaltén *p191*

There is a campsite at the southern end of Lago del Desierto and *refugios* at its northern end and at Laguna Diablo.

L **Hotel Lago del Desierto**, *T493010, www.lagodeldesierto.com*. Sleep 5, kitchen, also camping US$6 per person. Also has 3 cabañas on the shore of Lago del Desierto. Recomended. Bookings through *Hotel Lago del Desierto* in Chaltén.

B **El Pilar**, *T/F02962-493002, www.hosteriael pilar.com.ar*. A special place to stay a little way out of town, this simple country house in a spectacular setting on the confluence of Ríos Blanco and de las Vueltas, with views of Fitz Roy. A chance to sample the simple life with access to the less visited northern part of the national park and beyond. Spacious rooms, great food, recommended. Owner Miguel Pagani is an experienced mountain guide, and takes individuals and groups on individually tailored trekking tours.

Towards Torres del Paine *p199*

In La Esperanza, **Restaurant La Esperanza** has bunk beds, with bath. There are also 6-person *cabañas* at the YPF service station.

C **De La Frontera**, *4 km from Rio Turbio, Paraje Mina 1, T02962-421979.* The most recommended option.

C **Hostería Capipe**, *Dufour, 9 km from Río Turbio, T02962-482930, www.hosteriacapipe.com.ar.*

Eating

El Calafate *p189, map p201*

For cheap meals, there are two lively, packed places on the main street, *Libertador*, with good atmosphere and cheapish food: **Rick's Café**, *No 1105*, serving *tenedor libre* for US$5, and **Casablanca**, *Libertador and 25 de Mayo.* A jolly and welcoming place, serving omelettes, hamburgers and vegetarian food too, US$4 for steak and chips.

ΨΨΨ **La Posta** The restaurant at *Los Alamos Hotel* is undoubtedly the best in town. With elegant décor, slightly reminiscent of a traditional mountain lodge and a really superb menu, Patagonian lamb and rose hip sauce, king crab-stuffed raviolis, with a refined, but definitely not stuffy, atmosphere, and very friendly staff. Pricey but worth it. US$12 for 2 courses.

ΨΨΨ **Hotel Michelangelo** The restaurant *Espora y Gob Moyano* is excellent, US$10 for 2 courses, such as hare, steak and ink squid ravioli.

ΨΨ **El Hornito**, *Buenos Aires 155, just above the bus terminal.* A welcoming intimate place serving excellent pizzas and pastas.

ΨΨ **Pura Vida**. Recommended, for a relaxed place to eat well, with comfortable sofas, homemade Argentine food, lots of vegetarian options, and a lovely warm atmosphere with lake view.

Ψ **El Rancho**, *9 de Julio y Gob Moyano.* A tiny, cosy and popular place for big cheap pizzas.

Ψ **La Cocina**, *No 1245.* Pizzería, pancakes, pasta, salads, in cosy warm atmosphere.

Ψ **Mi Viejo**, *No 1111.* Popular *parrilla*, US$6 for *tenedor libre.*

Ice cream parlours

Heladería Aquarela, *No 1177.* You'll be glad to hear that it does get hot enough for ice cream, and the best is served up here – try the delicious (and beautifully coloured) *calafate.*

El Chaltén *p196, map p205*

ΨΨ **Restaurant Fuegia**, *San Martín.* Serves good food, with Patagonian dishes and some rather more imaginative options, such as curries and vegetarian food too.

ΨΨ **Ruca Mahuida**, *Lionel Terray s/n.* Widely regarded as the best restaurant in El Chaten, for imaginative and carefully prepared food.

Ψ **Domo Blanca**, *Costanera y D'Agostini.* Makes superb home made ice cream.

Ψ **Josh Aike** Excellent *confitería*, delicious homemade food, in a beautiful building. Recommended.

Ψ **Las Lengas**, *Viedma y Güemes.* Oposite the tourist office, this place offers plentiful meals, basic pastas and meat dishes. US$3 for 2 courses, one of the cheaper options.

Ψ **Pangea**, *Lago del Desiero 273 y San Martín.* Open for lunch and dinner, drinks and coffee, in calm comfortable surroundings with good music, a varied menu, from pastas to steak, trout and pizzas US$3 to US$7. Recommended.

Ψ **Patagonicus**, *Güemes y Madsen.* A lovely warm cosy stylish place with salads, home made pastas and fabulous pizzas for 2, US$4-7. Great family photos of mountain climbers on the walls. Open from midday to midnight. Recommended.

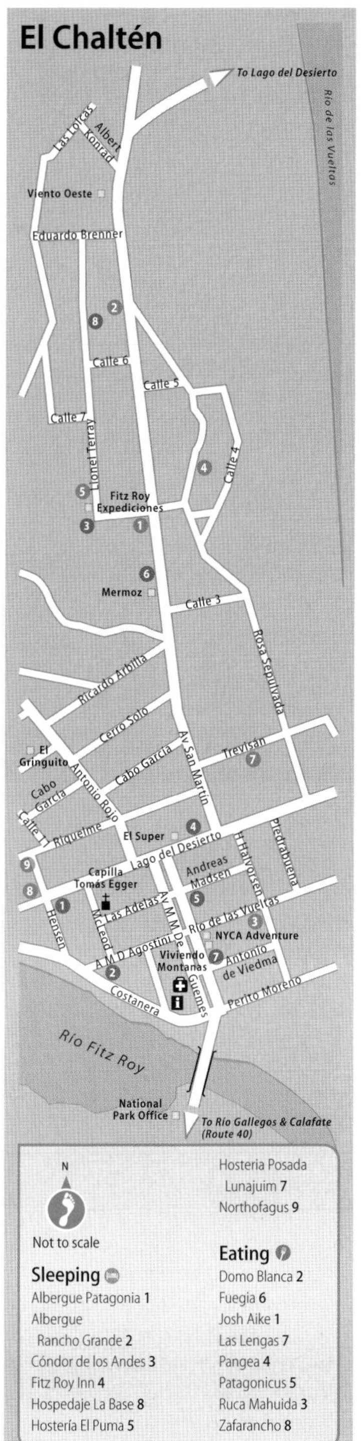

Zafarancho, *behind Rancho Grande*. A great bar-restaurant, serving a good range and reasonably priced. Also equipment rental and tours, see below.

Bars and nightclubs

El Calafate *p189, map p201*

Shackleton Lounge, *on the outskirts of town (US$1 in taxi)*, is highly recommended for a drink. It's a great place to relax, with lovely views of the lake, old photos of Shackleton, a great atmosphere and good music.

Tango Sur, *9 de julio 265, T02902-491550*. Live music and a tango show (US$5, Tue and Sun at 2030 and 2300), in a charming old-style house.

Festivals

El Calafate *p189, map p201*

There are couple of festivals worth seeing: people flock to the rural show on **15 Feb**, Lago Argentino Day, and camp out with live music, dancing and *asados*. There are also displays of horsemanship and *asados* on Día de la Tradición, **10 Nov**.

Shopping

El Calafate *p189, map p201*

All along Libertador there are souvenir shops selling the inevitable T-shirts and postcards, plus useful hats, fleeces and gloves, so that you can prepare yourself for those chilly boat rides to see the glacier. There are lots of fine quality handicrafts from all over Argentina – look out for Mapuche weavings and good woollen items. There are handicraft stalls on Libertador at around 1200. Everything is relatively expensive by Argentine standards.

Alas, *9 de Julio 59*. Supermarket with a wide choice.

Ferretería Chuar, *Libertador 1242*. The only place selling white gas for camping.

Los Glaciares, *Libertador y Perito Moreno*. Camping supplies.

El Chaltén *p196, map p205*

There are several small shops here, all are expensive and have little fresh food. There is a wider selection of goods in El Calafate.

El Gringuito, *Av Antonio Rojo*. The best choice for food. Fuel is available.

El Super, *Lago del Desierto y Av Güemes, T493039*. Rents and sells camping and climbing equipment, as well as maps, postcards, books and handicrafts.

Viento Oeste, *Av San Martín s/n, (at the end of town on the way to Camping Madsen) T02962-493021*. Handicrafts and equipment hire: tents, sleeping bags and everything else you'll need. Can also arrange mountain guides.

Zafarancho Restaurant, *Lionel Terray s/n T493093, www.chaltenoutdoor.com.ar /elranchito* For renting tents, good sleeping bags, heaters, cooking set, also general store.

Activities and tours

El Calafate *p189, map p201*

Ballooning

Hotel Kau Yatun, (details above). Organizes balloon trips over El Calafate and Lago Argentino, US$38 for 2½ hrs, US$65 for 5 hrs.

Birdwatching

Cecilia Scarafoni, *T02902-493196, ecowalks@cotecal.com.ar*. Expert-led birdwatching walks to Laguna Nimenez, lasting 2 hrs, US$4, Mon-Sat.

Boat trips

Fernández Campbell, *Av Libertador 867, T02902-491155*. The main operator for trips on Lago Argentino to both the Perito Moreno and Upsala glaciers.

Fishing

Fishing & Adventure, *Roca 2192, T/F02902-493050*. Offers fishing excursions, from half-day to 3-day expeditions.

Horse riding

Cabalgata en Patagonia, *Libertador 3600, T02902-493203, 156 20935, cabalgataen patagonia@cotecal.com.ar* US$12 for 2 hours, US$60 for full day, including lunch. Treks offered to Bahía Redonda, also 5-day excursion in Parque Nacional Los Glaciares.

Ice trekking

Hielo y Aventura, *Av Libertador 935, T02902-491053, hieloyaventura@cotecal.com.ar*, offers walking excursions through lovely lakeside *lenga* forests, followed by 90 mins 'minitrekking' on the Perito Moreno glacier with crampons (supplied and fitted). It's enormous fun (and not too physically challenging). Recommended for a close-up experience of the glacier. US$50.

Mountain bikes

Bike Way, *Espora 20, T02902-492180*. US$6 per hr, US$25 per day.

Rafting

Nonthue Aventura, *Libertador 1177, T02902-491179*. Rafting on the Río Santa Cruz, 0800, 1500, 4-5 hrs, US$30 without transport, US$40 with transport.

Offroading

Mil Outdoor Adventure, *Av Libertador 1029, T02902-491437, 491446, www.loslgaciares.com/miloutoors*. Offers a variety of excursions in 4WD vehicles, with excellent opportunities to visit otherwise inaccessible parts of the Patagonian steppe, short-trip US$40 per person, long-trip US$75 per person, recommended.

Tours and treks

Most agencies charge the same rates for excursions: to the **Perito Moreno Glacier** US$20; to **Lago Roca**, a full-day including lunch at *Estancia Anita*, US$30; horseriding to **Gualichó** caves, 2 hrs, US$20.

Albergue del Glaciar, *Los Pioneros 255, T/F02902-491243 www.glaciar.com.* This tour operator offers the best glacier trip, the 'Alternative Tour to Moreno Glacier'. It goes out by a different route, passing the Estancia Anita, and includes lots of information on the landscape and wildllife as you travel along the old road to the glacier. There's some light walking to approach the glacier along the lake shore, followed by the boat trip, to see it up close. US$25. Recommended constantly. They also do a great 2-day trip to El Chaltén, 'Supertrekking en Chaltén', a 2-day hiking trip, featuring the best treks in the Fitzroy massif, including camping and ice trekking. Highly recommended.

Chaltén Travel, *Libertador 1174, T02902-492212*. The most helpful, with huge range of tours: glaciers, *estancias*, trekking and trips to El Chaltén, also sells tickets along the Ruta 40 to Los Antiguos. English spoken. Highly recommended.

Hielos, *El Quijote hotel, Gob Gregores 1181, T02902-491017, www.patagonia adventure.com, www.hielos.com.ar*. Runs boat trips in El Chaltén, as well as flights from El Calafate over the glaciers.

Leutz Turismo, *Libertador 1341, T02902-492316, leutzturismo@cotecal.com.ar*. Daily excursion to Lago Roca 1000-1800, US$20 pp, plus US$11 for lunch at **Estancia Quien Sabe**, where strawberries and walnuts are grown.

Mundo Austral, *Libertador 1114, T02902-492365, F492116*. Offers all kinds of tours to the park and cheaper trips to the glaciers, with helpful bilingual guide Jorge Mendez, and can also books bus travel.

Upsala Explorer, *9 de Julio 69, T02902-491133, 491034, www.upsalaexplorer.com.ar*. Runs a truly spectacular (if pricey) tour to the Upsala glacier, US$100 (see p193). Bus transfers from El Calafate are not included but can be booked through the same company.

El Chaltén p196, map p205

Adventure tours and treks

Fitz Roy Expediciones, *Lionel Terray 212, (next to Hostería El Puma) T/F02962-493017, www.elchalten.com/fitzroy* This company is by far the best and most experienced, and are very professional. Owned by mountaineer and guide Alberto del Castillo. They organize trekking, rock climbing courses and ice-climbing courses (one day, US$38), adventure expeditions, including two-day ascents of Cerro Eléctrico and Cerro Solo (US$175pp), and 8-day trekking expeditions on the Campo de Hielo. Also organizes a circuit of the challenging terrain around Estancia El Pilar, ideal for everyone from kids to adults, including kayaking, mountain biking, rappelling, rope bridges, climbing. Great fun, safe, and well organized.

Viviendo Montanas, *De Agostini 141, T/F02962-493068, www.vivmont.com.ar, info@vivmont.com.ar*. A young company, organizing climbing schools and ice climbing expeditions (make sure you take sleeping bag and equipment), guides for trekking, too.

NYCA Adventure, *Av Güemes y Río de las Vueltas, T02962-493122, www.nyca.com.ar*. Organizes a great adventure circuit in the challenging terrain around Estancia El Pilar, ideal for everyone from kids to adults, including kayaking, mountain biking, rappel, rope bridges, climbing. Great fun, safe, and well-organized.

Boat trips

Chaltén Travel, *Av Gümes and Lago del Desierto, T493022*. Runs daily boat trips on Lago Viedma in summer on board *La Mariana II* departing from El Chaltén at 1030, 1330 and1630, 2 hrs, US$20. See also under El Calafate tours above.

Mermoz, *San Martín 493, T02962-493098*. Boat trips across Laguna del Desierto, including bus transfer and optional trekking. English spoken, helpful.

Viedma Discovery, *Av Güemes s/n, T02962-493103/493110, www.elchalten.com/viedmadiscovery*. Boat trips along Lago Viedma to see the Glaciar Viedma, including informative chat;

transfers US$10 extra. Also a good full day's trip along Lago Viedma, with ice trekking on Glaciar Viedma, US$15 plus transfer optional extra.

Horse riding

Guides for horseback treks include **El Relincho**, T02962-493007, and **Rodolfo Guerra**, T493020, who also hires out mules for climbing expeditions.

Transport

El Calafate *p189, map p201*

Air

El Calafate's international airport, *T02902-491220*, is 22 km east of town, and has a tourist information desk *T02902- 491230*. Aerolíneas Argentinas flies daily to/from **Buenos Aires**, with many more flights in summer. LADE (*Julio Roca 1004, T02902-491262, ladecalafate@cotecal.com.ar*) flies twice a week to **Río Gallegos** and **Río Grande**, and once a week to **Perito Moreno**. Aerovias Dap, finanzas@aeroviasdap.cl, flies to **Puerto Natales** in Chile daily in summer only (Oct-Mar). Airport charge for departing passengers is US$18.

Bus

The terminal is on Roca, 1 block up steep stairs from Libertador.

Long-distance To **Ushuaia** take bus to **Río Gallegos**, with Taqsa or Interlagos, several daily, US$11. To **El Chaltén**, with Cal-Tur or Chalten Travel, *Libertador 1174, T492212*, 3 daily, 4 hrs. To **Perito Moreno** and **Los Antiguos**, contact Chaltén Travel.

To **Bariloche** along Ruta 40 with Overland Patagonia, *www.overlandpatagonia.com*, 4 days via the Perito Moreno national park, Cueva de Las Manos, Estancia Melike, Río Mayo and Fitz Roy, US$95 plus accommodation at US$5 per day; bookings in El Calafate from Albergue del Glaciar, *T02902-491243, info@glaciar.com*.

To Chile To **Puerto Natales**, daily

with either Cootra *T02902-491444*, or Bus Sur *T02902-491631*, US$16, advance booking recommended (tedious border crossing). Bus Sur (Tue, Sat 0800) and Zaahj (Wed, Fri, Sun 0800) also run to Puerto Natales via **Cerro Castillo**, where you can pick up a bus to **Torres del Paine** in summer. Take your passport with you when booking a bus ticket to Chile.

Car hire

Adventure Rent a Car, *Libertador 290, T02902-492595, adventurerentacar@cotecal.com.ar*
Europcar, *Libertador 1711, T02902-493606, www.carletti.com.ar* Prices start at US$52 per day for a small car including insurance.

Taxi

To **Río Gallegos**, 4 hrs, US$100 irrespective of number of passengers, up to 5 people.

Perito Moreno glacier *p191*

The cheapest way to get to the glacier is on the regular daily **bus** services run by

Taqsa *T02902-491843*, and **Interlagos** *T02902-492197*, to the car park above the walkways. Many agencies in El Calafate (see Activities and tours, above) also run minibus **tours** (park entry not included) leaving 0800 and returning 1800, giving you three hours at the glacier; the return ticket is also valid if you come back next day (student discount available). See Albergue del Glaciar, above, for an extended alternative itinerary. **Boat** trips for up to 60 passengers are run by Fernandez Campbell (see above). 'Safari Náutico' offers the best views, US$10 per person, 1 hr. Boats leave from the tourist pier signposted from the carpark in Parque Nacional los Glaciares, bus travel is included. Out of season, trips to the glacier are difficult to arrange, but you can gather a party and hire a **taxi** (*remise* taxis T02902-491745/492005). These will charge US$45 for four passengers, round trip.

Upsala glacier *p193*

Tour boats usually run daily. The main operator is Fernández Campbell (see above) who charges US$25, including transfer bus and park entry fees. The bus departs at 0730 from El Calafate for Punta Bandera, with time allowed for lunch at the restaurant (not included, so take your own food) near the Lago Onelli track. The return bus to El Calafate is at 1930. A more expensive but also more spectacular trip is offered by Upsala Explorer, see Tour operators, above, and p193.

El Chaltén *p196, map p205*

Bus

In summer, buses fill quickly, so book ahead. The following are high-season services; they are less frequent in winter.

To **El Calafate**, daily, 4 hrs, US$7 one way, with Chaltén Travel, *T02962-493005*, and Caltur, *T02962-493062*. To **Los Antiguos** along Ruta 40, Itinerarios y Travesías, *T02962-493088*, runs overnight services on even dates (ie 2nd, 4th, 6th), including a stop at Cueva de las Manos in the early morning, returning south on odd dates (ie 3rd, 5th, 7th, etc), currently during summer only, but contact them to check about other times of year; Chaltén Travel, makes trips north on odd dates, returning on even dates. Both agencies charge US$40 single, bike US$5. Tickets are available from *Perito Moreno 152, T02962-493088*, and from Albergue Patagonia, *Av San Martín 495 T02962-493088, alpatagonia@ infovia.com.ar*. Book in advance.

Overland Patagonia does trips to **Bariloche** in 4 days, staying at *estancias* and visiting Cueva de las Manos.

Río Turbio *p199*

Bus

To **Puerto Natales**, 1hr, US$2, several daily with Cootra, *Tte del Castillo 01, T421448, cootra@oyikil.com.ar*; Bus Sur, *Baquedano 534, Pto Natales, T+56(0)61-411859, www.turismozaahj.co.cl*, and Lagoper, *Av de Los Mineros 262, T411831*. To **El Calafate**, same companies, also Expreso Pingüino and Taqsa, daily, US$7, 4½ hrs. To **Río Gallegos**, 4 hrs, US$5.

Directory

El Calafate *p189, map p201*

Banks You can change money at Thaler *Libertador 1311, T02902-493245, www.cambio-thaler.com*, but it's best to take cash as high commission is charged. There are ATMs at Banco de la Provincia de Santa Cruz, *Libertador 1285*, and at Banco de Tierra del Fuego, *25 de Mayo 34*. **Post office** *Libertador 1133*. **Telephone** Open Calafate, *Libertador 996*, is a huge *locutorio* and also has 20 fast internet computers, US$2 per hr, open 0800-2400.

Santiago

Introduction

If you are flying into Chile, you will probably arrive in Santiago. It is unlikely to prove a highlight of your Patagonian adventures – it's 1000km away for a start – but it's a good place to acclimatise and get over any jet lag. In a hollow surrounded by mountains with peaks over 5,000 m, no one can deny that the Chilean capital has a dramatic setting.

Santiago is a vibrant, progressive city. Its many parks, excellent museums, glittering high-rises and boutiques, not to mention ebullient nightlife, burst with possibilities. Santiago has grown to become the sixth largest city in South America, as well as the political, economic and cultural capital of Chile. But life isn't easy for everyone here. Many people, particularly those originally from rural areas, live in appalling *villas misérias* on the city's outskirts.

The region near the capital can be seen as a microcosm of the country as a whole. Coastal resorts are less than two hours away, and the city is within easy reach of the best ski resorts in South America, which are great spots for weekend hikes in summer. Meanwhile, the area south of Santiago is perhaps the best wine-producing area in Chile. Autumn is a particularly good time to visit the vineyards.

Ratings

Landscape
★★

Chillin'
★

Activities
★★★

Culture
★★★★

Costs
$$$$$

Ins and outs » p231

Getting there

Both international and domestic flights use **Aeropuerto Arturo Merino Benitez** ⓘ *26 km northwest, at Pudahue, international information T02-6901900/6018758, flight information T02-6763149*. It is a modern, safe and efficient terminal, with banks and ATMs, fast food outlets, tourist information with an accommodation booking service, a *casa de cambio* and car hire offices. Left luggage is US$2.50 per item per day for a maximum of 60 days. Outside customs there are kiosks for bus and taxi companies serving Santiago. » *For flights, see Essentials, p20 and p23.*

Frequent **bus** services between the airport and the city centre are operated by **Tur Bus** ⓘ *every 30 mins, US$2.50*; and **Centropuerto** ⓘ *T02-6019883, every 10 mins, first from centre 0600, last from airport 2230, US$2*. All airport buses stop at the new terminal at Metro Pajaritos, where buses also leave for the coast. En route to the airport, the buses also pick up at Estación Central and Terminal Santiago. Do not confuse these buses with the bus marked 'Aeropuerto' (these are yellow), which stops 2 km short of the airport. **Minibus** services between the airport and hotels or other addresses in the city (US$5 to/from the city centre, US$7 to/from Las Condes) are operated by **Transfer**, T02-7777707; **Delfos**,

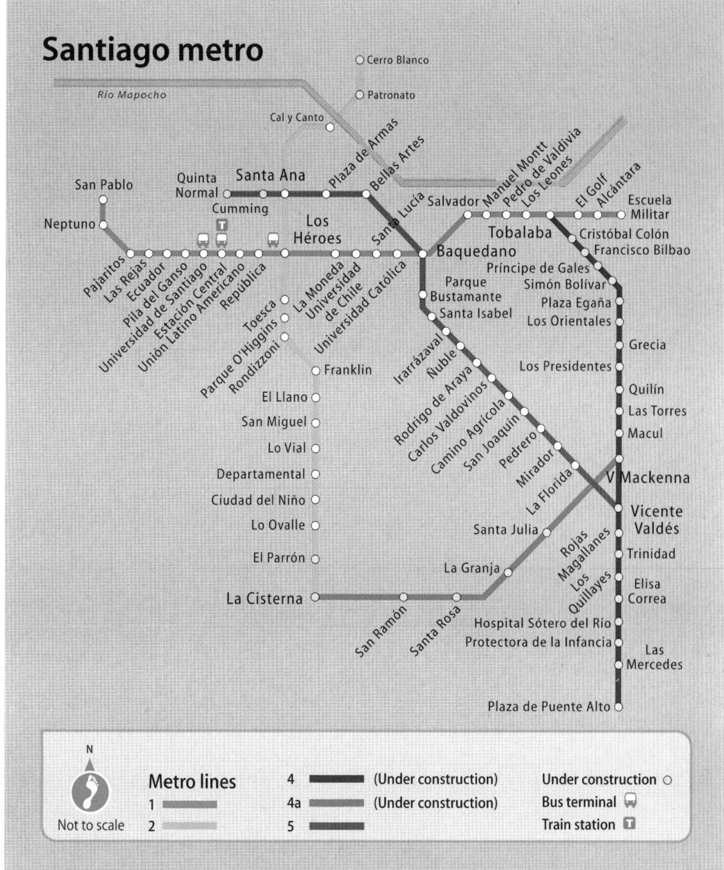

Playing it safe

Like all large cities, Santiago has problems of theft. Pickpockets and bagsnatchers operate in the central area, mostly on the metro, around the Plaza de Armas, in Barrio Brasil, near Cerro Santa Lucía and around the restaurants in Bellavista, and can easily be avoided with common sense. The biggest risk is in unwittingly entering a dangerous *barrio* away from the centre; avoid Pudahuel in the west, Conchalí in the north and Macul and La Pintana in the south. At night, take a public bus (*micro*) for safety in numbers or call for a radio taxi.

T02-6011111; **Turismo Bar-C** and **Navett**, T02-6956868, and should be booked the previous day. **Taxis** to/from centre cost around US$17, to/from Providencia US$20; agree the fare beforehand. There is a **taxi** office inside the international terminal.

Long-distance **buses** arrive at one of four terminals, all located close to each other, along Avenida Libertador Bernardo O'Higgins, Universidad de Santiago metro. The **train** station is at O'Higgins 3322. ▸▸ *For information on long-distance services, see Essentials, p24.*

Getting around

The city's main avenue, O'Higgins, is almost always referred to as the Alameda, and Plaza Baquedano is almost always known as Plaza Italia (in both instances, this book follows suit). Although parts of the centre can be explored on foot, you will need to master the city's fast but crowded three-line **metro** system. (A new Line 4 linking the south and east of the city will not be completed before the end of 2005.) Buses, known as **micros** also ply the city's streets but these can be confusing for foreign visitors and are slow during peak periods. It is not advisable to hail **taxis** on the street for night-time journeys. ▸▸ *Metro map, p 213.*

Tourist information

Sernatur (Servicio Nacional de Turismo) ⓘ *Av Providencia 1550, next to Providencia Municipal Library, T02-7318336, info@sernatur.cl, Metro Manuel Montt, Mon-Fri 0845-1830, Sat 0900-1400*. The national tourist board has maps, many brochures and posters. English is spoken. There is also an information office at the airport. For city information, visit the **Municipal Tourist Board** ⓘ *Casa Colorada, Merced 860, T02-336700, Metro Plaza de Armas*, which also offers walking tours of the city, on Wednesdays at 1500.

History

Santiago was founded by Pedro de Valdivia in 1541 on the site of a small indigenous settlement between the southern bank of the Río Mapocho and the Cerro Santa Lucía. During the colonial period, it was one of several Spanish administrative and cultural centres. Much of the fledgling city was destroyed by two earthquakes in 1647 and 1730 but following Independence, Santiago became more significant. In the 1870s, under Benjamín Vicuña MacKenna, an urban plan was drafted, the Cerro Santa Lucía was made into a public park and the first trams were introduced. As the city grew at the end of the 19th century, the Chilean elite built their mansions west of the centre around Calle Dieciocho. The spread of the city east towards Providencia began in 1895. In the latter part of the 20th century, Santiago grew rapidly as affluent residents moved east into new neighbourhoods in the foothills of the Andes and poorer neighbourhoods were established to the west of the centre.

The centre of the old city lies between the Río Mapocho and the city's main avenue, Alameda. From Plaza Italia, in the east of the city's central area, the river flows to the northwest and the Alameda runs to the southwest. From Plaza Italia, Calle Merced runs due west to the Plaza de Armas, the heart of the city, which lies five blocks south of the Río Mapocho.

Getting there International flights
Getting around Metro, micros, radio taxis and on foot.
Time required a couple of days at the start or end of your trip.
Weather Mediterranean climate, with long dry summers, showers in autumn and spring.
Sleeping 30% more expensive than the rest of Chile especially in Providencia and Las Condes.
Eating Bellavista is best for atmosphere and quality; great seafood at the Mercado Central.
Activities and tours Football matches, skiing nearby.
★ **Don't miss...** The view of the Andes from Cerro San Cristobal

Plaza de Armas

On the eastern and southern sides of the Plaza de Armas, there are arcades with shops; on the northern side is the post office and the Municipalidad; and on the western side the cathedral and the archbishop's palace. The **cathedral**, much rebuilt, contains a recumbent statue in wood of San Francisco Javier and the chandelier that lit the first meetings of Congress after Independence; it also houses an museum of

A view of Santiago from Cerro San Cristóbal

religious art and historical pieces. In the Palacio de la Real Audiencia is the **Museo Histórico Nacional**, ⓘ *Plaza de Armas 951, T02-638 1411, www.museo historico nacional.cl, Tue-Sun 1000-1730, US$0.80, free on Sun*, which covers the period from the Conquest until 1925 and contains a model of colonial Santiago.

Cathedral nave

Around the plaza

Southwest of the Cathedral are the courts and **Museo Chileno de Arte Precolombino** ⓘ *Bandera 361, www.precolombino.cl, open Tue-Sun 1000-1800, US$3, booklet, US$0.35*. Housed in the former Real Aduana, this is one of the best museums in Chile with an excellent representative exhibition of objects from the pre-Columbian cultures of Central America and the Andean region. Displays are well labelled in English. Two blocks west is **Palacio de la Alhambra** ⓘ *Compañía 1340, T02-6890875, www.snba.cl, Mon-Fri 1100- 1300, 1700-1930*, a national monument sponsored by the Society of Arts, with art exhibitions and a permanent display.

A few metres east of the Plaza de Armas is the Casa Colorada. Built in 1769, it was the home of the Governor in colonial days and then of Mateo de Toro, first President of Chile. It now holds the **Museo de Santiago** ⓘ *Merced 860, www.munistgo.cl/colorada, Tue-Sat 1000-1800, Sun and holidays 1100-1400, US$2, students free, booklet US$0.35*, which covers the history of Santiago from the Conquest to modern times with excellent displays, models and guided tours.

From the Plaza de Armas, Paseo Ahumada runs south to the Alameda, four blocks away. **Ahumada** is a pedestrianized street and the commercial heart of the centre. Ahumada and nearby **Calle Huérfanos** are always interesting places to come for a stroll, especially at night, when those selling pirated CDs or playing the three-card trick mix with evangelist preachers and satanists.

Four blocks north of the Plaza de Armas is the interesting **Mercado Central** ⓘ *Av 21 de Mayo y San Pablo*. This is the best place to come for seafood in Santiago (see page 226), and is so prominent in the Chilean psyche that it was the setting for a recent national soap opera, *Amores del Mercado*. The building faces the **Parque Venezuela**, on which is the Cal y Canto metro station, the northern terminus of Line 2, and, at its western end, the former Mapocho railway station, now a cultural centre and concert venue. If you head east from Mapocho station, along the river, you arrive at the **Parque Forestal**. The **Museo Nacional de Bellas Artes** ⓘ *www.mnba.cl, Tue-Sun 1000-1845, US$0.80*, is located in the wooded grounds and is an extraordinary example of neo-classical architecture. Inside is a large display of Chilean and foreign painting and sculpture; contemporary art exhibitions are held several times a year. In the west wing is the **Museo de Arte Contemporáneo** ⓘ *www/mac/uchile/cl, US$0.80*.

Along and around the Alameda

The Alameda runs through the heart of the city for over 3 km. It is 100 m wide, choked full of *micros*, taxis and cars day and night and ornamented with gardens and statuary.

At the eastern end of the Alameda is **Plaza Italia**, where there is a statue of General Baquedano and the Tomb of the Unknown Soldier. Four blocks south is the **Museo Nacional Benjamín Vicuña MacKenna** ⓘ *Av V MacKenna 94, www.dibam.cl/subdirec_museos/mbm_mackenna, Tue-Sat 0930-1300, 1400-1800, US$0.80*, which records the life and works of the 19th-century Chilean historian and biographer who became one of Santiago's most important mayors. It also has occasional exhibitions.

Between the Parque Forestal, Plaza Italia and the Alameda is the **Lastarria** neighbourhood (Universidad Católica metro). For those interested in antique furniture, pieces of art and old books, the area is worth a visit, especially the **Plaza Mulato Gil de Castro** (Calle Lastarria 305). Occasional shows are put on in the plaza, and surrounding it are restaurants, bookshops, handicraft and antique shops, an art gallery, the **Instituto de Arte Contemporáneo** and the **Museo Arqueológico de Santiago** ⓘ *Lastarria 307, Mon-Fri 1000-1400, 1530-1830, Sat 1000-1400, free*, with temporary exhibitions of Chilean archaeology, anthropology and pre-Columbian art. The museum also houses the **Museo de Artes Visuales** ⓘ *Tue-Sun 1030-1830, free.*

From here, the Alameda skirts **Cerro Santa Lucía**, a cone of rock rising steeply to a height of 70 m. It can be scaled from the Caupolicán esplanade, but the ascent from the northern side of the hill – wit h its statue of Diego de Almagro – is easier. On clear days you can see across to the Andes from the top and even when it is smoggy the sunset is good. There is a fortress, the **Batería Hidalgo** (closed to visitors) on the summit. The hill closes at 2100; visitors must sign a register at the entrance, giving their ID card number. It is best to descend the eastern side, to see the small **Plaza Pedro Valdivia** with its waterfalls and **statue of Valdivia**. The area is known to be dangerous after dark and you should beware of thieves.

Past the hill, on the right, the Alameda goes past the **Biblioteca Nacional** ⓘ *Moneda 650, www.dibam.cl, Mon-Fri 0900-1900, Sat 0900-1400, free*. Beyond, on the left, between Calle San Francisco and Calle Londres, is the oldest church in Santiago: the red-walled church and monastery of **San Francisco** (1618). Inside is the small statue of the Virgin that Valdivia carried on his saddlebow when he rode from Peru to Chile. Free classical concerts are sometimes given in the church in summer; arrive early for a seat. Annexed to the church, near the cloisters, is the **Museo Colonial** ⓘ *Londres 4, T02-6398737, www.museosanfransisco.cl, Tue-Sun 1000-1300, 1500-1800, US$1.50*. Containing displays of religious art and Gabriela Mistral's Nobel Prize medal.

Two blocks north of the Alameda is the **Teatro Municipal** ⓘ *Calle Agustinas, guided tours Tue 1300-1500 and Sun 1100-1400, US$3*. A little further west along the Alameda is the

The changing of the guard outside Palacio de la Moneda

Universidad de Chile and the **Club de la Unión**, an exclusive social club founded in 1864. The current building dates from 1925 and houses a restaurant where wonderful meals are served at exorbitant prices. Nearby, on Calle Nueva York, is the **Bolsa de Comercio** (stock exchange). The public are allowed access to view the trading, but you must have your passport checked in order to get inside.

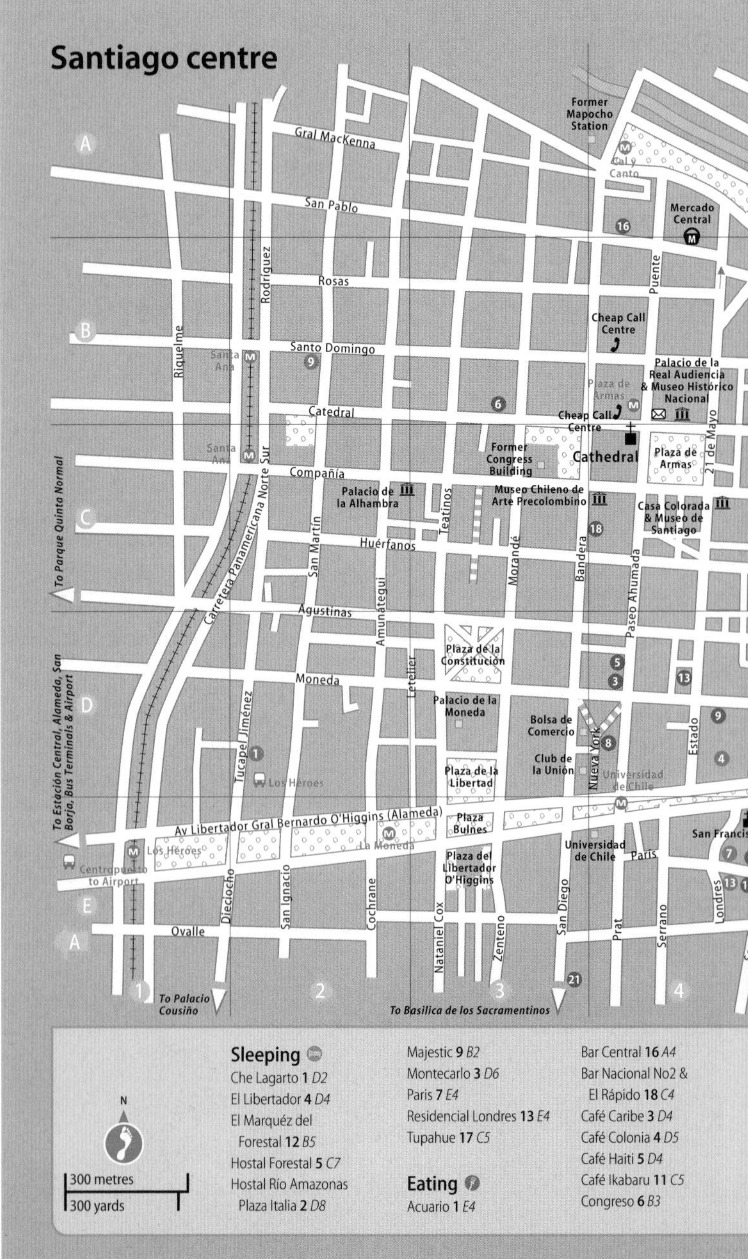

One block further west there are three plazas: **Plaza de la Libertad** to the north of the Alameda, **Plaza Bulnes** in the centre and **Plaza del Libertador O'Higgins** to the south. To the north of Plaza de la Libertad, hemmed in by the skyscrapers of the Centro Cívico, is **Palacio de la Moneda** ⓘ *Mon-Fri 1000-1800, guided tours of the palace 0900-1300 final Sun of every month* (1805), the Presidential Palace containing historic relics, paintings, sculptures and the elaborate

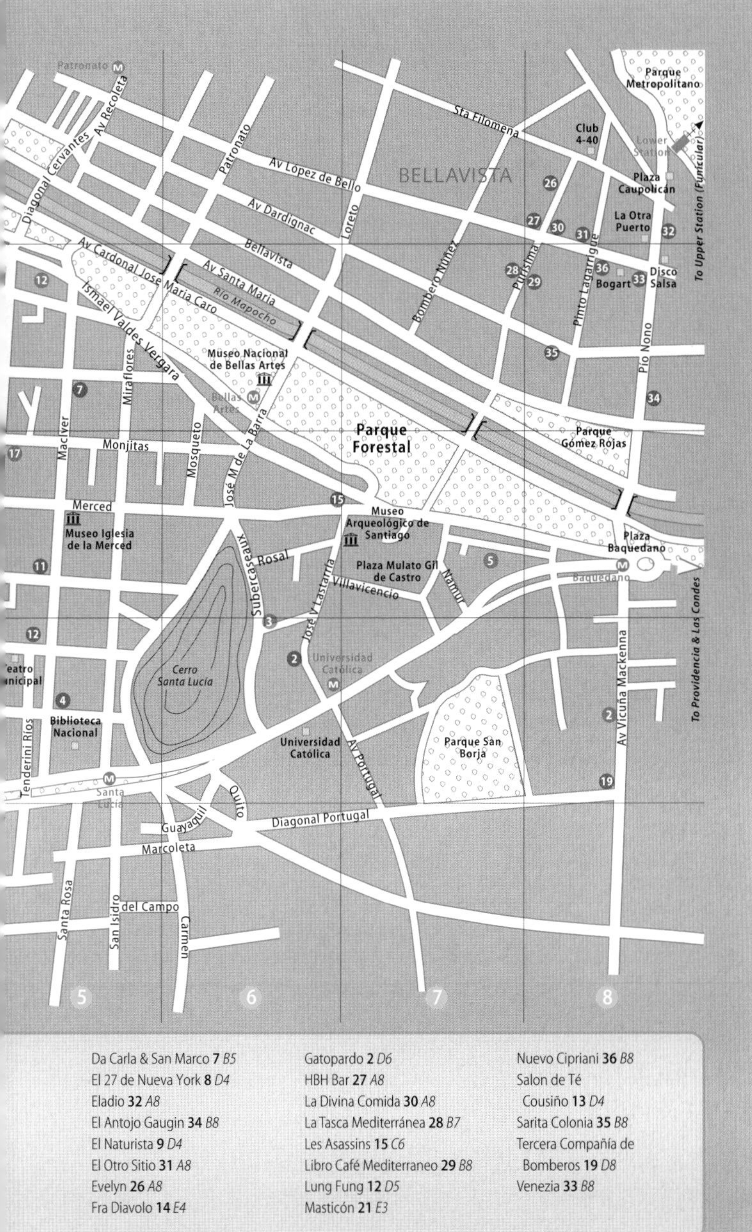

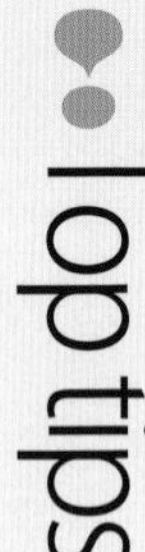

24 hours in the city

First, try to make sure you are here on a Saturday. Assuming you are staying in the centre, get up early and walk down to Calle San Diego for breakfast. Afterwards, walk down San Diego to the **Iglesia de los Sacrementinos** – Santiago's answer to Sacré Coeur – and then west through gardens until you reach the **Palacio Cousiño** in time for the first tour at 0930. This extraordinary building (see page 221) gives a real insight into the lives, customs and belief systems of the Chilean aristocracy and the opulence to which the upper classes became accustomed. Once the tour has finished, stroll to Toesca metro and head a few stops south to Franklin. Here you will find swarms of people all making their way to the **Mercado Bío Bío**. This market will show you how most of Santiago lives and it provides a striking contrast to Palacio Cousiño.

When you start feeling hungry, head back to Franklin metro and take the train north to **Cal y Canto**. On the opposite side of the Río Mapocho is the **Mercado Central**, where you will find some of the best **seafood restaurants** in Santiago.

After lunch, it's time to remind yourself that Santiago has one of the most dramatic settings of any of the world's major cities. Cross back over the Río Mapocho and stroll east towards the conical hill of **Cerro San Cristóbal**. If it's summer, the heat may be making you feel a little tired by now – if so, you could go up the hill on the **funicular railway**. If you are lucky and it is a clear day, you will have an unforgettable view of the Andes. Here you can stroll through lanes that are lined with trees – a world away from the clutter of the city. There are even swimming pools to cool off in and the chance to do some wine tasting. Towards dusk, have a drink in the café near the funicular railway station and watch the sun go down, lighting up the snows of the Andes.

After dark, go back down the hill by funicular railway (it's not advisable to walk here in the evening) in time to sample Santiago's nightlife. At the foot of Cerro San Cristóbal is **Barrio Bellavista**. Here you can take your pick of any one of dozens of excellent (and expensive) restaurants, before going out to one of the area's buzzing *salsotecas*. These don't really get going until midnight and you'll usually find that you don't leave much before five, so perhaps head back to your hotel room for some sleep after dinner and then go out dancing later on.

Salón Rojo used for official receptions. Although the Moneda was damaged by air attacks during the military coup of 11 September 1973 it has been fully restored. Only the courtyards are open to the public. In front of the palace is the statue of former President Arturo Alessandri Palma. Ceremonial changing of the guard every other day at 1000.

> "" In 1981, a thief made off with the statue of the Virgen del Carmen, but hastily returned it the next day after an earthquake rocked the city.

South of the Alameda

Four blocks south of Plaza del Libertador O'Higgins is **Parque Almagro**, notable for the **Iglesia de los Sacramentinos**, a gothic church loosely designed in imitation of Sacré Coeur in Paris, which is best viewed from the nearby Palacio Cousiño against the backdrop of the *cordillera*. **Palacio Cousiño** ⓘ *C Dieciocho 438, www.palaciocousino.co.cl, Metro Toesca, admission by guided tour only (Spanish or English), Tue-Fri 0930-1330, 1430-1700 (last tour 1600), Sat, Sun and holidays 0930-1330, US$2.40*, on the west side of the Parque Almagro and five blocks south of the Alameda, is a large mansion in French rococo style. It was built by Luis and Isadora Cousiño, part of a wealthy Chilean dynasty that made its money in the mining and wine industries. Furnished with tapestries, antiques and pictures imported from France, the palace startled Santiago society with its opulence and its advanced technology, including its own electricity generators and the first lift in the country. Even today, the word 'luxurious' falls short when describing the palace: one of the chandeliers is made with 13,000 pieces of crystal and the superb Italian staircase was built using 20 different types of marble. Look out also for the '*indiscretos*', three-seater armchairs designed for courting couples and a chaperone. Now owned by the Municipalidad, the palace is used for official receptions but is also open as a museum. A visit is highly recommended.

Parque O'Higgins lies about 10 blocks south of the Alameda. It has a small lake and many amusements including the racecourse of the **Club Hípico**, and an amusement park, **Fantasilandia** ⓘ *daily in summer, Sat and Sun only in winter, adults US$9, children US$7, unlimited rides*. There are kite-flying contests on Sundays and, during the Independence celebrations around 18 September, there are many good *peñas*. There are also three small museums in the park. It can be reached by Metro Line 2 to Parque O'Higgins station or by bus from Parque Baquedano via Avenida MacKenna and Avenida Matta.

Barrio Brasil

On the northern side of the Alameda, immediately to the west of the Panamericana, is the Barrio Brasil, a tranquil area in which many of the houses are brightly painted. This historic part of the city was the first area to be colonized by Santiaguinos away from the centre, at the end of the 18th century. It is now a more bohemian, studenty neighbourhood than the surrounding areas and has rich colonial architecture, inexpensive hotels and good restaurants. It is also a centre for nightlife with underground bars, clubs and Santiago's most radical shop, **La Lunita**, stocking feminist books and Santiago's only gay monthly, *Lambda News*.

The heart of the *barrio* is **Plaza Brasil**, easily reached by walking straight up calle Concha y Toro from the República metro stop. This is a narrow, winding cobblestone street that passes elegant old stone homes in rococo and German Gothic styles, before reaching the plaza, which is shaded by palms, lime trees and silk cottons. Just west of the plaza, on Compañía, is the **Basilica del Salvador**, a striking yellow- and rose-coloured church built between 1870 and 1872, with stained glass and a statue of the Virgen del Carmen. A little further along Compañía is the **Iglesia Preciosa Sangre**, a bright red church of neo-classical design, with impressive reliefs and twin towers.

Around Estación Central

The Alameda continues westwards across the Pan-American Highway towards the impressive railway station, **Estación Central**, which is surrounded by several blocks of market stalls. Opposite Estacíon Central is the **Planetarium** ⓘ *US$4.50*, while to the north on Avenida Matucana y Diego Portales is **Parque Quinta Normal**. The park was founded as a botanical garden in 1830, and is a pleasant, popular spot, which gets very crowded on Sundays with families and the street entertainers who vie with one another to get their pesos.

The park contains several museums. **Museo Ferroviario** ⓘ *www.corpdicyt.cl, Tue-Fri 1000-1800, Sat and Sun 1100-1900, US$1.20, free to over 60s, photography US$2*, contains the former Presidential stagecoach and 13 steam engines built between 1884 and 1953, including a rare surviving Kitson-Meyer. The **Museo Nacional de Historia Natural**, ⓘ *www.mnhn.cl, Tue-Sat 1000-1730, Sun and holidays 1100-1830,US$0.80, Sun free, students free*, was founded in 1830 and is one of Latin America's oldest museums. Housed in a neo-classical building, it has exhibitions on zoology, botany, mineralogy, anthropology, ethnography and aeology. **Museo Artequín** ⓘ *Av Portales 3530, Tue-Fri 0900-1700, Sat, Sun and holidays 1100-1800, US$1*, is housed in the Chilean pavilion built for the 1889 Paris International Exhibition. It contains prints of famous paintings and explanations of the techniques of the great masters. Recommended. Two blocks east of the park is the **Museo de la Solidaridad Salvador Allende**, ⓘ *Herrera 360, T02-6817542, www.mssa.cl, Tue-Sun 1000-1900, US$0.80*. Located in a beautiful listed building with a cobbled patio and palm trees with nesting birds, it houses a collection of over 400 art works produced by Chilean and foreign artists in support of the Unidad Popular government and in opposition to the Pinochet dictatorship. Artists include Alexander Calder, Joan Miró, Oswaldo Guayasamin and Roberto Matta. There are also videos of interviews (in Spanish) with survivors of the 1973 coup and an information sheet in English. You need to give four days' notice for guided tours, but they are recommended. The good café serves a cheap set lunch.

Bellavista and Cerro San Cristóbal

Santiago's bohemian face is most obvious in the **Bellavista** district, on the north bank of the Río Mapocho at the foot of **Cerro San Cristóbal**. This is the main focus of nightlife in the old city; the area around Pío Nono and López de Bello hums and buzzes, especially at weekends. In the bars you can see everything from live Cuban music to local imitations of Georges Brassens, while eating options range from classic Italian to sushi and West African palm-nut stew. There are also theatres, art galleries and craft shops specializing in lapis lazuli.

La Chascona ⓘ *Márquez de la Plata 192, T02-7778741, www.uchile.cl/neruda/chascona.html, Tue-Sun 1000-1300, 1500-1800, US$2 guided visits only, English guides can be booked*, is the house of the poet Pablo NAeruda. There are really three houses, built on a steep hillside and separated by gardens. It was completed in 1955 and Neruda lived here whenever he was in the capital. The house was fully restored after being damaged in the 1973 coup and is now the headquarters of the Fundación Pablo Neruda.

Virgen on the summit of San Cristóbal

Background

Moving mountains

In 2001, Santiago was rated the eighth most polluted city in the world. The principal reason is that it lies in a bowl, encircled by mountains, which means that the smog is trapped. This, combined with the centralization of Chilean industry in Santiago, the fact that many buses are not equipped with catalytic converters and the sheer volume of cars that choke the city's highways, conspires to create a pollution black spot. The smog is not too bad in spring, summer and autumn, but those who arrive here during winter are in for an unpleasant shock. After half an hour your throat will begin to itch and your eyes to water. Asthma rates among Santanguinos are high and older people sometimes die during the winter *emergencias*, when the pollution gets particularly bad. When Pedro de Valdivia founded the city in 1541, between the coastal mountains and the Andes, it must have seemed like a perfect site; he could never have imagined that the city would one day engulf the whole valley, and that the mountains would become a serious problem.

Over the years, all sorts of solutions have been proposed. A team of Japanese scientists once even suggested blowing up the part of the Andes nearest the city, so that the pollution could disperse more easily. Each weekday, cars that have number plates ending in one of two digits are prohibited from circulating. Pollution levels vary; the west and the old 'city centre' are much worse affected than the more expensive areas around Las Condes. Pollution is usually at its worst in July and at its lightest in September and October and after rainfall. Forecast levels of smog are published in the daily papers.

Parque Metropolitano

Bellavista lies at the foot of the **Cerro San Cristóbal**, which forms the **Parque Metropolitano** ⓘ *daily 0900-2100, vehicles US$3*, the largest and most interesting of the city's parks. On a clear day it provides excellent views over the city and across to the Andes. More usually, however, the views provide a graphic demonstration of Santiago's continuing smog problem. From the top, the **Cemeterio General** can also be seen, situated in the *barrio* of La Recoleta to the north. This cemetery contains the mausoleums of most of the great figures in Chilean history and the arts, including Violeta Parra, Victor Jara and Salvador Allende. There is also an impressive monument to the victims of the 1973-90 military government. There are two sectors, **sector Cumbre** on Cerro San Cristóbal and, further east, **sector Tupahue**. There are two entrances: west from Pío Nono in Bellavista and east from Pedro de Valdivia Norte. When the weather is good, the walk up the access road from Bellavista is very pleasant, providing unexpected views of distant and little-visited northern parts of the city. Near the Bellavista entrance is the **Jardín Zoológico** ⓘ *Tue-Fri 1000-1300, 1500-1800, Sat, Sun and holidays 1000-1800, US$2*, which has a well cared-for collection of animals. On Cerro Cumbre (300 m above the city), there is a colossal statue of the Virgin, which is floodlit at night; beside it is the astronomical observatory of the Catholic University, which can be visited on application to the observatory's director.

The Tupahue sector is reached by taxi either from the Bellavista entrance or on foot from the Pedro de Valdivia metro. This section of the park contains terraces, gardens and paths. One building houses the **Camino Real** (T02-2321758), a good, expensive restaurant with a splendid view from the terrace, especially at night, and an **Enoteca** of Chilean wines from a range of vineyards, which you can taste (US$1.50 per glass), or buy, although prices are higher than in shops. Nearby is the **Casa de la Cultura**, which has art exhibitions and free concerts at midday on Sunday. There are also two good **swimming pools** in the park. East of Tupahue are the **Botanical Gardens** ⓘ *daily 0900-1800, guided tours available*, with a collection of native plants.

If you don't want to walk to the top of Cerro San Cristóbal, take the **funicular** ⓘ *from Plaza Caupolicán at the northern end of Calle Pío Nono, every few minutes 1000-2000 daily, US$1.50 return, US$1 one way*, or the **teleférico** ⓘ *from Estación Oasis, Avenida Pedro de Valdivia Norte via Tupahue, summer only, Mon 1430-1830, Tue-Fri 1030-1830, Sat and Sun 1030-1900, US$3 combination ticket including funicular*. An open-top bus runs to San Cristóbal and Tupahue from the Bellavista entrance with the same schedule as the teleférico.

East to Providencia and Los Condes

East of Plaza Italia, the main east-west axis of the city is known as **Avenida Providencia**, as it heads towards the affluent areas of Providencia and Los Condes. On the south bank of the Mapocho is **Parque Baquedano**, also known as Parque Gran Bretaña. It is one of the more attractive parks in Santiago and houses the **Museo de los Tajamares** ⓘ *Av Providencia 222, Mon-Fri 0900-1400 and 1500-2100*, an exhibition of the 17th- and 18th-century walls built to protect the city from flooding by the river. There is also an exhibition of photographs.

South of Las Condes

Parque de la Paz, the new peace park in the southwestern suburb of Peñalolén, stands on the site of **Villa Grimaldi**, the most notorious torture centre during the Pinochet regime. The Irish missionary, Sheila Cassidy, has documented the abuses that she underwent when imprisoned without trial in this place. The walls are daubed with human rights' graffiti and the park makes a moving and unusual introduction to the conflict that has eaten away at the heart of Chilean society for the past 30 years. To reach the park, take a metro to Tobalaba and then any bus marked Peñalolén heading south down Tobalaba. Get off at the junction of Tobalaba y José Arrieta and then walk five minutes up Arrieta towards the mountains.

Sleeping

Expensive hotels in the city centre, Providencia and Las Condes tend to be slightly characterless but with good service. Most budget accommodation is located in the city centre or further west around the bus terminals. Decent *hostales* are also beginning to appear in Barrio Brasil and around Providencia. Another good option is to stay in a family-run guesthouse. Accommodation in Santiago tends to be more expensive than the rest of the country (see Essentials, p29).

Around the Plaza de Armas

p215, map p218

AL-A **Majestic**, *Santo Domingo 1526, T02-6958366, www.hotelmajestic.cl* Breakfast, pool, internet connection port in rooms. Excellent Indian restaurant. English spoken. Recommended.

B **Lira**, *Lira 314, T02-2222492, www.hotellira.co.cl* Old fashioned, friendly. Cheaper in pesos than in dollars.

Along and around the Alameda

p216, map p218

A-B **Libertador**, *O'Higgins 853, T02-6394212, www.hotellibertador.cl*

Helpful, stores luggage, good restaurant, bar, rooftop pool. Recommended.

B **El Marqués del Forestal**, *Ismael Valdés Vergara 740, T02-6333462, www.apart-hotel- elmarques.cl* Good value, apartments.

C **París**, *C París 813, T02-6640921, www.hotelparis.cl* With bath, quiet, clean, good meeting place, good value, breakfast extra, luggage store. Recommended. Book in advance.

Epp **Che Lagarto**, *Tucapel Jimenez 24, T02-6991493, www.chelagarto.com, infochile@chelagarto.com* Metro Los Héroes. Doubles and dorms, with breakfast. Some rooms with bath. New branch of the South American chain hostel. Comfortable common areas, kitchen facilities, internet.

Epp **Residential Londres**, *Londres 54, T02-6382215, unico54@ctcinternet.cl* Near San Francisco Church, former mansion, large old-fashioned rooms and furniture, some rooms with bath, few singles, no heating, English spoken, book exchange, great value, very popular, highly recommended, usually full, no advance bookings in season, arrive early.

Barrio Brasil *p221*

B **Ducado**, *Augustinas 1990, T02-6961948, hotelducado@entelchile.cl* With breakfast. Some rooms with kitchenette. Clean, quiet, reasonable value, nice area west of the Panamericana. Secure parking.

B **Happy House Hostel**, *Catedral 2207, T02-688 4849, www.happyhousehostel.cl* Also dormitories D per person. Luxury hostel in restored mansion with all mod-cons. Spacious kitchen and common areas, internet, pool table, bar, sauna, jacuzi, roof terrace. Full breakfast. Free tea and real coffee all day. Book exchange. English spoken, very friendly. Lots of info. Highly recommended.

B **Hostal Río Amazonas Barrio Brasil**, *Rosas 2234, T02-698 4092, www.hostalrioamazonas.cl.* With breakfast and bath, internet, good value. Friendly, helpful. Recommended.

Epp **Hostal Internacional Letelier**, *Cumming 77, T02-9656861*. Internet, without breakfast, also Spanish classes.

Around Estación Central *p222*

Staying in this area is convenient for those on a lightening visit or for those with an early or late start.

B **Tur Hotel Express**, *O'Higgins 3750, piso 3, in the Turbus Terminal, T02-6850100.* Comfortable business standard with breakfast, cable TV, air-conditioning, free internet. Particularly useful if you need to take an early flight as buses leave for the airport from here.

C **Res Mery**, *Pasaje República 36, off 0-100 block of República, T02-6968883, m.mardones@entelchile.net* Big green building down an alley, hot showers, quiet, good value. Recommended.

Dpp **Santiago Adventure**, *Cabo Arestey 2468 (off C España), T02-6715529. ULA metro.* Family run, friendly, tours, airport pick-up, English spoken. Recommended.

Bellavista and Plaza Italia *p222, map p218*

A **Presidente**, *Eliodoro Yáñez 867, T02-2358015, www.presidente.cl* Good value and good location.

A-B **Montecarlo**, *Subercaseaux 209, T02-6391569, www.hotelmontecarlo.cl* At foot of Cerro Santa Lucía in quiet street, modern but with "nice art deco touches", restaurant, stores luggage, helpful. Recommended.

B **Hostal Río Amazonas Plaza Italia**, *Vicuña Mackenna 47, T02-671 9013, www.hostalrioamazonas.cl* In a restored Mansion. With breakfast and bath, internet, good value. Friendly, helpful. Cheaper in dollars or euros than in pesos.

C **Casa Condell**, *Condell 114, T02-2092343 Salvador metro.* Also 4-bed dorms, E per person. Pleasant old house, central, quiet, nice roof-terrace. Shared baths, no breakfast, kitchen, free local phonecalls, friendly, English spoken. Recommended.

D-Epp **Bellavista Hostel**, *Dardignac 0184, T02-7328737, www.bellavistahostel.com* . In the heart of the lively Bellavista area. European-style hostel, sheets provided but make your own bed. With breakfast. Kitchen facilities, free internet. Good meeting place. Recommended.

D-Epp **Hostal Forestal**, *Coronel Santiago Bueras 120, T02-638 1347, www.hostalforestal.cl* . Dorms and doubles. With breakfast. Good location on a quiet side street near the plaza Italia. Comfy lounge with internet and big screen TV. Barbeque area, kitchen facilities, good information, friendly, English spoken. Recommended.

Providencia *p224*

AL-A **Orly**, *Pedro de Valdivia 027, T02-231 8947, www.orlyhotel.com Pedro de Valdivia metro.* Small, comfortable, convenient location. Also smaller and cheaper rooms, small café attached with cheap food. Recommended.

A-B **Lyon**, *Av Ricardo Lyon 1525, T02-2257732, hotelyon@gmr.met* With breakfast, small, intimate, good value, also has annex, B with breakfast.

B **Marilú's Bed and Breakfast**, *Rafael Cañas 246 C, T02-2355302, www.bedandbreakfast.cl* Comfortable, no credit cards, very friendly, good beds, English spoken. Highly recommended.

B **El Patio Suizo**, *Condell 847, T02-4941214, www.patiosuizo.com* Metro Parque Bustamante. Comfortable swiss run bed and breakfast in a quiet residential area. Rooms with bath, TV. Patio, internet. English spoken

Dpp **Santiago Hostel**, *Dr Barros Borgoño 199, T02-22649894. Hostelsantiago @yahoo.com* European style hostel, with dorms, breakfast, kitchen, garden, internet. Excellent skiing information.

Eating

El Mercurio's website has an excellent restaurant guide: www.emol.com. For cheap meals in the evening try the *fuentes de soda* and *schoperias* scattered around the centre.

Around the Plaza de Armas *p215, map p218*

For excellent cheap seafood make for the Mercado Central (Cal y Canto metro).

TTT-TT **Da Carla**, *MacIver 577*. Traditional Italian restaurant, good, expensive.

TTT-TT **Majestic**, *Santo Domingo 1526*. This hotel has an excellent Indian restaurant, good range of vegetarian dishes.

TTT-TT **San Marco**, *2 doors from Don Carla*, another Italian. Manages to pip its next-door neighbour to the post.

TT **Congreso**, *Catedral 1221*. Good meat and wines, popular at lunchtime.

TT **El 27 de Nueva York**, *Nueva York 027* International cuisine, good and varied.

TT **Lung Fung**, *Agustinas 715*. Delicious Oriental food, pricey, large cage in the centre with noisy parrots.

Bar Central, *San Pablo 1063*. Popular, noisy, good specialities, good value.
Bar Nacional No 2, *Bandera 317*. Good restaurants, popular, local specialities.
Círculo de Periodistas, *Amunátegui 31, piso 2*. Unwelcoming entrance, good-value lunches. Recommended.
El Naturista, *Moneda 846*. Vegetarian, excellent, closes 2100.
El Rápido, *next door to Bar Nacional No 2*. Specializes in *empanadas*, cheap, quick service, popular.

Cafés

Café Caribe and **Café Haití**, *Paseo Ahumada*, institutions among Santiago's business community and good places to see the people who make Chile tick; other branches in the centre and in Providencia.
Café Colonia, *MacIver 133*. Splendid variety of cakes, pastries and pies, fashionable and pricey, excellent.
Café Ikabaru, *Huérfanos 709*, another good coffee bar, popular and intimate.
Salón de Té Cousiño, *Cousiño 107*. Good coffee, snacks and *onces*, very popular.

Along and around the Alameda p216, map p218

Acuario, *París 817*. Excellent seafood and attentive service, good-value lunch.
Fra Diavolo, *París 836 (near Res Londres)*. Lunches only, excellent food and service.
El Rincón Español, *just off Rosal, Lastarria*. Spanish, good, reasonably priced, try the paella.
Gatopardo, *next door to El Rincón Español, Lastarria*. Mediterranean, good value. Highly recommended.
Confitería Torres, *O'Higgins 1570*. Traditional bar/restaurant, good atmosphere, live music at weekends. Cheap lunches are served in a large underground *comedor*.
La Caleta de Don Beno, *San Diego 397*. Excellent *parrilladas*, also seafood, popular, recommended.
Las Tejas, *San Diego 234*. Lively, rowdy crowd, very cheap cocktails and drinks such as *pisco sour* and *pipeño*, excellent *cazuelas* and other typical dishes.
Masticón, *San Diego152*. Good service, excellent value, popular, wide range.
Tercera Compañia de Bomberos, *Vicuña Mackenna 097, near the junction with Diagonal Paraguay*. Good food, very cheap, recommended.

Barrio Brasil p221

Las Vacas Gordas, *Cienfuegos 280, T02-6736962*. Excellent *parrillada*. Very popular, so book in advance.
Los Chinos Ricos, *Brasil 373, on the plaza*. Good Chinese.
Mansión de la Novia, *Agustinas 2859*. Chilean food, elegant.
Ostras Azócar, *Bulnes 37*. Specializes in oysters. Several reasonable seafood restaurants on the same street.
Café Universitario, *Alameda 395 y Subercaseaux (near Santa Lucía), Lastarria*. Good, cheap *almuerzos*, lively at night, separate room for lovers of rock videos.

Bellavista p222, map p218

Azul Profundo, *Constitución 111*. Typical Chilean with a touch of invention.
El Otro Sitio, *López de Bello 053, Bellavista*. Peruvian, excellent food, good service, elegant.
El Viejo Verde, *López de Bello 94, Bellavista*. Excellent vegetarian food.
Kilometre 11.680, *Dardignac 145, Bellavista*. French restaurant with one of Chile's best wine lists.
La Divina Comida, *Purísima 093, Bellavista*. Italian with 3 rooms - Heaven, Hell and Purgatory. Highly recommended.
Le Coq au Vin, *No 0110, Bellavista*. French, excellent cuisine, fairly priced.
Off the Record, *López de Bello 153, Bellavista*. Period design, nice atmosphere, cheaper set lunch.
Zen, *Dardignac 175, Bellavista*. Sushi restaurant. Recommended.
Aji Verde, *Constitución 284, Bellavista*. Chilean food, open for lunch.
Cava de Dardignac, *Dardignac 0191, Bellavista*. Portuguese cuisine with live *fado* music at night.

‡‡ **Etniko**, *Constitución 172, Bellavista.* Inventive Japanese cuisine.

‡‡ **La Tasca Mediterránea**, *Purísima 163, Bellavista*. Extensive menu including fish, seafood, good value. Recommended.

‡‡ **Michelle's**, *Arzobispo 0615, Bellavista*. Bistro with excellent seafood and fish dishes, recommended.

‡‡ **Tragaluz**, *Constitución 124, Bellavista, T02-738 2011*. Good Chilean, not cheap.

‡‡ **Venezia**, *Pío Nono y Lopez de Bello, Bellavista*. Large servings, good value.

‡ **Cafetería La Nona**, *Pío Nono 099*. Real coffee, good *empanadas* and cakes, fresh fruit juices. Recommended.

‡ **Empanatodos**, *Pío Nono 153*. Serves 25 different types of *empanadas*.

Providencia *p224*

‡‡‡ **El Giratorio**, *11 de Septiembre 2250, piso 16*. French food eaten while the city rotates outside. Recommended.

‡‡‡ **El Huerto**, *Orrego Luco 054, T02-2332690*. Recommended. Open daily, live music Fri and Sat evenings, varied menu, very good, popular.

‡‡‡ **La Pizza Nostra**, *Av Las Condes 6757*. Pizzas and good Italian food, real coffee, pricey. Also at *Av Providencia 1975* and *Luis Thayer Ojeda 019*.

‡‡‡ **Oriental**, *M Montt 584*. One of the best Chinese restaurants in Santiago.

‡‡‡ **Salvaje**, *Av Providencia 1177*. Excellent international menu, open-air seating, good-value lunches. Recommended.

‡‡ **A Pinch of Pancho**, *Gral del Canto 45*. Seafood and fish specialities, very good.

‡‡ **Café El Patio**, *Providencia 1652, next to Phone Box Pub*. Tofu and pasta as well as fish dishes, nice sandwiches, popular.

‡‡ **Gatsby**, *Providencia 1984*. American all-you-can-eat buffet and lunch/dinner, also coffees and snacks, open till 2400, tables outside in warm weather, good.

‡ **La Máquina**, *C Seminario, Salvador metro*. Nice vibe, music in the evening.

Las Condes *p224*

‡‡‡ **Cuerovaca**, *El Mañío 1659, Vitacura, T02-2468936*. Serves fantastic steaks, both Argentinian and Chilean. Recommended.

‡‡‡ **El Madroñal**, *Vitacura 2911, T02-2336312*. Excellent Spanish cuisine, one of the best, booking essential.

‡‡‡ **Sakura**, *Vitacura 4111*. Excellent sushi. Recommended.

‡‡‡-‡‡ **Diego Pizza**, *El Bosque Norte y Don Carlos*. Friendly, good cocktails, popular.

‡‡‡-‡‡ **Mare Nostrum**, *La Concepción 281*. Fine seafood.

‡‡ **Le Fournil**, *Vitacura 3841, opposite Cuerovaca, T02-2280219*. Excellent French bakery and restaurant. Popular for lunch.

Entertainment

For all entertainment, clubs, cinemas, restaurants, concerts, *El Mercurio Online* website has listings and a good search feature. Look under the *tiempo libre* section: www.emol.com There are also listings in weekend newspapers, including *Santiago What's On* (in English).

Bars and clubs

As in most of South America, a night out in Santiago begins late. Arrive in a restaurant before 2100 and you may be eating alone, while bars and clubs are often empty before midnight. There is a good selection of restaurants, bars, discos and *salsotecas* from the reasonably priced in **Bellavista** (Baquedano metro) to the smarter along Av Suecia and G Holley in **Providencia** (Los Leones metro). El Bosque Norte in **Las Condes** is lined with chic bars and expensive restaurants for the Chilean jetset (Tobalaba metro), while **Barrio Brasil** is popular with Chilean students (República metro). Most clubs and bars playing live music charge from US$2 (for student-orientated places) to US$1, usually with a drink included, although some clubs in Las Condes and Providencia may charge US$20 or more.

Cinemas

Cinema listings across the city are given in the 2 free newspapers, *La Hora* and *tmg*, given out at metro stations early on weekday mornings. Seats cost US$4-6 with reductions on Wed. There are many mainstream cinemas showing international films, usually in original English with Spanish subtitles. 'Ciné Arte' (arthouse cinemas that show quality foreign films), are also very popular and include:

Cine Arte Normandie, *Tarapacá 1181, T02-6972979*. Varied programme, altered frequently, films at 1530, 1830 and 2130 daily, students half price.

Performing arts

A great number of minor theatres around the city stage plays in Spanish; events are listed in *El Mercurio* and *La Tercera*.

Teatro Municipal, *Agustinas y San Antonio*. Performances by the Orquesta Filarmónica de Santiago and the Ballet de Santiago, throughout the year; on Tue at 2100 there are also free operatic concerts in the Salón Claudio Arrau; tickets from US$7 for a very large choral group with a symphony orchestra, and US$8 for the cheapest seats at the ballet, to US$70 for the most expensive opera seats. Some cheap seats are sold on the day.

Teatro Universidad de Chile, *Plaza Baquedano*. Home of the Orquesta y Coro Sinfónica de Chile and the Ballet Nacional.

Shopping

The shops in the centre and to the north of the Plaza de Armas are cheaper and more downmarket than the countless arcades and boutiques strung along Providencia, especially near Av Ricardo Lyon. Specialist shops tend to be grouped together, eg bikes and second-hand books on San Diego, new bookshops on Providencia, opticians on Mac Iver, lapis lazuli in Bellavista. Many stalls on Paseo Ahumada/Huérfanos sell overseas newspapers and journals.

Bookshops

Book prices are very high compared with Europe, even for second-hand books. There are many bookshops in the Pedro de Valdivia area on Av Providencia. Much better value but with a smaller selection are the bookshops in the shopping mall at Av Providencia 1114-1120. For cheap English-language books try the second-hand book kiosks on San Diego, 4 blocks south of Plaza Bulnes, next to the Iglesia de los Sacramentinos.

Camping and outdoors equipment

Club Andino and **Federación de Andinismo** (see p). Expensive camping goods; articles are imported.

Fabri Gas, *Bandera y Santo Domingo*. Camping gas cartridges.

Industria Yarur, *Rosas 1289 y Teatinos, T02-6723696*. Good value for money, discounts available.

Outdoors & Travel, *Encomeneros 206, Las Condes, T02-3357104*. Wide range of imported and local camping goods.

Patagonia, *Helvecia 210, Providencia, T02-3351796*. Good range of clothing and equipment, comparatively expensive.

Handicrafts

The Chilean gemstone, lapis lazuli, can be found in a few expensive shops in Bellavista but is cheaper in the arcades on the south side of the Plaza de Armas. Antique stores can be found in Plaza Mulato Gil de Castro and elsewhere on Lastarria (Merced end). Other craft stalls can be found in an alleyway, *1 block south of Av O'Higgins between A Prat and San Diego*; on the *600 to 800 blocks of Santo Domingo* and at *Pío Nono y Av Santa María* in Bellavista.

El Almacén Campesino, *Purísima 303, Bellavista*. Co-operative association sells handicrafts from all over Chile, including attractive Mapuche weavings, wood carvings, pottery and beautiful wrought copper and bronze. Prices similar to those in Temuco. Ask about shipping.

Plaza Artesanos de Manquehue, *Av Manquehue Sur, block 300-600, just off Apoquindo, Las Condes*. The biggest craft market in Chile. Modern crafts from ceramics to textiles, pleasant central piazza, watch the artisans at work. A cheaper market is held next to Pio Nono bridge in Bellavista, best at weekends.

Markets

For craft markets, see above.

Bío Bío flea market, *C Bío Bío*. Every Sat and Sun morning. This is the largest and cheapest flea market in the city and sells everything from spare parts for cars and motorbikes to second-hand furniture. Those trying to do up a new flat on the cheap, a car on the hoof, or who are simply interested in sharing a street with tens of thousands of others, should find their way here, just go to Franklin metro and follow the crowds. Beware rip-offs.

Mercado Central, *Puente y 21 de Mayo by the Río Mapocho. Cal y Canto metro.* An excellent range of goods and brilliant for seafood, with many places to eat cheaply, **Don Agusto** is recommended.

Activities and tours

Football

Colo Colo, play at the Estadio Monumental, reached by any bus to Puente Alto; tickets from *Cienfuegos 41, T02-6883244*.

Universidad de Chile, play at Campo de Departes, *Nuñoa, T02-2392793*. Estadio Nacional is the nearest metro station.

Universidad Católica, play at San Carlos de Apoquindo, reached by bus from Escuela Militar metro; tickets from *Andrés Bello 2782, Providencia, T02-2312777*.

Skiing

Ski equipment hire is much cheaper in Santiago than in the resorts.

Farellones, 1½ hours from the city, has good accommodation and facilities but can get very busy at weekends. Expect to pay US$40-50 for a combined ticket for the four resorts in the area. Buses organized by **Ski Travel**, *T02-2466881, www.skitotal.cl*, also rents equipment

Portillo, *www.skiportillo.cl*. Widely regarded as one of the best resorts in Chile. Only one hotel but extra activities are available, such as a visit to the Laguna del Inca. Any bus from Santiago to Mendoza will pass through Portillo.

Tour operators

Altue Expediciones, *Encomenderos 83, piso 2, Las Condes, T02-2321103, altue@entelchile.net* For wilderness trips including Patagonia and Chiloé.

Andina del Sud, *Bombero Ossa 1010, piso 3, of 301, T02-6971010, www.andinadelsud.com* Climbing and trekking in the Lake District and other areas.

Azimut 360, *Arzobispo Casanova 3, Providencia, T02-7358034, www.azimut.cl* Low prices. Adventure and eco-tourism throughout Chile. Highly recommended.

Cascada Expediciones, *Orrego Luco 040, Providencia, T02-2342274, www.cascada-expediciones.com* Activity tours in remote areas, including Torres del Paine.

Southern Cross Adventure, *Jose Miguel de la Barra 521, T02-6396591, www.scadventure.com* Climbing, biking, horseriding, trekking, archaeology, visits to volcanoes, fishing. English-speaking guides, camping gear provided.

Sportstours, *Moneda 970, piso 14 T02-5495200, www.sportstour.cl* German-run, helpful, 5-day trips to Antarctica.

Turismo Cabo de Hornos, *Agustinas 814, of 706, T02-6338481*. For **DAP** flights and Tierra del Fuego/Antarctica tours.

Boat/ferry operators Cruceros Australis, *El Bosque Norte 0440, T02-4423110, www.australis.com*, for Punta Arenas to Puerto Williams, Cape Horn and Ushuaia; **M/N Skorpios**, *Augusto Leguía Norte 118, Las Condes, T02- 2311030, www.skorpios.cl*, for Puerto Montt-Laguna San Rafael; **Navimag**, *Av El Bosque Norte 0440, of 1103, T02-4423120, www.navimag.cl* for Puerto Montt-Puerto Natales; **Patagonia Connection SA**, *Fidel Oteíza 1921, of 1006, Providencia, T02- 2256489, www.patagonia-connection.com*, for Puerto Montt- Coyhaique/Puerto

Chacabuco-Laguna San Rafael; **Transmarchilay**, *Agustinas 715, of 403, T02-6335959, www.transmarchilay.cl*, for Chiloé and the Carretera Austral.

Transport

Air

For details of the Aeropuerto Arturo Merino Benitez, see p213. For flights see Essentials, pp20-23. **Aerolíneas Argentinas**, *ofs Generales Tenderinoi 82, piso 6, T02-6393922*; **Air France**, *Alcantara 44, piso 6, Las Condes, T02-2909330, F02-2909340*; **Alitalia**, *El Bosque Norte 0101, of 21, T02-3788230*; **American**, *Huérfanos 1199, T02-6790000*; **British Airways**, *Isidora Goyenechea 2934, of 302, T02-3308600, airport T02-6010721*; **Continental**, *Nueva Tajamar 481, T02-2002100*; **Delta**, *Isidora Goyenechea 2939, of 601, T02-2002700*; **Iberia**, *Bandera 206, piso 8, T02-8701010*; **KLM**, *San Sebastián 2839, of 202, T02-2330011 (sales), T02-2330991 (reservations)*; **LACSA**, *Dr Barros Borgoño 105, piso 2, T02-2355500*; **LanChile**, *Américo Vespuccio 901, T02-526 2000, www.lanchile.cl*, other offices at *Huérfanos 926* and *Centro Comercial Alto Las Condes*; **Lufthansa**, *Moneda 970, piso 16, T02-6301655, www.lufthansa.cl*; **South African Airlines**, *11 de Septiembre 1881, of 713, T02-3769040*; **Sky Airline**, *Fuenzalida 55, Providencia, T600-6002828, www.skyairline.cl*; **United**, *El Bosque Norte 177, T02-3370000.*; **Varig**, *El Bosque Norte 177, piso 9, T02-7078001.*

Bus

Local Micros display their route in the windows. Routes are all numbered and buses will only halt at stops on main roads. Destinations are clearly marked at the stops. When you get on the bus, you should put exact change into the machine to get a ticket, but as the machines are unpredictible, you may have to pay the driver instead. Single fare US$0.50, but price rises are frequent.

Long distance There are frequent, good inter-urban buses to all parts of Chile (see Essentials p24). Fares from/to the capital are given in the text, see Transport for each destination. Bear in mind that on Fri in summer, when the night buses depart, the terminals are nightmarishly chaotic and busy.

Terminal Alameda, *O'Higgins 3712, T02-27071500*, has the best left luggage facilities in the city, and two of the best companies, **Tur Bus** (T02-6973541) and **Pullman Bus**, leave from here (serving Temuco, Pucón, Panguipulli, Osorno, Puerto Montt, Ancud and Castro).

Terminal Santiago, *O'Higgins 3878, T02-3761755, 1 block west of Terminal Alameda.* Sometimes referred to as the 'Terminal Sur', this terminal is used by services to and from the **south**, as well as buses to **Valparaíso** and **Viña del Mar**. It is the only terminal with services to **Punta Arenas** (48 hrs), and is also the centre for most international services.

Terminal Los Héroes, *Tucapel Jiménez, just north of the Alameda, T02-4200099. Los Héroes metro.* A smaller terminal for 8 companies to some useful destinations.

International Almost all international buses leave from the Terminal Santiago. There are frequent services via **Mendoza** to **Buenos Aires** and **Bahía Blanca**, but if you're going to destinations such as **Bariloche** or **Neuquén** in Argentine Patagonia, it is better to travel south to Temuco or Osorno and connect there. There are also services to destinations throughout the rest of South America; consult bus companies at the terminal.

Car

Driving in the city is restricted according to licence plate numbers; each day, certain plates are prohibited from circulating (numbers are given in the press).

Hertz, **Avis**, **Budget** and others are available from the airport; **Alameda**, *O'Higgins 4332, T02-7790609, Pila del Ganso metro*, very good value; **Automóvil**

Club de Chile, *Marchant Pereira 122, Providencia, T02-2744167*, discount for members of associated organizations; Avis, *San Pablo 9900, T02-6019757*, poor service reported; Hertz, *Costanera Andrés Bello 1469, T02-6010477 and at Hotel Hyatt T02-2455936*; Rosselot, *Francisco Bilbao 2032, Providencia, T02-3813690, www.rosselot.cl*, and airport, *T02-6901374*, Chilean firm with national coverage; Trekker Ltd, *www.trekkerchile.com, info@trekkerchile.com*, has camper vans, trucks and 4WD vehicles available; Verschae, *Manquehue Sur 660, T02-2027266, www.verschae.cl*, good value, branches throughout the country.

Colectivo/taxi

Collective taxis operate on fixed routes between the centre and the suburbs. They display destinations and route numbers. Fares vary, depending on the length of the journey, but are usually US$0.75-US$1.50. Higher fares at night.

Regular taxis (black with yellow roofs) are abundant, minimum charge US$0.30, plus US$0.10 per 200 m, more at night. Avoid taxis with more than 1 person in them, especially at night. For journeys outside the city arrange the charge beforehand. **Radio Taxis Andes Pacífico**, *T02-2253064/2888.*

Metro

The metro, www.metrosantiago.cl, is fast, quiet and very full. First train 0630 Mon-Sat, 0800 Sun and holidays; last train 2245. Fares US$0.55, 0715-0900 and 1800-1930, US$0.40 at all other times. Buy a *tarjeta Multivía*, US$4.70 from bigger stations, from which the appropriate fare is deducted for each journey. Metrobus (blue buses, US$0.40) connects Lo Ovalle, San Pablo, Las Rejas, Salvador, Cal y Canto, Escuela Militar, Pedrero and Bellavista de la Florida with outlying areas.

Train

For the Temuco service, see p256. Booking offices: *Alameda O'Higgins 853 in Galería Hotel Libertador, Local 21, T02-6322801*, Mon-Fri 0830-1900, Sat 0900-1300; *Escuela Militar metro, Galería Sur, Local 25, T02-2282983*, Mon-Fri 0830-1900, Sat 0900-1300; or *Estación Central, T02-6895718/6891682, www.efe.cl*, till 2230.

Directory

Banks and currency exchange

Redbanc ATMs (for Cirrus) are everywhere. Official exchange rates are published in *El Mercurio*, *La Nación*, and on *www.xe.com*. The best rates are offered by *casas de cambio* around Paso Ahumada and Huérfanos (Metro Universidad de Chile or Plaza de Armas). Most charge 3% commission to change TCs into dollars. Avoid street money changers (common on Ahumada and Agustinas).

American Express, *Andrés Bello 2711, piso 9, T02-3506700, Tobalaba metro*, also at *Blanco Viajes, Gen Holley 148, T02-2336164*, no commission but poor rates;

Turismo Tajamar, *Orrego Luco 023, T02-3368000*, Thomas Cook/Mastercard agent.

Embassies and consulates

Argentina, *Miraflores 285, T02-6331076.* Also Argentine consulate, *Vicuña MacKenna 41, T02-2226947*, open 0900-1400 (visa US$25, free for US citizens), if you need a visa for Argentina, get it here or in the consulates in Puerto Montt or Punta Arenas; Australians will need a letter from their embassy to get a visa here. **Australia**, *Isidora Goyenechea 3261, T02-5503500*; **Canada**, *Nueva Tajamar 481, Torre Norte, piso 12, T02-3629660*; **New Zealand**, *El Golf 99, of 703, T02-2909802*; **South Africa**, *Av 11 de Septiembre 2353, Edif San Román, piso 16, T02-2312862*; **UK**, *El Bosque Norte 0125, Casilla 72-D, T02-3704100*, will hold letters; **USA**, *Av Andrés Bello 2800, T02-2322600, www.embajadaeeuu.cl*, consulate at *Merced 230, T02-710133*, for visas.

Medical services

If you need to get to a hospital, take a taxi rather than waiting for an ambulance. **Clínica Central**, *San Isidro 231, T02-2221953*, open 24 hrs; **Emergency hospital**, *Marcoleta 377*, US$60, for vaccinations (not cholera); **Hospital de Urgencia**, *Portugal 125*, from US$125, cheapest public hospital; **Vaccinatoria Internacional**, *Hospital Luis Calvo, MacKenna, Antonio Varas 360.* **Emergency pharmacy**, *Portugal 155, T02-382439.*

Internet

Internet cafés are ubiquitous. Prices around US$0.60 to US$1 per hr.

Language schools

Escuela de Idiomas Violeta Parra, *Ernesto Pinto Lagarrigue 362A, Recoleta-Barrio Bellavista, T02-7358240, vioparra @chilesat.net*; **Instituto Chilena de la Lengua**, *Miraflores 590, piso 2, of 4, T02-6643114, www.cmet.net/ichil*; **Instituto Chileno Suizo de Cultura**, *San Isidro 171, T02- 6385414, chilenosuizo @tie.cl*; **Natalislang Language Centre**, *Vicuña Mackenna 06, piso 7, of 4, T02-2228721, info@natalislang.com*; **Pacifica**, *Guillermo Acuña 2884, Providencia, T02-2055129, pacifica@netline.cl*; **Top Language Services**, *Huérfanos 886, of 1107, T/F02-6390321.*

Post office

Plaza de Armas (open 0800-1900), poste restante (30 days max) is well organized with a list of post received on display (one list for men, another for women, indicate Sr or Sra/Srita on envelope), passport essential for collection. Sub offices in Providencia, *Av 11 de Septiembre 2092, Manuel Montt 1517, Pedro de Valdivia 1781, Providencia 1466*, and in *Estación Central shopping mall*, Mon-Fri 0900-1800, Sat 0900-1230. Paper, tape etc on sale, Mon-Fri 0800-1900, Sat 0800-1400.

Telephone

The cheapest call centres are on Bandera, Catedral and Santo Domingo, all near the Plaza de Armas. International calls from here are half the price of the main company offices: to the US, US$0.25 per min, to Europe, US$0.35 per min, eg at Catedral 1033 and Santo Domingo 1091. The main company offices are **Telefónica CTC**, *Moneda 1151*, closed Sun, and **ENTEL**, *Huérfanos 1133*, Mon-Fri 0830-2200, Sat 0900-2030, Sun 0900-1400, calls cheaper 1400-2200.

Useful addresses

Asatej Student Flight Centre, *Hernando de Aguirre 201, of 401, T02-3350395, chile@asatej.com.ar* Cheap flights, tours, car rental, ISIC cards, insurance, hotels. **Ministerio del Interior**, *Departamento de Extranjería, Teatinos 950 (near Estación Mapocho), T02-6744000.* Mon-Fri 0900-1200. For extension of tourist visa or any enquiries regarding legal status.

Chilean Lake District

Don't miss...
1 The feria at Temuco ▸▸ p240.
2 Volcán Villarrica ▸▸ p244.
3 Volcán Osorno ▸▸ p264.
4 Seafood in Angelmó ▸▸ p280.
5 The ferry to Puerto Natales ▸▸ p283.
40 km
40 miles
Pacific Ocean
CHILE
ARGENTIN
REGION IX
REGION X
Lago Lanalhue
Sauces
Contulmo
Purén
Collipulli
Lago Lleulleu
Cap Pastene
Victoria
Traiguén
Púa
Tirúa
Galvarino
Lautaro
Parque Nacional Tolhuaco
Termas de Tolhuaco
Lonquimay (2,865m)
Reserva Nacional Malalcahuello
Curacautín
Malacahuello
Lonquimay
Sierra Nevada
Chol Chol
Nehuentué
Nueva Imperial
Temuco
Carahue
Puerto Saavedra
Lago Budi
Barros Arana
Freire
Teodoro Schmidt
Río Toltén
Vilcún
Llaima
Lago Conguillo
Cherquenco
Vol Llaima (3,050m)
Parque Nacional Conguillío
Icalma
Melipeuco
Paso de Icalm
Lago Alumine
Moquehue
Los Laureles
Cunco
Radal
Río Colico
Lago Colico
Playa Negra
Lago Huilipilún
Lago Caburga
Caburga
Parque Nacional Huerquehue
Toltén
Villarrica
Lago Villarrica
Pucón
Termas de Palquin
Quillén
Loncoche
Villarrica (2,840m)
Mehuín
Lanco
Lican-Ray
Quetrupillán (2,009m)
Puesco
San José de la Mariquina
Lago Calafquén
Parque Nacional Villarrica
Paso Mamuil Malal
Río Cruces
Panguipulli
Coñaripe
Lago Panguipulli
Liquiñe
Lanín (3,768m)
Río Calle Calle
Riñihue
Lago Riñihue
Lago Neltume
Paso Carirriñe
Niebla
Antilhue
Corral
Valdivia
Los Lagos
Choshuenco
Puerto Fuy
Lago Huechulafquen
Parque Nacional Lanín
Lago Pirehueico
Manumento Natural Alerce Costero
Paillaco
Junín de los Andes
Futrono
Paso Hua Hum
Puerto Nuevo
Llifén
Lago Ranco
Lago Lacar
San Martí de los And
Río Bueno
La Unión
Lago Maihue
Trumao
Río Bueno
Lago Ranco
Río Cruces
Lago Huishué
Salto Pilmaiquén
Lago Gris
Osorno
Lago Constancia
Portezuela de Puyehue
Lago Puyehue
Río Golgol
215
Entre Lagos
Termas de Puyehue
Villa La Angostura
Río Negro
Rupanco
Lago Rupanco
Parque Nacional Puyehue
Parque Nacional Los Arrayanes
Islote
Parque Nacional Nahuel Huapi
Puerto Octay
Lago Nahuel Huapi
Punteagudo (2,490m)
Osorno (2,652m)
La Picada
Paso Pérez Rosales
Frutillar
Petrohué
Peulla
Bariloche
Río Negro
Lago Llanquihue
Lago Todos los Santos
Tronador (3,460m)
Cateral
La Poza
Ensenada
Parque Nacional Vicente Pérez Rosdales
Lago Mascardi
Calbuco
Cayutué
Villa Mascardi
Puerto Varas
Ralún
Lago Chapo
Puerto Montt
Pelluco
Cochamó
Parque Nacional Alerce Andino
Río Maullín
Isla Tenglo
Lenca
Puelo
p259
Maullín
La Arena
Carelmapu
Pargua
Calbuco
Isla Huar
Puelche
Faro Corona
Caulín
Contao
El Bolsón
Chacao
Norquinco
Río Negro/Hornopirén
Ancud
Golfo de Ancud
Los Repollos
Pumillahue
Linao
Parque Nacional Hornopirén
Vilcún
Belbén
Isla Caucahue
Isla Llancahué
El Mai
Chepu
Degán
Quemchi
Parque Pumalín
Parque Nacional Lago Puelo
Epuyén
Isla Butachauques
Península Huequi
Chiloé
Isla Mechuque
p275
Ayacara
Dalcahue
Tenaún
Castro
Achao
Isla Quinchao
Fiordo Reñihue
Fiordo Largo
Leptepu
Cholila
Leleq
Parque Nacional Chiloé
Nercón
Isla Chulin
Parque Pumalín
Vilopulli
Puqueldón
Isla Apiao
Chonchi
Caleta Gonzalo
Cucao
Teupa
Lago Menéndez
La Bolsa
Huillinco
Isla Lemuy
Isla Cahulinec
Caleta Santa Bárbara
Parque Nacional Los Alerces
Chiloé
Isla Talcán
Lago Futalaufquen
Queilén
Chaitén
Esquel
Isla Tranquil
Río Yelcho
Amarillo
Trevelin
Quellón
Trincao
Puerto Cárdenas
Lago Espolo
Corcovado (2,290m)
Futaleufú
Paso Futaleufú
Lago Yelcho
Puerto Piedra
Villa Santa Lucía
Carretera Austral
Paso Palena
Corcovado
Puerto Ramírez
Golfo de Corcovado
Nevada (2,042m)
Palena
Melinka
Lago General Vinttner
Lago Palena
Lago Vinttner
Río Palena
La Junta
Alto Río Pico
Lago Rosselot
Río Figueroa
Paso Las Pampas-Lago Verde
Río Pico

Introduction

Extending from the Río Biobío south to the city of Puerto Montt, the Lake District is one of the most popular destinations for both Chileans and visitors. The main cities are Temuco, Valdivia, Osorno and Puerto Montt, but the most attractive scenery lies further east where a string of lakes stretches down the western side of the Andes. Much of this region has been turned into national parks and the mixture of forests, lakes and snow-capped volcanoes is unforgettable.

In the north, the major resort is Pucón on Lago Villarrica, while, in the south, Volcán Osorno keeps watch over Lago Llanquihue and the Argentine border. Puerto Varas or the nearby city of Puerto Montt can both be used as a base for sea voyages south to Puerto Natales, Puerto Chacabuco and the San Rafael glacier, as well as east across the lakes and mountains to the Argentine resort of Bariloche.

Ratings

Landscape
★★★★

Chillin'
★★★★

Activities
★★★★

Wildlife
★★★★

Costs
$$$$

Northern lakes

Patagonia really starts with the southern lakes but there's plenty to see further north, including Volcán Villarrica, which has erupted 10 times in the last century. Popular resorts around Lago Villarrica provide access to the volcano and the opportunity for a wealth of outdoor activities. Temuco is a good starting point for any exploration of the region, providing an accessible gateway to some of the most beautiful spots in the Chilean Lake District.

Getting there Regular bus, train and plane services to Temuco or fly direct to Pucón for Volcán Villarrica.

Getting around Good bus services or hire a car.

Time required From 3 days for a whistle-stop tour to 2 weeks for an in-depth visit.

Weather Rain always possible but usually pleasant in summer.

Sleeping Plenty for all tastes and budgets.

Eating High class resort hotels, rough and ready in Temuco market.

Activities and tours Climbing, fishing, riding, rafting, skiing windsurfing. Spa treatments.

★ **Don't miss...** A guided ascent of Volcán Villarrica.

Ins and outs

Getting there 6 km southwest of Temuco is **Manquehue Airport**, with several daily flights north to Santiago and south to Puerto Montt. Taxis from airport to Temuco city centre cost US$4.50; there is no airport bus service. The airport 2 km east of Pucón on the Caburga road also has several flights a week to/from Santiago. There is a new long-distance **bus** terminal on the outskirts of Temuco, with connections to/from Santiago (many daily) and other large Chilean towns, including Valdivia and Puerto Montt (many daily), plus Neuquén and Bariloche in Argentina. There is also a nightly train to Santiago. Pucón is served by one or two daily buses from Puerto Montt, several daily from Santiago, as well as regular services from Temuco and Villarrica. » *Transport pp256-255.*

Getting around Temuco is the transport hub for the Lake District and its municipal bus station serves much of the region, as well as the communities towards the coast. Pucón is the main tourist centre on Lago Villarrica, offering tours and transport to nearby lakes and national parks.

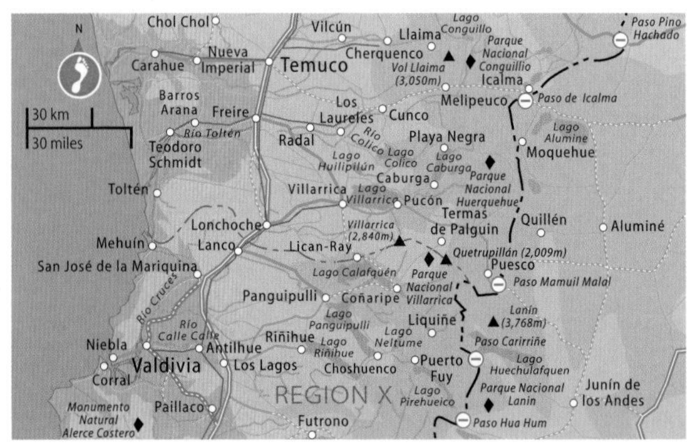

Background

The Mapuche

The largest indigenous group in southern South America, the Mapuche, take their name from the words for 'land' (*mapu*) and 'people' (*che*). They were known as Araucanians by the Spanish.

Never subdued by the Incas, the Mapuche successfully resisted Spanish attempts at conquest. At the time of the great Mapuche uprising of 1598 they numbered some 500,000, concentrated in the area between the Río Biobío and the Reloncaví estuary. The 1641 Treaty of Quilín recognized Mapuche autonomy south of the Biobío.

Although tools and equipment were privately owned, the Mapuche held land in common, abandoning it when it was exhausted by repeated use. This relatively nomadic lifestyle helps explain their ability to resist the Spanish. They became formidable guerrilla fighters and pioneered the use of horses by two men. Horses also enabled the Mapuche to extend their territory to the eastern side of the Andes and the Argentine pampas.

The conquest of the Mapuche was made possible by the building of railways and the invention of new weapons. The settlement of border disputes between Chile and Argentina allowed Argentine troops to occupy border crossings, while the Chileans subjugated the Mapuche.

Under the 1881 treaty, the Mapuche received 500,000 ha from the government. They were confined to reservations, most of which were situated near large estates for which they provided a labour force. By the 1930s, the surviving Mapuche, living in more than 3,000 separate reservations, had become steadily more impoverished and dependent on the government. Today Mapuche communities remain among the poorest in Chile and occupy only about 1½% of the lands they inhabited at the time of the Spanish conquest.

Between Temuco and the Pacific coast is the indigenous heartland of Chile, home to the largest Mapuche communities. Here you will find traditional thatched houses (*rucas*) and villages still fiercely proud of their traditions, hinting at the sort of country that the first *conquistadors* might have found. It is well worth making a trip to the dusty, friendly town of **Chol Chol**. Buses (Huincabus, 4 daily 1100-1800, 1 hr, US$1), laden with people and produce, make the 30 km journey from Temuco across rolling countryside. You will see people travelling by ox cart on the tracks nearby, and a few traditional round *rucas*. The town has a small museum dedicated to Mapuche culture.

Tourist information Sernatur ⓘ *Bulnes 586, T045-211969, infoaraucania@sernatur.cl, summer daily 0830-2030, winter Mon-Fri 0900-1200, 1500-1700,* in Temuco, has good leaflets in English. There is also a tourist kiosk in the market and an office of **CONAF** ⓘ *Bilbao 931, T045-234420.* Pucón's **tourist office** ⓘ *Municipalidad, O'Higgins 483*, provides information and sells licences for fishing on the lake. The **CONAF** office is at O'Higgins 669. Villarica's **tourist office** ⓘ *Valdivia 1070, T045-411162, daily in summer*, also has information and maps.

Temuco » pp247-257

At first sight, Temuco may appear a grey, forbidding place. However in reality it is a lively industrial and university town. For visitors, it is perhaps most interesting as a contrast to the more European cities in other parts of Chile. Temuco is proud of its Mapuche heritage, and it is this that gives it a distinctive character, especially around the *feria* (outdoor market). North and east of the city are national parks and reserves, and several hot springs.

Sights

The city is centred on the newly redesigned **Plaza Aníbal Pinto**, around which are the main public buildings including the cathedral and the municipalidad; the cathedral was destroyed by the 1960 earthquake, when most of the old wooden buildings in the city were also burnt down. On the plaza itself is a monument to 'La Araucanía' featuring figures from local history. Nearby are fountains and a small Sala de Exposiciones, which stages exhibitions. More compelling, though, is the huge produce **market** (*feria*) at Lautaro y Aníbal Pinto, which is always crammed with people (many of them Mapuche), who have come from the countryside to sell their produce (see page 254).

West of the centre, the **Museo de la Araucanía** ⓘ *Alemania 084, Mon-Fri 0900-1700, Sat 1100-1700, Sun 1100-1300, US$1, bus 1 from centre*, houses a well arranged collection devoted to the history and traditions of the Mapuche nation; there's also a section on German settlement.

On the northern edge of the city is the **Monumento Natural Cerro Ñielol** offering views of the city and surrounding countryside. The final peace treaty between the Chilean army and the Mapuche was signed on Cerro Ñielol in 1881, under 'La Patagua', a tree that can still be seen. It is a good spot for a picnic. There is an excellent visitors' centre ⓘ *0830-2030, US$1*, run by CONAF and a fine collection of native plants in their natural environment, including the *copihue rojo*, the national flower. Note that the hill has a one-way system for drivers (entry by Prat, exit by Lynch) and that bicycles are only allowed in before 1100.

Southeast of the centre is the predominantly Mapuche suburb of **Padre las Casas**. Here you will find the **Casa de la Mujer Mapuche** ⓘ *Corvalín y Almte Barroso, T09-1694682, Mon-Fri 0930-1300, 1500-1830, bus 8a/10, colectivo 13a*, which sells crafts and textiles made by a co-operative of 135 Mapuche weavers. The items are very good quality, but expensive.

Lago Villarrica » pp247-257

Backed to the southeast by the active and snow-capped Villarrica volcano (2,840 m), wooded Lago Villarrica, 21 km long and about 7 km wide, is one of the most beautiful lakes in the region. Its resorts – Villarrica and Pucón – are among the priciest in Chile and are busy with tourists in summer but those with the money will find them well worth the expense. Within easy reach is some of the most dramatic scenery in the Chilean Lake District, encompassing two lakes, two national parks and several hot spring resorts, perfect for relaxation after a hard day's trekking.

Villarrica

Pleasantly set at the extreme southwest corner of the lake, Villarrica can be reached by a paved road southeast from Freire, 24 km south of Temuco on the Pan-American Highway, or from Loncoche, 54 km south of Freire, also paved. Less significant as a tourist resort than nearby Pucón, it is also cheaper. Founded in 1552, the town was besieged by the Mapuche in the uprising of 1599: after three years the surviving Spanish settlers, 11 men and 13 women, surrendered. The town was refounded in 1882.

Going further

Parque Nacional Conguillio

One of the most popular national parks in Chile lies 80 km east of Temuco and is a good stopping point en route to the Argentine border at Paso Pino Hachado (see page 90). At the centre of the park is the still-active Volcán Llaima. It is possible to climb the volcano, hike throughout the park and also ski. The best means of visiting is with a hired 4WD or as part of a tour. The three park entrances are accessible from Curacautín, Melipeuco and Cherquenco, respectively. There is a visitor centre at the entrance by Lago Conguillio. Open December to March, US$5.

There is a small museum, the **Museo Histórico** ⓘ *Pedro de Valdivia 1050 y Zegers, Mon-Sat 0900-1730, 1800-2200, Sun 1800-2200, reduced hrs in winter, US$0.25*, containing a collection of Mapuche artefacts. Next to it is the **Muestra Cultural Mapuche**, featuring a Mapuche *ruca* and stalls selling good quality handicrafts in summer. There are good views of the volcano from the *costanera*; for a different perspective over the lake, go south along Aviador Acevedo and then taek Poniente Ríos towards the **Hostería de la Colina**.

Pucón

On the southeastern comer of the lake, 26 km east of Villarrica, Pucón is one of the most popular destinations in the Lake District, famous above all as a centre for visiting Volcán Villarrica (2,840 m), which lies to the south. Built across the neck of a peninsula, it has two black sand beaches, which are popular for swimming and watersports. Whitewater rafting is also offered on the nearby rivers and excursions can be made into the Parque Nacional Huerquehue and Parque Nacional Villarrica, which both lie east of the town.

The Pucón of today is very different from the town of 30 years ago, when it was a small, pleasant, quiet village with seasonal Chilean tourism, but no foreign backpackers. It is now a thriving tourist centre, full of Chileans in summer and gringos in the autumn. Neon signs are forbidden and roadsigns and telephone kiosks are made of wood, but the streets are full of bars,

Volcán Villarrica

restaurants and *artesanía*. The commercial centre lies between **Avenida O'Higgins**, the main thoroughfare, and the **Gran Hotel Pucón**. Private land (ask for permission at the entrance) leads west from the centre to **La Peninsula**, where there are views of the lake and volcano, as well as pony rides and golf. There is also a nice walk, along the **Costanera Otto Gudenschwager**, starting at the northern end of Calle Ansorena and following the lakeside to the north.

Boat trips ⓘ *daily 1500 and 1900, summer only, 2 hrs, US$4*, on the lake leave from the landing stage at La Poza at the western end of O'Higgins. Walk a couple of kilometres north along the beach from here to the mouth of the Río Pucón for views of volcanoes. Or take a boat ⓘ *summer only, US$12*, to the mouth of the river from near the Gran Hotel.

From the road to the Villarrica volcano, a *ripio* road branches off for 5 km to some privately managed *cuevas volcanicas* (**volcanic caves**) ⓘ *US$10*, surrounded by a small attractive park with tunnels and a museum, as well as paths through the forest. Entry to the site is expensive, but it's recommended as a bad-weather option.

Lago Caburga and around » pp 247-257

Lago Caburga (spelt locally Caburgua) is a very pretty lake in a wild setting 25 km northeast of Pucón. It is unusual for its beautiful white sand beach (other beaches in the area have black volcanic sand), and is supposedly the warmest lake in the Lake District. The western and much of the eastern shores are inaccessible to vehicles, but the village of **Caburga**, at the southern end of the lake, is reached by a turning off the main road to Argentina, 8 km east of Pucón.

If walking or cycling, there is a very pleasant alternative route: turn left 3 km east of Pucón, cross the Río Pucón via Puente Quelhue, then turn right and follow the track for 18 km through beautiful scenery. (From the bridge, there are also pleasant walks along the north shore of Lago Villarrica to the Mapuche settlement of **Quelhue** and the village of **Trarilelfú**.) Just off the main road from Pucón, Km 15, are the **Ojos de Caburga** ⓘ *US$0.50*, beautiful pools fed from underground, which are particularly attractive after rainfall.

The northern tip of Lago Caburga can be reached by a road from Cunco, which runs east along the northern shore of **Lago Colico**. This is one of the less accessible lakes, and lies north of Lago Villarrica in a remote setting.

Parque Nacional Huerquehue

ⓘ *open officially Jan-Mar, but you can get in at other times, US$3, parking 1½ km along the track, US$1*. Located a short distance east of Lago Caburga, Parque Nacional Huerquehue covers 12,500 ha at altitudes rising to 1952 m at the **Picos del Caburgua**. It also encompasses about 20 lakes, some of them very small, and many araucaria (monkey puzzle) trees. The entrance and administration is on the western edge, near **Lago Tinguilco**, the largest lake in the park. From the entrance there is a well-signed track north up a steep hill to **Lago Chico**, where the track divides left to **Lago Verde** and right to **Lago Toro**. The lakes are surrounded by trees and are very beautiful. The tracks rejoin at **Lago Huerquehue**, where a further 20 km of trails begin. None of the routes is particularly taxing, making the park a good warm-up for the volcán Villarrica hike. An adequate map is available at the entrance and the warden is very helpful. People in the park rent horses and boats but take your own food.

Reserva Forestal Cañi

ⓘ *Information from Fundación Lahuén, Urrutia 477, Pucón, T045-441660, lahuen@interaccess.cl. Access by guided tour only, US$17 per person (take lunch), plus transport. Also a 2-day tour with basic accommodation, US$34 per person.* Situated south of Parque Nacional Huerquehue and covering 500 ha, this is a private nature reserve owned by the **Fundación Lahuén**, and only

... and relax

More than a third of all the thermal spas in Chile are concentrated in the Lake District and further south, thanks to the high level of volcanic activity in this area. There are several east of Pucón, ranging from luxurious hotel complexes with extensive spa treatments to rustic bathtubs in the forest and natural pools or rivers. Easing your aching muscles in thermal water is the perfect way to recover after an arduous volcano trek.

The most expensive and ostentatious are the **Termas de Huife**, Km 33, T045-1975666, www.termashuife.cl, US$9, reached via a turning off the Pucón-Caburga road. The complex has three modern pools on the banks of the river Liucura. Overnight guests at the Hostería Termas de Huife (L) stay in upmarket cabins on site and can indulge in various treatments. Closer to Pucón and rather more low-key are the **Termas de Quimey-Co**, Km 29, T045-441903, US$5, with a hotel (A), campsite and two cabins. Further on are the **Termas los Pozones**, Km 35, US$5 per day, US$7 at night, which have six natural rock pools but little infrastructure and are very popular with backpackers.

Termas de Palguín, T045-441968, www.termasdepalguin.cl, US$6, are situated in a beautiful spot in the Quetrupillán section of the Villarrica national park, close to the spectacular Saltos del Puma and del León. They have a swimming pool, private baths and cabins.

Termas de San Luis, T045-411388/T045-412880, termasdesanluis@entelchile.net, US$9, are reached north off the Curarrehue road at Km 23. There's an indoor and outdoor pool, a sauna and well-equipped cabañas (AL), plus a pick-up service for overnight guests from Pucón. At Km 35, another turning leads north for 15 km to the **Termas de Pangui**, US$10, where there are three pools beautifully situated in the mountains. Accommodation is in a lodge (C-D) or in 3-person teepees right next to the hot pools. There are also camping facilities, good vegetarian meals, trekking and aromatherapy; contact O'Higgins 555, of 2, Pucón, T045-442039, ingeluz@yahoo.com

accessible on a guided tour – it is definitely worth a visit. The reserve contains 17 small lakes and is covered by ancient native forests of coigue and lenga; it also has some of the oldest araucaria trees in Chile. From its highest peak, **El Mirador**, (1,550 m) there are panoramic views over neighbouring parts of Argentina and Chile, including four volcanoes: Lanín, Villarrica, Quetrupillán and Llaima. As the reserve is above the snowline, tours are normally restricted to summer, though visits in winter are sometimes possible.

Parque Nacional Villarrica » pp247-257

This park, which covers 61,000 ha, stretches from Pucón to the Argentine border near Puesco. There are three sectors: around Volcán Villarrica; around Volcán Quetrupillán and the Puesco sector, which includes the slopes of the Lanín volcano on the Argentine

Volcán Villarrica

frontier. Each sector has its own entrance and ranger station. Between July and November it is possible to ski at the **Pucón resort**, which is situated on the eastern slopes of Villarrica and reached by a badly maintained track (see page 254).

Climbing Villarrica

The Villarrica volcano, 2,840 m high and still active, lies 8 km south of Pucón. Due to accidents, access to the volcano, US$3.50, is restricted only to groups with a guide – several agencies offer excursions (see Activities and tours, page 254) – and to individuals who can show proof of membership of a mountaineering club in their own country. Tours from Pucón cost US$30-40, including park entry, guide, transport to park entrance and hire of equipment (no reduction for those with their own equipment). Bargain for group rates. Entry is refused if the weather is poor. Good boots, crampons and ice picks are essential; these can be rented for US$4 per day from tour operators. You should also take sunglasses, sun block, plenty of water and chocolate or some other snack; equipment is checked at the park entrance.

It is a three- to four-hour trek to the summit, but you can skip the first 400 m by taking the ski lift (US$4). At the summit look down into the crater at the bubbling molten lava below, but beware of the sulphur fumes; the better tour agencies provide gas masks, otherwise take a cloth mask moistened with lemon juice. On exceptionally clear days you will be able to see six other volcanoes. Conditions permitting, groups may carry ski and snowboard equipment for the descent; otherwise just slide down.

Towards Paso Mamuil Malal

From Pucón a road runs southeast along the southern bank of the valley of the Río Traniura to the Argentine border at Paso Mumuil Malal/Tromen (see page 245) and on through Parque Nacional Lanín to Junín de los Andes. Unless the pass is closed by snow, this is the route used by international buses from Temuco. The road provides access en route to thermal springs and a number of hikeable waterfalls (*saltos*) in the Quetrupillán and Puesco sectors of the Villarrica national park.

Traversing the ice cap on Villarrica

At Km 18, a *ripio* road heads south 10 km to the Quetrupillán section of the park. On the edge of the park are the **Termas de Palguín** ⓘ *US$6*, and the spectacular **Saltos del Puma** and **del León** ⓘ *also accessible at Km 27 on the Pucón-Curarrehue road, US$1.50 for both*. From the springs a very rough dirt road, great for horse riding, runs south across the national park to Coñaripe (see page 246). Palguín is also the starting point for a four- to five-day hike to Puesco (see below), with vistas over the Villarrica and Lanín volcanoes.

Back on the Curarrehue road, at Km 23, a turning leads north to the indoor and outdoor pools at **Termas de San Luis** ⓘ *US$9*, from where it is 30 minutes' walk to **Lago del León**. At Km 24, the **Salto Palguín** can be seen (but not reached), and beyond that is the impressive **Salto China** ⓘ *Km 26, US$1*, where there's a restaurant and camping. At Km 35 another turning leads north for 15 km to the **Termas de Pangui** ⓘ *US$10*, where there are three pools beautifully situated in the mountains.

Beyond the small town of **Curarrehue**, 36 km east of Pucón, the road deteriorates as it turns south to the customs post in the Puesco sector of the park. The road then climbs via **Lago Quellelhue**, to reach the border at **Paso Mamuil Malal** (Paso Tromen). To the south of the pass rises the graceful cone of **Volcán Lanín** (3,747 m), one of the world's most beautiful mountains (see page 99).

Seven Lakes » pp247-257

Heading south from Villarrica, you can rejoin the Pan-American highway towards Valdivia and Osorno or take a more leisurely route southeast to Lican Ray and the 'Siete Lagos'. These lakes tend to be less developed than the resorts to the north and south. They form a picture-postcard necklace of water, with a backdrop of thick woods and distant snows. Six of the lakes lie in Chile, with the seventh, Lago Lacár, in Argentina. After the final peace settlement of 1882 the area around these lakes was reserved for Mapuche settlements. Most of the lakes have black-sand beaches, although as the water level rises in spring, these all but disappear.

Lago Calafquén and around

The most northerly of the seven lakes, **Lago Calafquén** is a popular tourist destination, readily accessible by a paved road from Villarrica, along which there are fine views of the Villarrica volcano. Wooded and dotted with small islands, the lake is reputedly one of the warmest in the region and is good for swimming. A partly paved road runs around the lake.

The major resort on the lake is **Lican-Ray**, named after a legendary Mapuche woman (see page 247). It is 30 km south of Villarrica on the north shore, and although crowded in summer, most facilities close by April. There are two beaches, one on each side of the peninsula. Boats can be hired (US$2 an hour) and there are catamaran trips (US$3 per hr or US$11 to the islands). Some 6 km to the east is the river of lava formed when the Villarrica volcano erupted in 1971. There is a **tourist office** on the plaza ⓘ *daily in summer, Mon-Fri in winter*.

Coñaripe, lies 21 km southeast of Lican-Ray with a black sand beach surrounded by mountains. The **tourist office** on the plaza ⓘ *mid Nov-mid Apr daily; late Apr-early Nov Sat and Sun only*, can arrange excursions to local thermal springs. From Coñaripe a road (mostly *ripio*) around the lake's southern shore leads to **Lago Panguipulli**, 38 km west, with views over Volcán Villarrica.

Another route heads southeast towards the Argentine border at **Paso Carirriñe**. As it crosses the steep Cuesta Los Añiques, there are views of **Lago Pellaifa**, a tiny lake with rocky surroundings and a small beach. The **Termas de Coñaripe** ⓘ *Km 16, T063-411407*, has four pools, accommodation, restaurant, cycles and horses for hire. Further south are the **Termas de Liquiñe** ⓘ *Km 32, T/F063-317377, US$4-7 per person*, with eight thermal springs and accommodation (but little other infrastructure), surrounded by a small native forest. About 8 km north of Liquiñe is a road going southwest (20 km) along the southeast shore of **Lago Neltume** to meet the Choshuenco-Puerto Fuy road.

Lagos Panguipulli and Pirehueico

Covering 116 sq km, Lago Panguipulli, the largest of the seven lakes, is reached by paved road from Lanco or Los Lagos on the Pan-American Highway or by *ripio* roads from Lago Calafquén. A road leads along the beautiful northern shore, which is wooded with sandy beaches and cliffs.

The site of a Mapuche settlement, **Panguipulli**, meaning 'hill of pumas', is situated on a hillside at the northwest corner of the lake and is the largest town in the area. On Plaza Prat is the Iglesia San Sebastián, built in Swiss style, with three bells from Germany. The plaza also has a tourist office (open Dec-Feb only). In summer, catamaran trips are offered on the lake and excursions can be made to Lagos Calafquén, Neltume, Pirehueico and Riñihue.

Choshuenco lies 45 km east of Panguipulli on the Río Llanquihue, at the eastern tip of the lake and can only be reached by road from Panguipulli or Puerto Fuy. To the south is the **Reserva Nacional Mocho Choshuenco** (7,536 ha), which has two volcanoes: Choshuenco (2,415 m) and Mocha (2,422 m). On the slopes of Choshuenco the **Club Andino de Valdivia** runs a small ski resort and three *refugios*. From Choshuenco a road leads east to Neltume and Lago Pirehueico, via the impressive waterfalls of **Huilo Huilo**. The falls are three hours' walk from Choshuenco, or take the Puerto Fuy bus and get off at **Alojamiento Huilo Huilo**.

Border with Argentina

Paso Carirriñe across the Argentine border is open between 15 October and 31 August, and is reached by unpaved road about 15 km from the Termas de Liquiñe. On the Argentine side the road continues through the Parque Nacional Lanín to Junín de los Andes (see page 100). This route is only used by international buses, when Paso Tromen is closed with snow. **Chilean immigration and customs** ⓘ *0800-2000 daily*. **Argentine immigration and customs** ⓘ *0800-2000 daily*.

Background

The legend of Lican-Ray

At the height of the wars between the Spanish and the Mapuche a young Spanish soldier was lost and strayed into the forests near Lago Calafquén. He came across a beautiful young Mapuche woman drying her hair in the sun and singing. He began to sing along and as they exchanged glances, they fell in love. She called him Allumanche, which means white man in Mapuche, and, pointing to herself, indicated that her name was Lican Rayan, meaning the flower of magic stone. They began to live together near the lake.

Lican Rayan's father, Curtilef, a powerful and fearsome chief, feared she might be dead. One day a boy came to him and said: "Lican Rayan is alive. I have seen her near the lake with a white man but she is not a prisoner: it is clear they are in love".

Lican Rayan saw the warriors coming to look for her. Knowing her father she feared what might happen, so she persuaded the soldier that they should flee. They escaped by riding on logs to one of the islands. There they felt safe, but they could not light a fire against the cold because the smoke would give them away. The weather grew cooler, the north wind blew and it rained heavily. After several days, unable to bear the cold and thinking that the warriors would have given up the search, they lit a fire. The smoke was spotted by Curtilef's men, so Lican Rayan and the solider fled to another island further away but again they were discovered and had to escape. This happened so many times that, although they were never caught, they were never seen again.

In the town of Lican-Ray, it is said that on spring afternoons it is sometimes possible to see a distant column of smoke from one of the islands, where Lican Rayan and the soldier are still enjoying their love after over 400 years.

Abridged and translated from *Lengua Y Costumbres Mapuches* by Orietta Appelt Martin, Imprenta Austral, Temuco, 1995.

Lago Pirehueico is a 36-km long, narrow and deep glacial lake surrounded by virgin *lingue* forest. It is beautiful and largely unspoilt, although there are plans to build a huge tourist complex in Puerto Pirehueico. There are two ports on the lake: **Puerto Fuy** at the northern end and **Puerto Pirehueico** at the southern end. The ports are linked by a ferry service (the crossing is beautiful; see page 257) and can also be reached by the road that runs east from Neltume to the Argentine border crossing at **Paso Hua Hum** (see page 101). The road south from Puerto Fuy, however, is privately owned and closed to traffic.

Sleeping

Temuco *p240, map p248*

A **Don Eduardo**, *Bello 755, T045-214133, deduardo@ctcinternet.cl* Suites in tower block with kitchen and parking, recommended.

A-B **Bayern**, *Prat 146, T045-276000, www.interpatagonia.com/hotelbayern* 3-star. Small rooms, but clean and helpful.

B **C'est Bayonne**, *Vicuña MacKenna 361, T045-234119, netchile@entelchile.net* With breakfast, small, modern, German and Italian spoken.

B **Continental**, *Varas 708, T045-238973, continental@ifrance.com* Popular with business travellers, old-fashioned building, old beds, excellent restaurant, the bar is popular with locals in the evening, cheaper rooms without bath.

D pp **Hostal Argentina**, *Aldunate 864*. With breakfast, hot water, clean.

D pp **Hostal Las Espigas**, *Miraflores 315, T045-881138, rivaseugenia@hotmail.com* Good rooms with bath, kitchen, breakfast, dinner available on request.

E pp **Casa Blanca**, *Montt 1306 y Zenteno, T045-277799, www.hostalcasablanca.cl* With breakfast, friendly, slightly run down, but good value for rooms with bath.

E pp **Hosp Aldunate**, *Aldunate 187, T045-213548*. Friendly, cooking facilities, also cheaper dormitory accommodation.

E pp **Hosp Maggi Alvarado**, *Recreo 209, off Av Alemania, T045-263215*. Small rooms, but very clean, friendly, helpful.

E pp **Oriente**, *M Rodriguez 1146, T045-233232, h-oriente@hispavista.com* Clean, recommended,

E pp **Turismo**, *Tarapacá 140, T045-881116*. Clean, good food, comfortable, best value.

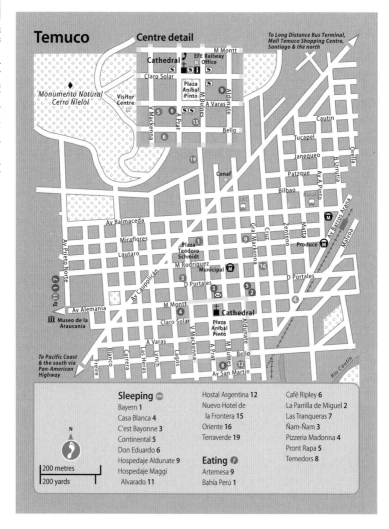

Temuco

Centre detail

Sleeping

Bayern **1**
Casa Blanca **4**
C'est Bayonne **3**
Continental **5**
Don Eduardo **6**
Hospedaje Aldunate **9**
Hospedaje Maggi Alvarado **11**
Hostal Argentina **12**
Nuevo Hotel de la Frontera **15**
Oriente **16**
Terraverde **19**

Eating

Artemesa **9**
Bahía Perú **1**
Café Ripley **6**
La Parrilla de Miguel **2**
Las Tranqueras **7**
Ñam-Ñam **3**
Pizzeria Madonna **4**
Pront Rapa **5**
Temedors **8**

200 metres
200 yards

Villarrica *p240*

Price codes are based on high season (Jan- Feb); off-season is 30-40% lower.

AL-A **El Ciervo**, *Koerner 241, T045-411245, www.hotelelciervo.cl* 4-star. Beautiful location, pool. Recommended.

AL-B **Hostería de la Colina**, *Las Colinas 115, overlooking town, T045-411503, aldrich@ entelchile.net.* With breakfast, large gardens, good service, good restaurant. Recommended.

A **Hostería Bilbao**, *Henríquez 43, T045-411186, www.7lagos.com/bilbao* Clean small rooms, pretty patio, good restaurant.

A **Hotel y Cabañas El Parque**, *3 km east on Pucón road, T045-411120, www.hotelparque.cl.* Lakeside with beach, tennis courts, breakfast, good restaurant with set meals. Highly recommended.

A **Hotel-Yachting Kiel**, *Koerner 153, T045-411631, www.villarrica.com /yachting* Off season, lakeside, clean, friendly, good.

B **Bungalowlandia**, *Prat 749, T045-411635, www.villarrica.com /bungalowlandia* *Cabañas* for 2, with *comedor*, good facilities.

B **Cabañas Traitraico**, *San Martín 380, T/F045-411064*, 100 m from lake, sleep 6, TV, heating, kitchenette, parking.

C **Kolping**, *Riguelme 399, T/F045-411388.* Good breakfast, recommended.

E **La Torre Suiza**, *Bilbao 969, T045-411213, www.torresuiza.com* Price per person. Excellent breakfast, kitchen and laundry facilities, camping, cycle rental, German, English spoken.

E **Villa Linda**, *Valdivia 678, T045-411392.* Price per person. Hot water, clean, basic, cheap, good restaurant.

E pp **Parque Natural Dos Ríos**, *13 km west of Villarrica, T09-4198064/ 09-9581887, www.dosrios.de* Tranquil 40 hectare nature park with *cabañas* on the banks of the Río Toltén (there is a white sand beach), horseback riding, bird-watching, children-friendly, German, English spoken.

E pp **Sra Nelly**, *Aviador Acevedo 725, T045-412299.* Hot water all day, good value, camping, recommended.

Camping

Many sites east of town on Pucón road, but these are open in season only. Those nearest to town are **El Edén**, *1 km southeast of centre, T045-412772*, US$4 per person, recommended, and **Los Castaños**, *T045-412330*, US$11 per site.

Pucón *p241*

Rooms may be hard to find in high season (Dec-Feb), but there are plenty of alternatives in Villarrica. There are also rooms in private houses – look for the signs or ask in bars/restaurants. Price codes are based on high season rates; off-season prices are 20-40% lower and it's often possible to negotiate.

LL-L **Antumalal**, *2 km west of Pucón, T045-441011, www.antumalal.com, info@antumalal.com* Picturesque chalet-style accommodation with magnificent views of the lake. Meals available. Lovely gardens with tennis. Open year round. Excellent.

A **Araucarias**, *Caupolicán 243, T045-441286, www.araucarias.cl* Clean, comfortable, indoor pool.

A **La Posada Plaza-Pucón**, *Valdivia 191, T045-441088, www.hotelplazapucon.cl* With bath, cheaper without, full board available, also spacious cabins.

A **Munich**, *Alderete 275, T/F045-442293.* Modern, spacious, English spoken.

B **Geronimo**, *Alderete 665, T045-443762, johanavillagran@hotmail.com* Comfortab le, friendly, quiet, cable TV, with restaurant, bar and terrace.

C-D **Hosp La Casita**, *Palguín 555, T045-441712, lacasita@entelchile.net* Clean, laundry and kitchen facilities, English and German spoken, large breakfast, garden, motorcycle parking, ski trips, Spanish classes.

C-D **La Tetera**, *Urrutia 580, T045-441462, www.tetera.cl* Rooms with and without bath. Good breakfast with real coffee,

German and English spoken, good Spanish classes, book swap, Navimag reservations, informative. Highly recommended, book in advance.

C-E **Hostería école**, *Urrutia 592, T045-441675, www.ecole.cl* Price per person without breakfast, also dormitory accommodation and rooms with bath, discount for Hostelling International members, good vegetarian and fish restaurant, ecological shop, forest treks, rafting, biking, information, language classes, massage, recommended.

E **Hostal Backpackers**, *Palguín 695, T045-441373, hostal@politur.com* Kitchen facilities, internet, information, 10% discount on Politur excursions.

E pp **Hostal Carlos Alfredo Richard**, *Arauco 171, parque_huerquehue@hotmail.com* Central location, shared rooms, use of kitchen, internet, also at Parque Huerquehue (see below).

E pp **Res Lincoyán**, *Av Lincoyán 323, T045-441144, www.lincoyan.cl* With bath, cheaper without, clean and comfortable.

E pp **Tr@vel Pucón**, *Blanco Encalada 190, T045-444093, pucontravel@terra.cl* English, German, French spoken, near Turbus terminal, garden, kitchen facilities, Spanish classes.

There are also plenty of people who meet the buses with offers of accommodation in private houses, generally E or F per person.

Camping

La Poza, *Costanera Geis 769, T045-441435*. Hot showers, clean, quiet, good kitchen facilities, open all year. Recommended.

L'etoile, *Km 2 towards Volcán Villarrica, T045-442188*. Attractive forest site.

Lago Caburga and around p242

C **Hostería Los Robles**, *3 km from Caburga village, T045-236989*. Lovely views, good restaurant; also campsite, expensive in season, cheap out of season.

C-D **Refugio Tinquilco**, *3½ km from park entrance, T02-7777673, patriciolanfranco*

@entelchile.net Doubles with bath, meals served, cooking facilities, heating.

D **Landhaus San Sebastián**, *east of Lago Caburga, F045-1972360, www.landhaus-chile.com* With bath and breakfast, tasty meals, laundry facilities, good walking base, English and German spoken, Spanish classes.

Dpp **Hostal Carlos Alfredo Richard**, *southwest shore of Lago Tinquilco, 2 km from park entrance, parque_huerquehue @hotmail.com* Breakfast included. Large rooms, private bathrooms with hot water, restaurant, rowboats to hire.

Camping

The southern end of Lago Caburga is lined with campsites, but there are no shops, so take your own food. There are also 2 sites north of Lago Colico and 2 campsites at the entrance to Parque Nacional Huerquehue, US$8, but no camping is allowed in the park.

Parque Nacional Villarrica *p243*

Avoid the refugio 4 km inside the park towards Volcán Villarrica, which is insecure and in desperate need of renovation. There is a CONAF campsite at Puesco and another, near Lago Tromen, free, but no facilities.

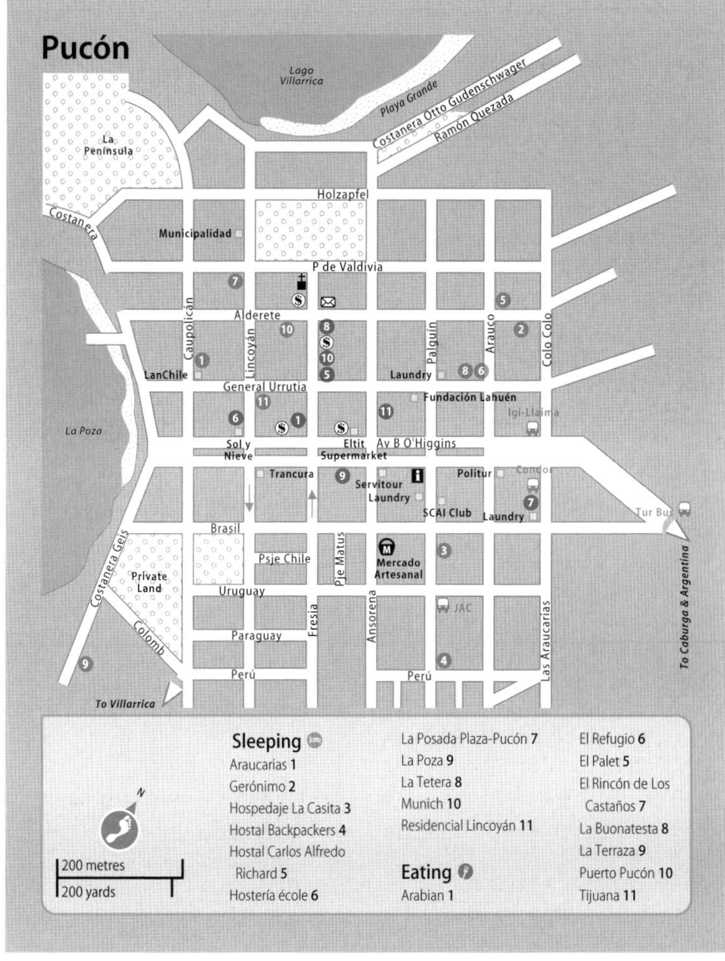

Towards Paso Mamuil Malal p244

E **Kila Leufu**, *Km 20, Pucón-Curarrehue road, T09-7118064, www.kilaleufu.cl* Price per person. Rooms on the Martínez family farm, contact daughter Margot in advance, friendly, English spoken, full board available including spit-roast lamb in the *ruca*, also offers trekking information, horseriding and mountain bike hire. Recommended.
E **Rancho de Caballos**, *36km SE of Pucón on the dirt road to Coñaripe, T045-441575.* Price per person. Restaurant with vegetarian dishes, laundry and kitchen facilities; also *cabañas* and camping, self-guided trails, horseriding excursions US$50 per day, English and German spoken, recommended.

Lago Calafquén and around p246

App **Termas de Liquiñe**, *Km 32 , T/F063-317377.* Full board, cabins, restaurant, tours offered.
C **Hostería Inaltulafquen**, *Casilla 681, Playa Grande, Lican-Ray, T045-431115, F045-410028.* With breakfast and bath, English spoken.
D **Cabañas Cacique Vitacura**, *Urrutia 825, Playa Grande, Lican-Ray, T02-2355302, tradesic@inter media.cl* For 2, also larger cabins with kitchen.
E pp **Hosp Chumay**, *on Plaza, Coñaripe, T063-317287 turismochumay@hotmail.com* Restaurant, internet, tours.

Camping

Isla Llancahue, *5 km east, T063-317360.* Campsite with *cabañas* on an island in Río Llancahue. There are also several campsites on the north and south sides of the lake, US$15 per site.

Lagos Panguipulli and Pirehueico p246

Beds are available in private houses around Lago Pirehueico, and free camping is possible on the beach.
B **Hostal España**, *O'Higgins 790, Panguipulli, T063-311166, hostal_espana @elsitio.com* Rooms with breakfast.
B **Hostería Quetropillán**, *Etchegaray 381, Panguipulli, T063-311348.* Comfortable.
E pp **Hosp Familiar**, *Los Ulmos 62, Panguipulli, T063-311483.* English spoken, kitchen facilities, helpful, good breakfast.
E pp **Hostería Rayen Trai**, *María Alvarado y O'Higgins, Choshuenco.* Former yacht club serving good food, open all year.
E pp **Hotel Central**, *Valdivia 115, Panguipulli, T063-311331/09-8823955.* Clean rooms, with breakfast.

Eating

Temuco p240, map p248

Those on a very strict budget should make for the **Mercado Municipal**, *Aldunate y Portales*, where there are several restaurants and fierce touting for business. *Humitas* are on sale in the street in summer/autumn.
ΨΨ **Bahía Peru**, *Alemania y Recreo, near the Mall Mirage, about 10 blocks west of centre.* One of several good mid-priced restaurants on Av Alemania (take bus 1), Peruvian food, good pisco sours.
ΨΨ **Caletas Restaurante**, *Mercado Municipal, Aldunate y Portales.* Seafood.
ΨΨ **La Cumbre del Cerro Ñielol**, *Cerro Ñielol.* Food and dancing on top of the hill, not always open.
ΨΨ **La Parrilla de Miguel**, *Montt 1095.* Good for meat and wine .
ΨΨ **Pizzeria Madonna**, *Montt 670.* Good atmosphere, good pizzas, reasonable.
ΨΨ **Las Tranqueras**, *Alemania 0888.* Meat specialists, great grills, but vegetarian options also available.
Ψ **Artemesa**, *Aldunate 620, 8th floor.* Vegetarian restaurant with views.
Ψ **Cafetería Ripley**, *Prat y Varas.* Real coffee.
Ψ **Ñam-Ñam**, *Portales 802.* Good sandwiches and snacks.
Ψ **Restaurante Temedors**, *San Martín 827.* Good-value lunch.

Villarrica p240

ΨΨΨ **El Tabor**, *Epulef 1187.* Excellent but pricey.

Temuco market

TT **El Rey de Mariscos**, *Letelier 1030*. Good seafood.
TT **Rapa Nui**, *Vicente Reyes 678*. Good and cheap end of the range, closed Sun.
TT **The Travellers**, *Letelier 753*. Varied menu including vegetarian and Asian food, bar, English spoken.
TT **Chito Fuentes**, *Reyes 665*. Fast food.
T **Café 2001**, *Henríquez 379*. Coffee and ice cream, good.

Pucón p241, map p251
There are a couple of German cafés, Holzapfel Backerei and La Tetera, recommended for coffee and snacks. For other options see Sleeping, above. Vegetarians should check out the delicatessen at O'Higgins y Fresia, which serves fresh vegetarian food. For eating options in the national parks and lakes east of Pucón, see Sleeping, above.
TTT **Ana María**, *O'Higgins 865*. Classic Chilean food.
TTT **En Alta Mar**, *Urrutia y Fresia*. Fish and seafood, very good.
TTT **Puerto Pucón**, *Fresia 251*. Spanish, stylish.
TT **Arabian**, *Fresia 354-B*. Good Arab food.
TT **Brasil**, *Fresia 477*. Chilean food.
TT **El Palet**, *Fresia 295*. Authentic local food, clean, friendly service, reasonably priced. Recommended by local people.
TT **El Refugio**, *Lincoyán 348*. Some vegetarian dishes, expensive wine.
TT **El Rincón de Los Castaños**, *Colo-Colo 450*. Chilean food.
TT **La Buonatesta**, *Fresia 243*. Good pizzeria.
TT **La Maga**, *Fresia 125*. Uruguayan Parillada serving possibly the best steak in Chile.
TT **Nau Kana**, *Fresia*. Good Oriental food.
TT **Tijuana**, *Fresia 303*. Mexican.
T **La Terraza**, *O'Higgins 323*. Pleasant terrace, cheap lunches.

Lago Calafquén and around p246
TT-T **Café Ñaños**, *Urrutia 105, Lican-Ray*. Very good, reasonable prices, helpful.
TT-T **Restaurant-Bar Guido's**, *Urrutia 405, Lican-Ray*. Good value.
T **Coyote**, *on the plaza, Lican-Ray*. Cheap, open off-season.

Lago Panguipulli p246
TT **Didáctico El Gourmet**, *Ramón Freire s/n*. Restaurant linked to a hotel school. Excellent food and wine, mid price but high quality, school terms only.
TT-T **Café Central**, *M de Rozas 750*. Good cheap lunches, expensive evening meals.
TT-T **El Chapulín**, *M de Rozas 639*. Good food, good value, friendly.

Festivals and events

Villarrica p240
Many events are organised in Jan and Feb, including music, regattas, triathlon, rodeo and the **Festival Cultural Mapuche**, with a market, based around the Muestra Cultural Mapuche, usually in 2nd week of Feb.

Shopping

Temuco p240, map p248

Crafts

Mapuche crafts and textiles are sold inside and around the **Mercado Municipal**, *Aldunate y Portales*, and also in the **Casa de la Mujer Mapuche** (see Sights above).

Food

Temuco feria, *Lautaro y Aníbal Pinto*. This is one of the most fascinating markets in Chile, where people from the surrounding countryside come to sell their wares. You will find excellent cheap fruit and vegetables, local spices like *merquén* (made from smoked chillies), fish, grains, cheese and honey; there are many inexpensive bars and restaurants nearby.

Activities and tours

Note that travel agencies will not start a trek to **Volcán Villarrica** if the weather is bad and some travellers have experienced difficulties in obtaining a refund: establish in advance what terms apply in the event of cancellation and be prepared to wait a few days. For information on individual guides, all with equipment, ask for recommendations at the tourist offices. There are plenty of tour operators in Temuco, but it is far better to book with a company in Villarrica or Pucón. Check with the local tourist office for the latest information, as prices, schedules and operators can change very quickly in this popular tourist area.

Villarrica p240

Tour operators

Operators include: **Karina Tour**, *Letelier 825, T045-412048*; **Politur**, *Henriquez 475, T045-414547*; **Turismo Coñaripe**, *P Montt 525, T045-411111*, or **Turismo Repu-Pehuén**, *Pedro de Valdivia 565, T/F045-412065*. Prices are fairly standard: to Parque Nacional Villarrica, US$13; to climb Volcán Villarrica, US$30-40; to Valdivia US$25; to Termas de Coñaripe US$22.

Pucón p241, map p251

Aerial sports

Fabrice Pini, *Colo Colo 830, T09-4111072*. Paragliding US$50 for ½ hr; also hydrospeed watersports, US$20 for the morning.

Fishing

Pucón and Villarrica are celebrated as bases for fishing on Lago Villarrica and on the beautiful Lincura, Trancura and Toltén rivers. The local tourist office will supply details on licences and open seasons etc. Some tourist agencies also offer trips.

Mario's Fishing Zone, *O'Higgins 581, T045-444259, www.pucon.com/fishing Expensive, but good fishing guide.*

Off Limits, *Fresia 273, T045-441210, offlimitspucon@hotmail.com* Fishing specialists, English spoken, offer fly-fishing excursions US$100 per day, max 3 people. Also fishing boat excursions from US$190 for 2 people.

Horse riding

Horse hire is about US$35 half day, US$55 full day; enquire at **La Tetera** in Pucón, or try **Rancho de Callabos** at the Termas de Palguín; for both see Sleeping above.

Centro de Turismo Ecuestre Huepil, *T09-4534212*. Small groups, local excursions and 3-day trips to Argentina.

Skiing

Pucón resort, *20 km from Pucón on the slopes of Villarrica, www.skipucon.cl*. It has 20 pistes, 9 lifts, ski schools, equipment rental, restaurant, bar and other facilities. Piste preparation can be mediocre but the view across the lakes is incredible. For details of lift passes, consult the website.

Tour operators

All operators can arrange a variety of trips. Prices vary, as well as the quality of guides and equipment, so shop around: climbing Villarrica, 12 hrs, US$30-40 including park entry and equipment; ski hire and transport to slopes US$20 per person; tours to Termas de Huife, US$20 including entry. To reach the falls, lakes and *termas* it is usually cheaper for groups to flag down a taxi and negotiate a price. In addition to the following, try **Hostería école**, see Sleeping above.

Ronco Track, *O'Higgins, esq. Arauco, T045-449597*. Quadbike excursions.

Sol y Nieve *O'Higgins, esq Lincoyán, T/F045-441070, www.solynieve.cl.* Previously held in high esteem, with guides and equipment, but now some mixed reports about organisation. Most guides speak English.

Sur Expediciones, *O'Higgins 660*. New but good reputation.

Watersports

Equipment for water-skiing (US$10 for 15 mins), dinghy sailing (lasers US$11 per hr) and windsurfing (sailboards US$10 per hr) can be hired at Playa Grande. Outlets on La Poza beach are more expensive and not recommended. Whitewater rafting is popular on the **Río Trancura**, east of Pucón; many agencies offer trips: Trancura Baja (basic, grade III) US$15; Trancura Alta (advanced, grade IV) US$25.

Aguaventura expediciones, *Palguín 336, T045-444246, www.aguaventura.com* Rafting, plus canoe trips on Río Liucura, US$10 per person, and kayaking. French run, English spoken.

Lagos Panguipulli and Pirehueico

p246

Fishing

Good spots on Lago Panguipulli include: **Puntilla Los Cipreses** at the mouth of the Río Huanehue, 11 km east of Panguipulli, 30 mins by boat; and the mouth of the **Río Niltre**, on the east side of the lake. Boat hire US$3, licences from the **Municipalidad**, **Librería Colón**, *O'Higgins 528* or from the **Club de Pesca**.

Whitewater rafting

Good rafting on the **Río Fuy**, grade IV-V; **Río San Pedro**, varying grades, and on the **Río Llanquihue** near Choshuenco.

Transport

Temuco *p240, map p248*

Air

LanChile and **Sky** fly to **Manquehue Airport** from **Santiago**, 1¼ hrs, **Osorno**, 40 mins, and **Puerto Montt**, 45 mins. **Airline offices** LanChile, *Bulnes 687, on Plaza, T045-272138*; **Sky Airline**, *T600-600 2828* for information; **Varig**, *Bello 870, T045-213120.*

Bus

Regional Services to neighbouring towns leave from **Terminal Rural**, *Pinto y Balmaceda* or from bus company offices nearby: **Erbuc**, *Miraflores y Bulnes*; **JAC**, **NarBus** and **Igi Llaima**, *Balmaceda y Aldunate*; **Tur Bus**, *Lagos 549*.

JAC runs buses to **Villarrica** and **Pucón**, many daily 0705-2045, 1½ hrs, US$3, and to **Coñaripe**, 3 hrs, and **Lican Ray**, 2 hrs. To **Panguipulli**, **Power** and **Pangui Sur**, 3 hrs, US$3. **Pangui Sur** also has services to **Loncoche**, US$1.50 and **Los Lagos**, US$2.50.

Long distance The terminal is north of city at *Pérez Rosales y Caupolicán*; to get there, take buses 2 or 10 from the centre. To **Santiago**, several companies, 9hrs, most overnight, US$8 (*salón cama* US$22); to **Valdivia** 2½hrs, US$3; to **Osorno** 4hrs, US$4; to **Puerto Montt**, **Cruz del Sur**, 10 daily, 5½ hrs, US$6; to **Castro** (Chiloé), **Cruz del Sur**, 3 daily; also buses to cities further north.

To Argentina To **Neuquén** via Pucón, Paso Tromen and Junín de los Andes, **Buses San Martín**, 3 a week, US$15. To **Neuquén** via Curacautín, Lonquimay and the Paso Pino Hachado, **Igi Llaima**, **Buses Caraza** and **Buses El Valle**, daily between them, US$20; see p for onward services from Neuquén. To **Bariloche** via Osorno, **Tas Choapa**, daily, US$18; see p129 for onward services.

Car hire

Automóvil Club de Chile, *Varas 687, T045-248903* and at airport; **Budget**, Lynch 471, T045-214911; **Euro**, *MacKenna 426,*

T045-210311, helpful, good value; **Full Famas**, *at airport and in centre T045-215420*, recommended. Several others.

Train

The **station** is at *Barros Arana y Lautaro Navarro, T045-233416*. There is also another ticket office at *Bulnes 582, T045-233522*, open Mon-Fri 0900-1300, 1430-1800, Sun 0900-1300. To **Santiago**, overnight service on a modern train, daily 2200, 9 hrs, *Preferente* US$30, *salón* US$20. There is a connecting bus service from Pucón at 1900. There are no trains south of Temuco.

Villarrica *p240*

Bus

The main terminal is at *Pedro de Valdiva y Muñoz*; JAC has 2 terminals, at *Muñoz y Bilbao*, (long-distance) and opposite for Pucón and Lican-Ray (local). Other services leave from the **Terminal Rural**, *Matta y Vicente Reyes*.

Buses to **Santiago**, 10 hrs, US$9, several companies; to **Pucón**, both **Vipu-Ray** (main terminal) and **JAC**, every 15 mins in summer, 40 mins, US$0.75; to **Puerto Montt**, US$6; to **Valdivia**, JAC, 5 a day, 2½ hrs, US$3.50; to **Lican-Ray** services in summer, JAC and Vipu-Ray, US$1; to **Coñaripe**, US$1.50, and **Liquiñe** at 1600 Mon-Sat, 1000 Sun; to **Temuco**, JAC, every 30 mins in summer, US$3; to **Loncoche** (Route 5 junction for hitching), US$1.50. There are also occasional direct buses to **Panguipulli**, via Lican Ray.

To Argentina Buses from Temuco to Junín de los Andes stop in Villarrica en route to Paso Tromen; fares are the same as from Temuco, see p255. There are no services from Villarrica when the Tromen pass is blocked by snow; buses go via Paso Carirriñe instead.

Pucón *p241, map p251*

Air

Lan Express flies to **Santiago**, 4 times weekly in summer. The **LanChile** office is at *Urrutia 103 y Caupolican, T045-443516*, open Mon-Sat 1000-1400, 1800-2200.

Bus

There is no municipal terminal; each company has its own: **JAC**, *Uruguay y Palguín*; **Tur Bus**, *O'Higgins 910, east of town*; **Igi Llaima** and **Condor**, *Colo Colo y O'Higgins*.

To **Villarrica**, JAC, every 15 mins, US$0.75; to **Valdivia**, JAC, 5 daily, US$4.50; to **Temuco** hourly, 2 hrs, US$3, or *rápido*, 1 hr, US$3.50; to **Puerto Montt**, 6 hrs, US$8, daily with **Tur Bus**, or change at Valdivia. To **Santiago**, morning and evening, 10 hrs, US$11; *salón cama* service by **Tur Bus** and **JAC**, US$30.

To Argentina Buses from Temuco to **Junín de los Andes** arrive in Pucón at 1000; for fares see Temuco, p255. There are no services from Pucón, when the Tromen pass is blocked by snow.

Car hire

Prices from$27 per day: **Christopher Car**, *O'Higgins 335, T/F045-449013*; **Hertz**, *Fresia 220, T045- 441664*, more expensive; **Pucón Rent A Car**, *Camino Internacional 1395, T045-441922, kernayel@ cepri.cl*; **Sierra Nevada**, *Palguín y O'Higgins*, cars and 4WDs, reasonable.

Taxi

Taxis are useful for out-of-town trips: **Cooperative**, *T045-441009*.

Lago Caburga and around *p242*

JAC runs buses from Pucón to **Caburga**, several daily, US$1; there are also minibuses every 30 mins from *Ansorena y Uruguay* in Pucón; a taxi day trip costs US$25 return. Tour agencies arrange transport for groups to **Parque Nacional Huerquehue**, US$8. Taxis cost US$34 return. Minibuses from *Ansorena y Brasil*.

Towards Paso Mamuil Malal *p244*

Several minibuses daily to **Curarrehue** from Pucón, also daily bus from Pucón to

border, 1800, 2 hrs, US$2, returns to Pucón 0700.

Lago Calafquén and around *p246*

From Lican-Ray, buses leave from offices around the plaza to **Villarrica**, JAC, frequent, 1 hr, US$0.75; to **Santiago**, Tur Bus and JAC, 10 hrs, US$12, *salón cama* US$25; to **Temuco**, JAC 2½ hrs, US$3.50; to **Coñaripe**, 4-7 daily.

From Coñaripe, buses run to **Panguipulli**, 7 daily (4 off season), US$1.50; to **Villarrica**, 16 daily, US$1; to **Lican-Ray**, 45 mins, US$0.75. Also a nightly bus direct to **Santiago** run by Tur Bus and JAC, 10½ hrs, US$12, salón cama in summer US$25.

Lagos Panguipulli & Pirehueico *p246*

Bus

The bus terminal in Panguipulli is at *Gabriela Mistral y Portales*. To **Santiago** daily, US$12; to **Valdivia**, Mon-Sat, 4 only on Sun, several companies, 2 hrs, US$3; to **Temuco**, frequent, Power and Pangui Sur, US$2; to **Puerto Montt**, US$5; to **Calafquén**, 3 daily at 1200, 1545 and 1600; to **Choshuenco**, **Neltume** and **Puerto Fuy** (3 hrs), 3 daily, US$3; to **Coñaripe**, for Lican-Ray and Villarrica, 4-7 daily.

Ferry

The *Hua Hum* ferry sails across Lago Pirehueico from Puerto Fuy to Puerto Pirehueico, twice daily in summer, daily at other times, 2-3 hrs, foot passengers US$1, cars US$15; vehicles should reserve a space in advance at the Hotel Quetropillán in Panguipulli. The ferry connects with buses to **San Martín de los Andes** (Argentina), via Paso Hua Hum, daily in summer, weekly in winter (out Sat 0930, return Sun 1330).

Directory

Temuco *p240, map p248*

Banks and currency exchange ATMs at several banks on or around Plaza A Pinto also at the new JAC bus terminal. There are many *cambios* around the Plaza; all deal in dollars and Argentine pesos. **Honorary consulate** Netherlands, *España 494*, honorary consul, Germán Nicklas, is friendly and helpful. **Internet** *Gral. MacKenna 445*; several others, generally US$0.75 per hr. **Laundry** Alba, *Zeneto 480*, opposite the church, and at *Aldunate 324* and *Aldunate 842*; Marva, *M Montt 415 and 1099*, Mon-Sat 0900-2030. **Post office** *Portales 839*. **Telephone** CTC, *A Prat just off Claro Solar and plaza*, Mon-Sat 0800-2400, Sun and holidays 1030-2400; Entel, *Bulnes 303*. daily 0830-2200; also call centres at *Lautaro 1311* and *Montt 631*.

Villarrica *p240*

Banks and currency exchange There are ATMs at the major banks. Rates at *casas de cambio* are generally poor. Exceptions are: Central de Repuestos, *Muñoz 415*, and Cristopher, *Valdivia 1061*, for TCs. **Internet** Cybercafé Salmon, *Letelier y Henríquez*. **Laundry** Lavacenter, *Alderete 770*; Lavandería y Lavaseco Villarrica, *Andrés Bello 348*. **Post office** *Muñoz y Urrutia*, Mon-Fri 0900-1300, 1430-1800, Sat 0900-1300. **Telephone** CTC, *Henríquez 544*; Chilesat, *Henriquez 473*; Entel, *Henríquez 440 and 575*.

Pucón *p241, map p251*

Banks and currency exchange ATMs in Banco Santander and Eltit supermarket, both on O'Higgins. Change TCs before arriving as rates poor. Several *casas de cambio* on O'Higgins. **Bicycle hire** US$1.50 per hr or US$10 per day from several travel agencies, many on O'Higgins; shop around as quality varies. **Internet** several on O´Higgins. **Laundry** at *Urrutia 520*; *Palguín 460*; *Fresia 224*; *Colo-Colo 475* and *478*, several others. **Post office** *Fresia 183*. **Telephone** CTC, *Gen Urrutia 472*; Entel, *Ansorena 299*.

Going further

Going further... Valdivia

For a complete contrast to the rural communities around the lakes, visit the lively student city of Valdivia to the west. It's a good place to rest after arduous treks in the mountains. Founded in 1552 by Pedro de Valdivia, the city was abandoned as a result of the Mapuche insurrection of 1599 and was not refounded until 1645 when it became the only Spanish mainland settlement south of the Río Biobío. The Spanish fortified the area throughout the 1600s but the defences proved of little avail during the Wars of Independence, when the Chilean naval squadron under Lord Cochrane seized control of Valdivia's forts in two days. Until the 1880s Valdivia remained an outpost of Chilean rule, reached only by sea or by a coastal route. In 1960, a devastating earthquake and tidal wave caused the land around Valdivia to drop by 3 m, creating new lagunas to the north of the city.

Getting there There are daily flights to the airport 29 km north of the city from Santiago, as well as numerous buses from Santiago, Puerto Montt and Temuco. Access from the Panamericana is via Loncoche (toll US$2.50), Paillaco or by *ripio* road from Los Lagos. **Tourist information** (Prat 555, T063-342300).

Don't miss...

Cervecería Kunstmann, T063-292969, www.cerveza-kunstmann.cl Tour the working brewery and museum before tucking into German food and five types of beer.

Plaza de la República The heart of the city and the site of the cathedral museum, for four centuries of Christian history

Isla Teja This island is home to the university, the botanical gardens and two good museums.

Santuario de la Naturaleza Río Cruces Boat trips from the city dock run north to this flooded nature reserve, which now attracts many bird species.

Niebla and Corral Take a boat downstream to visit two of the most important 17th-century Spanish forts. The boat also stops midstream at Isla Mancera, a small island dominated by the Castillo de San Pedro de Alcántara, the earliest of the Spanish forts.

Semana Valdiviana This festival in mid February, culminates in Noche Valdiviana, when a procession of elaborately decorated boats sail past the Muelle Fluvial.

Sleeping and eating

C-E **Aires Buenos**, Gral Lagos 1036, T063-206304. Price per person. Some rooms with bath. Kitchen facilities, bar, internet, tours, Spanish and tango lessons, Argentinian run, English spoken, recommended. TTT **Restaurante Camino de Luna**, Prat s/n. A floating restaurant next to the costanera, unique in Chile.

Southern lakes

The southern lakes are the real gateway to Patagonia. The virgin forest becomes thicker, the volcanoes more remarkable, the settlements fewer. In spite of the fact that tourism is booming on Llanquihue and Todos los Santos, there are numerous spots where you can still escape to the old heart of Patagonia. And with activities from windsurfing and horse trekking to ice climbing, this region will keep even the most active traveller happily occupied.

Getting there Long-distance buses to Osorno or flights to Puerto Montt, also buses from Bariloche.
Getting around Plenty of buses to Puerto Varas; limited services around Llanquihue.
Time required 2-5 days.
Weather Stunning sun or stunning rain.
Sleeping From luxury tourist hotels to campsites.
Eating Try the German pastries for a reminder of the early settlers.
Activities and tours Fishing, hiking, riding and rafting
★ **Don't miss...** The guided ascent of Volcán Osorno.

Ins and outs

Getting there Osorno is a key crossroads for bus routes in southern Chile and to the Argentine Lake District. Passengers heading for Bariloche, Neuquén, Coyhaique or Punta Arenas will pass through here before making for the Puyehue Pass into Argentina. There are hourly local services to Puerto Montt and frequent services north to Temuco and Valdivia. Puerto Varas is the main centre on Lago Llanquihue and is served by shuttle buses from Puerto Montt every few minutes; there are connections north to Osorno, Valdivia, Temuco and Santiago and east across Lago Todos los Santos to Bariloche. A taxi to Puerto Varas from Puerto Montt airport costs US$16.

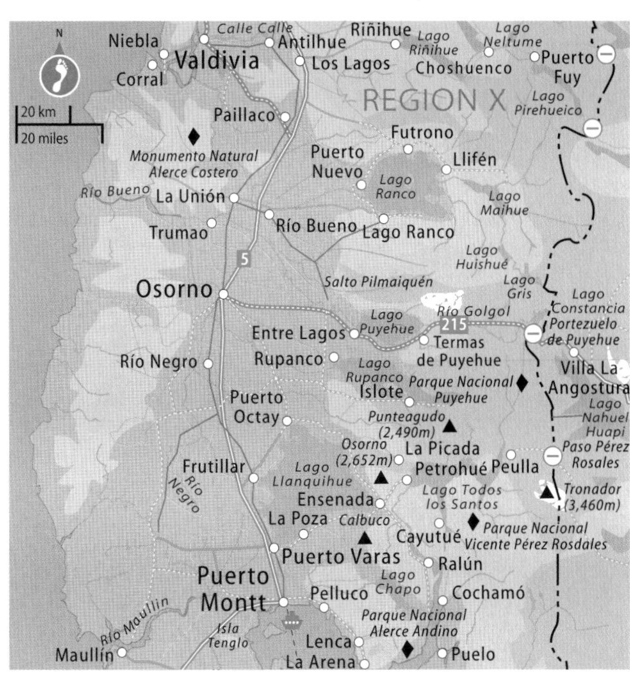

 Getting around There are local bus services around Lago Llanquihue but the eastern shore is difficult to visit without your own transport. Beyond Las Cascadas, the road is narrow with lots of blind corners, necessitating speeds of 20-30 kph at best in places. There is almost no public transport on this section and hitching is very difficult. Minibuses run along the southern shore of the lake to Ensenada for access to the Parque Nacional Vicente Pérez Rosales. » *For further details, see Transport, page 273.*

Tourist information Information is available in Osorno from the provincial government office of **Sernatur** ⓘ *Plaza de Armas, O'Higgins s/n, p 1, left, T064-234104,* and from **CONAF** ⓘ *Rosas 430, T064-234393.* Puerto Varas tourist office is in the **Municipalidad** ⓘ *San Fransisco 413, T065-321330, secturismo.puertovaras@ munitel.cl* Other places in town also claim to offer information, but may only give information about their paying members' services. There is no general information centre for Lago Llanquihue, but each town has its own municipal tourist office.

Osorno and around » *pp267-274*

Situated at the confluence of the Ríos Rahue and Damas, Osorno is grey and nondescript and has little to attract tourists, but if you're travelling by bus, you're likely to just pass through it. Founded in 1553, the city was abandoned in 1604 and was refounded by Ambrosio O'Higgins and Juan MacKenna O'Reilly in 1796. It later became one of the centres of German immigration to Chile. The municipal **tourist office** is based in the bus terminal and in a kiosk on the Plaza de Armas, both open December to February, and offers free **city tours** ⓘ *Mon-Fri 1500 and 1700, Jan-Feb only, book in advance.*

Sights

On the large **Plaza de Armas** stands the modern, concrete and glass cathedral, with many arches and a tower that is itself an open, latticed arch with a cross superimposed. West of the centre on a bend overlooking the river is the **Fuerte María Luisa**, built in 1793 and restored in 1977; only the river front walls and end turrets are still standing. East of the main plaza along Calle MacKenna are a number of late 19th-century wooden mansions built by German immigrants, now preserved as national monuments. Two blocks south of the Plaza is the **Museo Histórico Municipal** ⓘ *Matta 809, Mon-Sun 1100-1900 in summer; Mon-Fri 0930-1730, Sat 1500-1800 in winter, US$1,* which has displays on natural history, Mapuche culture, the refounding of the city and German colonization. The **Auto Museo Moncopulli**, ⓘ *Route 215, 25 km east of Osorno, T064-204200, 1000-1900 daily, bus towards Entre Lagos,* is the best motor museum in Chile. Exhibits include a Studebaker collection from 1852 to 1966. There is also a 1950s-style cafeteria.

East of Los Lagos

The southernmost of the Seven Lakes, **Lago Riñihue**, is most easily reached from Los Lagos on the Pan American Highway. **Riñihue**, a beautiful but small and isolated village at its western end, is worth visiting but the road around the southern edge of the lake from Riñihue to Enco is closed and there is no road around the northern edge of the lake.

South of Lago Riñihue is **Lago Ranco**, one of the largest lakes in the region, covering 41,000 ha. It has a rough road round its edge, characterized by lots of mud and animals, including oxcarts. However it is worth taking the opportunity to witness an older lifestyle and to see the beautiful lake, starred with islands, and the sun setting on the distant volcanoes. There is excellent fishing on the southern shore around the ugly town of **Lago Ranco** and to the west around **Puerto Nuevo**; several hotels organize fishing expeditions. The main town on the northern shore is **Futrono**, which has a daily boat service to **Huapi**, the island in the middle of the lake. On the eastern shore is **Llifén**, Km 22, a picturesque place, from where it is possible visit **Lago Maihue**, 33 km further east. From Llifén the road around Lago Ranco continues via the Salto de Nilahue (Km 14) to **Riñinahue**, Km 23, with access to beaches.

Lago Puyehue and around

Surrounded by relatively flat countryside, 47 km east of Osorno, **Lago Puyehue** extends over 15,700 ha. The southern shore is much more developed than the northern shore, which is accessible only by unpaved road from **Entre Lagos** at the western end. On the opposite side of the lake are the **Termas de Puyehue**, an upmarket spa resort with extensive facilities (see page 267). Two thermal swimming pools are open to day visitors ⓘ *0900-2000 daily, US$3.50 outdoor, US$15 indoor*. From the *termas*, route 215 heads northeast to the Anticura sector of Parque Nacional Puyehue and on towards the border, while another road leads southeast to the Aguas Calientes and Antillanca sectors of the park.

Parque Nacional Puyehue

Stretching east from Lago Puyehue to the Argentine frontier, **Parque Nacional Puyehue** covers 107,000 ha, much of it in the valley of the Río Golgol. On the eastern side are several lakes, including Lago Constancia and Lago Gris. There are two volcanic peaks: **Volcán Puyehue** (2,240 m) in the north (access via a private track US$10) and **Volcán Casablanca** (also called Antillanca, 1,900 m). Leaflets on walks and attractions are available from the park administration at Aguas Calientes and from the ranger station at Anticura.

Four kilometres southeast of the Termas de Puyehue, in a thickly forested valley beside the Río Chanleufú, is **Aguas Calientes**, where you'll find the park administration and a dirty, open-air pool ⓘ *Mon-Fri 0830-1230, 1400-1800 in summer only; Sat, Sun and holidays 0830-2030 all year; outdoor pool US$2, children US$1; indoor pool US$6, children US$3*, with very hot thermal

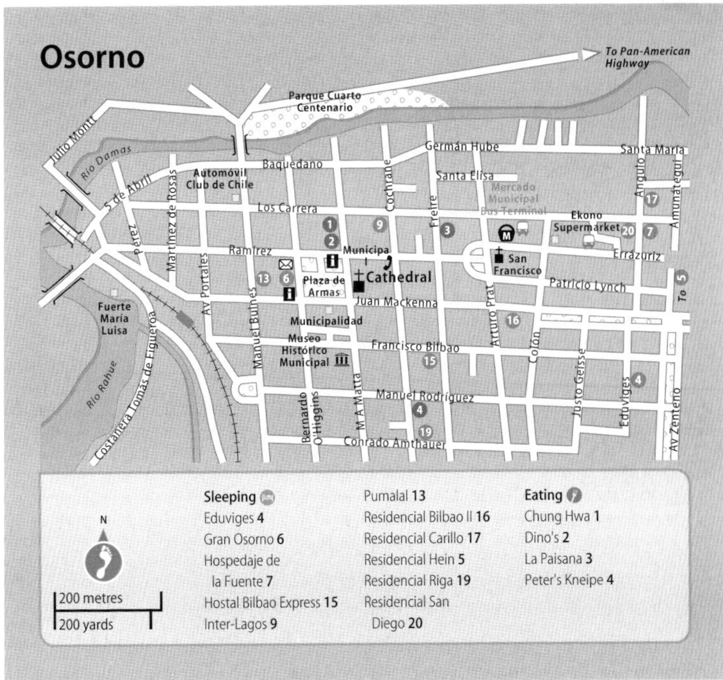

water. From Aguas Calientes the road continues 18 km past three small lakes and through forests to the ski resort at **Antillanca** on the slopes of Volcán Casablanca. In winter (and sometimes summer, depending on the weather) a one-way traffic system operates on the last 8 km of the narrow and icy road: ascending traffic from 0800 to 1200 and 1400 to 1730; descending traffic from 1200 to 1400 and after 1730. This is a particularly beautiful area of the park, especially at sunrise, with views over Lago Puyehue to the north and Lagos Rupanco and Llanquihue to the south, as well as the snow-clad peaks of Calbuco, Osorno, Puntiagudo, Puyehue and Tronador forming a semicircle. From Antillanca it is possible to climb Casablanca for even better views; there's no path and the hike takes about seven hours there and back; information from **Club Andino** in Osorno.

The paved Route 215, meanwhile, heads northeast from the Termas de Puyehue to **Anticura**. In this section of the park are three waterfalls, including the spectacular 40-m wide **Salto del Indio**. Legend has it that an Indian, enslaved by the Spanish, was able to escape by hiding behind the falls. Situated just off the road, the falls are on a marked path through dense forest which includes a 800-year-old Coihue tree known as 'El Abuelo'. The **Argentine border** at Paso Puyehue is reached 26 km east of Anticura (see page 112).

Lago Rupanco

Lying south of Lago Puyehue and considerably larger, this lake covers 23,000 ha and is far less accessible and less developed for tourism than most of the other larger lakes. Access from the northern shore is via two unpaved roads that branch off Route 215. **El Paraíso** (aka Marina Rupanco), at the western tip of the lake, can be reached by an unpaved road south from Entre Lagos. A 40-km dirt road runs along the southern shore, via **Laguna Bonita**, a small lake surrounded by forest, and **Piedras Negras** to **Bahía Escocia** at the eastern end. From the south, access is from two turnings off the road between Osorno and Las Cascadas.

Puerto Varas and Lago Llanquihue » pp267-274

The second largest lake in Chile and the third largest natural lake in South America, Lago Llanquihue is one of the highlights of the Lake District. Three snowcapped volcanoes can be seen across the vast expanse of water: the perfect cone of Osorno (2,680 m), the shattered cone of Calbuco (2,015 m) and the spike of Puntiagudo (2,480 m), as well as, when the air is clear, the distant Tronador (3,460 m). On a cloudless night with a full moon, the snows reflect eerily in the lake and the peace and stillness are hard to match.

Situated on the southwestern corner of the lake, Puerto Varas is the commercial and tourist centre of Lago Llanquihue. In the 19th century Puerto Chico (on the southern outskirts) was the southern port for shipping on the lake. With the arrival of the railway the settlement moved to its current location and is now a resort, popular with South American tourists. Despite the numbers of visitors, it has a friendly, compact feel and its location near centres for trekking, rafting, canyoning and fly fishing make it one of the best bases for exploring the southern Lake District. It can also be used as an alternative to Puerto Montt for catching the Navimag ferry.

Around town

Parque Philippi, on top of a hill, is a pleasant place to visit, although the views are a bit restricted by trees and the metal cross at the top is unattractive. To reach the summit walk up to **Hotel Cabañas del Lago** on Klenner, cross the railway and the gate is on the right. The centre lies at the foot of the hill, but the town stretches east along the lake to **Puerto Chico**, where there are hotels and restaurants. The imposing **Catholic church** was built by German Jesuits in 1918 in Baroque style as a copy of a church in the Black Forest. North and east of the **Gran Hotel Puerto Varas** (1934) are a number of German-style mansions.

The southern shore

Puerto Varas is a good base for trips around the lake. A paved road runs along the south shore to Ensenada on the southwestern corner of the lake. Two of the best beaches are **Playa Hermosa**, Km 7 and **Playa Niklitschek**, Km 8, where an entry fee is charged. At Km 16 narrow channels overhung with vegetation lead south from Lago Llanquihue to the little lake of **La Poza**. There are boat trips (US$1.50) to the beautiful **Isla Loreley**, an island on the lake, and a channel leads from La Poza to yet another lake, the **Laguna Encantada**. At Km 21 there is a watermill and a restaurant run by the Club Alemán.

Frutillar and the western shore

Lying about half-way along the western side of the lake, Frutillar is in fact two towns: **Frutillar Alto**, just off the main highway, and **Frutillar Bajo**, beautifully situated on the lakeside, 4 km away. The latter is possibly the most attractive and expensive town on the lake, with superb views from the *costanera* over the water with volcanoes Osorno and Tronador in the background. The town's atmosphere is very German and somewhat snobbish, but the **tourist office** ⓘ *on the lakeside, T065-420198, open summer only*, is helpful. In the square opposite is an open-air chess board and the **Club Alemán** restaurant. A new concert hall has recently been built on the lakeside to host the town's prestigious music festival in late January (see Festivals and events, page 272).

Away from the waterfront, the appealing **Museo Colonial Alemán** ⓘ *off Prat, summer 1000-1930 daily; winter 1000-1330, 1500-1800 Tue-Sun, US$2*, is set in spacious gardens, with a watermill, replicas of two German colonial houses with furnishings and utensils of the period and a blacksmith's shop selling personally engraved horseshoes for US$5. It also has a *campanario*, a circular barn with agricultural machinery and carriages inside, as well as a handicraft shop. At the northern end of the town is the **Reserva Forestal Edmundo Winckler**, run by the Universidad de Chile and extending over 33 ha, with a guided trail through native woods. Named after one of the early German settlers, it includes a very good collection of native flora as well as plants introduced from Europe.

Twenty kilometres south of Frutillar, **Llanquihue** lies at the source of the Río Maullín, which drains the lake. The site of a large dairy processing factory, this is the least touristy town on the lake, and makes a cheaper alternative to Puerto Varas and Frutillar. It has uncrowded beaches and hosts a German-style beer festival at the end of January.

The sun sets on the snows of Volcán Osorno

Puerto Octay

Puerto Octay is a small town at the north tip of the lake. It's 56 km southeast of Osorno, set amid rolling hills, hedgerows and German-style farmhouses with views over the Osorno volcano. Founded by German settlers in 1852, the town enjoyed a boom period in the late 19th century when it was the northern port for steamships on the lake: a few buildings survive from that period, notably the church and the enormous German-style former convent. Since the arrival of railways and the building of roads, the town has declined. Much less busy than Frutillar or Puerto Varas, Puerto Octay offers an escape for those seeking peace and quiet.

Museo el Colono ⓘ *Independencia 591, Tue-Sun 1000-1300, 1500-1900, Dec-Feb only*, has displays on German colonization. Another part of the museum, housing agricultural implements and machinery for making *chicha*, is just outside town on the road towards **Centinela**. This peninsula, about 3 km south (taxi US$1.50 one way) along an unpaved road has accommodation, camping, a launch dock, bathing beaches and watersports. It is a very popular spot in good weather, especially for picnics, with fine views of the Osorno, Calbuco and Puntiagudo volcanoes.

Eastern shore

The eastern lakeside, with the Osorno volcano on your left is very beautiful. From Puerto Octay two roads run towards Ensenada, one *ripio* along the shore, and one paved. (They join up after 20 km.) At Km 10 along the lakeside route is **Playa Maitén**, a lovely beach, often deserted, with a great view of Volcán Osorno. Continue for another 24 km past **Puerto Fonck**, which has fine 19th century mansions, and you'll reach **Las Cascadas**, surrounded by picturesque agricultural land, old houses and German cemeteries. To reach the waterfalls that give the village its name follow signs along a *ripio* road east to a car park, continue along a footpath over two or three log bridges over a stream, and after a final wade across you will arrive at a 40-m high natural cauldron, with the falls in the middle. The round trip takes about one-and-a-half hours.

Volcán Osorno

The most lasting image of Lago Llanquihue is the near perfect cone of Volcán Osorno, situated north of Ensenada on the eastern edge of the lake. Although the peak is on the edge of the Parque Nacional Pérez Rosales (see page 265), it is climbed from the western side, which lies outside the park. Access is via two roads that branch off the Ensenada-Puerto Octay road along the eastern edge of Lago Llanquihue: the northern one at Puerto Klocker, 20 km south of Puerto Octay; the other 2 km north of Ensenada (turning unmarked, high clearance vehicle necessary).

Guided ascents of the volcano – with transport from Puerto Montt or Puerto Varas, food and equipment – are organized by agencies in Puerto Varas (see page 272), weather permitting ⓘ *US$150 per person, payment in advance, minimum group 2, maximum 6 with 3 guides*. Weather conditions are checked the day before and a 50% refund is available if the climb is abandoned due to weather. Guided ascents start from the *refugio* at **La Burbuja**, from where it is six hours to the summit. Those climbing from La Burbuja must register with CONAF and show they have suitable equipment. The volcano can also be climbed from the north (La Picada); this route is easier and may be attempted without a guide, although only experienced climbers should attempt the summit as ice climbing equipment is essential.

Ensenada

Despite its lack of a recognizable centre, Ensenada is beautifully situated at the southeast corner of Lago Llanquihue, almost beneath the snows of Volcán Osorno. A good half-day trip from Ensenada is to **Laguna Verde**, about 30 minutes from **Hotel Ensenada**, along a beautiful circular trail behind the lake (take first fork to the right behind the information board), and down the road to a secluded campsite at Puerto Oscuro on Lago Llanquihue.

Parque Nacional Vicente Pérez Rosales » pp267-274

ⓘ CONAF administration, Petrohue. Also a guardeparque office in Peulla. Hourly minibuses in summer from Puerto Montt, Puerto Varas and Ensenada to Petrohué; it is impossible to reach the national park independently out of season.

Established in 1926, this is the oldest national park in Chile, stretching east from Lago Llanquihue to the Argentine frontier. The park is covered in woodland and contains a large lake, Lago Todos Los Santos, plus three major volcanic peaks: Osorno, Puntiagudo and Tronador. Several other peaks are visible, notably Casablanca to the north and Calbuco to the south. Near the lake are the Saltos de Petrohué, waterfalls on the Río Petrohué. A memorable journey by road and water takes you through the park from Puerto Montt to Bariloche in Argentina (see pages 119 and 283). A combination of walking and hitching rides in locals' boats is the best way to explore the park. No maps of treks are available in the park; buy them from a tour agency in Puerto Varas (see page 272). In wet weather many treks in the park are impossible and the road to Puerto Montt can be blocked.

Lago Todos los Santos

The most beautiful of all the lakes in southern Chile, Lago Todos los Santos is a long, irregularly shaped sheet of emerald-green water, surrounded by a deeply wooded shoreline and punctuated by several small islands that rise from its surface. Beyond the hilly shores to

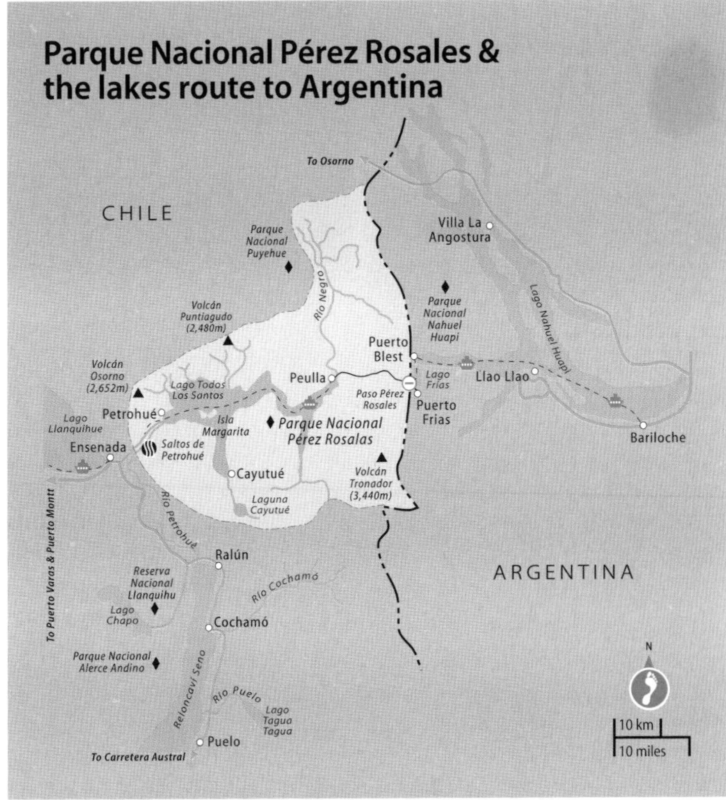

the east are several graceful snow-capped mountains, with the mighty Tronador in the distance. To the north is the sharp point of **Cerro Puntiagudo**, and at the northeastern end **Cerro Techado** rises cliff-like out of the water. The lake is fed by several rivers, including the Río Peulla to the east, the ríos Techado and Negro to the north, and the Río Blanco to the south. At its western end the lake is drained by the Río Petrohue. The lake is warm and sheltered from the winds, and is a popular location for watersports, swimming and for trout and salmon fishing. The only scheduled vessel on the lake is the **Andina del Sud** service between Petrohue and Peulla, with connections to Puerto Montt and Bariloche. There are no roads round Lagos Todos Los Santos and only those with houses on the lakeshore are allowed access by boat, but private launches can be hired for trips.

Petrohue falls

Petrohué and around

At the western end of the lake, 16 km northwest of Ensenada, **Petrohué** is a good base for walking tours with several trails around the foot of Volcán Osorno, or to the *miradors* that look over it, such as Cerro Picada. The Petrohué office of **CONAF** incorporates a visitors' centre, small museum and 3D model of the national park.

Near the Ensenada-Petrohué road, 6 km west of Petrohué, is the **Salto de Petrohué** ⓘ *US$1.50*, which was formed by a relatively recent lava flow of hard volcanic rock. Near the falls are a snack bar and two short trails, the Sendero de los Enamorados and the Sendero Carileufú. Boat trips from Petrohué visit **Isla Margarita**, the largest island on the lake, with a lagoon in the middle of it, in summer only, and boats can also be hired to visit the **Termas de Callao** – actually two large Alerce tubs in a cabin – north of the lake. The boat will drop you at the uninhabited El Rincón (arrange for it to wait or collect you later), from where it's a three-and-a-half-hour walk to the baths through forest beside the Río Sin Nombre. The path twice crosses the river by rickety hanging bridges. Just before the baths is a house, doubling as a comfortable *refugio*, where you collect the keys and pay.

Peulla and around

Peulla, at the eastern end of the lake, is a good starting point for hikes in the mountains. The **Cascadas Los Novios**, signposted above the **Hotel Peulla**, are a steep walk away, but are stunning once you reach them. There is also a good walk to **Laguna Margarita**, which takes four hours. Peulla is also the location of Chilean immigration and customs for those crossing into Argentina via the **Paso Pérez Rosales**, see page 120.

Cayutué and around

On the south shore of Lago Todos Los Santos is the little village of **Cayutué**, reached by hiring a boat from Petrohué, US$30. From Cayutué (no camping on the beach but there are private sites) it is a three-hour walk to **Laguna Cayutué**, a jewel set between mountains and surrounded by forest, where you can camp and swim. From the laguna it is a five-hour hike south to **Ralún** on the Reloncaví Estuary (see page 277): the last half of this route is along a *ripio* road built for extracting timber and is part of the old route used by missionaries in the colonial period to travel between Nahuel Huapi in Argentina and the island of Chiloé.

Sleeping

Osorno p260, map p261

A **Gran Hotel Osorno**, *O'Higgins 615, T064-232171, granhotelosorno @entelchile.net* Cable TV, well furnished.

B **Inter-Lagos**, *Cochrane 515, T064-234695, www.hotelinterlagos.cl* With breakfast, garage, restaurant.

B **Eduviges**, *Eduviges 856, T/F064-235023, www.hoteleduviges.cl* Spacious, clean, quiet, attractive, gardens, also *cabañas*. Cheaper to pay in pesos than in dollars. Recommended.

B-C **Pumalal**, *Bulnes 630, T064-242477, pumalal@entelchile.net* With breakfast, modern, airy, clean.

C **Res Riga**, *Amthauer 1058, T064-232945, resriga@telsur.cl* Clean, pleasant. Highly recommended but heavily booked in high season.

C-D **Hostal Bilbao Express**, *Bilbao 1019, T064-262200, pazla@telsur.cl* With breakfast, parking, restaurant. Also **Res** Bilbao II, *MacKenna 1205, T/F064-264444*.

C-D **Res Hein**, *Errázuriz 1757, T064-234116*. Old-fashioned, spacious, family atmosphere.

East of Los Lagos p260

B **Huequecura**, *Llifén, Lago Ranco, T09-6535450*. Good meals and fishing services.

C **Hostería Huinca Quinay**, *3 km east of Riñihue, Lago Riñihue, T063-461347, F063-461406*. *Cabañas* and restaurant.

C **Riñimapu**, *Lago Riñihue, T063-311388*. Comfortable, good value, excellent food.

D **Hosp Futronhue**, *Balmaceda 90, Futrono, Lago Ranco, T063-481265*. Good breakfast.

Camping

There are campsites all around Lago Ranco as well as several on Lago Maihue, but many are open in summer only and prices are very high.

Lago Puyehue and around p261

L **Hotel Termas de Puyehue**, *T064-232157*, was built in 1910 and is now a large-scale resort, with many facilities, including gym, tennis courts, children's playroom and a well-stocked wine cellar. It also organizes adventure activities and trips. Relaxation packages (aromatherapy, fangotherapy, mudbaths, sauna and milk and honey baths) are available. Heavily booked Jan-Feb (cheaper May to mid-Dec).

A **Cabañas No Me Olvides**, *Entre Lagos, T064-371633*. Cabins with kitchen, also camping US$10 per site.

B **Motel Ñilque**, *on the southern shore, T064-231177*. Cabins (half-price May-Oct), fishing, watersports, car hire.

B-C **Hostería Entre Lagos**, *Ramírez 65, Entre Lagos, T064-371225*. Rooms with lake view.

C **Hostería Isla Fresia**, *access from the southern lakeshore, T064-236951*. Located on own island, transport provided.

E pp **Hosp Millaray**, *Ramirez 333, Entre Lagos, T064-371251*. With breakfast, excellent, clean, friendly.

F pp **Ruta 215**, *Ramirez 333, Entre Lagos, T064-371251*. Good breakfast. Clean, friendly, German spoken.

Parque Nacional Puyehue p261

B-C **Hotel Antillanca**, *at foot of Volcán Casablanca, T064-235114, www.skiantillanca.com* Includes free mountain biking and parapenting, access to ski resort, restaurant/café, pool, sauna, friendly club-like atmosphere, also *refugio*.

Camping

Chanleufu, *Aguas Calientes, T064-236988*. US$25 per site with hot water, also *cabañas*, expensive café, small shop.
Los Derrumbes, *1 km from Aguas Calientes*. No electricity, US$20 per site.

There is also a CONAF *refugio* on Volcán Puyehue (check with CONAF in Anticura whether it is open) and a campsite beside the Río Chanleufú (US$4 pp).

Lago Rupanco p262

There are several campsites on the southern shore.
L-AL **Puntiagudo Lodge**, *Bahía Escocia, T064-1974731, www.puntiagudolodge.cl* With breakfast, very comfortable, good restaurant, fly fishing, riding, boat trips.
B **Refugio Club de Pesca y Caza**, *sector Islote, 7 km east of Piedras Negras, T064-232056*. Basic *refugio* with breakfast and bath.

Puerto Varas p262, map p270

There are many hotels all along the lake front, but in high season they tend to be tourist traps. Camping wild and having barbecues is forbidden on the lake shore.
AL **Bellavista**, *Pérez Rosales 060, T065-232011, www.hotelbellavista.cl*. Cheerful with good views over the lake, restaurant parking, recommended.
AL **Cabañas del Lago**, *Klenner 195, T065-232291, www.cabanasdellago.cl* On Philippi hill overlooking lake, superb views. Also self-catering *cabañas* sleeping 5 (good value for groups), cheaper rates in low season, heating, sauna. Cheaper to pay in pesos than in dollars.
AL **Terrazas del Lago**, *Pérez Rosales 1571, T/F065-232622, www.terrazasdellago.cl*. Good breakfast, views over Osorno volcano, restaurant.
AL-A **Licarayén**, *San José 114, T065-232305, www.hotelicarayen.cl*. Overlooking lake, comfortable, clean, 'the perfect place for bad weather or being ill', recommended. Book in season.
AL-A **Los Alerces**, *Pérez Rosales 1281, T065-232060, www.hotellosalerces.com* 4-star, with breakfast, also new cabin complex, attractive.
A **Cabañas Ayentemo**, *Pérez Rosales 0950, T065-233412, www.ayentemo.cl* Clean, comfortable, friendly.
B **The Outsider**, *San Bernardo 318, T065-232910, outsider@telsur.net* With bath, real coffee, meals, friendly, comfortable, English spoken, book ahead.
C-E **Las Dalias**, *Santa Rosa 707, T065-233277*. Doubles with bath or simpler rooms (price per person). Peaceful , clean, good breakfast with real coffee, parking, German spoken.
D pp **Hosp Carla Minte**, *Maipo 1010, T065-232880, www.interpatagonia.com /carlaminte*. With breakfast, cable TV, very comfortable.
D pp **Hosp Las Carmelas**, *Imperial y Rosario*. Excellent, helpful, good meals, lends books including some in English. Recommended.
E pp **Amancay**, *Walker Martínez 564, T065-232201, c_bittner_amancay @chile.com* With breakfast. Some rooms with bath. Friendly, German spoken, also *cabañas*, sleep 4. Recommended.
E pp **Canales del Sur**, *Pasage Ricke 224, T065-346121, www.canalesdelsur.com* Very friendly and helpful, tours arranged.
E **Casa Azul**, *Manzanal 66 y Rosario, T065-232904, www.casaazul.net* German/Chilean owners, homemade muesli for breakfast, large kitchen, good beds with duvets, central heating, internet, book exchange, comfortable common area, English and German spoken, tours organised, friendly, helpful. Highly recommended.
E **Colores del Sur**, *Santa Rosa 318, T065-231850, colores_del_sur @hotmail.com* Kitchen facilities, hospitable, good meeting place.
E **Compass del Sur**, *Klenner 467, T065-232044, www.compassdelsur.cl* Chilean-Swedish run, kitchen facilities,

internet, cable TV in comfortable lounge, breakfast with muesli and real coffee, friendly, helpful, lots of information, tours, German, English, Swedish spoken. Highly recommended. Also camping.

E pp **Ellenhaus**, *Walker Martínez 239, T065-233577, www.ellenhaus.cl* Kitchen and laundry facilities, luggage stored, lounge, German and English spoken. Recommended.

E-F pp **Hosp Don Raúl**, *Salvador 928, T065-234174, hospedajedonraul @hotmail.com* Laundry and cooking facilities, very friendly, garden with hammock, clean. Recommended. Camping by main road.

Frutillar and around *p263, map p272*

During the annual music festival accommodation should be booked well in advance; alternatively stay in Puerto Varas. There are several cheap options along Carlos Richter (main street) in Frutillar Alto and numerous campsites on the lake to the north and south.

A **Salzburg**, *Playa Maqui, 7 km north of Frutillar Bajo, T065-421589, www.salzburg.cl.* Excellent restaurant, sauna, mountain bikes, tours and fishing.

B **Los Maitenes**, *3 km north of Frutillar Bajo, T065-330033, www.interpatagonia .com /losmaitenes* Old country house in 16 hectares by the lake (private beach), fishing trips, free pick-up from terminal.

A **Residenz am See**, *Philippi 539, Frutillar Bajo, T065-421539, www.frutillarsur.cl /publicid/alojar/residenz/ramsee.html* Good German-style breakfast.

B **Apart Hotel Frutillar**, *Philippi 1175, Frutillar Bajo, T065-421388.* Self-contained flats sleeping 4.

B **Winkler**, *Philippi 1155, Frutillar Bajo, T065-421388.* Discount to Hostelling International members, cabins, friendly.

D *Perez Rosales 590, Frutillar Bajo. Cabañas* and excellent breakfast.

D pp **Hosp Vivaldi**, *Philippi 851, Frutillar Bajo, T065-421382.* Quiet, comfortable, excellent breakfast and lodging, also family accommodation. Recommended.

E pp **Hosp Tia Clara**, *Perez Rosales 743, Frutillar Bajo, T065-421806.* Kitchen facilities, very friendly, good value, recommended.

F pp **Hosp Juana Paredes**, *Anibal Pinto y Winkler, Frutillar Alto, T065-421407.* Recommended, also *cabañas* for up to 5 and parking.

Puerto Octay *p264*

Several farms on the road around the north and east side of the lake offer rooms. Camping is also possible.

AL **Hotel Centinela**, *T064-391326, www.hotelcentinela.cl* Built in 1914 as a summer mansion, this hotel has been recently restored. It is idyllically situated and has superb views, also *cabañas*, restaurant with grand minstrels' gallery and bar, open all year.

E pp **Hostería Irma**, *on lake, 2 km south of Las Cascadas, T064-396227.* Attractive former residence, good food, very pleasant.

E pp **Hostería La Baja**, *Centinela, T064-391269/09-1656280, irisbravo1 @hotmail.com* With breakfast and bath. Beautifully situated at the neck of the peninsula.

E pp **Zapato Amarillo**, *35-mins' walk north of town, T064-391575, www.zapato amarillo.8k.com* Doubles and shared rooms. Excellent for backpackers, spotless kitchen, great breakfasts with homemade bread, very friendly, German and English spoken. Lots of information, mountain bikes, tours, canoes and sailing boat, luggage storage, phone for free pick up from town. Main house has a grass roof or there's the round house next door. Highly recommended.

Volcán Osorno *p264*

D There are two *refugios*, both of them south of the summit and reached from the southern access road: **La Burbuja**, the former ski-club centre, 14 km north of Ensenada at 1,250 m) and **Refugio Teski Ski Club**, just below the snow line. Price per person, meals served. **Refugio La**

Picada marked on the northern slopes on many maps burned down years ago.

Ensenada *p264*

There are several campsites in the vicinity.
AL-B **Cabañas Brisas del Lago**, *T065-212012, www.brisasdellago.cl* On beach, sleep 2-6, good restaurant nearby, supermarket next door. Recommended.
A **Ensenada**, *Casilla 659, Puerto Montt, T065-222017, www.hotelensenada.cl* With bath, old-world style, good food, good view of lake and Volcán Osorno, runs tours, hires mountain bikes (guests only).
A **Hotel Puerto Pilar**, *west of Ensenada on Puerto Varas road, T065-335378, www.hotelpuertopilar.cl Price per person, also cabañas*, situated away from the road with good views of Volcán Osorno and good service. Recommended.
C **Hosp Arena**, *T065-212037*. With breakfast. Recommended.
C **Pucará**, *2 km from town*. With good restaurant (the steaks are recommended).
D-E pp **Hosp Ensenada**, *T065-338278*. Very clean, great breakfast.
E pp **Hosp Opazo**. With breakfast, very friendly.
Fpp **Hosp Toqui**, *above grocery shop*. Cheapest in town, basic, quiet, hot water, kitchen, beach at the bottom of the back yard, recommended.

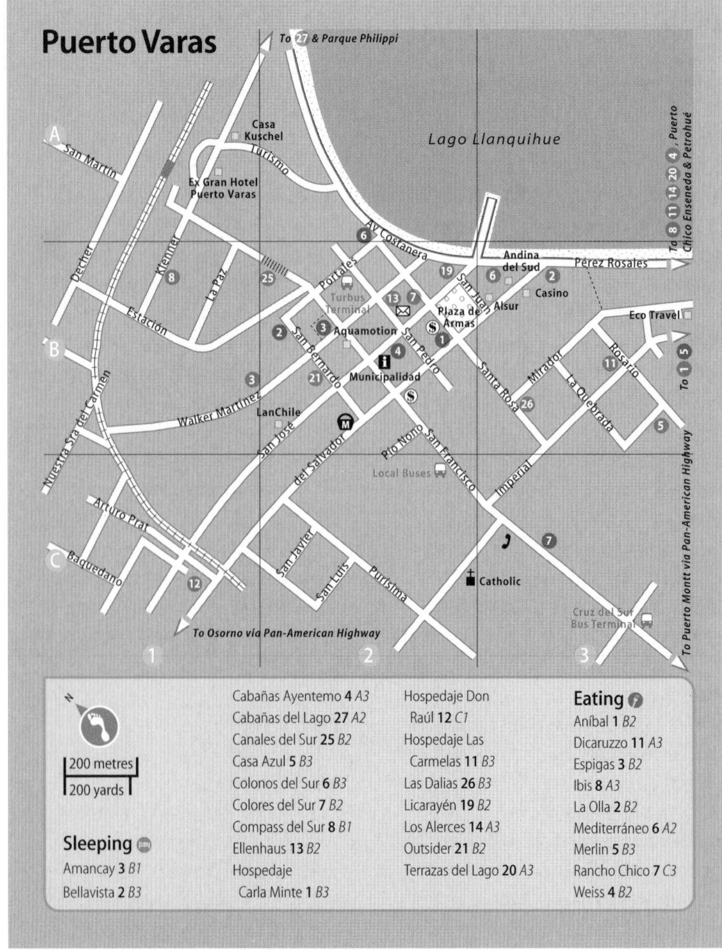

Petrohue *p265*
The CONAF office in Petrohué can help find cheaper family accommodation. Camping wild and picknicking forbidden.
L **Fundo El Salto**, *near Salto de Petrohué, T065-233585, rioazul@chilesat.net* Very friendly, run by New Zealanders, mainly a fishing lodge, good home cooking, fishing trips arranged.
L-AL **Hotel Petrohué**, *T/F065-212025, www.petrohue.com*. Burned down in 2002, but now rebuilt with bath, excellent views, log fires, cosy. The owner, Franz Schirmer, is a former climbing guide, who can advise on activities around the lake.

Peulla
L **Hotel Peulla**, *T065-258041/ 02-8891032,* hpeullareservas@terra.cl Price includes dinner and breakfast, cheaper out of season. Beautiful setting by the lake, but often full of tour groups on the lakes crossing, poor restaurant, bar and shop.
D **Res Palomita**, *50 m west of Hotel Peulla*. Price per person for half board, lunches available. Family-run, simple, comfortable but not spacious, separate shower, book ahead in season.

Eating

Osorno *p260, map p261*
The bakery at *Ramírez 977* sells good wholemeal bread.
ŸŸ **Dino's**, *Ramírez 898, on the plaza*. Good restaurant, bar/café downstairs.
ŸŸ **La Paisana**, *Freire 530*. Arab specialities.
ŸŸ **Peter's Kneipe**, *M Rodríguez 1039*. Excellent German restaurant.
Ÿ **Chung Hwa**, *Matta 517*. Chinese.

Puerto Varas *p262, map p270*
ŸŸŸ **Merlin**, *Imperial 0605, east out of town, T065-233105, www.merlinrestaurant.cl*. Has the reputation as one of the best restaurants in the Lake District. Often recommended, but some adverse reports.
ŸŸ **La Olla**, *San Bernado y Martinez*. Seafood and traditional Chilean cuisine. Recommended. There is another branch on the *costanera* going east.
ŸŸ **Mediterráneo**, *Santa Rosa 068*. On the lakefront, varied menu, good.
ŸŸ **Dicaruzzo**, *Costanera 01071*. Recommended.
ŸŸ **Espigas**, *Martínez 417, local 3*. Vegetarian.
ŸŸ **Ibis**, *Costanera 1117*. Very good.
Ÿ **Aníbal**, *Del Salvador y Santa Rosa*. Pizzas, cheap, tasty.
Ÿ***Barómetro**, San Pedro 418. Cosy bar serving Kuntstman beer and food.*
Ÿ **Rancho Chico**, *San Francisco opposite the church*. Menus for US$3.
Ÿ **Pim's**, *San Francisco near Calle Imperial*. Spacious US-style pub with food.
Ÿ **Weiss**, *San José 415*. Great value, very good meat, seriously cheap.

Cafés
Café Danés, *Del Salvador 441*. Good coffee and cakes.
El Molino, *on road to Ensenada 22 km east*. Café next to an old water mill.

Frutillar and around *p263, map p272*
There are several German-style cafés on Calle Philippi, including **Salón de Te Frutillar** and **Guten Apetit**.
ŸŸ **Andes**, *Philippi 1057, Frutillar Bajo*. Good set menus and à la carte.
ŸŸ **Club Alemán**, *Av Philippi 747*. Good but not cheap, and hostile to backpackers.
ŸŸ **Selva Negra**, *Varas 24 y Philippi, Frutillar Bajo*. Located in a traditional German mill, with scores of toy witches hanging from the ceiling, open 1100-2300.
Ÿ **Casino de Bomberos**, *Philippi 1060, Frutillar Bajo*. Upstairs bar/restaurant, open all year, memorable painting caricaturing the firemen in action. Great value but service can be poor.

Puerto Octay *p264*
There are some good, cheap restaurants on Germán Wulf.
ŸŸ **El Rancho del Espanta-Pajaros**, *6 km south on the road to Frutillar, T065-339141*. In a converted barn with wonderful views

over the lake, serves all kind of spit roasted meat. All you can eat, with drinks included, for US$10. Also arranges horseriding trips. Recommended.

Ensenada *p264*

Latitude 42, *Yan Kee Way resort, T065-212030.* Excellent restaurant in a plush fishing resort. Varied cuisine and very good quality wine list.

Festivals and events

Frutillar and around *p263, map p272*

A highly regarded classical **music festival** is held in the town between Jan and early Feb; tickets must be booked well in advance from the Municipalidad, *T065-421290*. A German-style **beer festival** with oom-pah music is held in Llanquihue at the end of Jan.

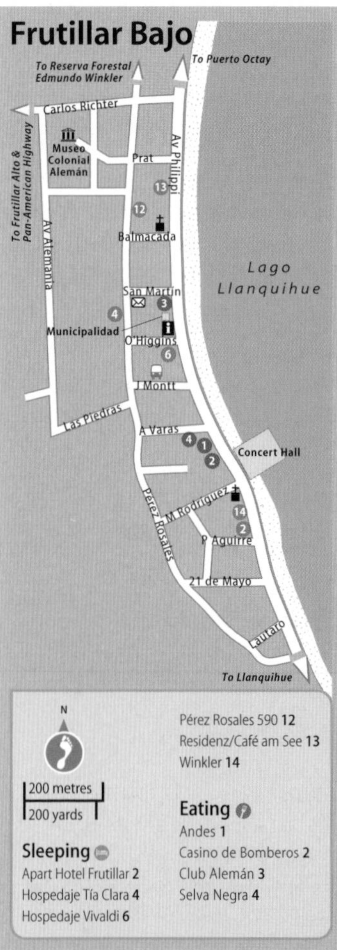

Activities and tours

Lago Rupanco *p262*

Fishing

Lago Rupanco is very popular for fishing. **Bahía Escocia Fly Fishing**, offers excursions fromthe Puntiagudo Lodge (see Sleeping, above); advance booking required. In Osorno, fishing tackle is available from **Climet**, *Angulo 603*, and **The Lodge**, *Los Carrera 1291, local 5.*

Puerto Varas *p262, map p270*

Fishing

A licence (obligatory) is obtainable from the Municipalidad. Fishing expeditions are organised by many operators (see below). The Río Pescado (25km east of Puerto Varas) is a good easy alternative for those who don't want to hire a guide.

Horseriding

Cabañas Puerto Decher, *Fundo Molino Viejo, 2 km north of Puerto Varas, T065-338033.* Guided tours, horseriding, minimum 2 people, mixed reports.

Campo Aventura, *San Bernardo 318, T065-232710, www.campo-aventura.com, info@campo-aventura.com.* English and German spoken, offer 1, 3 and 10-day trips on horseback (see Cochamó, p277).

Mountain biking

Bikes available from many tour operators, see below, for around $US14 per day; check equipment carefully

Tour operators

Alsur, *Del Salvador 100, T065-232300, www.alsurexpeditions.com* Rafting on Rió Petrohue. Official tour operator to the Parque Pumalín. Sells trekking maps.

Andina del Sud, *Del Salvador 72, T065-232811.* Operates 'lakes' trip to

Bariloche via Lago Todos los Santos, Peulla, Cerro Tronador, plus other trips.
Aqua Motion, *San Fransisco, T065-232747, www.aquamotion.cl* Rafting, trekking, mountain biking, fishing. Ludwig Godsambassis, who works for Aqua Motion, also works independently as a trekking guide out of season and is very knowledgeable.
Kokayak, *San José 320, T065-346433*, French/Chilean run, offers bike hire, white-water rafting and sea kayaking.
Tranco Expeditions, *Santa Rosa 580, T065-311311, www.trancoexpediciones.cl* Trekking, rafting and climbing, Norwegian and English spoken, good equipment.
Travel Art, *Imperial 0661, T065-232198, www.travelart.cl*. Biking and hiking tours.
Turismo Biker, *Café Terranova, on Plaza, turismobiker@yahoo.es*. Specialists in downhill mountain bike trips.

Transport

Osorno *p260, map p261*

Air

LanChile, *E Ramirez 802, T064-314949*, flies daily to **Santiago**; not recommended.

Bus

Main terminal 4 blocks from Plaza de Armas at *Errázuriz 1400*, bus from centre, US$0.30. Left luggage open 0730-2030.

Long distance To **Santiago**, frequent, 11½ hrs, US$13, *semi cama* US$30; to **Temuco**, US$6; to **Panguipulli**, Buses Pirehueico, 4 a day; to **Pucón** and **Villarrica**, Tur Bus, frequent, US$7; to **Valdivia**, frequent, 2 hrs, several companies, US$3, but **Igi Llaima** only US$1.80; to **Frutillar**, US$1.50, **Llanquihue**, **Puerto Varas** and **Puerto Montt**, every 30 mins, US$3; to **Puerto Octay**, Vía Octay, 6 daily 0815-1930 (return 0800-1930) Mon-Sat, 5 daily 0800-2000 Sun, (4 return buses), US$2; to **Lago Ranco** (town), 6 a day, Empresa Ruta 5, 2 hrs, US$2; to **Punta Arenas**, several each week, US$55; to **Anticura**, daily at 1620, 3 hrs .

To Argentina Several buses run daily services from Puerto Montt via Osorno to **Bariloche** via Paso Puyehue (see p282).

Local Some local services leave from the **Mercado Municipal terminal**, 1 block west of the main terminal. To **Entre Lagos**, frequent in summer, reduced service off-season, **Expreso Lago Puyehue**, *T064-234919*, and **Buses Puyehue**, 45 mins, US$1; buses by both companies also continue to **Aguas Calientes**, off-season according to demand, 2 hrs, US$2. To **Puyehue**, 4-5 daily, 1½ hrs, US$2.50, but the buses don't stop by the lakeside (unless you want to get off at **Hotel Termas de Puyehue** and clamber down).

Bus from Osorno to **Piedras Negras** from the main terminal, leaves 1230 Mon-Fri, 1630 on Sat, returns from Piedras Negras early morning.

Lago Ranco *p260*

Buses from Valdivia to **Llifén** via Futrono, **Cordillera Sur**, 4 daily, US$2.50; to **Riñihue** via Paillaco and Los Lagos, frequent. To **Osorno**, **Empresa Ruta 5**, 6 daily.

Parque Nacional Puyehue *p261*

Expreso Lago Puyehue, *T064-23499*, and **Buses Puyehue**, run from Osorno to **Aguas Calientes**, according to demand, 2 hrs, US$2. There is no public transport from Aguas Calientes to **Antillanca**; hitching is always difficult, but it is not a hard walk. Buses run from Osorno to **Anticura**, daily at 1620, 3 hrs.

Puerto Varas *p262, map p270*

Minibuses to **Ensenada** and **Petrohué** leave from *San Bernardo y Martínez*; regional buses stop on *San Fransisco 500 block*; long distance buses leave from their own terminals.

To **Santiago**, **Turbus**, **Igi Llaima**, **Cruz del Sur** and several others, US$13, *semi cama* US$20, *salón cama* US$30. **Thaebus**, **Full Express** and others have services to **Puerto Montt**, every 15 mins, 30 mins, US$0.70; same companies, same frequency to **Frutillar**, 30 mins, US$0.75, and **Osorno**, 1 hr, US$2.50. Same companies hourly to **Petrohue**, US$3. To **Valdivia**, 3 hrs, US$4.50; to **Temuco**, US$8; to **Cochamó** via Ensenada, 5 a day, US$2. Services from Puerto Montt to **Bariloche** (Argentina) via Puyehue also stop here. For the Andina del Sud lakes route via Lago Todos Los Santos, see p283.

Car hire

Adriazola Expediciones, *Santa Rosa 340, T065-233477*; Turismo Nieve, *Gramado 560, T065-346115.*

Frutillar and around *p263, map p272*

Colectivos run between the two towns, 5 mins, US$0.50. Most buses to other destinations leave from opposite the Copec station in Frutillar Alto. Thaebus and others have frequent services to **Puerto Varas**, US$0.75, and **Puerto Montt**, US$1.25. To **Osorno**, Turismosur, 1¼ hrs, US$1.50; to **Puerto Octay**, Thaebus, 5 a day.

Puerto Octay *p264*

Buses to **Osorno**, 9 a day, US$2; to **Las Cascadas** Mon-Fri 1730, return next day 0700. Thaebus runs 5 daily services to **Frutillar**,1 hr, US$0.90, **Puerto Varas**, 2 hrs, and **Puerto Montt**, 2¼ hrs, US$2.

Ensenada *p264*

Frequent minibuses run from **Puerto Varas** in summer. Buses from Puerto Montt to **Cochamó** also stop here.

Lago Todos los Santos *p265*

Boat

The Andina del Sud catamaran sails between **Petrohué** and **Peulla**, departing Petrohué 1030 Mon-Sat, departing Peulla 1500 Mon-Sat, 2 hrs, US$22 per person one way, bicycles free (book in advance); most seating indoors, no cars carried, commentaries in Spanish and English, expensive refreshments. It is no longer possible to get a day return from Petrohué to Peulla, so you have to stay overnight in Peulla, which is expensive. This is the only public service across the lake and it connects with the Andina del Sud/Cruce de Lagos tour bus between Puerto Montt and Bariloche (see p283). Local fishermen also make the trip across the lake and for a group this can be cheaper than the public service, allow 3½ hrs.

Bus

Minibuses from **Puerto Varas** to Ensenada continue to **Petrohué** in summer; last return bus from Petrohue to Puerto Varas, 1800. Note that apart from the Andina del Sur service from Puerto Montt, there is no transport from Peulla to the border at Paso Pérez Rosales.

Directory

Osorno *p260, map p261*

Banks and currency exchange Several banks and *casas de cambio* in the centre. **Internet** Chat-Mail MP3, *Patricio Lynch 1334*; Dream House, *Matta 510*, opposite Chung Hwa Restaurant; Pub Sa Tanca, *Patio Freire 542.* **Laundry** *Prat 678*, allow at least a day. **Post office** *O'Higgins 645.* **Telephone** *Ramírez at central plaza, Juan MacKenna y Cochrane.*

Puerto Varas *p262, map p270*

Banks Good exchange rates at Banco Osorno, *Del Salvador 399*. Also numerous *casas de cambio.* **Camera and film** Foto Kodak, *Del Salvador*; Foto Master, *San José 301*. **Internet** Ciber Service, *Salvador 264, local 6-A*; George's, *San Ignacio 574*; also at *Gramado 560, piso 2* and *San José 380, piso 2*. **Laundry** *Gramado 1090*; Lavanderia Delfin, *Martínez 323*, expensive. **Medical emergencies** Clinica Alemana, *Otto Bader 810, T232336, emergencies T065-232274*, usually has English- speaking doctors. **Post office** *San José y San Pedro; Del Salvador y Santa Rosa.* **Telephone** Bellsouth, *San Bernardo 555*; CTC, *Salvador 320*; Telefónica del Sur, *Del Salvador 314*; Entel, *San José 314.*

Puerto Montt and around

The capital of Región X (Los Lagos), Puerto Montt lies on the northern shore of the Seno de Reloncaví 1,016 km south of Santiago. The jumping-off point for journeys south to Chiloé and southern Patagonia, it is a busy modern city, the fastest growing in Chile, flourishing with the salmon-farming boom. It was founded in 1853, as part of the German colonization of the area, on the site of a Mapuche community known as Melipulli, meaning four hills. There are good views over the city and bay from outside the Intendencia Regional on Av X Region. There is a wide range of accommodation here, but you might prefer to stay in Puerto Varas, which is more picturesque and only 20 minutes' away by bus.

Getting there Flights from Santiago or overnight buses.
Getting around Puerto Montt is the terminus for ferry services south and also marks the start of the Carretera Austral.
Time required 2 days to 1 week.
Weather Can rain at any time, but summer can be lovely.
Sleeping All budgets and tastes.
Eating Wonderful seafood at Angelmó.
Activities and tours Sailing, sea kayaking, riding and trips to Chiloé.
★ **Don't miss...** The ferry to Puerto Natales.

Ins and outs

Getting there El Tepual Airport is 13 km northwest of town, served by **ETM** buses from the bus terminal ⓘ *T065-294292, 1½ hrs before departure, US$0.75*; there's also a minibus service to/from hotels, US$4 per person. There are several daily **flights** north to Santiago and Temuco, and south to Coyhaique and Punta Arenas. **Ferries** serve Chaitén (four times weekly) and Puerto Chacabuco (four times weekly); there's also a weekly service south to Puerto Natales. Puerto Montt is the departure point for **bus** services south to Coyhaique and Punta Arenas, and for buses north to Santiago and all the intermediate cities. ▸▸ *Transport p282.*

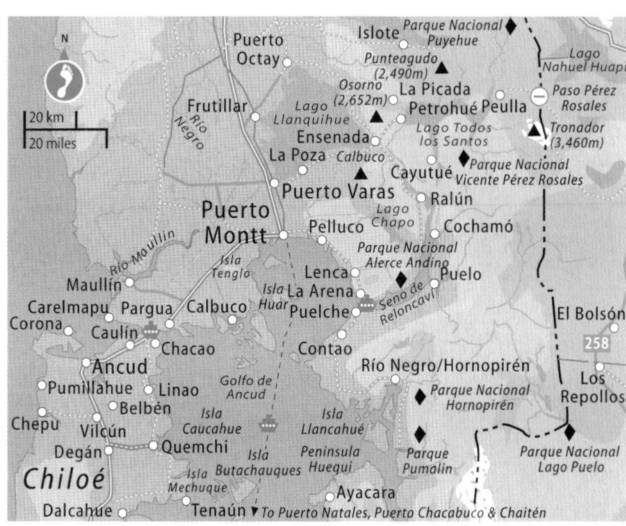

Tourist information Sernatur ⓘ *Gobernación Provincial, Plaza de Armas, summer daily 0900-1300, 1500-1900; winter Mon-Fri 0830-1300, 1400-1800*. Ask for information on Chiloé here as this is often difficult to obtain on the island. **Regional tourist office** ⓘ *Intendencia Regional, Av Décima Región 480 (p 3), Casilla 297, T065-254580*. There's also an information kiosk on the Plaza de Armas, which has town maps, but little information on other destinations. **CONAF** is at Ochogavia 458. Information on the Parque Pumalín (see page 292) is available from *Buin 356, T065-250079, www.pumalinpark.org*.

Sights

The **Plaza de Armas** lies at the foot of steep hills, one block north of Av Diego Portales, which runs east-west parallel to the shore. The **Palacio del Arte Diego Rivera** ⓘ *Quillota 116, off the Plaza de Armas, T065-261817*, hosts temporary exhibitions, concerts and plays.Two blocks west of the square is the **Iglesia de los Jesuitas** on Calle Gallardo, dating from 1872, which has a fine blue-domed ceiling; behind it on a hill is the **campanario** (clock tower). Further west, near the bus terminal, is the **Museo Regional Juan Pablo II** ⓘ, *Diego Portales 997, 1030-1800 daily, US$1*, documenting local history. It has a fine collection of historic photos of the city and memorabilia of the Pope's visit in 1988. ▸▸ *For Parque Nacional Alerce Andino, see page 291.*

Angelmó

The little fishing port of Angelmó, 2 km west along Av Diego Portales (a pleasant 30-minute walk) has become a tourist centre thanks to its dozens of seafood restaurants and handicraft shops, but it is also the site of an enormous mountain of wood chips that are shipped off to Japan every week and then replenished – a stark reminder of the deforestation in this area. Launches depart from Angelmó for the wooded **Isla Tenglo**, a favourite place for picnics, with views from the summit. The island is famous for its *curanto*, served by restaurants in

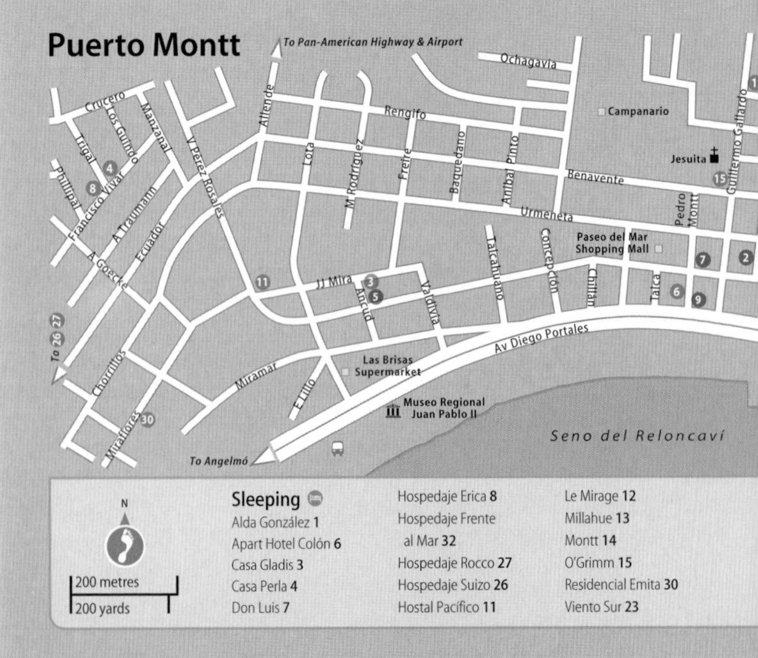

summer. Boat trips round the island from Angelmó last for 30 minutes and cost US$8. A longer boat trip (2 hrs) will take you to **Isla Huar**.

Towards Chiloé

The road west from Puerto Montt is very beautiful. **Chinquihue** (the name means 'place of skunks'), beyond Angelmó, has many seafood restaurants, oysters being a speciality. Further south is **Calbuco**, scenic centre of the fishing industry. It is on an island linked to the mainland by a causeway and can be visited direct by boat or road. West of here is the Río Maullin, which drains Lago Llanquihue, and has some waterfalls and good salmon fishing. At its mouth is the fishing village of **Maullín**, founded in 1602. On the coast to the southeast is **Carelmapu**, with an excellent beach and *cabañas* at Playa Brava, about 3 km away. At the southern tip of the mainland, **Pargua** is the departure point for car ferries to Chiloé (see page 285).

Seno de Reloncaví » *pp267-274*

The Seno de Reloncaví situated east of Puerto Montt and south of the Parque Nacional Pérez Rosales, is the northernmost of Chile's glacial inlets. It is a quiet and beautiful estuary, often shrouded in mist, but stunning nonetheless, and recommended for its wildlife, including sea lions and dolphins, and for its peaceful atmosphere. It is relatively easily reached by a road that runs along the wooded lower Petrohué valley south from Ensenada and then follows the eastern shore of the estuary for almost 100 km to join the Carretera Austral.

Ralún and around

A small village situated at the northern end of the estuary, Ralún is 31 km southeast from Ensenada by a poorly paved road. There is a village shop and post office, and on the outskirts are **thermal baths** ⓘ *US$2, reached by boat, US$2.50 across the Río Petrohué*. Ralún is the departure point for a five-hour walk north to **Laguna Cayutué** in the Parque Nacional Vicente Pérez Rosales (see above). From Ralún you can either travel along the eastern shore of the estuary to Cochamó (see below) or take the road that branches off and follows the western side of the estuary south, 36 km to Lago Chapo and the Parque Nacional Alerce Andino (see page 291).

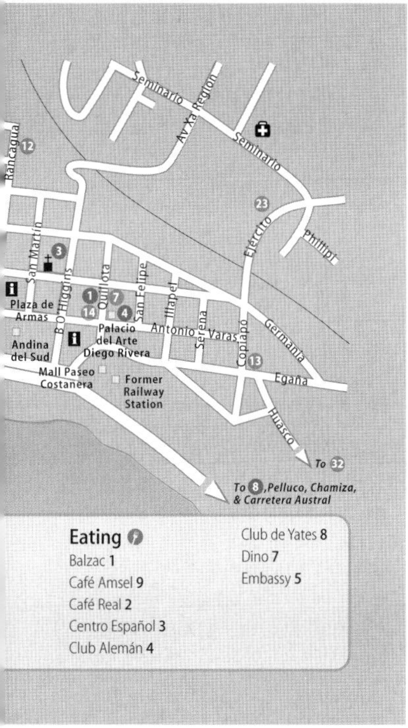

Eating
- Balzac 1
- Café Amsel 9
- Café Real 2
- Centro Español 3
- Club Alemán 4
- Club de Yates 8
- Dino 7
- Embassy 5

Cochamó and further south

Some 17 km south of Ralún along a poor *ripio* road is the pretty village of Cochamó. It's situated in a striking setting, on the east shore of the estuary with the volcano behind, and has a small, frequently deserted waterfront, where benches allow you to sit and admire the view. Cochamó's fine wooden church dates from 1900 and is similar to those on Chiloé. It has a clock with wooden hands and an unusual black statue of Christ.

A ferry weaves its way through the ice-bergs in the southern fjords.

Further south, on the south bank of the Río Puelo (crossed by a new bridge) is **Puelo**, a most peaceful place. From here the road continues 36 km further southwest to Puelche on the Carretera Austral (see page 291). The Gaucho Trail east from Cochamó to **Paso León** on the Argentine frontier was used in the colonial period by the indigenous population, Jesuit priests and later by *gauchos*. It runs along Río Cochamó to La Junta, then along the north side of Lago Vidal, passing waterfalls and the oldest surviving Alerce trees in Chile at El Arco. The route takes three to four days by horse, five to six days on foot.

Sea routes south of Puerto Montt » p283

Puerto Montt is the departure point for several popular voyages along the coast of southern Chile. All sailings are from Angelmó; timetables should be checked carefully in advance as schedules change frequently.

To Puerto Natales

One of the highlights of many journeys to Chile is the 1,460-km voyage between Puerto Montt and the southern port of **Puerto Natales**, made by the *M/V Magallanes*; it is quicker to fly and cheaper to go by bus via Argentina but the voyage by boat is spectacular. The route south from Puerto Montt crosses the Seno de Reloncaví and the Golfo de Ancud, then continues south through the Canal Moraleda and the Canal Errázuriz, which separate the mainland from the outlying islands. It then heads west through the Canal Chacabuco to Bahía Anna Pink and across the open sea and the infamous Golfo de Peñas (Gulf of Sorrows) to reach a series of channels, which provide one of the narrowest routes for large shipping in the world. There are spectacular views of the wooded fjords, weather permitting, particularly at sunrise and sunset, and a sense of desolate peace pervades everything except the ship, which is filled with cows in transport containers mooing day and night, and people having a good time.

The only regular stop on this route is at the fishing village of **Puerto Edén** on Isla Wellington, one hour south of the Angostura Inglesa. It has three shops, one off-licence, one café, and a *hospedaje* (open intermittantly) for up to 20 people. The population of 185, includes a few remaining native Alacaluf people. **Isla Wellington** is largely untouched, with stunning mountains. If you do stop here, take all food; maps (not very accurate) are available in Santiago. The onward fare to Puerto Natales is US$50.

This is a cargo ferry rather than a cruise liner; standards of service and comfort vary, depending on the number of passengers and weather conditions. Economy class is basic, cramped and near the engine room, in 24-berth dormitories; book a cabin instead. The food is variable, and, apart from videos, entertainment on board is limited. However, wine is available and you are welcome to bring your own. »» *Travellers' tale p331.*

To Puerto Chacabuco and Laguna San Rafael

A weekly catamaran service sails between Puerto Montt and **Puerto Chacabuco**, 80 km west of Coyhaique. This beautiful voyage passes forested cliffs, seemingly within touching distance, and offers glimpses of distant snows. However, taking this route south means that travellers miss out on the attractions of the Carretera Austral. The Navimag ferry *M/N Edén* also sails this route, continuing (September to April only) from Puerto Chacabuco to visit **Laguna San Rafael** (see page 304). However, it may well be cheaper, and is certainly more comfortable, to take a catamaran service direct to the Laguna from Puerto Chacabuco (see page 304) or to charter a small plane from Coyhaique (see page 306). A luxury alternative is to board *Skorpios II* for a cruise to Chiloé and Laguna San Raphael. Generally service is excellent, the food superb and, at the laguna, you chip ice off the face of the glacier for your whisky. After San Rafael the ship visits **Quitralco fjord**, where there are thermal pools and boat trips. There are also four- to six-day tours from Puerto Montt with **Patagonia Connection**, which visit Puerto Chacabuco, Laguna San Rafael and the Termas de Puyuhuapi (see page 301).

To Chaitén

The sea route to Chaitén through the Golfo de Ancud is quicker and more reliable than the Carreterra Austral but you'll miss much of the spectacular scenery encountered along the way. However, if you are pushed for time, **Navimag** and **Transmarchilay** both offer ferry services on a weekly basis. The journey normally takes 10 hours. **Catamaranes del Sur** and **Aysen Express** also run a much faster cataraman service six times weekly.

Sleeping

Puerto Montt *p275, map p276*

Accommodation is expensive in season, much cheaper off season. There are lots of *cabañas*, on the outskirts of the city and in **Pelluco**.

AL **Apart Hotel Colón**, *Pedro Montt 65, T065-264290, aparthotelcolon@entelchile.net*. Fully furbished apartments, good value.

AL **Don Luis**, *Quillota 146, T065-259001, www.hoteldonluis.cl*. Four-star hotel and very good restaurant.

AL **Viento Sur**, *Ejército 200, T065-258701, www.hotelviento.cl* Excellent 4-star, good restaurant, sauna, gym and great views.

A **O'Grimm**, *Gallardo 211, T065-252845, www.ogrimm.com*. With breakfast, cosy restaurant with occasional live music, central.

B **Le Mirage**, *Rancagua 350, T065-255125, F065-256302, hlemirage@telsur.cl*. With breakfast, small rooms, clean.

B **Montt**, *Varas 301 y Quillota, T065-253651*. With or without bath, clean, friendly, good value, good restaurant.

C **Millahue**, *Copiapó 64, T065-253829*. With breakfast, modern, good restaurant, also apartments at *Benavente 959, T/F065-254592*.

C-E **Hostal Pacífico**, *J J Mira 1088, T065-256229, www.hostalpacifico.cl*. With or without bath, breakfast included, cable TV, parking, comfortable.

E **Casa Perla**, *Trigal 312, T065-262104, www.casaperla.com*. Price per person with breakfast. Near the bus terminal, helpful, friendly, meals, laundry, internet, pleasant garden, English spoken, Spanish classes, good meeting place. Recommended.

E **Hospedaje Erica**, *Trigal 309, T065-259923*. Price per person. Kitchen, TV, big bathroom, good views, uphill from the bus terminal.

E **Hosp Frente al Mar**, *Huasco 6, T065-260126*. Price per person with breakfast, kitchen, also *cabañas*.

E **Hosp Rocco**, *Pudeto 233, T065-272897, www.hospedajerocco.cl* Price per person with breakfast, but without bath, real coffee, English spoken, friendly atmosphere.

E **Hosp Suizo**, *Independencia 231, T/F065-252640*. Price per person, with breakfast. More expensive rooms with bath. Attractive house near the bus terminal, clean, German and Italian spoken, painting and Spanish classes.

E **Res Emita**, *Miraflores 1281, T065-250725*. Price per person with breakfast, including homemade bread. Some rooms with bath. Clean, friendly, safe, near the bus terminal.

E-F **Alda González**, *Gallardo 552, T065-253334*. Price per person with or without bath, breakfast included, cooking facilities, English and German spoken, good value, near the Plaza de Armas.

F **Casa Gladis**, *Ancud y Mira*. Price per person for dorms, some double rooms, kitchen and laundry, near bus terminal.

Camping

Anderson, *11 km west*. American run, hot showers, private beach, home-grown fruit, vegetables and milk products.

Municipal, *Chinquihue, 10 km west*. Open Oct-Apr, fully equipped with tables, seats, barbecue, toilets and showers, small shop, no kerosene, bus service from town.

Seno de Reloncaví p277

C **Campo Aventura**, *4 km south of Cochamó, Bookings: San Bernardo 318, Puerto Varas, T065-232910, www.campo-aventura.com, info@campo-aventura.com* For riding, trekking and fly-fishing tours, see Activities and tours. Accommodation is offered at the base camp (signpost on road). Price per person with great breakfast, kitchen, sauna. Camping is also possible. Fresh milk from Campo Aventura's cow, herb garden, good food using local produce, vegetarian also available, book exchange, Spanish classes. There's another base in a renovated mountain house in the valley of La Junta.

Epp **Cochamó**, *T065-216212*. Basic but clean, friendly, often full of salmon farm workers, good meals, recommended.

E-Fpp **Hosp Edicar**, *Cochamó*. With or without breakfast. Without bath, spacious, recommended.

E-Fpp **Hosp Maura**, *JJ Molina 12, Cochamó*. With or without bath. Beautifully situated, good food.

Eating

Puerto Montt p275, map p276

For seafood enthusiasts, the only place to go is **Angelmó**, where there are many small, very popular seafood restaurants in the old fishing port by the market, serving excellent lunches only. There is fierce touting for business. Look out for local specialities such as *curanto* and *picoroco al vapor*, a giant barnacle whose flesh looks and tastes like a crab, and ask for *té blanco* (white wine; the stalls are not legally allowed to serve it). There are more good seafood restaurants on the other side of the city in **Pelluco** (see p291). In Puerto Montt itself, try the following:

TTT **Balzac**, *Urmeneta y Quillota*. Very good.

TTT **Centro Español**, *O'Higgins 233*. Expensive but very good.

TTT **Club Alemán**, *Varas 264*. Old-fashioned, good food and wine.

TTT **Club de Yates**, *Juan Soler s/n*. Excellent seafood.

TT **Café Amsel**, *Hotel Burg, Pedro Montt y Portales*. Superb fish, not cheap, real coffee.

TT **Embassy**, *Ancud 106*. Very good, upper end of range.

TT **Puerto Café**, *Angelmó 2456 (above Travellers)*. Real coffee, vegetarian dishes, English spoken, recommended.

Café Real, *Rancagua 137*. For *empanadas, pichangas, congrío frito* and cheap lunches.

Dino, *Varas 550*. Restaurant upstairs, snacks downstairs (try the lemon juice).

Las Antiqüedades, *Av Angelmo*. Attractive, unusual décor, real coffee, interesting menu.

Cafés

Asturias, *Angelmó 2448*. Limited menu but often recommended.

Café Alemana, *Rancagua 117*. Real coffee, good.

Café Plaza, *Urmeneta 326*. Good location, friendly, pool/billiards.

Seno de Reloncaví *p277*

Eateries in Cochamó include **Donde Payi,** opposite the church and **Reloncaví**, on the road down to the waterfront. On the seafront there is a cheap fish/seafood restaurant, which also hires out canoes, US$1 for 30 mins.

Activities and tours

Puerto Montt *p275, map p276*

There are many agencies. Most offer 1-day excursions to **Chiloé** (US$20) and to **Puerto Varas**, Isla Loreley, Laguna Verde, and the Petrohué falls: these tours are cheaper from bus company kiosks inside the bus terminal. Some companies offer 2-day excursions along the Carretera Austral to **Hornopirén**, US$76, with food and accommodation.

Alsur, *Antonio Varas 445, T/F065-287628*. Rafting and water sports

Andina del Sud, *Varas 437 (very close to central tourist kiosk), T065-257797*. Sells a variety of tours, and through its subsidiary Cruce de Lagos (www.lakecrossing.cl) also offers the lakes trip to Bariloche (see p283).

Eureka Turismo, *Varas 449, T065-250412, www.chile-travel.com/eureka.htm* Helpful, German and English spoken.

Kayaking Austral, *T09-6980951, or book through Casa Perla*. Guided sea kayaking.

Marina del Sur (MDS), *Chinquihué, T/F065-251958*, . Sailing courses, notice board for crew (*tripulante*) requests, modern building with bar and restaurant. The MDS charters office specialises in chartering boats for cruising the Patagonian channels: US$2,200-8,500 per week depending on size of boat.
Patagonia Verde, *Diego Portales 514, T065-286990*. Mountaineering, fishing, trekking, horse riding.
Petrel Tours, *Benavente 327, T065-251780, petrel@telsur.net* Recommended.
Travellers, *Av Angelmó 2456, T065-262099, www.travellers.cl, www.daytours.cl* Booking office for **Navimag** ferry to Puerto Natales, bespoke excursions, also day trips, book swap ("the best south of Santiago"), map display, TV, real coffee, English-run.

Seno de Reloncaví *p277*

Campo Aventura, *Bookings: San Bernardo 318, Puerto Varas, T065-232910, www.campo-aventura.com, info@campo-aventura.com*. Specializes in all-inclusive riding and trekking expeditions with packhorses along the Gaucho trail between the Reloncaví estuary and the Argentine frontier, 2-10 days, US$97 per person, per day; good guides, spectacular scenery, English, French and German spoken, highly recommended. It also organises other activities including fly-fishing and combined sea kayaking-horseriding trips with **Kokayak** in Puerto Varas.
Sebastian Contreras, *Calle Morales, Cochamó, T065-216220*. An independent guide who offers tours on horseback and hires out horses, recommended.

Transport

Puerto Montt *p275, map p276*

Air

LanChile and **Sky** have several flights daily to **Santiago**, from US$100 return (one way more expensive); to **Balmaceda** for Coyhaique, from US$80 return; to **Punta Arenas**, from US$130 return. In Jan, Feb and Mar you may be told that flights are booked up, however, cancellations are sometimes available from the airport. To **Chaitén**, Aeropuelche, daily, US$40. To **Bariloche** and **Neuquén** (Argentina), TAN, 2 weekly, 40 mins; to **Port Stanley** (Falkland Islands/Islas Malvinas), from Santiago via Punta Arenas, **LanChile**, Sat, US$600 return.

Airline offices Aeropuelche, *Copiapó 106, T065-435827*; **LanChile**, *O'Higgins 167, T065-253315*; **Sky**, *T600-600 2828*.

Bus

The very crowded terminal on the seafront at *Diego Portales y Lota*, has telephones, restaurants, a *casa de cambio* and left luggage (US$1.50 per item for 24 hrs).

Expreso Puerto Varas, Thaebus and Full Express run minibuses every few minutes to **Puerto Varas**, US$0.80, **Llanquihue** and **Frutillar**, US$1.25, and to **Osorno**, US$1.50. Buses and *colectivos* nos 2, 3 and 20 ply the route to **Angelmo**, US$0.30 each way.

To **Ensenada** and **Petrohué**, several companies, hourly; to **Ralún**, **Cochamó** and **Puelo**, Buses Fierro and Buses Bohle, 4 daily via Puerto Varas and Ensenada; to **Pucón**, several daily, 6 hrs, US$6; to **Santiago**, several companies, 13 hrs, US$13, *semi cama* US$20, *salón cama* US$30; to **Temuco**, US$5; to **Valdivia**, US$4. To **Ancud**, 2 hrs, US$4.50, and **Castro**, 3 hrs, US$4.50, on Chiloé, regular services with **Cruz del Sur** and others.

To **Punta Arenas**, Pacheco and Queilén Bus, 1-3 weekly, 32-38 hrs, approximately US$35 (bus goes through Argentina via Bariloche; take US$ cash to pay for meals etc in Argentina); book well in advance in Jan-Feb and book any return journey before setting out. To **Coyhaique** via Bariloche, 2 weekly, **Turibus**, US$46.

International Buy tickets for international buses from the bus terminal, not through an agency. **Andes Mar** has through-services to Buenos Aires, Neuquén and Bahía Blanca; less in winter.

To **Bariloche** via Osorno and the Puyehue pass, daily, 7hrs, **Andes Mar**, **Rio de la Plata** and **Tas Choapa**, US$12. **Andina del Sud** (see p281) in partnership with **Cruce de Lagos** in Bariloche, runs services to **Bariloche** via Lago Todos Santos and Paso Pérez Rosales, depart company offices in Puerto Montt daily at 0800, US$140 one way (plus US$140 May-Aug for overnight stay in the **Hotel Peulla**; for a cheaper alternative see p271). The trip may be cancelled if the weather is poor; there are reports of difficulty in obtaining a refund. If you have time but are short of money, you can buy tic+kets for the boat in Puerto Montt or Puerto Varas and do the rest of the trip independently, but bear in mind that there is no transport from Peulla to the border, 26 km.

Car hire

Automotric Angelmó, *Talca 79*, cheap and helpful; **Automóvil Club de Chile**, *Ensenada 70, T065-254776, and at airport*; **Autovald**, *Diego Portales 1330, T065-256355*, cheap rates; **Avis**, *Urmeneta, 1037, T065-253307, and at airport*; **Budget**, *Gallardo 450, T065-254888 and at airport*; **Dollar**, *Hotel Vicente Pérez Rosales, Antonio Varas 447*; **Egartur**, *Benavente 575, loc. 3, T065-257336, egartur@telsur.cl*, good service, will deliver your car to your hotel for free; **First**, *Antonio Varas 447, T065-252036*; **Full Famas**, *Diego Portales 506, T065-258060, F065-259840, and airport, T065-263750*, friendly, helpful, good value, has vehicles that can be taken to Argentina; **Hertz**, *Antonio Varas 126, T065-259585*, helpful, English spoken; **Travicargo**, *Urmeneta 856, T065-257137*.

Seno de Reloncaví p277

Bus

Buses Fierro and **Bohle** from Puerto Montt via Puerto Varas and Ensenada, to **Ralún**, **Cochamó** and **Puelo**, 4 daily.

Boat

In summer boats sail up the estuary from **Angelmó**. Contact the **Sernatur** office in Puerto Montt.

To Puerto Natales p278

This route is run year round exclusively by **Navimag**, *Terminal Transbordadores, Av Angelmó 2187, T065-253318, www.navimag.cl*.

Schedule The *Magallanes* departs Puerto Montt once a week, Nov-Apr, Mon 1600, returning from Puerto Natales Fri 0400 (although departures are frequently delayed, or even advanced, by weather conditions). The journey takes 3½ days.

Prices High season (Oct-Apr): economy from US$275 per person (take sleeping bag), private cabin with view US$1590; fares 10-20% lower in Oct and Apr. Low season (May-Sep) economy from US$200, private cabin US$720. All prices include meals; 10% discount for ISIC holders in cabin class only.

Reservations Book well in advance for cabin class departures Dec-Mar (more than 2 weeks in advance in Feb), especially for the voyage south; Puerto Natales to Puerto Montt is less heavily booked. It is worth putting your name on the waiting list for cancellations at busy periods. Tickets can be bought in advance through **Travellers** in Puerto Montt (see Activities and tours, above), from **Navimag** offices in Puerto Montt, Puerto Natales and Punta Arenas, from travel agencies throughout the country, or online at www.navimag.cl

To Puerto Chacabuco p279

Aysen Express, *O'Higgins 167, Of 307, T065-437599, www.aysenexpress.cl*, operates a weekly catamaran service, departs Puerto Montt Fri, 11 hrs, US$43. **Navimag**, *Terminal Transbordadores, Av Angelmó 2187, T065-253318, www.navimag.cl* operates the *M/N Edén* ferry on this route throughout the year, once or twice a week, 24 hrs, bunks from US$70, reclining seat US$25, cars US$150, motorcycles US$35, cycles US$20. In the summer (Sep-Apr) it continues once a week (usually at the weekend) to Laguna San Rafael, 21-24 hrs, return fare Puerto Montt-Laguna San Rafael US$325-US$650; for fares from Puerto Chacabuco to Laguna San Rafael see p304.

To Laguna San Rafael p279

For boats to the glacier from Puerto Chacabuco, see p308 and Navimag, above. Compañía Naviera Puerto Montt, *Diego Portales 882, Puerto Montt, T/F065-252547*. Runs 6-day, 6-night tours to the Laguna, via various routes, on board the *Quellon*, US$900. Office in Santiago at *Alameda B O'Higgins 108, local 120, T02-6330883*, and in Puerto Aisén/Puerto Chacabuco. Pamar, *Pacheco Altamirano 3100, T065-256220*. Sails Sep-Mar only. Patagonia Connection SA, *Fidel Oteíza 1921, Oficina 1006, Providencia, Santiago, T02-225 6489, www.patagonia-connection.com*, operates all-inclusive 6-day tours, from Puerto Montt to Laguna San Rafael, US$1300-2100, including the *Patagonia Express* catamaran service from Puerto Chacabuco, with accommodation at Termas de Puyuhuapi (see p301) and a day excursion to Laguna San Rafael. Raymond Weber, *Av Chipana 3435 Pasaje 4, T02-8858250, www.chilecharter.com*, charters luxury sailing catamarans to visit Golfo de Ancud and Laguna San Rafael. Skorpios Cruises, *Angelmó 1660 y Miraflores (Castilla 588), T065-252619, www.skorpios.cl*. Luxury ship *Skorpios 2* leaves Puerto Montt Sat 1100 for a 6-day cruise to Laguna San Rafael, returning to Puerto Montt Fri, double cabin from US$680 per person; the fare varies according to season, type of cabin and number of occupants. For further details (and information about routes sailed by *Skorpios 1* and *3*), consult the website.

To Chaiten and elsewhere p279

Bohemia, *Antonio Varas 947, T065-254675*. To Río Negro, Isla Llancahué, Baños Cahuelmó and Fiordo Leptepu/Coman on the Carretera Austral, *m/n Bohemia*, 6 days/5 nights, US$545-720 per person depending on season. Catamaranes del Sur, *Diego Portales 510, T065-267533, www.catamaranesdelsur.cl*, and Aysen Express, *O'Higgins 167, Of 307, T065-437599, www.aysenexpress.cl*, 6 catamarans weekly between them to Chaiten, 4½ hrs, US$35 including transfer to port from company offices. Navimag, *Terminal Transbordadores, Av Angelmó 2187, T065-253318, www.navimag.cl*, 1 ferry per week to Chaiten, 10 hrs, passengers US$23, *literas* US$33, cars US$90, bicycles US$11. Transmarchilay, *Transbordadores, Angelmó 2187, T065-270416, www.transmarchilay.cl*, 3 ferries weekly to Chaiten, prices similar to Navimag.

Directory

Puerto Montt p275, map p276

Banks and currency exchange For Visa visit Corp Banca, *Pedro Montt y Urmeneta*, good rates; commission charges for TCs vary widely; good rates at Galería Cristal, *Varas 595*; Afex, *Portales 516*. **Consulates** Argentina, *Cauquenes 94, piso 2, T065-253996*, quick visa service; Germany, *Antonio Varas y Gallardo, piso 3, Oficina 306*, Tue-Wed 0930-1200; Netherlands, *Chorillos 1582, T065-253003*; Spain, *Rancagua 113, T065-252557*. **Internet** *Antonio Varas 629*; also upstairs in bus terminal and several on Av Angelmo. **Laundry** Nautilus, *Av Angelmó 1564*, cheap, good; Yessil't, *Edif Caracol, Urmeneta 300*, service washes. **Medical services** *Seminario s/n, T065-261134*. **Post office** *Rancagua 126*, open 0830-1830 Mon-Fri, 0830-1200 Sat. **Telephone** Many call centres around town.

Going further

Chiloé

The mysterious archipelago of Chiloé is one of the most fascinating areas of Chile. Isolated from mainstream Spanish development for 200 years, Chiloé is different to the mainland and retains many unique traditions, including the belief in witchcraft and local mythical figures such as 'El Trauco', an ugly, smelly creature who is said to seduce virgins and the 'La Fiura', who attracts men with her colourful clothes before putting them to sleep with her foul breath.

Chiloé consists of one main island, Chiloé Grande (180 km long), and numerous islets. There are two main towns, Ancud and Castro, in which most of the island's 116,000 people live, and a number of small villages. The Parque Nacional de Chiloe covers extensive areas of uninhabited temperate rainforest on the wild western side of the island. At Cucao, an immense 20 km long beach a is battered by thundering Pacific surf. The more sheltered east coast and offshore islands are covered with wheat fields and dark green plots of potatoes and the roads are lined with wild flowers in summer. There are often dolphins playing in the bay, and, on a clear day, views across to Corcovado volcano on the mainland. The Humboldt Current ensure a wide variety of fresh shellfish are available all year; try *curanto* (a stew, traditionally cooked in a hole in the earth). Chiloé is famous for its painted churches, now designated UNESCO World Heritage sites. The earliest example from 1730 is in Achao on the island of Quinchao.

Ferry and catamaran services connect the island with Chaitén and the Carretera Austral (see page 295), but the main sea link is the frequent vehicle ferry service between Pargua on the mainland (55 km southwest of Puerto Montt) across the Chacao straits to Chacao (30 minutes, cars US$11.40 one way, foot passengers US$1). Frequent bus services meet the ferries, linking Ancud and Castro with Puerto Montt and beyond. Local services, however, can be crowded and slow. Mountain bikes and horses are ideal for travelling through the more remote parts of Chiloe; there are also limited opportunities for hiking.

The agrotourism network (T065-628333) enables visitors to stay with a local family and share their way of life. Prices per person are all E/F with breakfast. Further information can be obtained from the tourist office in Ancud, Libertad 665, **T** 065-622665, Mon-Fri 0900-1300, 1430-1730.

Carretera Austral

Don't miss...
1 Cycling along the Carretera Austral ▸▸ p290.
2 Parque Pumalin ▸▸ p292.
3 Whitewater rafting at Futaleufú ▸▸ p297.
4 Cruising to the San Rafael glacier ▸▸ p304.
5 Trekking around Chile Chico ▸▸ p311.
50 km
50 miles
Pacific Ocean
CHILE
ARGENTINA
REGION XI
p309
Puerto Montt
Puerto Varas
Bariloche
Chiloé
Castro
Ancud
Quellón
Chaitén
Futaleufú
Esquel
Coyhaique
Puerto Aisén
Balmaceda
Chile Chico
Los Antiguos
Cochrane
Tortel
Villa O'Higgins
Golfo de Corcovado
Golfo de Peñas
Archipiélago de las Chonos
Carretera Austral
Parque Nacional Laguna San Rafael
Campo de Hielo Norte
Lago General Carrera
Lago Buenos Aires

Introduction

Travelling along the Carretera Austral (also known as the Camino Austral) is one of the greatest journeys South America has to offer. The Carretera is a largely unpaved *ripio* road stretching over 1,000 km through ever-changing spectacular scenery. Before the opening of the Carretera, this part of Chile was largely inaccessible; it remains breathtaking. Deep tree-lined fiords penetrate into the heart of a land of spiralling volcanoes and sparkling glaciers, rushing rivers, crystal blue lakes and temperate rainforest, rich with southern Chile's unique flora.

The only town of any size, Coyhaique, lies in the valley of the Río Simpson. South of Coyhaique are Lago General Carrera, the largest lake in Chile, and the Río Baker, one of the country's longest rivers. Further south still is Villa O' Higgins and the icefields of the Campo de Hielo Sur, which feed several magnificent glaciers and prevent further road building, although a route (by boat and on foot or mountain bike) exists to El Chaltén in Argentina. Coyhaique enjoys good air connections with Puerto Montt and Santiago, while nearby Puerto Chacabuco can be reached by ferry or catamaran from Puerto Montt, Chaitén and Chiloé. The most appealing parts of this region, however, can only be visited by travelling along the Carretera Austral.

Ratings

Landscape
★★★★★

Chillin'
★★

Activities
★★★★

Wildlife
★★★★

Costs
$$$

Ins and outs

Remember to take enough cash. There are Cirrus and Mastercard ATMs in Chaitén and Cochrane, but Coyhaique is the only place after Puerto Montt that has Visa ATMs.

Getting around

The road can be divided into three sections: **Puerto Montt to Chaitén** (242 km), including two or three ferry crossings; **Chaitén to Coyhaique** (435 km); and **Coyhaique to Villa O'Higgins** (582 km), including one ferry crossing. There is also a branch that runs along the southern shore of **Lago General Carrera** from Puerto Guadal to Chile Chico. The Puerto Montt-Chaitén section can only be travelled in summer, when the ferries are operating, but an alternative route, through Chiloé to Chaitén, exists year round (see page). The road is paved around Coyhaique, from Puerto Chacabuco to Villa Cerro Castillo.

Bus Most of the buses that ply the Carretera Austral are minibuses (and in more than one case converted transit vans) operated by small companies and often driven by their owners. Services are less reliable than elsewhere in Chile and timetables change frequently. Booking your ticket in advance means that if your bus does not leave for whatever reason, the company is liable to pay for your accommodation until the bus is ready to depart. Complaints should be directed to SERNAC, the governent consumer rights department, in Coyhaique.

Driving Some sections of the road can be difficult or even impossible after heavy rain or snowfall, so check the weather carefully and be prepared to be stuck in one place for a few days while conditions improve. Take a four-wheel-drive vehicle and fill up your tank whenever possible. Although tourist infrastructure is growing rapidly and unleaded fuel is available all the way to Villa O'Higgins, you should protect windscreens and headlamps and carry adequate spare fuel and parts, especially if you are intending to detour from the main route. **Hitching** is popular in summer, but extremely difficult out of season, particularly south of Cochrane. Watching the cloak of dust thrown up by the wheels from the back of a pick-up, while taking in the lakes, forests, mountains and waterfalls, is an unforgettable experience, but be prepared for long delays and allow at least three days from Chaitén to Coyhaique.

Cycling The Carretera Austral is highly recommended for cycling as long as you have enough time and are reasonably fit. A good mountain bike is essential and a tent is an advantage. Most buses will take bicycles for a small charge. An excellent online guide to cycling the Carretera, can be found at www.salamandras.cl

Best time to visit

January and February are probably the best months for a trip to this area. From April to September it is bitterly cold inland; roads are subject to snowfall or flooding, and some ferry services are suspended.

Puerto Montt to Chaitén

This 242-km section of the Carretera Austral is the most inaccessible and secluded stretch along the entire route, passing through two national parks and the private Parque Pumalin. Beautiful old trees close in on all sides, the rivers and streams sparkle and, on (admittedly rare) clear days, there are beautiful views across the Golfo de Ancud to Chiloé.

Getting there Drive, or get the ferry direct to Chaitén.
Getting around Minibus, car and ferry. Very difficult in winter.
Time required 3-5 days.
Weather Heavy showers; snow in winter.
Sleeping Plenty of choice in Chaitén; *cabañas, residenciales* and camping elsewhere.
Eating Decent restaurants in Chaitén, basic elsewhere
Activities Trekking, fishing, horse riding.
★ **Don't miss...** Parque Pumalin

Parque Nacional Alerce Andino

ⓘ *entrances 2½ km from Correntoso (35 km west of Puerto Montt) and 7 km west of Lenca (40 km south of Puerto Montt), US$5.* This national park covers 39,255 ha of steep forested valleys between the beautiful Seno de Reloncaví (see page 277) and Lago Chapo, and contains ancient alerce trees, some over 1,000 years old (the oldest are estimated to be 4,200 years old). There are also some 50 small lakes and many waterfalls in the park. Wildlife includes *pudú*, pumas, *vizcachas*, condors and black woodpeckers. There are ranger posts at Río Chaicas, Lago Chapo, Laguna Sargazo and at the north entrance and a map is available from CONAF in Puerto Montt.

Hornopirén and around

Forty-six kilometres south of Puerto Montt (allow one hour), **La Arena** is the site of the first ferry, across the Reloncaví estuary to **Puelche**. From Puelche there is an unpaved road north to Puelo but the Carretera Austral continues 58 km south to **Hornopirén**, also called Río Negro, which lies at the northern end of a fjord. At the mouth of the fjord is **Isla Llancahué**, a small island with a hotel and thermal springs. The island is reached by boat ⓘ *T09-6424857, US$25 one way shared between group*; look out for dolphins and fur seals on the crossing. From

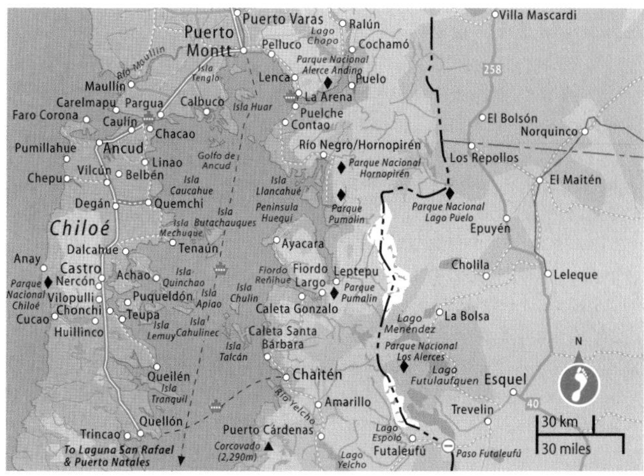

Background

The long road south

Although the first town in this area, Balmaceda, was founded in 1917, followed by Puerto Aisén in 1924, the first road, between Puerto Aisén and Coyhaique, was not built until 1936. It was not until the 1960s, when new roads were built and airstrips were opened, that this region began to be integrated with the rest of the country.

The Carretera Austral has helped transform the lives of many people in this part of Chile, but the motivation behind its construction was mainly geopolitical. Ever since Independence, Chilean military and political leaders have stressed the importance of occupying the southern regions of the Pacific coast and preventing any incursion by Argentina. Building the Carretera Austral was seen by General Pinochet as a means of achieving this task: a way of occupying and securing territory, just as colonization had been in the early years of the 20th century.

Begun in 1976, the central section of the Carretera Austral, from Chaitén to Coyhaique, was opened in 1983. Five years later, the northern section, linking Chaitén with Puerto Montt, and the southern section, between Coyhaique and Cochrane, were officially inaugurated. Since then, the Carretera has been extended south of Cochrane to Puerto Yungay and Villa O'Higgins. Work is continuing, building branch roads and paving the most important sections.

Hornopirén, excursions can be made to the Hornopirén volcano (1,572 m), Lago Cabrera and the **Parque Nacional Hornopirén**. The park lies 16 kilometres east by *ripio* road and encompasses the Yates volcano (2,187 m) as well as the basins of two rivers, the Blanco and the Negro. The park protects some 9,000 ha of alerce forest as well as areas of mixed native forest including lenga and coigue. From the entrance a path leads 8 km east up along the Río Blanco to a basic *refugio*.

Parque Pumalin and around

ⓘ *T/F02-7358034, www.pumalin.org, free*. Hornopirén is the departure point for the second ferry, to **Caleta Gonzalo**, situated on the southern edge of the Fiordo Reñihue. This is the base for visiting **Parque Pumalin**, seen by many as one of the most important conservation projects in the world. Created by the US billionaire Douglas Tompkins, this private reserve extends over 320,000 ha and is in two sectors, one just south of the Parque Nacional Hornopirén and the other stretching south and east of Caleta Gonzalo to the Argentine border. Its purchase aroused controversy, especially in the Chilean armed forces, which saw it as a threat to national sovereignty, but now the park has nature sanctuary status.

Covering large areas of the western Andes, most of the park is occupied by temperate rainforest and is intended to protect the lifestyles of its inhabitants as well as the physical environment. Tompkins has established a native tree nursery, producing 100,000 saplings of endangered species, and developed apiculture; in 2002 the Pumalin bee stations produced 30,000 kg of honey. There are treks ranging from short trails into the temperate rainforest to arduous hikes lasting for several days. Three marked trails lead to Cascadas Escondidas; to an area of very old alerce trees; and to Laguna Tronador. The Carretera Austral runs through the

Ancient trees in Parque Nacional Alerce Andino

park, climbing steeply before reaching two lakes, Lago Río Negro and Lago Río Blanco. The coast is reached at **Santa Bárbara**, 48 km south, where there is a black sand beach, good campsite and swimming. Do not camp close to the water.

Chaitén

The capital of Palena province, Chaitén lies in a beautiful spot, with a forest-covered hill rising behind it, and a quiet inlet leading out into the Patagonian channels. The town is important as a port for catamarans and ferries to Puerto Montt and to Chiloé (see page 295), and is a growing centre for adventure tourism. There is excellent fishing nearby, especially to the south in the ríos Yelcho and Futaleufú and in lagos Espolón and Yelcho. Fishing licences are sold at the Municipalidad. Visits are also possible to an offshore sea-lion colony on **Isla Puduguapi**.

Sleeping

Parque Nacional Alerce Andino *p291*
There are basic *refugios* at Río Pangal, Laguna Sargazo and Laguna Fría, and campsites at Río Chaicas and at the northern entrance; no camping is permitted within the park boundaries.

Hornopirén and around *p291*
B **Termas de Llancahuée**, *Llancahue island, T09-6424857*. Full board, good food, pool.
C-D **Hornopirén**, *Carrera Pinto 388, T065-217256*. Good rooms, also *cabañas*.
E **Holiday Country**, *O'Higgins 637, T065-217220*. Restaurant, also *cabañas*.

Camping

There's a good site next to the **Hostería Setca**, US$14 per site, and 4 more sites south on the road to Pichanco.

Parque Pumalin and around *p292*
There is a restaurant, *cabañas* and a campsite in Caleta Gonzalo. Camping is available in the park at several well-run sites from US$8 per tent.

Chaitén *p293, map p294*
Ferries from Chiloé are met by people offering accommodation.
A **Brisas del Mar**, *Corcovado 278, T065-731284, cababrisas@telsur.cl* Good *cabañas*.

A-B Schilling, *Corcovado 320, T065-731295*. With breakfast, heating, restaurant.

B Mi Casa, *Av Norte, T065-731285, hmicasa@telsur.cl* On a hill offering fine views. Sauna, gymnasium and restaurant with good-value set meal. Recommended.

C Cabañas Tranqueras del Monte, *Av Norte s/n, T065-731379, tranqer@telsur.cl* Furnished, English spoken, recommended.

D El Triángulo, *Juan Todesco y Corcovado, T065-731312*. Without bath or breakfast.

E Casa Rita, *Rivero y Prat*. Use of kitchen, clean, open all year, heating. Recommended. Camping also available.

E Hospedaje Ancud, *Libertad 105*. Price per person. Use of kitchen, very friendly.

E Hospedaje Recoba, *Libertad 432, T065-731390*. Price per person with breakfast. Clean, friendly, good meals.

E Hospedaje Watson, *Ercilla 580, T065-731237*. Price per person including use of kitchen. Clean.

E Hostería Llanos, *Corcovado 378, T065-731332*. Price per person with breakfast. Basic, without bath, good beds, friendly, restaurant.

E Hostería San Sebastián, *Riveros 163, T065-731225*. Price per person. Some with bath, with breakfast.

E Martín Ruiz, *Carretera Austral, 1 km north of Chaitén*. Price per person with breakfast. Friendly, nice views.

Eating

South of Puerto Montt p291

Pazos, *Pelluco, T065-252552*. Serves the best *curanto* in the Puerto Montt area.

Chaitén p293, map p294

Las Brisas del Mar, *Corcovado 278*. Good fish dishes.

Corcovado 448. Decent food

El Quijote, *O'Higgins 42*. Bar snacks.

Flamengo, *Corcovado 218*. Popular.

Activities and tours

Chaitén p293, map p294

Chaitur, *Diego Portales 350, T/F065-731429, nchaitur@hotmail.com* Travel agent for bus and boat tickets, excursions, trekking, horseriding, fishing and trips to Pumalín park. English spoken, friendly and helpful. Information and internet access. Highly recommended. Another branch in the bus station.

Transport

Before setting out, it is imperative to check when the ferries are running and, if driving, to make a reservation for your vehicle: do this at **Transmarchilay** in Puerto Montt (see Directory page 284).

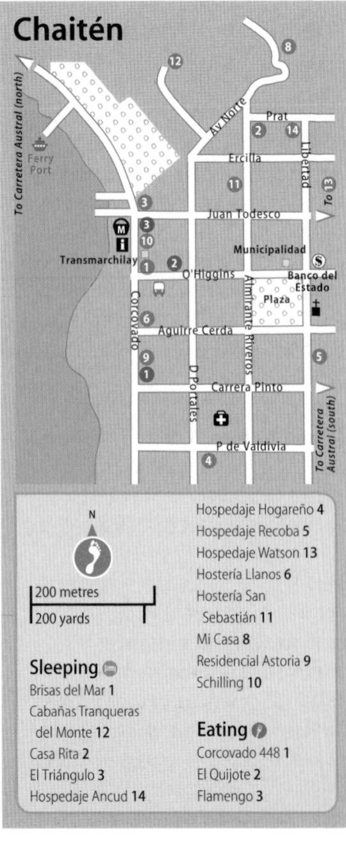

Parque Nacional Alerce Andino p291

To reach the northern entrance, take **Fierro** or **Río Pato** bus from Puerto Montt to **Correntoso** (or **Lago Chapo** bus which passes through Correntoso), several daily except Sun, then walk. To reach the southern entrance, take any **Fierro** bus to Chaicas, La Arena, Contau and Hornopirén, US$1.50, get off at **Lenca** sawmill, then walk (signposted).

A **ferry** makes the 30-min crossing, from La Arena to **Puelche**, 10 daily Dec-Mar, reduced service off season. Arrive 30 mins early for a place; buses have priority, cars US$5.

Hornopirén and around p291

Bus

Fierro 2 buses daily from Puerto Montt. No buses south from Hornopirén.

Ferry

In Jan and Feb only, the **Transmarchilay** ferry *Mailen* sails from Hornopirén to **Caleta Gonzalo**, 1600 daily, 6 hrs, return departures 0900 daily, cars US$83 one way, foot passengers US$13, bicycles US$8. Advance booking required: there can be a 2-day wait. **Chaitur** organizes connecting transport between the ferry port in Caleta Gonzalo and Chaitén (see Activities and tours, above).

Chaitén p293, map p294

Air

Flights to **Puerto Montt** by **Aerosur**, **Aeropuelche** and **Aeromet**, daily 1200, 35 mins, US$50. **Aeroregional** also flies to **Castro**, irregular service. Bookings through **Chaitur** (see Activities and tours).

Bus

Terminal at O'Higgins 67. Several companies run minibuses along the Carretera Austral to **Coyhaique**, most days direct in summer, 2 a week with overnight stop in La Junta or Puyuhuapi in winter, departures usually 0800-0900. Minibuses usually travel full, so can't pick up passengers en route. Chaitur acts as an agent for all these services (see Activities and tours). **Buses Norte**, *Libertad 432, T065-731390*, has buses to **Coyhaique**, US$25, and intermediate points such as La Junta (US$9) and Puyuhuapi. To **Futaleufú**, 4 hrs, with **Chaitur**, 1530 Mon-Sat, US$8; with **B y V**, 0900 daily, US$9; with **Buses Ebenezer**, Mon-Sat 1530, Sun 1700.

Sea

The ferry port is about 1 km north of town. Schedules change frequently and are infrequent off season. **Transmarchilay**, *Corcovado 266, T065-731273, www.transmarchilay.cl*; **Navimag**, *Carrera Pinto 108, T065-731570, www.navimag.cl*; **Catamaranes del Sur**, *Todesco 180, T065-731199, www.catamaranesdelsur.cl*

To **Chiloé**, **Navimag** and **Transmarchilay** have services to Castro or Quellón, 4 per week in summer (Dec-Mar), reduced service off season, 5hrs, passengers US$16 one way, cars US$85, bicycles US$9. **Aysen Express** and **Catamaranes del Sur** catamarans run the same route, 5 weekly in summer, less regular off season, 2 hrs, US$18.

To **Puerto Montt**, **Navimag** and **Transmarchilay**, 4 weekly, 10 hrs, passengers US$23, car US$93, bike US$9; **Catamaranes del Sur** and **Aysén Express**, 5 weekly, 3 hrs, US$30. To **Puerto Chacabuco**, **Aysén Express** 2 weekly, 7 hrs, US$32.

Directory

Chaitén p293, map p294

Banks Banco del Estado, *O'Higgins y Libertad*, charges US$10 for changing TCs, ATM accepts Mastercard and Cirrus but not Visa. Rates in general are poor along the Carretera Austral; change money in Puerto Montt.

Chaitén to Coyhaique

This section of the Carretera Austral, 422 km long, runs through long stretches of virgin rainforest, passing small villages, the still white waters of Lago Yelcho and the Parque Nacional Queulat, with its glaciers and waterfalls. Roads branch off east to the Argentine frontier and west to Puerto Cisnes and Puerto Aisen. Near Coyhaique, the road passes huge tracts of land destroyed by logging, where only tree-stumps remain as testament to the depredations of the early colonists. Founded in 1929, Coyhaique is the administrative and commercial centre of Region XI and is the only settlement of any real size on the Carretera Austral. A lively city, it provides a good base for excursions in the area.

Getting there Plane or bus to Coyhaique. Ferry or catamaran to Puerto Chacabuco.
Getting around Bus or car.
Time required 3 days for travel, up to 2 weeks for activities.
Weather Wet, with frost, snow and fog up high.
Sleeping Plenty for all budgets, some good camping.
Eating Most choice in Coyhaique.
Activities and tours Fantastic fishing, hiking, skiing, whitewater rafting, canoeing, horse riding.
★ **Don't miss...** Cruising to the San Rafael glacier.

Ins and outs

» *For further details, see Transport, page 306.*

Getting there Coyhaique is the transport hub for Region XI. There are two **airports** in the area: **Tte Vidal**, 5 km southwest of Coyhaique, which handles only smaller aircraft, and **Balmaceda**, 56 km southeast of Coyhaique, near the Argentine frontier. Flying to Balmaceda is the most direct way to reach

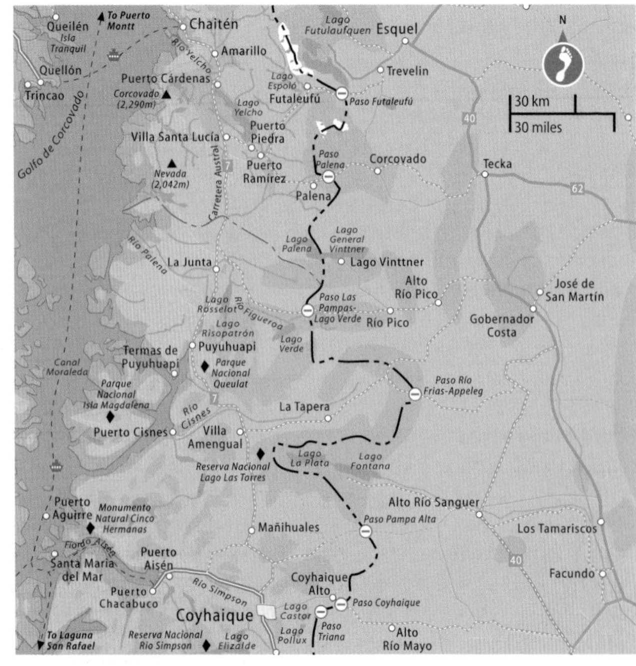

Coyhaique, with three or four flights daily from Santiago and Puerto Montt and a weekly flight to/from Punta Arenas. Minibuses, known as 'transfers', run between Balmaceda and Coyhaique, collecting/delivering to hotels; contact **Travell** ⓘ *Parra y Moraleda, T067-230010, US$3.50* and **Transfer** ⓘ *Lautaro 828, T067-233030, US$3.50*. A taxi takes 1 hour, US$6. **Long-distance buses** (several weekly) from Puerto Montt to Coyhaique do not travel along the Carretera Austral, using instead the long and expensive route via Argentina. Another enjoyable way to reach this part of the country is to take the **boat** from Puerto Montt to Puerto Chacabuco (see page 283).

Lago Yelcho and the border

Surrounded by forest, 45 km south of Chaitén, **Puerto Cárdenas** lies on the northern tip of **Lago Yelcho**, a beautiful glacial lake on the Río Futaleufú surrounded by hills and the beautiful Yelcho glacier. The lake is frequented by anglers. At Puerto Cárdenas, there is a police post where you may have to register your passport. Further south at Km 60, a path leads to the **Yelcho glacier**, a two-hour walk. The Argentine frontier is reached at Futaleufú and Palena, along a road that branches off the Carretera Austral at **Villa Santa Lucía** (Km 81). The road to the border is single track, *ripio*, best with a good, strong vehicle. At **Puerto Ramírez**, at the southern end of **Lago Yelcho**, the road divides: the north branch runs along the valley of the Río Futaleufú to Futaleufú, while the southern one continues to Palena. The border is 8 km east of both Futaleufú and Palena. Both crossings lead to the Welsh settlement of **Trevelin** (45 km east of Futaleufú, 95 km east of Palena; see page 136) and **Esquel** (23 km northeast; see page 135). » *For full details, see page 135.*

Futaleufú

Only accessible by road since 1982, Futaleufú (big river in the Mapuche language) has now established itself as the centre for the finest whitewater rafting in the southern hemisphere. Every year, hundreds of fanatics travel to spend the southern summer here and there is no shortage of operators offering trips. The river is an incredible deep blue colour and offers everthing from easy grade II-III sections downstream to the extremely challenging grade V Cañon del Infierno (Hell Canyon), surrounded by spectacular mountain scenery.

The village, hemmed in by mountains and the Río Espolón, is peaceful, with wide streets and Chilote-style houses. Information is available at the **tourist office** ⓘ *O'Higgins y Prat, T065-721370*. **Lago Espolón**, west of Futaleufú, is reached by a turning 41 km northeast of Puerto Ramírez. It is a beautiful lake and enjoys a warm microclimate: 30°C in the day in summer, 5°C at night. It's even warm enough for a quick dip, but beware of the currents.

La Junta and around

From Villa Santa Lucía, the Carretera Austral follows the Río Frío and then the Río Palena to **La Junta**, a tranquil, nondescript village at the confluence of Río Rosselot and Río Palena, 151 km south of Chaitén. Fuel is available here. From La Junta roads head northwest to **Puerto Raúl Marín Balmaceda** on the coast and east for 9 km to **Lago Rosselot**, surrounded by forest and situated at the heart of a *reserva nacional* (12,725 ha). From Lago Rosselot the road continues for 74 km to a border crossing at **Lago Verde** towards Las Pampas and Gobernador Costa in Argentina, ⓘ *summer 0730-2200; winter 0800-2000.*

Puyuhuapi and around

The Carretera Austral continues south from La Junta, along the western side of Lago Risopatrón, past several waterfalls, to **Puyuhuapi** (also spelt Puyuguapi). Located in a beautiful spot at the northern end of a fjord, the village is a tranquil stopping place between Chaitén and Coyhaique. It was founded by four Sudeten German families in 1935 and its

Ciudad de los Césares was a fabulously wealthy mythological city built between hills made of gold and diamonds and inhabited by immortal beings.

economy is based around fishing, tourism and the factory where Puyuhuapi's famous handmade carpets are produced. From Puyuhuapi, the road follows the eastern edge of the fjord along one of the most beautiful sections of the Carretera Austral, with views of the **Termas de Puyuhuapi** on the other side (see page 301).

Covering 154,093 ha of attractive forest around Puyuhuapi, the **Parque Nacional Queulat** ⓘ *administration at the CONAF office in La Junta, T067-314128*, is, supposedly, the former location of the legendary Ciudad de los Césares. According to myth, the city was protected by a shroud of fog and hence was impossible for strangers to discover. The Carretera Austral passes through the park, close to **Lago Risopatrón**, where boat trips are available. Twenty-four kilometres south, a two-hour trek leads to the **Ventisquero Colgante** hanging glacier. From here the Carretera Austral climbs out of the Queulat valley through a series of hairpin bends offering fine views of the forest and several glaciers.

Río Cisnes

Stretching 160 km from the Argentine border to the coast at Puerto Cisnes, the Río Cisnes is recommended for rafting or canoeing, with grand scenery and modest rapids – except for the horrendous drop at Piedra del Gato, about 60 km east of Puerto Cisnes. Good camping is available in the forest. Possibly the wettest town in Chile, **Puerto Cisnes** is reached by a 33-km winding road that branches west off the Carretera Austral about 59 km south of Puyuhuapi. The **Argentine border** is reached via a road that follows the Río Cisnes east for 104 km, via La Tapera. On the Argentine side, the road continues via Río Frías to meet up with Route 40, the north-south road at the foot of the Andes (see page 182). **Chilean immigration** ⓘ *12 km west of the frontier, open daylight hrs only.*

Towards Coyhaique

The **Reserva Nacional Lago Las Torres** is 98 km south of Puyuhuapi and covers 16,516 ha. It includes the wonderful Lago Las Torres, which offers good fishing and a small CONAF

Termas de Puyuhuapi

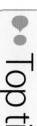

Top tips

Angling for a catch

The rivers around Coyhaique provide the greatest fishing in Chile; each summer the international fishing fraternity converge on the town for the season, which runs from 15 November to 15 April. Rivers range from the typically English slow chalk stream to the fast-flowing Andean snowmelt torrents, requiring a variety of angling techniques.

On the outskirts of Coyhaique, the spectacular **Río Simpson** teems with both rainbow and brown trout. It is renowned for its evening hatches (sedge and mayfly), which take place throughout the season. Catches in excess of five pounds are frequent and rainbow trout weighing over 12 pounds have been landed.

Located near the Argentine border, a scenic one-hour drive from Coyhaique, **Río Nirehuao** is a fly-fisher's dream. Throughout the season the brown trout feed voraciously on grasshoppers and dragonfly. The easy wading and moderate casting distances make this river an all-time favourite.

South of Coyhaique, the **Río Baker** offers anglers a unique fishing experience in its turquoise blue water. The Baker is huge and intimidating, as are its fish: rainbows up to 12 pounds lurk here and anglers regularly take fish in the four to seven pound range. The **Río Cochrane,** a gin-clear tributary of the Baker, also holds large rainbows. The Cochrane is mainly a 'sight-fishing' river, which requires skill, patience and an experienced guide.

campsite. Further south, at Km 125, a road branches east to El Toqui where zinc is mined. From here the Carretera Austral is paved.

Coyhaique and around » pp 300-308

Located 420 km south of Chaitén, Coyhaique (also spelt Coihaique) lies in the broad green valley of the Río Simpson. The city is encircled by a crown of snowcapped mountains and, for a few hours after it has rained, the mountainsides are covered in a fine layer of frost – a spectacular sight. Although a visit to the tourist office will throw up far more attractions outside Coyhaique than in the town itself, this is a pleasant, friendly place, perfect for relaxing for a couple of days or as a base for day trips. The town is centred around an unusual pentagonal plaza, built in 1945, on which stand the cathedral, the Intendencia and a handicraft market. Further north on Baquedano is a display of old military machinery outside the local regimental headquarters. In the Casa de Cultura the **Museo Regional de la Patagonia Central** ⓘ *Baquedano s/n, Tue-Sun 0900-2000 (summer), 0830-1730 (winter), US$1*, has sections on history, mineralogy, zoology and archaeology, as well as photos of the construction of the Carretera Austral. English is spoken at Coyhaique's very helpful **Sernatur** office ⓘ *Bulnes 35, T067-231752, infoaisen@sernatur.cl, Mon-Fri 0830-1700*, which has bus timetables. **CONAF** is at ⓘ *Ogana 1060*. Maps (photocopies of 1:50,000 IGM maps) are available from **Dirección de Vialidad** on the plaza.

From Coyhaique there are two routes into Argentina: via Coyhaique Alto and Paso Huemules (see page 183). The former route takes you past the **Monumento Natural Dos**

“” Puerto Aisén is much wetter than Coyhaique – local wags say that it rains for 370 days a year.

Lagunas ⓘ *25 km east of Coyhaique, entry US$1, camping US$12 per site*, a small park that encompasses Lagos El Toro and Escondido. The latter route passes Balmaceda airport.

Around Coyhaique

There are two national reserves close to Coyhaique: 5 km northwest off the Carretera Austral is **Reserva Nacional Coyhaique**, which covers 2,150 ha of forest (mainly introduced species), while west of Coyhaique (take any bus to Puerto Aisén) is the **Reserva Nacional Río Simpson**, covering 40,827 ha of steep forested valleys and curiously rounded hills rising to 1,878 m. One of these, near the western edge of the park, is known as *'El Cake Inglés'*. There are beautiful waterfalls, lovely views of the river and very good fly fishing here. The southeastern sector of the reserve is designated as the **Reserva Nacional Río Clara** and is one of the best places to see the native huemul (see page 313), although visitors must be accompanied by a warden. Other wildlife includes pudú and pumas, and a variety of birds ranging from condors to several species of ducks. Administration is 32 km west of Coyhaique, just off the road.

Puerto Aisén and Puerto Chacabuco

Puerto Aisén lies at the confluence of the rivers Aisén and Palos. First developed in the 1920s, the town grew as the major port of the region until the silting up of the Río Aisén forced the port to move 15 km further downriver to Puerto Chacabuco. Today boats lie high and dry on the bank when the tide is out and the foundations of buildings by the river are overgrown with fuchsias and buttercups. To see any maritime activity you have to walk to **Puerto Aguas Muertas** where the fishing boats come in. There is a helpful **tourist office** in the Municipalidad ⓘ *Prat y Sgto Aldea, Dec-Feb only*.

The town is linked to the south bank of the Río Aisén by the Puente Presidente Ibañez, once the longest suspension bridge in Chile. From the far bank a paved road leads to **Puerto Chacabuco**, from where ferry services depart for Puerto Montt and **Laguna San Rafael** (see page 304).

A good 10 km walk north along a minor road from Puerto Aisén leads to **Laguna Los Palos**, calm, deserted and surrounded by forested hills. **Lago Riesco**, 30 km south of Puerto Aisén, can be reached by an unpaved road that follows the Río Blanco. In season, the *Apulcheu* sails regularly to **Termas de Chiconal** ⓘ *US$30*, about one hour west of Puerto Chacabuco on the northern shore of the Seno Aisén, offering a good way to see the fjord.

Sleeping

Lago Yelcho and the border *p297*

L-A **Cabañas Yelcho en La Patagonia**, *7 km south of Puerto Cardenas, T065-731337*. Cabins and rooms on the lake shore. Also camping and cafeteria.

AL **Cabanas CAVI**, *nr Puerto Cárdenas*. Sauna, restaurant, video room, laundry. Six *cabañas* with private bathrooms, hot water, kitchen facilities. Also campsite with electricity, hot showers, laundry , barbecue area and fishing boats for hire. Book via **Turismo Austral Ltda**, *Santa Magdelena 75, of 902, Providencia, Santiago,T02-3341309*.

B **Termas de Amarillo**, *T065-731326*. Camping and *cabañas*.

C **Res Yelcho**, *Puerto Cárdenas, T065-264429*. Clean, full board available.

Budget buster

Termas de Puyuhuapi

Situated on the western edge of the fjord, 18 km southwest of Puyuhuapi, are the Termas de Puyuhuapi, T067-325103, US$15 per person, under-12s US$10. This resort, accessible only by boat (US$3 each way, 10-min crossing) has several 40°C springs filling three pools near the beach. Accommodation at the resort (L) includes use of the pools and the boat transfer. Price depends on the season and type of room. The hotel restaurant is good; full board US$40 extra. The resort can be visited on a four- or six-day tour with Patagonia Connection SA (see page 284); alternatively, transport to the hotel can be arranged independently via hydroplane from Puerto Montt.

Futaleufú p297

There are *cabañas* and a campsite on the shore of Lago Espolón, US$3.75 for a motor home.

AL-A **Hostería Río Grande**, *O'Higgins 397, T065-721320*. The best place in town. Comfortable, en-suite bathrooms, friendly, bar, restaurant, tours and activities.

E pp **Continental**, *Balmaceda 397, T065-721222*. Basic, hot water, clean. Recommended. Cheap restaurant.

E **Hospedaje Adolfo**, *O'Higgins 302, T065-721256*. Nice and friendly, though basic.

E **Residencial Yamara**, *O'Higgins s/n*. Without bath. Recommended.

La Junta and around p297

A-B **Hostal Espacio y Tiempo**, *T067-314141, www.espacioytiempo.cl* Attractive garden, English spoken, good restaurant, fishing expeditions.

Epp **Residencial Valderas**, *Varas s/n, T067-314105*. Breakfast, bath, good value.

Puyuhuapi and around p297

There's a CONAF campsite at Lago Risopatrón.

L **Cabañas El Pangue**, *Lago Risopatrón, Km 240, Parque Nacional Queulat, T067-325128, cpangue@entelchile.net* Cabins sleep 4, private bathrooms, hot water, heating, telephone, parking, swimming pool, fishing trips, horseriding, mountain bikes. Recommended.

AL-A **Cabañas Fiordo Queulat**, *Seno Queulat, Parque Nacional Queulat, T067-233302*. Good reputation, hikes and fishing trips. Campsite nearby, US$3.50.

C-D **Hostería Alemana**, *Av Otto Uebel 450, T067-325118*. A large, comfortable, wooden house on the main road. Highly recommended, closed in winter.

D pp **Casa Ludwig**, *Av Otto Uebel s/n, south of Puyuhuapi, T067-325220, www.contactchile.cl/casaludwig* Excellent. English spoken. Highly recommended.

Camping

CONAF, *reservations T067-212125*, runs a basic campsite (cold water) 12 km north of Puyuhuapi on Lago Risopatrón, and another near the Ventisquero Colgante.

Río Cisnes p298

B **Cabañas Río Cisnes**, *Costanera 101, T067-346404*. Cabins sleep 4-8. Owner, Juan Suazo, has a boat and offers good sea trout/salmon fishing.

Epp **Hostería El Gaucho**, *Holmberg 140, T067-346514*. With breakfast, dinner available, hot water.

Coyhaique p299, map p303

Look out for notices in windows, since any place with fewer than 6 beds does not have to register with the authorities.

A **Cabañas La Pasarela**, *Km 1.5, T067-234520*. Good atmosphere, *comedor*.
A **Cabañas Río Simpson**, *Km 3, T067-232183, riosimpsoncab@hotmail.com* Fully equipped cabins for 4-9 people. Horseriding, fishing and tours. Several tame alpacas in the grounds.
A **El Reloj**, *Baquedano 828, T067-231108, www.aisen.org/elreloj* In a former saw-mill. Good restaurant, nice lounge, some rooms have wonderful views. English spoken. Highly recommended.
A **San Sebastian**, *Baquedano 496, T067-233427*. Small, views, good breakfast, recommended.
A-B **Hotel y Apart Hotel Austral**, *Colón 203, T067-232522*. Clean, English spoken, tours arranged, friendly. Recommended.
B **Libanés**, *Simpson 367, T067-234242, hlibanes@entelchile.net* Rooms with TV, phones, heating, also laundry and café.
B **Hostal Araucarias**, *Vielmo 71, T067-232707*. Large rooms, good view, also hires out cars.
B-G **Cabañas Ogana**, *Av Ogana Pasaje 8, 185, T067-232353*. Breakfast and kitchen facilities, also camping and *cabañas*.
C **Hostal Bon**, *Serrano 91, T067-231189*. With breakfast, friendly, clean, also *cabañas*, good meals. Recommended.
E **Hospedaje Baquedano**, *Baquedano 20, T067-232520*. Room in family home by the river, use of kitchen, bathroom and laundry. Wonderful views. Friendly, helpful, English spoken, breakfast served with homemade bread, recommended.
F **Hospedaje Natti**, *Av Simpson 417, T067-231047*. Clean, very friendly, kitchen facilities, breakfast. Highly recommended.
F-Gpp **Albergue Las Salamandras**, *2 km south of town, T067-211865, www.salamandras.cl* Double rooms, dormitories, *cabañas* and camping in attractive forest location. Kitchen facilities, winter sports, trekking and tours. Maps and cycling information provided. English spoken. Excellent budget choice.
F-G **Hospedaje Lautaro 269**, *T067-238116*. Parking, internet and kitchen facilities. English spoken. Recommended.

Campsites

Sernatur in Coyhaique has a full list of all sites in Region XI. There are several in Coyhaique and on the road to Puerto Aisén. In the Reserva Nacional Coyhaique, there are basic campsites, US$4, at Laguna Verde and at Casa Bruja and a *refugio*, US$1, 3 km from the entrance. There's also a campsite near the turning to Santuario San Sebastián, US$5, in the Reserva Nacional Rio Simpson.

Puerto Aisén and around *p300*

AL **Parque Turístico Loberías del Sur**, *Carrera 50, Puerto Chacabuco, T067-234520*. Recently rebuilt 5-star complex, serving the best food in the area. Have a drink or a meal overlooking the boats and the mountains before boarding your ferry. Car hire available.
B **Hotel Caicahues**, *Michimalonco 660, Puerto Aisén, T067-336633*. With bath, heating, telephone and internet.
E **Roxy**, *Aldea 972, Puerto Aisén, T067-332704*. Price per person. Friendly, clean, large rooms, restaurant. Rooms at the back are quieter and have a view. Good.

Eating

Puyuhuapi and around *p297*

TT **Café Rossbach**, *Costanera, Puyuhuapi*. Limited menu, including excellent salmon; also good for tea and Küchen; building is in German Black Forest style.

Coyhaique *p299, map p303*

TTT **Café Restaurant Histórico Ricer**, *Horn 48 y 40 2o Piso*. Regional specialities, historical exhibits, recommended.
TT **Casona**, *Vielmo 77*. Traditional food. Recommended.
TT **El Reloj**, *Baquedano 828*. Uses all local ingredients, recommended.
TT **La Casona**, *Obispo Vielmo 77*. Good lamb and fish dishes, recommended.
TT **La Olla**, *Gen Prat 176*. Great Spanish food, good-value lunches.
TT **Piel Roja**, *Moraleda y Condell*. Friendly bar with laid-back atmosphere and meals.

Café Alemana, *Condell 119*. Excellent cakes, coffee, vegetarian dishes.

Casino de Bomberos, *Gen Parra 365*. Wide range, large portions, good value.

El Mastique, *Bilbao 141*. Seriously cheap but good. Recommended.

La Fiorentina, *Prat*. Cheap pizzas, good.

Puerto Aisén p300

The best restaurant is the **Parque Turístico Loberías del Sur**, see Sleeping.

La Cascada, *Km 32 between Coyhaique and Puerto Aisén*. Waterfalls nearby. Recommended for meat and fish.

Martina, *Av Municipal, near bridge, Puerto Aisén*. Good Chilean fare. Probably the best in town.

There are many cheap places on Aldea in Puerto Chacabuco, between Municipal and Dougnac.

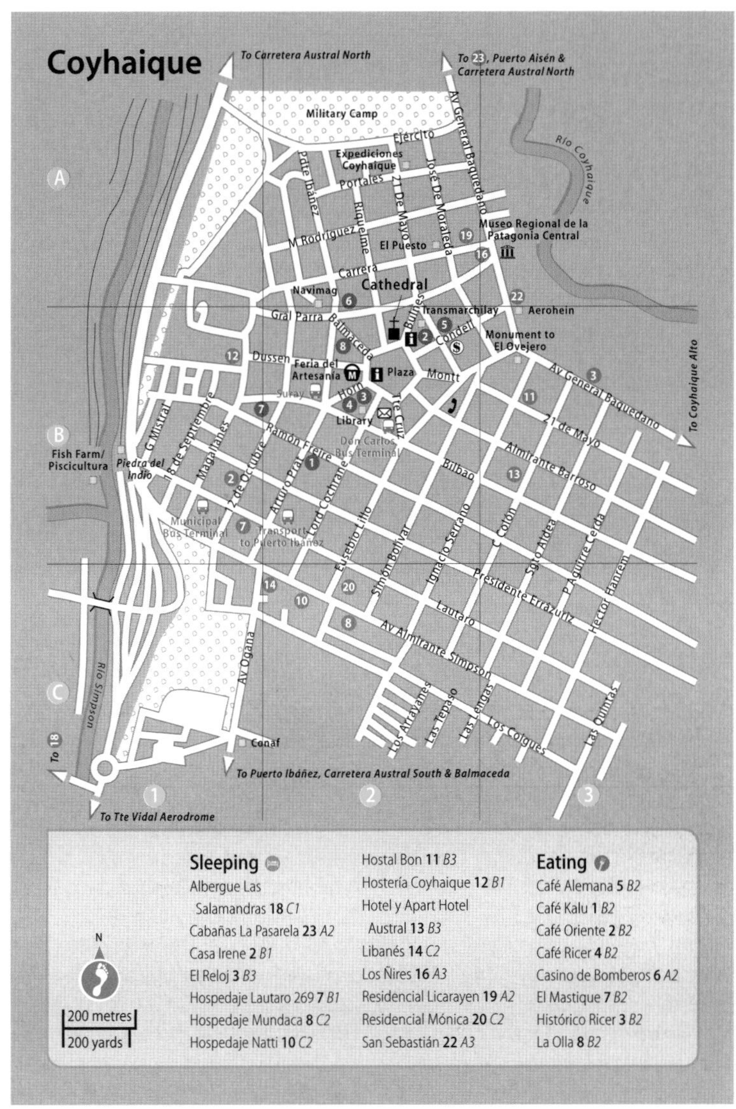

Going further

Glaciar San Rafael

Situated some 200 km south of Puerto Chacabuco, the San Rafael glacier is one of the highlights for many travellers to Chile. About 45 km in length and towering 30 m above water level, the deep blue glacier groans and cracks as it carves off icebergs, which are carried across the Laguna San Rafael and out to sea via the Río Tempano. Around the shores of the laguna is thick vegetation and above are snowy mountain peaks.

The San Rafael is one of many glaciers flowing from the giant **Campo de Hielo Norte**, which covers much of the 1,740,000-hectare **Parque Nacional Laguna San Rafael** (entry fee US$6). In the national park are puma, pudu, foxes, dolphins, occasional sea-lions and sea otters, and many species of bird.

There is a small ranger station on the shore of Laguna San Rafael, which provides information on the national park. Walking trails are limited (about 10 km in all) but a lookout platform has been constructed, with fine views of the glacier. The rangers are willing to row you out to the glacier in calm weather: an awesome three-hour adventure, past icebergs and swells created when huge chunks of ice break off the glacier and crash into the laguna.

The San Rafael glacier is rapidly disintegrating and is likely to have disappeared entirely by 2011. Some place the blame for the speed of deterioration on the waves created by motorised tourist boats that go too close to the glacier. If the glacier is to be preserved, it is vital that travellers take a pro-active stance on this issue and insist that the boats do not go too close to the glacier and further damage this fragile environment.

Activities and tours

Lago Yelcho and the border *p297*

Fishing

Isla Monita Lodge, near Puerto Cardenas, offers packages for anglers and non-anglers on a private island on Lago Yelcho (see p297), as well as fishing in many nearby locations; contact **Turismo Grant**, *PO Box 52311, Santiago, T02-6395524, F02-6337133.*

Puerto Cisnes *p298*

Fishing

There are good opportunities for fishing in this area; contact **German Hipp**, *Costanera 51, T067-346587* or **Cabañas Río Cisnes** (see above). Further information from **Turismo Lago Las Torres**, 130 km Carretera Austral Norte, T067-234242.

Futaleufú *p297*

All tour operators in Futaleufú can arrange whitewater rafting. The Hostería Río Grande (see above) also offers good trips. There's good fishing on Río Futaleufú and Lago Espolón.

Earth River, *www.earthriver.com/futaleufu.htm* Excellent for river-rafting and kayaking trips, book in advance.

Expediciones Chile, *www.exchile.com* Offers the best multi-day trips. Book in advance. Day trips can be booked on site.

Futaleufú Expediciones, *O'Higgins 397,*

Getting there

Air Aerohein and Don Carlos provide air taxis from Coyhaique, US$200 each for party of 5; some pilots in Puerto Aisén will also fly to the glacier for about US$95 per person, but many are unwilling to land on the rough airstrip. Other air-tour options available from Coyhaique. See page 306.

Boats from Puerto Montt Slow service with Navimag (via Puerto Chacabuco); official cruises by Skorpios; tours with Patagonia Connection; also private yacht charters. See page 279.

Boats from Puerto Chacabuco Slow service with Navimag; one- or three-day trips with Catamaranes del Sur; luxury catamaran cruises with Iceberg Express. Local fishing boats from Puerto Chacabuco/Puerto Aisén (enquire at the port) take about 18-20 hrs each way and charge the same as the tourist boats. Note that they may have neither adequate facilities nor a licence for the trip. Out of season, trips are very difficult to arrange. See page 307.

T/F065-258634. Rafting, canyoning, trekking and horseriding expeditions.

Coyhaique *p299, map p303*

A full list of specialist tours and fishing guides is available from **Sernatur**. Excursions and trekking information is available from **Albergue Las Salamandras** (see Sleeping).

Fishing

For fishing in the area, see Angling for a catch, p299.

Patagonia Travel Service, *Condell 149, T067-237795*. Offers fishing tours on Lago Riesco and near Puerto Chacabuco.

Turismo Aysén, *Barroso 626, T067-238036*. Fishing and horseriding.

Scenic flights

Patagonia Explorer, *T09-8172172, stonepiloto@hotmail.com* Pilot Willy Stone offers charter flights to the Laguna San Rafael, US$200 per person, recommended.

Skiing

El Fraile, *office in Coyhaique at Dussen y Plaza de Armas 376, T067-231690*. 29 km southeast of Coyhaique, near Lago Frío, 5 pistes, 2 lifts, a basic cafetería and equipment hire (season Jun-Sep).

Tour operators

Baltazar Araneda, *T067-231047 or*

through Hospedaje Natti (see Sleeping). Horseriding trip to Lagos Palomo, Azul and Desierto, US$240 per person for 4 days, US$300 for 5 days. Recommended.

Encounter Patagonia, *Colon 166, T067-215001, info@encounterpatagonia.com* Small specialist agency with strong local contacts, eco aware, English-speaking. Highly recommended.

Geo Turismo, *Lillo 315, T067-237456, www.geoturismo.cl* Wide range of tours throughout the region, English spoken, professional, recommended.

Turaustralis, *Moraleda 589, T067-239696, hsaldivia@hotmail.com* Fishing, horseriding, bird watching, tours.

Turismo Prado, *21 de Mayo 417, T067-231271, www.turismopradopatagonia.cl* Tours of local lakes and other sights, Laguna San Rafael trips and historical tours. Also offers general tourist information and accepts TCs.

Puerto Aisén *p300*

Turismo Rucaray, *on the plaza, rucaray@entelchile.net* Recommended for local tours. Internet access.

Transport

Lago Yelcho and the border *p297*

Transporte Patagonia Norte, *T065-741257*, runs a weekly bus from Palena to **Puerto Montt** via Argentina, Mon 0630, 13 hrs, US$28.

Futaleufú

Bus

To **Chaitén**, daily, 5 hrs; to **Puerto Montt**, Tue and Fri, US$33; to the **Argentine border** Mon and Fri 0900 and 1800 from *Balmaceda 419*, 30 mins, US$3; on the Argentine side there are connecting services to **Trevelin** and **Esquel**.

La Junta and around *p297*

There is no bus terminal in La Junta. All minibuses should be booked in advance. To **Puerto Cisnes**, Empresa Entre Verde, *T067-314275*, Mon and Fri, US$7. To **Coyhaique**, Buses Emanuel, Tue and Sat, US$12; Buses Daniela, *T067-231701*, 2 weekly, US$12; Buses Norte, 3 weekly; Buses Becker, Mon-Sat, US$13. To **Chaitén**, Buses Emanuel, Mon to Sat, US$8; Transportes Lago Verde, *Varas s/n, T067-314108*, 3 weekly, US$8; Buses Norte, 3 weekly. To **Lago Verde**, Buses Daniela, 2 weekly.

Puyuhuapi and around *p297*

Daily buses from Puyuhuapi north to **Chaitén** and south to **Coyhaique**, plus 2 weekly to **Lago Verde**.

Río Cisnes *p298*

Transportes Terra Austral, *T067-346757*, runs services from Puerto Cisnes to **Coyhaique**, Mon-Sat 0600, US$9; **Buses Norte**, *T067-346440* offers the same route once a week, US$8.

Coyhaique *p299, map p303*

Air

Airline offices Sky, *Prat 203, T067-240826, local calls 600-6002828*; LanChile, *Moraleda 402, T067-231188, local calls 600-5262000*; Don Carlos, *SubTte Cruz 63, T067-231981*.

Tte Vidal airport To **Chile Chico** with Don Carlos, Mon-Sat, US$42, or with Aerohin, *Baquedano 500, 252177*, Mon-Sat, from US$30. **Don Carlos** also flies to **Cochrane**, Mon and Thu, 45 mins, US$71, and to **Villa O'Higgins**, Mon and Thu, US$107, only for those who have strong stomachs or are in a hurry. There are also flights to **Tortel**, Wed, US$33, but these are for residents of the village.

Balmaceda airport LanChile and Sky to **Santiago**, several daily, US$130-250 return plus tax; to **Puerto Montt**, several daily, US$75-150 return plus tax. LanChile also to **Punta Arenas**, Sat, US$75-150 return plus tax. One-way fares are usually more expensive. For transport to/from the airport, see p296. For flights to Laguna San Rafael, see page 304.

Bus

The main terminal is at *Lautaro y Magallanes*. In the terminal are: **Bus Sur**, *T067-211460, www.bus-sur.cl*; **Giobbi**, *T067-232607*; **Los Ñadis**, *T067-211460*; **Interlagos**, *www.turismointerlagos.cl*, recommended; **Acuario 13**, *T067-240990*; **Queilén Bus**; **Transportes Terra Austral**, *T067-254475*. Other companies are: **Don Carlos**, *Subteniente Cruz 63, T067-232981*; **Suray**, *Prat 265, T067-238387*; **Turibus**, *Baquedano 1171, T067-231333*; **Bus Norte**, *Parra 337, T067-232167*; **Buses Daniela**, *Baquedano 1122, T067-231701*.

Carretera Austral north Suray, Interlagos and Don Carlos to **Puerto Aisén** every 15 mins, 1 hr, US$2. To **Chaitén** via Puyuhuapi and La Junta, **Buses Norte**, Mon, Thu, Sun, 12 hrs, US$20; **Buses Becker**, **Chaitur** and **B y V**, US$25. To **Lago Verde** via La Junta, **Buses Daniela**, Tue, Sat, US$18; **Transportes Bronco**, Wed and Sat, US$16. To **Puerto Cisnes**, **Transportes Terra Austral** and **Alegria**, Mon-Sat, US$10.

Carretera Austral south To **Cochrane**, with intermediate stops, **Interlagos**, 0930 Mon, Wed, Thu, Sat, Sun, US$12, recommended; **Don Carlos**, 0830 Tue, Sat, US$14; **Acuario 13**, 1000 Wed, Sat, US$11; and **Los Ñadis**, 1000 Tue, Thu, Sun, 8 hrs, US$11. *Colectivos* to **Puerto Ibáñez**, 2 hrs, book the day before, US$6, pick up at 0700 from your hotel to connect with **El Pilchero** ferry to Chile Chico: **Dario Figueroa Castro**, *T067-233286*, **Tour Aisen**, *09-8982643*, **Colectivos Sr Parra**, *T067-251073*, Sat and Sun only; **Minibus Don Tito Segovia**, *T067-250280*; **Sr Yamil**, *T067-250346*, and **Humberto Gomez**, *T067-423262*.

Long distance To **Puerto Montt**, via Bariloche, all year, **Turibus**, Tue and Sat 1700, US$25; **Queilén Bus**, Wed, Sat, US$33, onward connections, often heavily booked. To **Comodoro Rivadavia** (Argentina), 12 hrs, US$30, **Turibus**, Mon, Fri; **Giobbi**, Tue, Sat, from terminal. To **Punta Arenas** via Coyhaique Alto and Comodoro Rivadavia, **Bus Sur**, Tue, US$50.

Car

Car hire **Automóvil Club de Chile**, *Carrerra 333, T067-231649*, jeeps and other vehicles; **Río Baker**, *Balmaceda airport, T067-272163*; **Sur Nativo Renta Car**; *Baquedano 457, T067-235500*; **Traeger-Hertz**, *Baquedano 457, T067-231648*; **Turismo Prado**, *21 de Mayo 417, T/F067-231271*. Hire cars may be taken across the border and returned to an office in Argentina, but you should buy fuel at a station in Coyhaique.

Puerto Aisén /Puerto Chacabuco p300

Bus

Suray runs buses between the two ports every 20 mins, US$0.75. **Interlagos** and **Suray** have frequent services to **Coyhaique**, 1 hr, US$2.

Ferry

Agemar, *Tte Merino 909, Puerto Aisén, T067-332716*; other operators are all in Puerto Chacabuco. Boat information is posted at **Turismo Rucaray**.

To Puerto Montt **Transmarchilay**, *Av O'Higgins s/n, T067-351144, www.transmarchilay.cl*, and **Navimag**, *Terminal de Transbordadores, T067-351111, www.navimag.cl*, year-round ferry services via the Canal Moraleda once a week in summer, irregular off-season, 24 hrs, US$40. **Aysén Express** weekly catamaran service via Chaitén and Chiloé, 11 hrs, US$43.

To Laguna San Rafael It is best to make reservations for this trip at the ferry's offices in Puerto Montt, Coyhaique or Santiago (or, for **Transmarchilay**, in Chaitén or Ancud).

Catamaranes del Sur, *Carrera 50, T067-351112, www.catamaranesdelsur.cl*, 1-3 weekly Sep-Apr, 1-day trips US$299, 3-day trips from $550.

Compañía Naviera Puerto Montt, *Sgto Aldea 679, Puerto Aisén, T067-332908 /3511066*. Motorized sailing boats, the *Odisea* and the *Visun*, sail Dec-Mar on 6-day trips to the Laguna San Rafael.

Iceberg Express, *Av Providencia 2331, of 602, Santiago, T02-3350580*. 12-hr luxury catamaran cruises.
Navimag, *Terminal de Transbordadores, T067-351111, www.navimag.cl*. Official services, all year, reduced service off season, 24 hrs, from US$259.

Directory

Futaleufú *p297*

Banks Banco de Chile, changes US dollars and Argentine pesos.

Coyhaique *p299, map p303*

Banks Several with Redbanc ATMs in centre, for dollars, TCs and Argentine pesos. Casa de Cambio Emperador, *Bilbao 222*; Lucia Saldivia, *Baquedano 285*. **Hospital** *Calle Hospital 068, T067-233172*. **Internet** Ciber Patagonia, *21 de Mayo 525*, best value; Entel, *Prat 340*; Hechizos, *21 de Mayo 460*, also cheap; several others. **Language schools** Baquedano International Language School, *Baquedano 20, T067-232520, www.patagoniachile.cl/bils, pguzmanm@entelchile.net* US$300 per week, including 4 hrs one-to-one tuition daily, lodging and all meals, other activities organized at discount rates, friendly, informative, suitable for all ages and levels, highly recommended. **Laundry** Lavaseco Universal, *Gen Parra 55*. QL, *Bilbao 160*. **Post office** *Cochrane 202*, open Mon-Fri 0900-1230, 1430-1800, Sat 0830-1200. **Shipping offices** Aysen Express, *Condell 149, of 203, T067-240956, aysenexpress@123.cl*; Navimag, *Ibáñez 347, T067-233306, www.navimag.cl*; Transmarchilay, *21 de Mayo 447, T067-231971, www.transmarchilay.cl*.

Puerto Aisén *p300*

Banks Banco de Crédito, *Prat*, for Visa; Banco de Chile, *Plaza de Armas*, only changes cash, not TCs. Redbanc ATM in Puerto Chacabuco. **Post office** *south side of bridge*. **Telephone** *Plaza de Armas, next to Turismo Rucuray*; ENTEL, *Libertad 408*, internet access.

Lago General Carrera and beyond

The section of the Carretera Austral around the north and western sides of Lago General Carrera is reckoned by many to be the most spectacular stretch of all. Straddling the frontier with Argentina, the lake is the largest in South America after Lake Titicaca and is believed to be the deepest on the continent, with a maximum depth of 590 m. The region has 300 days of sunshine a year and rainfall is low. In general, the climate has more in common with Argentine Patagonia than with the rest of the Carretera Austral.

South from Cochrane, the scenery becomes increasingly remote and dramatic. The final stretch of the Carreterra Austral leads to the small town of Villa O'Higgins at the end of the road.

Getting there Direct buses and flights to Cochrane.
Getting around Ferries across Lago General Carrera but little public transport; hire a 4WD.
Time required At least 1 week to allow for the lack of public transport.
Weather Lots of sunshine and little rain.
Sleeping From plush *cabañas* to basic hostels and campsites.
Eating Limited restaurants, but *hosterías* offer good food.
Activities and tours Fishing, horse riding, rafting, canoeing.
★ **Don't miss...** Trekking around Chile Chico.

Ins and outs

Getting there and around There are direct buses and flights to Cochrane from Coyhaique. Minibuses also run along the Carretera Austral in summer to Puerto Ibañez (five weekly), from where, a ferry connects with Chile Chico. Overland routes between Coyhaique and Chile Chico are much longer, passing either through Argentina via Los Antiguos, or along the Carretera Austral and west around the lake. Public transport is scarce: air taxis link the small towns but there are only two weekly buses from Chile Chico to Cochrane and from Cochrane to Villa O'Higgins. A four-wheel-drive makes getting around much easier. p317.

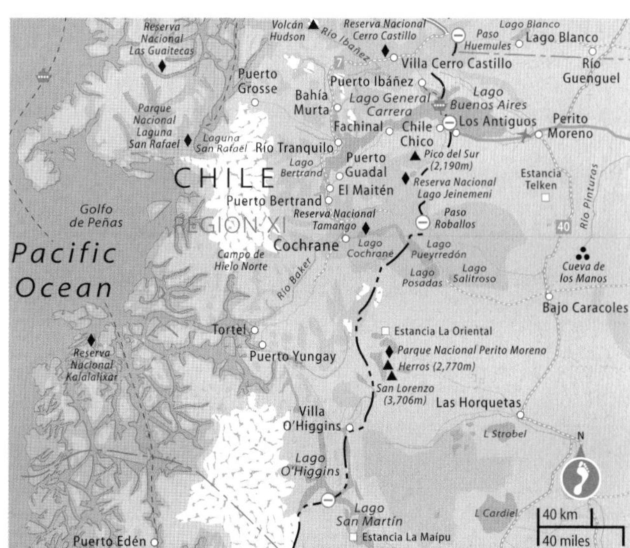

Reserva Nacional Cerro Castillo

Beyond Coyhaique, the Carretera Austral runs southwest through the Reserva Nacional Cerro Castillo, which extends over 179,550 ha. The park is named after the fabulous **Cerro Castillo** (2,675 m), which resembles a fairytale castle with rock pinnacles jutting out from a covering of snow. It also includes Cerro Bandera (2,040 m) just west of Balmaceda and several other peaks in the northern wall of the valley of the Río Ibañez. There is a *guardería* at the northeastern end of the park near Laguna Chinguay and a CONAF campsite nearby ⓘ *T067-237070, US$5 per site*. At Km 83 the road crosses the Portezuelo Ibañez (1,120 m) and drops through the Cuesta del Diablo, a series of bends with fine views over the Río Ibañez.

Puerto Ibañez and around

At **Bajada Ibañez**, 97 km south of Coyhaique, a branch road heads southeast for 31 km to **Puerto Ibáñez** (officially Puerto Ingeniero Ibáñez), the principal port on the Chilean section of Lago General Carrera. From here boats depart for Chile Chico on the southern shore; this is a very cold crossing even in summer, so take warm clothing. The Carretera Austral, meanwhile, continues from Bajada Ibañez 8 km to **Villa Cerro Castillo**. Near the village is the **Monumento Nacional Manos de Cerro Castillo**, where traces of ancient rock paintings, estimated to be 10,000 years old, have been found. The road climbs out of the valley, passing the emerald-green **Laguna Verde** and the Portezuelo Cofré, before descending to the boggy Manso valley.

Lago General Carrera

» *pp 314-317*

Known as General Carrera in Chile and as Buenos Aires in Argentina, this lake is a beautiful azure blue, surrounded at its Chilean end by predominantly Alpine terrain and at the Argentine end by dry pampa. The eruption of Volcán Hudson in 1991 (south of Chile Chico) polluted parts of Lago General Carrera and many rivers and, although the waters are now clear, the effects can still be seen in some places.

The western shore

Some 5 km from the Carretera Austral, at Km 203, **Bahía Murta** is situated on the northern tip of the central 'arm' of Lago General Carrera. This village dates from the 1930s, when it exported timber to Argentina via Chile Chico. From here, the road follows the lake's western shore to **Río Tranquilo** (228 km from Coyhaique), where buses stop for lunch and fuel is

available. Close to Río Tranquilo is the unusual **Catedral de Mármol**, a peninsula made of marble, with fascinating caves that can be visited by boat ⓘ *10 mins, US$25 to hire a boat with guide*. The village also has an unusual cemetery. A new branch of the Carretera Austral heads northwest from Río Tranquilo to **Puerto Grosse** on the coast at Bahía Exploradores.

The southern shore

At the southwestern tip of Lago General Carrera, at Km 279, is **El Maitén**, from where a road branches off east along the south shore of the lake towards Chile Chico. Ten kilometres east of El Maitén, **Puerto Guadal** is a picturesque town that is a centre for fishing. It also has shops, accommodation, restaurants, a post office and petrol. Further east, just past the village of **Mallin Grande**, Km 40, the road runs through the **Paso de las Llaves**, a 30-km stretch carved out of the rock-face on the edge of the lake. The road climbs and drops, offering wonderful views across the water and the icefields to the west. At Km 74, a turning runs to **Fachinal**. A further 8 km east, there is an open cast mine, which produces gold and other precious metals.

Chile Chico and around

Chile Chico is a quiet, friendly but dusty town situated on the lake shore 122 km east of El Maitén, close to the Argentine border. The town dates from 1909 when settlers crossed from Argentina and occupied the land, leading to conflict with cattle ranchers who had been given settlement rights by the Chilean government. In the showdown that followed (known as the war of Chile Chico) the ranchers were driven out by the settlers, but it was not until 1931 that the Chilean government finally recognized the town's existence.

Now the centre of a fruit-growing region, it has an annual festival at the end of January and a small museum open in summer; outside is a boat that carried cargo on the lake before the opening of the new road along the southern shore. There are fine views from the **Cerro de las Banderas** at the western end of town. The **tourist office** ⓘ *Municipalidad, O'Higgins 333*, can help in arranging tours. From Chile Chico a road runs 2 km east to the border and on for 5 km to **Los Antiguos** (see page 184)

The country to the south and west of Chile Chico provides good walking terrain, through weird rock formations and dry brush scrub. The northern and higher peak of Cerro Pico del Sur (2,168 m) can be climbed by the agile from Los Cipres (beware dogs in the farmyard). You will need a long summer's day and the 1:50,000 map. From the summit you'll enjoy indescribable views of the Lake and the Andes. Twenty kilometres south of Chile Chico towards Lago Jeinimeni is the **Cueva de las Manos**, a cave full of Tehuelche paintings, the most famous of which are the *manos azules* (blue hands). The path is difficult, and partly hidden, so you're recommended to take a guide.

Reserva Nacional Lago Jeinemeni

ⓘ *53 km south of Chile Chico, open all year but access limited between Apr and Oct due to high river levels, admission US$1.50, camping US$3.* This park covers 160,000 ha and includes two lakes, **Lago Jeinemeni** and **Lago Verde**, which lie surrounded by forests in the narrow valley of the Río Jeinemeni. Impressive cliffs, waterfalls and small glaciers provide habitat for huemul deer, pumas and condors. Activities include fishing for salmon and rainbow trout, trekking and rowing. Access is via an unpaved road, which branches south off the road to Los Antiguos and crosses five rivers. At Km 42, there is a small lake, **Laguna de los Flamencos**, where large numbers of flamingos can be seen. The park entrance is at Km 53; just beyond is a ranger station, a campsite and fishing area at the eastern end of Lago Jeinemeni. Take all supplies, including a good map.

Towards Cochrane » pp 314-317

South of El Maitén, the Carretera Austral becomes steeper and more winding; in winter this stretch is icy and dangerous. **Puerto Bertrand**, 5 km away, is a good place for fishing. Beyond Puerto Bertrand, the road climbs up to high moorland, passing the confluence of the rivers Neff and Baker, before winding south along the east bank of the Río Baker to Cochrane. The road is rough but not treacherous and the scenery is splendid all the way. Watch out for cattle and hares on the road (and huemuls in winter) and take blind corners slowly.

Cochrane and around

Sitting in a hollow on the northern banks of the Río Cochrane, 343 km south of Coyhaique, Cochrane is a simple place, good for walking and fishing. The **tourist office** ⓘ *Mon-Sat 0900-1300, 1430-2000*, is open in summer only; in winter go to the Municipalidad at Esmeralda 398. Excursions can be made from the town to **Lago Cochrane**, which covers over 17,500 ha, straddling the frontier with Argentina (the Argentine section is called Lago Puerredón). On the northern shore is the **Reserva Nacional Tamango** ⓘ *Dec-Mar 0830-2100, Apr-Nov 0830-1830, US$3, guided visits to see the huemal, Tue, Thu, Sat, US$60 for a group of 6 people*, a lenga-forest reserve that is home to one of the largest colonies of rare huemul as well as guanaco, foxes, woodpeckers and hummingbirds. There are several marked trails affording views over the town, the nearby lakes and even to the Campo de Hielo Norte to the west. Tourist facilities, however, are rudimentary.

Some 17 km north of Cochrane, a road runs east for 78 km through Villa Chacabuco to the border at **Paso Roballos**. On the Argentine side the road continues to **Bajo Caracoles**, a very isolated settlement on Ruta 40 (see page 185). There isn't any public transport along this route and, although the road is often flooded in spring. » *Border crossing, p185.*

South of Cochrane » pp 314-317

Travelling by bus on the final 224-km stretch of the Carretera Austral from Cochrane to Villa O'Higgins can be frustrating, as you will want to stop every 15 minutes to marvel at the views. From **Vagabundo**, Km 98, boats sail regularly down the Río Baker to Tortel. This is a beautiful trip through thick forest, with vistas of snow-capped mountains and waterfalls.

Tortel

Built on a hill at the mouth of the river 135 km from Cochrane, Tortel has no streets, only wooden walkways and became famous in October 2000 as the place where British Prince William spent three months working for **Raleigh International**; it is also where Rosie Swale ended her epic horseback journey through Chile, as recorded in *Back to Cape Horn*. A branch of the Carretera Austral, beginning 2 km south of Vagabundo and reaching south to Tortel, was completed in 2003, so the village is now accessible by road, and the repercussions on its character will be enormous. From Tortel, you can hire a boat to visit two spectacular glaciers: **Ventisquero Jorge Montt**, five hours southwest, or **Ventisquero Steffens**, on the edge of the Parque Nacional San Rafael. On the Río Baker nearby is the **Isla de los Muertos**, where some hundred Chilote workers died under mysterious circumstances early in the 20th century.

The Carretera continues southwards to **Puerto Yungay**, a tiny village with a military post and a pretty church. This section of the road is hilly and in places very bad; don't drive along it at night. From Puerto Yungay, there is a regular **ferry** to Río Bravo, from where the road continues through more spectacular scenery – lakes moors, swamps, rivers and waterfalls – before arriving at its final destination.

Background

Deer, oh deer

The Andean **huemul** (pronounced 'way-mool') is a shy mountain deer native to southern Chile and Argentina. It's a medium-sized, stocky creature, adapted to survival in rugged terrain. Males grow antlers and have distinctive black face masks. Although it used to range from just south of Santiago to the Straits of Magellan, human pressures have pushed the huemul to the brink of extinction, with current numbers estimated at just 1,000-1,500. Your best chance of seeing one is in the Reserva Nacional Río Claro, just outside Coyhaique (see page 300), or the Reserva Nacional Tamango, near Cochrane (see page 312). To visit either of these you will need to be accompanied by a warden.

The Carretera Austral area is also one of the best places for trying to spot the equally rare **pudu**. This miniature creature, around 40 cm tall and weighing only 10 kg, is the smallest member of the deer family in the world. Native to southern Argentina and Chile, the pudu is vulnerable to extinction, largely due to habitat loss, but also because its unique appearance (the males grow two short spiked antlers) has made it a target for poaching for zoos. Reddish-brown in colour, the pudu is ideally adapted to the dense temperate rainforests of Patagonia, scooting along trails through the undergrowth, leaving behind minuscule cloven tracks.

Villa O'Higgins

Situated at the southernmost end of the Carretera Austral, Villa O'Higgins has the atmosphere of a frontier town. It lies 2 km from a northerly 'arm' of **Lago O'Higgins**, which straddles the Argentine border as Lago San Martín. The lake is dotted with numerous icebergs that have split off the Campo de Hielo Sur to the west; these can be visited by boat from **Bahía Bahamóndez**, 7 km south. **Tourist information** ⓘ *T067-211849, www.villaohiggins.cl*, is available in the plaza in summer or from the Municipalidad, which can also provide guides and information on trekking. Behind the town, a *mirador* affords spectacular views of nearby mountains, lakes and glaciers.

It is now possible, if arduous, to get from Villa O'Higgins to **El Chaltén** in Argentina on foot or by horse. From **Bahía Bahamóndez**, a boat sets off across Lago O'Higgins ⓘ *T067-670313, www.villaohiggins.cl, 3 times per week Dec-Mar, 3 hrs, US$25*, to **Candelario Mancila** on the southern shore. Here you'll find accommodation, horses and guides for hire (US$17) and **Chilean immigration** ⓘ *open winter 0800-2000, summer 0800-2200. Prior permission to cross must be sought from the international police at Coyhaique (Condell 14)*. From Candelario Mancila, it is 15 km to the Argentine border and a further 5 km to the Argentine immigration post on **Lago del Desierto** (see page 199); allow two days on foot with a guide. You can catch a boat across the lake, 45 Argentine pesos per person, or walk the 15 km to the southern shore, from where there is transport in summer to El Chaltén. With the opening of this route, it is now possible to travel along the whole of the Carretera Austral and on to Torres del Paine without having to double back on yourself.

Sleeping

Puerto Ibañez and around p310

E **Residencial Villaricia**, *O'Higgins 59, Villa Cerro Castillo*. Accommodation, good mid-price meals and a grocery store. Cheap meals are also available at Restaurante La Querencia, *O'Higgins s/n, Villa Cerro Castillo*.

F pp **Residencial Ibáñez**, *Bertrán Dixon 31, Puerto Ibañez, T067-423227*. Clean, warm, hot water. Similar next door at no 29.

F pp **Vientos del Sur**, *Bertrán Dixon 282, Puerto Ibañez, T067-423208*. Cheap meals available, good.

The western shore p310

B **Hostal Los Pinos**, *2 Oriente 41, T067-411576, Río Tranquillo*. Family run, well maintained, good mid-price meals. Recommended.

E pp **Hostería Carretera Austral**, *1 Sur 223, Rio Tranquillo, T067-419500. Also serves mid-range/cheap meals.*

E pp **Cabañas Jacricalor**, *1 Sur s/n, Río Tranquillo, T067-419500. Cabañas.*

Free camping is possible in Bahía Murta, with good views of Cerro Castillo.

Chile Chico and around p311

AL-C **Terra Luna Lodge**, Santiago office: *General Salvo 159, Providencia, T02-2351519*. Lodge: *km 1.5 Carretera Austral to Chile Chico, Puerto Guadal, T067-431263, www.terra-luna.cl, info@terra-luna.cl*. A good variety of accommodation options (including a main lodge and a few private bungalows) on private land at the edge of Lago General Carrera. Also all-inclusive adventure programs and excursions (from 1 to 7 days) including trekking, kayaking, fishing, mountain biking and horse riding.

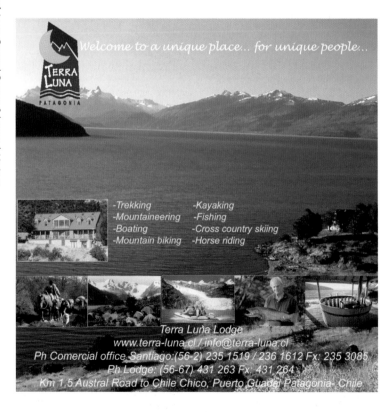

D pp **Hostería de la Patagonia**, *Camino Internacional s/n, T067-411337*. Full board

available. Clean, excellent food, English spoken, trekking, horseriding and whitewater rafting, also camping.
E pp **Casa Quinta No me Olvides**, *Camino Internacional s/n* . Without bath. Clean, cooking facilities. Also camping. Tours to Lago Jeinimeni and Cueva de las Manos.
E pp **Plaza**, *O'Higgins y Balmaceda, T067-411510*. Basic, clean. Recommended.
E pp **Residencial Don Luis**, *Balmaceda 175, T067-411384*. Clean, meals available.

Camping

Free campsite at **Bahía Jarra**, 5 km from Chile Chico, then 12 km north. Also **Camping del Sol** at the east end of town.

Towards Cochrane p312

AL **Mallín Colorado**, *2 km west of El Maitén, T067-2741807, chile@patagonia-pacific.cl* *Cabañas*, horseriding, rafting, fishing, English spoken.
C **Hostería Campo Baker**, *Puerto Bertrand, T067-411477*. *Cabañas*, sleeps 5.
E pp **Doña Ester**, *Puerto Bertrand*. Rooms in a pink house. Good.
F pp **Hostería Puerto Bertrand**, *Sector Costanera, Puerto Bertrand, T067-419900*. Meals, *cabañas* and activities (see below).

Cochrane p312

A **Ultimo Paraíso**, *Lago Brown 455, T067-522361*. Regarded as the best place to stay. Also arranges fishing trips.
A **Wellmann**, *Las Golondrinas 36, T067-522171*. Hot water, comfortable, warm, good meals. Recommended.
B **Cabañas Rogery**, *Tte Merino 502, T067-522264*. Cabins sleep 4, with kitchen facilities. Breakfast included.
D pp **Hostal Latitud 47 sur**, *Lago Brown 564*. Clean, hot water, internet, tours.
D pp **Residencial Cero a Cero**, *Lago Brown 464, T067-522158, ceroacero@ze.cl* With breakfast, cheaper without bath, welcoming, recommended.
D pp **Residencial Rubio**, *Tte Merino 4, T067-522173*. Breakfast included, lunch and dinner extra. With bath. Very good.
E pp **Residencial Cochrane**, *Dr Steffens 451, T067-522377*. Good meals, camping available. Recommended.
E pp **Residencial El Fogón**, *San Valentín 651, T067-522240*. Its pub is one of few eating places open in the low season.

Camping

In the Reserva Nacional Tamango, there are campsites at **Los Correntadas**, US$10 per site, also *cabañas*, and **Los Coigües**, US$13 per site, also *cabañas*. Details and booking through CONAF, *main plaza in Cochrane, T067-422164*.

South of Cochrane p312

E pp **Apocalipsis 1:3**, *Villa O'Higgins, T067-216927*. Without bath, friendly, serves food.
E pp **Hospedaje Costanera**, *Tortel, T067-234815*. With breakfast (also open to non-residents). Clean, warm, with attractive garden, recommended.
E pp **Hospedaje Patagonia**, *Villa O'Higgins, T067-234813*. Without bath.

Eating

Hosterías are your best bet for food in this region (see Sleeping, above), although you may also want to try the following:

Chile Chico and around p311

ǂǂ **Café Holiday**, *Calle Gonzalez*. Good coffee, friendly service.
ǂǂ **Cafetería Loly y Elizabeth**, *Gonzalez 25, on the plaza*. Serves coffee, delicious ice cream and cakes.

Cochrane p312

ǂ **La Costa**, *plaza*. A friendly cheapie. There are also a couple of mid-range options on Tte Merino and San Valentín

Tortel p312

ǂ **Café Celes Salom**. Basic cheap meals and a disco every Sat with occasional visiting bands.

Activities and tours

Lago General Carrera p310

Fishing

El Puesto Expediciones, *Lagos 258, Río Tranquillo, T067-233785, elpuesto@entelchile.net* Fishing trips and other excursions.

Hacienda Tres Lagos, *Sector El Maitén, Puerto Guadal, T067-411323*. Fishing trips.

Towards Cochrane p312

Jonathan Leidich, *Puerto Bertrand, T067-411330*. Lives on the edge of the lake, and is highly recommended for rafting, horseriding and other activities.

La Red de Turismo Río Baker, *Hostería Puerto Bertrand, Sector Costanera, Puerto Bertrand, T067-419900*. Organises rafting, horseriding and other activities.

Patagonia Baker Lodges, *Orillas del Río Baker, Puerto Bertrand, T067-411903*. Fishing trips on the lake.

Cochrane p312

Fishing

Lago Cochrane offers excellent fishing all-year round; boats can be hired for US$12 per person; fishing trips are run by Hotel Ultimo Paraíso (see Sleeping).

Tour operators

Excursions can be arranged through Guillermo Paso at Transportes Los Ñadis (see below, Transport).

Red de Turismo Río Baker, *San Valentin 438, T067-522646, trural@patagonia chile.cl* Tours of all kinds.

Samuel Smiol, *T067-522487*. Tours to the icefields and mountains, English spoken.

Tortel p312

Charter boats can be arranged through the *Municipalidad, T067-211876*. To **Ventisquero Jorge Montt**, speedboat 2 hrs, US$100 per person; *lancha* 5 hrs, US$120. To **Ventisquero Steffens**, speedboat 1 hr, US$60 per person; *lancha* 2½ hrs, $70.

Villa O'Higgins p313

Villa O'Higgins Expediciones, *Carretera Austral km1240. T/F067-670313, www.villaohiggins.cl*. Boat trips to the Campo Hielo Sur on board the *Quetru*, via Candelario Mancilla, Nov-Mar, 12 hrs round trip, US$65.

Transport

Puerto Ibañez and around p310

Buses and jeeps meet the ferry in Puerto Ibáñez for connections to **Coyhaique**, 2 hrs, US$5. There is also a road from Puerto Ibáñez to **Perito Moreno** in Argentina, but no public transport. Transportes Amin Ali, *O'Higgins s/n, Villa Cerro Castillo, T067-419200*, provides transport from Villa Cerro Castillo to **Coyhaique**, US$5.

Ferry

The car ferry, *El Pilchero*, sails from Puerto Ibáñez to **Chile Chico**, daily Mon, Wed-Fri, Sun 1000, return departures 1700 (Sun 1200), 2¾ hrs, cars US$30, passengers US$3, motorbikes and bicycles US$5. The number of passengers is limited to 70; arrive 30 mins before departure, reservations possible.

Chile Chico and around p311

Air

Don Carlos flies to **Coyhaique** (Tte Vidal airport), 5 weekly, US$35, from an airstrip just outside Chile Chico.

Bus

Transportes Ales, *T067-411739*, runs minibuses along the south side of the lake to **Puerto Guadal**, Wed, Sat, US$8, and **Cochrane**, US$15. Additional services to Puerto Guadal are provided by Sr Sergio Haro Ramos, *T067-411251*, Wed, Sat, US$10, and Transportes Seguel, 2 weekly, US$9. Minibuses from Chile Chico to **Los Antiguos** (Argentina), 45 mins including formalities, US$2 (payable in Chilean pesos only), are run by Arcotrans, *T067-411841*, and Transportes Padilla, *T067-411904*. The buses depart when they are full – usually about 5 times daily each. For onward transport, see p187.

Ferry

For services to Puerto Ibáñez, see above.

Cochrane *p312*

Air

Don Carlos flies to **Coyhaique**, Mon, Thu, US$57, from an airstrip just north of town.

Bus

To **Coyhaique**, Don Carlos, *Prat 344, T/F067-522150*, 2 weekly, US$14; **Inter Lagos**, 6 weekly, US$12, recommended; Los Ñadis, *Los Helechos 490, T/F067-522196*, 3 weekly, US$11; **Acuario 13**, *Río Baker 349, T/F067-522143*, 3 weekly, US$19. To **Vagabundo**, US$7, Los Ñadis, 3 weekly; Acuario 13, 4 weekly. To **Villa O'Higgins**, Los Ñadis, 1 service Mon, US$11; **Acuario 13**, 1 weekly, US$11. To **Chile Chico**, Transportes Ale, Thu and Sun, US$17. To **Tortel**, Acuarcio, 4 weekly, US$8.

Tortel *p312*

Air

Don Carlos to **Coyhaique** (Tte Vidal), Mon and Wed, US$25. This is a subsidized price for residents of the village. Other travellers must buy a standby ticket and should expect to pay much more.

Boat

To **Vagabundo**, Tue, Sun 0900, 5 hrs, US$2 one way; return trip Tue, Sun 1500, 3 hrs. There is also a boat once a fortnight from Tortel to **Puerto Yungay**, or you can arrange a charter for 6-10 people by contacting Viviana Muñoz or Hernán Ovando at the *Municipalidad, T067-211876*, 8 hrs, US$110 return.

Villa O'Higgins *p313*

Don Carlos air taxi flies to Villa O'Higgins from **Coyhaique**, via Cochrane, Mon, Thu, US$75. There are also 2 buses weekly to **Cochrane**, US$8. Boats across Lago O'Higgins depart from Bahía Bahamóndez.

Directory

Chile Chico and around *p311*

Banks Generally it's best to change money in Coyhaique or Argentina, but dollars and Argentine pesos can be changed in small amounts (at poor rates) at shops and cafés in Chile Chico, including Café Loly y Elizabeth. **Camera and films** Rene Villegas, *O'Higgins 424*. **Car hire** Jaime Acuña Vogt, *Grosse 150, T/F067-411553*. **Hospital** *Lautaro s/n, T067-411334*.

Cochrane *p312*

Banks Banco del Estado, *on the plaza*, changes dollars. ATM accepts Mastercard and Cirrus but not Visa. **Car hire** Marcel Moya Diaz, *Dr Steffens 147, T067-522276*. Petrol is available at the Copec station. **Internet** There are 2 on the plaza, one run by nuns (closed Sun). **Supermarket** Melero, *Las Golondrinas 148*.

Tortel *p312*

Banks There is no bank in the village but a mobile bank comes by air twice per month. **Medical services** Medical centre staffed by doctors, nurses and dentists visits monthly. **Post office** open Mon-Fri 0830-1330, post leaves Tortel weekly by air. **Telephone** *T067-234815*.

Far South

Villa O'Higgins
L Strobel
Lago O'Higgins
Lago San Martín
L Cardiel
Estancia La Maípu
Estancia La Angostu
Puerto Edén
Isla Wellington
Fitz Roy (3,405m)
El Chaltén
40
Glaciar Viedma
Lago Viedma
Estancia Helsingfors
Tres Lagos
Cerro Norte
Estancia La Leona
Parque Nacional Los Glaciares
Glaciar Upsala
Golfo Trinidad
Leona
Lago Argentino
Río Santa Cruz
Puerto Bandera
Estancia Arice
Río Bote
Gendarme Barreto
Parque Nacional Bernardo O'Higgins
Glaciar Perito Moreno
El Calafate
Estancia Alta Vista
ARGENTINA
Estancia Nibepo Aike
El Cerrito
Fuentes del Coyle
Lago Sarmiento
Pacific Ocean
Parque Nacional Torres del Paine
5
p340
La Esperanza
Paso Cancha Carrera
Cerro Castillo
REGION XII
Gobernac Mayer
4
Río Coig
Ferry to Puerto Montt
Balmaceda (2,035m)
Seno Ultima Esperanza
Paso Dorotea
Río Turbio
Paso Casas Viejas
Monumento Nacional Cueva Milodón
El Turbio
Río Gallegos
Cordillera Sarmiento
Puerto Natales
Bel
El Zurdo
N
Morro Chico
CHILE
9
40 km
40 miles
Villa Tehuelches
Río Verde
Monur Los
Cordillera Riesco
Parque Nacional Alacalufes
Mag
Seno Otway
2
Reserva Forestal Magallanes
1
p333
Punta Arenas
Reserva Forestal Laguna Parillar
Fuerte Bulnes
Estrecho de Magallanes
p322
Isla Dawson
Parque Nacional Alberto de Agostini
Don't miss...
1 Skiing at Cerro Mirador ▶▶ p325.
2 Penguins at Seno Otway ▶▶ p326.
3 A cruise to Tierra del Fuego ▶▶ p332.
4 A boat trip to Parque Nacional Bernardo O'Higgins ▶▶ p334.
5 Trekking 'El Circuito' ▶▶ p344.

Introduction

A spectacular land of fragmenting glaciers and teetering icy peaks, southern Patagonia feels like nowhere else on earth. Although Chileans posted here will often say that they are a "long way from Chile", this is the country's most popular destination for visitors. The jewel in the crown is the Parque Nacional Torres del Paine, a natural magnet for travellers from all over the world. The 'towers', three distinctive columns after which the park is named, point vertically upwards from the Paine massif like fingers, surrounded by imposing glaciers, turquoise-coloured lakes and thick forests of native trees.

Puerto Natales is the base for exploration of Torres del Paine and for boat trips to the glaciers in the Parque Nacional Bernardo O'Higgins. It also provides access to the Parque Nacional Los Glaciares in Argentina. Further south, Punta Arenas is a European-style city with a lively Chilote community and remnants of earlier English and Croatian influences.

Ratings

Landscape
★★★★★

Chillin'
★★

Activities
★★★

Wildlife
★★★★

Costs
$$$$

Punta Arenas and around

Capital of Región XII, Punta Arenas lies 2,140 km due south of Santiago. The city was originally named 'Sandy Point' by the English, but adopted the Hispanic equivalent under Chilean colonization. A centre for the local sheep farming and fishing industries, it is also the home of La Polar, the most southerly brewery in the world. Although Punta Arenas has expanded rapidly, it remains a tranquil and pleasant city. The climate and architecture give it a distinctively northern European atmosphere, quite unlike anywhere else in Chile.

Getting there Expensive flights from Santiago or long-distance buses from Argentina.
Getting around Bus or 4WD.
Time required 2 days is sufficient.
Weather High winds all year; very cold in winter and watch out for the strong sun.
Sleeping Plenty of choice.
Eating Basic fare and great chocolates
Activities Fishing in Parrillar.
★ **Don't miss...** The penguins at Seno Otway and Isla Magdalena.

Ins and outs

Getting there Punta Arenas is cut off from the rest of Chile. The only road connections are through Argentina: either via Comodoro Rivadavia and Río Gallegos to Coyhaique and the Carretera Austral or via Bariloche to Puerto Montt. It is quicker, and often cheaper, to take one of the many daily flights to/from Puerto Montt or Santiago instead. There are also direct flights to Porvenir, Puerto Williams and Ushuaia. **Carlos Ibáñez del Campo Airport** is 20 km north of town; **Buses Transfer** and **Buses Pacheco** are scheduled to meet flights, US$2. A taxi costs US$9. The many buses from Punta Arenas to Puerto Natales, 247 km north, will only stop at the airport if they are scheduled to pick up passengers there. For ferry routes to Tierra del Fuego, see page 354. ▸▸ *Transport p330.*

Tourist information The municipal **tourist office** on the plaza is good, T061-200610, or try **Sernatur** ⓘ *Magallanes 960, T061-225385*, and **CONAF** ⓘ *Menéndez 1147, piso 2, T061-223841, open Mon-Fri.*

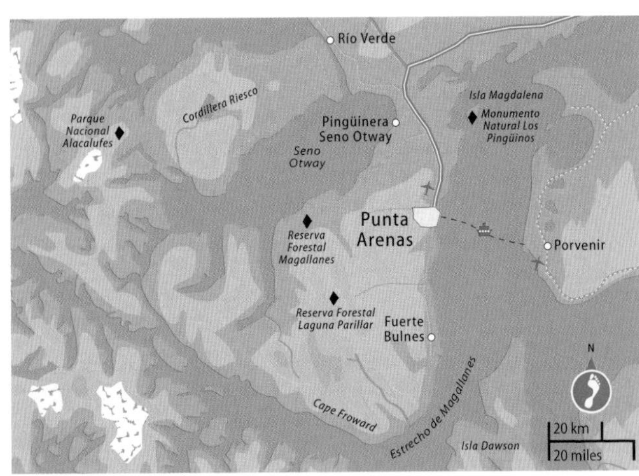

Background

Shackleton and the rescue from Elephant Islan

Shackleton's 1914-16 Antarctic expedition is one c polar exploration. Shackleton's vessel, *Endurance*, England in August 1914 with 28 men aboard, beca pack-ice in January 1915. After drifting northwards ... the ice for eight months, the ship was crushed by the floes and sank. With three boats, supplies and the dogs, the group camped on an ice floe which continued to drift north for eight months. In April 1916, after surviving on a diet largely of seals and penguins, the party took to the boats as the ice broke up. After seven days at sea they reached Elephant Island. From there Shackleton and five other men sailed 1,300 km in 17 days to South Georgia, where there were whaling stations. On reaching the south shore of South Georgia, Shackleton and two men crossed the island (the first such crossing and achieved without skis or snowshoes) to find help. Shackleton, from whom nothing had been heard by the outside world since leaving the island 18 months before, was not at first recognized.

The British government sent a rescue vessel to Elephant Island, but the delays involved led Shackleton to seek help locally. After ice had prevented three rescue attempts – the first from South Georgia, the second from the Falkland Islands/Islas Malvinas and the third from Punta Arenas – Shackleton persuaded the Chilean authorities to permit a fourth attempt using the tug *Yelcho*. Leaving Punta Arenas on 25 August 1916, the small vessel encountered thick fog but, unusually for the time of year, little ice and it quickly reached Elephant Island where the men, who had endured an Antarctic winter under upturned boats, were down to four days of supplies.

Although the expedition failed to cross Antarctica, Shackleton's achievement was outstanding: despite the loss of *Endurance*, the party had survived two Antarctic winters without loss of life. Shackleton himself returned to the region in 1921 to lead another expedition but, in January 1922, aged only 47, he suffered a fatal heart attack in South Georgia.

History

After its foundation in 1848, Punta Arenas became a penal colony modelled on Australia. In 1867, it was opened to foreign settlers and given free port status. From the 1880s, it prospered as a refuelling and provisioning centre for steam ships and whaling vessels. It also became a centre for the new sheep *estancias* since it afforded the best harbour facilities. The city's importance was reduced overnight by the opening of the Panama Canal in 1914. Most of those who came to work in the *estancias* were from Chiloé; many people in the city have relatives in Chiloé and feel an affinity with the island (the *barrios* on either side of the upper reaches of Independencia are known as Chilote areas); the Chilotes who returned north took Patagonian customs with them, hence the number of *maté* drinkers on Chiloé.

❞ People from Punta Arenas tell visitors that they often have four seasons in one day. Frequently, however, the only season appears to be winter.

Sights » pp326-332

Punta Arenas is not a huge city and walking about is a pleasant way of getting to know it. Around the attractive **Plaza Muñoz Gamero** are a number of mansions that once belonged to the great sheep-ranching families of the late 19th century. A good example is the **Palacio Sara Braun** ⓘ *Tue-Sun, US$1.50*, built between 1894 and 1905 with materials from Europe; the Palacio has several elegantly decorated rooms open to the public and also houses the **Hotel José Nogueira**. In the centre of the plaza is a statue of Magellan with a mermaid and two Fuegian Indians at his feet. According to local wisdom, those who rub or kiss the big toe of one of the Fuegians will return to Punta Arenas.

Just north of the plaza is the **Museo de Historia Regional Braun Menéndez** ⓘ *Magallanes 949, T061-244216, museoregional1001@chilnet.cl, Mon-Sat 1030-1700, Sun 1030-1400 (summer) or 1100-1300 (winter), US$1.50, children half-price*, the opulent former mansion of Mauricio Braun, built in 1905. A visit is recommended. Part of the museum is set out as a room-by-room regional history; the rest of the house has been left with its original furniture. Guided tours are in Spanish only but a somewhat confusing information sheet in English is also available. One block further north is the **Teatro Cervantes**, now a cinema with an ornate interior.

Punta Arenas

Three blocks east, the **Museo Naval y Maritimo** ⓘ *Pedro Montt 981, T061-205479, terzona@armarda.cl, Tue-Sun 0930-1230, 1400-1700, US$1,* houses an exhibition of local and national maritime history, with sections on naval instruments, cartography, meteorology and shipwrecks. There is a video in Spanish and an information sheet in English. West of the plaza, on Waldo Seguel are two reminders of British influence in the city: the **British School** and **St James's Anglican Church** next door. Nearby on Calle Fagnano is the **Mirador Cerro de La Cruz** offering a view over the city and the Magellan Straits complete with its various shipwrecks.

North of the centre along Bulnes is the excellent **Museo Regional Salesiano Mayorino Borgatello** ⓘ *Colegio Salesiano, Av Bulnes 374, entrance next to church, Tue-Sun 1000-1800, hours change frequently, US$2,* which covers the history of indigenous peoples, with sections on local animal and bird life and other interesting aspects of life in Patagonia and Tierra del Fuego. Three blocks further on, the **cemetery** ⓘ *Av Bulnes, 0800-1800 daily,* is one of the most interesting places in the city, with cypress avenues, gravestones in many languages, which bear testimony to the cosmopolitan provenance of Patagonian pioneers, and many mausolea and memorials to pioneer families and victims of shipping disasters. Look out for the statue of Indicito, the little Indian, on the northwest side, which is now an object of reverence, bedecked with flowers. Further north still, the Instituto de la Patagonia houses the **Museo del Recuerdo** ⓘ *Av Bulnes 1890, Km 4 north (opposite the zona franca), T061-207056, Mon-Fri 0830-1130, 1430-1815, Sat 0830-1300, US$2, children free,* an open-air museum with artefacts used by the early settlers, pioneer homes and botanical gardens.

On 21 de May, south of Independencia, is Chile's only Hindu temple, while further along the same street, on the southern outskirts of the city, the wooded **Parque María Behety**, features a scale model of Fuerte Bulnes, a campsite and children's playground, popular for Sunday picnics. In winter, there is an ice rink here.

Around Punta Arenas

Reserva Forestal Magallanes

ⓘ *7 km west of town, administration at CONAF, Menéndez 1147, piso 2, Punta Arenas, T061-223841, open Mon-Fri, admission US$2.* Known locally as the Parque Japonés, this forest reserve extends over 13,500 ha and rises to 600 m. **Viento Sur** (see Activities and tours, below) offers a scheduled transport service to the reserve, but it can also be reached on foot or by bike: follow Independencia up the hill and take a right turning for Río de las Minas, about 3 km from the edge of town; the entrance to the reserve is 2 km beyond. Here you will find a self-guided nature trail through lenga and coigue trees. The road continues through the woods for 14 km passing several picnic sites. From the top end of the road a short path leads to a lookout over the **Garganta del Diablo** (Devil's Throat), a gorge with views over Punta Arenas and Tierra del Fuego. From here a slippery path leads down to the Río de las Minas Valley and then back to Punta Arenas. Also within the reserve, **Cerro Mirador** is one of the few places in the world where you can ski with a sea view (see page 330). There's also a good two-hour hike here in summer; the trail is clearly marked and flora is labelled.

Fuerte Bulnes and south

About 25 km south of Punta Arenas, a fork to the right leads to the very peaceful Reserva Forestal Laguna Parrillar, surrounded by snowcapped hills. It has older forest than the Magallanes Reserve and sphagnum bogs, and offers excellent salmon trout fishing. There is a three-hour walk to the tree-line along poorly marked, boggy paths, and fine views from the Mirador. Camping is forbidden but there are sites for cooking on gas stoves. Note that there is no public transport to the reserve; a radio taxi will cost about US$50.

Fifty-six kilometres south of Punta Arenas, **Fuerte Bulnes** is a replica of the wooden fort erected in 1843 by the crew of the Chilean vessel *Ancud*. Built in the 1940s and originally designed to house a museum, nearly all the interesting exhibits and artefacts were moved to museums in Punta Arenas and Santiago in 1986 and now only the empty shells of the various buildings remain.

Nearby is **Puerto Hambre**, where there are ruins of the church built in 1584 by a group of ill-fated Spanish colonists led by Sarmiento de Gamboa. Disaster struck the fledgling colony when their only remaining ship, with Sarmiento on board, was blown into the Atlantic, leaving many men stranded on land. Sarmiento organized two rescue missions, but was captured by the English and imprisoned. When the English corsair Thomas Cavendish sailed through the Straits in 1587 he found only 18 survivors. Only one of them trusted Cavendish enough to set sail with him; the rest of the men were left to die and Cavendish named the place Port Famine as a reminder of their grisly fate. This is a very beautiful area with views towards the towering ice mountains near Pico Sarmiento; it was of Puerto Hambre that Darwin wrote: "looking due southward... the distant channels between the mountains appeared from their gloominess to lead beyond the confines of this world".

Bypassing Fuerte Bulnes, the road south continues past a memorial to Captain Pringle Stokes, Captain of the *Beagle* before Fitz Roy, who committed suicide here in 1829, before running out 5 km further on at San Juan. Beyond is the southernmost point of the continent of South America at **Cape Froward**.

North of Punta Arenas

Seventy kilometres north of Punta Arenas, **Seno Otway** is the site of a colony of Magellanic penguins, which can be visited ⓘ *Oct-mid Mar, US$4*. There are beautiful views across the sound to the mountains to the north and rheas, skunks and foxes can also be seen. Several agencies offer trips to the colony, lasting five hours (US$14 at peak season); if you wish to visit independently, a taxi from Punta Arenas will cost US$40 return.

A small island, 30 km northeast, Isla Magdalena is the location of the **Monumento Natural Los Pingüinos**, a colony of 150,000 penguins, administered by CONAF. Deserted apart from during the breeding season from November to early February, Magdalena is one of a group of three islands visited by Drake (the others are Marta and Isabel), whose men killed 3,000 penguins for food. Boat trips to the island are run by **Comapa** ⓘ *Tue, Thu, Sat, 1600 (Dec-Feb), 2 hrs each way, with 2 hrs on the island, US$30, subject to cancellation if windy; full refund given.* Tours are also organized by several operators in Punta Arenas.

Beyond, Route 255 heads northeast via Punta Delgada to the **Argentine frontier** and then along Route 3 to Río Gallegos. For routes to El Calafate, see page 335.

Sleeping

Punta Arenas *p322, map p327*

Hotel prices are substantially lower during winter months (Apr/May-Sep). Most hotels include breakfast in the room price. Accommodation is also available in many private houses; ask at tourist office. There are no campsites in or near the city.

LL **José Nogueira**, *Bories 959, in former Palacio Sara Braun, T061-248840, www.hotelnogueira.com* Beautiful *loggia*, good food, lovely dining room, parking, great atmosphere. Probably the best hotel in town. Recommended.

L **Tierra del Fuego**, *Colón 716, T061-226200, www.patagoniahotels.com* Good breakfast, parking. Some rooms with kitchenette. Recommended. **Café 1900** is downstairs.

AL **Plaza**, *Nogueira 1116, piso 2, T061-241300, www.chileaustral.com/hplaza* Pleasant, good breakfast.

A **Cóndor de Plata**, *Colón 556, T061-247987, F061-241149*. Clean, good breakfast. Often used by polar expeditions.

A **Mercurio**, *Fagnano 595, T061-242300, mercurio@chileaustral.com* TV and phone, good restaurant and service. Recommended.

A **Savoy**, *Menéndez 1073, T061-241951, www.hotelsavoy.cl* Pleasant rooms but

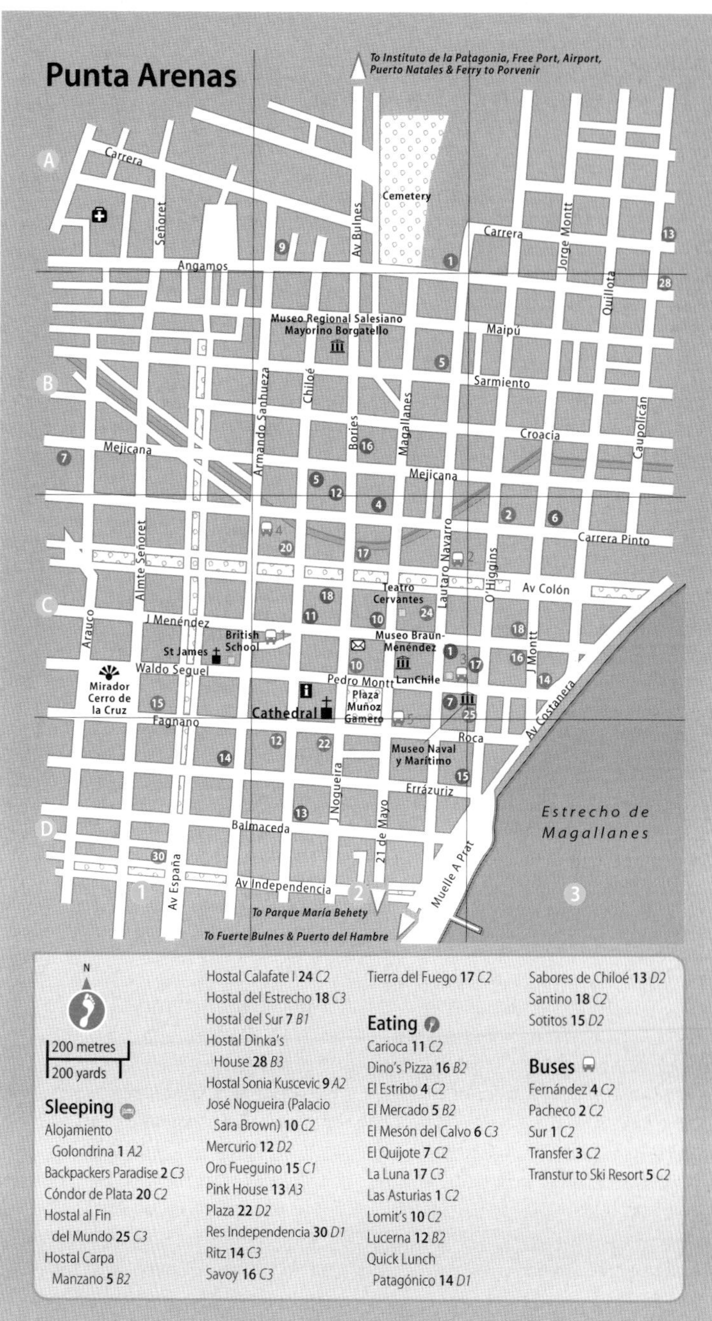

some lack windows, good place to eat.

A-B **Hostal Carpa Manzano**, *Lautaro Navarro 336, T061-242296, F061-248864, carpamanzano@tie.cl*. Clean, quiet, recommended, but not the most central.

B **Hostal Sonia Kuscevic**, *Pasaje Darwin 175 (off Angamos 500 block), T061-248543, www.hostalsk.50megs.com* With bath, breakfast, kitchen facilities, hot water, heating, parking. Good discount with Hostelling International card.

B **Oro Fueguino**, *Fagnano 356, T061-249401, www.orofueguino.cl* Recently refurbished, TV and phone, recommended. Often fills up with with groups so book ahead.

B-C **Ritz**, *Pedro Montt 1102, T061-224422*. Old, clean and cosy. Recommended (Bruce Chatwin stayed here: check out his name in the guest book).

B-C **Hostal Calafate I**, *Lautaro Navarro 850, T061-248415, www.calafate.cl* Rooms with TV, cheaper without bath, internet access, clean. **Calafate II**, *Magallanes 926, T061-241281, www.calafate.cl* is the same price but more impersonal.

B-C **Hostal Del Estrecho**, *Menéndez 1048, T061-241011, www.chileanpatagonia.com /estrecho* With large breakfast and bath (cheaper without), cable TV.

C **Hostal del Sur**, *Mejicana 151, T061-227249, F061-222282*. Large rooms and excellent breakfast. Recommended.

C-D **Hostal Dinka's House**, *Caupolicán 169, T061-226056, www.dinkashouse.cl* With bath, breakfast, use of kitchen, laundry.

E **Al Fin del Mundo Hostal** , *O'Higgins 1026, T061-710185, alfindelmundo@123.cl*. Price per person with breakfast. Shared baths, spacious, central, helpful, laundry facilities, internet, English spoken, recommended.

E **The Pink House**, *Caupolicán 99, T061-222436, www.chileanpatagonia.com /pinkhouse* Price per person. Clean rooms with or without bath, breakfast included, friendly and helpful.

E **Alojamiento Golondrina**, *Lautaro Navarro 182, T061-229709*. Price per person. Kitchen facilities, meals served, friendly, English spoken, hot water, internet access, good large breakfast. Recommended.

F **Backpackers Paradise**, *Carrera Pinto 1022, T061-240104, backpackersparadise@hotmail.com* Price per person. Basic. Dormitories, cooking facilities, limited bathroom facilities, good meeting place, luggage store, internet access. Recommended.

F **Res Independencia**, *Independencia 374, T061-227572, www.chileaustral.com/independencia* Price per person, with breakfast, kitchen facilities, laundry service, and camping. Also good value cabañas away from the centre.

Eating

Punta Arenas *p322, map p327*

Note that many eating places in Punta Arenas are closed on Sunday.

ΨΨΨ-ΨΨ The hotels **Tierra del Fuego** and **José Nogueira** each have excellent restaurants (see Sleeping above).

ΨΨΨ-ΨΨ **Sotitos**, *O'Higgins 1138*. Good service and excellent cuisine. Elegant, expensive. Recommended.

ΨΨ **El Estribo**, *Carrera Pinto 762*. Specializes in local and exotic dishes, such as guanaco.

ΨΨ **El Mercado**, *Mejicana 617*. Open 24 hrs, reasonable set lunch, expensive à la carte.

ΨΨ **El Mesón del Calvo**, *Jorge Montt 687*. Excellent, seafood, lamb, small portions, pricey. Recommended.

ΨΨ **La Luna**, *O'Higgins 974*. Fish and shellfish including local specialities, good.

ΨΨ **Las Asturias**, *Navarro 967*. Basque seafood specialities, good food and atmosphere, recommended .

ΨΨ **Quick Lunch Patagónico**, *Armando Sanhueza 1198, Esquina Errazuriz*. Vegetarian, Mexican and Chinese food.

ΨΨ **Santino**, *Colón 657, T061-220511*. Good pizzas, large bar, good service.

Ψ **Carioca**, *Menéndez 600 y Chiloé*. Cheap lunches, snacks and beer, good service.

Ψ **Dino's Pizza**, *Bories 557*. Good pizzas, huge sandwiches. For something different,

Fishy business

Visitors to Punta Arenas and the surrounding region should be especially wary of eating shellfish. In recent years, the nearby waters have been affected by a **marea roja** (red tide) of poisonous algae. Infected molluscs can kill humans almost instantly, so never pick up mussels along the shore of Punta Arenas. However, all shellfish sold in restaurants have been inspected and so are theoretically safe.

There are seasonal bans on **centolla** (king crab) fishing to protect dwindling stocks; do not purchase *centolla* out of season.

try their rhubarb juice. Recommended.

El Quijote, *Lautaro Navarro 1087*. Good sandwiches and fish dishes. Recommended.

Lomit's, *Menéndez 722*. Cheap snacks and drinks, open when the others are closed, popular with tourists.

Lucerna, *Bories 624*. Excellent meat, reasonably priced, good.

Restaurant de Turismo Punta Arenas, *Chiloé 1280*. Good, friendly. Recommended. Also serves beer and 26 varieties of sandwiches, open 24 hrs.

Sabores de Chiloé, *Chiloé esq Balmaceda*. Chilote food.

Cafés and bars

Casa del Pastel, *Carrera Pinto y O'Higgins*. Very good pastries.

Olijoe, *Errazuriz 970*. Reasonably plush British-style pub, leather interior, recommended.

Pancal, *21 de Mayo 1280*. Excellent *empanadas*, bread and pastries.

Pub 1900, *Av Colón esq. Bories*. Friendly, relaxed atmosphere.

Shopping

Punta Arenas *p322, map p327*

Zona Franca, *3½ km north of the centre, on the right-hand side of the road to the airport, take bus E or A from Plaza Muñoz Gamero or a colectivo*. Punta Arenas has certain free-port facilities. Cheap electrical goods are especially worth seeking out, as is camping equipment. The quality of most other goods is low and the prices little better than elsewhere. Open Mon-Sat 1000-1230, 1500-2000.

Handicrafts and local products

Punta Arenas is famous for the quality of its handmade **chocolate**, sold at several shops on Calle Bories.

Chile Típico, *Carrera Pinto 1015*. Chilean souvenirs at good prices; also available from outdoor stalls at the bottom of Independencia, by the port entrance.

Patagonia Gourmet, *Mejicana 608*. Local marmalades and other specialities.

Pingüi, *Bories 404*. Crafts and books on Tierra del Fuego, Patagonia and Antarctica.

The Wool House Patagonia, *Fagnano 675, by the plaza*. Good quality, reasonably priced woollen clothes.

Activities and tours

Punta Arenas *p322, map p327*

Tour operators

Arka Patagonia, *Magallanes 345, T061-248167, www.arkaoperadora.com* All types of tours, rafting, fishing, etc.

Sandy Point, *Pedro Montt 840, T061-222241*. Offer transport to Seno Otway and Fuerte Bulnes with or without guide. Also has airport shuttlebuses that will pick you up from your lodgings, US$3.

Turismo Aonikenk, *Magallanes 619, T061-228332, www.aonikenk.com* Expensive but very good bespoke excursions. Recommended.

Turismo Aventour, *Nogueira 1255, T061-241197, aventour@entelchile.net* English spoken, specialize in fishing trips, also organize tours to Tierra del Fuego.

Turismo Comapa, *Magallanes 990, T061-200200, www.comapa.com*. Tours to Torres del Paine, Tierra del Fuego and Isla Magdalena, also for trips to the Falklands /Malvinas, Ushuaia and Cape Horn.

Turismo Nueva Galicia, *Sarmiento 845, T061-220409, www.nuevagalicia.com* Organizes boat trips from Puerto Natales to PN Bernardo O'Higgins (see p334).

Turismo Pehoé, *Menéndez 918, T061-244506, www.pehoe.com* Organizes tours and hotels; enquire here about catamaran services.

Turismo Viento Sur, *Fagnano 565, T061-226930, www.vientosur.com* For camping equipment, fishing excursions, sea kayaking, cycle hire, English spoken, good tours, recommended.

Skiing

Cerro Mirador, *9 km west of Punta Arenas in the Reserva Nacional Magallanes.* Season Jun to Sep, weather permitting. Daily lift-ticket, US$7; equipment rental, US$6 per adult. There's a mid-way lodge with food, drink and equipment.

For cross-country skiing facilities, contact the **Club Andino**, *T061-241479, www.clubandino.tierra.cl*. **Transtur** buses to the ski resort depart 0900 and 1400 from in front of Hotel Cabo de Hornos, US$3 return, taxi US$6. Skiing is also available at **Tres Morros**.

Transport

Punta Arenas *p322, map p327*

Transport is heavily booked from late Dec to Mar; advance booking is advised.

Air

Airline offices Aerovías DAP, *O'Higgins 891, T061-223340, www.dap.cl*, open 0900-1230, 1430-1930; **LanChile**, *Lautaro Navarro 999, T061-241232, www.lanchile.cl*

National To **Balmaceda** (for Coyhaique), with **LanChile** (LanExpress), Sat, US$80, or daily via Puerto Montt (more expensive). To **Puerto Montt**, with **LanChile** (LanExpress), 3-6 daily, US$150 one way; it's sometimes cheaper to buy a return ticket. To **Santiago**, **LanChile** (LanExpress), several daily, US$160 return, via Puerto Montt. When no tickets available, go to airport and get on standby waiting list. To **Porvenir**, Aerovías DAP, 2 daily Mon-Sat, US$26 one way, plus other irregular flights, with Twin-Otter and Cessna aircraft. To **Puerto Williams**, Aerovías DAP, daily in summer, US$70 one way. To **Ushuaia** (Argentina), **Aerovías DAP**, twice weekly in summer, 1 hr, US$110 one way; reserve in advance from mid-Dec to Feb. To **Falkland Islands/Islas Malvinas**, LanChile, Sat, US$500 return. International Tours & Travel, *T+500-22041, www.falklandstravel.com*, serve as LanChile agents on the Falkland Islands.

Bus

Buses depart from the company offices as follows: Bus Sur, *Menéndez 565 T061-227145, www.bus-sur.cl*; **Buses Transfer**, *Pedro Montt 966, T061-229613*; **Cruz del Sur**, **Pingüino** and **Fernández**, *Sanhueza 745, T061-242313, www.busesfernandez.com*; **Gesell**, *Menéndez 556, T061-222896*; **Ghisoni**, *Lautaro Navarro 971, T061-222078, www.ghisoni.terra.cl*; **Los Carlos**, *Plaza Muñoz Gamero 1039, T061-241321*; **Pacheco**, *Colón 900, T061-242174, www.busespacheco.com*; **Turbus**, *Errázuriz 932, T061-225315*.

Services and frequencies change every year, so check on arrival at the helpful Sernatur office. Timetables are also printed daily in *El Austral*. The services detailed below are for high season only.

Fernández, Transfer (cheapest), Buses Pacheco and Buses Sur, all run several services each day to **Puerto Natales**, 3 hrs, last departure 2000, US$4 one way, US$7.50 return (although this means you have to return with the same company).

Travellers' tales

The ferry to Puerto Montt

Two things stand out on the ferry from Puerto Natales to Puerto Montt: good scenery and *vino tinto*.

The scenery is not easily forgotten. Not long after you've pulled out of Natales, the town is already a distant speck amid the channels. The air is still, the sides of the fjords thick with virgin forest, offering glimpses of snowy peaks. There are occasional breaks: the empty rolling skies around the Golfo de Penas, the sudden barrage of noise near the village of Puerto Edén, the ghost ship in the middle of the channel. But for the most part, just silence – except, of course, at night.

That's where the *vino* comes in. These are long nights on the ferry, and if you're not among the masses being sick overboard, you have to do something to settle the stomach. *Rebecca Stern*

Buses will pick up at the airport with advance notice.

To **Coyhaique**, 20 hrs, Buses Sur, 1 per week via Argentina, US$45, meals not included. Cruz del Sur, Queilen Bus and Pacheco have services through Argentina to **Osorno**, **Puerto Montt** and **Castro**, several weekly, 36 hrs to Castro, US$50.

To Argentina To **Río Gallegos**, regular services with Pingüino, Ghisoni, Pacheco, all cost US$14 and take about 5 hrs. For services to **Buenos Aires** it is cheaper to go to Río Gallegos and buy an onward ticket from there. Pacheco and Ghisoni also have buses most days to **Río Grande** via Punta Delgada, 8hrs, US$18, heavily booked. Tecni Austral (from Ghisoni office), US$28, and Pacheco, US$42, run alternate days to **Ushuaia** via Punta Delgada, 12-14 hrs, book any return at same time.

Car

Bargain if you want to hire a car for several days. Autómovil Club, *O'Higgins 931, T061-243675*, and at airport;Budget, *O'Higgins 964, T061-241696*; Hertz, *O'Higgins 987, T061-229049*, English spoken; also at airport *T061-210096*; Internacional, *Seguel 443* and at airport, *T061-228323*, recommended; Lotus Rentacar, *Mejicana 694, T061-241697*;

Budget buster

Cruising to Tierra del Fuego

The Chilean company, **Crucero Australis** offers spectacular luxury cruises around the fjords and islets south of Punta Arenas. The *Magellanes* departs Punta Arenas on Saturdays in season (5 days, 4 nights, US$785-1903 per person) stopping to explore remote glaciers and wildlife colonies en route to Puerto Williams and Ushuaia. The cruise from Ushuaia departs on Wednesdays and takes the more southerly route back to Punta Arenas (4 days, 3 nights, US$490-1649) via the end of the world at Cape Horn.

For further information and advance bookings, contact **Cruceros Australis**, Miraflores 178, piso 12, Santiago, T02-6963211, www.australis.com (Buenos Aires office T011-4325 4000).

Lubac, *Magallanes 970, T/F061-242023*; **Magallanes Rent a Car**, *O'Higgins 949, T/F061-221601;* **Paine Rent a Car**, *Menéndez 631, T/F061-240852*, try bargaining, friendly; **Willemsen**, *Lautaro Navarro 1038, T061-247787*.

Sea

For ferry services to Tierra del Fuego, see p354. All tickets on ships must be booked in advance for Jan and Feb.

Visits to the beautiful fjords and glaciers south of Punta Arenas are a highlight. **Comapa** runs a fortnightly 22-hr, 320-km round trip to the 30-km **fjord d'Agostino**, where many glaciers descend to the sea. **Cruceros Australis SA**, runs 5-day luxury cruises from Punta Arenas to **Ushuaia** (see Budget buster, p330).

Most **cruise ships** to Antarctica (see p378) leave from Ushuaia.

Shipping offices Comapa (Compañía Marítima de Punta Arenas), *Magallanes 990, T061-200200, www.compapa.com*; **Navimag**, *Magallanes 990, T061-244400, www.navimag.cl*.

Taxis

Ordinary taxis have yellow roofs. Reliable service is available from **Radio Taxi Austral**, *T061-247710/244409. Colectivos* (all black) run on fixed routes within the city, US$0.50 for anywhere on the route.

Directory

Punta Arenas *p322, map p327*

Banks and currency exchange Several banks around Plaza Muñoz Gamero, all have ATMs. Argentine pesos can be bought at **Cambio Gasic**, *Roca 915, Of 8, T061-242396*. **Consulates** Argentina, *21 de Mayo 1878, T061-261912*, open weekdays 1000-1530, visas take 24 hrs; UK, *Catarates de Niaguara 01325, T061-211535*, helpful, information on Falkland Islands. For others, ask the tourist office. **Hospitals** Hospital Regional Lautaro Navarro, *Angamos 180, T061-244040*; Clínica Magallanes, *Bulnes 01448, T061-211527*, private clinic; minimum US$45 per visit. A list of English-speaking doctors is available from Sernatur. **Internet** Lots of places offer access, including at *Magallanes y Menendez*, and below Hostal Calafate on *Magallanes, ½ block north of Plaza*. Prices are generally US$1 per hour. **Laundry** Lavasol, *O'Higgins 969*, the only self-service laundry, Mon-Sat 0900-2030, Sun (summer only) 1000-1800, US$6 per machine, wash and dry, good but busy. **Post office** *Bories 911 y Menéndez*, Mon-Fri 0830-1930, Sat 0900-1400. **Telephone** There are several call centres in the centre (shop around as prices vary).

Puerto Natales and around

From Punta Arenas a good paved road runs 247 km north to Puerto Natales through forests of southern beech and prime pastureland; this is the best sheep-raising area in Chile. Ñandúes and guanacos can be seen en route. Founded in 1911, the town grew as an industrial centre and, until recent years, its prosperity was based upon employment in the coal mines of Río Turbio, Argentina. Today, Puerto Natales is the starting point for trips to the magnificent Bernardo O'Higgins and Torres del Paine national parks and also provides access across the border to the Parque Nacional Los Glaciares. Unsurprisingly, tourism is the mainstay of the town's economy.

Getting there Bus from Punta Arenas or El Calafate; boat from Puerto Montt.
Getting around Organized tours to surrounding wilderness areas.
Time required 2 days.
Weather Can be cold at any time of year.
Sleeping Lots of choice.
Eating Basic fare.
Activities and tours Tours to Torres del Paine and Bernardo O'Higgins national parks.
★ **Don't miss...** The boat trip along the Seno de Ultima Esperanza

Ins and outs

Getting there Puerto Natales is easily reached by daily buses from Punta Arenas and from El Calafate (less frequent in winter) via Río Turbio or Cerro Castillo (both roads *ripio*). There are also two buses weekly from Río Gallegos. The town is the terminus of the *Magallanes* ship from Puerto Montt (see page 339). If driving between Punta Arenas and Puerto Natales make sure you have enough fuel. **Tourist information** ⓘ *Av Pedro Montt y Phillipi, T061-412125*; information is also available from the **Municipalidad** ⓘ *Bulnes 285, T061-411263*, and from **CONAF**, *O'Higgins 584*.

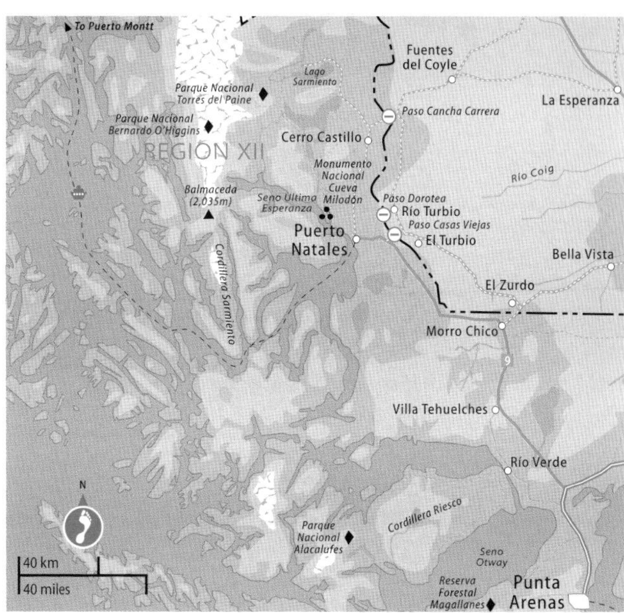

“ ” Cueva Milodón near Puerto Natales was the end point of Bruce Chatwin's travelogue, *In Patagonia*.

Sights

Puerto Natales lies on the eastern shore of the Seno Ultima Esperanza (Last Hope Sound), over which there are fine views, weather permitting, to the Peninsula Antonio Varas. The colourful old steam train in the main square was once used to take workers to the the biggest meatpacking factory in Patagonia at **Puerto Bories**, 6 km north of town; although much of the old plant was destroyed by fire, the English-style administration buildings and housing can be visited. The slab-like **Cerro Dorotea** dominates the town, with superb views of the whole Seno Ultima Esperanza. It can be reached on foot or by any Río Turbio bus (recommended, as the hill is further than it seems).

Monumento Nacional Cueva Milodón

ⓘ *25 km north of Puerto Natales, US$4. Buses JB US$5, taxi US$18 return.* The cave, a massive 70 m wide, 220 m deep and 30 m high, contains a plastic model of the prehistoric ground-sloth whose remains were found there in 1895. The remains are now in London, although there is some talk of returning them to the site. Evidence has also been found here of occupation by Patagonians some 11,000 years ago. Nearby, there is a visitors' centre, with summaries in English. Most tours to Torres del Paine stop at the cave.

Parque Nacional Bernardo O'Higgins

Often referred to as the **Parque Nacional Monte Balmaceda**, this park covers much of the Campo de Hielo Sur, plus the fjords and offshore islands further west. A three-hour boat trip from Puerto Natales up the Seno de Ultima Esperanza takes you to the southernmost section, passing the **Glaciar Balmaceda**, which drops from the eastern slopes of Monte Balmaceda (2,035 m). The glacier is retreating; in 1986 its foot was at sea level. The boat docks one hour further north at **Puerto Toro**, from where it is a 1-km walk to the base of the **Glaciar Serrano** on the north slope of Monte Balmaceda. On the trip, dolphins, sea-lions (in season), black-necked swans, flightless steamer ducks and cormorants can be seen. Take warm clothes, including a hat and gloves.

Puerto Natales

Balmaceda glacier

There is a route from Puerto Toro along the Río Serrano for 35 km to the Torres del Paine administration centre (see page 341); guided tours are available. It is also possible to travel to the Paine administration centre by boat or zodiac ⓘ *5 hrs, US$90*; details from **Casa Cecilia** in Puerto Natales (see Sleeping below), or from Onas tour operator; advanced booking essential.

Towards Argentina

From Puerto Natales, the Argentine frontier can be crossed at three points: Paso Casas Viejas, Paso Dorotea and Paso Cancha Carrera (see page 198). They all eventually meet Route 40, which runs north to El Calafate and east to Río Gallegos. All buses use the Río Turbio crossing, but if you're driving to El Calafate, the Cerro Castillo crossing is a shorter route. » *For onward routes from the border to El Calafate, see page 208.*

Sleeping

Puerto Natales *p333, map p336*
Most prices include breakfast. Hotels in the countryside are open only in the summer months; specific dates vary. In season, cheaper accommodation fills up quickly after the arrival of the *Magallanes* from Puerto Montt.

LL-L **Costaustralis**, *Pedro Montt 262, T061-412000, www.costaustralis.com* Modern, comfortable, good views, popular cafeteria. Much cheaper off-season. Recommended.

L **Martín Guisinde**, *Bories 278, T061-412770, www.austrohoteles.cl/martingusinde.html* Pub, restaurant, modern. Recommended.

AL **Glaciares**, *Eberhard 104, T061-411208, F411209, www.hotelglaciares.com* New hotel with snack bar.

AL-A **Aquaterra**, *Bulnes 299, T061-412239/ 09-4499075, www.aquaterrapatagonia.cl* New hotel, with restaurant and alternative therapy centre.

AL-A **Hostal Sir Francis Drake**, *Phillipi 383, T061-411553, www.chileaustral.com/ francisdrake*. Good views, quiet, snack bar, tours offered. Recommended.

AL-A **Lady Florence Dixie**, *Bulnes 655, T061-411158, www.chileanpatagonia.com/florence* . Modern, friendly. Recommended.

B **Concepto Indigo**, *Ladrilleros 105, T061-413609, www.conceptoindigo.com* Private rooms and dormitory accommodation (C per person), exceptional views, rock climbing courses and tours, good meeting place, slide shows, good pizzeria and vegetarian restaurant plus bar. Internet access.

B **Lago Sarmiento**, *Bulnes 90, T061-411542, www.hotellagosarmiento.galeon.com* Go od value, good views, restaurant, parking, slightly run down.

B **Res Oasis**, *Señoret 332, T061-411675, resoasis@hotmail.com* Comfortable rooms, with bath, cable TV. Some rooms without windows.

B-C **Hostal Bulnes**, *Bulnes 407, T061-411307, www.hostalbulnes.com.* Price per person, with breakfast, some rooms with bath, laundry facilities, luggage store.

C **Blanquita**, *Carrera Pinto 409, T061-411674.* Quiet, with bath, heating and breakfast, friendly. Recommended.

C **Natalino**, *Eberhard 371, T061-411968.* Clean and very friendly. Rooms with bath, breakfast. Tours to Milodón Cave arranged, parking.

C-E **Casa Cecilia**, *Tomás Rogers 60, T061-411797, redcecilia@entelchile.net* With breakfast, clean, cooking facilities, English, French and German spoken,

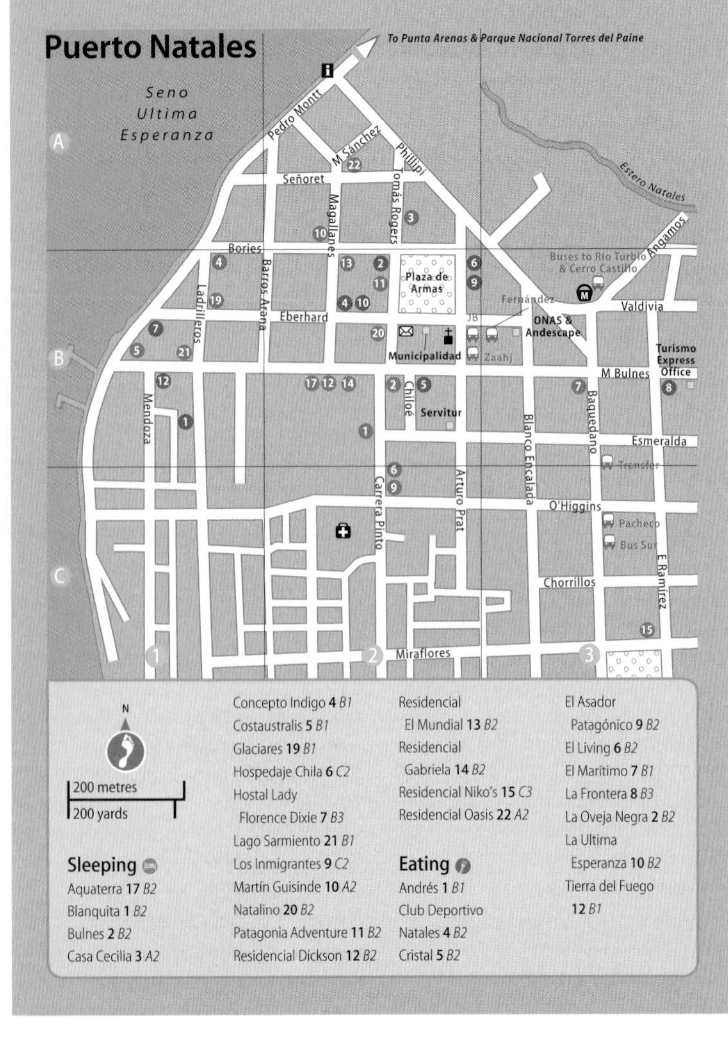

heating, luggage store, camping equipment and bike hire, information on Torres del Paine, tours organised, bus tickets sold, credit cards accepted. Price per person with or without bath. Warmly recommended.
E **Patagonia Adventure**, *Tomás Rogers 179 on Plaza, T061-411028, patagonia_adventure@ terra.cl*. Price per person. Dormitory style and double rooms, friendly, clean, use of kitchen, breakfast, English spoken, camping equipment and bike hire, luggage store, book exchange, interesting bicycle and kayak tours, recommended.
E **Res Niko's**, *Ramirez 669, T061-412810*. Price per person, with breakfast, good meals, some rooms with bath, recommended, also at *Phillipi 528, T061-411500*.
F **Res Gabriela**, *Bulnes 317, T061-411061*. Price per person. Clean, good breakfast, helpful, luggage store. Recommended.
F **Res Mundial**, *Bories 315, T061-412476, omar@fortalezapatagonia.cl*. Price per person, with or without bath. Use of kitchen, good-value meals, luggage stored. Recommended.
F **Hosp Chila**, *Carrera Pinto 442, T061-412328*. Price per person. Use of kitchen, welcoming, laundry facilities, luggage store, bakes bread. Recommended.
F **Los Inmigrantes**, *Carrera Pinto 480, T061-413482, losinmigrantes@hotmail.com*. Price per person. Good breakfast, clean, kitchen facilities, equipment rental, luggage store. Recommended.
F **Res Dickson**, *Bulnes 307, T061-411871, lodgin@chileaustral.com*. Price per person. Good breakfast, clean, helpful, cooking and laundry facilities, internet. Recommended.

Around Puerto Natales p334

Along the road from Punta Arenas are several hotels, including:
L **Hostal Río Penitente**, *Ruta 9, Km 138, T061-331694, www.hosteriariopenitente.com*. In an old *estancia*. Recommended.
L-AL **Cisne de Cuello Negro**, *6 km north of town, near Puerto Bories, for bookings contact: Av Colón 782, Punta Arenas, T061-244506, www.pehoe.com/cisne.html* Clean, reasonable, excellent cooking. Recommended.
AL **Hotel 3 Pasos**, *40 km north of Puerto Natales towards Torres del Paine, T061-225167, 02-1969631, www.hotel3pasos.cl*. Simple and beautiful.
A **Hostería Llanuras de Diana**, *Ruta 9, Km 215 (30 km south of Puerto Natales), T061-410661, llanuras_de_diana@123mail.cl*. Hidden from road, beautifully situated. Recommended.
A **Hostería Río Verde**, *Ruta 9, Km 90, east off the highway on Seno Skyring, T061-311122, www.chileaustral.com/rioverde*. Private bath, heating. Recommended.
C **Hotel Río Rubens**, *Ruta 9, Km 183, T061-226916, 09-6401583*. Popular for fishing.

Camping

There is free camping at **Monumento Nacional Cueva Milodón** once the US$4 entrance fee has been paid.

PN Bernardo O'Higgins p334

Although the park is uninhabited, guest accommodation is available at
L **Hostería Monte Balmaceda,** *T061-220174*.

Eating

Puerto Natales p333, map p336

El Asador Patagonico, *Prat 158 on Plaza*. Specializes in spit-roast lamb. Recommended.
El Marítimo, *Pedro Montt 214*. Seafood and salmon, good views, popular. Recommended.
El Rincón de Don Chicho, *Luiz Cruz Martinez 206*. All-you-can-eat *parillada*. Vegetarian options on request. Recommended.

La Ultima Esperanza, *Eberhard 354*. Recommended for salmon, seafood, enormous portions, not cheap but worth the experience.

Andrés, *Ladrilleros 381*. Excellent, good fish dishes, good service.

Club Deportivo Natales, *Eberhard 332*. Very cheap, decent meals

Cristal, *Bulnes 439*. Tasty sandwiches and salmon, good value.

La Caleta Economica, *Eberhard 261, T061-413969*. Excellent seafood, also meat and chicken dishes, good value for money.

La Oveja Negra, *Tomas Rogers 169, on Plaza*. Typical Chilean dishes, good, book swap.

Tierra del Fuego, *Bulnes 29*. Cheap, good.

Cafés

El Living, *on Plaza*. Cosy, British run, with English newspapers and magazines. Wide variety of cakes, good tea and coffee, wine and vegetarian food. Book exchange.

Bars and clubs

Puerto Natales *p333, map p336*

There are a couple of discos on Blanco Encalada.

El Bar de Ruperto, *Bulnes 371*. Good, English-run pub with cheap internet access, games and live music at weekends.

Kaweshkar, *Bulnes 43*. Relaxed bar, food served.

La Esquina, *Magallanes y Eberhard*. Good bar.

Shopping

Puerto Natales *p333, map p336*

Everything tends to be more expensive than in Punta Arenas.

Camping equipment

Balfer, *Bulnes y Pedro Montt*. Camping gear and fishing tackle, but more expensive than the Zona Franca in Punta Arenas. Camping gas is available in hardware stores. **Patagonia Adventure** and **Casa Cecilia** hire out good-quality gear (for both, see Sleeping, above).

Activities and tours

Puerto Natales *p333, map p336*

Reports of the reliability of trips to Torres del Paine National Park with some agencies are very mixed. It is better to book tours direct with operators in Puerto Natales than through agents in Punta Arenas or Santiago, where huge commissions may be charged.

Some agencies offer 1-day tours to the **Perito Moreno** glacier in Argentina (see pxxx) but, unless you're very short of time, it is better to organize a tour from El Calafate.

Bigfoot Expediciones, *Bories 206, T061-414611, www.bigfootpatagonia.com*. Sea kayaking and ice-hiking trips on the Grey glacier. Recommended.

Chile Nativo, *Barros Arana 176, casilla 42, T061-411835, www.chilenativo.com* Specializes in multi-day and bespoke tours of Torres del Paine.

Estancia Rosario, *Peninsula Antonio Varas, on the western side of the Seno Ultima Esperanza, T061-411273, estancia_rosario@hotmail.com*, offers lunches, horseriding and other activities, US$30 for a full day including transport across the sound. Book in advance.

Estancia Travel, *Casa 13-b, Puerto Bories, Puerto Natales, Chile. T/F061-412221, www.estanciatravel.com*. Based at Estancia Puerto Consuelo, 25 km north of Puerto Natales. Horseriding trips from 1 to 10 days around southern Patagonia and Torres del Paine, with accommodation at traditional estancias. Also kayaking trips. British run. Bi-lingual guides, recommended.

Onas and **Andescape**, *Eberhard 595, T061-412707, www.onaspatagonia.com, T061-412592, www.andescape.cl* Tours of Torres del Paine and kayak trips. Onas offer transport to the park by boat and zodiac. Andescape also runs many

refugios in the park (see p348).
Sendero Aventura *Hostal Patgonia Adventure, Tomás Rogers 179, T061-415636, sendero_aventura@terra.cl.* Trekking to Torres del Paine, boats to Parque Nacional Balmaceda, camping equipment and bike hire. Recommended.
Tour Express, *Bulnes 769, T061-411639, www.tourexpress.cl* Recommended for tours to Torres del Paine.
Turismo 21 de Mayo, *Eberhard 560, T061-411476, www.turismo21demayo.cl* Organizes boat trips to Parque Nacional Bernado O'Higgins, see Transport below.
Turismo Zaahj, *Prat 236, T061-412260*. 1 day tours of Torre del Paine cost around US$25, excluding park entry.

Transport

Puerto Natales *p333, map p336*

Air

Aerovías DAP *www.dap.cl*, flies daily in summer to **El Calafate**, US$54.

Bus

There are buses to **Punta Arenas** by Bus Fernández, *Eberhard 555, T061-411111*; Bus Sur, *Baquedano 534, T061-411325*; and Bus Transfer, *Baquedano 414, T061-421616*; several daily, 3 hrs, US$4, book in advance. Bus Sur runs to **Coyhaique**, Mon, US$45. For details of buses to **Torres del Paine**, see p.

To Argentina Bus Sur has 3 weekly direct services to **Río Gallegos**, US$14. Lagoper (Baquedano y Valdivia), Turisur, Bus Sur and Cootra run hourly services to **Río Turbio** (change bus at border), 2 hrs (depending on customs), US$4. To **El Calafate**, Bus Sur and Zaahj Bus, 5 hrs, US$22; Cootra also runs a service via Río Turbio, 7 hrs, reserve at least 1 day ahead.

Boat

The Navimag ferry *Magallanes* sails every Fri in summer to **Puerto Montt**, less often off season (see p278 and p331); confirmation of reservations is advised.

Shipping offices Comapa, *Hotel Coastaustralis, Bulnes y Pedro Montt, T061-414300*; Navimag, *Pedro Montt 262, Loc B, Terminal Marítimo, T061-411421*.

Car hire

Avis, *Bulnes 632, T061-410775*; Motor Cars, *Blanco 330, T061-415593, www.motorcars.cl*; Ultima Esperanza, *Blanco Encalada 206, T061-410461*. Hire agents can arrange permission to drive into Argentina, but this is expensive and takes 24 hrs to arrange.

PN Bernardo O'Higgins *p334*

The cutter *21 de Mayo* and the sailing boat *Nueva Galicia* sail every morning from Puerto Natales to **Parque Nacional Bernardo O'Higgins** in summer and on Sun only in the winter, US$60 per person, minimum 10 passengers. Book through Casa Cecilia (see Sleeping), or Turismo 21 de Mayo (see Activities and tours). Lunch extra, so take own food; snacks and drinks available on board. The trip can be combined with a visit to Torres del Paine. Pay the full return fare on the boat.

Directory

Puerto Natales *p333, map p336*

Banks and casas de cambio Some *casas* offer very poor rates (much better to change money in Punta Arenas). Banco Santiago, *Bulnes y Blanco Encalada*, Mastercard and Visa, ATM; Enio America, *Blanco Encalada 266*, Argentine pesos can be changed here. Others on Bulnes and Prat. **Internet** Concepto Indigo, *Hosp María José* (see Sleeping, above). El Rincón de Tata, *Prat 236*, Patagonianet, *Blanco 330*. **Laundry** Lavandería Catch, *Bories 218*, friendly service. **Post office** *Eberhard 417*, open Mon-Fri 0830-1230, 1430-1745, Sat 0900-1230. **Telephone** CTC, *Blanco Encalada 23 y Bulnes*; Entel, *Baquedano y Bulnes*, phone and fax; Telefonica, *Blanco Encalada y Phillipi*.

Parque Nacional Torres del Paine

Covering 242,242 ha, 145 km northwest of Puerto Natales, this Chilean national park is a UNESCO Biosphere Reserve and a must-visit thanks to its diverse wildlife and spectacular surroundings. Taking its name from the Tehuelche word *Paine*, meaning 'blue', the park encompasses some truly stunning scenery, with constantly changing panoramas of peaks, glaciers and icebergs, vividly coloured lakes of turquoise, ultramarine and grey, and quiet green valleys filled with wild flowers. In the centre of the park is one of the most impressive mountain areas on earth, a granite massif from which rise oddly shaped peaks of over 2,600 m, known as the *Torres* (towers) and *Cuernos* (horns) of Paine.

Getting there Tour from Puerto Natales.
Getting around Trekking
Time required up to 10 days to explore the park properly.
Weather Unpredictable.
Sleeping From tents to hotels. Note that at the top end, you're paying for location not quality.
Eating Campstove cuisine
Activities Hiking, glacier walking, boat trips.
★ **Don't miss...** The 'circuit'.

Los Cuernos

In total, there are 15 peaks above 2,000 m, of which the highest is Cerro Paine Grande (3,050 m); few places can compare to its steep forested talus slopes topped by 1,000-m vertical shafts of basalt with conical caps. These are the remains of frozen magma in ancient volcanic throats, everything else having been eroded. On the western edge of the park is the enormous Campo de Hielo Sur icefield; four main glaciers – Grey, Dickson, Zapata and Tyndall – branch off it, their meltwater forming a complex of lakes and streams, which lead into Pacific fjords. Two other glaciers, Francés and Los Perros, descend on the western side of the central massif.

Ins and outs

Getting there Several national and international agencies offer organized or bespoke tours to Torres del Paine (see page 42). Once you're in the far south, however, the most practical way to get to the national park is with one of the many bus or tour companies that leave Puerto Natales daily. Hiring a pick-up from **Budget** in Punta Arenas is an economical alternative for a group: US$415 for four days. The road from Puerto Natales is being improved but it currently takes three hours from Puerto Natales to the administration. Petrol is available at Río Serrano, but fill up when you set off, just in case. ▸▸ *Transport, p349.*

Getting around Allow a week or 10 days to see the park properly. Most visitors will find that they get around on foot, however, there are minibuses between the CONAF administration and Guardería Laguna Amarga, as well as boats across Lago Pehoé. Roads inside the park are narrow and bendy with blind corners. Rangers keep a check on the whereabouts of all visitors: you are required to register and show your passport when entering the park or setting off on any hike.

Visitor information ⓘ *Entrances at Laguna Amarga, Lago Sarmiento and Laguna Azul, entry fee foreigners US$11 (proceeds are shared between all Chilean national parks).* **CONAF** *administration centre at the northern end of Lago del Toro, T061-691931, open daily 0830-2000 in summer, 0830-1230, 1400-1830 off season.* It provides a good slide show at 2000 on Saturday and Sunday and there are also excellent exhibitions on the flora and fauna of the park in Spanish and English. There are six ranger stations (*guarderías*) in the park staffed by *guardaparques*, who give advice and also store luggage (not at Laguna Amarga). A basic map is provided with your park entrance ticket; other maps (US$4) are obtainable at CONAF offices in Punta Arenas or Puerto Natales but most are unreliable. The maps produced by **Cartographia Digital** and **Patagonia Interactiva** have been recommended as more accurate.

Best time to visit The weather in the park can change in a few minutes. The warmest months are December to March, although it can be wet and windy at this time of year. Most visitors come to the park during January and February, which, if possible, should be avoided due to overcrowding and the unpredictability of the weather. Many parts of the park are now open all year round, although after mid-March, there is less public transport and trucks are irregular. October and November are recommended for wild flowers, and visiting in winter is increasingly popular as there is little wind. Snow may prevent access but well-equipped hikers can do some good walking, when conditions are stable. Rain and snowfall are heavier the further west you go and bad weather sweeps off the Campo de Hielo Sur without warning. For information in Spanish on weather conditions, phone the administration centre.

Wildlife

The park enjoys a micro-climate especially favourable to plants and wildlife. Over 200 species of plants have been identified and, although few trees reach great size, several valleys are thickly forested and little light penetrates. There are 105 species of birds in the park, including

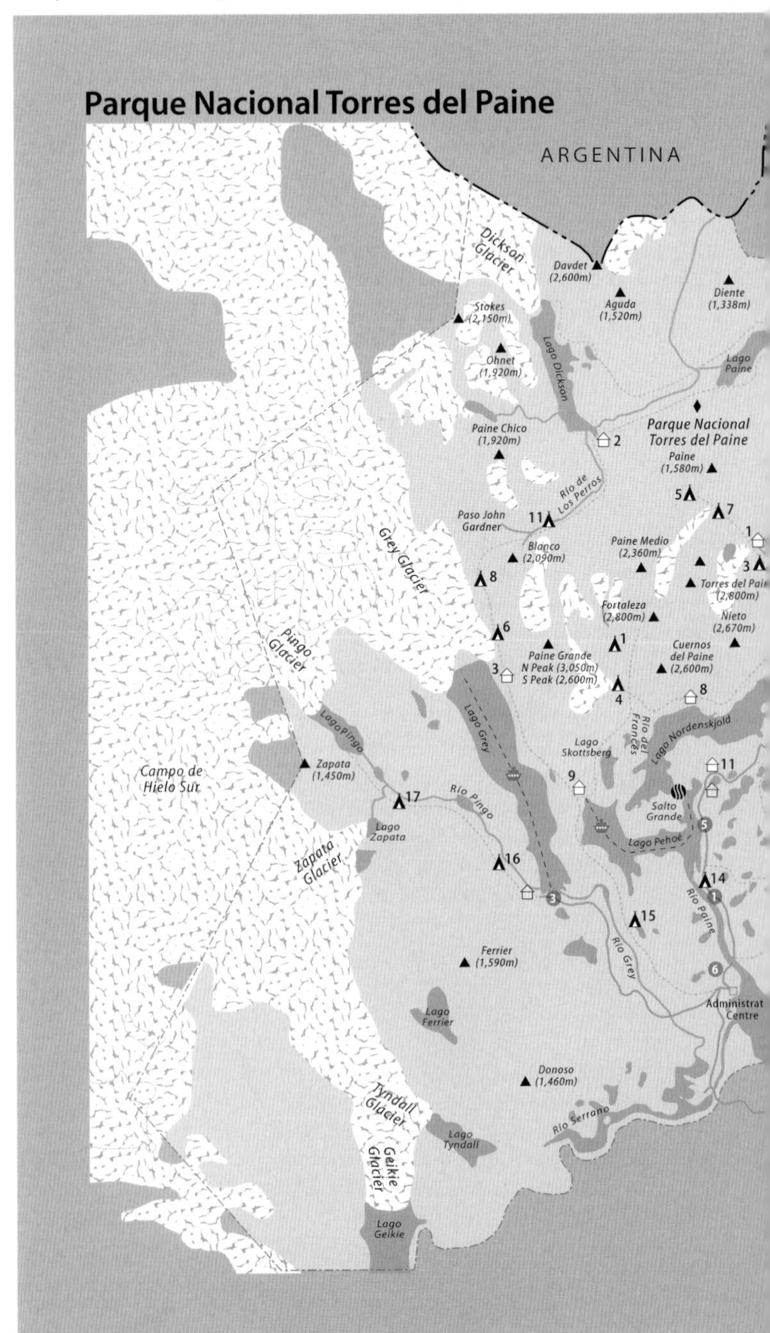

Far South Parque Nacional Torres del Paine

18 species of waterfowl and 11 birds of prey. Particularly noteworthy are condors, blacknecked swans, rheas, kelp geese, ibis, flamingos and austral parrakeets. The park is also one of the best places for viewing rheas and guanacos. Other mammals include hares, foxes, skunks, huemules (see page 313) and pumas (the last two only very rarely).

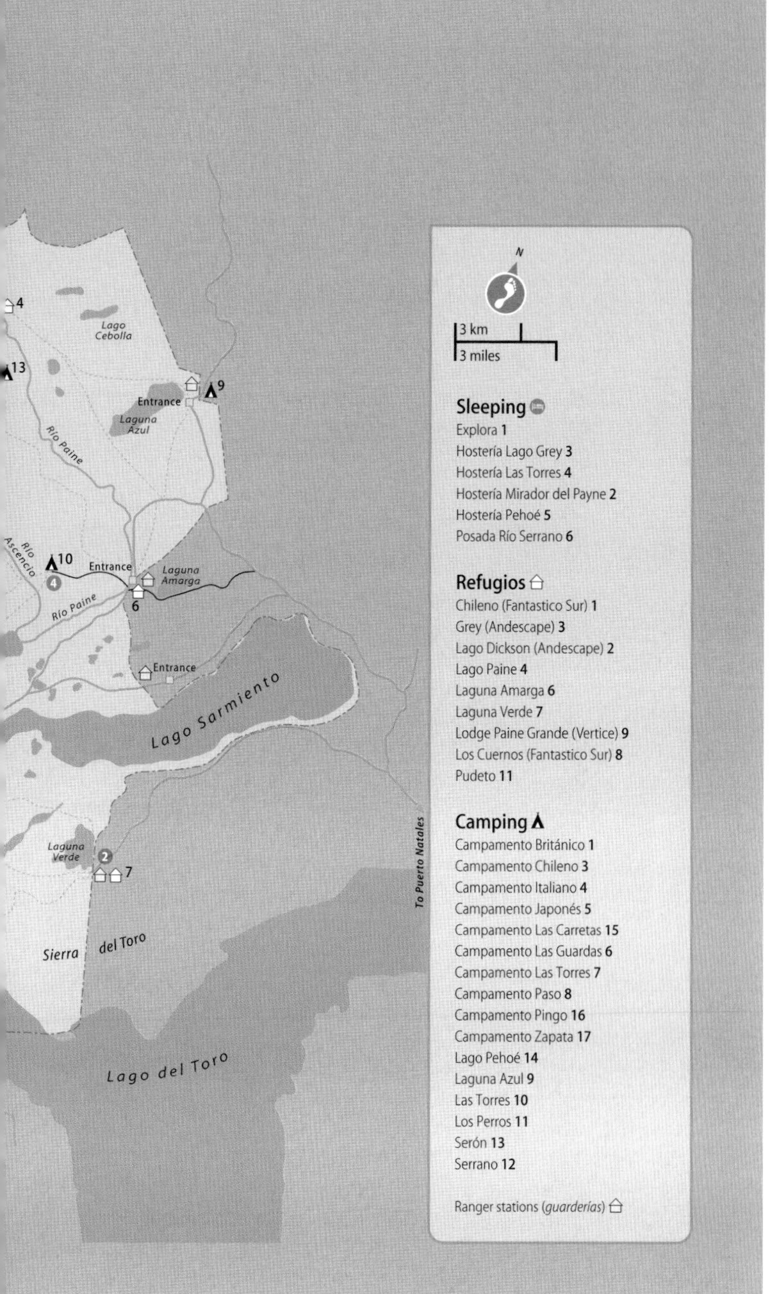

Tourists del Paine

Torres del Paine has become increasingly popular with foreigners and Chileans alike: receiving around 70,000 visitors in 2002. Despite efforts to manage the ever-growing numbers, the impact of such a large influx is starting to show.
Litter has become a problem, especially around *refugios* and camping areas; please take all your rubbish out of the park, including all toilet paper; human waste should be buried.
Bring all necessary equipment and your own food from Puerto Natales; don't rely on the shops at the Andescape *refugios* within the park, which are expensive and have a limited selection.
The wind tends to increase in the evening so, if you're camping, it is a good idea to pitch tents early (by 1600).
Rats and mice are occasionally a problem around campsites and *refugios*, so do not leave food in your pack (which may be chewed through), instead, hang food in a bag on a wire.

Forest fires are a serious hazard; you are not allowed to build fires in the park. Bring a stove if camping.

Trekking

There are about 250 km of well-marked trails. Visitors must keep to the trails: cross country trekking is not permitted. It is vital not to underestimate the unpredictability of the weather, nor the arduousness of some stretches on the long hikes. Some paths are confusingly marked and it is all too easy to end up on precipices with glaciers or churning rivers awaiting below; be particularly careful to follow the path at the Paso John Gardner on the *Circuito* (see below). The only means of rescue are on horseback or by boat; the nearest helicopter is in Punta Arenas and high winds usually prevent its operation in the park. It is essential to be properly equipped against cold, wind and rain. A strong, streamlined, waterproof tent is essential if doing El Circuito (although you can hire camping equipment for a single night at most *refugios*). Also essential are protective clothing, strong waterproof footwear, compass, good sleeping bag and sleeping mat. In summer also take shorts and sunscreen.

El Circuito

The most popular trek is a circuit round the Torres and Cuernos del Paine. It is usually done anticlockwise starting from the *guardería* at **Laguna Amarga** and, although some people complete the route in less time, it normally takes five to six days. The circuit is often closed in winter because of snow; major rivers are crossed by footbridges, but these are occasionally washed away. From Laguna Amarga the route is north along the western side of the Río Paine to **Lago Paine**, before turning west to follow the lush pastures of the valley of the Río Paine to the southern end of **Lago Dickson** (it is possible to add a journey to the *campamento* by the Torres on day one of this route); the *refugio* at Lago Dickson lies in a breathtaking position in front of the icy white lake with mountains beyond. From Lago Dickson the path runs along the wooded valley of the **Río de los Perros**, past the Glaciar de los Perros, before climbing through bogs and up scree to **Paso John Gadner** (1,241 m, the highest point on the route), then dropping steeply through forest to follow Glaciar Grey

Trekkers by Laguna Amarga

southeast to **Lago Grey**, continuing to **Lago Pehoé** and the administration centre. There are superb views en route, particularly from the top of Paso John Gadner.

The longest stretch is between Refugio Laguna Amarga and Refugio Dickson (30 km, 10 hours in good weather; two campsites on the way at Serón and Cairon), but the most difficult section is the very steep, slippery slope from Paso John Gadner down to the Campamento Paso; the path is not well signed at the top of the pass, and some people have got dangerously lost and ended up on Glaciar Grey itself. Camping gear must be carried, as some *campamentos* (including Campamento Paso and Campamento Torres) do not have *refugios*.

The W

A popular alternative to El Circuito, this four- to five-day route can be completed without camping equipment as there is accommodation in *refugios* en route. It combines several of the hikes described separately below. From Refugio Laguna Amarga the first stage runs west via **Hostería Las Torres** and up the valley of the **Río Ascensio** via Refugio Chileno to the base of the **Torres del Paine** (see below). From here return to the Hostería Las Torres and then walk along the northern shore of **Lago Nordenskjold** via Refugio Los Cuernos to Campamento Italiano. From here climb the Valley of the **Río del Francés** (see below) before continuing to Lodge Paine Grande. From here you can complete the third part of the 'W' by walking west along the northern shore of **Lago Grey** to Refugio Grey and the Grey Glacier before returning to Lodge Paine Grande and the boat back across the lake to the Refugio Pudeto.

Valley of the Río del Francés

From Lodge Paine Grande this route leads north across undulating country along the western edge of **Lago Skottberg** to Campamento Italiano and then follows the valley of the Río del Francés, which climbs between Cerro Paine Grande and the Ventisquero del Francés (to the west) and the Cuernos del Paine (to the east) to Campamento Británico; the views from the mirador an hour's walk above Campamento Británico are superb. Allow two and a half hours from Lodge Paine Grande to Campamento Italiano, two and a half hours further to Campamento Británico.

Travellers' tales

A near miss

It was our first day in the park. We decided that we were going to get off the bus from Puerto Natales at Laguna Amarga and trek to the base of the Torres. Everything was great for the first two hours, as we trekked through the fields to the base of the narrow gorge leading up to the campsite.

Then we made our mistake. Leaving the campsite, we pressed up a shoulder of the mountains; the path slowly petered out but we carried on, until about half an hour later we saw a group of people making their way on horseback up the path – on the other side of the gorge.

Instead of doing the sensible thing and turning back, we decided to try and make our way down the gorge to cross the river, and rejoin the path on the other side. About halfway down, I slipped trying to cross a scree slope and fell down towards the river – my fall was only broken by a dead tree trunk lying across the scree. Two metres the other side and I would have gone straight down. The only thing I lost was my one pair of glasses. *Toby Green*

Treks from Guardería Grey

Guardería Grey, 18 km west by road from the administration centre, is the starting point for a five-hour trek to Lago Pingo. From the *guardería* follow the **Río Pingo**, via Refugio Pingo and Refugio Zapata (four hours), with views south over Ventisquero Zapata (look out for plenty of wildlife and for icebergs in the lake) to reach the lake. **Ventisquero Pingo** can be seen 3 km away over the lake. Two short signposted walks from Guardería Grey have also been suggested: one is a steep climb up the hill behind the ranger post to **Mirador Ferrier**,

Lago Grey

from where there are fine views; the other is via a suspension bridge across the Río Pingo to the peninsula at the southern end of **Lago Grey**, from where there are good views of the icebergs on the lakes.

To the base of the Torres del Paine

From Refugio Laguna Amarga, this six-hour route follows the road west to **Hostería Las Torres** (one and a half hours), before climbing along the western side of the **Río Ascensio** via Refugio Chileno (two hours) and Campamento Chileno to Campamento Las Torres (two hours), close to the base of the **Torres del Paine** (be careful when crossing the suspension bridge over the Río Ascensio near Hostería Las Torres, as the path is poorly marked and you can end up on the wrong side of the ravine). The path alongside the Río Ascensio is well marked, and the Campamento Las Torres is in an attractive wood (no *refugio*). A further 30 minutes up the morraine takes you to a lake at the base of the towers themselves; they seem so close that you almost feel you could touch them. To see the Torres lit by sunrise (spectacular but you must have good weather), it's well worth carrying your camping gear up to Campamento Torres and spending the night. One hour beyond Campamento Torres is Campamento Japonés, another good campsite.

To Laguna Verde

From the administation centre follow the road north 2 km, before taking the path east over the **Sierra del Toro** and then along the southern side of **Laguna Verde** to the Guardería Laguna Verde. Allow four hours. This is one of the easiest walks in the park and may be a good first hike.

To Laguna Azul and Lago Paine

This route runs north from Laguna Amarga to the western tip of **Laguna Azul**, from where it continues across the sheltered **Río Paine** valley past Laguna Cebolla to the Refugio Lago Paine at the western end of the lake. Allow eight and a half hours.

Sleeping Map p342

LL **Explora**, *Salto Chico on edge of Lago Pehoé, T061-411247, reservations from Av Américo Vespucci 80, piso 7, Santiago, T02-2066060, www.explora.com* Ugly building but the most luxurious and comfortable hotel in the park, offering spectacular views, pool, gym, tours and transfer from Punta Arenas.

LL **Hostería Lago Grey**, *T061-410172, reservations T061-225986, www.austrohoteles.com* Small rooms on edge of Lago Grey with views of the Grey Glacier, average restaurant.

LL-L **Hostería Lago Tyndall**, *T061-221303, www.hosterialagotyndall.com* Expensive, cafeteria-style restaurant, electricity during the day only, good views. Not recommended.

LL-L **Hostería Las Torres**, *head office Magallanes 960, Punta Arenas, T061-710050, www.lastorres.com* Nice rooms, good restaurant, English spoken, horseriding, transport from Laguna Amarga ranger station.

LL-L **Hostería Pehoé**, *5 km south of Pehoé ranger station, 11 km north of park administration, T061-411390 www.pehoe.com*. On an island with spectacular view across the lake to Cerro Paine Grande and Cuernos del Paine, this place does not make the most of its stunning location, rundown, overpriced. Reservations from Turismo Pehoé in Punta Arenas. Closed Apr-Oct.

L **Hostería Mirador del Payne (Estancia Lazo)**, *on the eastern edge of the park, reservations from Fagnano 585, Punta Arenas, T061-228712, F061-410498, www.miradordelpayne.com* Beautifully situated on Laguna Verde with spectacular views and good fishing, restaurant. Recommended but an inconvenient base for visiting the park; own transport essential, or you can trek to it from within the park.

AL-A **Posada Río Serrano**, *reservations through Baqueano Zamora, Baquedano 534B, Puerto Natales, T061-412911, www.baqueanozamora.com*. An old *estancia*, much improved recently, some rooms with bath, some with shared facilities, breakfast extra, near park administration, with expensive but good restaurant and a shop.

Private refugios

Three companies between them run half the refugios in the park: **Andescape**, *Eberhard 599, Puerto Natales, T061-412877, www.andescape.cl*; **Fantastico Sur**, *book through Las Torres, T061-710050, albergue@lastorres.com*; and **Vertice Patagonia**, *T061-414300, www.vertice patagonia.cl*. They provide dorm space only (bring a sleeping bag, or hire one for US$6). US$20-27 per person, full board about US$25 extra. Refugios have kitchen facilities, hot showers, and space for camping. Andescape refugios hire tents for US$11 per night. Most refugios close in winter, one or two may stay open, depending on the weather. Advance booking essential in high season.

Refugio Grey (Andescape). On the eastern shore of Lago Grey. Guided glacier walks including ice climbing, US$50.

Refugio Lago Dickson (Andescape). On the northern part of the circuit.

Refugio Chileno (Fantastico Sur). In the Valley of the Río Ascencio, at the foot of the Torres.

Refugio Las Torres (Fantastico Sur). Next to the Hostería Las Torres (see above).

Refugio Los Cuernos (Fantastico Sur). On the northern shore of Lago Nordenskjold.

Lodge Paine Grande (Vertice Patagonia). Opened September 2004 on the northwestern tip of Lago Pehoé.

Other refugios

In addition, there are 6 free CONAF *refugios*: Zapata, Pingo, Laguna Verde, Laguna Amarga, Lago Paine and Pudeto. Most have cooking areas (wood stove or fireplace) but Laguna Verde and Pingo do not. These two are in very poor condition.

Campsites

For camping regulations, see Tourists del Paine, p344. The wind tends to increase in the evening so it is a good idea to pitch tents early (by 1600). Equipment can be hired in Puerto Natales (see above).

In addition to sites at the **Andescape** *refugios*, there are the six managed sites within the park: **Los Perros**, run by **Andescape**, with shop and hot showers; **Laguna Azul**, hot showers; **Lago Pehoé**, run by **Turismo Río Serrano**, US$20 per site, max 6 persons, hot showers, beware mice; **Serrano**, run by **Turismo Río Serrano**, US$15 per site, max 6 persons, cold showers, basic. **Las Torres** and **Serón**, both run by **Estancia Cerro Paine**, US$4, hot showers. Free camping is permitted in 7 other *campamentos*.

Activities and tours

Before booking a tour check all the details carefully and get a copy in writing, as there have been increasingly mixed reports of the quality of some tours. Many companies who claim to visit Glaciar Grey, for example, only visit Lago Grey (you see the glacier in the distance).

Several agencies in Puerto Natales including Servitur, Zaahj, Onas and Tour Express (see p338) offer 1-day tours by minibus, US$25 plus park entry; these give a good impression of the lower parts of the park, although you spend most of the day in the vehicle and many travellers would argue that you need to stay several days, or at least overnight, in the park to appreciate it fully. Cheaper tours are also available, but both guide and vehicle may not be as good as the established operators.

Hostería Grey (see Sleeping, above)

provides excusions by boat to the face of the Grey Glacier at 0900 and 1500 daily, 3½ hrs, US$60 per person.

Onas Turismo, (see p338), runs trips down the Río Serrano in zodiac boats to the Serrano glacier in the Parque National Bernardo O'Higgins, and from there on the tour boats to Puerto Natales, US$90 each all inclusive. Book in advance.

Transport

Bus

From early Nov to mid-Apr daily bus services run from Puerto Natales to the park, leaving between 0630 and 0800, and again at around 1430, 2½ hrs to Laguna Amarga, 3 hrs to the administration centre, US$7 single, US$12 open return (return tickets are not always interchangeable between different companies); return departures are usually around 1300 and 1800. Generally, buses will drop you at Laguna Amarga and pick you up at the administration centre for the return. The buses wait at Refugio Pudeto until the 1200 boat from Refugio Lago Pehoé arrives. Travel between 2 points within the park (eg Pudeto–Laguna Amarga) is US$3. Services are provided by **Bus Sur**, *Baquedano 534, T061-411325*; **JB**, *Prat 258, T061-412824*; and **Fortaleza**, *Prat 258, T061-410595*. In season there are also minibus services from Laguna Amarga to the **Hostería Los Torres**, US$4, and from the administration centre to **Hostería Lago Grey**.

At other times, services by travel agencies are subject to demand; arrange your return date with the driver and try to coincide with other groups to keep costs down; **Luis Díaz** has been recommended, about US$12, minimum 3 persons.

In season, there is a direct bus service from Torres del Paine to **El Calafate** (Argentina), with **Chaltén Travel**, US$40. At other times you must either return to Puerto Natales and catch a bus, or get a ride from the park to Villa Cerro Castillo and try to link with the Natales–El Calafate bus schedule.

Boat

A boat service runs across Lago Pehoé from Refugio Lago Pehoé to Refugio Pudeto, daily, 30 mins, US$14 1 way with 1 piece of baggage free, tickets available on board. Departures from Pehoé 1000, 1230, 1830; from Pudeto 0930, 1200, 1800. Reduced service off season, no service May-Sep.

Tierra del Fuego

Don't miss...

1. Fishing at Lago Blanco ▸▸ p358.
2. Hiking to the Dientes de Navarino ▸▸ p359, or Bahía Lapataia ▸▸ p368.
3. The view from Cerro Martial ▸▸ p366.
4. A boat trip to Estancia Harberton ▸▸ p367.
5. Staying on a pioneer estancia ▸▸ p370.

Introduction

At the southern end of Patagonia and at the very end of the world lies its last remaining wilderness, the island of Tierra del Fuego. The eastern half belongs to Chile, an almost untamed expanse of immense sheep farms and virgin mountains, dotted with remote lagoons, including Lago Blanco, which offers the world's best fly fishing. The only settlement is the tiny town of Porvenir.

Argentine Tierra del Fuego boasts a welcoming city with a splendid setting: Ushuaia nestles below the mighty Darwin Range at the very tail of the Andes and looks out over the Beagle Channel to the jagged peaks of Isla Navarino beyond. Visit in autumn, and you'll think the island's name, 'Land of Fire', derives from the blaze of scarlet and orange beech forest covering the mountains but, in winter, the slopes of Cerro Castor offer good powder snow and spectacular views. Head to Parque Nacional Tierra del Fuego for excellent hikes for every ability or be inspired by original pioneer Thomas Bridges to sail forth along the Beagle Canal, past islands covered with basking fur seals, to Estancia Harberton. And if this isn't remote enough, take a boat from Ushuaia to Cape Horn or even Antarctica.

Ratings

Landscape
★★★★

Activities
★★★★

Wildlife
★★★★★

Costs
$$$$

Ins and outs » *Ins and outs, p357 and p363; Transport, p361 and p376*

There are frequent flights into Porvenir, Río Grand and Ushuaia, but all land access to Tierra del Fuego is via the Chilean side of the island. Transport to the island is heavily booked in summer, especially in January, and even the buses fill quickly, so this part of your journey requires some careful forward planning.

Getting there

Air There are flights to **Río Grande** and **Ushuaia** in Argentine Tierra del Fuego, from Buenos Aires and El Calafate, and flights from many other towns in Patagonia with the army airline LADE. There are also daily flights from Punta Arenas to **Porvenir** in Chilean Tierra del Fuego and, less frequently, to **Puerto Williams** on Isla Navarino. Ushuaia is the best entry point for most visitors, with hiking, boat trips and winter sports all nearby; Río Grande provides access to some fantastic estancias, while Porvenir is better for exploration of the remote Chilean plains and isolated lakes.

Ferry There are two ferry crossings to Tierra del Fuego: from **Tres Puentes**, just north of Punta Arenas, to **Porvenir**; and from **Punta Delgada** across the Primera Angostura (First Narrows) to the tiny port of **Punta Espora**. All buses from mainland Argentina and most services from Punta Arenas use the quicker and more frequent Punta Delgada crossing, which is 59 km south of the Argentine border at **Monte Aymond** (see page 173) and 170 km northeast of Punta Arenas, via RN255. There's a cosy tea room on the northern side, with hot snacks and toilets.

Getting around

The only legal crossing between the Chilean and Argentine parts of Tierra del Fuego is 142 km east of Porvenir. There are two settlements called **San Sebastián**, one on each side of the border, but they are 14 km apart and taxis are not allowed to cross the frontier, which means you must travel on one of the scheduled buses or with your own transport. **Chilean immigration and customs** ⓘ *San Sebastián (Chile), open 0800-2200.* **Argentine immigration and customs** ⓘ *San Sebastián (Arg), open 24 hrs daily.* From Argentine San Sebastián Route 3 heads east to Río Grande and then south to Ushuaia. This is the main route

Making the most of Tierra del Fuego

Avoid visiting in January. Beds and buses are full, and Tierra del Fuego is not at its most tranquil. March and April are blissful.

To save time and avoid disappointment, arrange hiking trips before you arrive, with a reputable adventure tourism company, like Compania de Guias de Patagonia or Canal Fun. See page 375.

Tolhuin has a fabulous bakery that's open 24 hours. It's worth a detour to see the tranquil lakeside, too. See page 364.

Agency tours will only allow you two hours at Estancia Harberton. For a fuller experience of pioneer life and the chance to walk around the beautiful coastline, hire a car and drive. See page 367.

Boat trips from Ushuaia along the Beagle Channel are much more pleasant on board the charming old *Barracuda* than on the modern catamarans, and the commentary is better too. See page 375.

Parque Nacional Tierra del Fuego is best in the late afternoon when the tour buses have gone, particularly Lago Roca and Bahía Lapataia. But make sure you allow enough daylight to get back! See page 368.

through the Argentine half of the island and is surfaced apart from a 50 km section between Ushuaia and Tolhuin. Other roads on Tierra del Fuego are narrow and gravelled. Fuel is available in Porvenir, Cerro Sombrero and Cullen (Chile) and Río Grande, Ushuaia and San Sebastián (Argentina). There are scheduled buses linking Punta Arenas with Río Grande and Ushuaia in summer; a few travel via Porvenir. However, there is no guaranteed public transport along the *ripio* roads either south of Porvenir or east of Ushuaia to Harberton and Estancia Moat on the south coast.

Tourist information

Information on Chilean Tierra del Fuego is best sought from tour operators in Punta Arenas (see page 329) or from **Sernatur** (www.sernatur.com). The excellent tourist office in Ushuaia (see page 365) is a good source for information on the Argentine side of the island. See also www.tierradelfuego.org.ar

Best time to visit

Summer is best for trekking, when daytime temperatures can reach 20°C but more often hover around 15°C. Try to avoid Ushuaia in January, however, when it is swamped with tourists. There are also very stiff winds at this time of year, particularly further north, around Río Grande, where they can gust up to 200 kph. Ushuaia is at its most beautiful in autumn, when the dense forests all around are turned rich red and yellow, and there are many bright clear days. The ski season is from mid-June to October, when temperatures hover around zero, but the wind drops.

The people of Tierra del Fuego

Human habitation on Tierra del Fuego dates back some 10,000 years; four indigenous groups inhabited the island until the early 20th century. The most numerous, the **Onas** (also known as the Selk'nam), were hunter-gatherers in the north, living mainly on guanaco and several species of rodents. The southeastern corner of the island was inhabited by hunter-gatherers known as the Haus or **Hausch**, while the Yaganes or **Yámanas** lived along the Beagle Channel and on the islands further south. A seafaring people who survived mainly on seafood, fish and seabirds, they developed strong upper bodies for rowing long distances. The fourth group, the **Alacalufe**, lived in the west of Tierra del Fuego as well as on the Chonos Archipelago, surviving by fishing and hunting seals.

The first Europeans to visit the island came with the Portuguese navigator **Fernão Magalhães** (Magellan), who, in 1520, sailed through the channel that bears his name. He saw fires lit on shore and so named the island 'Tierra del Fuego' ('the land of fire'). However, numerous maritime disasters meant that the indigenous population were left undisturbed for three centuries.

Robert Fitzroy and Charles Darwin visited in 1832 and 1833 and several disastrous attempts to convert the indigenous groups followed but it wasn't until 1869 that the first successful mission was finally established. In 1884, the **Reverend Thomas Bridges** (see page 366) founded a mission at Ushuaia and soon many Yámana had settled nearby. Bridges learnt the Yámana language and compiled a Yámana-English dictionary to ease the conversion process. Charles Darwin had written that the Yámana language "barely deserves to be called articulate" but, in fact, it turned out to have an extraordinarily rich vocabulary: the dictionary had 32,000 words and was not complete at the time of Bridges' death in 1898.

The work of the missionaries was disturbed by the discovery of gold in 1887 and the growth of sheep farming. The gold rush began when Julio Popper, a German settler, founded the successful El Paramó mine at San Sebastián. He was followed by treasure seekers from north America and Europe, including many Croatians, whose descendents still live on the island. Sheep farms were created as the Argentine and Chilean governments attempted to populate the island following a border settlement in 1883. The Ona hunted the 'white guanacos' and the colonists responded by offering two sheep for each Ona that was killed (proof was provided by a pair of Ona ears). The indigenous groups were further ravaged by epidemics of European diseases. Despite the efforts of Salesian missionaries in the early 20th century, the Ona went into terminal decline; the last Ona died in 1999. The Hausch have also died out. One old Yámana lady survives near Puerto Williams and there is a handful of Alacalufe at Puerto Edén in the Chonos Archipelago.

Chilean Tierra del Fuego

Chilean Tierra del Fuego forms part of Región XII (Magallanes), of which the capital is Punta Arenas. It is a wild spot, less populated than the Argentine side of the island, and is characterised by a mixture of thick forests, wide rolling pampas and imposing glaciers. There are peaks of well over 2,000 m and numerous lakes and rivers, rich in trout and salmon. To the south of Tierra del Fuego, across the Beagle Channel, Isla Navarino is even more remote and inaccessible.

Getting there Ferry from Punta Delgada
Getting around Difficult without own transport; hire a car in Punta Arenas
Time required Minimum 1 day plus 2 days for Isla Navarino
Weather Wild and windy
Sleeping Limited options; camping is possible but chilly.
Eating Limited choice but good lobster in Porvenir; food is expensive on Isla Navarino
Activities and tours Salmon and trout fishing, hiking.
★ **Don't miss...** Lago Blanco

Ins and outs

Visitors to Chilean Tierra del Fuego arrive either by air to Porvenir or by ferry to Porvenir or Punta Espora. The ferry is recommended for occasional views of porpoises following the ships, though arriving by air gives a memorable view of the island. From the Porvenir ferry, buses (US$1.50) and taxis (US$5) run to the town's bus terminal, where local buses depart for Cameron and the Argentine side of the island. There is no local bus service to or from Punta Espora. The only reliable way of reaching Isla Navarino is by air from Punta Arenas.

Porvenir

Chilean Tierra del Fuego has a population of 7,000, most of whom live in Porvenir. Founded in 1894 as a port serving the sheep *estancias* of the island, this is the only town on the Chilean side of the island. It is quiet and pleasant, with painted zinc houses and tall trees lining the main avenue. Many inhabitants are descended from Croatian goldminers who came to seek their fortune during the gold boom of the 1890s; the signpost at the port marks the distance to Croatia. There is a small museum, **Museo Fernando Cordero Rusque** ⓘ *Samuel Valdivieso 402, T061-580098*, with archaeological and photographic displays on the Ona people, sections on natural history and gold mining, and a small **tourist annexe**.

Although it's small and not geared up for tourism, Porvenir is the base for exploring the wonderful virgin territory of western Tierra del Fuego and for fly fishing for brown trout, sea run brook trout and steelheads in the island's richly stocked lakes and rivers.

Beyond Porvenir

About 90 km east of Porvenir, roads head north to San Sebastián and south to **Cameron**. This large farm settlement is the only other community of any size on the Chilean part of the island and lies 149 km southeast of Porvenir on the opposite shore of windswept Bahía Inútil. Nearing Cameron, the southern mountains loom ahead and the road passes secluded canyons and bays, interspersed with a few farms.

From Cameron a road runs southeast for a further 40 km before splitting north to San Sebastián and south to **Sección Río Grande** (7 km from the

Travellers' tales

Everyone said that hitchhiking on Tierra del Fuego was insanity...

I arrived in Porvenir with two friends on the ferry from Punta Arenas and we waited at the edge of town for a lift. We wanted to go right down to Lago Blanco, where the roads stop. We soon got a lift with a jeep full of army conscripts to a base a few miles out of town and then the waiting began.

Waiting on Tierra del Fuego is an interesting experience if you're in the right frame of mind but hell if you're not. An icy wind tears across the plains, and your lips get terribly chapped. Dust is blown along the unmade *ripio* roads and gets into everything.

After an hour the first car came; it gave us a lift for 50 km or so, and then we waited another three hours for another car to come along. It was like that all the way to Lago Blanco: outside Cameron, we waited in an abandoned police post; in other places the wind was so severe that we burrowed down under a mound by the roadside to stop being blown along like everything else.

But it was all worth it. In the evening, we walked along a track towards the lake, and were suddenly startled by a herd of guanacos bounding across the deserted road, from one area of virgin forest to the next. *Andrew Chadwick*

junction) – there is very little traffic here. The road south climbs into the hills, through woods where guanacos hoot and run off into glades and the banks are covered with red and purple moss. The north shores of **Lago Blanco** can be reached by cutting through the woods from Sección Río Grande, with superb views of the mountains surrounding the lake and the snows in the south. In the centre of the lake is Isla Victoria, which has accommodation (see Sleeping below). The lake area can be very cold, even in mid-summer, when biting winds sweep in from the south, so wrap up warmly.

Isla Navarino and Cape Horn » p 360-362

Situated on the southern shore of the Beagle Channel, Isla Navarino is unspoilt and beautiful, and encompasses great geographical diversity: the **Dientes de Navarino** range has peaks over 1,000 m, covered with southern beech forest up to 500 m, while, to the south, stretch great plains covered with peat bogs and lagoons abundant in flora. Wildlife is prolific: guanacos and condors can be seen inland, as well as large numbers of beavers, which were introduced to the island and have done a lot of damage. The island was the centre of the indigenous Yámana culture, and has 500 archaeological sites, dating back 3,000 years. The flight from Punta Arenas – the only reliable way of reaching the island – is beautiful, with superb views of Tierra del Fuego, the Cordillera Darwin and the islands stretching south to Cape Horn.

Puerto Williams

The only settlement of any size on the island is Puerto Williams, a Chilean naval base situated about 50 km east of Ushuaia (Argentina). Puerto Williams is the southernmost permanently inhabited town in the world; Puerto Toro, 50 km east-south-east, is the world's southernmost permanently inhabited settlement. Due to the long-running border dispute with Argentina

> Standing above the Murray Narrows, with petrels floating over the icy waters and the tree-covered cliffs of Hoste Island rising in the distance, the senses sharpen. Everything can be seen, touched, smelt: nowhere is as alive as this.

here, Puerto Williams is controlled by the Chilean Navy. Outside the Naval headquarters, you can see the bow section of the *Yelcho*, the tug chartered by Shackleton to rescue men stranded on Elephant Island (see box, page 323).

Museo Martín Gusinde ⓘ *Mon-Thu 1000-1300, 1500-1800, 1500-1800 Sat and Sun, US$1*, known as the Museo del Fin del Mundo ('End of the World Museum') is full of information about vanished indigenous tribes, local wildlife and famous voyages by Charles Darwin and Fitzroy of the *Beagle*. A visit is highly recommended. There is a **tourist office** ⓘ *Municipalidad de Cabos de Hornos, Pres Ibañez 130, T061-621011, closed in winter*, near the museum, which can provide maps and information on hiking. A kilometre west of the town is the yacht club (one of Puerto Williams' two nightspots), whose wharf is made from a sunken 1930s Chilean warship. The last of the Yámana people live at **Villa Ukika**, 2 km east, where there are beaver dams and waterfalls.

Exploring the island

For superb views, climb **Cerro Bandera**, which is reached by a path from the dam 4 km west of the town (a steep three- to four-hour round trip). A challenging 53 km circuit of the **Dientes de Navarino** begins here. This is the southernmost trail in the world and passes through impressive mountain landscapes, frozen lagoons and snowy peaks. It takes four to five days and is possible only between December and March; ask at the Puerto Williams tourist office for further information. At the southernmost point of the walk, there are views of Cape Horn in clear weather, but conditions change quickly and it can snow on the hills, even in high summer, so take warm clothes.

Magellanic penguins

Beyond Cerro Bandera, a road leads 56 km west of Puerto Williams towards Puerto Navarino. There is little or no traffic on this route and it is very beautiful, with forests of lengas stretching right down to the water's edge. At **Mejillones**, 32 km from Puerto Williams, is a graveyard and memorial to the Yámana people. At **Puerto Navarino** there are a handful of marines and an abandoned police post, where you may be allowed to sleep. There are beautiful views across to Ushuaia and west to icebound Hoste Island and the Darwin Massif. A path continues to a cliff above the Murray Narrows: blue, tranquil and utterly calm.

Cape Horn

It is possible to catch a boat south from Isla Navarino to Cape Horn (the most southerly piece of land on earth apart from Antartica). There is one pebbly beach on the north side of the island; boats anchor in the bay and passengers are taken ashore by motorized dinghy. A rotting stairway climbs the cliff above the beach, up to the building where three marines run the naval post. A path leads from here to the impressive monument of an albatross overlooking the wild, churning waters of the Drake Passage below. ▸▸ *Transport, p362.*

Sleeping

Porvenir *p357*

A **Hostería Los Flamencos**, *Tte Merino 018, T061-580049, www.hosterialosflamencos.com.* Comfortable, nice restaurant, best in town.

C **Rozas**, *Phillippi 296, T061-580088.* With bath, hot water, heating, restaurant and bar, internet, laundry facilities. Recommended.

E **España**, *Croacia 698, T061-580160.* Price per person. Some rooms with bath, breakfast extra. Good restaurant with fixed-price lunch.

E **Miramar**, *Santos Mardones 366.* Price per person. Full board also available. Clean, friendly, heaters in rooms, hot water, panoramic views, good.

E-F **Hosp Guaignio**, *Santos Mardones 333, T061-580491, wshere@hotmail.com* Price per person without bath, including breakfast. Friendly and helpful, use of kitchen, clean, good value.

Beyond Porvenir *p357*

If you get stuck in the wilds, note that it is almost always possible to camp or bed down in a barn at an *estancia*.

B-E **Hostería de la Frontera**, *San Sebastián, T061-224731, 09-4995331, frontera@entelchile.net.* Rooms with bath and decent restaurant. Avoid the basic, dirty accommodation in an annexe.

B-E **Hostería Tunkelen**, *Cerro Sombrero, 46 km south of Primera Angostura, T061-212757, hosteria_tunkelen@hotmail.com.* Rooms and dormitory accommodation. Recommended.

E **Posada Las Flores**, *Km 127 on the Porvenir-San Sebastián road.* Reservations via **Hostal de la Patagonia** in Punta Arenas.

F **Pensión del Señor Alarcón**, *Cerro Sombrero, 46 km south of Primera Angostura.* Good, friendly.

F **Refugio Lago Blanco**, *Lago Blanco, T061- 241197.* The only accommodation on the lake.

Puerto Williams *p358*

You can also stay at private houses.

A-B **Hostería Wala**, *on the edge of Lauta bay, T061-621114, 2 km out of town.* Splendid walks in the area. Very hospitable.

C **Pensíon Temuco**, *Piloto Pardo 224, T061-621113.* Price per person for full board, comfortable, good food, hot showers. Slightly overpriced, but recommended.

D **Hostería Camblor**, *T061-621033, hosteriacamblor@terra.cl.* Price per person for full board. Gets very booked up.

E **Hostal Yagan**, *Piloto Pardo 260, T061-621334, hostalyagan@hotmail.com.*

Price per person. Single and double rooms. Good meals available. Clean and comfortable, friendly, tours offered.

E **Jeanette Talavera**, *Maragaño 168, T061-621150, www.simltd.com* Small dormitories, shared bathrooms, kitchen and laundry facilities, also organizes sailing trips, treks and other activities.

E **Residencial Onashaga**, *Uspashun 15, T061-621564, run by Señor Ortiz - everyone knows him*. Price per person. Cold, rundown, but good meals, helpful, full board available.

Eating

Porvenir *p357*

There are many lobster fishing camps nearby, where fishermen will prepare lobster on the spot.

TT **Club Croata**, *Senoret y Phillippi*. On waterfront, good food, lively.

TT-T **Restaurante Puerto Montt**, *Croacia 1169*. Recommended for seafood.

T **Miramar**, *Croacia s/n*. Large portions, good value.

Puerto Williams *p358*

There are several grocery stores; prices are very high because of the remoteness. Away from the **Club Naútico**, nightlife in Puerto Williams is at the **Dientes de Navarino**, a bar in the plaza.

Activities and tours

Porvenir *p357*

Turismo Cordillera de Darwin, *Croacia 675, T061-580206, www.explorepatagonia.cl* For tours of the island from a day to a week.

Puerto Williams *p358*

There is no trekking/outdoors equipment available on Isla Navarino, so stock up in Punta Arenas before you arrive.

Sailing

Captain Ben Garrett offers recommended adventure sailing in his schooner *Victory* in Dec and Jan, including special trips to Ushuaia, cruises in the canals and voyages to Cape Horn, the glaciers, Puerto Montt and Antarctica. Write to Victory Cruises, Annex No 1 Puerto Williams; or call collect to Punta Arenas and leave a message with the Puerto Williams operator.

Transport

Porvenir *p357*

Air

Aerovías DAP, *Señoret s/n, Porvenir, T061-580089, www.aeroviasdap.cl*, fly from Punta Arenas (weather and bookings permitting), twice daily Mon-Sat, US$23 one way. Heavily booked so make sure you have your return reservation confirmed.

Bus

Buses from Punta Arenas to Ushuaia don't take on passengers here. **Transportes Gessell**, *Duble Almeyda 257, T061-580488* (also in Punta Arenas at *José Menéndez 556, T061-222896*) runs buses to **Río Grande** (Argentina), Tue and Sat 1400, 5 hrs, US$15; return service Wed and Sun 0800. Local buses run to **Cameron** from Manuel Señor, in theory Mon and Fri 1700, US$10.

Ferry

The *Melinka* sails from **Tres Puentes** (5 km north of Punta Arenas; catch bus A or E from Av Magallanes, US$1; taxi US$3) to **Bahía Chilota**, 5 km west of Porvenir, Tue-Sun 0900 with an extra afternoon sailing Tue-Thu in season, 2½ hrs, pedestrians US$6, cars US$40. The boat returns from Porvenir in the afternoon Tue-Sun.

Timetable dependent on tides and subject to change: check in advance. The crossing can be rough and cold; watch for dolphins. Reservations are essential especially in summer (at least 24 hrs in advance for cars); obtainable from **Transbordadora Austral Broom**, *Bulnes 05075, Punta Arenas, T061-218100 (T061-580089 in Porvenir), www.tabsa.cl*.

The ferry service from **Punta Delgada** on the mainland to **Punta Espora**, 80 km north of Porvenir, departs usually every 40 mins 0830-2300 (schedules vary with the tides) and takes just 15 mins, pedestrians US$2, cars US$18. This is the principal route for buses and trucks between Ushuaia and mainland Argentina. Before 1000 most space is taken by trucks.

Puerto Williams *p358*

Air

Aerovías DAP, *Centro Comercial s/n, T061-621051, www.aeroviasdap.cl*, flies 20-seater Cessna aircraft from Punta Arenas Mon-Sat, departure time varies, 1¼ hrs, US$64 one way. Book well in advance; there are long waiting lists. Luggage allowance 10 kg (US$2 per kg extra). **Aeropetrel** will charter a plane from Puerto Williams to Cape Horn (US$2,600 for 8-10 people).

Ferry

Despite its proximity, there are no regular sailings to Isla Navarino from Ushuaia (Argentina). The following all depart from **Punta Arenas**: Austral Broom ferry *Cruz Australis, www.tabsa.cl,* once a week, 36 hrs, US$120 for a reclining seat, US$150 for a bunk, meals included; *Navarino* (contact Carlos Aguilera, *21 de Mayo 1460, Punta Arenas, T061-228066*), 3rd week of every month, 12 passengers, US$150 one way; *Beaulieu* cargo boat, once a month, US$300 return, 6 days. Some cruises to Ushuaia also stop at Puerto Williams.

Cape Horn *p360*

Crucero Australis cruises from Ushuaia stop at Cape Horn (see Budget buster p332). In addition, the naval vessel *PSG Micalvi*, which sails once every 3 months from Punta Arenas via Puerto Williams, may take passengers to Cape Horn for US$250 (letters of recommendation will help). Navy and port authorities in Puerto Williams may deny any knowledge, but everyone else knows when a boat is due; ask at the *Armada* in Punta Arenas (see p332). Otherwise ask at the yacht club about hitching a ride to Cape Horn.

Directory

Porvenir *p357*

Currency exchange Available at Estrella del Sur, *Santos Mardones*.

Puerto Williams *p358*

Post office closes 1900.
Telephone CTC, Mon-Sat 0930-2230, Sun 1000-1300, 1600-2200.

Argentine Tierra del Fuego

Argentine Tierra del Fuego belongs to the province of Tierra del Fuego, Antártida y Las Islas del Atlántico Sur, the capital of which is the welcoming tourist centre Ushuaia. The population of the Argentine sector is around 85,000, most of whom live in the two towns of Río Grande and Ushuaia. Both bigger and more developed than the Chilean side of the island, it provides good territory for guided explorations of the wilderness.

Getting there Easiest by air
Getting around Organized tours or 4WD required for remote areas
Time required 3 days
Weather Strong winds in summer, snow in winter
Sleeping Lots of accommodation in Ushuaia, heavily booked in summer; excellent estancias.
Eating Full range of restaurants in Ushuaia; less choice in Río Grande
Activities and tours Fishing, hiking, horse riding, skiing.
★ **Don't miss...** Estancia Harberton

Ins and outs » *Transport, p377.*

Getting there The main point of entry is **Aeropuerto Internacional Malvinas Argentinas** ⓘ *4 km from Ushuaia, on a peninsula in the Beagle channel, T02901-423970,* which receives daily **flights** from Buenos Aires (4 hrs), frequent flights from El Calafate and Punta Arenas, as well as weekly flights with army airline LADE from many towns in Patagonia. This is by far the easiest way to get to the Argentine side of the island and the view from the plane as you land over jagged mountains onto the quiet channel below is magical. From the airport, a taxi to the centre of town costs US$2. There is another airport at Río Grande with flights to/from Buenos Aires and Ushuaia. **Buses** from mainland Argentina and from Punta Arenas in Chile travel to Río Grande and Ushuaia via Punta Delgada and San Sebastián. There are also buses from Porvenir to Río Grande.

Getting around If you fly in and out of Ushuaia, you can probably get around fine by bus and boat for the National Park and visits along the Beagle Channel, including Haberton. However, if you want to visit Lago Fagnano or remoter estancias or hike in places not visited by the many adventure tourism companies, you could consider hiring a car. Buses from Río Grande and Ushuaia are frequent, but are heavily booked in summer. There are abundant tours from Ushuaia to suit most needs, and some great hiking adventures on offer too.

Río Grande

Río Grande is a sprawling modern coastal town, the centre for a rural sheep-farming community, which grew rapidly in the oil boom of the 1970s and suffered when tax benefits were withdrawn in recent years, leading to increasing unemployment and emigration and leaving a rather sad, windy town today. The people are friendly but there's little culture, and you're most likely to visit in order to change buses. There are a couple of good places to stay, however, and two small museums: the **Museo de Ciencias Naturales y Historias** ⓘ *El Cano 225, Tue-Fri 0900-1700, Sat/Sun 1500-2000*, and the **Museo de la Ciudad** ⓘ *Alberdi 555, T02964-430414, open Tue-Fri 1000-1700*, which recounts the city's history through sheep, missions, pioneers and oil. In the

Ushuaia - the world's southernmost town

blue-roofed hut on the plaza is the small but helpful **tourist office** ⓘ *Rosales 350, T02964-431324, www.tierradelfuego.org.ar, Mon-Fri 0900-2100, Sat 1000-1700.*

The Salesian mission **La Candelaria** ⓘ *11 km north on Route 3, T02964-421642, open Mon-Sat 1000- 1230, 1500-1900, Sun 1500-1900, US$1.50, afternoon teas, US$3,* was founded in 1893 by José Fagnano to try to protect the Ona people from gold prospectors and sheep farmers. It now houses displays of natural history and indigenous artefacts, with strawberry plantations, piglets and an aviary too.

South of Río Grande

A fan of roads spreads out south and west from Río Grande to numerous *estancias*; these are unpaved and best attempted in a 4WD vehicle. **Estancia Viamonte**, on the coast 40 km south, is a working sheep farm with a fascinating history. Here, Lucas Bridges, son of Tierra del Fuego's first settler, built a home to protect the large tribe of indigenous Onas, who were fast dying out. The *estancia* is still inhabited by his descendents, who can take you riding and to see the life of the farm. Accommodation is also available. It's highly recommended for an insight into Fuegian life and a cosy place to read '*Uttermost part of the Earth*'.

The paved road south, Route 3, continues across wonderfully open land, more forested than the expanses of Patagonian steppe further north, and increasingly hilly as you near Ushuaia. After around 160 km, you could turn left along a track to the coast, to find **Estancia Cabo San Pablo**, 120 km from Río Grande. This simple working *estancia* is in a beautiful position, surrounded by native woodland for walking and riding, birdwatching and fishing. It's open all year, but reserve in advance.

Route 3 then climbs high above **Lago Fagnano**, a large expanse of water at the heart of Tierra del Fuego, which straddles the border with Chile. In the small settlement of **Tolhuin** there's a YPF service station just off the main road and a tiny, friendly **tourist office**. Drive into the village to visit the famous bakery **La Union**, where you can buy all kinds of bread, great *empanadas* and delicious fresh *facturas* (pastries), before heading down to the tranquil lake shore, where there's a quiet, unexploited stretch of beach and a couple of good places to stay.

Further along Route 3, 50 km from Ushuaia, a road to the right swoops down to **Lago Escondido**, a long, fjord-like lake with steep green mountains descending into the water on all sides. There are cabañas and a couple of hosterias, one with a good restaurant for lunch.

Ushuaia » p 369-377

Ushuaia's setting is spectacular. Its brightly coloured houses look like toys against the dramatic backdrop of snow-coverd Cerro Martial to the north. Opposite are the forbidding peaks of Isla Navarino, and between flows the green Beagle Channel. Sailing these waters, it is easy to imagine what it was like when Darwin arrived here in 1832 and when the Bridges family first settled here in 1871. Although the town has expanded in recent years, sprawling untidily along the coast, Ushuaia still retains the feel of a pioneer town, isolated and expectant. There are lots of places to stay, which fill up entirely in January, a fine museum, and some great fish restaurants. There is dramatic landscape to be explored in all directions, with good treks in the Parque Nacional Tierra del Fuego just to the west of the city and more adventurous expeditions into the wild heart of the island, trekking, climbing or riding. There's splendid cross-country skiing nearby in winter, as well as downhill skiing at Cerro Castor. And to the east, along a beautiful stretch of coastline is the historic *estancia* of Harberton, which you can reach by a boat trip along the Beagle Channel.

Tourist information ⓘ *San Martín 674, corner with Fadul, T/F02901-432000, www.tierradelfuego.org.ar, Mon-Fri 0800-2200, Sat, Sun and holidays 0900-2000*. Quite the best tourist office in Argentina. The friendly and helpful staff speak several languages and will find you somewhere to stay, even in the busiest period. They also have a great series of leaflets in English, French, German and Dutch about all the things to see and do, including bus and boat times. There's also an office at the airport, T02901-423970. **Tierra del Fuego National Park Office** ⓘ *San Martín 1395, T02901-421315*, has a useful little map of the park.

History

Missionary Thomas Bridges first established a mission here in 1884 and the fledgling settlement soon attracted pioneers in search of gold. A penal colony, on nearby Staten Island, moved to the town in 1902 and Croatian and Spanish immigrants, together with shipwreck survivors, began to settle here. However, the town remained isolated until planes arrived in 1935. When the prison closed it was replaced by a naval base and, in the 1970s, a wave of new inhabitants arrived, many of them from Buenos Aires, attracted by reduced income taxes and cheap car prices. Now the city is capital of Argentina's most southerly province and, although fishing still plays a key role in the local economy, Ushuaia has become an important tourist centre as the departure point for voyages to Antarctica.

Sights

It's easy to walk around the town in a morning, since all its sights are close together. You'll find banks, restaurants, hotels and shops along Calle San Martín, which runs parallel to the shore, a block north of the coast road, Maipú. Boat trips leave from the **Muelle Turistico** (tourist pier) by a small plaza, 25 de Mayo, on the seafront. There are several museums worth looking at, if bad weather forces you indoors. The most fascinating is **Museo del Fin del Mundo** ⓘ *on the seafront at Maipú y Rivadavia, T02901-421863, daily 1200-1900, US$3.50, students US$1*, in the 1902 bank building, which tells the history of the town through a small collection of carefully chosen exhibits on the indigenous groups, missionaries, pioneers and shipwrecks. There's also a stuffed collection of Tierra del Fuego's birdlife and an extensive reference library. Further east, the old prison, Presidio, at the Naval Base, houses the **Museo Marítimo** ⓘ *Yaganes y Gob Paz, daily 0900-2000, closed winter, US$ 5 for foreigners*, which has models and artefacts from seafaring days, and, in the cells, the **Museo Penitenciario**, which details the history of the prison. **Museo Yámana** ⓘ *Rivadavia 56, T02901-422874, daily 1200-1900 high season, otherwise closed lunchtime, US$2*, has interesting scale models of everyday indigenous life.

Background

Building Bridges

The story of the first successful missionary to Tierra del Fuego, **Thomas Bridges**, is one of the most stirring in the whole history of pioneers in Argentina. An orphan from Bristol, Thomas Bridges was so called because he was found as a child under a bridge with a letter 'T' on his clothing. Bridges arrived in Tierra del Fuego from the Falkland Islands in 1871 with his wife, young daughter and his adoptive father, Reverend Despard. Despard left Tierra del Fuego following the massacre of Christians by indigenous inhabitants but Thomas remained, living near the shores of the Beagle Channel until his death in 1898. He created the new settlement of Ushuaia and then was granted land at Harberton (see page 367), where he devoted his life to the Yámana people (Yaganes) and compiled a dictionary of their language.

Thomas's son **Lucas** (1874-1949), one of six children, spent his early life among the Yámanas and Onas, living and hunting as one of them, learning their language, and even, almost fatally, becoming involved in their blood feuds and magic rituals. Lucas became both defender and protector of the indigenous people whose culture he loved, creating a haven for them at Harberton and Estancia Viamonte (see page 370), at a time when most sheep farmers were more interested in shooting them. His compelling memoirs, *Uttermost Part of the Earth* (1947) trace the tragic fate of the native population with whom he grew up; it is now out of print, but can still be found in second-hand bookshops.

For exhilirating views along the Beagle Channel and to Isla Navarinho beyond, don't miss a trip on the chair lift up to **Cerro Martial** ⓘ *daily 1000-1800, US$2.20*, about 7 km behind the town. From the top of the lift, you can walk for 90 minutes through lenga forest to Glaciar Martial, where there's limited skiing in winter. There's also a splendid tea shop, *refugio* and *cabañas* at the Cerro. Several companies, including **Lautaro** and **Kaupen**, run minibus services from the corner of Maipu and Roca to the bottom of the chairlift, hourly in summer, US$ 2-4 return, last buses return at 1900 and 2100. Otherwise it's a 1½ hour walk from town via Magallanes.

The **Tren del Fin del Mundo** ⓘ *T02901-431600, www.trendelfindelmundo.com.ar, 3 departures daily in summer, 1 in winter, US$16/17 return, kids US$6, plus US$4 park entrance and the station, La Estación del Fin del Mundo, is 8 km west of town. Buses from Maipu and Roca. Taxi US$3, bus US$2*, is the world's southernmost steam train, running new locomotives and carriages on track first laid by prisoners to carry wood to Ushuaia. It travels from the Fin del Mundo station, 8 km west of Ushuaia, into the Tierra del Fuego National Park (see page 368) and is an unashamedly touristy experience with relentless commentary in English and Spanish. However, it might be fun for children and is one way of getting into the national park to start a walk. Sit on the left on the outbound journey for the best views. Tickets are available at the station or from the **Tranex** kiosk in the port.

Views of Harberton

Estancia Harberton

ⓘ *85 km east of Ushuaia (2hrs drive), T02901-422742, estanciaharberton@tierradelfuego.org.ar, open daily. Tour of the estancia US$3, museum entrance US$2.* In a land of extremes and superlatives, Harberton still stands out as special. The oldest *estancia* in Tierra del Fuego was built in 1886 on a narrow peninsula overlooking the Beagle Channel by the missionary Thomas Bridges (see above). He was granted the land by President Roca for his work with the indigenous peoples and for rescuing victims of shipwrecks in the channels. Harberton is named after the Devonshire village where Thomas's wife Mary was born; the farmhouse was pre-fabricated by her father in England and assembled on a spot chosen by the Yámana. The English connection is evident in the neat garden of lawns, shrubs and trees between the jetty and the farmhouse; behind the buildings is a large vegetable garden, a real rarity on the island.

Still operating as a working farm, Harberton is run by Thomas Goodall, great-grandson of the founder. Visitors receive an excellent guided walk (bilingual guides) through protected forest around the *estancia*, where there are reconstructions of the Yámana dwellings, plus a tour of the impressive **Museo Acatushun** www.acatushun.com, founded by Thomas' wife, Natalie Goodall. The museum is the result of 23 years' scientific investigation into the area's rich marine life and contains the complete skeletons of dolphins, whales and seals. Tea or lunch (if you reserve ahead) are served in the room overlooking the bay. You can camp free, with permission from the owners, or rent one of the two simple cottages on the shore. There are wonderful walks along the coast, and noticeably more wildlife here than in the Tierra del Fuego National Park, probably owing to the *estancia*'s remoteness. ▸▸ *Transport, p377.*

Beagle Channel

A sea trip along the Beagle Channel can be rough but is highly recommended. Excursions can be booked through most agencies and leave from the Muelle Turistico in Ushuaia. Destinations include the sea lion colony at **Isla de los Lobos**, **Isla de los Pájaros**, **Les Eclaireurs lighthouse** and the **penguin colony at Isla Martillo**. You can visit Estancia Harberton by boat but always check that your tour actually includes the *estancia* and not just Harberton bay. ▸▸ *Activities and tours, p375.*

Parque Nacional Tierra del Fuego » p 369-377

ⓘ *Administration San Martín 1395, Ushuaia, T02901-421315, www.parquesnacionales.gov.ar, tierradelfuego@apn.gov.ar. Park entrance 11 km west of Ushuaia, open all year round, US$4 for non-Argentines. Note there are no legal crossing points to Chile from the national park.* Covering 63,000 ha of mountains, lakes, rivers and deep valleys, this small but beautiful park stretches west to the Chilean border and north from Bahía Lapataia on the Beagle Channel to beyond Lago Fagnano. Large areas are closed to tourists to protect the environment, but there are marvellous walks for every level fitness. Lower parts of the park are forested with lenga, ñire and coihue and are rich in birdlife, including geese, the beautiful torrent duck, Magellanic woodpeckers and austral parakeets. Even if you have just a couple of hours to spare, take a bus or taxi to Lago Roca or Bahía Lapataia

Walking in the park

You'll be given a basic map with marked walks at the entrance. More detailed topographical maps are sold in Ushuaia at **Oficina Antárctica**, Maipú and Laserre, or consult the Ushuaia tourist office. All walks are best attempted in the early morning or afternoon to avoid the tour buses. Wear warm, waterproof clothing: in winter the temperature drops to as low as -12°C and in summer, although it can reach 25°C, evenings can be chilly. For a longer hike and a really rich experience of the park, go with guides who know the territory well and can tell you about wildlife. » *Activities and tours, p375.*

1 Senda Costera (6.5 km, 3 hrs each way) This lovely easy walk along the shore of the Beagle Channel gives you the essence of the park: its rocky coastline, edged with a rich forest of beech trees and glorious views of the low islands and steep mountains. Start at **Bahía Ensenada** (where the bus can drop you off and where boats leave for trips to Bahía Lapataia, daily 1000-1700, 2 hrs, US$15, reservation essential). Walk along a well-marked path along the shoreline and then rejoin the road briefly to cross Río Lapataia (ignoring signs to Lago Roca to your right). After crossing the broad green river and a second stretch of water (where

there's a small camping spot and the *gendarmería*), it's a pleasant stroll inland to the beautifully tranquil **Bahía Lapataia**, an idyllic spot, with views across the sound.

2 Lago Roca or Sendo Hito XXIV (4 km, 90 mins one way). Another easy walk, this time alongside peaceful Lago Roca, where there's a very helpful *guardaparque*, plus camping and a confiteria .. It takes in lovely pebble beaches and dense forest, with lots of bird life and is especially recommended in the evening, when most visitors have left. Get off the bus at the junction for Lago Roca, turn right along the road to the car park (passing the *guardaparque*'s house) and follow the lake side.

3 Cerro Guanaco (4 km, 4 hrs one way). Starting at the car park for Lago Roca, this is a challenging, steep hike up through forest to a mirador with splendid views over Lago Roca, the Beagle Channel and far-off mountains. The ground is slippery after rain: take care and don't rush. Allow plenty of time to return in daylight, especially in winter.

 Sleeping

Río Grande *p363*

Book ahead, as choice is limited.

B **Hotel Atlantida**, *Belgrano 582, T02964-431914, atlantida@netcombbs.com.ar* A modern, rather uninspiring place, with plain comfortable rooms, with bath and cable TV, good value with breakfast.

B **Posada de los Sauces**, *Elcano 839, T02964-432895, info@posadadelos sauces.com.ar* By far the best choice. Breakfast included, beautifully decorated and comfortable rooms, good restaurant and cosy bar. Recommended.

C **Apart Hotel Keyuk'n**, *Colón 630, T02964-424435, aparthotelkeyukn @speedy.com.ar*. A good apart hotel, with simple well equipped flats for 2-4.

F pp **Hotel Argentina** , *San Martín 64, T02964-422546, hotelargentino @yahoo.com* The best cheap place. Much more than the backpackers youth hostel it claims to be, in a beautifully renovated 1920s building close to the sea front. Kitchen facilities, a bright sunny dining room with space to sit, owned by the welcoming Graciela, who knows all about the local area. Highly recommended.

Camping

Club Naútico Ioshlelk-Oten, *Montilla 1047, 2 km from town on river*. Clean, cooking facilities, camping inside heated building in cold weather. YPF petrol station has hot showers.

South of Río Grande *p364*

See also Budget buster, p370.

A **Hostería Petrel**, *Lago Escondido, RN 3, km 3186, T02901-433569, hpetrel@infovia.com.ar*. Decent rooms with bath in a secluded, forest on a tranquil beach. It is the only place to stay in this idyllic spot. The good restaurant overlooks the lake and serves delicious lamb, US$7, open to non-residents. There are also tiny basic *cabañas* right on the water, US$40 for 2-4 people.

D **Cabañas Khami** , *Lago Fagnano. T02964-15-611243, T/F02964-422296 www.cabaniaskhami.com.ar* Isolated in a lovely open spot at the head of Lago Fagnano on low-lying land, very comfortable and well equipped *cabañas*, nicely decorated, and with great views of the lake. Good value at US$40 per day for 6. Recommended.

D **Terrazas del Lago**, *Route 3, km 2938, T02964-15-604851, terrazas@uol.com.ar* A little way from the shore of Lago Fagnano, smart wooden *cabañas*, well decorated, also a *confiteria* and *parrilla*.

D **Parador Kawi Shiken**, *4 km south of Tolhuin on RN3, km 2940, T02964-15-611505, www.hotelguia.com/hoteles /kawi-shiken/* A rustic place with 3 rooms, shared bathrooms, *casa de té* and restaurant. Ring ahead to arrange for local *cordero al asador* (barbecued lamb). Also horse riding.

Budget buster

Estancia living at the end of the world

Working sheep farms are the essence of Patagonia, and you'll never forget your experience here: a warm welcome, hiking and riding, organic Patagonian lamb cooked on a fire, and the grandeur of the great outdoors. www.estanciasdesantacruz.com

LL **Estancia María Behety**, *15 km from Río Grande.* Very exclusive, for keen fly fishermen only. This 19th-century estancia is located on a 40 km stretch of river that has become legendary for brown trout. Comfortable accommodation and good food. At US$5,350 per week, this is one of the country's priciest fishing lodges.

L **Estancia Rivadvia**, *100 km south of Río Grande on route H, T02901-492186/15-616813, www.estanciarivadavia.com, myrna@estanciarivadavia.com*. A 10,000 ha sheep farm, owned by descendents of the Croatian pioneer who built the place. Luxurious accommodation and good food in a splendid house at the heart of Tierra del Fuego. See wild horses and guanacos and trek to the trout lake of Chepelmut and Yehuin.

L **Estancia Rolito**, *Route 21, km 14, T02901-492007, rolitotdf@hotmail.com*. A magical place on the Beagle channel with sweeping views of the coast, cosy accommodation and friendly hosts. Book through Turismo de Campo, 25 de Mayo 50, T02901-432419, www.turismodecampo.com.ar. Day visits also possible.

L **Estancia Viamonte**, *40 km southeast of Río Grande, on the coast, T02964-430861, www.estanciaviamonte.com*. Built in 1902 by Lucas Bridges, writer of *Uttermost Part of the Earth*, to protect the indigenous Ona peoples, this working estancia is run by his descendants. It has traditional, beautifully furnished rooms, with bathrooms and delicious meals. Join in the farm activities, read the famous book by blazing fires or ride horses over the estate. Reserve a week ahead. (US$150 per day, full board and all activities).

A **Estancia Cabo San Paolo**, *120 km south of Río Grande, T02964-15-610630, www.estanciasdesantacruz.com/cabosanpablo*. Set on the shore in an amazing landscape. Two beds in the main house plus a guest house. Fishing, horse riding, pioneer hiking, good company and great comfort.

A pp **Estancia Harberton**, *90 km east of Ushuaia, along RN 3 and 33, T02901-422742, harberton@tierradelfuego.org.ar*. Two impeccably restored buildings on the tranquil lakeside, give you space and privacy away from the main house. Simple accommodation but wonderful views and beautiful walks on the estancia's coastline.

Camping

Camping Hain del Lago, *Tolhuin, T02964- 425951, T02964-15-603606, robertoberbel @hotmail.com* Lovely views, barbeques, hot showers, *quincho*.

Camping La Correntina, *T02964-15-605020, 17 km from Tolhuin.* In woodland, with bathrooms, and horses for hire.

Ushuaia *p365, map p372*

The tourist office has accommodation lists and can help find you somewhere to stay but in Jan reserve in advance, www.tierradelfuego.org.ar/ushuaia. Many people offer rooms in private houses.

L **Cap Polonio**, *San Martín 748, T02901-422140, cappolonio@tierradelfuego.org.ar.* A smart central modern city hotel with very comfortable minimalist rooms, all with bath, phone, TV, internet; some have views of the canal. There's a chic restaurant-cafe downstairs.

AL **Canal Beagle**, *Maipú y 25 de Mayo, T02901-430370.* Comfortable rooms with great views over the Beagle Channel. Right on the waterfront, the newly renovated ACA is good value and welcoming.

A **Apart Hotel Cabo San Diego**, *25 de Mayo 368, T02901-435600, www.cabosandiego.com.ar.* Really comfortable and spacious apartments, very spick and span, well-equipped for cooking, good bathrooms. Great for couples or families.

A **César**, *San Martín 753, T02901-421460, www.hotelcesarhostal.com.ar.* Very central, this big tourist place is often booked by groups, but is reasonable value. Simple rooms with bath, breakfast included.

A **Los Ñires**, *Av de los Ñires 3040, T02901-443781, www.tierradelfuego.org.ar/losnires.* The setting is the feature here, with lovely views, comfortable rooms in simple rustic style and a good restaurant. Transfers and breakfast included.

A **Tolkeyen**, *Del Tolkeyen 2145, 4 km west towards national park, T02901-445315, www.tolkeyenhotel.com.ar.* A lovely rustic place in a superb setting, with open views from its rooms, which vary between plain and flouncy, but are all comfortable. Close to the national park, with free buses into town. Also an excellent restaurant, serving king crab and Fuegian lamb. Very relaxing. Recommended.

B **Cabañas del Martial**, *L F Martial 2109, T02901-430475, cabanasdelmartial@speedy.com.ar.* Wonderful views from these comfortable and well-equipped *cabañas*. US$65 for 5 people.

A **Hostería Posada Fin del Mundo**, *Valdez 281, T02901-434847, reservas@posadafindelmundo.com.ar.* A relaxed family atmosphere, homely rooms and friendly staff. Good value.

D **Albergue Kayen**, *Gob. Paz 1410, T02901-431497, www.alberguekayen.com.ar.* Good value, friendly place with family attention, in an elevated position with fine views over channel. Rooms have shared bath, self service breakfast.

D **B&B Nahuel**, *25 de Mayo 440, T02901-423068, byb_nahuel@yahoo.com.ar.* A delightful house with views over the channel, with brightly painted and tastefully decorated rooms, and a lovely welcome from the owner. Great value. Recommended.

D pp **El Nido de Cóndores**, *Gob. Capos 795 y 9 de Julio, T02901-437753, www.compania deguias .com.ar.* Simple rooms with shared bath, but a really excellent breakfast in this friendly place with a lovely relaxing café below. The owners are Ushuaia's best walking guides, and can arrange superb trekking. Recommended.

D **Galeazzi-Basily**, *Gdor Valdez 323, T02901-423213, fbasily@quasarlab.com.ar.* Private rooms in this cosy and stylish family home, with incredibly welcoming owners, Francis and Alejandro, who speak excellent English. Pleasant residential area just 5 blocks from the centre. Delicious breakfast included. There is also a 5-bed *cabaña* in the garden. Highly recommended.

F pp **Familia Velasquez**, *Juana Fadul 361, T02901-421719.* Basic rooms in cosy cheerful family home, where the kind owners look after you. Excellent value.

G pp **Amanecer de la Bahia**, *Magallanes 594, T02901-424405, amanecerdelabahia@arnet.com.ar.* A light, spacious, impeccably kept hostal, with shared

rooms for 4 and 6, also double and triples. Internet, living rooms, breakfast included.
G pp **Albergue Cruz del Sur**, *Deloqui 636, T02901-434099, xdelsur@yahoo.com.* There's a very friendly atmosphere in this relaxed small hostal, with cosy dorms, use of kitchen, and a lovely quiet library room for reading. A place to make friends. Recommended.

Parque Nacional Tierra del Fuego

p368, map p368

Camping Lago Roca, *21km from Ushuaia.* By the forested shore of tranquil Lago Roca, this is a beautiful site with good facilities, reached by bus Jan-Feb, expensive small shop, cafetería. Park entry fee US$4; camping fee US$4 per tent.

There are also various sites with no facilities at **Bahía Ensenada**, 16 km from Ushuaia, **Camping Las Bandurrias** and **Camping Laguna Verde**, both 20 km from Ushuaia.

Eating

Río Grande *p363*

La Nueva Colonial, *Fagnano 669.* Half a block from the plaza, next to Casino Club, where the locals go for delicious pasta in a warm family atmosphere.

La Nueva Piamontesa, *Belgrano y Mackinlay, T02964-423620*, to the side of the charming 24 hr grocery store. Cheap

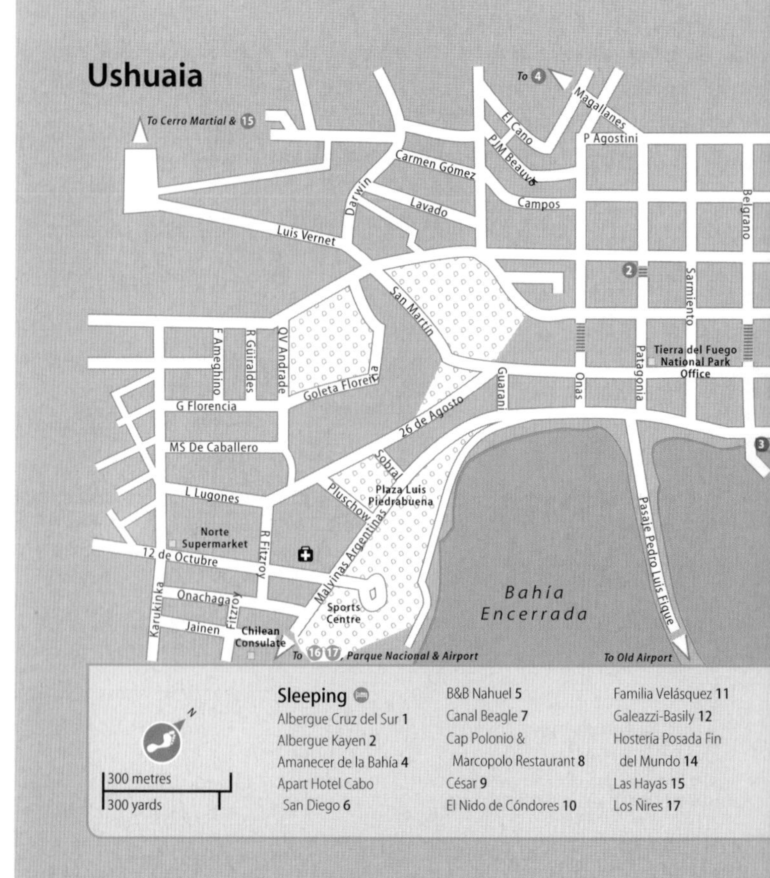

set menus and also delivers food.

🍴 **La Rueda**, *Islas Malvinas 954, first floor*. Excellent *parrilla* in a welcoming place.

South from Río Grande *p364*

The following are all in Tolhuin.

🍴 **La Posada de los Ramirez**, a cosy restaurant and *rotisería*, where 3 courses will cost you US$4, open weekends only, lunch and dinner.

🍴 **La Union**. Excellent bakery open 24 hrs daily except Mon midnight to Tue 0600.

🍴 **Parrilla La Victoria**, *Koshten 324, T02964-492297*. Open daily, with beef and lamb on the *asado* and pizzas; call ahead for delicious Fuegian lamb.

Ushuaia *p365, map p372*

🍴🍴🍴 **Marcopolo**, *San Martín 748, T02901-430001*. A chic modern international-style café restaurant for seafood and everything else. Soothing décor, good service. Tango show Fri 2200.

🍴🍴 **Los Pioneros, Bodegon Fueguino**, *San Martín 859, T02901-431972*. In a stylishly renovated 1896 house in the main street, this stands out from the crowd by serving *picadas*, with delicious and imaginative dips, and unusual *cazuelas*. A buzzy atmosphere and welcoming staff.

🍴🍴 **El Rancho**, *San Martín y Rivadavia*. A *parrilla* with Argentine live music, and rather atmospheric, despite the obvious

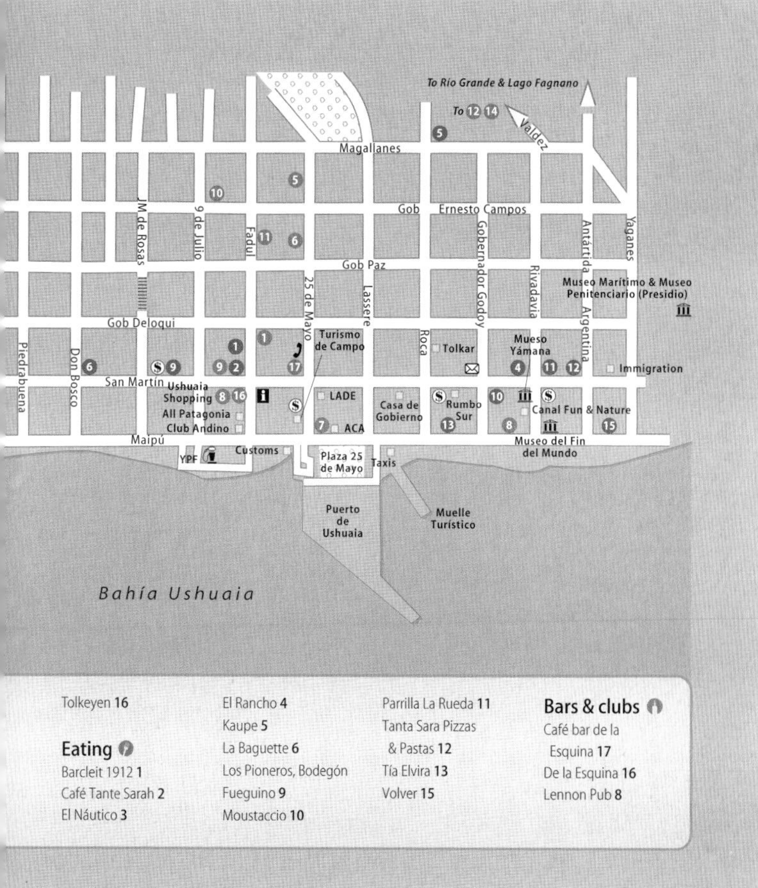

Budget buster

LL **Las Hayas**, *Camino Glaciar Martial, km 3, T02901-430710, www.lashayas hotel.com*. Ushuaia's only 5-star hotel is in a spectacular setting, high up on the mountainside en route to the Martial glacier, with outstanding views over the Beagle channel. Light, tasteful, impeccable rooms. Breakfast included and use of pool, sauna, gym, squash court, 9-hole golf course, shuttle from town and transfer from airport. A lovely calm atmosphere, friendly staff, recommended.

ΨΨΨ **Kaupe**, *Roca 470 y Magallanes, T02901-422704*. The best restaurant in town with exquisite food. King crab and meat dishes all beautifully served, in a lovely environment – a great treat.

appeal to tourists. Good steaks too.

ΨΨ **Tante Sara Pizzas and Pastas**, *San Martín 175, T02901-435005*. A brightly-lit functional place with tasty filling food.

ΨΨ **Tia Elvira**, *Maipu 349, T02901-424725*. Retains its reputation for excellent seafood, with a good choice of fresh fish and good views.

ΨΨ **Volver**, *Maipu 37, 02901-423977*. In an atmospheric old 1898 house, with ancient newspaper all over the walls, so that you can read intriguing fragments while you eat. Cosy stoves and an intimate atmosphere. Delicious salmon and *arroz con mariscos*.

Ψ **Barcleit 1912**, *Fadul 148, T02901-433015*. Serves good cheap Italian food, 3 courses for US$2.50, pizzas and pastas.

Ψ **El Nautico**, *Maipu y Belgrano, T02901-430415*. For a good lunch, ask for the US$4 set menu here, served in a great setting on the waterfront.

Ψ **Moustaccio**, *San Martín 298, T02901-423308*. Long established, good for cheap fish in a cosy atmosphere.

Ψ **Parrilla La Rueda**, *San Martín y Rivadavia, T02901-436540*. Of the 2 good *tenedor libres* on *San Martín*, this is the best at US$5.20 for great range including lamb *asador al palo*.

Cafés and bars

Bar de la Esquina, *Fadul y San Martín*. French bistro, delicious sandwiches, cakes and *picadas* with drinks.

Café Bar de la Esquina, *25 de Mayo y San Martín*. Light meals and drinks, in a good atmosphere.

Café Tante Sarah, *Fadul y San Martín, opposite the tourist office*. The most appealing of the cafés on *San Martín*. Smart and modern with an airy feel, serving good coffee and tasty sandwiches.

La Baguette, *Don Bosco y San Martín*. The best fresh takeaway sandwiches, and also delicious *empanadas* and *facturas* (pastries).

Lennon Pub, *on Maipu*. A lively friendly atmosphere and live music.

Festivals and events

Río Grande p363

The **sheep shearing festival** in **Jan** is definitely worth seeing, if you're in the area. There's a **rural exhibition** with handicrafts, **2nd week of Feb**.

Shepherd's day, with impressive sheepdog display, is the first week in **Mar**.

Winter solstice, the longest night with fireworks and ice skating contests takes place **Jun 20/21**, although this is a very inhospitable time of year.

Tourists and sealions in the Beagle Channel

Activities and tours

Ushuaia *p365, map p372*

Boat trips

Excursions along the Beagle Channel can be booked through most agencies and leave from the Muelle Turistico.

Patagonian Adventure, by catamaran to Isla de los Lobos, Isla de los Pájaros and Les Eclaireurs lighthouse, 4½ hrs including 1 hr trekking on Bridges island, US$22, including hot drink.

Alternatively the charming old boat **Barracuda** sails to Isla de los Lobos, Isla de los Pájaros, Les Eclaireurs lighthouse and the Isla Martillo penguin colony, with excellent commentary, highly recommended, 4½ hrs, US$18.

The third option takes you past the Isla de los Lobos, Isla de los Pájaros, Isla Martillo penguin colony and Les Eclaireurs lighthouse and then visits Estancia Harberton, 8 hrs round trip on catamaran, Tue, Thu, Sat only, US$45, includes packed lunch and entrance fee.

Tour operators

Lots of companies offer adventure tours that include trekking, canoeing, birdwatching and horse riding. All agencies charge the same fees: Tierra del Fuego National Park, 4 hrs, US$12 (entry fee US$4 extra); Lagos Escondido and Fagnano, 8 hrs, US$22 with lunch.

All Patagonia, *Juana Fadul 26, T02901-430725, www.allpatagonia.com/Eng*. A wonderful range of tours, sailing, hiking, birdwatching around Ushuaia. Ask about the birdwatching trip to the centre of the island and the 6-day trip crossing the Fuegian *cordillera*. Also Antarctic trips. Well-organized and recommended.

Canal Fun & Nature, *Rivadavia 82, T02901-437395, www.canalfun.com.* Huge range of activities, horse riding, 4WD excursions. Recommended.

Rumbo Sur, *San Martín 350, T02901-421139, www.rumbsur.com.ar.* Flights, buses and all the conventional tours, Harberton, plus wonderful Antarctic expeditions, mid Nov to mid Mar (around US$2500 pp), friendly, English spoken.

Tolkar Turismo, *Roca 157, T02901-431412, www.tolkarturismo.com.ar.* Flights, bus tickets to Punta Arenas and Río Gallegos, conventional and adventure tourism, mountain biking to Lago Fagnano.

Travel Lab, *San Martín y 9 de Julio, T02901- 436555, travellabush @speedy.com.ar.* Buy tickets at platform 2 for *Tren del fin del Mundo*, unconventional tours, mountain biking, trekking. English and French spoken, helpful.

Turismo de Campo, *25 de Mayo 34, T02901-437351, www.turismodecampo.com.ar.* Adventure tourism in small groups with English-speaking guides. Boat and trekking in the national park, visits to Estancia Rolito (see Sleeping, above, full board US$60pp), birdwatching tours, horseriding in Monte Susanna, sailing in the Beagle Channel. Also trips to Antarctica. Highly recommended.

Fishing

The lakes and rivers of Tierra del Fuego offer great fishing for brown and rainbow trout, and stream trout in Lago Fagnano. Both flycasting and spinning are allowed, and permits must be bought. The trout season is 1 Nov-31 Mar, licences US$10 per week, US$5 per day. For information, contact **Asociación de Caza y Pesca**, *Maipú y 9 de Julio*, which has a museum.

Hiking and climbing

For hiking, climbing (and cross-country skiing) contact **Club Andino**, *Fadul 5*. To get to the remoter areas, go with a tour operator (see above).

Compañia de Guias de Patagonia, *Hostal El Nido de los Condores, Gob Campos 785, y 9 de Julio, T02901-437753, T02901-15-618426, www.compania deguias.com.ar.* The best walking guides. Well-run expeditions for all levels to the national park and more inaccessible places, all equipment and food included. Also ice climbing, with training and equipment. Professional, friendly and knowledgeable. Highly recommended.

Skiing

Ushuaia is popular as a winter sports resort, especially for cross-country skiing, with several centres in the vicinity. There's good powder snow, thanks to the even temperatures (between 5 and -5°C). The season runs mid Jun-mid Oct but late Aug-late Sep is recommended for longer days. Various new centres have sprung up along Route 3, northeast of Ushuaia.

Cerro Castor, *27 km northeast on RN3, T02901-15-605595, www.cerrocastor.com.* The most developed resort in Tierra del Fuego, 22 km of pistes of all grades and a vertical drop of 760 m. Also excellent for cross-country skiing. Equipment rental (from US$10 per day) for skiing, snowboarding and snowshoeing, plus a ski school, cafés and a hotel. Also restaurants on the pistes. Ski pass US$25-18 per day, depending on season. 3 buses daily from Ushuaia.

Haruwen, *35 km northeast on RN 3.* Cross-country skiing, snow-shoeing and other activities. Equipment and lessons.

Martial Glacier, *7 km from the centre.* A single piste for beginners.

Tierra Mayor, *21 km northeast on RN3, T02901-437454.* A beautiful wide valley that's recommended for cross-country skiing. Also half- and full-day husky excursions and snow shoeing. There's a cosy restaurant with wood stoves on site. **Antartur** runs buses to the resort.

Transport

Book ahead in summer, as flights fill up fast. In winter, poor weather often causes delays. Passport needed to buy tickets.

Río Grande p363

Air

The airport is 4 km west of town, *T02964-420600*. A taxi to the centre costs US$2. To **Buenos Aires**, **Aerolíneas Argentinas**, *San Martín 607, T02901-424467*, daily, 3½ hrs direct. **LADE** flies to **Ushuaia**, once a week and to other Patagonian towns.

Bus

Buses leave from the terminal *Elcano y Güemes, T02964-420997*, or from the office of **Tecni Austral**, *Moyano 516, T02964-430610*. To **Porvenir** (Chile), 5 hrs, **Gesell**, Wed and Sun 0800, US$9, passport and luggage control at San Sebastián. To **Punta Arenas** (Chile), via Punta Delgada,

10 hrs, **Pacheco**, Tue, Thu, Sat 0730, US$15. To **Río Gallegos** for connections to **El Calafate**, **Tecni Austral**, 3 times a week, US$15. To **Ushuaia**, **Tecni Austral**, 3-4 hrs, 2 daily (heavily booked in summer), US$12; also **Tolkeyen**, US$7.

Ushuaia *p365, map p372*

Air

Schedules tend to change from season to season, so call airline offices for times and prices: **Aerolíneas Argentinas**, *Roca 116, T02901-422267, www.aerolineas.com.ar*; **Aerovias DAP**, *25 de Mayo 64, T02901-431110*; **LADE**, *San Martín 542, Loc 5, T02901-421123, www.lade.com.ar.*

Aerolíneas and LADE fly to **Buenos Aires**, 3½-5 hrs depending on whether service is direct, and **El Calafate**, 1¼ hrs. Also flights to **Río Gallegos**, 1 hr, and **Río Grande**, 1 hr, but check with agents. To **Punta Arenas** (Chile), **Aerovias DAP**, 1 hr.

Bus

Long distance Buses arrive at offices around town: **Tecni Austral/Tolkar**, *Roca 157, T02901-431412*; **Líder**, *Gob Paz 921, T02901-436421*; **Tolkeyen**, *Maipú 237, T02901-437073*. To **Buenos Aires**, 36 hrs, US$70, **TAC**, **Don Otto**, **El Pinguino** and **Transportadora Patagonica**. To **Río Grande**, 4 hrs, **Tecni Austral** and **Líder**, both US$12, 2 daily; **Tolkeyen**, US$10. No through services from Ushuaia to **Río Gallegos**; instead, go to Río Grande, and change (total 8-10 hrs); book a ticket for the journey with **Tolkar** in Ushuaia, US$18.

To **Punta Arenas** (Chile), via Punta Delgada (15-min ferry crossing), 12 hrs, **Tecni Austral**, Mon, Wed, Fri 0600, US$23; **Tolkeyen/Pacheco**, Tue, Thu, Sat, 0630, US$25; also less frequent via **Porvenir**, 12 hrs (2½-hr ferry crossing), US$50.

Local **Ebenezer** and **Bella Vista**, daily to **Lago Escondido**, US$10 return, and **Lago Fagnano**, US$12. In summer, various companies, hourly to **Lago Roca**, US$3 return, and **Bahía Lapataia**, US$7, from the tourist pier; last return 2000 /2100. **Ebenezer** and **Gonzalo** to the **Fin del Mundo station** (see p 366) 0800, 0900, 1400; return 1700, US$3. For services to Harberton, see below.

Car hire

Most companies charge US$45 per day including insurance and 150 km per day. **Hertz**, *at the airport, T02901- 432429.* **Localiza**, *San Martín 1222, T02901-430739.*

Sea

For cruises to Cape Horn and Punta Arenas, see Budget buster, p332. For trips to Antarctica, see Going further, p378

Taxi

Remise Carlitos, *T02901-422222*; **Tienda Leon**, *San Martín 995, T02901-422222.*

Estancia Harberton *p367*

Access by car is along a good unpaved road which branches off Route 3, 40 km east of Ushuaia. Marvellous views en route but no petrol beyond Ushuaia. **Boat** trips twice weekly in summer from the Muelle Turistico, US$20 for a day trip. Daily **minibuses**, **Bella Vista** and **Lautaro**, from Maipu and Juana Fadul, US$14 return. **Tours**, US$40 plus entrance.

Directory

Río Grande *p363*

Banks and currency exchange 4 banks with ATMs on San Martín between 100 and 300. **Post office** *Piedrabuena y Ameghino*. **Telephone** *Locutorio* at *San Martín 170 and 458.*

Ushuaia *p365, map p372*

Banks and currency exchange
ATMs are plentiful along San Martín. Changing TCs is difficult but possible at Banco de Tierra del Fuego, *San Martín 396.* **Consulate** Chile, *Malvinas Argentinas y Jainen, Casilla 21, T02901- 421279.* **Internet and telephone** Cyber cafes and *locutorios* along San Martín. **Post office** *San Martín*, Mon-Fri 0900-1300, 1700-1900, Sat 0830-1200.

Antarctica

Ushuaia is the starting point for a number of excellent expeditions to Antarctica. These usually run from mid-November to mid-March and last between eight and 11 days, taking in the Antarctic peninsula and the Wedell sea. Some offer extra activities, such as camping and kayaking. Its not exactly a luxury cruise: trips are usually made in non-tourist boats used for scientific exploration, so the accommodation is informal and simple and the food is reasonable but not excessive. The expedition leader organizes lectures during the three-day journey to reach the Antarctic, with at least two disembarkations a day in a zodiac to see icebergs and penguins. When selecting your trip, bear in mind that there's most ice in November and December, more baby penguins in January and February, and whales in March. The landscape, however, is always impressive.

A longer trip of 18 to 19 days, combines the Antarctic with the Malvinas/Falklands and South Georgia islands. There are weekly departures in season. It's worth turning up in Ushuaia and asking the major tour operators for availability; there's a 30% discount if you book last minute in Ushuaia, when the price is around US$2500pp.

For further information and bookings contact **Rumbo Sur**, **Turismo de Campo** and **All Patagonia**, see Activities and tours, page 375. Seats can also sometimes be purchased on Chilean Naval supply vessels heading for Antarctica, though this requires patience and a long period of waiting in Punta Arenas, see Transport, page 332, for further details.

Index » *Entries in red indicate a map*

Index

Advertisers' index

Administration

- Capital city
- Other city/town

- International border
- Regional border
- Disputed border

Roads and travel

- Highway (paved)
- Highway (unpaved)
- Primary road (paved)
- Primary road (unpaved)
- Secondary road (paved)
- Secondary road (unpaved)
- Track
- Footpath
- Railway with station
- Airport
- Bus station
- Metro station
- Cable car
- Funicular
- Ferry

Water features

- River, canal
- Lake, ocean
- Seasonal marshland
- Beach, sand bank
- Waterfall

Topographical features

- Contours (approx)
- Mountain/volcano
- Mountain pass
- Escarpment
- Gorge
- Glacier
- Salt flat
- Rocks

Cities and towns

- Main through route
- Main street
- Minor street
- Pedestrianized street
- Tunnel
- One way street
- Steps
- Bridge
- Fortified wall
- Park, garden, stadium
- Sleeping
- Eating
- Bars & clubs
- Entertainment
- cp Casa particular
- Building
- Sight
- Cathedral, church
- Chinese temple
- Hindu temple
- Meru
- Mosque
- Stupa
- Synagogue
- Tourist office
- Museum
- Post office
- Police
- Bank
- Internet
- Telephone
- Market
- Hospital
- Parking
- Petrol
- Golf
- A Detail map
- A Related map

Other symbols

- Customs
- Archaeological site
- National park, wildlife reserve
- Viewing point
- Campsite
- Refuge, lodge
- Castle
- Diving
- Deciduous/coniferous/palm trees
- Hide
- Vineyard
- Distillery
- Shipwreck
- Historic battlefield

Credits

Footprint credits

Editor: Sophie Blacksell
Assistant editors: Angus Dawson, Nicola Jones
Text: Christabelle Dilks, Toby Green, Janak Jani
Map editor: Sarah Sorensen
Picture editor: Kevin Feeney

Publisher: Patrick Dawson
Editorial: Alan Murphy, Felicity Laughton, Laura Dixon, Claire Boobbyer, Sarah Thorowgood
Cartography: Robert Lunn, Claire Benison, Kevin Feeney, Angus Dawson, Thom Wickes, Esther Monzon
Advertising: Debbie Wylde
Finance and administration: Sharon Hughes, Elizabeth Taylor, Lindsay Dytham

Photography credits

Front cover: Alamy (Mount Fitz Roy, Los Glaciares National Park)
Inside: South American Pictures (Danny Aeberhard, Hillary Bradt, Mike Harding, Jason P Howe, Kathy Jarvis, Sue Mann, Katie Moore, Tony Morrison, Frank Nowikowski, Chris Sharp, Karen Ward), Christabelle Dilks, James Sturcke
Back cover: Alamy (Magellanic penguins, Seno Otway National Park)

Print

Manufactured in Italy by Printer Trento
Pulp from sustainable forests

Footprint feedback

We try as hard as we can to make each Footprint guide as up to date as possible but, of course, things always change.

If you want to let us know about your experiences – good, bad or ugly – then don't delay, go to www.footprintbooks.com and send in your comments.

Publishing information

Footprint Patagonia
1st edition

February 2005
ISBN 1 904777 26 0
CIP DATA: A catalogue record for this book is available from the British Library

Published by Footprint

6 Riverside Court
Lower Bristol Road
Bath BA2 3DZ, UK
T +44 (0)1225 469141
F +44 (0)1225 469461
discover@footprintbooks.com
www.footprintbooks.com

Distributed in the USA by

Publishers Group West

Neither the black and white nor colour maps are intended to have any political significance.

Every effort has been made to ensure that the facts in this guidebook are accurate. However, travellers should still obtain advice from consulates, airlines etc about travel and visa requirements before travelling. The authors and publishers cannot accept responsibility for any loss, injury or inconvenience however caused.

Publishing stuff

The South American Handbook: 1924-2005

It was 1921

Ireland had just been partitioned, the British miners were striking for more pay and the federation of British industry had an idea. Exports were booming in South America – how about a Handbook for businessmen trading in that far away continent? The *Anglo-South American Handbook* was born that year, written by W Koebel, the most prolific writer on Latin America of his day.

1924

Two editions later the book was 'privatized' and in 1924, in the hands of Royal Mail, the steamship company for South America, became *The South American Handbook*, subtitled 'South America in a nutshell'. This annual publication became the 'bible' for generations of travellers to South America and remains so to this day. In the early days travel was by sea and the Handbook gave all the details needed for the long voyage from Europe. What to wear for dinner; how to arrange a cricket match with the Cable & Wireless staff on the Cape Verde Islands and a full account of the journey from Liverpool up the Amazon to Manaus: 5898 miles without changing cabin!

1939

As the continent opened up, *The South American Handbook* reported the new Pan Am flying boat services, and the fortnightly airship service from Rio to Europe on the Graf Zeppelin. For reasons still unclear but with extraordinary determination, the annual editions continued through the Second World War.

1970s

From the 1970s, jet aircraft transformed travel. Many more people discovered South America and the backpacking trail started to develop. All the while the Handbook was gathering fans, including literary vagabonds such as Paul Theroux and Graham Greene (who once sent some updates addressed to **"The publishers of the best travel guide in the world, Bath, England"**.)

1990s

During the 1990s Patrick and James Dawson, the publishers of *The South American Handbook* set about developing a new travel guide series using this legendary title as the flagship. By 1997 there were over a dozen guides in the series and the Footprint imprint was launched.

2000s

In 2003, Footprint launched a new series of pocket format guides focusing on short-break European cities. The series grew quickly so that at the end of 2004 there were over 100 Footprint travel guides covering more than 150 destinations around the world. In January 2004, *The South American Handbook* reached another milestone: 80 annual editions. A memorable birthday party was held at Stanfords in London to celebrate.

The future

There are many more guides and pocket guides in the pipeline. A Lifestyle series was launched in 2004 with *Surfing Europe,* packed with 500 full-colour photographs and 70 maps and charts and a Backpackers' series is planned for 2005. To keep up-to-date with new releases check out the Footprint website for all the latest news and information, **www.footprintbooks.com.**